D0856064

THE
Music Lover's
HANDBOOK

The Music Lover's

Lawrence Abbott
Louis Armstrong
Robert Bagar
Béla Bartók
Marion Bauer
Louis Biancolli
Felix Borowski
Wallace Brockway
John N. Burk
Gilbert Chase
Carlos Chávez
Aaron Copland
Olin Downes
Carl Engel
David Ewen
George Gershwin
Lawrence Gilman
Benny Goodman
Herbert Graf
John Tasker Howard
A. Eaglefield Hull
Schima Kaufman
Lincoln Kirstein

Paul Landormy
Hugo Leichtentritt
Eugenie Lineva
Daniel Gregory Mason
Douglas Moore
C. Hubert H. Parry
Ethel Peyser
Sergei Prokofiev
Romain Rolland
Pitts Sanborn
Winthrop Sargeant
Dorothy Scarborough
Percy Scholes
Harold C. Schonberg
Cecil Sharp
Grigori Shneerson
Dmitri Shostakovich
Nicolas Slonimsky
Igor Stravinsky
Davidson Taylor
Deems Taylor
George P. Upton
Herbert Weinstock

Ralph Vaughan Williams

Handbook

EDITED BY

Elie Siegmeister

WILLIAM MORROW AND COMPANY

NEW YORK — 1943

★ VICTORY EDITION ★
*The typographical size and
format of this book are in
accordance with the paper con-
servation orders of the War
Production Board.*

WILLIAM MORROW & CO.
Publishers

PRINTED IN THE UNITED STATES OF AMERICA
BY H. WOLFF, NEW YORK

TO THE MEMORY OF MY FATHER

WILLIAM SIEGMEISTER

Contents

vii

THE
Music Lover's
HANDBOOK

Prelude

When the writer was smaller, he was, disgracefully enough, no child prodigy. Rather—let it be confessed right now—he had a strong, healthy suspicion of all forms of "good" music then known to him. Every day, at four-fifteen promptly, he would stop digging up buried treasure, scalping Indians, or holding down first base on the gang's punchball team, go into the house, seat himself on a rather hard stool, and dutifully start practising *The Poet's Dream, Dance of the Buttercups, Valse No. 4 in B Flat,* and other eminent masterpieces.

But after about ten minutes of esthetic uplift (carefully regulated by the tick of a tireless metronome), the yells of the gang scalping another Indian, finding the treasure, or going down to defeat in the abandoned punchball game would begin to pierce through the fog of wrong notes, and—shameful to relate—the writer, without a thought of his artistic future, would sneak *pianissimo ma prestissimo* down the back stairs, and out to freedom, with a whoop.

The boy, now a grown-up and reasonably cheerful musician, wonders, looking back—was there something wrong with him—lack of moral fiber and all that sort of thing? Or was it the fault of the musical environment that gave him *The Poet's Dream* to cut his musical teeth on?

For we American kids liked music, when it was *our* kind. Any day we might be found playing *Turkey in the Straw* on a piece of tissue paper stuck in a comb, or blowing *Si and I Went to the Circus* through a battered five-cent kazoo. And when the Fourth of July parade came boom-booming down the street we'd all join in with our own special ta-ta-ra-toodles and *The Monkey Wrapped His Tail Around the Flag Pole.* In purest Bel Canto, of course.

What held for those kids was also more or less true, twenty years ago, of most American adults, especially those out of range of the

3

"best" neighborhoods of the big cities. Visiting lecturers might bemoan "Yankee coldness" and "insensitivity to great music." The ordinary American with horse sense knew that if you had to change your name from plain Mary Hickenlooper to Olga Samaroff to break into "classical" music, there must be something wrong up there. He'd rather stick to ballads, waltzes, jazz, Stephen Foster and John Philip Sousa, keep his hair short, and his feet on the ground. But was he unmusical? Ever since 1625, when the New England divine John Cotton thundered against "lascivious dancing to wanton ditties," the plain American has loved a fiddle-tune, a breakdown, a lively ballad; and, later, a minstrel song, a spiritual, a blues song—some of the best, even though simplest, music the world has ever known.

But the classics? It was the French dancing masters and German court musicians who first brought them over, and they've been surrounded with an aura of gentility, luxury, wing collars, and deep-bosomed "ladies." European musicians, who until not so long ago still ran all our orchestras, operas, and concert managements, had brought with them the age-old traditions of two kinds of music: one, the "educated music" of refined patronage and prestige; and the other, the "cheap, vulgar" popular music of everybody else. This old-world cleavage had no place in a democracy—the man in the street sensed that. He left culture to the big-wigs.

Today this is all gone. With the growth of radio, good music, for so long an aristocratic privilege, has won its way into the hearts of Americans everywhere. When Beethoven is heard in hot-dog stands, César Franck in filling stations between changes of oil, and Stravinsky played in every fifteen-cent movie house throughout the country (what matter if it be through the medium of Disney's grinning dinosaurs?) it is clear that the old bars are down—once and for all. In the country where Paul Bunyan and Johnny Appleseed once walked, Brahms and Prokofiev are now household terms, and kids on sand-lots a thousand miles from Carnegie Hall whistle the intervals of Tchaikovsky's First Piano Concerto. Serious music, released from the hot-house, has broadened its audience a hundredfold. It has entered the main stream of American life.

With the enormous increase in the amount of music played and heard, with the development of a vast new audience, there was bound to come a deep-seated change in musical attitudes, tastes and ideas. The new radio, record, and movie public, and that of concerts in the army camps, do not have the prejudices of pride and tradition of the old substantial Back Bay and Academy of Music subscribers and patrons. They have never learned, for instance, that "hot" rhythms or spicy harmonies are undignified and "not art," or that music begins and ends with the Three B's. With the coming of a democratic musical public, the genteel tradition in music went by the board, and a great breath of fresh air blew into the musical universe.

In the last ten years we have begun to hear, via radio and on records—but also occasionally in the concert hall—a vastly wider range of music: Javanese gamelan music and American Indian songs, Renaissance madrigals and the latest works of Schönberg, Prokofiev and Marc Blitzstein. The narrow boundaries of nineteenth-century European concert art have been stretched to include music from a dozen different centuries and parts of the globe. Ozark Mountain songs, hot jazz, and the music of ancient Mexico, pre-revolutionary William Billings, harpsichord music, the swing version of the *Nutcracker Suite,* a newly discovered serenade by Mozart and the first performance of an *American Symphonette* by Morton Gould drift into our homes side by side, and are listened to with equal curiosity.

Our generation has, in consequence, the opportunity for a broader outlook on the world of music than any previous one in history, a truer picture than any heretofore available of the almost infinitely varied kinds of music made by man.

But with this fountain of wealth comes also an embarrassment of riches. Obviously, among so many different conflicting styles the old "eternal standards" of "good" and "bad" music held with such confidence only a generation ago are as out of date as the Model-T Ford. One cannot listen for the same thing in Bach, Boogie-woogie, and Balinese music! This cosmopolitan mixture can easily lead to musical indigestion, and we see the result in the often bitter sectarian arguments of the musical cultists that enter the correspondence columns of the Sunday music pages. There we meet the fervent devotees of neoclassicism, atonality, le jazz hot, pure form, and a dozen other proposed roads to musical salvation. Then there are the adherents of this or the other modern composer: Prokofiev, Béla Bartók, Duke Ellington, or Charles Ives. And perhaps here is the reason for a book such as this. Sensitiveness to music and the ability to appreciate genuine expressions in whatever style can never, of course, come simply from reading a book. Music is an art of sound, and only constant and intelligent listening, day-to-day familiarity with the actual materials of music, can mold those indefinable things we call musical taste and judgment. It is therefore hoped that the music mentioned in this book will first of all be listened to—and read about only afterward.

But in the complex world of today, music is no isolated thing. Its forms, tone colors, expressive qualities do not come out of nowhere; they come out of life itself. They are, of course, often to be enjoyed simply for themselves alone, for the joy and richness they give, in the concert hall or in one's armchair. But many times they have deeper meanings than the notes themselves reveal. They may tell of human strivings, experiences, struggles. They may give an insight into personality and society, into our lives or those far removed from our own in time and place—an insight no other art can give in this way.

All this cannot be deduced simply "from the notes themselves." An orchestral conductor who wishes to understand all there is to know about a great composer's style not only studies his scores down to the last quarter-note and phrasing mark; but also the forms in which the music is cast; he scans the orchestration minutely, reads the man's letters and biography, what others have said about the work. In short, he tries every avenue of approach to penetrate the meaning of music, which often far transcends the actual notes the composer was able to set down on paper.

Take Bach, for example. Here was a man whose thought and emotions were as manifold and subtle as any history has produced. Yet the musical notation of his day was rough and approximate. It provided for only the most general indications of loud and soft. Some of his greatest masterpieces were left without so much as a mention of the speed at which they should be played. Yet anyone knows that to take a work at a wrong tempo or with wrong inflections is to ruin its essential meaning.

A musician who wishes to penetrate the works of a master cannot go by mere musical hearsay—by how they are *generally* done, by so-and-so's traditional "interpretation." He will search every source of information, consult every conflicting opinion and authority, and then, out of all this material, form his own opinion. If he is a gifted and sincere musician he will end up by finding the truth.

If this is true of the musician, how much more important for the untrained listener. The listener must first use his ears and his heart. But they will not get him very far unless he also uses his head as well, unless he knows enough about the instruments of the orchestra to recognize them; can tell the difference between a fugue and a sonata; can recognize broad differences in style; knows something about the lives of the composers and the development of their work in relation to the world about them.

Then, although his problems will be far from solved—they may be just beginning—he will at least have certain standards of comparison, a deeper sense of enjoyment, and a more intimate participation in the world of music.

THE MUSIC LOVER'S HANDBOOK makes no attempt to solve everyone's difficulties or to cover everything that is to be known in the vast field of music. There is little here of interest to fact-collectors and antiquaries—absolutely nothing on the viola da gamba, ancient Greek music, Guillaume de Machaut, or other worthies whose art no longer has meaning for twentieth-century ears. This is a handbook, rather, of living music, of yesterday and today; its aim, to discuss some of the varied aspects and outstanding works of music in such a way as to stimulate the reader to go out and hear them. Naturally, not everyone's choice of "outstanding works" will be the same, and I know very well that another editor might prepare just as valuable a volume with quite different contents. That is testimony to the greatness and variety of the world of music.

This book, therefore, does not presume to say the final word about music. But it does present a meeting of minds that should give the listener not only information but also, it is hoped, richness and pleasure. Included are many sorts of writing—scholarly, gay, intimate, casual, passionate, full of conviction. Here are some of the outstanding figures of the present day, including composers, radio commentators, performers, jazzmen, critics and historians of music, folk-song enthusiasts, and just plain musicians. If the opinions expressed are sometimes contradictory, so much the better.

This book looks at music not as something that is dead and gone, but as a living and growing art, one for all to partake of. Alongside the more important classics, as much space as possible is given to contemporary American music, its role in the life of the nation, its problems and prospects. It is assumed here that there is no fundamental cleavage between serious music and jazz, or between these two and folk music. In a generation reaching out with enthusiasm for new musical fields to conquer, all manifestations of native music are important and alive. In a time when long-haired composers have grown scarcer than hen's teeth—and a good thing it is—music of all kinds plays a part in the creative life of our nation.

And with the growth of non-professional orchestras, of concerts for the armed forces, of talented American composers by the wagon-load, the problems of American music today are the vital concern not only of the musicians themselves, but of the entire musical audience, and indeed, in the long run, of all the people of our nation. It was Walt Whitman who said, "Great art needs great audiences," and if that was ever true, it is true today. American music will grow only when Americans call for it, when all the people can hear it and make it their own.

This HANDBOOK is designed for casual or for serious use. It can be opened at the middle, the beginning, or the end. Or some hardy souls may even choose to read it from cover to cover! If it contributes towards a live and sympathetic understanding of the music of the present as well as the past, it will have more than fulfilled its aim.

ELIE SIEGMEISTER

May 15, 1943

Introduction by Elie Siegmeister

DURING the past two generations, deep and far-reaching changes have taken place in the world of music. Ideals of pleasing harmony, beautiful tone, and "pure" expression, held sacred for hundreds of years, have slowly but definitely broken down. The concert hall, hitherto the *sanctum sanctorum* of high romantic emotion, has opened its doors to the violence and challenge of the world outside. Timbres, rhythms, and motives unknown to a previous age—the beat of the honky-tonk, the noise of the city, the rhythms of jazz and mills and motors, the thunder of the people's war—all these have found their way into symphonic works. In addition to the dignified "legitimate" sonorities of the traditional orchestra, composers have added to their scores the moan of the blues, the squealing clarinet, "hot" trumpet, saxophone, and drums, the twanging Kentucky fiddle and guitar—and these scores have been performed in the most distinguished concerts by Koussevitzky, Stokowski, and Toscanini himself.

The composer, no longer only an artist but also a citizen of our time, has become aware of the new audience and the new outlets for music: radio and the movies, the schools, theaters, and army camps— as important today as the concert hall itself. The old dividing lines between "serious" and "popular" music, once so sharply drawn, have grown indistinct. With the serious musicians turning to the more "commercial" outlets, and the tunesmiths of Tin Pan Alley working their way up towards the symphonic field, such divisions may soon cease to have any meaning whatsoever. A new concept and style of music is definitely emerging.

Yet, as in all great periods of musical change, the ideas and common notions of what music is have lagged behind the actual practice. Teachers, commentators, and critics, with eyes fixed on the works of the old masters, cling to beliefs that apply rather to the music of a hundred years ago than to that of our own time.

9

For example, it is commonly believed that there are only two kinds of music—"great" and unimportant. Great music—so the story goes—is created only by "genius"; it is in a category by itself, clearly separated from other kinds of music; its forms are timeless and eternal. The true composer follows only his "inner life"; outside conditions and events do not affect him, for his world is isolated from the common one we know.

These ideas, formerly accepted as gospel truth, are beginning to be looked upon as dubious half-truths. For we know today that nothing is more permanent in music than change. Compositions once considered timeless and eternal are today remembered only in textbooks, while others (such as the *St. Matthew Passion*) once considered quite unimportant are now ranked as masterpieces. Musical styles and forms widely used at one time are now historical relics. Who writes sarabandes or ricercares or coloratura arias nowadays?

"Genius," too, is a very slippery category, into which men enter and from which they fall with the waning years. Was Bach in 1800 thought the genius we now hold him to be? And the "immortals" of another day, the Telemanns, Jommellis, Hummels, and Spohrs—once fêted by the crowned heads of Europe—where are they on our modern lists?

If we turn to music itself, we find that here, too, constant change is the basic law. One century favors serious contrapuntal forms—fugues and the like; another will have none of the fugue—but only light, entertaining melodies and melodic pieces. One generation goes opera-mad; another prefers the instrumental virtuoso. Program music is all the rage for fifty years or so, and then is all but forgotten in the return to high-minded counterpoint.

What sense can be made out of this constant change? Does it mean that music is all chaos, accident, and "divine madness"?

Well, to a certain extent it is, but in addition it is order, discipline, logic, and an understandable part of the march of history and human life. In recent years both composers and the public have begun to accept the idea that music, besides reflecting the inner being of man, also has its place in the outer world—that it forms part of the normal processes of life as well as the rare, inscrutable ones.

Besides being inspiration, music is construction. It is a craft and activity which the composer pursues as a man among other men. The musician no longer regards himself as a high priest contemplating the ethereal realms. He is an American, a Mexican, an Englishman, a Russian, living in the year 1943, making music for his fellowmen to hear, writing for the musical public and outlets of our time, just as an author writes for the reading public and publishing outlets that actually exist here and now.

Thus, moved by the events of the war, with shellfire sounding not far away, Shostakovich writes his *Leningrad Symphony.* The Mexican, Revueltas, incorporates the rhythms of the village dances in *Redes,* a film dealing with the poor fishermen of his native land. And in Connecticut an insurance broker, Charles Ives, chants the glory of firecrackers, parades, and village bands in his *Fourth of July Symphony.* Music becomes both personal and a reflection of the thoughts and feelings of all men—an "inner" and an "outer" expression all rolled into one. The artist and his work are joined to the moods of our time, indistinguishable and inseparable from the conditions, events, joys, and terrors that affect the lives of all of us today.

Thus the era of the composer who fled from the life about him and disdained "vulgar" reality is passing, if not already gone. But, even more important, the old isolationist doctrines that pictured music as an art unrelated to the world of common men—they are going, too, and good riddance unto them!

For when they are completely gone, we shall begin to think and hear music with clearer heads and hearts. We shall see that what holds true of our living music was also true of the living art of former days. In Palestrina's time, and in Bach's, Mozart's, Tchaikovsky's, the composer reflected the temper of life about him as well as the one "inside."

To the great classic masters, composing was a way of functioning as well as expressing oneself. And as the patterns of life changed, the men of music changed with them. In ages of religion they wrote ritual music. In a time of pleasure and sensuous indulgence, their art was entertainment and emotional excitement. In the days of imperial pomp and majesty, composition became an art for royalty, full of stateliness, form, and dignity. When a rising democracy raised the cry "Back to Nature!" musicians, too, stripped their art of artifice and useless ornamentation, striving to attain in the realm of sounds that same simplicity and directness which other men sought in dress, speech, manners, architecture, economics, and every other department of life.*

Every composer, consciously or not, writes for an audience. Some-

---

* It is not implied that every piece of music in a given age follows a single pattern, but simply that each age and place has certain dominant values, which music by and large follows.

times it is a dream audience, but more often than not it has been a very real, flesh-and-blood audience of live human beings. And even in those cases where the musician writes *against* his audience, they, in a sense, make the music as much as the man who actually sets the notes down on paper. For no individual springs from a vacuum, and no artist, full of genius though he may be, arises without roots in his time, his environment and people.

In our own land we can see this most clearly in a composer like George Gershwin. Gershwin produced almost every one of his compositions for a definite purpose and audience. His popular songs were made for the Tin Pan Alley market, his musical comedy scores for Broadway production, and—as everyone probably knows—these outlets place precise limits on the composer. The "commercial" popular song must always be thirty-two measures long, with the Chorus divided into four exactly equal sections, and these in turn arranged according to a fixed pattern.* The standard musical comedy is still, for the most part, just as cut-and-dried, with so many love songs, chorus numbers, duets, dance routines and all the rest.

Gershwin grew up in the Broadway environment and accepted its formulas as a matter of course. He knew his market and audience, and wrote for them—whether "on inspiration" or "to order," it matters little. The fact remains that he was able to produce popular music of distinction with consistent regularity.

When he turned to the opera form or to that of the concerto, Gershwin accepted their conventions too, although he added a type of rhythmic and melodic idea familiar to and beloved by the American people. To be sure, he wrote music of a highly personal character, as will every gifted artist. But he never felt any conflict between his own musical impulse and the needs of his market—the American people, from which he sprang and of which he remained a part. Who knows or cares whether Gershwin's music is "great" or "eternal"? The important thing is that it gives musical pleasure of a very satisfying sort not only to the "great unwashed" but also to the distinguished musicians who have recently begun to perform it.

But, you say, Gershwin's music was light and playful, and could of course easily be written to order. The truly "great" and "serious" composer, however, must stand above the limitations of time and place, . . . etc., etc.

* The formula is "Strain"—"Repeat"—"Release"—"Strain"; or, in technical terms, the familiar AABA.

What then of Mozart's operas and serenades, Haydn's string quartets, Palestrina's *Missa Papae Marcelli,* Bach's church Cantatas, Stravinsky's *Petroushka* and *Le Sacre,* Falla's *Three-Cornered Hat,* Beethoven's *Rasumovsky* quartets and a thousand other works of classical and modern masters—all written to order, for specific patrons and occasions? Are they any less great because they conformed to external requirements as well as to the inner needs of the composer himself? Mozart even wrote many of his operas with particular singers in mind, employing notes which he knew sounded well in their voices, and his concertos incorporated the favorite technical devices of individual clarinet, horn, or bassoon players he knew. The larger part of Palestrina's music was fashioned for the Sistine Chapel choir. Both in subject matter and in style it was consonant with the ideals and dictates of the Church of which the Italian fur merchant was a faithful and devoted appointee.

If we could survey the whole history of music, we should see it as part of the great human procession. Musical styles arise and composers function as part of one or another movement of human history. Individuals grow out of the mass, always stimulated by the needs and desires of their time, of the people with whom they live and work.* Among a people enamored of the dance (as Americans are today) dance rhythms are strongly cultivated and tend to spread into many different fields of music. Thus, syncopation, the Charleston rhythm, and the improvisatory quality of swing are felt in many an American sonata, symphony, and choral work, as well as in music that is actually danced to. In similar manner, popular dance rhythms and patterns penetrated, as we shall see, into art music in Renaissance times, laying the foundation for the suite, rondo, variations, and other "classical" forms of European music.

Born among a people for whom chants, hymns, or spirituals carry the greatest meaning in life, a composer will grow up with the patterns of religious song in his music. Bach's magnificent Cantatas, Chorale Preludes, and Passions did not grow out of one man alone; they were the climax of a hundred years of Protestant composers, who shaped and molded the ritual melodies and forms that the Eisenach master naturally and inevitably came to use in his work. He is the peak; but

---

* Often a composer is ahead of the accepted convention of his time; though even then he is usually part of an advanced minority—if not of musicians, then of people in other fields who think as he does. Beethoven, Debussy, Mussorgsky, Ives have been examples of this type.

a thousand mute musicians formed the bedrock on which he stands. And beyond the musicians themselves, Bach is inconceivable without the whole movement of Lutheranism, the plainness and fervor of generations, the folk poetry and spirit of which all the music was but a part.

Music is allied and indebted to the dance and to religion. What is true of these holds also for a score of other human activities which have at one time or another been united with music, and which have contributed greatly towards shaping its spirit, structure, and style.

Thus, together with the new music of today, a new concept of music arises, in which the greater and smaller masterpieces are seen as part of the movement and meaning of life as a whole. And, as we shall see in various sections of this HANDBOOK, the works of individual masters take power and meaning from their roots in the people. Starting with the simplest folk song, growing through the various forms of dance, concert, opera, ballet music, in "classic," "romantic," and "modern" periods, right up to present-day America, we shall see music as an art rooted in the ideals and aspirations that have moved men and women in successive ages, and those that move all of us today.

PART ONE

Fiddle Strings and Ballads

I. Fiddle Strings and Ballads

How did music ever get started? This is a question that most of us have asked at some time or other, and it has been variously answered. According to one story, the art of music was stolen by Prometheus and by him communicated to men. Or—a nymph once pursued by Pan, finding herself cornered near a river bank, transformed herself into a reed; whereupon, to console himself, Pan cut the reed and played a mournful tune, thus inventing the first flute. Again, we are told that music was invented by hunters of old who, delighted by the twang of their bowstrings, decided to sit down and make themselves some fiddles.

Though all these are engaging stories, nobody, of course, actually knows or ever can know how music began. Nor is it of serious importance, because, after all, music is here, and who cares what happened thousands of years ago? However, this much is clear: that music was undoubtedly started by people who knew nothing at all about it, who probably didn't even realize that what they were making *was* music.

Long before the earliest recorded compositions by professional music-makers, the plain people sang and danced, chanted lullabies and work songs and prayers to their gods. All over the world, in ancient times as today, people unable to read or write a note of music have been and are rich in their feeling for melody and rhythm. Their music-making defies the rules of the schools, and in many ways it may sound rough and crude to the sophisticated ear; but if all the evidence of history is worth anything, it goes to show that before there ever was such a thing as a trained musician, music was an art and a practice well known and deeply loved by the humble of the earth.

At various times in different parts of the world, professional musicians and professional art music arose; and eventually an invidious distinction grew up between the various kinds of music. The theory was that everything good and beautiful—including music—emanated from

17

the gifted few, and never from the vulgar crowd.* The rigid distinction between "art music" and the "crude doggerel" of the masses was characteristic of every age in which caste ruled human society; though it never struck anyone as odd that those who expressed contempt of the people and all their works continued to borrow all the best productions of the people—its finest folk melodies, dance rhythms, scales, instruments.

Some ideas have a way of persisting for generation after generation until they are openly challenged. Thus the low regard for the people's music and the traditional misconceptions regarding it have hung on in some quarters right up to today, though it is nearly a hundred years since the Russian composer Glinka said, "It is the people who create; we only record and arrange." Even in our own time, it is widely believed still that folk music is something cute—charming—archaic; that it has historical interest only; that it really was not a creation of the people at all, but a crude reflection of art music, which peasants heard somewhere and imitated in their own benighted way. "The people are not creators, but wonderful imitators," wrote the French composer Vincent d'Indy (which did not prevent him from borrowing a folk song for his *Symphony on a French Mountain Air*). And a scholarly history of music says: "In the days of romanticism it was believed that folk music is entirely a creation of the people. It has since been recognized that poetic or musical creation demands an originality that the crowd cannot possess."

Fortunately, we are saying good-bye to all that, and beginning to break down the barriers that have for so long prevented us from knowing and appreciating the world's heritage of folk music. Still further, we are for the first time getting an accurate picture of what that music really is.

Ask any chance acquaintance to whistle a few folk songs and you are likely to get "Santa Lucia," "Home on the Range," "Die Lorelei," "Clementine," "Otchi Chornaya," "Comin' Thro' the Rye," and others of the same type. You might even get a snatch from a Liszt *Hungarian Rhapsody*, Brahms's "Lullaby," or Foster's "Old Folks at Home" ("Swanee River")—whose very titles reveal that they were written by professional composers. At any rate, this sort of music—excellent in

---

* We know today that the first recorded aristocratic music in history—that of the medieval Troubadours—was largely based on a continuous borrowing and adaptation of folk melodies.

its own right—is not, and never was, created by the people themselves; much that has passed for "folk" was in reality a smoothed-out
and prettified version of the real thing. In the past few decades, some
of the world's finest musicians—Béla Bartók in Hungary, Pedrell in
Spain, Cecil Sharp and Vaughan Williams in England—have gone
into the backwoods of their respective countries and dug up a wealth
of hitherto unsuspected folk music, quite different from anything we
had ever heard from those countries, and far more beautiful. Listening
to those authentic ballads, lullabies, dance melodies, and work songs,
we realize that this is one of the richest, most exciting types of music
on earth; and far from being "simple" or "crude," it is often molded
with a taste, sensitivity, and craftsmanship that are the envy of the
professional musician.

Take a song like "Poor Wayfaring Stranger," sung in this country
for over a hundred years by lumberjacks, backwoodsmen, housewives,
pioneers, country preachers, and other American folks—very few of
whom ever "knew anything about music." Here's a version sung to
me by an old farmhand in New York's Catskill Mountains last year:

This is a simple, bare piece of music, without any ornaments,
trimmings, or fancy orchestration—not even any chords to support the
melody. Yet I have seen audiences of thousands throughout the country listen in rapt silence to its quiet dignity, its unquestionable right-
ness and beauty. There are thousands of others—some grand like
"Poor Wayfaring Stranger," others tender, rollicking, tragic, playful,
or dramatic. Among them you will of course find some that are dull
(just as you will in concert music, too); but a far larger proportion
have been molded by generations to a chiseled perfection. I can think

of many pieces of music that are grander and more impressive, but none more perfect *within their own scheme* than "Poor Wayfaring Stranger," "Old Joe Clarke," "The Twa Corbies," "Ay, Manuela," "Renaud, Renaud," and many another I could name. Sung in straightforward fashion by an Alabama servant girl, a Tyrolese mountaineer, or a Mexican farmer (the list is inexhaustible), folk music is an authentic art whose quality is not duplicated by any other music that has ever been made.

Because it springs from common life, folk music does not have any special locale. There is scarcely a people on earth (except those whose national life has been blotted out by force) that does not have a distinctive style and tradition of its own. And in many lands this art of the people is thriving vigorously, with the old tunes flourishing, being constantly remade, and a new crop coming up every year. It is not possible in the following essays to give more than the merest taste of the many varieties of folk music existing in the world. The field is enormous and the diversity of style and feeling equally so. Each region has its own unique qualities not reproduced anywhere else. There are the wonderful rhythmic complexities of African and of East and West Indian folk music; the high development of folk counterpoint in Russia and the Balkans; the rich melodic ornamentation and subtle vocal arabesques of Spanish *flamencos,* Palestinian songs, Arab and Persian folk music; the foursquare heartiness of Dutch and German tunes; the dignity and grandeur of the old English ballads, the devil-may-care fantasy of American mountain tunes, and so on. And, be assured, these characterizations are but the merest generalities, for within each national group there are usually a dozen distinctly different types of folk music. It is impossible in one book to give more than the merest feeling of the world's folk music; only hearing the actual music itself can do that.

The musical qualities of folk song no longer need defense, for in recent years great progress has been made towards making the best examples known on the radio, in the more progressive schools, and on recordings. But, while the people's music has won a place in the musical scheme of things, one of the old misconceptions about it still persists: that art music and folk music dwell in separate worlds, that each is all right in its own sphere, but that never the twain shall meet.

A modern understanding of music history reveals the incorrectness of this view. Most musicians of today recognize no hard and fast

barrier between the creation of the people and that of the artist, but rather a continuous interplay between the two. The following essays therefore deal not only with what folk music is, and how and where it is found, but also with its relation to the great traditions of art music. It would be impracticable in a book of this nature to cover comprehensively the folk music of the entire world; there is room for but a few types—English, Negro, Russian, Mexican (and, in Part VII, American)—which may induce the reader to pursue further this truly inexhaustible subject.—E. S.

Hunting for English Ballads
By Cecil Sharp

Extracts from A. H. Fox-Strangways, "Cecil Sharp"

[*Sitting in a village inn at midday with a dozen men and women resting drowsily, he addressed a woman who entered with a basket of fruit and eggs:*]

"I, TOO am going to market, but to buy, not to sell. The fact is I have a great fancy for the old-fashioned songs. Perhaps you can tell me of a singer I could get one or two from." Silence! "Or there may be some one in this room. . . . You [to an old man] look like a singer." The old man didn't deny this, but said he hadn't "tuned a zong" this many a long day, and he didn't suppose he could "zay a zong right through, even if I gave him a quart of zider."

I took the hint, ordered the cider, and returned to the assault. "Did you ever hear sing 'John Barleycorn'?" I asked. "I've a 'eered 'un, but I never used to zing he," was the reply. I then turned round to the rest of the company and suggested that one of them could remember the song. They all knew the song, but no one would venture to sing it. I explained that I only wanted one verse, as I knew all the words. Then up spoke an old man, who until now had been silent. "If it's only the tune you do want, I can sing you the first verse, and that, I reckon, will be enough." And then, without further pressing, he broke forth into song. He had an extraordinarily beautiful voice, rich and resonant, and he held onto the last note of the refrain with

consummate art, swelling it to a fortissimo, and then allowing it gradually to die away into silence. I saw at once that I had captured a fine
tune. I called upon the landlord to fill up his mug, while I prevailed
upon the old man to sing the verse once again, in order that I might
write it down in my pocket book. Having done this I sang the verse
myself that he might see whether I had written it down correctly—
much to the amazement of the company, and their amusement, too, I
expect. Once again I made him repeat the verse, partly for my own
pleasure—it was glorious to listen to him—and partly that I might
revise my manuscript. He told me that he was a coal miner, that he had
heard the song when he was a boy, fifty or sixty years ago; that it was
sung by a tramp who was passing through the village; that it had
pleased his fancy, and that he had never forgotten it.

WHERE THE SONGS ARE FOUND

In the out-of-the-way districts—on the heights of Mendip, for
example—I often take singers whom I have found in the fields into
public houses; for their homes are far off and there is nowhere else
to go. But the majority of the songs have been taken in cottages, in
barns, by the roadside, or in the open fields.

I once took down two excellent songs from a "bird-starver." It
was his business to guard a patch of mangold seeds from being eaten
by birds, and this he did by hammering a tea tray. He was quite prepared to sing, but his conscience would not allow him to neglect his
duty.

So we arranged that he should hammer his tray between each
verse of his songs, and thus combine business with pleasure; and we
accomplished this to our mutual satisfaction and to the amusement
of passers-by.

On another occasion I recovered a good song from the proprietor
of a cocoa-nut pitch at Cheddar Cliffs, when business was slack; and
I have many times sat by the side of stone-breakers on the wayside and
taken down songs—at the risk, too, of my eyesight, for the occupation
and the song are very often inseparable.

One singer in Langport could only sing a song when she was
ironing, while another woman in the same court sang best on washing
day! I remember an amusing incident which happened to me at the
house of the latter. I was in her wash-house sitting on an inverted tub,
notebook in hand, while my hostess officiated at the copper, singing

the while. Several neighbours congregated at the door to watch the strange proceeding. In one of the intervals between the songs one of the women remarked, "You be going to make a deal o' money out o' this, sir?" My embarrassment was relieved by the singer at the wash-tub, who came to my assistance and said, "Oh! 'tis only 'is hobby." "Ah, well," commented the first speaker, "we all do 'ave our vailin's!"

Letter from Alabama

By Elie Siegmeister

I HAD just walked into her lovely old antebellum mansion for the first time a half-hour before, but already Mary Louise (tall, white-haired, about sixty, but all animation, and spry as a fox) was talking about Vera Hall, "Dock" Reed, Aunt Molly MacDonald, and all the other folk singers around Livingston. Whereupon I interposed, "How can I hear these singers?"—and Mary Louise:

"Well, let's get in the car, and go hear them now."

We drove over to the colored "café" behind the town. Clapboards, garbage lying all around, the front covered with billboards—but lively sounds coming out, dark Negroes gaily dressed and laughing loudly, white teeth gleaming in the twilight.

"Say, boy, have you seen Vera Hall?"

"No'm—I ain't done seen Vera."

All the laughing stopped, the Negroes suddenly sober as deacons in church. But as soon as we turned away, it resumed as though it had not been interrupted.

At the next "café" we picked up Vera—a robust, smiling colored woman of about thirty-five—and drove back to Mary Louise's place.

Then the singing began. Vera has a lovely contralto full of sweet-ness, velvet, and the rich Negro timbre, flowing up occasionally into a high falsetto with delicate slides and twists. She sang play-party songs, "shoutin' " spirituals, funny songs, and "O Death" in a powerful Negro version; then some "moans"— "Job, Oh Job," and "De Black Cat Say to de White Cat" (a lively, gay dance song with alternating major and minor tones), and a beautiful slow blues, "Black Woman." Here are a few bars of this last one:

Vera's husband came in and sang chain-gang songs. I wrote and wrote as fast as I could, and we stayed till eleven at night.

On Monday morning at nine Mary Louise was at the door:

"Come on, hurry up—we've got to get out on the railway to the section gang!"

I hurried into my clothes, shaved, and dragged out the rest of the music paper, downed an orange and a glass of milk—and there was Mary Louise with a brand-new car she had borrowed for the occasion, shouting:

"I can't understand it! What's the matter with this generation? I'd 've been up at six to go after them, and you just getting out. . . ."

We drove down the road. Mary Louise stopped an old Negro grandma in red bandanna, horn-rimmed spectacles, and worn gingham dress.

"Auntie, have you seen the section gang?" And, while waiting for it: "Say, do you know the old songs you used to sing for me?"

Right then and there, with the car parked in the middle of the road, old Sally Ann Johnson sang "Jesus Gonna Make up Mah Dyin' Bed."

"You got to feel it," she said; "you jus' cain' sing it when you's not warmed up to it." And old Auntie Johnson trundled off.

Then we climbed over a half-mile of muddy scrub, with indefatigable Mary Louise of course in the lead—talking, laughing, and raving about "Rich" Amberson, another folk singer, who is also a "conjure" man, a preacher, teller of fantastic tales, and handy man about town.

We came to the railroad track and there—about a quarter-mile off in the bright sun—was the section gang: fifteen Negroes bent over the track working away. Going nearer we heard the sound of singing, and, as we were right by them, the rhythmical movements of the shovels, tamping the gravel under the ties. The Caller, a very dark Negro in blue work jeans, intoned a melody so weird that it was almost impossible to write down. The words I could not make out at the time, but got shortly afterward. The men were poised in position with their shovels.

Caller: "Boys, is yuh right?"
All: "Yes, de bes' I know."
Caller: "Oh, ketch 'em up solid—*Lawd, Lawd!* [tamping starts]
          Oh, solid an' soun'!
          So de Double-six-ninety *—*Lawd, Lawd!*
          Cap'n won't knock 'em down.

          "Oh, on de udder railin'—*Lawd, Lawd!*
          On de udder tah [tie]—
          Oh, on de udder railin', *Lawd,*
          Cap'n whar de dolluh lie.

          "Cap'n got a big gun—*Lawd, Lawd!*
          Try to play bad;
          Ah'm gonna take it, *Lawd,*
          If you make me mad."

—And on and on. I got fifteen verses down; there are hundreds—the men all digging their shovels in absolute precision timed to the singing, as in that African film *Dark Rapture.*

Later I got a "Lining Chant" as the men moved the whole railbed over with steel lining bars, in sudden rhythmical spurts. Keeping time to the Caller's chant, they tapped on the rails with their bars—then, all in unison, a great "throw"—and the track moved a couple of inches west.

Well, I could spend two weeks in Livingston instead of three days—but I got about thirty songs noted down and the most wonderful introduction to some fine people and exciting music in the Deep South.

* The name of a train.

Peasant Songs of Old Russia

Extracts from "Peasant Songs of Great Russia" (1900)*

By Eugenie Lineva

As I think of them, these folk singers and improvisers, singers of whom our country may well be proud, they seem to pass before me like a pageant or procession. Clad in rough homespun, in torn kaftans which have lost in hard work every vestige of color, with uncombed beards and unwashed hands, half confused and half proud, they stand there, when rumor reaches them of the song lover and collector. Full of an original and attractive roughness, as if excusing themselves, they say, "Dear, dear, it is only our village songs that we know." They wag their heads with good-humored mistrust when they hear the answer: "That is just what we want!" "What for?" they wonder. They shift about from one foot to the other. "Of course we can sing," they say; "but what is it wanted for? Won't they arrest us?"

I laugh. "What for?"

"Well, for the songs—who knows?"

I assure them that no harm can come to them from singing the songs—only praise; and I explain to them, as well as I can, my purpose in collecting them. They begin to calm down. The idea appeals to them of preserving the old songs, the worth of which everyone accepts, even the young people. "Ah, they come to the old things. Isn't this before the end?" I heard a woman's voice say, full of apprehension.

Women and children stand round me in a dense circle and observe me with searching eyes. In the first row stand the girl-nurses with babies in their arms. They are the most curious gossips of the village, acting the roles of post and newspaper. I feel that they all want to find out about me, to "place me." Here everybody knows all about everybody else. They do not like anything not quite clear. That I am collecting old songs for the Imperial Geographical Society tells them

* Folk music in Tsarist Russia, as depicted in this article, was vastly different from the Russian people's music today. The old songs are still sung, but they have been largely superseded by the modern folk and Red Army songs, with their stirring, vigorous spirit. This change strikingly illustrates the close relation between the life of a people and the spirit of its music.—E. S.

nothing. After listening to my explanation, they begin to question me in their turn, to clear up the mystery.

Influenced by an acquaintance with the peasant singers and their life, the questions begin to stir us unconsciously: How is the folk song born? How does it develop? How does it die out? What is this sphinx, this "unconscious collective creative power" embracing a whole country and variable as life itself? Can it be "unconscious" if it serves as reflection both of the souls of separate persons and of the soul of the people?

"Song is truth," according to the peasant saying. It is the expression of the soul in poetic-musical form. We remember how Anisia Elisarovna composed her first lament when the parents married her against her will: "I thought it all over," she said, "and told it—relieved my soul." These words show very clearly that emotion and thought [had] acted together: "I thought it all over, and told it—relieved my soul." This example shows better than anything the influence of separate individuals on the people's creativeness. Personal initiative brought out by dramatically complicated circumstances appears as the beginning, as the foundation of the lament.

There are great numbers of laments; composed for special occasions, they were repeated in similar circumstances and came into general use.

Alterations and adaptations go on all the time in the wedding laments till they constitute a part of the marriage ritual. But latterly, since the *samohodki* (free marriages) have come into use and young people wed of their own free choice—sometimes even eloping without engagement or other customary rites and ceremonies—the laments begin to be forgotten and to die out. This stream of the people's creative genius dries up, as it were. For as soon as a certain feature disappears from life, it ceases to reflect on the musico-dramatic creative power of the people in lament and song.

The peasant singers have no idea of major or minor keys, as we understand them, although they use the word *laad* (accord, agreement; in music, a general scheme of sounds which form the scale of a given melody). They say, "You are not in the proper *laad,* you do not sing this song right,"—meaning that each song has its own *laad*. The special qualities of the musical build of the song are difficult to define, because the fancy of the peasant singer follows his free will and he constantly introduces unexpected changes in the rendering of the song.

The sense of rhythm is very strong in peasants. Anyone may have observed when a building is being erected by a whole *artel*, or at the loading and unloading of a vessel, the rhythm of the work under the influence of song. The power of joint, rhythmical singing, whilst at work, seems miraculous; enormous weights are moved and hoisted up with the song, as it were. I remember once on the Volga, at Kamyshim, the dockers were hauling up huge baskets of fish out of the hold. When they lifted a basket up out of the hold and threw it, the weight seemed enormous. Before putting it on the boards over which the baskets were dragged to the landing, the dockers stood still and, beginning the song: "It'll go of itself," tried to pull up the basket. As one group sang this, the other answered, "It doesn't!"—and so on up to the moment when by their united efforts they moved the basket from its place with the exclamation, "There goes!" Then they all easily and quickly pulled at it in time with the songs, drawing it up to the landing stage where they laid it in a row of similar baskets. Here is the melody of the song, constantly varied, of course:

I had a chance to observe a remarkable sense of rhythm even in play songs of peasant children. I recollect once passing through one of the Novgorod villages, where a crowd of children were playing. They were divided into two groups, girls and boys. The girls, taking each other by the hand, advanced toward the boys quickly, almost running, in time to the song they were singing: "We have sown the millet, the millet"—and as quickly retreated, repeating the words. In just as good order and stamping with their feet, the boys approached the girls, singing: "We shall stamp out the millet, the millet." Here is the melody:

Mexican Popular Music

Abridged from "Mexican Music"

By Carlos Chávez and Herbert Weinstock

BEFORE Europeans arrived on this continent there flourished in Mexico civilizations or cultures which present-day archeology and history are learning to understand and relate to each other. Among the Aztecs, music achieved the marks of a true artistic culture. It filled a role of real social importance in government, religion, and war. It was a true state institution, and was the object of special study and cultivation.

Among the Aztecs also music played a purely lyric part. Fray Bernardino de Sahagun preserved Aztec poetry which tells us of the contemplative and delicate interior life of the Indian poets. All this poetry was sung.

Besides the chroniclers, we have another unquestionably reliable source of information: the archeological instruments preserved in museums. The study of these instruments indicates the existence of true musical culture among the ancient Mexicans. [The instruments are large wooden drums, rattles, whistles, flutes, rasps, and various other percussion instruments.]

It will be understood that a musical tradition so strong, complete, and rooted could not easily be overthown or supplanted. The conquistador did not combat it. From the beginning he accepted the continuation of the pagan rites, merely adapting them to Christianity. For this reason it is still possible, in the atria of many churches in small towns, and in the great religious processions, to hear the Indians playing the *huehuetl,* the *teponaxtle,* and their little flutes. Nor could the conquistador have battled against the custom of singing the traditional hymns of which we still hear some. The military music, of course, disappeared for natural reasons.

But the conquistador brought in a real wealth of new music, new instruments, new melodies, new forms. This torrent of music began little by little to usurp the place of the aboriginal music. In this brief exposition it will only be possible to mention, without comment, the general lineaments of the music brought into Mexico by the Spaniards.

In the first place, there was music for religious services, of which

29

the most important was plainsong, which was taught to the Indians from the first days of the Conquest. Catholic music in Mexico followed the same course as in other parts of the world, in accordance with papal regulations. Its general influence throughout Mexico was as enormous as the power of the Church itself.

Popular and peasant music and dances were introduced by the Spaniards (coming from many districts of Spain) into all the chief regions of Mexico. From this source our peasant dances, such as the *jarabe,* the *huapango,* and many others, probably come. Practically all the music known under the generic name of *son* shows a Spanish origin.

The Spanish *romance* was widely diffused at an early date. It took root because of its resemblance to native Indian songs, and has become the Mexican *corrido.*

The profane songs and dances of picaresque character—the gay street songs, and even those of the courtly festivals—must have had enormous importance, if we can judge by the testimony taken during innumerable trials conducted by the Inquisition for the sin of singing, playing, and dancing unchurchly music. We can find a concrete example in the invention in Mexico, in the sixteenth century, of the *pavan,* which takes its name and its aspect of gallantry from the courtship of the turkey (Spanish, *pavo*).

Thus, by the phrase "Mexican music" we mean the Indian music of the ancient Mexicans; the music of Spanish or other origin implanted in Mexico, and, finally, the production in Mexico of a mixture of these elements. The Indian branch and the Spanish branch differ in that Indian music from the Conquest on remained static, while Spanish music has undergone constant evolution.

The Indian music best preserving its purity is not what remains of Aztec culture, but that of more or less primitive or nomad tribes which never, properly speaking, achieved a culture. Such are the Yaquis, the Seris, and the Huicholes.

I do not think that the qualities of Mexican music depend on its proportion of Indian and Spanish ancestry, but on the existence of many new, local factors—historical, geographic, and ethnic circumstances which work directly on the artistic phenomenon.

CORRIDOS MEXICANOS

The modern Mexican *corrido* is a true folk ballad. Its simple, artless, narrative verses have long served, particularly in remote sections of Mexico, in lieu of newspaper, post, telegraph, and newsreel.

Professional *corrido* singers, arriving in a remote village, bring in the only available news of the outside world. Similarly, it is from these singers that other parts of the world learn of the occurrences in remote mountain fastnesses and desert plains. Printed versions of these ballads have served to spread and perpetuate highly colored retellings of crimes, violent deaths, bandit raids, natural catastrophes, railroad wrecks, wars, and heroic deeds.

Corridos are sung at fairs and fiestas, or in village plazas to loiterers and passers-by. A lone guitarist may do the singing, or he may be joined by a woman who will also vend sheets of colored paper containing the printed words of his most popular ballads. Less often, two men may sing, or even be joined by a woman. When there are two voices the interval between them is most commonly a third or a tenth.

The texts of the *corridos* are usually the anonymous creations of the musician who sings them. However, some of these verses have been polished by passing time into a variety of set versions. They frequently begin with an invitation to listen, and end with a farewell strophe of thanks, stating that such and such a story has been told. Recently, students of the *corrido* have come to know some of the best present-day *corrido* singers, and are thus able to add an author's name to a few of the ballads.

SONES MARIACHI

Mariachi is the name given to an instrumental ensemble found chiefly in the Mexican state of Jalisco, and to a lesser extent and in varied form in Colima, Michoacán, Nayarit, and even Mexico City itself. Fundamentally, a *mariachi* consists of two violins, a large five-stringed guitar, a small guitar, and a five-octave harp. In modern ensembles, the harp is frequently omitted, while clarinet and trumpet are added.

The characteristic music of a *mariachi,* like that played during a *huapango,* is called a *son,* though *mariachis* also accompany the popular ballads known as *corridos,* as well as *canciónes.* The *son mariachi* is frequently a type of primitive round. It is both sung and danced. If the occasion is a religious fiesta, the *mariachi* is likely to take up its place at the door of the church. For secular festivities, such as weddings, birthday parties, celebrations of memorable dates, or gaieties attending a good harvest, however, it usually plays out of doors in an arbor of branches or wide banana leaves.

The *son mariachi* is basically rhythmic, of complex and intertwining beats. The singers are always the men who play the instruments. They use a high falsetto voice, and traditionally keep a third or a sixth apart. The verses sung are almost invariably gay, frequently picaresque in character.

The instrumentalist-singers likewise dance. Never moving on heel or toe, they keep their feet flat to the ground. Movement is confined almost entirely to the legs, and particular point is made of not moving the head at all. A specialty of some *mariachi* dancers in Vera Cruz is a number in which a bottle is balanced on top of the head.

HUAPANGOS

Huapango is the name of a type of fiesta celebrated in the states of Vera Cruz, Tamaulipas, San Luis Potosí, Hidalgo, Tabasco, and Puebla, particularly along the shores of the Gulf of Mexico and in the adjacent tropical lowlands. It consists of instrumental music, singing, and dancing.

Whole communities participate in *huapangos,* only the instrumentalists being professionals. In its purest form, the music, called a *son,* was played on a tiny five-stringed guitar and a harp. In the more or less hybrid and decadent forms in which the music is usually heard today, this ensemble has widened to include large four- and six-stringed guitars and violins. Rhythm, constantly created by instrumentalists, singers, and dancers, is the most important element in this music, and is infinitely varied. Most *sones* are in 3/4, 2/4, or 6/8 time, often rapidly alternating, and even combined. The melodies, almost certainly derived from sixteenth-century Spanish music, are not likely to be used in more than one locality, or even by more than one singer: they are personal and seem improvisatory. The harmonies are likewise of such ever-shifting complexity, such variety from region to region— and even ranch to ranch—that simple definitive statements about them are all but impossible.

The singing of a *son* is done by the community, divided into groups and soloists of special abilities. The verses are made up of rhyming stanzas of four, five, six, or ten lines. All but a few of them deal with two universal subjects: women and nature. They are romantic, insinuating, often humorous, and almost never weakly sentimental; incline, in truth, to burlesque the sentimental.

The dancing of a *huapango* is done on a high wooden platform. A man and woman, pairs of men and women, or women alone, are the principal dancers, though children and the village elders may join in if sufficiently talented and strong. The steps are fast and dazzlingly complicated in rhythm. In certain popular *sones,* trick steps are traditional. In *La Bamba* (the music of which has an unmistakable Negro tang), the dancer, to gain applause, balances a glass of water on his head without spilling a drop. Or the man may loop a silk scarf with his feet without losing the rhythm. If successful in this difficult trick, he places the looped scarf on the head of a chosen girl—very often with important results in their lives. As a genre, the *huapango* reflects the vivacious gaiety of the inhabitants of the Gulf Coast of Mexico, so different in their laughter and song from the more somber Mexican of highland and desert.

The Nature and Evolution of Folk Song

Abridged from two chapters in *"National Music"*

By Ralph Vaughan Williams

IN PRIMITIVE times before there were newspapers to tell us the news, history books to teach us the past, and novels to excite our imagination, all these things had to be done by the ballad singer, who naturally had to do it all from memory. To this end he cast what he had to tell into a metrical form and thus the ballad stanza arose. As a further aid to memory and to add to the emotional value of what he had to say he added musical notes to his words, and it is from this that the ordinary folk tune of four strains arose. Folk music, you must always remember, is an applied art. The idea of art for art's sake has happily no place in the primitive consciousness. I have already told you how the country singer is unable to dissociate the words and tune of a ballad. Song then was to him the obvious means of giving a pattern to his words. But this pattern is influenced by another form of applied music, that of the dance, the dance in which the alternation of strong and weak accents and precision of time are essential.

Before I go any further I had better give you some actual examples of what I mean by folk song, and try and persuade you that I am not telling you of something clownish and boorish, not even something inchoate, not of the half-forgotten reminiscences of fashionable music mouthed by toothless old men and women, not of something archaic, not of mere "museum pieces," but of an art which grows straight out of the needs of a people and for which a fitting and perfect form, albeit on a small scale, has been found by those people; an art which is indigenous and owes nothing to anything outside itself, and above all an art which to us today has something to say—a true art which has beauty and vitality in the twentieth century. Let us take a few typical examples of English folk-song: "The Cuckoo," "My Bonny Boy," "A Sailor from the Sea," or "It's a Rosebud in June."

Can we not truly say of these as Gilbert Murray says of that great national literature of the Bible and Homer, "They have behind them not the imagination of one great poet, but the accumulated emotion, one may almost say, of the many successive generations who have read and learned and themselves afresh re-created the old majesty and loveliness. . . . There is in them, as it were, the spiritual life-blood of a people."

A folk song is at its best a supreme work of art, but it does not say all that is to be said in music; it is limited in its scope and this for various reasons.

(1) It is purely intuitive, not calculated. (2) It is purely oral, therefore the eye does not help the ear and, prodigious though the folk singer's memory is, owing to the very fact that it has not been atrophied by reading, it must be limited by the span of what both the singer and hearer can keep in their minds at one stretch. (3) It is applied music, applied either to the words of the ballad or the figure of the dance. (4) Folk music, at all events European folk music, and I believe it is true of all genuine folk music, is purely melodic.* These limitations are not without corresponding advantages. (a) The folk singer, being unselfconscious and unsophisticated and bound by no prejudices or musical etiquette, is absolutely free in his rhythmical figures. If he has only five syllables to which to sing notes and those syllables are of equal stress he makes an unit or what in written music we should call a bar of five beats (to put it into the language of scientific music). If he is singing normally in a metre of 6/8 and he wants to dwell on one particular word he lengthens that particular phrase to

---

* Vaughan Williams's statement is truer of Western European folk music than of that of other regions. Russian, African, American Negro folk music are full of the most fascinating effects of part singing and their own special kind of harmony.—E. S.

a metre of 9 beats. If he is accompanying a dance and the steps of the dance demand it he will lengthen out the notes to just the number of long steps, regardless of the feelings of the poor collector who is afterwards going to come and try and reduce his careless rapture to terms of bars, time signatures, crotchets and quavers.* We are apt to imagine that bars of five and seven, irregular bar-lengths, and so on are the privilege of the modernist composer: he is probably only working back to the freedom enjoyed by his ancestor. (b) To pack all one has to say into a tune of some sixteen bars is a very different proposition from spreading oneself out into a symphony or grand opera, especially when these sixteen bars have to be repeated over and over again for a ballad of some twenty verses. We have often experienced music which at first seemed attractive but of which we wearied after repetition. The essence of a good folk tune is that it does not show its full quality till it has been repeated several times, and I think a great deal of the false estimates of folk melodies which are current are due to the fact that they are read through once, or possibly hummed through without their words, or worse still strummed through once on the piano and not subjected to the only fair test, that of being sung through with their words.

The fact that folk music is entirely oral and is independent of writing or print has important and far-reaching results. Scholars are too apt to mistrust memory and to pin their faith on what is written. They little realize how reading and writing have destroyed our memory. Cecil Sharp gives amazing examples from his own experience of the power of memory among those who cannot read or write. The scholars look upon all traditional versions of a poem or song as being necessarily "corrupt"—as a matter of fact corruptions are much more likely to creep in in the written word than in the spoken. Any alteration in a written copy is likely to be due to carelessness or ignorance, whereas when we do find variations in versions of traditional words and music these are as often as not deliberate improvements on the part of later reciters or singers.

There is no "original" in traditional art, and there is no particular virtue in the earliest known version. Later versions are as likely as not developments and not corruptions.

There is a well-known saying of the folk-lorist Grimm that "A folk song composes itself." Others replied to this with the common-

* British crotchets and quavers = American quarter and eighth notes.—E. S.

sense view that "It only takes one man to make a folk song." Böhme, in the Introduction to his *Alt-deutsches Liederbuch,* says, "First of all one man sings a song, then others sing it after him, changing what they do not like." In these words we have the clue to the evolution of the folk song. Let me quote you also from Allingham's *Ballad Book.* "The ballads owe no little of their merit to the countless riddlings, siftings, shiftings, omissions, and additions of innumerable reciters. The lucky changes hold, the stupid ones fall aside. Thus with some effective fable, story, or incident for its soul and taking form from a maker who knew his business, the ballad glides from generation to generation and fits itself more and more to the brain and ear of its proper audience."

According to Gilbert Murray even a written book could be ascribed in primitive times to a communal authorship. Thus, the *Iliad* and the *Odyssey* are both the products of a long process of development. If this be true of the book, how much more so of purely oral music and poetry.

Cecil Sharp, in his book on English folk song, argues strongly in favour of the communal authorship of traditional music and poetry, but it must be noted that he does not claim a communal *origin.* He writes: "The folk song must have had a beginning and that beginning must have been the work of an individual. Common sense compels us to assume this much, otherwise we should have to predicate a communal utterance that was at once simultaneous and unanimous. Whether or not the individual in question can be called the author is another matter altogether. Probably not, because the continual habit of 'changing what they do not like' must in course of time ultimately amount to the transference of the authorship from the individual to the community."

This then is the evolution of the folk song. One man invents a tune. (I repeat that I grant this much only for the sake of argument.) He sings it to his neighbours and his children. After he is dead the next generation carry it on. Perhaps by this time a new set of words have appeared in a different metre for which no tune is available. What more natural than to adapt some already existing tune to the new words? Now where will that tune be after three or four generations? There will indeed by that time not be one tune but many quite distinct tunes, nevertheless, but all traceable to the parent stem.

To sum up, let me quote Cecil Sharp's definitions of art music and folk music. "Art music," he writes, "is the work of the individual, it is composed in, comparatively speaking, a short period of time, and being committed to paper it is for ever fixed in one unalterable form. Folk music is the product of a race and reflects feelings and tastes that are communal rather than personal; it is always in solution; its creation is never completed, while at every moment of its history it exists not in one form but in many."

So you see the individual has his share in the creation of the folk song, and the race has its share. If I may venture to give my own definition of a folk song I should call it "an individual flowering on a common stem." We folk-song collectors are often asked "what is the origin" of a particular tune or "how old" it is. There is no answer to either of these questions; there is no original version of any particular tune; any given tune has hundreds of origins. Nor can we say how old it is; in one sense any particular tune is as old as the beginnings of music, in another sense it is born afresh with the singer of today who sang it. Sometimes we are laughed at: the scoffer says: "I expect that is not an old tune at all; the old man who sang it to you invented it himself." Quite possibly to a certain extent he did. It is not the age but the nature of the tune which makes it a folk song.

Some Reflections on Folk Song

Extracts from "The English Folk Song: Some Conclusions"

By Cecil Sharp

WE HAVE defined the folk song as "the song created by the common people." This definition involves the assumption that the folk song is the unaided composition of the unskilled; and to some it will seem fantastic to credit the unlettered peasant with the capacity to compose music, good, bad, or indifferent. Surely, it will be argued, it is far more probable that the folk song is only the fashionable song of a bygone day, the composition of the skilled musician, which found its way into the country villages where, although long ago forgotten in the town or city of its origin, it has since been preserved.

Unfortunately [this explanation] does not square with facts. For, if the music of a common people originated in the towns, the sheet music and song books of the past would surely bear evidence of the fact. And this they fail to do. To search for the originals of folk songs

amongst the printed music of olden days is mere waste of time. Moreover, there is a further difficulty. Composed music differs generically
from folk music; it belongs to a different order. Folk music, as we shall
presently see, is distinguished by certain technical peculiarities which
are absent from art music; while, on the other hand, art music possesses many musical attributes which are not to be found in the music
of the common people, or in that part of it which we call folk music.
But, apart from technical differences, the extreme naturalness, the
spontaneity, freshness, and unconventionality of folk music are just
those qualities which are conspicuously absent from the popular song
music of past centuries. Indeed, folk music is as distinct from art music
as is the wild flower of nature from the gorgeous blooms of the cultivated garden. As well search for a wild rose in a well-kept garden, as
for a folk song in the song books of the past.

All products of the primitive mind that are orally preserved and
are not written down are in a perpetual state of flux. The very conditions of their existence postulate change and growth. The collector of
folk songs, for instance, knows that it is only very rarely that two singers
will be found to sing the same song in precisely the same form. These
several forms are not corruptions in varying degree of one original.
They are the changes which, in the mass, engender growth and development. Nor are these different forms necessarily or widely distinct from
each other.

Moreover, although the variations are very numerous they will not
all be preserved. Manifestly, those alterations will alone survive which
commend themselves to other singers and narrators and are imitated
by them. Consequently, the folk tale or song, throughout its life history, will always be approaching a form which will accurately express
the taste and feeling of the community; what is purely personal will
be gradually but surely eliminated.

There is reason to believe that the primitive ballad was not only
communal in authorship but communal in performance also, and that
it was danced as well as sung. Some writers maintain that the game of
ball also formed an integral part of the performance, and derive from
the root *ball* the etymology of the words *ballet* and *ballad*. As time
went on, dance and song become divorced, each taking on a separate
and independent existence, and developing along its own lines. With
this separation the words *ballet* and *ballad* became differentiated, the

former being applied to the dance only, and the latter to the song. Curiously, the synonymous use of these two words still survives. The English peasant will often say that he has learned a particular song "off a ballet," meaning thereby a "ballad-sheet"; or, "Never had no ballet to it"—as a singer once said to me.*

Very soon after the separation of the song and the dance had taken place, the former became less communal in its performance. A "leader" of the ballad made his appearance, between whom and the crowd the performance was apportioned. As time went on, the part allotted to the multitude, which at first was of considerable importance, gradually diminished until it had dwindled down to the chanting of certain stereotyped phrases at regular intervals, the whole of the narrative portion being supported by the leader. Hence the solo and chorus —or refrain—with which we are all familiar. Nowadays, the crowd has been dispossessed altogether, and both narrative and chorus are sung by the soloist.†

Attention must be drawn to the conventional method of singing adopted by folk singers. During the performance the eyes are closed, the head upraised, and a rigid expression of countenance maintained until the song is finished. A short pause follows the conclusion, and then the singer relaxes his attitude and repeats in his ordinary voice the last line of the song, or its title. This is the invariable ritual on formal occasions. It does not proceed from any lack of appreciation. The English peasant is by nature a shy man and undemonstrative, and on ceremonious occasions, as when he is singing before an audience, he becomes very nervous and restrained, and welcomes the shelter afforded by convention. I have never seen women sing in this way; but then they never perform in public, and only very rarely when men are present. A man will sing naturally enough, and without any formality, by his own fireside. I have known him, on such occasions, to get quite excited when he is singing a song that moves him, and to rise from his chair and gesticulate and, perhaps, beat the table to enforce the rhythm of the tune. One old woman sang to me out in the open

---

* The traditional use of the word still persists in our own South. Aunt Molly Jackson, of Harlan, Kentucky, always speaks of singing a "ballet."—E. S.

† It is interesting to note that the disappearance of the "crowd"—*i.e.*, the communal performance of folk music—occurred not only in England, but also in most of western Europe, where agricultural work has become largely an individual affair. Wherever close community life still prevails—as in the Balkans, on plantations in our South, in Russia, and in Africa, not only is folk song communal and choral, but the connection between group singing and dancing is still strong.—E. S.

fields, where she was working, and between the verses of her song she seized the lapel of my coat and looked up into my face with glistening eyes to say, "Isn't it beautiful?"

Singers have often said to me, "When I were young I used to dance thicky zong, but I be too old now"—an interesting survival of the days before the sister arts of singing and dancing were divorced. "The Keys of Heaven" is a song that often used to be danced and sung with dramatic action by a man and his wife.

The repertoires of many of the old singers are very extensive. I have taken down as many as a hundred genuine folk songs from a single singer, and to recover as many as thirty or even forty is no unusual experience. These figures, moreover, must be doubled to arrive at the number of songs such singers really know; for, for every song that the collector will take from them, they know another that he does not want, either because he has already noted it down from someone else, or because it is not a folk song. Miss Lucy Broadwood writes of a Sussex singer, Mr. Henry Burstow: "He is proud of knowing four hundred songs, and keeps a valuable list of their titles, of which he allowed me to make a copy. He once, by request, sang all his songs to a gentleman; 'it took a month to do it!'."

The Folk Song and the Composer

Extracts from "National Music"

By Ralph Vaughan Williams

I WANT to discuss the importance of [folk music] to us, not as antiquarians or mere researchers but as musicians living in the twentieth century. Has it anything to say to us as creative artists? Well, I would suggest that, to say the least of it, it acts as a touchstone. In the folk song we find music which is unpremeditated and therefore of necessity sincere, music which has stood the test of time, music which must be representative of our race as no other music can.

This, then, or something like this is the foundation, it seems to me, on which all our art must rest, however far from it we spread and however high above it we build.

But what do we mean when we talk of building up a national art on the basis of folk song? I, for one, assure you that I do not imagine that one can make one's music national merely by introducing a few folk tunes into it. Beethoven did not become a Russian because he introduced two Russian folk songs, out of compliment to the Russian Ambassador, into his Rasumovsky Quartets. Nor does Delius become an Englishman because he happens to use an English folk tune introduced to him by his friend, Percy Grainger, as a canto fermo in one of his purely Nordic inspirations. So I am far from suggesting that anyone can make his music "national" by adding a few touches of local colour. Nevertheless I do hold that any school of national music must be fashioned on the basis of the raw material of its own national song.

The great masters of music have never hesitated to build on folk-song material when they wished to. Certain musical critics cannot get out of their heads that it is a source of weakness in a composer to use what they call "borrowed" material. I remember one writer saying unctuously that Bach never needed to borrow from folk song. He could have known very little about Bach. I think he was an organist, which may account for it. As you probably know, about three-quarters of Bach's work is built up on the popular hymn-tunes which he loved so well—in fact, "borrowed" material. Not all of these hymn-tunes are, of course, folk songs in the technical sense of the word, though many of them are adaptations from traditional melodies.

But let us start a little further back.

Through all the ecclesiastical music of the fifteenth and early sixteenth centuries runs the mysterious figure of *"L'Homme armé,"* a secular tune which it became the fashion to introduce as a canto fermo into masses and motets.

Now why did these early choral composers introduce this and other secular airs into their Masses? As I daresay you know, the thing became a scandal and was prohibited because the congregations, when they heard the sound of the tunes they knew proceeding from the choir, would join in singing, not the words of the Mass but the words proper to the tune, which were often, I believe, not for edification.

I think these old composers felt that they must keep in touch with real life, that they believed, unconsciously, that music which is vital must preserve the popular element. If we look down the ages this is true of all great music. Could anything be more "popular" than a fugue subject of the "Cum Sancto" in Bach's B minor Mass, or the opening of the Finale of Beethoven's C minor? When hearers complained to Beethoven that his later quartets did not please, he did not reply that he was the high priest of an esoteric cult or that art was for the few, but he said, "They will please one day."

To return to *"L'Homme armé."* The practice was discontinued by papal edict in the sixteenth century, but I think we can trace the influence in the "tuney" bits which Palestrina occasionally introduces into his motets and masses, when the metre of the words allows it, as at the "Osanna." A little later than Palestrina we find the Elizabethan Virginal composers doing much the same thing; and we owe our knowledge of such tunes as "Sellenger's Round," "Carman's Whistle," "John, Come Kiss Me Now," and dozens of others—in fact our whole knowledge of what was being sung in the streets of London in the reign of Elizabeth—to the fact that these Virginal composers introduced these songs into their compositions. Little they cared about "originality"—perhaps they felt, as we felt in modern England about twenty-five years ago, that these tunes must not remain unrecorded, that the fashionable English ladies who played on their virginals and were then, as now, apt to look with an exaggerated reverence on anything that came from overseas, would be all the better for a good honest English tune.

Do we find the folk-song influence in the classical period— Mozart, Beethoven, Schubert?

One would at first be inclined to say no. I hope I shall not be accused of inventing a paradox if I say that it is not noticeable because it is so very plain. If we look at a collection of German Volkslieder we are apt to be disappointed because the tunes look exactly like the simpler Mozart, Beethoven, and Schubert tunes. The truth, of course, is the other way about: the tunes of Mozart, Beethoven, and Schubert are so very much like Volkslieder.

We talk of the "classical tradition" and the "grand manner." This really means the German manner, because it so happened that the great classical period of music corresponded with the great line of German composers.

What we call the classical idiom is the Teutonic idiom, and it is absolutely as narrowly national as that of Grieg or Mussorgsky. But

there is one composer of the classical period whose case is different—
Joseph Haydn. Haydn's themes, indeed the whole layout of his work,
has really nothing in common, except purely superficially, with that
of Mozart, though they have the same technical background and show
some of the conventions of the polite music of the period. Sir Henry
Hadow in his interesting essay on Haydn's nationality, called "A
Croatian Composer," proves definitely, I think, that he was not a
Teuton, but a Slav of Croatian nationality.* It is a curious comment
on the strength of the German influence on all music that up till quite
lately, we habitually spoke not only of Haydn, but even of the Hungarian Liszt and of the Polish Chopin, as "German" composers.

That Haydn's musical ancestry is different from that of his German so-called compatriots is obvious in all his characteristic work. Of
course before he attained maturity he followed the lead of his teachers, and even in later life, in the enormous amount of his output, there
is a certain proportion of mere journeyman work, and it is noticeable
that in these the national characteristics are not so apparent. It is when
he is most himself that he owes most to the music of his own country.

Some explanation surely is required of all the irregular metres
and characteristic phrases which distinguish Haydn's music. They derive from nothing in the music of Emanuel Bach or any other of his
Teutonic forerunners. What is their ancestry? These themes and many
others are found to be nearly identical with certain Croatian folk tunes.

It goes without saying that Hadow has been accused of charging
Haydn with plagiarism. This is what he writes on the subject:

"No accusation could be more unfounded or more unreasonable. He
poached upon no man's preserve, he robbed no brother artist, he simply
ennobled these peasant tunes with the thought and expression of which he
was most nearly in accord. . . . No doubt he was not only the child of his
nation, he had his own personality, his own imaginative force, his own message to deliver in the ears of the world, but through all these the national
element runs as the determining thread. . . . No doubt there are other
factors; [besides nationality] the personal idiosyncrasy that separates a man
from his fellows and again the general principles, fewer perhaps than is
commonly supposed, that underlie all sense of rhythm and all appreciation

---

* Recent scholars—especially the Germans, of course—claim to have proved that
Haydn *was* after all of "pure Teutonic stock." However, it makes little difference which
theory is correct, because the important thing is not a composer's "race" but what kind
of music he wrote. And it is incontestable that Haydn, who spent his life in close contact with Czechs, Croats, Bohemians, was strongly influenced by Slavonic folk music,
and his art is as much "Slavonic" as German, if not more so.—E. S.

of style. But to say this is only to say that the artist is himself and that he belongs to our common humanity. In everything, from the conception of a poem to the structure of a sentence, the national element bears its part with the other two; it colours the personal temperament, it gives a standpoint from which principles of style are approached, and wherever its influence is faint or inconsiderable the work of the artist will be found to suffer in proportion. . . . It is wholly false to infer that music is independent of nationality. The composer bears the mark of his race not less surely than the poet or the painter, and there is no music with true blood in its veins and true passion in its heart that has not drawn inspiration from the breast of the mother country."

The debt of the Russian nationalist school of composers to their own folk song I need hardly dwell on—it meets us at every turn.

Chopin wrote national dances, the Mazurka and the Polonaise; Mussorgsky and Borodin frankly made use of folk songs. Grieg and Dvořák avowedly and Smetana less frankly imitated them. In each case they have made the so-called "borrowed" tunes their own.

In the eighteenth century an enterprising Scottish publisher commissioned Beethoven to harmonize some Scottish melodies. The result was curious and not satisfactory, but the strange thing is that the accompaniments added by the great master gave a decidedly German tinge to the tunes.

In the nineteenth century Brahms harmonized a collection of his own German Volkslieder—they sound exactly like Brahms, but here there is no misfit because the composer felt at home with his material.

I will not give you any more detailed examples, but I will try and tell you what I mean by the connection between the composer and the folk song of his country. Supreme art is not a solitary phenomenon; its great achievements are the crest of the wave; it is the crest which we delight to look on, but it is the driving force of the wave below that makes it possible. For every great composer there must be a background of dozens of smaller ones. Professor Dent has given us examples of a crowd of small practitioners in Vienna, who, so to speak, went to make up one Schubert.

There never has been and never will be a great artist who appeared as a "sport"; a supreme composer can only come out of a musical nation, and at the root of the musical quality of a nation lies the natural music whose simplest and clearest manifestation is the folk song.

Folk Music, Haydn, and Beethoven

Extracts from the article "The Relation of Folk Song to . . . Art Music . . ."
from "The Sackbut" for June 1921

By Béla Bartók

PEASANT music, in the strict sense of the word, must be regarded as a natural phenomenon. It is just as much a natural phenomenon, for instance, as the various manifestations of Nature in fauna and flora. Correspondingly it has, in its individual parts, an absolute artistic perfection—a perfection in miniature forms which, one might almost say, is equal to the perfection of a musical masterpiece of the largest proportions. It is the classical model of how to express an idea musically in the most concise form, with the greatest simplicity of means, with freshness and life, briefly yet completely and properly proportioned.

When I speak of the influence of peasant music, I do not mean a mere whitewash of it, as it were, or the mere adaptation of peasant melodies or snatches of melodies and their piecemeal incorporation in musical works, but rather the expression of the real spirit of the music of any particular people which is so hard to render in words. The manner in which the spirit is interpreted in the compositions is closely dependent upon the personality and musical talent of the particular composer, so that it is of little use for a blockhead or a man with no musical talent to run to "the people" in order to get inspiration for his thin ideas.

The practice of employing peasant music in the attempt to put life into works of art music is not entirely new. In fact, many symphonic themes (especially in last movements) of the Viennese classics— Haydn, Mozart, and Beethoven—suggest peasant music; in their cases it would seem to be a matter of Slavonic peasant instrumental music. In order to make some of these interesting cases known more widely in musical circles I will quote [some examples from] the collection.

The first melody is identical with the main theme of Haydn's D major Symphony (finale).

"Oj Jellena"   CROATIAN PEASANT SONG

Finale, London Symphony   JOSEPH HAYDN

The second and third melodies constitute the main theme of the first passage of the *Pastoral* Symphony. The theory that this was Beethoven's own theme and that it penetrated to the Croatian peasantry with the popularization of the symphony is quite untenable. The peasantry is capable of taking up only such melodies as it hears repeated to the point of satiety at village dances or other meetings. Nobody can imagine that Beethoven's symphonies achieved such widespread popularity in the villages of eastern Europe. One has only to consider that in the country districts of eastern Europe the very name of Beethoven is unknown even to the gentry—that these circles indeed lack the slightest acquaintance with the higher music of any period. It is much nearer the truth to say that Beethoven heard his melody from a bagpipe played in western Hungary, where Croats also are settlers and where he often stayed. Before strangers, peasants play on an instrument much more naturally than they sing melodies from a text. The tune appealed to Beethoven, and as it seemed to give a picture of rural life he used it in his symphony without acknowledgment—as was usual at the time. Bars 16 to 25, which constantly repeat the selfsame one-bar motif,

are in fact a very faithful imitation of the bagpipe interlude-passages as they can still be heard in our day. Thus, for instance, the interlude occurs as the eight- or tenfold repetition of the motif in a melody which I heard played on the bagpipes of a Hungarian peasant. My theory is strengthened by the bagpipe-like accompaniment of the theme.

The Past and Future of Folk Music

By Elie Siegmeister

THE foregoing essays have given a glimpse of a few of the many different kinds of folk music in the world. Perhaps most people will grant the attractiveness and beauty of this music and the "learned" works inspired by it. But still the question persists: "Is this not something remote and archaic? Is not folk music part of a dying way of life? Will it not inevitably disappear when civilization spreads to outlying regions? Then, except as a relic, what meaning can it have for us today and in the future?"

It is first of all necessary to realize that folk songs are more than music. They are, in the deepest sense, part of the life of the people—not an *added* part that could be dispensed with if need be, but a very basic and organic part of common life. To the peoples of a hundred nations, folk music is inseparable from almost every act of daily living; in each of them it has played a vital role. It has helped men to work, fight, pray, and make love. With it, mothers have sung their children to sleep, given their daughters away in marriage, celebrated the birth of infants, buried the dead.

Folk songs have been the lamentation of the people, their anger, their strength in a time of oppression, an instrument of aspiration, struggle, and bitter war. They tell us more about the heart of a nation than a hundred history books, for their language is simple, direct, and unmistakable. In every act of community life, music has had its role. It has lent dignity to ceremonies, recorded the legends and traditions of a people, brought men together in planting and harvesting, joy and catastrophe, prayer and struggle—in every moment of shared emotion and activity.

If it were possible to add up the history of all folk music, it would be a history of the race, for there is not an experience that the people have gone through that has not come out, in one way or another, in their songs. Folk music records the wars, struggles, migrations, Crusades, uprisings, pestilences, droughts, and famines; and also the people's hours of triumph and emancipation.

Not only are the words, melodies, stories, and dance steps inseparable in much folk music, but in many cases the songs and instrumental pieces cannot be detached from other acts of life of which they are a part. Cecil Sharp reports the exclamation of one Appalachian singer who could not remember a song: "Oh, if I were only driving the cows home it would come quickly enough!" Just a few weeks ago, when I asked a section hand in Alabama to repeat a "lining chant" I had heard him sing that morning, he had to take a shovel in his hand and go through the movements of "tamping" before the words and music would come. It is impossible to look at folk songs, therefore, as so many "charming," "delightful," or "picturesque" items. They are part of the breath and substance of all of us.

Undoubtedly, there is much in the people's music that mirrors the past. The lords and ladies that people the Kentucky ballads, the "conjure" words that occur in Creole and Haitian songs, the magic incantations still traceable in the melodies of Spain, Tunisia, and Brazil—all these recall an age that is irretrievably gone (for us in modern cities, that is,—not for many millions elsewhere on earth). Also, it is undoubtedly true that among certain "educated" nations—France, England, Belgium—and in most "educated" regions of our own land, folk music is now the exclusive property of specialists and professors at universities. The spreading of academic music study, the smattering of do-re-mi learned at school, the wide acceptance of the "genius" theory of music, have served to smother the natural creativeness present in the child and the untutored man.

Yet once we remove the barriers between music and the people, once we recognize the unbroken continuity between the common man's creation and that of the artist, there is no reason why the creative ability of the ordinary person cannot bloom again. That is why it is so important to rewrite the story of music to include folk as well as art music, and all the points of contact between the two. The world of music is one whole, with "folk" and "art" two essential, and often closely related, parts.

We must understand that the influence of folk on art music is not confined simply to the use of folk tunes in an extended composition. Far more important than this are the absorption by a composer of the folk style, and his own original creations based on the common language. Every folk singer is constantly reworking inherited material —why not the artist, too, who feels himself a continuator of the people's traditions? In his case, of course, we expect not a mere chewing of the old cud, but grander works, in which the folk style finds a broader extension and fulfillment.

In addition to the composers cited by Mr. Vaughan Williams and Mr. Bartók, there are a host of others who consciously or unconsciously stemmed from popular sources. Mozart's *Don Giovanni* and *The Magic Flute* contain more than one melody that was as "popular" in style as any other music of their time.

Beethoven did not disdain the absolutely simple and folklike either. Think of the theme of the Finale of the *Eroica*—originally conceived as a Contradanse; or the unadorned Volkslied pattern of the *Alle Menschen werden Brüder,* on which the magnificent choral movement of the Ninth is based:

One could cite almost innumerable compositions of Schubert, Weber, Chopin, Grieg, Tchaikovsky, Borodin, Rimsky-Korsakov,

Mahler, and Bizet solidly rooted in the folk spirit of their respective peoples. Compare Brahms's "Lullaby" (which has become virtually a folk song) with the second theme of his D major Symphony and you will find an identity of spirit as well as of mere notes. As a matter of fact, Brahms loved folk music intensely—German, Austrian, Hungarian—and utilized it in countless arrangements, settings, variations, and improvisations. It is not surprising that folk themes and folklike themes appear in his symphonies, sonatas, and chamber music.

Wagner, in some ways the most intellectual and self-conscious of composers, found himself when he turned to the study of the folk myths and traditions of his native Germany. All the subjects of his great music-dramas were drawn from folk lore, and much of the music has an unmistakable German folk spirit.

It would be hard to tell whether this is a "folk" or a "composed" song, did we not know it as the "Shepherd's Song" from the first act of *Tannhäuser.* Many of the *leitmotivs* of the *Ring* are distinctly folklike in character: think of Siegfried's horn call, for instance. Even in the ultra-subjective *Tristan,* the folk element intrudes itself in Kurwenal's mocking ballad in Act I.

But it was in his most perfect work, *Die Meistersinger,* that Wagner achieved the greatest exaltation of the native folk style. Germanic in every note, this drama is solidly rooted in the songs and dances, the chorales, waltzes, trade songs, street cries, and ballads of early Germany. *Die Meistersinger* represents not only a re-creation of the people's music, but a wonderfully imaginative extension of the spirit of folk life and folk poetry, equaled perhaps by only one other composer of the nineteenth century, the Russian, Mussorgsky.

Mussorgsky's melodies were so closely modeled on those of the Russian peasantry that it is sometimes almost impossible to tell where "folk" leaves off and "composer" begins. It is not only the technical similarity between the two that is striking, but also the profound penetration of Mussorgsky into the quality and "scent" of the people's music. The choruses from *Boris Godunov* seem more folklike than many folk songs themselves. Their communicative power was such that after the first performances of the work, it is said, crowds of students tramped the streets of St. Petersburg singing them. Mussorgsky felt himself one of the people; his music was a shoot from the common stock.

It is hardly necessary to give further examples of the interpenetration of folk and art traditions. Suffice it to say that in our own time, Stravinsky has based his finest works—*The Fire-Bird, Petroushka, Le Sacre,* and *Les Noces*—on the native music of his homeland; Falla, on the folk lore of Spain, Bartók on that of Hungary, and Bloch on Jewish traditional music. A host of American composers have been closely drawn to the music of our own common people.

Two tendencies appear today: the approach of art music to the folk, and the growth of folk music into art. It is certain that the age of "naive" folk music is drawing to a close with the spread of universal education, radio music, the contracting boundaries of the world. But folk music itself need not die out; in fact, it may take a new lease on life. It is not education in itself that is deadly to the folk spirit—it is *false* education.

With the spreading of a new attitude towards music, and of the idea that music is once more a part of common life, folk creation is coming up fresh and strong once more. In the songs of the European underground, of the guerrilla fighters of Yugoslavia and Norway; in the mighty battle songs of Russia and China; in the American war ballads and the blues of Leadbelly, Joshua White, Woody Guthrie, Aunt Molly Jackson, and many others, a new kind of folk music is being born. It is the folk music of those who can read and write, who have even been to concerts and heard the works of "learned" composers there as well as on the radio, but who still retain the idea that common folk have something to say in music even today.

Once we have begun to understand that the impulse behind folk and behind art music is one impulse expressing itself in two different forms, there is no reason why we cannot welcome and encourage the further development of both, side by side. In the true democracy we are working and fighting for, music must again become an essential part of community life, and the values of art and those of common living brought together once more as they have been in the great ages of the past.

PART TWO

How Music Is Made

II. How Music Is Made

THE making of music, like many other highly skilled professional occupations, often appears awesome and mysterious to the layman. Just as the doctor who diagnoses your case as "chronic idiopathic hypertension" is bound to make a much greater impression than the one who merely says you have high blood pressure, so the composer who describes his latest brain child as a "sonata in passacaglia form, in the Mixolydian mode, *allegro con fuoco,* followed by a crab canon in double counterpoint *andante* and a *basso ostinato* in ternary form, with the theme in augmentation and diminution" seems far more impressive than the fellow who simply says he's written a new piece.

Every profession has its own particular air of secrecy and wonder, but composing has retained this much longer than most others. Ever since prehistoric times when music was a part of magic rituals and the musician and magician were one and the same person, the tradition has remained that the act of composition is mysterious and uncanny. Like the primitive wizard or the prophets of old, the composer has been pictured as a highly keyed-up, unstable, unworldly person, likely to be seized by the divine fever at any moment and fall into a *raptus* or trance in which the outside world completely ceases to exist. When picture magazines do a feature story on the composer he is almost invariably shown working at midnight, his hair mussed up, collar askew, a whisky bottle or a big pot of black coffee on the piano, a slightly drugged look in his eye, and bits of scrawled, ink-blotted manuscripts littering the floor.

Now I hate to give away trade secrets (and I hope ASCAP will not blacklist me for this) but quite a number of composers I know are perfectly sane, hard-working, normal people who get up by an alarm-clock every morning, prefer soft drinks to hard, and keep their hair reasonably neat. Some are even married and remain in love with their own wives. Most of them hate to work at midnight and never wait for trance or ecstasy before beginning to compose. They work regular hours and just as much and as often as they get a chance. And they are, in my humble opinion, among the most distinguished creative talents in America today.

What is true of today's composers was probably equally true of most of the great musicians of the past. We know that many of them toiled and struggled, often sweated blood over their music. We have only to look at Beethoven's sketch-books to see how he chiseled and hammered away, wrote and rewrote most of his greatest compositions, before he got them right. Bach, asked what was the secret of his art, responded, "I have worked hard." There is no question that he and all the great masters labored constantly and with intense application— they had to, in order to get all that work done.

Even Wagner, whose autobiography tends to give the impression that his life was one endless series of adventures, intrigues, love affairs, and his music the product of the famous *raptus,* must have spent years and years sitting stock-still at his desk or piano. The sheer labor of setting down the hundreds of thousands—if not millions—of notes contained in the orchestral scores of the *Ring* alone is appalling, and could never have been achieved without the months and years of patient, systematic work old Richard put in.

Besides the capacity for hard work, of course, a man must have talent. Without it, years of drudgery and the most profound technical knowledge in the world can never produce one bar of real music. Musicians know the type of ambitious composer who fancies himself the modern Beethoven; he spends fourteen hours a day at his piano or desk, turns out three huge symphonic works and six intricately written string quartets every year—only it is all about as exciting as last month's newspaper, and we would willingly swap it all for one decent Tin Pan Alley tune.

But to get back to the question: How is music made? I have already mentioned the hard work and the talent. Besides that, there's an immense amount of skill involved. Perhaps this makes the whole process seem too formidable. Really it's not essentially mysterious or even unfamiliar in a way to the average person.

Have you ever felt exceptionally good when getting up in the morning and found yourself humming while taking a shower or shave? Or did you ever burst into a kind of spontaneous singing while walking down a country road on a lovely spring morning? Nine times out of ten you were probably humming or singing something you had heard somewhere—but the tenth time you may have been humming one of those fragmentary bits of melody that people often make up themselves quite unconsciously. My father, who was completely untrained in music, used to hum such meandering, wayward melodies with great zest while playing chess, and I knew he was laying a particularly nasty trap for me by the way his voice would spiral up into a jubilant, satisfied rhythm. Today I often hear my three-year-old daughter vocalising— passionately off-key!—while drawing pictures on our newly painted woodwork.

This sort of rhapsodic, spontaneous singing or humming is in essence the first step in all composing. It is basically the way most composers begin when they have to write a piece—except that instead of vocalising or humming, some play about with tones, rhythms, and pitches on a piano keyboard; and others, with mental images of these in their minds. In some cases, this habit of mental improvisation becomes so strong that a composer can indulge in it under the strangest circumstances. I have watched a very gifted composer friend of mine who works as editorial consultant in a Broadway publishing house carry on a business conversation, ask and answer questions, talk on the telephone—all the while working out musical passages in his mind and writing them into an orchestral score he had before him. I personally find the subway quite conducive to thinking up new ideas—the purring, rumbling noise furnishes a sort of neutral sound curtain against which melodies can stand out in bold relief. Shostakovich is said to be able to continue composing in a room full of people, with his children clambering on to his lap.

Let us admit then that the first step in composition is this more or less conscious sort of random improvising. What then? If almost anyone can do this, what is the distinctive mark of the composer? It is this: *shaping* the material thus discovered. The layman or amateur musician improvises as a rule quite aimlessly. One idea may follow another in quick succession, forming a series of more or less unconnected melodic fragments. This may be fun for the maker, but is generally deadly for anyone who may happen to be listening.

The composer, in addition to a given theme or mood, starts with a certain *plan* in mind. He knows by experience that a work of music, besides carrying charming, interesting, or stirring ideas (or themes), must be organized in such a way that these themes are set forth and driven home to full advantage. He does this by repeating, varying, alternating, contrasting, or combining the ideas with which he starts, in various skilful ways he may have picked up from previous composers or thought up himself. The planning and organization of a musical work, especially a large one, we call *form*. Knowledge of musical form, and the ability to handle it freely and naturally, are absolutely essential for any composer who wishes to write compositions more than three or four minutes long. Even with the greatest inborn gift and "inspiration" in the world, a composer cannot put together a long work unless he has developed this technique.

Three questions may still remain in the reader's mind: (1) How does the composer get from the idea he starts with to a large work? (2) What exactly are the materials he works with? (3) Why are there so many different musical forms—and what is the nature of each?

The first question is the subject of the essays "How the Composer Works" and "Putting a Composition Together." The second is discussed in "About Voices and Instruments," "Listener's ABC," and "Tempo Marks." And the third is taken up in the articles on the Fugue, Sonata, and various other musical forms.

But a word may be said here as to the reason for the variety of musical forms. It is the same as the reason why there are so many different languages, religions, modes of dress, etc., among the peoples of the earth. The music we hear today did not spring up all at once like a shooting star in the heavens or a new fashion in hats. It was a long time a-growing. In different ages and nations music catered to the tastes, customs, and ideas of many peoples. It served religion, labor, the dance, war, magic, love-making, and entertainment. Each of these activities demanded and produced a special kind of music, special rhythms, styles, and forms.

In the course of time, and with the continual interchange among various peoples, the many styles and forms were gathered into one great cultural heritage. Patterns, techniques, and mannerisms coming from many corners of the earth—from peasant dances, church services, and court minuets—all came together and entered into the general language of music, which we today interpret according to our own lights. It is fascinating to know about the many different forms and styles of music, where they came from, how they arose, and how they came to be used as we use them today.   —E. S.

How the Composer Works

The chapter "The Creative Process in Music" in "What to Listen for in Music"

By Aaron Copland

MOST people want to know how things are made. They frankly admit, however, that they feel completely at sea when it comes to understanding how a piece of music is made. Where a composer begins, how he manages to keep going—in fact, how and where he learns his trade—all are shrouded in impenetrable darkness. The composer, in short, is a man of mystery to most people, and the composer's workshop an unapproachable ivory tower.

One of the first things most people want to hear discussed in relation to composing is the question of inspiration. They find it difficult to believe that composers are not as preoccupied with that question as they had supposed. The layman always finds it hard to realize how natural it is for the composer to compose. He has a tendency to put himself into the position of the composer and to visualize the problems involved, including that of inspiration, from the perspective of the layman. He forgets that composing to a composer is like fulfilling a natural function. It is like eating or sleeping. It is something that the composer happens to have been born to do; and, because of that, it loses the character of a special virtue in the composer's eyes.

The composer, therefore, confronted with the question of inspiration, does not say to himself: "Do I feel inspired?" He says to himself: "Do I feel like composing today?" And if he feels like composing, he does. It is more or less like saying to yourself: "Do I feel sleepy?" If you feel sleepy, you go to sleep. If you don't feel sleepy, you stay up. If the composer doesn't feel like composing, he doesn't compose. It's as simple as that.*

Of course, after you have finished composing, you hope that everyone, including yourself, will recognize the thing you have written as having been inspired. But that is really an idea tacked on at the end.

---

* Sometimes, though, especially when you are working on a commission—as Mr. Copland frequently does—you *must* compose, to meet a deadline, whether you feel like it or not. I have written some of my best things when under this sort of pressure, and I suspect that Mr. Copland also has.   —E. S.

Someone once asked me, in a public forum, whether I waited for inspiration. My answer was: "Every day!" But that does not, by any means, imply a passive waiting around for the divine afflatus. This is exactly what distinguishes the professional from the dilettante. The professional composer can sit down day after day and turn out some kind of music. On some days it will undoubtedly be better than on others; but the primary fact is the ability to compose. Inspiration is often only a by-product.

The second question that most people find intriguing is generally worded thus: "Do you or don't you write your music at the piano?" A current idea exists that there is something shameful about writing a piece of music at the piano. Along with that goes a mental picture of Beethoven composing out in the fields. Think about it a moment and you will realize that writing away from the piano nowadays is not nearly so simple a matter as it was in Mozart or Beethoven's day. For one thing, harmony is so much more complex than it was then. Few composers are capable of writing down entire compositions without at least a passing reference to the piano. In fact, Stravinsky in his *Autobiography* has even gone so far as to say that it is a bad thing to write music away from the piano because the composer should always be in contact with *la matière sonore.* That's a violent taking of the opposite side. But, in the end, the way in which a composer writes is a personal matter. The method is unimportant. It is the result that counts.

The really important question is: "What does the composer start with? Where does he begin?" The answer to that is, Every composer begins with a musical idea *—a *musical* idea, you understand, not a mental, literary, or extramusical idea. Suddenly a theme comes to him. (Theme is used as synonymous with musical idea.) The composer starts with this theme; and the theme is a gift from Heaven. He doesn't know where it comes from—has no control over it. It comes almost like automatic writing. That's why he keeps a book very often and writes themes down whenever they come. He collects musical ideas. You can't do anything about that element of composing.

The idea itself may come in various forms. It may come as a melody—just a one-line simple melody which you might hum to yourself. Or it may come to the composer as a melody with an accompani-

---

* This is too sweeping a statement. Some composers—particularly writers of opera, ballet, religious, theater, and movie music—certainly start with a mood, an image, a story, or an idea, and evolve the *musical* idea only later.—E. S.

ment. At times he may not even hear a melody; he may simply conceive an accompanimental figure to which a melody will probably be added later. Or, on the other hand, the theme may take the form of a purely rhythmic idea. He hears a particular kind of drumbeat, and that will be enough to start him off. Over it he will soon begin hearing an accompaniment and melody. The original conception, however, was a mere rhythm. Or a different type of composer may possibly begin with a contrapuntal web of two or three melodies which are heard at the same instant. That, however, is a less usual species of thematic inspiration.

All these are different ways in which the musical idea may present itself to the composer.

Now, the composer has the idea. He has a number of them in his book, and he examines them in more or less the way that you, the listener, would examine them if you looked at them. He wants to know what he has. He examines the musical line for its purely formal beauty. He likes to see the way it rises and falls, as if it were a drawn line instead of a musical one. He may even try to retouch it, just as you might in drawing a line, so that the rise and fall of the melodic contour might be improved.

But he also wants to know the emotional significance of his theme. If all music has expressive value, then the composer must become conscious of the expressive values of his theme. He may be unable to put it into so many words, but he feels it! He instinctively knows whether he has a gay or a sad theme, a noble or diabolic one. Sometimes he may be mystified himself as to its exact quality. But sooner or later he will probably instinctively decide what the emotional nature of his theme is, because that's the thing he is about to work with.

Always remember that a theme is, after all, only a succession of notes. Merely by changing the dynamics—that is, by playing it loudly and bravely or softly and timidly—one can transform the emotional feeling of the very same succession of notes. By a change of harmony a new poignancy may be given the theme; or by a different rhythmic treatment the same notes may result in a war dance instead of a lullaby. Every composer keeps in mind the possible metamorphoses of his succession of notes. First he tries to find its essential nature, and then he tries to find what might be done with it—how that essential nature may momentarily be changed.

As a matter of fact, the experience of most composers has been that the more complete a theme is, the less possibility there is of seeing it in various aspects. If the theme itself, in its original form, is long enough and complete enough, the composer may have difficulty in seeing it in any other way. It already exists in its definitive form. That is why great music can be written on themes that in themselves are insignificant. One might very well say that the less complete, the less important, the theme the more likely it is to be open to new connotations. Some of Bach's greatest organ fugues are constructed on themes that are comparatively uninteresting in themselves.

The current notion that all music is beautiful according to whether the theme is beautiful or not doesn't hold true in many cases. Certainly the composer does not judge his theme by that criterion alone.

Having looked at his thematic material, the composer must now decide what sound medium will best fit it. Is it a theme that belongs in a symphony, or does it seem more intimate in character and therefore better fitted for a string quartet? Is it a lyrical theme that would be used to best advantage in a song; or had it better be saved, because of its dramatic quality, for operatic treatment? A composer sometimes has a work half finished before he understands the medium for which it is best fitted.

Thus far I have been presupposing an abstract composer before an abstract theme. But actually I can see three different types of composers in musical history, each of whom conceives music in a somewhat different fashion.

The type that has fired public imagination most is that of the spontaneously inspired composer—the Franz Schubert type, in other words. All composers are inspired, of course, but this type is more spontaneously inspired. Music simply wells out of him. He can't get it down on paper fast enough. You can almost always tell this type of composer by his prolific output. In certain months, Schubert wrote a song a day. Hugo Wolf did the same.

In a sense, men of this kind begin not so much with a musical theme as with a completed composition. They invariably work best in the shorter forms. It is much easier to improvise a song than it is to improvise a symphony. It isn't easy to be inspired in that spontaneous way for long periods at a stretch. Even Schubert was more successful in handling the shorter forms of music. The spontaneously inspired man is only one type of composer, with his own limitations.

Beethoven symbolizes the second type—the constructive type, one might call it. This type exemplifies my theory of the creative process in music better than any other, because in this case the composer really does begin with a musical theme. In Beethoven's case there is no doubt about it, for we have the notebooks in which he put the themes down. We can see from his notebooks how he worked over his themes—how he would not let them be until they were as perfect as he could make them. Beethoven was not a spontaneously inspired composer in the Schubert sense at all. He was the type that begins with a theme; makes it a germinal idea; and upon that constructs a musical work, day after day, in painstaking fashion. Most composers since Beethoven's day belong to this second type.

The third type of creator I can only call, for lack of a better name, the traditionalist type. Men like Palestrina and Bach belong in this category. They both exemplify the kind of composer who is born in a particular period of musical history, when a certain musical style is about to reach its fullest development. It is a question at such a time of creating music in a well-known and accepted style and doing it in a way that is better than anyone has done it before you.

Beethoven and Schubert started from a different premise. They both had serious pretensions to originality! After all, Schubert practically created the song form singlehanded; and the whole face of music changed after Beethoven lived. But Bach and Palestrina simply improved on what had gone before them.

The traditionalist type of composer begins with a pattern rather than with a theme. The creative act with Palestrina is not the thematic conception so much as the personal treatment of a well-established pattern. And even Bach, who conceived forty-eight of the most varied and inspired themes in his *Well-Tempered Clavichord,* knew in advance the general formal mold that they were to fill. It goes without saying that we are not living in a traditionalist period nowadays.

One might add, for the sake of completeness, a fourth type of composer—the pioneer type: men like Gesualdo in the seventeenth century, Mussorgsky and Berlioz in the nineteenth, Debussy and Edgar Varèse in the twentieth. It is difficult to summarize the composing methods of so variegated a group. One can safely say that their approach to composition is the opposite of the traditionalist type. They clearly oppose conventional solutions of musical problems. In many ways, their attitude is experimental—they seek to add new harmonies, new sonorities, new formal principles. The pioneer type was the characteristic one at the turn of the seventeenth century and also at the beginning of the twentieth century, but it is much less evident today.

But let's return to our theoretical composer. We have him with his idea—his musical idea—with some conception of its expressive nature, with a sense of what can be done with it, and with a preconceived notion of what medium is best fitted for it. Still he hasn't a piece. A musical idea is not the same as a piece of music. It only induces a piece of music. The composer knows very well that something else is needed in order to create the finished composition.

He tries, first of all, to find other ideas that seem to go with the original one. They may be ideas of a similar character, or they may be contrasting ones. These additional ideas will probably not be so important as the one that came first—usually they play a subsidiary role. Yet they definitely seem necessary in order to complete the first one. Still that's not enough! Some way must be found for getting from one idea to the next, and it is generally achieved through use of so-called bridge material.

There are also two other important ways in which the composer can add to his original material. One is the elongation process. Often the composer finds that a particular theme needs elongating so that its character may be more clearly defined. Wagner was a master at elongation. I referred to the other way when I visualized the composer's examining the possible metamorphoses of his theme. That is the much-written-about development of his material, which is a very important part of his job.

All these things are necessary for the creation of a full-sized piece —the germinal idea, the addition of other lesser ideas, the elongation of the ideas, the bridge material for the connection of the ideas, and their full development.

Now comes the most difficult task of all—the welding together of all that material so that it makes a coherent whole. In the finished product, everything must be in its place. The listener must be able to find his way around in the piece. There should be no possible chance of his confusing the principal theme with the bridge material, or vice versa. The composition must have a beginning, a middle, and an end; and it is up to the composer to see to it that the listener always has some sense of where he is in relation to beginning, middle, and end. Moreover, the whole thing should be managed artfully so that none can say where the soldering began—where the composer's spontaneous invention left off and the hard work began.

Of course, I do not mean to suggest that in putting his materials together the composer necessarily begins from scratch. On the contrary, every well-trained composer has, as his stock in trade, certain normal structural molds on which to lean for the basic framework of his compositions. These formal molds have all been gradually evolved over hundreds of years as the combined efforts of numberless composers seeking a way to ensure the coherence of their compositions. What these forms are and exactly in what manner the composer depends on them will materialize later.

But whatever the form the composer chooses to adopt, there is always one great desideratum: The form must have what in my student days we used to call *la grande ligne* (the long line). It is difficult adequately to explain the meaning of that phrase to the layman. To be properly understood in relation to a piece of music, it must be felt. In mere words, it simply means that every good piece of music must give us a sense of flow—a sense of continuity from first note to last. Every elementary music student knows the principle, but to put it into practice has challenged the greatest minds in music! A great symphony is a man-made Mississippi down which we irresistibly float from the instant of our leave-taking to a long-foreseen destination. Music must always flow, for that is part of its very essence, but the creation of that continuity and flow—that long line—constitutes the be-all and end-all of every composer's existence.

Putting a Composition Together

Abridged from the chapter "Design in Music" in "The Listener's Guide to Music"

By Percy Scholes

CONSIDER yourself a composer, with the wish to bring into the world a piece of some length—say five minutes or fifty. You are fortunate in that a kind heaven has sent you a happy initial idea, a little tune which you feel to be expressive of something deeply felt within you. Such a tune lasts, perhaps, half a minute (few tunes in themselves last much longer). You write it down, gloat over it with artistic pride, and then say—What next?

Perhaps you decide that the half-minute tune is so good that you will repeat it. You now have a minute-long piece. You can stop there if you like, but it does not seem a very satisfactory thing to do. Then shall you make up your five-minute "Song without Words" by ten

repetitions of that tiny tune, or your fifty-minute Symphony by one
hundred such repetitions? Heaven (which sent you the tune) forbid!
No audience would stand it. The best of tunes will outstay its welcome
when thus persistent. Such vain repetitions are only permitted in church,
where the congregation is so devoutly absorbed in the words of its
hymns and psalms that the recurrence of the same tune for many verses
passes unnoticed, or amongst the country-folk who so lose themselves
in the tale the ballad singer tells that his tune becomes to them its mere
vehicle. And you are writing not for church, nor for the bar-parlour of
the village inn, but for the Queen's Hall. Mere repetition, then, will
not work. You must try another dodge.

This time you put your heaven-sent tune on paper and then wait
for heaven to send down another. In an hour or two, or in a few days,
it comes—and on to the paper it goes. One and a half or two minutes
of your five or your fifty minutes is now provided for. You wait for
a third tune, and a fourth and a fifth, and, when they come to you, you
add them. At this point it seems wise to try the piece on some friend
—or enemy. You find it does not "go down." There are two reasons
for this. Firstly, there is a certain expenditure of nervous force in
enjoying a new tune, and a succession of five different new tunes,
straight off the reel, makes too great a call on that nervous force. Secondly, when the thing is done, it sounds not like one thing, but like
five. Devise four nice little connecting passages to join up the five tunes
and, though improved, still it does not sound a whole.

Your experiments have shown you the truth of the matter. The
first one proved to you the necessity of *variety*, the second the necessity of *unity*. You think it all over, and sleep on it before deciding
what to do next. It comes to you in a flash when you wake up next
morning. Happy thought! You now take your first tune, follow it with
your second and *return* to your first. It works! You have hit on the very
form of a Mozart Minuet and that in which ninety per cent. of the
minuets, short songs, "Songs without Words," Nocturnes, Dances, and
similar delicious trifles are composed. The mind after hearing the first
tune (which we will call I) is ready for a change and welcomes the
second (which we will call II). After that it does not want further
change for the moment, but is ready to welcome again its old friend I.*

You now take three of your tunes, which we will call respectively,
I, II, and III, and arrange them as follows:

I II I III I.

* This pattern is known as Three-part Form, or ABA.—E. S.

That, too, you find, is acceptable. You extend this and get:

$$\overbrace{\text{I}\ \ \text{II}}\ \text{I}\ \ \ \text{III}\ \ \overbrace{\text{I}\ \ \text{II}}\ \text{I}.$$

Then you have discovered the very plan of a Beethoven Rondo!

All you need now is to remove any crudities due to your lack of experience in composition. You feel a little dissatisfied still and appeal to a musical friend, who tells you that the feeling of sameness that still remains is due to your three tunes all being in what he calls "the same key." Or he points out that they are too similar in "rhythm." Or he says that they are too far removed in "key" or in rhythm, and so forth. But you have at least grasped the right *principle*—Variety and Unity, diversity of material relieved by repetition of material. Your plan will still not reach to the fifty minutes allotted, but you are *on the way* to discover how to write a fifty-minute piece. Having found the principle of the Minuet and the Rondo you have found the principle of all European and American music.

Listener's ABC

Adapted from the chapter "Some Simple Necessary Terms Explained" in "The Listener's Guide to Music"

By Percy Scholes

IT IS impossible to explain musical form without the use of the names of notes, the names of keys, and the names of "times."

NOTES

The sounds of nature range from "low" to "high" (to use purely conventional terms), proceeding by a mere smooth incline (to follow out the idea of those conventional terms). When a dog howls, a cat mews, or a cow moos, it is merely using a section of that incline, beginning at the lowest point of which its vocal cords are capable and proceeding to the highest, or vice versa. Birds do not glide like cats, they hop: their song, too, as it happens, proceeds not by a smooth movement but from point to point in the "incline" of sounds. In other words, birds use notes—and so do humans, birds and humans being the only two truly musical families of the world's creatures.

SCALES AND KEYS

A bird inherits a little combination of notes from its ancestors and contents itself with repeating this over and over again as long as it lives. Man invents new combinations in infinite variety; consequently man needs a working system. He fixes on a certain series of notes with a definite relation to each other and makes his tunes out of these. Such a series is called a scale. A scale is simply the regiment of the notes used in a human tune, drawn up on parade, and made to number off.

It is found, as an acoustical fact, that any given note recurs at higher and lower pitches (of which the upper is said to be an octave above the lower), so that the whole long staircase of notes is divided into a number of short flights of stairs, and these become the scale-units of music.

In normal European and American music each of these scale-units is divided into twelve equal parts,* of which seven † are chosen for chief service, the others being called on as auxiliaries. These seven may be chosen out of the twelve according to two systems. The one system produces what we call the major scale, the other the minor scale.

The twelve notes are divided from each other by intervals called "semitones"; two semitones make a tone. On the piano keyboard any two adjacent notes are a semitone apart; any two notes next-but-one to each other are a tone apart (whether white or black has nothing to do with it; there is no social distinction of colour—all enjoy equal rights of citizenship).

The major scale can be begun from any of the twelve notes by proceeding upwards as follows (I = tone; ½ = semitone):

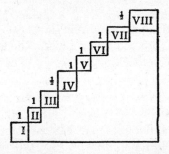

---

* Many of the statements in this essay are practical rather than scientifically exact.
† Eight, instead of seven, if the main note be included both at top and bottom—hence the term Octave.

The minor scale can be begun by proceeding upwards as follows:

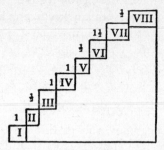

[The arrangement of the notes VI and VII is sometimes varied slightly.]

The essential difference between the major and the minor scales is that in the lower part of the major scale the semitone occurs between III and IV, and in the lower part of the minor scale between II and III. Play a few scales major and minor, beginning on any note of the pianoforte and proceeding according to the diagrams just given, and the great difference of effect will be realized.

For convenience letter-names are given to the white notes of the piano as follows: A, B, C, D, E, F, G. The note next above any of these white notes is called its sharp, the one next below, its flat. A glance at the piano will show that on the keyboard sharps and flats generally fall on black notes, but that in two or three cases they fall on white notes, which white notes have thus not only their own proper names but also an additional name acquired from another note. (This is simple enough: you may speak of a man as Tom Brown, or you may speak of him as Bill Jones's neighbour.)

The object of our explanation so far has been to enable a reader who did not know a fact about our tonal system when he began this article to understand in future what is meant by such terms as "C major" or "D minor," "G sharp minor" or "B flat major." A piece "in" the key of C major is one of which the main prevailing choice of notes is made by the use of those found in the major scale beginning on the note C, and so forth.

Hardly any piece, however tiny, stays in one key. Even an Anglican chant to which the psalms are sung in church, with its mere ten notes, generally moves to another key about half-way through—that is to say, some flat or sharp is introduced in place of one of the original notes, and thus the key is altered. Such an alteration we call a modulation.

A modulation, or a series of modulations is, however extended, merely an incident; the piece returns before its end to the key in which it started—which is felt to be *the* key of the piece.

A piece may modulate from any key to any key, but there are certain close relationships of key within which it is easier and apparently more natural to modulate. Thus we speak of "related keys," and in a quite short piece it is likely that all modulations which occur will be to keys closely related to the main key of the piece.

RHYTHM AND TIME

The whole universe moves in rhythm, suns revolve and seasons change, tides rise and fall, flowers appear and die, hearts beat and horses trot according to a periodic system which we call by that name. Poems are written and declaimed (or ought to be declaimed) in rhythms. Regular beats or pulses and recurring accents can be felt in a line of poetry, and these occur also in music. These accents divide the line of poetry or phrase of music into rhythmic units. In both poetry and music there are felt to be either two beats or three beats, as the case may be, to each unit. If a phrase of music seems to have four beats to a unit these will be found to be really two units of two beats each, making together the larger group of four. Similarly, six beats fall into two sets of three, or three sets of two, and twelve beats into four sets of three.

The reader is now in a position to understand the "time-signatures" he sometimes sees quoted in concert programmes. The indication of 3/4 means that there are three beats to a unit, or measure,* 2/2 has two beats, 6/8 has two sets of three beats, and so forth.

Within each unit (or measure) there may be, and generally are, smaller combinations—groups of half-beat notes or quarter-beat notes, two-beat notes, three-beat notes, one-and-a-half-beat notes, etc. There is thus possible an infinite variety of long and short notes and combinations of such, but underlying these shifting note-rhythms the regular rhythmic pulsation of the beats and measures can be felt.

Another part of the rhythmic system of music is the use of "phrases" or "sentences." In addition to its shifting rhythms of short notes and long ones, and its regular rhythms of beats and measures, any tune you may hear will be found to fall into equal or fairly equal lengths of (say) two or four measures apiece. Thus, *America* † has the

---

* The author here and later uses the British term *bar,* for which I have substituted the American term *measure.*—E.S.

† The reader should here be notified that the original passage here dealt with *God*

time-signature of 3/2, *i.e.,* its measure-rhythm consists of groups of three beats each. But its measures also fall into groups as follows:

<table>
<tr><td>3 phrases making one sentence</td><td>{</td><td>My country, 'tis of thee,
(2 measures)
Sweet land of liberty,
(2 measures)
Of thee I sing!
(2 measures)</td></tr>
<tr><td>4 phrases making another sentence</td><td>{</td><td>Land where my fathers died,
(2 measures)
Land of the Pilgrims' pride,
(2 measures)
From ev'ry mountain-side
(2 measures)
Let Freedom ring!
(2 measures)</td></tr>
</table>

The reader is now in a position to understand the words *beat, measure, phrase,* and *sentence* when he meets them in annotated concert programmes.

MELODY, HARMONY, AND COUNTERPOINT

The poet and the plain man often use the words "melody" and "harmony" interchangeably. By either they mean merely pleasant sound.

Technically used, as in a concert programme, the words have distinct meanings, melody being a simple string of notes such as you could whistle or sing by yourself, and harmony a combination of notes such as you could play with your hands on the piano. A handful of notes, whether sung by a choir or played by instruments, is called a "chord." When you sing *America* you are uttering melody; if you sit down and accompany yourself by "chords" on the piano you are also producing "harmony." Despite the poets, neither melody nor harmony necessarily connotes anything pleasant—in fact poor melody and bad harmony are very common. Moreover, new styles of melody and harmony are constantly being introduced to which many people object very much until they get used to them.

"Counterpoint" is simply a combination of melodies. A com-

Save the King—the author being a Briton. Since, however, American readers are more familiar with *America* (which uses the same tune), it has been thought advisable to "translate" the passage into American.—E. S.

poser might take *America,* leaving the existing tune for you to sing as before, but fit with it two or three other tuneful parts for two or three other voices to sing at the same time. You would then be singing your old "melody," each of the other voices would have its melody, and the whole would be a piece of counterpoint; and, further, since the voices sounding together would produce a series of chords, there would be "harmony."

It may be well to call attention to the adjective from "counterpoint," frequently used. It is *contrapuntal.** *America* as sung by one person is "melodic"; as usually sung by a choir, or accompanied at the piano, it is *also* "harmonic"; as just arranged in imagination in the last paragraph it is, *further,* "contrapuntal."

OPUS NUMBERS

The word *opus* will be found occasionally in this book, and frequently in concert programmes (often reduced to "Op."). Modern composers of the serious sort generally number their works as they produce them "Op. 1," "Op. 2," etc. Frequently several pieces are brought into one opus, and they are then numbered Op. I, No. 1; Op. I, No. 2, etc. It is always worth while to notice an opus number, as it gives an idea whether the work represents its composer's early tentative stages or his maturity. In hearing an Op. 5, for instance, you must generally be a little indulgent. On the other hand, an Op. 50 or Op. 100 has no claim on your charity, and must be content to bear your fiercest criticism.

The use of opus numbers is associated by the general public with the performance of what it calls "classical" music, since the more commonplace compositions are rarely numbered by their makers. On the day this essay was written the author overheard in the train a conversation illustrating this fact. Two men were arranging together the holding of a suburban concert, and the guiding principle of the construction of the programme was laid down in these words: "No classical music, all good popular stuff—*none of them ops!"*

* Another word for *contrapuntal* is *polyphonic*—meaning "many-voiced."—E. S.

About Voices and Instruments

Adapted from "Approach to Music"

By Lawrence Abbott

IF MUSIC existed only in the mind's ear—in the form of notes, representing tones of various pitches, which our imaginations could reconstruct and enjoy without having to hear them performed—this essay would go unwritten. But music doesn't exist that way. It has to be either sung or played. Although trained musicians can sit in silence before a printed score and enjoy the flow of melodies and the sounds of harmonies with as much relish as if the four walls were re-echoing to the sound of the music, their enjoyment is not one of creation but of re-creation, of imaginative retrospect. For such persons the printed music recalls intervals, progressions, and dissonances which at past times have invaded their eardrums. Had it not been for those previous occasions the notes would convey no sensation at all—any more than we could recall with pleasure the flavor of a maple walnut sundae if we had never in our lives tasted maple syrup or walnuts.

The very fact that music has to be sung or played opens up a new source of pleasure in our measure-by-measure listening—a sensuous enjoyment of the quality of the tones themselves. Middle C played successively by a violin, English horn, trombone, and xylophone has four different sounds which are easily distinguishable. In all four cases the pitch is identical: 261.6 cycles per second. The difference lies in what might be called tonal texture or tone color. The French have a word for it: *timbre*.

Back in ancient times, when primitive people first started to sing and to fashion crude instruments from hunter's bows and animal horns, they instinctively groped towards ways of achieving new beauty and variety of tone in the music they made. Down through the ages they have continued to do this, constantly developing and perfecting new instruments, and at the same time developing and perfecting their own ability to make agreeable musical sounds in their throats. Today, as a result, we have a bewildering array of machines and gadgets for making music and a whole army of men and women who have trained themselves to bellow with terrific intensity without producing sounds so disagreeable as to cause musical audiences to flee—which would happen if you or I tried to make as much noise as that.

During the next few pages we shall survey briefly the field of musical instruments, both animate and inanimate. This survey will be a modern bird's-eye view, not a historical discussion, for it would be more confusing than enlightening to burden you with descriptions of primitive, obsolete instruments which we meet today only in museums, as battered and silent relics of the past.

VOICES

The simplest and, in some ways, the most fundamental of all instruments is the human voice. Since Nature has endowed men and women with different altitudes of pitch—the two sexes sing roughly an octave apart—voices are divided first of all into men's and women's. In each division we find high, medium, and low voices: among women, sopranos, mezzo-sopranos, and contraltos (or, to use the abbreviated form, altos); among men, tenors, baritones, and basses. The word "bass" has the same meaning as "base" or "bottom," for it refers in general to the lowest part in any musical composition, and can be applied to abstract music or to the deepest notes on a piano or to instruments of low compass, as well as to bass voices. Either for this reason, or else to sound more erudite, musicians sometimes use the Italian word _basso_ when referring to the lowest of voices.

In four-part choral music only the four chief vocal divisions are listed: soprano, alto, tenor, and bass. Singers with medium-pitched voices have to cast their lot with whichever part takes them least out of their own natural range. Even in music for women's voices alone the term mezzo-soprano doesn't usually appear, the four parts being labeled first soprano, second soprano, first alto, and second alto. Men's choruses and glee clubs, similarly, are divided into first and second tenors, and first and second basses. It is in solo work, in the recital hall and on the operatic stage, that mezzo-sopranos and baritones are permitted to shine under their own colors. In this field altos also stand more on their dignity, and are invariably called contraltos. Some singers whose voices are pitched a little lower than the usual baritone range term themselves bass-baritones.

The highest voices—sopranos and tenors—occupy the most coveted positions in vocaldom. Their brilliant upper tones are more easily capable of "bringing down the house" than the less sensational tones of equally gifted but lower-voiced singers. As a result they always receive the leading roles in operas, leaving to the contraltos and baritones the less inspiring parts of servants, villains, and dullards. The results are not always esthetically satisfying—as, for instance, in Verdi's musical setting of Shakespeare's *Othello,* in which the Moor declaims in a high penetrating voice while crafty Iago booms out as a resonant baritone. But this is the public's fault, not the composer's. Opera audiences have always demanded it that way, and few composers have had the courage to throw operatic convention overboard.* Perhaps if our present crop of attractive contraltos and handsome baritones grows larger, and if our audiences come to indicate a preference for artistry over display, we may yet attend operas featuring deep-voiced heroes and shrill villainesses.

Within each range of pitch, voices may be found that differ from each other in quality and style. Among sopranos three types deserve our notice: the coloratura soprano, whose voice is light, agile, and capable of ascending to great heights, where it can dazzle audiences with flute-like runs, trills, and other kinds of ornamental passages; the dramatic soprano, powerful and resonant, ideally suited for singing Wagnerian roles above the surging accompaniment of a hundred-piece orchestra; and the lyric soprano, whose clear, sweet tone quality is better suited to sustained, songlike melodies, such as are found in the French and Italian operas. Among tenors there are likewise the dramatic tenor, sometimes called robust or heroic tenor, and the lighter and more flexible voice known as lyric tenor. And there are two types of bass voice: the *basso cantante,* which means a "singing" or lyric bass; and the *basso profundo,* noted for its depth of pitch.

Because they are human, voices radiate a personal warmth and intensity of feeling which cannot be duplicated by any man-made instrument. And they have another advantage in that they can sing words as well as tones, thus being able to stir us doubly—through poetic thoughts linked with expressive music. But in several other ways voices are inferior. They have not the capacity for accuracy or nicety of tone which other instruments have; we tolerate a singer's being off key to a far greater degree than we would a violinist's deviation from true pitch. They cover only a limited range, compared with a piano, organ, or symphony orchestra. They are far from agile; rapid runs and skips, which any piano student can play with ease, are next to impossible for

---

* Mozart did. The roles of both Don Giovanni and Figaro—his greatest heroes—were written for baritone.—E. S.

even the best singers, and when accomplished by a virtuoso coloratura soprano arouse audiences to incredulous oh's and ah's. It might be mentioned also that voices are subject to catarrhal complaints and other forms of "indispositions" to which inanimate objects are not subject. For these reasons, as well as for the additional one of providing variety, man-made instruments are a boon.

INSTRUMENTS

Roughly speaking, there are only three possible ways of producing musical sounds without the aid of the human voice. To illustrate, let us imagine that we are at home, without a musical instrument in the house, and afflicted with such a sore throat that we cannot sing, yet are obsessed with a desire to make musical sounds. What to do about it? We must resort to crude, primitive devices—as we would if asked to start a fire without matches. First, we might find a ball of strong twine, tie one end to the arm of a chair, and stretch the twine to the other arm. Then, by wrapping it several times around the arm and pulling with all our strength, we might make the twine taut enough so that when we tapped it with a pencil or plucked it with our finger it would give out a definite musical tone. After that good start we might hunt in the kitchen for other tone-producing devices. Let us imagine that we find an empty ginger-ale bottle and blow across the top of it. A musical tone! Experimenting further, we might take down a skillet from its hook and hit it with a spoon. If it is solid cast iron or aluminum it will give out a clear, resounding tone. If not, we could try the spoon on other pieces of kitchenware—a Pyrex baking dish, or a drinking glass—until we found one (which we eventually would) with a clear, bell-like tone. In this way we could demonstrate each of the three different ways of creating musical sounds: (1) making a string vibrate, (2) making a column of air vibrate inside a pipe or tube, and (3) making a solid object vibrate. This sounds simple enough. And it is. Even in practice, instruments fall naturally into these three classifications. The two dozen or so different kinds of instruments in a symphony orchestra are arranged on the concert platform as three separate sections: (1) stringed instruments, (2) wind instruments, and (3) percussion instruments. The members of the last-named group are sometimes spoken of as the battery. Neither term refers to the kind of material which is made to vibrate, but rather to the way the instruments are played—the percussion instruments in all cases being hammered instead of being plucked, bowed, or blown *—but it happens that these instruments are also alike in the other respect. In every case the vibrating material is an object, either solid or hollow, and not a string or a column of air inside a tube.

THE PIANO

The most universal of instruments is the piano. The reason why it occupies this position is easy enough to discover. Most instruments, like voices, can play only one melody at a time and are unable to sound the simultaneous tones of a chord. A flute player, or trumpeter, or violinist, cannot produce satisfying performances of music by himself; he needs at least a couple of other fellows who will join with him to produce the necessary harmonies. A pianist, on the other hand, can play tunes, chords, and contrapuntal passages with ease. Most professional violinists, 'cellists, flutists, and other instrumentalists know how to play the piano, for they find it invaluable to be able to perform music single-handed at times. The piano is, of course, *the* instrument for composers since it can reproduce the tones of choral compositions, string quartets, and other instrumental combinations, leaving nothing to the composer's imagination but the instrumental coloring—which, of course, a piano cannot duplicate.

For the same reason the piano is also *the* instrument of the home. In Victorian days no well-dressed parlor was complete without its ornate upright and its inevitable swivel stool. The 1920's saw a decline in the piano's popularity—perhaps because interest had turned to that exciting new invention, radio, or perhaps because so many heads of households retained unpleasant memories of tedious boyhood hours, learning to play music by rote under unimaginative teachers who never thought of training them to enjoy it through understanding. The past decade, however, has seen the piano restored to favor again. Nowadays we are more apt than not to find a sleek, curved grand in any living room which has sufficient *lebensraum* to hold it, or else an upright or one of the graceful little spinet-type pianos which have lately blossomed into style. But are our modern homes so very different in this respect from the well-equipped European homes of a thousand years ago, or even those of Greece or Egypt twenty-five hundred years ago? Not fundamentally so, for in those ancient and medieval households an honored corner was always set aside for the harp. And what is our twentieth-century

---

* Not *all* percussion instruments are hammered. The cymbals are clashed, and the castanets, tambourine, and maraca (gourd rattle) are shaken.—E. S.

piano but a harp fitted inside a wooden box and equipped with a row of padded hammers plus a keyboard to operate them, thus relieving us of the necessity of plucking or hitting the strings by hand? Look inside a piano, and you will recognize the harplike shape of its construction. We must therefore consider it for what it is: a modern adaptation, befitting our mechanical age, of a historical instrument of Biblical antiquity.

The piano is the lion of all stringed instruments. Its eighty-eight notes cover a range of seven and one-third octaves—even greater than that of a full symphony orchestra. Its full name, pianoforte (Italian for "soft-loud"), testifies to its dynamic range—from a gentle tinkle to a reverberating roar. It has one great limitation: it cannot produce sustained, singing tones. When a great pianist like Hofmann sits down at the keyboard, and critics afterwards write about his "marvelous singing effects" and of his tone as having a "singing quality in music of a sustained and lyric character which would be difficult to rival," they don't really mean what they say. They are just trying to tell us how nearly Hofmann came to accomplishing the impossible. A skilled pianist can create the illusion of a sustained tone, nothing more. Yet this limitation is one of the piano's priceless assets. Every tone it produces is like that of a bell—a sudden, sharp splash of sound that grows gradually fainter and fainter. Whenever you hear a piano, think of these "drops" of tone as falling on our ears like raindrops in a pool. Only how much more subtly and beautifully!

THE HARP

The present-day concert harp is far larger and has many more strings than the harps of King David's time or even those of the seventeenth-century Irish bards. But its principle is the same. Its forty-seven strings, stretched with great tension on its frame, cover a range of about six and a half octaves. In this respect it is markedly superior to a quartet of mixed voices, which has a combined range of less than four octaves. The harp is played by plucking the strings with the fingers. It is almost needless to add that harpists carefully cultivate their calluses! They use the thumb and three fingers on each hand, and so can sound eight tones at once. They can also play rapid successions of tones, which produce those rippling "broken" chord effects known as *arpeggios* (an Italian word which cannot be paraphrased exactly in English without coining a word such as "harpifications"). This effect is so characteristic of the harp that any broken chord has come to be called an *arpeggio,* even when played on other instruments.

THE HARPSICHORD

Some centuries ago, when the idea of putting a harp into a box and playing it by means of a keyboard was first conceived, the technique of plucking the strings was retained through the use of quills, which were actuated by the keys. Thus originated the harpsichord, with its delicate mandolinlike tone. During the period of such composers as Bach, Scarlatti, and Gluck the harpsichord was the most widely used keyboard instrument. Today it is chiefly of historical interest and would not have been mentioned in this chapter at all but for the fact that it has recently undergone a revival, and may occasionally be heard in performances of seventeenth- and eighteenth-century music.*

THE VIOLIN FAMILY

We could mention a number of other stringed instruments whose tones are produced by plucking or hammering, such as the Spanish guitar, Hawaiian ukulele, and Hungarian czimbalom, but although these instruments have added to the musical gaiety of nations they hardly ever enter the realm of art music. In this field it is a different type of stringed instrument which shares equal honors with the piano, and on many occasions completely eclipses it: the family of bowed instruments, frequently called the violin family after its most important member. In the recital halls of our nation pianists and violinists together make up about 95 per cent of our instrumental soloists. In a symphony orchestra bowed strings form about a two-thirds majority, and dominate it in texture as well as numbers, for string tone is the most constantly used timbre in the palette of orchestral colors. The violin family is unique among all stringed instruments in its ability to produce —at the wave of a magic wand—steadily sustained tones, and even tones which become louder as they continue. The wand which does the trick is called a bow. It is nothing more than a modification of a hunter's bow, having instead of a string many dozens of fine white horsehairs that are coated with rosin to give their surface some friction. This non-skid surface when drawn across a string sets it vibrating. By this device a player can control the intensity, quality, and duration of the tones he produces with amazing precision.

If the description just given has piqued your curiosity to such an extent that you are resolved to pick up a violinist's bow at the first favor-

* It has even been used, with stunning effect, in swing ensembles, on radio and records.—E. S.

able opportunity and examine it—take care. Unless you want to arouse a combination of fury, anguish, and hysteria on the part of its owner, don't touch the rosined surface, or even the slight amount of natural oil on your finger or thumb is enough to make the spot you touch more slippery than the rest of the bow, and so ruin it for him.

All the members of the violin family are alike in general construction: each has four strings, tuned approximately half an octave apart, which are stretched over a small bridge above a hollow wooden box of peculiar shape, which acts as a resonator, making what would otherwise be a feeble tone full and rich. You are undoubtedly familiar with the usual way of playing a violin or 'cello, so we won't burden you with a detailed description of its fundamentals. But there are a number of special effects possible on stringed instruments which are useful items for a concert-goer to tuck away in his mind. Ordinarily a violinist has to be careful not to let his bow touch more than one string at a time, but through the process known as double-stopping he can bow two strings at once and by fingering the proper tone on each obtain chord effects. Triple- and quadruple-stopping are also possible, but since the bow cannot touch more than two strings at once, the chords obtained in this way are arpeggiolike and cannot be sustained. Usually the bow scrapes along the string at a comfortable distance of two inches or so from the bridge. By bowing very near the bridge (*sul ponticello* is the Italian direction for it) the tone becomes very thin and ghostly. By doing the opposite, bowing near the finger board (*sulla tastiera*), the customary brilliance of tone gives way to a soft, almost lustreless mellowness. A still more efficacious way of altering the instrument's tone is by placing a small wooden clip, called a mute or sordine, on the bridge. A soft, sweet, veiled tone results. Sometimes the stroking motion of the bow is abandoned for other ways of setting the strings vibrating. A rarely used method is to tap the strings with the wooden back of the bow (*col legno*), producing a strange, barbaric effect. Far more common is the device of plucking the strings with a finger, harp fashion (*pizzicato*); the "plunk, plunk" sounds made in this way give a pleasant rhythmic accent to the music but lack singing quality, dying away even more quickly than piano tones.

One more effect remains to be described: those pale, ethereal tones known as harmonics. As the name implies, they are actually harmonics, or overtones, of the strings on which they are played. In many instances harmonics are written into a composition merely to show off the performer's skill in playing them, but they are also used for legitimate artistic effects, as in the beginning of Wagner's Prelude to *Lohengrin* where four violins in harmonics convey an atmosphere of celestial purity.

Bowed instruments are made in four different sizes, forming a "choir" which corresponds roughly to the four types of voices found in a church choir: violin (soprano); viola (alto); violoncello, or 'cello (tenor); and bass viol, or double bass (bass).

Because the range of these instruments is so much greater than that of voices the correspondence is only a rough one. In a string quartet, for instance, the parts are allotted to the four solo instruments in this way: violin (soprano), another violin (alto), viola (tenor), 'cello (bass).

THE VIOLA

The violin and the viola are the two chin-sized members of the string choir. The viola may be described as an overgrown violin which has had its highest string removed and a correspondingly lower string added at the opposite side. It is only slightly larger than the violin, and so is a bit hard to distinguish from its smaller cousin when the sixty or seventy string players in a symphony orchestra are sitting together on the stage. The two instruments are nearly alike in tone, too; the violin tone is apt to be clearer, sharper, more brilliant, the viola mellower and throatier.

THE 'CELLO

To differentiate the 'cello is far easier. Because of its greater bulk it is held between the knees. Its tone, while warm and mellow, has a penetrating quality in its upper range which is lacking in the viola; it almost approaches a buzzing effect at times. Its deeper tones are rich and resonant.

THE DOUBLE BASS

A close companion to the 'cello is the giant member of the string choir, the bass viol, frequently called double bass, contrabass, string bass, or just plain bass. Its bullfrog tones are about an octave lower than those of the 'cello. Whereas the other strings are tuned in fifths, the bass viol, because of its ponderous size, is tuned in fourths. Basses are chiefly useful as orchestral instruments; double-bass recitals are freakish rarities, and hardly less rare are appearances of these instruments in chamber-music groups. In orchestral music they spend most of their time supplying the lowest part of the harmony. Only occasionally do they have a chance to play a real tune. Yet their deep reverberating tones, which set the very walls of a concert hall vibrating, form so solid and satisfying a foundation that we should feel lost without them. Perhaps one of the chief reasons why radio and phonograph reproductions of symphonic music—remarkable as they are—don't sound quite like the real thing is because the deepest bass-viol tones are lost.

Possibly some few readers may be wondering why no mention has been made of that important member of the orchestral family, the second violin. To which the only truthful reply is that the second violin is not an instrument, but a condition of servitude. It is a perfectly ordinary violin whose player is condemned forever to perform the less exciting and less exacting parts. Its range is mezzo-soprano instead of soprano. But do not feel too sorry for second violinists, since in the great works of art music they have highly important and interesting roles in which they often exchange chitchat with the first violins on a basis of full equality.

If timbre is considered the "color" of musical sounds, piano music may be thought of as black-and-white reproductions of sound—equivalent to pencil sketches and etchings in the graphic arts. Continuing the analogy, string quartet or string orchestra music can be considered monochromatic, like paintings composed entirely of various shades of a single hue—all blues, or all browns. In both music and the graphic arts singleness of color is in many ways an asset. It gives an effect of purity. It enables us to focus our attention almost completely on a work's contour and design. Its very severity makes it wear well. Yet we would not willingly deprive ourselves of the beauty of color—of a multihued sky at sunset, or of the variegated blues and greens in the ocean on a summer's day, or of the colors in masterpieces of oil painting. Musical coloring is an equal source of delight. It is mainly to obtain variety of tonal color that we supplement the string choir of an orchestra or chamber group with wind instruments.

WIND INSTRUMENTS

There are two wind families—the wood-wind instruments and the brass instruments. Both classes may be described as consisting of pipes or tubes which make musical sounds when blown into. Their difference is partly a matter of materials. Brass instruments are made of either brass or a similar type of metal, such as nickel-silver, while most of the wood winds are made of wood—in fact, until comparatively recent years all of them were. Yet there is a more fundamental difference. All brass instruments are long, uninterrupted tubes, ending in a cup-shaped or funnel-shaped mouthpiece; their tones are produced by blowing into the mouthpiece with almost closed lips, so that they vibrate as the air is forced past them; and variations in pitch are achieved mostly by the way the player tightens or relaxes his lip muscles. The wood-wind instruments, on the other hand, have relatively short tubes into which holes have been bored along the side; their tones are varied chiefly by opening and closing the holes. Wood winds are simply glorified versions of the humble tin whistle. If you have ever tried to play a penny whistle, you will remember that the first thing to do is to cover each of the holes with a finger tip. Then, when you blow, you get a fairly low tone. By lifting up the finger which is farthest from your mouth you obtain a slightly higher tone. By lifting the next finger the tone is raised still further. In this way you can play a scale. By opening one hole after another you are successively shortening the length of the closed part of the tube, just as the violinist shortens the length of the vibrating section of a string by stopping it with his finger. Wood-wind instruments used to be played exactly in this way, by placing fingers over the holes, but a hundred years or so ago a Bavarian by the name of Böhm figured out a mechanical way of opening and closing the holes through a complicated system of keys, springs, levers, and felt pads. This made it a great deal easier for wood-wind players to execute difficult, fast passages. Today all wood-wind instruments are equipped with keys, most of them arranged according to Böhm's system, and for this reason their holes are invisible.

THE WOOD WINDS

Unlike the violin family, the wood-wind instruments do not form a single, unified choir, but are of three kinds: (1) instruments of the flute type, played by blowing across a hole—the same idea as blowing across the top of an empty bottle; (2) instruments of the clarinet type, played by blowing through a mouthpiece with a reed fastened to it— like the method of blowing on a blade of grass cupped in our hands, and (3) instruments of the oboe type, played by blowing through the crack formed by two reeds fastened together—as if we held two blades of grass between our lips. The first method, that of blowing across a hole, gives a clear, pure tone; the second method, letting the lips vibrate against a reed, gives a full, mellow, brilliant tone; and the third, making two reeds vibrate, produces a nasal, penetrating tone.

THE FLUTE

The flute family is not a complete choir in itself. It has no tenor or bass member. In fact, only two treble-voiced instruments appear at all frequently: the piccolo (high soprano) and the flute (soprano).

The flute is the coloratura soprano among the wood winds. It is ideally suited to the playing of runs and trills and other kinds of music that speed along trippingly. It is equally at home in gentle, melodious passages. Its upper tones are clear and birdlike, its lower ones soft and hollow. The piccolo is merely a baby-sized flute, half as large and sounding an octave higher. Its shrill tone makes it stand out over a whole orchestra. Both instruments are easy to recognize by sight, for they are held sideways, while all other wind instruments are held out or downwards, the player blowing straight into the tube instead of across it.

Once in a blue moon you will hear a bass flute. The term bass flute is a misnomer, however, for this instrument is actually an alto flute, having the same relation to an ordinary flute as a viola has to a violin.

THE CLARINET

The clarinet family has two members: the clarinet (soprano, equivalent to the violin), and the bass clarinet (tenor, equivalent to the 'cello).

Swing enthusiasts who are familiar with Benny Goodman, Artie Shaw, Ted Lewis, and other jazz clarinettists, need no introduction to the timbre of this instrument—although they may have a distorted idea of its style possibilities. In art music it plays as agile a role as in swing, yet its agility is meticulous rather than flamboyant. Its high tones are brilliant and penetrating, its middle register full and mellow, and its lowest tones have a peculiar quality that can best be compared to the sound of a boat whistle in a fogbound harbor.

The bass clarinet looks like a large-sized clarinet with a turned-up end in the manner of a saxophone, or of an elephant's trunk when lifted. It sounds like a deep-voiced edition of its soprano cousin. Because of its lower pitch it is somewhat mellower.

When we come to the double-reed group we find—for the first time among wood winds—a complete choir: the oboe (soprano, corresponding to the violin); English horn (alto, corresponding to the viola); bassoon (tenor, or baritone, corresponding to the 'cello); and the contrabassoon (bass, corresponding to the bass viol).

THE OBOE

The oboe's tone is hard to describe—as, in fact, are all timbres—but it is unmistakable once it has become familiar. It is a good deal like the tone of Scottish bagpipes and those of strange Oriental instruments played by snake-charmers and beggars in Bombay, Baghdad, and such places. And with good reason, for all three of these types of instruments belong to the double-reed family and are fundamentally the same. Bagpipes consist of an oboe-type mouthpiece separated from three oboelike pipes by a bag to hold a reserve supply of wind. The Oriental instruments are simply crude oboes. The characteristic tone of the oboe has been variously described as nasal, salty, pungent, acrid, penetrating; its upper tones are especially thin and piercing. From this description you may get an impression that its sound is distinctly ugly. Perhaps it is. Yet its bitter-sweet quality wears well, and its harshness is softened by a plaintiveness, a pathos, which endears it to most listeners.

THE ENGLISH HORN

Even a greater misnomer than *bass flute* is the name *English horn*. It is almost as classic an example of inappropriateness in nomenclature as *Holy Roman Empire,* for it is neither English nor a horn, but an alto oboe which first became popular in France. Some musicologists have suggested that its French name, *cor anglais,* may have come into being as a misspelling of *cor anglé,* which means "angled horn," referring to the fact that, instead of being straight like an oboe, it has a bend near the mouthpiece. In fairness to the French, who may not like to have their prowess at spelling impugned, it must be added that other musical authorities suggest that the cor anglais was similar enough to the hornpipe (a crude instrument of Chaucer's time whose name survives today only as the name of a dance) to have been dubbed an "English hornpipe." At any rate, if you should wish to pick out the English-horn player at a symphony concert, don't look among the horns but among the double reeds. An English horn has a deeper, more expressive, and even more plaintive tone than that of the oboe. In its lusciousness it runs a close second to the 'cellos; in fact it is the only wind instrument whose timbre approaches the emotional quality of string tone.

THE BASSOON

Far beneath it in dignity, yet a highly useful instrument notwithstanding, is the tenor member of the family, the bassoon. In shape it resembles several round pieces of wood fastened together, out of which protrudes a curved metal tube. It appeared that way to the Italians, too, and so they named it *fagotto* ("bundle of sticks"). Its tone has a grotesque flavor which approaches the comical whenever it plays quick, skipping melodies. This has prompted many composers to write clownish passages for it. Yet it has its serious side, too. Its uppermost tones are gentle and expressive, like those of a tenor singing in a half-voice.

The lowest, gruffest member of the choir is the contrabassoon, sometimes called double bassoon. In fact it is the deepest-toned of any instrument except the piano. Whereas the piano's lowest notes sound like barks, the contrabassoon's can best be compared to snores or grunts. Three bassoons and a contrabassoon make an effective "male quartet" of double reeds, and the contrabassoon also performs a useful if minor function in symphony orchestras by playing along with the bass viols, making their tones sound fuller and stronger.

BRASS INSTRUMENTS

We are now ready to turn our attention from the instruments of the tin-whistle type to a family of quite a different sort, whose members look for all the world like the handiwork of an imaginative master plumber. These are the instruments of the brass choir. They consist of convolutions of metal piping and tubing, full of U-turns and elbow joints, and all but one of them have valves which can be opened or closed. Equally noticeable is their lack of reeds, holes, and keys. The four important members of the brass choir are: the trumpet (soprano), horn (alto), trombone (tenor), and tuba (bass).

THE TRUMPET

The trumpet, being so closely related to the bugle, has the same bold, martial quality and intensity of volume that make the bugle so desirable an instrument for military use outdoors. When the violins are bowing their heads off, and the wood winds are all out of breath, and the composer wants to lift the music to a greater climax, he lets the trumpets ring out. This instrument has other uses too. Played softly, it has a round tone that is fuller and richer than any wood-wind tone. Like the violin, it can be muted. This is accomplished by inserting a conical object in its bell-shaped open end. The mute sets up so much interference in the air waves that the trumpet's customarily noble tone is changed entirely, assuming a pinched, nasal, "tin horn" quality which is not altogether unlike the voice of Donald Duck.*

THE FRENCH HORN

The alto member of the brass family, the horn, is the most individual of the four. Its warm, mellow, liquid tone has a romantic charm all its own. It does not have to depend on other families of instruments for support; often four horns play together in "close harmony," forming a separate little choir of their own. Yet it also blends beautifully with the other brasses, and it goes equally well with the wood winds when the other brasses are silent. All in all, it is a highly popular member of the orchestra. Slow, sustained melodies are best suited to it; even these are difficult to play, however, and we must forgive horn players for occasional impurities and wobbly tones which would be inexcusable in any other instrument. When muted, the horn is transformed from a suave, dignified Dr. Jekyll into a sinister Mr. Hyde, with a harsh, croaking voice that has even more of a tin-horn quality than the muted trumpet. In appearance as well as tone the horn is distinctive, because of its circular shape and its extremely flaring bell which faces downward and away from the audience. The horn is frequently called "French horn" to distinguish it from the English horn and also from the saxhorn and flügelhorn, types of band instruments about which we need not concern ourselves.

THE TROMBONE

The one brass instrument which has no valves is the trombone, the " 'cello" of the brass choir. It is a direct descendant of an ancient instrument which the Moors called a sackbut (Moorish for "pump") and which was played in the same picturesque way as a trombone, by moving a sliding section of U-shaped tubing back and forth. The trombone is about an octave lower in pitch than the trumpet. Its tone is impressively powerful; it has the trumpet's bold, ringing quality, but being deeper has also a sonorous nobility which no other instrument can quite equal.

---

* In recent years half a dozen different types of mutes have been developed, mainly by jazz trumpeters. Used in symphonic music, these mutes produce a wide variety of tone colors, some of which are expressive, poetic, and not at all Donald Ducky.—E. S.

THE TUBA

Largest and deepest of the brass instruments is the tuba, whose cavernous throat—at least, in the minds of juvenile spectators at street parades—forms so inviting a target for peanut shells. In its secluded rear-row position in a symphony orchestra, however, its dignity is unassailable. Its round, mellow, and powerful tone provides an effective bass for the brass choir. Frequently it joins forces with three trombones to form a deep-voiced quartet—an unbeatable combination for portraying music of solemnity and majestic grandeur.

THE SAXOPHONE

One popular family of wind instruments remains to be described: the saxophone. Like the violin family it comes in all sizes, from soprano to contrabass. But it is a peculiar type of instrument. It belongs partly to the wood winds and partly to the brasses, for it is a hybrid combination of both. Its metal tubing is like that of a bugle, yet its mouthpiece and arrangement of holes and keys are patterned after the clarinet. Its velvety, emotional tone is a staple article in the modern dance band, but only on rare occasions is it permitted in a symphony orchestra. Probably the reason why it is not more popular as a purveyor of art music is that its personality is so distinctive and dominating that it does not blend successfully with other instruments, but stands out "like a sore thumb."* As Deems Taylor once put it, the saxophone is a prima donna among instruments, and its failure to win acceptance as an orchestral instrument proves that "if you insist on being a prima donna all the time you can't expect to get a job in the chorus."

PERCUSSION INSTRUMENTS

If you recall our imaginary search among kitchen utensils for ways of producing musical sounds, you will remember that the third method we discovered—after making a home-made harp by stretching a piece of twine tight and a home-made flute by blowing across the top of an empty bottle—was to set a solid or hollow object vibrating by hitting it with a spoon. This third method was a crude illustration of the one family of orchestral instruments which has not yet been discussed: the

* I have to disagree on this point. Many contemporary composers have used it in symphonic scores; it seems to me a beautifully neutral tone that blends very well indeed. Probably the reason it hasn't been used more is the good old one—inertia.—E. S.

percussion instruments. As their name implies, they are all played by being struck—either directly, with sticks or hammers or the hands, or by being knocked about through shaking. Some percussion instruments can produce musical tones, but many of them simply make noises. Yet all are useful members of the orchestra, serving a purpose which no other choir can accomplish nearly so well—that of accenting the rhythms.

Since percussion instruments form such a motley crew—they come in all different designs and shapes—it may help us to keep them straight if we divide them into three classifications: (1) drum-type (parchments stretched over round frames); (2) cymbal-type (plates or discs of sheet metal), and (3) bell-type (lengths of metal or wood, which produce definite musical tones and are graduated in size to form a scale).

There are in addition a few miscellaneous noisemakers which defy classification.

THE DRUMS

Among the drums are two familiar members of every military band: the bass drum which, when struck with a padded hammer, produces a deep, reverberating "boom"; and the snare drum (sometimes called "side drum" or "military drum") which takes its name from the snares, or strings of catgut, that vibrate against the lower head when the upper head is hit, and give it its distinctive crisp, rattling sound. More useful in a symphony orchestra than either of these is the kettledrum.* As its name implies, it is a large bowl-shaped piece of copper, like a kettle, over the top of which is stretched a head of vellum. Its great advantage over all other drums lies in its ability to sound deep resonant tones of definite pitch, which can be varied by tightening or loosening the head. The kettledrum player of an orchestra usually surrounds himself with three or four kettledrums of assorted sizes, so that he has several tones constantly at hand. He can also produce still others at a moment's notice by changing the tension on his drum. If you have attended symphony concerts you may perhaps have noticed the kettledrummer vigorously turning thumbscrews during a performance, then leaning over a drum and tapping very softly to verify the correctness of its new pitch. Another drum-type instrument is the tambourine—a little hand drum encircled with jingling pieces of metal,

---

* The common (Italian) name for the kettledrums is *timpani.*—E. S.

which can be played in three different ways: by thumping, shaking, and rubbing with the thumb. It is practically a "must" in Spanish music.

THE CYMBALS AND THE GONG

In brass bands another instrument is always to be found along with the drums: the cymbals. In symphony orchestras cymbals are used more sparingly, for their resounding metallic clash makes such a terrific noise —sounding for all the world as if the cook had dropped a couple of dishpans—that the rest of the orchestra is half smothered by it. They are ideal instruments for a composer to use when capping a tremendous musical climax, as at the end of the great crescendo in Wagner's Prelude to *Lohengrin*. They are also appropriate in wild, orgiastic music. Another instrument, like a cymbal in principle but quite different in effect, is the gong, or tam-tam, a noise-maker of Chinese origin consisting of a broad circular plate of hammered metal about three feet in diameter. Its sound is as unique as it is strange and imposing—a deep, muffled, shuddering roar. The proper dramatic moment for the gong to sound is not at the height of a climax, but afterwards, when the music is subsiding into deathlike mutterings. So startling and fateful is its tone that the composer who makes use of it more than once in an orchestral work is inviting a dangerous anticlimax.

BELLS, XYLOPHONE, CELESTA

Among the percussion group are four bell-like instruments: (1) orchestra bells, known also by their German name *Glockenspiel*—metal bars arranged in two rows, like the black and white keys of a piano, to form a scale. They are struck with wooden hammers and have clear, high, bell-like tones; (2) the xylophone, similar to orchestra bells except that its bars are made of wood. Its tones are dull and clanking; (3) the celesta, which Tchaikovsky once described as "something between a piano and a glockenspiel." It looks like a miniature upright piano with a half-size keyboard, and it actually has the same type of action and hammers as a piano, but the hammers strike metal bars which are placed over hollow wooden boxes. Its sweet, vibrant, bell-like tones have a celestial quality—at least, so its inventor, M. Mustel of Paris, thought. Hence its name. And (4) chimes, sometimes called tubular bells—long metal tubes, suspended from a frame. Its tones are intended to approximate the sound of great church bells. This task is one to which they are not quite equal, but since the only alternative would be to bring into our concert halls, opera houses, and broadcasting studios bells of cast bronze weighing twenty or thirty tons, we may consider ourselves lucky in having even an approximation.

OTHER PERCUSSION INSTRUMENTS

A few percussion instruments remain outside these three classifications: the triangle—a triangular steel rod which is struck with a straight steel rod, producing a high, metallic ring of uncertain pitch; castanets, those little shell-like pieces of wood which are associated chiefly with Spanish music; the rattle—a ratchet which is whirled on the end of a stick (an instrument better suited to Election Day parades and New Year's Eve parties than to symphonic music)—and a few other noise-making gadgets that appear only on rare occasions.*

THE ORGAN

No survey of instruments would be complete without mention of the organ. Its myriad tubes and pipes make it a wind instrument, but it occupies a field all its own. It is like the piano in that it can play harmonies and contrapuntal passages as well as melodies, and like the orchestra in its ability to produce many varieties of tone color. Its range is greater than that of any other instrument—even greater than that of the entire symphony orchestra. What it lacks is the subtlety of which the orchestra is capable. Since it is played by a single person, its tones and rhythms are too sharp and clear, so that imperfections stand out. It lacks the soft-focus quality of massed strings, which have a roundedness comparable to the slightly blurred outlines in an artistic photograph. And since it is not responsive to variations of touch, as is the piano, and cannot make one tone slide to another, as strings and voices can, it sounds mechanical and stiff compared to most other instruments. Unless it is played with great skill, the successive tones of a melody are apt to sound disjointed, or else jumbled and confused through overlapping. It also lacks the percussive quality of a piano or symphony orchestra. Yet it is a noble instrument, of a grandeur and power which has brought it a wide following, and much fine music has been written for it which is missed by those who stay away from organ recitals.

ELECTRONIC INSTRUMENTS

Our modern age of electrical marvels has witnessed the development of a number of musical instruments whose tones are produced

---

* Among those familiar to jazz fans are the wood block, temple blocks, the tom-toms, etc.—E. S.

synthetically through electrical impulses. This is not a reference to radios, phonographs, and auditorium amplifiers—which are *reproducing* instruments rather than musical instruments in the true sense of the term—but electronic contrivances which do away, wholly or partly, with the conventional ways of producing sounds through vibrations that depend on the length and tautness of a string, or the length of a column of air, or the size and shape of a metal bar. In building these instruments electrical engineers are merely doing for music what modern chemists have already done for the textile and confectionery industries in producing synthetic fabrics, dyes, and flavors.

Prominent among the electronic instruments are the Hammond organ and the Novachord, pipeless keyboard instruments whose tones are produced by electromagnets and rotating discs, and the Theremin, a strange creation that looks like a radio receiving set and sounds like an overgrown 'cello. The Theremin's sounds are produced by moving one's hands back and forth through the air a foot or two in front of it, as if performing some trick of black magic. Other new instruments have been built which are semi-electronic—pianos, violins, guitars, and others, whose conventional sounding boards have been omitted and whose weak tones are amplified instead by microphones and loud-speakers.

Considerable interest and enthusiasm have been aroused by these inventions. A noted radio authority recently said: "Most familiar musical instruments are merely evolutions of the crude noisemakers of our tribal ancestors. Even today the making of music depends upon the accidental agglomeration of nondescript materials such as wood, brass, horsehair, skins, and the intestines of animals. With the advent of the radio tube, new magic in music creation has suddenly become possible. Tones of exquisite beauty, never before heard, can now be summoned without the performer having to saw on a string or blow himself blue in the face." This is a pretty theory. But the fact remains that the value of an instrument lies in the beauty, subtlety, and flexibility of its tone, and not in the social standing of the materials out of which it is made. So far, electronic instruments have won acceptance for economic rather than musical reasons; they have yet to achieve any new heights of musical beauty. It will be interesting to see if they ever progress beyond this stage. Let us hope that they do, for new kinds of beauty are always welcome—but if they are to put a symphony orchestra to shame, they have a long road to travel.

CHAMBER-MUSIC COMBINATIONS

Instruments may be heard singly or in all sorts of combinations. We often find them in pairs: one melodic instrument assisted by another which is capable of playing harmonies and can therefore serve as accompanist—as for instance violin and piano, or flute and harp. We also find them in a variety of small, intimate groupings which form a category called—for want of a better term—"chamber music." As you can guess, this term means "room music" or "house music" as opposed to auditorium music. The timbre of chamber-music groupings may be monochromatic, as in a string quartet; or almost so, as in a wood-wind ensemble; or it may be a decided mixture of colors, as in Beethoven's septet for clarinet, bassoon, horn, and four stringed instruments.*

THE SYMPHONY ORCHESTRA

Going beyond the pale of chamber music, we reach the crowning instrumental combination of all—the symphony orchestra, ranging in size from about 80 to 110 players. Two factors determine its precise size: first, the number of men allotted to each of the five string parts—which is purely a matter of policy on the part of the orchestra's management, since the strings form a chorus, and each part may be reinforced by as many players as is deemed wise; and second, the number of different wind-instrument parts, which, since each part is played by only one man, depends entirely on the "instrumentation" of the music—something decided by the composer when the music was written. In general, orchestras are two-thirds strings, with the balance divided about fifty-fifty between wood winds and brasses, except for a trifling number of percussion players.

Curiously enough, the most popular of all instruments, the piano, is only an occasional member of the symphony orchestra—and a relatively unimportant one at that. This phenomenon is not difficult to explain. The piano's chief asset is that it is a whole orchestra in one. When a ninety-piece orchestra is already at hand, the asset ceases to be of any great value. At the same time its chief drawback—the fact that it cannot play truly sustained tones—is brought into high relief; it suffers by comparison with the stringed and wind instruments as a pur-

* Small jazz ensembles sometimes bring together unorthodox but highly interesting combinations. Benny Goodman's quartet consisted of clarinet, piano, electric vibraphone, and percussion.—E. S.

veyor of melodies. The piano's percussive, bell-like quality makes it admirably suited to the role of supplying rhythmic accents and rippling embellishments, but even in this field it has a competitor in the harp, and for some reason the harp's tone blends more harmoniously with the rest of the orchestra than does that of the piano.

An "average" symphony orchestra (if there were such a thing) would be composed as follows:

Strings:
- 32 violins (16 firsts and 16 seconds)
- 14 violas
- 12 'cellos
- 10 bass viols
- 1 harp

Wood Winds:
- 2 flutes and 1 piccolo
- 2 clarinets and 1 bass clarinet
- 2 oboes and 1 English horn
- 2 bassoons and 1 contrabassoon

Basses:
- 4 horns
- 3 trumpets
- 3 trombones and 1 tuba

Percussion:
- 1 kettledrum player
- 2 or 3 others who take turns at various instruments

This imposing aggregation of instruments gives the composer almost unlimited scope. He can let his music sound in pure colors— giving one phrase to the strings alone, another to oboes and bassoons, and so on; or he can mix his timbres—having a melody played by violas, bassoons, and oboe together, or doubling 'cellos with horns, or making the flute play two octaves above a low clarinet passage. These blended flavors can be fascinating, although too much of them can give the music a muddy tone.

In vocal music the possible combinations are limited, since there are so few kinds of voices compared with instruments. Yet even here quite a range is at the composer's disposal, from solo or duet with piano accompaniment up to chorus of mixed voices with soprano, contralto, tenor, and bass soloists on the side, and orchestral support into the bargain.

ARRANGING

All music may be arranged (or transcribed, as it is also called), so that it can be performed by some instrumental or vocal combination different from the one originally planned by the composer.* Schubert composed his "Serenade" as a song, but Liszt transcribed it for piano solo, and countless others since his time have made transcriptions for harp, organ, mixed chorus, salon orchestra, military band, and Heaven knows what.

INSTRUMENTATION

Some music is more amenable to transcription than others. Schumann's symphonies sound well when played by four hands on the piano, for although they were written for orchestra they were conceived by a composer who was far more familiar with the piano than with orchestral instruments as a medium for musical performance. Most likely his instinctive musical thoughts were abstract, and it took a conscious effort on his part to decide what instruments should play what parts. Brahms, too, had a far stronger feeling for melody, harmony, and counterpoint than for the instrumental investiture of his music. His Quintet in F Minor for piano and strings, for example, was first conceived as a quintet for violins, viola, and 'cellos, and then rewritten as a sonata for two pianos, before it finally emerged in the form in which we know it best today. With Wagner, on the other hand, musical thoughts went hand in hand with the appropriate instrumental coloring. In the opening act of *Tristan,* when the Cornish knight first appears before Isolde, there is a striking passage in which a heroic theme sounds in the brasses, and, while its last note is being sustained, a number of heavily accented chords are bowed by the strings. This music is so wedded to its instrumentation that hearing it played on the piano can give us no true conception of its dignity and power. Chopin's piano music, likewise, is so inextricably bound up with its medium that orchestral transcriptions cannot do it justice and, undoubtedly for this reason, have never come into favor on symphony programs.

*Arranging (mostly for dance orchestra) has become one of the most highly skilled—and well paid—professions in music today. Many fine composers, notably Morton Gould and Russell Bennett, win far greater economic return for their arrangements than for their original music.—E. S.

Now that we have pretty well surveyed the field of instrumental coloring, we may be tempted to ask ourselves, "Of what use is all this information? What advantage is there in being able to recognize timbres?" There are several ways in which a knowledge of instruments can add to the listener's satisfaction in music. For one thing, there is a certain rudimentary pleasure in being familiar with the various types of voices and instruments, as there is in being able to recognize various kinds of wild animals in a menagerie. It gives us a friendly sense of acquaintanceship with what we hear. It is also satisfying to be able to pick out the different strands of a complex work through the contrasting tone colors in which they are presented. In Wagner's *Ride of the Valkyries,* for instance, three different things are going on simultaneously —sweeping passages in the violins, agitated flutterings in the wood winds, and a stentorian theme in the brasses. Yet each stands out distinctly by virtue of the differences in timbre. The better we know these timbres the clearer music of this sort becomes for us. And we gain a still deeper pleasure by becoming conscious of the fitness of the instrumental coloring to the music we hear. It is satisfying to be able to note the artistic effectiveness of somber chords clothed in dark, veiled colors, dramatic moments accented by sudden pizzicato effects, refreshing contrasts in color between one section of a composition and its neighbor, passages for solo instruments that are written with a felicitous regard for the instrument's personality, and so forth. It is true that we also become conscious of passages which don't "come off" so effectively as they might because of inferior scoring. Yet even these produce satisfactions of a sort, not the least of which (though not the greatest) is a self-important feeling of being able to put one's finger on a human failing in some illustrious composer.

Tempo Marks

Abridged from the chapter "Measure by Measure" in "Approach to Music"

By Lawrence Abbott

TEMPO indications confront audiences on almost every program: verbal instructions, like *allegro di molto* or *andante quasi allegretto.* These are occasionally in German, French, or English, but usually they are in Italian, for Italian is the accepted international language of music, just as Latin is the accepted language of horticulture and of medicine.

Verbal tempo indications must not be confused with titles. They don't belong in the same category as *Albumblatt,* or *Serenata,* or *Rapsodie espagnole,* which are actually the names of pieces. Words like *allegro* and *andante* are, like metronome marks, primarily intended as instructions to the performer; we listeners are faced with them only because so many pieces and movements of pieces have no other name or "handle" by which they can be identified. When we find a medicine bottle on the shelf with the label "One tablespoonful every two hours" we don't fall into the error of supposing that that is the name of the medicine; we know those are merely the directions as to how it should be taken. Likewise, *allegro ma non troppo* isn't actually the name of a symphonic movement, but merely the directions as to the speed at which it should be taken. It may be translated as "briskly, but not too much so," or "Play this music fast enough to make it sound cheerful, but be careful not to overdo it."

Mere words, of course, cannot describe tempo with any great precision; all they can do is tell us, in a general way, the character of a piece: whether it is fast and jolly or slow and majestic. As far as the listener is concerned that is ample. He can leave it up to the performer to choose with intelligence the exact tempo that will bring out the music's characteristics to best advantage, feeling free to disagree if that rate of speed fails to carry full conviction. Even for performers verbal directions are usually adequate. They are like the admonitions of the motorcycle cop who, after stopping a speeder on the highway, tells him to "take it easy." The policeman doesn't say in so many words "Keep down to forty miles an hour," but his remark means approximately that. Anyone who sits down at the piano and rattles off the opening movement of Beethoven's Sonata in G, Opus 49, No. 2, at breakneck speed deserves to be stopped by some musical traffic officer with the equivalent admonition: "Allegro, ma non troppo!"

These are the principal tempi in music, ranging from the slowest to the fastest:

Largo: extremely slow (literally, "broadly").
Lento: very slow.
Adagio: still very slow, though slightly less so than *lento.*
Andante: moving along, but at a slow, leisurely pace.

Moderato: at a moderate pace (an aggravatingly indefinite direction).
Allegretto: fairly quickly, but unhurried.
Allegro: fast, briskly (literally, "happy," "cheerful").
Presto: extremely fast.

One of these terms, *allegretto,* is merely a modification of *allegro.* Being an Italian diminutive, it means "a little allegro"—in other words, "not quite as fast and brisk as allegro." Through modifications of this sort many other gradations in tempo are indicated. *Larghetto* is a tempo which is "broad, but not quite so slow as largo." *Andante quasi allegretto* is a compromise between the two tempi named. *Allegro moderato* means "moderately fast"—a trifle slower than plain *allegro.* *Allegro di molto* means "very fast." *Prestissimo* means "as fast as possible—and then some."

Sometimes adjectives are coupled with tempo terms not for purposes of clarifying the rate of speed but as indications of style. *Allegro vivace* is not necessarily any faster or slower than *allegro con fuoco.* One means "quick, vivacious," the other "quick with fiery spirit."

Form and the Listener

By Elie Siegmeister

IT SHOULD be quite clear by now why the man who writes a piece of music has to think about the question of form. But why must the *listener* bother himself with it? You don't have to understand the mechanics of cobbling to enjoy wearing a good pair of shoes; why should it be necessary to understand the mechanics of musical cobbling, as it were, to enjoy a good piece of music?

In many cases, of course, it isn't. Almost anyone can listen to Brahms's *Hungarian Dances,* Tchaikovsky's *Nutcracker Suite,* many operatic arias, Falla's *Three-Cornered Hat,* and other pieces of comparatively simple construction and enjoy them to the full. It is where the musical pattern becomes more elaborate—in fugues, concerti, sonatas, symphonies, Wagner's music dramas, etc.—that the listener's troubles begin. A composer may have put in two weeks, six months (or in extreme cases as much as ten years,*) on a work of monumental proportions or subtle character, in which musical ideas are not merely stated, but combined and interwoven in various complex ways. He does not go to all this trouble merely in order to make things harder; but because he has something big to say, something so universal and important that it can not be stated simply in terms of a few pretty tunes or easily grasped bits of tone color.

I remember the first time I heard Brahms's First Symphony—it was in my second year of concert-going. I knew that Brahms was one of the top composers and that the C minor was one of the master-works of all music, and went to the concert anticipating a wonderful experience.

I was bitterly disappointed. Instead of the attractive melodies and luscious orchestral effects I had expected, here was a long-drawn-out, abstruse, and rather somber exercise in tones. The few brief snatches of melody which struck my ears seemed to be immediately swallowed up in a morass of complicated and very dull musical gymnastics, which made no sense whatsoever to my unsophisticated ears.

Of course, I was only fourteen at the time, but a very self-assured music critic. After a few years and a half dozen more hearings of this Brahms work, I began to see how little I had really heard that first time. For what had struck me as complicated musical gymnastics, lack of melody, etc., was of course a superb human utterance, in which deep emotion was combined with the keenest intellectual handling. Here, it was not so much the individual melodies that mattered— though beautiful in themselves—as the way in which they were treated. This architectural treatment of musical ideas, this superb marshaling, building up, and driving home of grand thoughts and emotions is not easy for the composer to achieve or for the unprepared listener to grasp. It requires a certain amount of sensitivity, knowledge, and musical experience. (Only in recent years has Brahms become one of the top concert favorites, and Wagner first-rate box-office at the opera.) In other words, it requires a certain awareness of the build-up of music, its architecture or form. This is not textbook knowledge; it can be grasped only through the ear. But a little information never hurts, and in the long run it may increase one's pleasure in listening to fugues, oratorios, symphonies, and modern compositions that perhaps seem forbiddingly complex.

* Brahms worked on his First Symphony over a period of ten years.

Variations, Chaconne, Suite

Adapted from two chapters in "Approach to Music"

By Lawrence Abbott

In theory the simplest musical pattern is the *theme and variations*. Music in this form starts with a melody which is then repeated a number of times, each time with changes or additional features. The form should not be difficult to master, for it is encountered frequently in plain everyday music. When someone sings a popular ballad and the pianist alters the style of his accompaniment with each verse to suit the changing mood of the words, he is playing "variations" on the first verse. When an expert dance orchestra swings into one of the song hits of the day, repeating the refrain over and over again, these musicians also play variations—for, having a sense of showmanship, they don't repeat the tune the same way each time. First a trio of saxophones will croon the melody, then the trumpet will take it up while the pianist indulges in fancy tricks on the side, then the clarinetist will occupy the center of the stage, and instead of playing the tune as written he will embellish it almost beyond recognition—and so on. In this way the music retains a sparkle and freshness.

In art music the form is the same, but even greater flexibility is permitted. The composer usually chooses a brief and distinctive theme so that it can be recognized through its subsequent disguises; then he proceeds to elaborate or simplify its contours, weave ornamental figures above and below it, change its rhythm and tempo, carry it from major into minor or vice versa, and harmonize it in various ways. Haydn, Mozart, Beethoven, and their contemporaries wrote variations which usually deviate only slightly from the original tune, and are therefore easy to follow. Composers of more recent times have been less kind to their audiences, though perhaps more stimulating; often their variations wander far afield, so that only by the wildest stretch of the imagination can we find anything in common between them and the original tune.* When you hear a "theme with variations" you must

---

* An exception is Ravel's *Bolero,* in which the theme is repeated precisely, almost the sole variation being changes in orchestration.—E.S.

not expect too much of a melody to begin with, for composers usually choose a simple and unassuming one, in order to impress us with the variety of effects and heights of beauty which they subsequently draw out of such apparently unpromising material.

THE CHACONNE

One of the earliest ways in which composers made use of the theme-and-variations form was in the old classic dance form known both as the *passacaglia* and the *chaconne.* This slow, stately dance in ¾ time required music in which a short theme was obstinately repeated over and over again, usually in the bass,* while other melodies and figurations were played above it. Down through the years composers have made effective use of this rigid form. Outstanding examples are the massive Passacaglia in C Minor by Bach and the towering final movement of Brahms's Fourth Symphony, consisting of thirty-four variations on an eight-note theme.

THE SUITE

Have you ever been to a dance at which the music was so superlative that hosts of young people stopped dancing entirely to crowd in around the musicians and listen with undivided attention? Since the 1920's, when virtuoso American jazz orchestras began creating complex, exhilarating music out of simple fox-trot tunes, this has become a more and more commonplace occcurrence. The top-flight orchestras, such as Benny Goodman's, frequently play to dance floors filled with motionless, spellbound listeners. Many years ago a similar sort of thing undoubtedly took place. Some noble lord, perhaps, delighted with several of the minuets, sarabandes, and galliards which his private orchestra played during balls at the palace, ordered them performed some evening as part of an after-dinner concert. Thus was born a form of music which is now an indispensable item on the concert-goer's bill of fare: the suite. Today the suite is accepted by musicians as one of the important musical forms at the disposal of composers of art music. Yet its similarity to the simple little dance piece from which it sprang still remains apparent. A suite by Bach, Handel, or Bizet is not greatly different in its basic conception from a fifteen-minute radio program of dance music, in which fox trots alternate with rhumbas, tangos, and

---

* The technical term for this process is *basso ostinato.* A recent example is the "Fascist" section in Shostakovich's Seventh Symphony.—E. S.

waltzes. The individual pieces of a Bach suite naturally show an artistic excellence which is not to be matched by any random collection of modern dance tunes; yet in both cases the fundamental pattern into which the pieces have been arranged as a group is identical.

Back in the period when art music was first branching away from simple, everyday tunes toward more elaborate art forms, suites were invariably sets of dance pieces—sarabandes, minuets, jigs, gavottes, rigadoons, and the like—arranged with a sense of showmanship so as to provide agreeable contrasts of tempo and time, and often preceded by an overture in the French style, having a slow introduction and a fugal allegro. When you hear suites by Bach, Handel, Purcell, Corelli, and other masters of their time, expect to hear a prelude followed by a set of dances. The intervening years have seen a gradual extension of the term "suite" to include collections of almost any type of music. For instance, when a composer writes an opera, ballet, or incidental music to a play, he hates to see his beloved creation gathering dust on the shelf between infrequent stage performances. So he picks out a few outstanding excerpts and rearranges and edits them so that they form an effective succession of concert pieces—a suite.

The older composers frequently used other names that mean practically the same thing as suite. A composition which bears the title "serenade," or "partita," or "divertimento," or "cassation," may be trusted to be a series of short contrasted movements.*

Overture, Prelude, Concerto

Abridged from the chapter "Arabesques and Architecture" in "Approach to Music"

By Lawrence Abbott

THE word "overture" means, literally, an opening piece. It was first used years ago to denote a musical introduction to an opera. This meaning it still retains, of course, but it can also mean the introduction to a play or to a set of musical numbers, and is even applied to independent concert pieces composed in the style of an operatic overture.

* For further discussion of the Suite, see pp. 143 and 303.—E. S.

When it occupies its rightful role in the theater or opera house, the overture is supposed to put us in the proper mood to enjoy the drama to come. It may simply set the tone—inform us that we are in for an evening of gaiety, or romance, or melodrama, or whatever the case may be. Or it may foreshadow the plot through musical suggestion, as Beethoven has done in his second and third overtures to *Leonore* by the interpolation of an off-stage trumpet call to symbolize the arrival of the seventeenth-century Spanish equivalent of "the marines."

Overtures started out as formless little pieces. Then, about three hundred years ago, a French court musician named Lully * developed a definite structural plan which came to be known as the French overture form: a slow introduction followed by a quick fugue, with sometimes a closing section in slower tempo again. This type of overture was in vogue for a century or so until it was crowded into oblivion by the development of sonata form. Since then composers have written their overtures either in sonata form—having two contrasted themes, a development section, and a restatement of the themes—or else in a free style.

Opera overtures are likely to contain themes which are to appear later in the opera—presenting the cast of musical characters, as it were, in advance. Since there is presumably plenty of drama to come, the composer does not always feel it necessary to arrange the themes in a symmetrical pattern or to develop them. He may introduce them in a rambling fashion, forming a medley or potpourri—one theme strung out after another with appropriate transition passages between them, and perhaps a return at the end to the most important theme of the opera. When a work of this type is written for the concert hall instead of the theater it more often bears the label "rhapsody" or "fantasy" or "fantasia"—an admission on the composer's part that the music follows his own whim rather than any set form.

The term *prelude* means the same thing as *overture*—an introductory piece. It is often applied to operatic introductions which are not so extended as overtures, and to music which precedes a single act of an opera or introduces an instrumental piece such as a fugue. Yet it frequently appears as a title for short independent pieces, just as the overture has been applied to longer independent pieces.

* Actually Italian, not French, though he lived in Paris throughout his professional career and is customarily classed with the French school.—E. S.

THE CONCERTO

Just what is a concerto? It may be described as a composition for two opposing and unequal forces. The large force is the full symphony orchestra, called the *tutti,* while the small force pitted against it is usually a single instrument—a violin, or 'cello, or piano, or a wind instrument. A *double concerto* features a pair of solo instruments, and a *concerto grosso* features a group of soloists, usually three or four, known as the *concertino.* Some writers define a concerto as a composition for solo instrument or instruments "with orchestral accompaniment." But this is no more accurate than to say that a sonata for violin and piano is a composition for violin "with piano accompaniment." In the case of a sonata the two instruments are supposed to be on an equal footing. Likewise the soloist and the orchestra are supposed to share the honors equally. You will find this true if you listen closely to a concerto. At one moment the soloist commands our attention while he announces a theme, and the orchestra remains in the background, playing its soft accompaniment; yet a few moments later the roles are reversed: the orchestra surges to the forefront while the soloist either lapses into silence or assumes a subordinate position, perhaps embellishing the melody with little ornamental figurations. Throughout a concerto this interchange takes place. The biggest moment of all for the soloist is the part known as the *cadenza,* which comes at the end of the recapitulation in the first movement. The orchestra stops, and the solo instrument is permitted to entertain the audience alone for a while with dazzling passages and difficult technical feats. In some concertos this section is nothing more than a gaudy display of acrobatics, yet a cadenza is supposed to contain real thematic development as well as the inevitable stunt passages. In this respect it has the same difficult dual task that confronts the concerto as a whole —that of presenting music on a lofty plane and at the same time exhibiting the virtuosity of the soloist.

Most concerti grossi are archaic works, composed before sonata form was evolved. Hence their form corresponds to that of a suite. They are usually in three or four movements; the first is often a slow introduction followed by a fugal allegro. Bach's famous *Brandenburg* Concertos are actually concerti grossi.

Listening to Polyphonic Music

Extracts from the chapter "Musical Texture" in "What to Listen for in Music"

By Aaron Copland

MUSIC that is polyphonically written makes greater demands on the attention of the listener, because it moves by reason of separate and independent melodic strands, which together form harmonies. The difficulty arises from the fact that our listening habits are formed by music that is harmonically conceived, and polyphonic music demands that we listen in a more linear fashion, disregarding, in a sense, those resultant harmonies.*

No listener can afford to ignore this point, for it is fundamental to a more intelligent approach toward listening. We must always remember that all music written before the year 1600 and much that was written later was music of polyphonic texture, so that when you listen to music of Palestrina or Orlando di Lasso, you must listen differently from the way you listen to Schubert or Chopin. That is true not only from the standpoint of its emotional meaning but also, technically, because the music was conceived in an entirely different way. Polyphonic texture implies a listener who can hear separate strands of melody sung by separate voices, instead of hearing only the sound of all the voices as they happen from moment to moment, vertical fashion.

The reader cannot expect to grasp this point thoroughly without listening to the same piece of music over and over again, making a mental effort to disentangle the interweaving voices. Here we must confine ourselves to a single illustration: the well-known chorale prelude by Bach Ich ruf' zu Dir, Herr Jesu Christ.

This is an example of three-voiced polyphony. As a bit of laboratory work, you should listen to this short piece four times, hearing first the part that is always easiest to hear—the top, or soprano, part. Now listen again, this time for the bass part which moves in a well-poised manner, making use of repeated notes. The alto, or middle voice, should be listened for next. This voice is a kind of figurated

---

* All the musical forms discussed so far fall into the category of harmonic (or *homophonic*) music, distinguished by different patterns of grouping melodies *one after the other*. The contrapuntal (or *polyphonic*) forms are distinguished by different patterns of grouping melodies *one above* (or *below*) *the other*.—E. S.

melody, but it is distinguishable from the others because of its sixteenth-note (faster) motion. Now hear all three voices together, keeping them well apart in your mind: the soprano with its sustained melody, the alto with the more flowing inner melody, and the bass with its poised line. A supplementary experiment might consist of hearing two voices at a time: soprano and bass, alto and soprano, bass and alto, before hearing all three voices together.

In carrying out this little experiment, you will be doing a very valuable thing for yourself. Until you can hear all polyphonic music in this way—in terms of voice against voice, line against line—you will not be listening properly.

Polyphonic texture brings with it the question of how many independent voices the human ear can grasp simultaneously. Opinions differ as to that. Even composers have occasionally attacked polyphony, holding it to be an intellectual idea that has been forced upon us—not a natural one. Nevertheless, I think it can safely be maintained that with a fair amount of listening experience, two- or three-voiced music can be heard without too much mental strain. Real trouble begins when the polyphony consists of four, five, six, or eight separate and independent voices. But, as a rule, listening polyphonically is aided by the composer because he seldom keeps all the voices going at the same time. Even in four-voiced polyphony, composers so manage that one voice is usually silent while the other three are active. This lightens the burden considerably.

There is also this to be said for polyphonic music: that repeated hearings keep up your interest better than music of homophonic texture. Even supposing that you do not hear all the separate voices equally well, there is every likelihood that when you return to it again, there will be something different for you to listen to. You can always hear it from a different angle.

The Round and the Canon

Abridged from the chapter "Arabesques and Architecture" in "Approach to Music"

By Lawrence Abbott

ANYONE who has ever joined in the sportive pastime of singing rounds, such as "Three Blind Mice," or "Frère Jacques," or "Oh, How Lovely

Is the Evening," has already experienced the pleasures of canon form. For the round is a simple form of canon. Its tune consists of three or four melodic phrases of equal length, so arranged that they harmonize perfectly when sung simultaneously. "Frère Jacques," for instance, is composed of four phrases: (A) *Frère Jacques,* (B) *Dormez vous,* (C) *Sonnez les matines,* and (D) *Din-dan-dou.* These can be combined melodically (placing one after another) and at the same time contrapuntally (placing one above the other) by the simple process of having four singers or instrumentalists perform the piece as if they were running a handicap race, one person being allowed to start ahead of the others, the second having to wait until the first has reached the quarter-way mark, and the other two spaced at similar intervals behind. The result is a two-dimensional pattern:

First voice: A B C D A B C D A B C D, etc.
Second voice: A B C D A B C D A B C, etc.
Third voice: A B C D A B C D A B, etc.
Fourth voice: A B C D A B C D A, etc.

Music of this sort can go on forever—in fact, it ends only when the performers arbitrarily stop at some prearranged signal, or else drop out one by one from sheer exhaustion.

A canon is likewise a handicap race, but instead of being a simple run around a circular track it is a difficult cross-country affair, and, to make it harder, the second melody starts almost on the first one's heels. For these reasons it would be an insuperably complex job for the composer to lay out a course over which three or four melodies could race without tripping over each other; and, even if he succeeded, the result would be too confusing for us listeners to follow with pleasure. So a canon features only two contestants. It consists of a continuously flowing melody which is chased by its own counterpart. The melody is called the "subject," and its reflection or shadow, which keeps always the same distance behind, is called the "imitation." The imitation may copy the melody tone for tone, either at the same pitch or an octave higher or lower, or it may be an approximate copy, starting at a different point in the scale (four tones higher, let us say, or three tones lower) and then following the melody's outline, always remaining the same number of tones higher or lower. The imitation may follow the subject at any distance, but in most canons it is only one or two beats behind.

The Fugue

By Elie Siegmeister

WHAT is a fugue? Certainly it has a bad reputation—that of being the driest, most forbidding, technical kind of music. We may recall the old definition: "A fugue is a piece of music in which the voices come in one after another and the audience go out one after another."

But what's this I hear? A quartet of saxophones playing a tricky piece of dance music. One of them, a high soprano, starts off with an impudent, hopping melody; a second picks up the tune; the two play about for a while like cat and mouse. Then here's the third, a mellow "tenor," with the tune lower down (the first two still scampering about up above). And pretty soon the last, a low, growling fellow, comes in with the same thing way down deep.

The four of them chatter and cackle away, tossing the phrase back and forth from one to the other. Sometimes one or two of the players drop out for a moment, as if to catch their breaths. When each comes back in, he is sure to have the melody to himself, blowing away for all he's worth. The excitement mounts; the repetitions of the tune come faster and faster—the players are practically stepping on one another's toes. Climax, pause, and *finis*.

"A fugue, did you say? Come on, professor—this is *real music!*"

Yes, and it was real music in Johann Sebastian's time. Dance music? Well, not quite—but wasn't that fugue in the last movement of one of his *French Suites* called a Jig (fancy spelling: *Gigue*)? Shades of Walt Disney and Leopold Stokowski! Wasn't it they who took the famous D minor Toccata and Fugue and convinced millions of people that old Bach was human? And isn't the fugue after all, the most *democratic* form of composition? In it everybody gets a chance: each voice has equal rights and ownership in the theme, each gets his moment to shine, all come out even at the end of the race.

This all may not be so far-fetched as it sounds. For the fugue does in fact go back to the old round, sung by members of communal groups for hundreds of years before Bach. And in carrying out the independence of the voices, this form is reaching back to the independence of each individual man in the village round, who chimes in with his voice at his appointed time, just as lusty and important as all the rest. Perhaps in reviving the fugue form (relatively neglected for a while after Bach's death), Mozart, Beethoven, Brahms, Hindemith, and Shostakovich simply re-asserted the old idea that making music is the job of many men working together in a close common bond, in which each counts.

Now all this, of course, gives you very few actual data on the *structure* of a fugue. If you wish a technical description, here it is:

The most important thing about the Fugue is the Subject—usually a short, compact melody—which is announced at the beginning of the piece. It is immediately taken up by a second voice entering at a certain fixed pitch relationship to the first voice,* which meanwhile takes up a contrasting melody known as the Counter-subject. Fugues may be in three, four, or five voices, each entering in turn with the Subject—always a given number of tones higher or lower than the previous "entry." This whole process is known as the "Exposition." It is always characterized by a sense of cumulative growth, because each voice, after it has completed the subject, continues to weave an independent melody of its own. The end of the Exposition thus leaves us with three, four, or five voices, blended perfectly together.

From this point on, the composer has freedom to develop his Subject by a number of different devices. He may (and almost always does) introduce it in different keys. He may use the device called "double counterpoint"—which simply means that the music has been turned topsy-turvy. (The Subject, which may have been *above* the Counter-subject originally, now appears *below* it, or vice versa.) The Subject may be changed in ways termed Inversion (upside down); Augmentation (twice as slow); and Diminution (twice as fast). One more typical fugue device may be named: the Stretto. It generally occurs near the end of the composition and consists of a series of interlocking entries of the subject arranged in cumulative, climactic fashion.

Any such series of technical terms is bound to make the fugue sound like a musical crossword puzzle, and in a sense that is what it is. In a well-written fugue, every note must be in its place, and practically each one must have a good reason for being where it is. Certainly it requires intellect and a certain mathematical turn of mind to become a successful writer of fugues.

All the more reason, then, why we marvel at men such as Bach,

* Either five scale steps above, or four below.

who took this abstruse, scholastic pattern and made it into music. Certain movements of the B minor Mass are so stirring emotionally that you never realize that they are fugues unless you stop to think about it. Other compositions of Bach in fugue form are dreamy, poetic, or charged with grief; meditative, stormy, playful, or grandiose. To the old master, handling the fugue was as natural as writing tuneful melodies was to Schubert.

Yet, paradoxically enough, it is not because of the fugue alone that all this technical information is important. For the various fugal devices passed from the fugue itself into the general technical storehouse of the musical art. Knowing the various ins and outs of fugal writing is as essential to the serious composer as is a knowledge of complex strategy to a general. Although he may never write a fugue, this knowledge will stand the composer in good stead in almost any other type of work he may undertake. It is essential to the writer of symphonies and string quartets, where fugal-type sections often occur, and it can even help the writer of operas and ballet music. For it teaches the composer that basic principle of all art—how to make the most out of the smallest materials.

Sonata Form

By Elie Siegmeister

SONATA form is one of the most important forms of composition, for it is the pattern not only of works actually entitled "Sonata" but of string quartets, trios, quintets, symphonies, and most overtures as well. First developed about two centuries ago, it is still widely used —even by some of our most rabid modernists—and no form has yet appeared that seems likely to take its place.

The form of a sonata's first movement (the only part of it that I shall discuss right now) is in many ways like a three-act play, with Exposition, Conflict, and Dénouement. In most sonatas, the main character (in musical language, Theme I) enters right on the stage and plunges directly into the action. However, the sonata may begin instead with a short prelude, in which apparently nothing of great importance happens, but in which the stage is being set, as it were, for the main business which is shortly to begin. This is like those plays which open with the butler and maid engaged in a very casual conversation. You just know that right in the middle of it somewhere the hero will suddenly burst in and things will get going.*

The first thing every good playwright knows is that each of his *dramatis personae* must have a distinct character of his own. In the sonata, too, Themes I and II (also III and IV, if any) must have their marked personalities, each sharply distinguished from the others. If the opening theme is vigorous and dramatic, for instance, the second is likely to be more contemplative, or at least lyrical and songlike. Listen to the first idea of Beethoven's Fifth Symphony (the "Fate-knocks-at-the-door," or "V" theme). Note its sharp, gruff, rhythmic character.

The second theme, on the other hand,

has the tender, "yielding" quality that Beethoven's second themes were famous for.

Of course, not all first themes are gruff and vigorous, nor all succeeding ones tender. Mozart's beautiful G minor Symphony opens with one of the most melancholy themes in all music:

Only afterwards does the orchestra launch into a sharp, rhythmic melody that contrasts beautifully with the first:

—which just goes to show that there are many ways of writing a sonata.†

Now we've met our main characters—Themes I and II, and per-

* In some cases, however, the prelude may create a tragic and beautiful mood of anticipation or suspense. Examples are the opening of Beethoven's *Egmont* and *Leonore* Overtures, comparable in their psychological effect to the first page of *Hamlet* in which two soldiers stand guard and talk of nothing very important; but one knows that the Ghost is coming.

† Strictly speaking, this is the "bridge passage," not the second theme itself; but the principle is the same.

haps two or three subordinate ones; we're all set for things to happen. Curtain on Act I (or "Exposition," if you prefer technical language).

Act II. Just as in the play, the leading characters get involved in all sorts of complicated intrigues. They enter and leave abruptly and in rapid succession. Musically speaking, the themes are broken up, twisted about, drawn out, combined with each other. They appear in many guises and disguises. Various aspects of their characters which we had never before suspected are now revealed. Under the stress of the action, one and the same theme appears in different moments as forceful, hesitant, meditative, humorous, or noble.

All along, the pace of this Act II ("Development section") is constantly shifting. Little climaxes are built up, agitation suddenly shifting to quiet—and then, when you are least expecting it, to a dramatic mood all over again. Finally the big climax really appears. All the forces are gathered for action, the music builds powerfully— and what happens?

Act III. In the drama, the complications would be reaching their height here. But in music, it is generally such an effort to follow the leading themes through all the distortions and disguises they have assumed in Act II (the development) that the composer usually decides to present them once more in a clear and straightforward manner. The dénouement in music ("recapitulation") consists in hearing all the themes of Act I again in more or less their original form. We're very glad to find they have come through the fracas of Act II safe and sound. I say "more or less" original form because the themes never return exactly the same as when they started. There is something about them now that wasn't quite there before—something richer and stronger, a sense of added growth and importance. With this, and a short final flourish (the "coda," or tailpiece), the early Sonata writers would bring their argument to a close.

But along about the time of the French Revolution, when the ideas of conflict, aspiration, and struggle-to-the-end became uppermost in many men's minds, composers—especially Beethoven—began to be dissatisfied with this way of bowing the characters out in a polite happy ending. He felt something bigger and more affirmative was needed with which to close.

And so he introduced something new: Act IV (or the "Final development"). Having brought his themes back more or less intact, Beethoven now proceeds to put them through a second and more intense conflict, from which one—almost always the first theme—emerges as the pinnacle and capstone of the entire work. So end the first movements of all Beethoven's symphonies after the Fourth (and also most symphonies since Beethoven's time). The circle is completed: the dramatic process attains its goal with the very opening thought now completely resolved at the end.

This, then, is the basic pattern of the Sonata's first movement as understood by Beethoven, Schumann, Chopin, Brahms, Debussy, and many more recent masters. Of course, there is much more detail that could be added—about "bridge passages," "modulations," subthemes, "codettas" and what not. Also it must be remembered that free treatments of the Sonata pattern are to be encountered almost as frequently as the original pattern itself. But all these details are comparatively unimportant for most purposes; if the reader will bear the general outline in mind, he will have enough to keep him busy for quite a while.

So much for the Sonata form itself. Remember, what we have been talking about thus far is the form of only the *first* movement of a sonata or a symphony. What of the other movements?

In many four-movement works the Sonata pattern is used in every movement, except the third (the Minuet or Scherzo). But, though the technical design may be more or less the same, the substance and spirit of the various movements rarely is—that would produce unbearable monotony. Broadly speaking, the plan of a typical Sonata, Quartet, or Symphony since Beethoven's time is roughly the following: *

First Movement: commonly the longest and most serious of the four. It is usually lively and vigorous—though the quiet, slow opening is now being used often. As a "keynote" movement, it should challenge the listener, make him "sit up and take notice"—both emotionally and intellectually.

Second Movement: in nine cases out of ten the slow movement. After the arresting, taxing nature of the opener, it gives the listener a chance to relax and bask in a long, expansive melody. The second movement relies more on mood than on construction. It is a test of the composer's power to create a poetic or lyrical "line" that flows on almost endlessly (unfortunately it is sometimes a test also of the listener's power to stay awake). Sometimes, instead of Sonata form,

---

* Of course, the exceptions are legion. Also one must not forget that the four-movement scheme is not always employed. Very often there are only three movements; sometimes five, or even six or seven.

this movement consists of a Theme and Variations—or, simpler yet, a Three-Part form: a mood, a contrasted one, the first again.

Third Movement: This is the one part of the Sonata or Symphony that almost never employs Sonata form. After the quiet, sustained, and often meditative quality of the slow movement, something light and refreshing is decidedly in order. The third movement is almost always a dance, full of rhythm and animal spirits. In the old days, it was a Minuet, lusty or elegant; with Beethoven it is a racy, prankish Scherzo; in Brahms's symphonies, a folklike *allegretto;* in Tchaikovsky's Fifth, a Waltz; in some of Mahler's symphonies, a homely Austrian *Ländler;* and in a recent symphony by Harl McDonald a Rhumba was used as Third movement. Even in Shostakovich's realistic and serious *Leningrad* Symphony, the composer felt it necessary to relax the mood and to introduce his Third movement with a light, Scherzo-like subject.

Fourth Movement: This is the last and least predictable of all. Sometimes, as in Haydn, it is a brisk and playful Rondo, a cheerful "good-bye." Beethoven did all sorts of things with the fourth movement: in the *Eroica* it is a set of variations on a contradanse; in the Fifth, a paean to struggle and victory; in the Seventh it becomes the famous "apotheosis of the dance"; in the Ninth, the great "Ode to Joy" dominates—voices, soloists, and chorus joining the orchestra in Schiller's hymn of universal brotherhood.

Since Beethoven's time, composers have been quite at a loss to know what to do with their last movements. Some, like Mahler, have kept the Chorus idea; others have reverted to the light mood of Haydn; still others, like César Franck, have thought it wise to bring the theme of the very first movement back again in full glory. But, whatever the form, the last movement usually closes in a strong mood. Tchaikovsky is the only composer who dared introduce a note of mournful despondency in his Finales. Composers of recent sonatas and symphonies have proceeded on the idea that audiences wish to leave the concert hall with a feeling of "lift" and exhilaration.

The Symphony

Abridged from two chapters in "Listening to Music"

By Douglas Moore

IT IS customary to call the last half of the eighteenth century the classic period of music. The reason is that during these years instrumental forms were definitely fixed. Not only do we find here the framework upon which all subsequent music has been built, but we also discover that here for the first time instrumental groupings, such as the symphony orchestra, the string quartet and the chamber ensemble, were standardized.

THE CLASSIC SYMPHONY ORCHESTRA

It seems hard to realize that the symphony orchestra as we know it did not come at once. On the contrary, the orchestras which accompanied the early operas varied enormously. The basis of the orchestra was the harpsichord; the players were kept together when necessary by signals from the harpsichordist much in the fashion that the obsolescent theater orchestra is directed by a pianist who occasionally raises a free hand to give a down beat to his colleagues. To one or several harpsichords the composer would add those instruments which he thought necessary for the dramatic effects of the work. It was not until Lully (1633-1687) assembled a group of winds and strings that a body somewhat like our symphony orchestra came into being.

Even after Lully, orchestras depended somewhat upon the purse of the noble who kept the players as a part of his retinue. Bach in his work at Cöthen where he was court composer, or at Leipzig where he provided church music, never had what we should recognize as a full orchestra. You will notice this if you watch the grouping of players used to accompany the Mass in B minor or to play one of the *Brandenburg* concertos.

Haydn (1732-1809), however, was so fortunate as to be employed by the wealthy Prince Esterházy, who gave him enough players so that he was able to standardize certain groups and write works for them which served as the basis for all succeeding compositions. To the typical orchestra of Haydn, consisting of flutes, oboes, bassoons, trumpets, horns, strings, and kettledrums, Mozart added the clarinets * and the trombones; thus we have the model for the great Wagnerian orchestra of the nineteenth century.

Some time before the appearance of Haydn, the viol family had been definitely displaced by the louder and more effective violin type. In Haydn's time the harpsichord gave way to the louder and more rhythmic piano. Practically all the instruments which we have today existed in fairly complete form in the classic age. The brass instruments were made without valves and consequently were unable to play all the notes of the scale, but this limitation was somewhat compensated for by the skill and adroitness of the classic composers in using them. The classic symphony orchestra, which today is often reproduced in the concert hall for performances of the Haydn and Mozart symphonies, differs chiefly in volume from the one required for modern works. There was no distinction made between chamber music and music for large orchestra. Doubling of parts, whatever the nomenclature of the composition, was the usual practice, and as we have seen, the number of players available usually determined the size of the ensemble.

We have then, in Haydn's time, the first genuine distinction made between chamber and orchestral music. In the category of chamber music we find the trio, quartet, quintet, and sonata for one or more instruments. In the realm of the orchestra we find the symphony, the overture, and the concerto.

The general design and the forms employed in this new music greatly resembled one another. They represent a fusion and extension of preceding forms: the French and Italian overture, the concerto, the suite, and the fugue. These forms were developed and standardized by the composers of the so-called Mannheim School—Stamitz, Richter, and others—and the Viennese composers Haydn and Mozart. Although modifications are to be observed in succeeding composers, the principles of the classic composers, once established, have continued as the basis of all instrumental music in the larger forms.

THE CLASSIC SYMPHONY

In listening to the classic symphony we must bear in mind that it is entirely different in scope from the symphony of Beethoven and

---

* Until this time, the clarinet was considered a vulgar instrument, fit only for the lower-class dances and weddings where it was commonly used. Mozart's introduction of it into his symphonies was a distinctly "modern" step somewhat analogous to the use of the saxophone in serious music some years ago.—E. S.

Brahms, and was conceived for a very different audience. The late eighteenth century was an age of formalism where deep feeling was somewhat distrusted. Had one of Prince Esterházy's audiences been given a performance of such a work as the *Pathetic* Symphony of Tchaikovsky, it would have been much surprised by its length, noisiness, and excess of emotion. Tchaikovsky's music was prepared for by the great expansion of musical form and content which Beethoven and his successors provided. If we are at first inclined to regard the classic symphony as cold and formal, we should try to imagine ourselves back in an age which preferred more restrained expression. The gracefulness, good taste, and elegant proportions of classic music are qualities which wear well.

The classic symphony was much shorter than the symphony of the nineteenth century. This explains the difference in volume of output between Haydn and Mozart on the one hand, and Beethoven and Brahms on the other. Haydn wrote about one hundred and forty-three symphonies during his long life, Mozart in a much shorter span wrote forty-one. Mozart wrote so fast, we are told, that he composed his three most popular symphonies, the G minor, the E flat major, and the C major, in the space of six weeks one summer. Beethoven wrote only nine symphonies and Brahms four. Brahms worked for ten years on his first symphony before he gave it to the public. Undoubtedly the classic symphonies were often perfunctorily made. They were intended for a single occasion and many of them were not repeated. The idea of printing and wide circulation was very far from the composers' minds.

Among Haydn's and Mozart's works, and indeed in the case of later composers, we find short collections of pieces under a single heading which are really little symphonies and resemble the larger type in general construction. Such works are called Serenades or Divertimentos. A very famous example of this is Mozart's serenade, *Eine Kleine Nachtmusik*.

THE SYMPHONY OF THE NINETEENTH CENTURY

It would not be possible to include within the scope of this study even a bare outline of the history of the symphony of the nineteenth century. What particularly concerns us is the symphonic framework, not its history. Perhaps it is easier to study this framework as it was built up from composer to composer, confining ourselves to those men who were responsible for its growth.

There is not a single tendency of the nineteenth century which we do not find at least suggested in the works of Beethoven (1770-1827). He is to the symphony what Bach is to the fugue. If we can understand the large symphonic canvas of Beethoven, no other symphonies written before or since should lie beyond our grasp.

BEETHOVEN

Beethoven studied composition for a time with Haydn and, as might be expected, his early compositions show the clear imprint of his teacher's hand. The first two symphonies follow not only the design, but the style, of the Haydn symphony; all the movements are in Sonata form with the exception of the third movement of each. The third movement of the First Symphony suggests a typical Haydn minuet, but the third movement of the Second Symphony is a scherzo somewhat more characteristic of Beethoven's own personality. Although the form of the scherzo is like that of the minuet, its character undergoes a profound metamorphosis. The gay minuet of Haydn and Mozart is nothing like the impetuous, headlong Beethovenian scherzo. The word scherzo means jest; Beethoven's jesting is what you would expect from the man himself—rough and uncouth, but tremendously vital. His jesting reaches a climax in the scherzo of the Ninth Symphony, which is playful somewhat as a Jove is playful, hurling thunderbolts at mortals below.

From the Third Symphony on, Beethoven writes out the third section of the scherzo instead of indicating by the sign da capo that the first part is to be repeated literally. The Fifth Symphony scherzo has a third section in which the presentation of the first section material is greatly changed; also this scherzo does not come to an end, but is joined to the last movement. The Eighth Symphony, which is a reversion to the classic pattern, is an exception to the above, and the third movement has again the characteristic features of the Haydn minuet, with the use of the da capo sign for literal repetition of the first part.

The changed aspect of the third movement had a somewhat disturbing effect upon the proportions of the symphony as conceived by Haydn. The lilting, tuneful rondo followed very naturally after the dignified dance rhythm of the minuet, but the scherzo steals some of the fire of the classic rondo and leaves the last movement with the necessity of establishing another mood. As a result the last movement grew in importance until, in some cases, it was sufficiently serious to compete with the first movement. In the Ninth Symphony Beethoven put the scherzo movement second so that the joyful finale comes as a marked contrast to the lyric and leisurely third movement.

But it is in Sonata form itself that the greatest change is to be noticed. We find great expansion of length, the inclusion of additional material and yet a greater degree of compactness of design. This compactness is a result of Beethoven's conception of form as something dramatic, and his use of thematic contrasts which furnish material for lengthy development. Even in the longest Sonata-form movements of Beethoven, nothing is included which does not serve the main idea. The general procedure is to alternate the moods of themes: a rhythmically vigorous idea is usually succeeded by an expressive one of melodic character. The most salient of these themes are selected for treatment in the development section. There is no padding; no episodes are included merely because they sound well. The main purpose of the movement is always in view.

The first section of the form, that devoted to statement of the themes, is different from that of Haydn and Mozart because of greater clarity of themes. You will never be in doubt as to what constitutes the principal theme of one of Beethoven's movements in Sonata form. When the theme has been stated he proceeds at once to the bridge where we often find an idea of much thematic importance. With the arrival of the new key a second theme is stated, generally lyric in character. This theme is sometimes regarded merely as a lyric interlude to form a contrast with the principal theme, but seldom to appear in the development section.

The Third Symphony (Eroica), one of the longest, has an innovation which only appears once in all the symphonies, an innovation which has caused endless trouble to explain. He introduces a new theme in the middle of the development section. It bears no resemblance to anything contained in the exposition section. Perhaps it does as well as anything to say that at that point Beethoven needed another theme to contrast with his powerful first theme; there was no place to include it in the exposition, so he simply stated it when he was ready to use it for development. It is a singularly lovely theme, one that you will easily recognize if you play through the movement.

The Beethovenian coda assumes great proportions; sometimes it is even more interesting than the development section. He regards it as a second development: further conclusions to be drawn about his material after it has been restated in the recapitulation.

Here is the general plan of Beethoven's treatment of Sonata form as found in a number of his larger works:

1. Exposition of principal themes stated in terms of contrast.
2. Development of the most important themes.
3. Recapitulation showing variation of themes as affected by development.
4. Further development completely establishing one theme as victor.

All forms and all movements suffer changes at the hands of Beethoven. In the second movement there is a tendency away from Sonata form to song form. In three of the symphonies, the Fifth, Seventh, and Ninth, the slow movement is a theme or double theme and variation. These are nothing like the loosely connected pieces of the classic age; the divisions are carefully concealed, and the relation of variation to theme is often very subtle. The third movement, as described above, was changed from the Second Symphony on from minuet to scherzo, retaining in general the form of the minuet. In the last movement we find Sonata form, rondo-sonata, or theme and variations. For the finale of the Ninth Symphony, which is a theme and variations of great length, a chorus is employed for the first time in the history of the symphony; the text is Schiller's *Ode to Joy*.

The use of voices as an additional resource of the symphony was regarded by Beethoven's contemporaries as very daring. Indeed, of the later composers of the nineteenth century only Mahler has employed this innovation, but this step of Beethoven's was of profound influence in the case of Wagner.

CYCLIC FORM

So much for the separate movements of the Beethoven symphonies. They are not hard to follow provided you hear the exposition section frequently enough to become familiar with the themes. It is interesting as you listen to one of these expositions to speculate upon the choice of themes for development and what their role will be. In this way you will gain much insight into the mind of the composer.

In the problem of relationship of the movements constituting the symphony, Beethoven evidently felt an impulse toward unification. Early in the century potpourri symphonies with movements collected from different works were often played. The inter-relationship of movements of the symphony, linking them not only by means of tonality but by certain resemblances of themes, served to make the succession of movements more logical. This is what we call the *cyclic* treatment of themes in the symphony. There are a few traces of this in some of the early works of Beethoven; for example in the *Pathetic* Sonata, Opus 13, the second theme of the first movement is the basis for the rondo refrain of the finale. In the scherzo of the Fifth Symphony there appears a theme which is rhythmically similar to the principal motive of the first movement. The relation between this scherzo and the finale is very close: the scherzo does not end but leads into the finale, and in the course of this movement it reappears as a part of the development section.

It is in the Ninth Symphony, however, that we have the most surprising cyclic treatment of themes. In the long introduction to the last movement, one by one the themes of the preceding movements appear, led by a sort of conductor theme, until finally the theme proper ushers in the main body of the movement. This statement of the most important previous themes seems to sum up the whole symphony and tie it together.

Whether or not Beethoven intended to prescribe this unification as necessary to the symphony is not known. Certain composers who succeeded him, notably César Franck and his school, seized upon the idea as one of great importance and used themes interchangeably between movements. When carried too far, this leads to monotony. If a theme is much developed in the first movement, we are glad to pass on to fresh material when we come to the second. But if used with reticence, as Beethoven himself employed it, theme reminiscence from movement to movement adds to the unity of the whole work.

Beethoven's form tended to be increasingly subjective; it became the expression of his own thoughts, something personal and suited to his individual style of subject matter. He dominated every composer who came after him and seemed to exemplify every discovery of the century. When we think that we have grasped the essential nature of his method, we are sure to come upon a work which refuses to be included in such a system. Many composers who have found in Beethoven their chief inspiration also give evidence that they did not neglect the basic principles of Haydn and the classic Sonata form.

Of these composers of the symphony, Brahms (1833-1897) is easily the most important. Many of the romantic composers such as Schubert (1797-1828), Schumann (1810-1856), and Mendelssohn

(1809-1847) composed symphonies which if less important than those of Beethoven, especially from an architectural point of view, have won an enduring place in the concert repertory.

SCHUBERT

Schubert wrote eight symphonies. The first six are classic in style and bear closer relationship to the symphonies of Haydn than to those of Beethoven. They are, however, of great lyric beauty and it is surprising that they appear so seldom on concert programs. The Eighth Symphony in B minor, known as the *Unfinished* Symphony, is an extraordinary composition in two movements. These combine Schubert's genius for melody and for the dramatic. For some reason he never added the third and fourth movements although sketches exist which indicate that he had planned to do so.

The Seventh Symphony in C major, composed after the Eighth, is the longest and most important of his works in this form. The texture of the writing is less compact than that of Beethoven, and the material lacks his power of concentration; but the themes are so beautiful that questions of form and style become rather futile when applied to a consideration of the work. From beginning to end this symphony is marked by sustained and joyous lyricism.

SCHUMANN

The four symphonies of Schumann contain much beautiful music which is somewhat handicapped by his comparative lack of skill in orchestration. Schumann's genius for form which is everywhere evident in his shorter works seems less adapted to the extended lengths of the symphony. Particularly in his treatment of first-movement form we feel that like Schubert he is somewhat at a disadvantage, often confused or even pedantic. Generally the slow movements and the scherzo are where he excels, but even there he is not always effective orchestrally. Schumann's greatest work for orchestra is his piano concerto, where his natural gift for writing for the instrument gives momentum and authority to the whole. Many musicians consider this the finest piano concerto in the literature of music.

MENDELSSOHN

The two most frequently played symphonies of Mendelssohn are the *Scotch* and the *Italian* Symphonies. Mendelssohn was considered a classicist by his contemporaries. It was he who discovered some of the forgotten choral works of Bach and gave them to the public. He was a skilled and erudite composer, an artist of subtle delicacy and aristocratic charm. His symphonies are written with an almost perfect understanding of the resources of the orchestra. If, in general, the texture is not so compact nor the development so interesting as the symphonic style of Beethoven, the first movement of the *Italian* Symphony must be cited as an exception. This entire movement is related to, and penetrated by, the joyous, youthful motive which begins it.

BRAHMS

With the appearance of Brahms some years later, the symphony came into a great renaissance. Not since the time of Bach had there been a composer who had so thoroughly assimilated all forms and styles of his predecessors. In the midst of the Romantic movement, in the very shadow of Wagner's overwhelming popularity, Brahms coolly surveyed the music of all the ages, including that of his own, and selected those elements which seemed to him most congenial. At a time when program music was the rage, he furnished no explanatory material about his work and confined himself to objective forms.

From Bach and the sixteenth-century masters he selected polyphonic treatment as opposed to the homophony in vogue. From the Middle Ages he gained his interest in the ancient modes, often flavoring his melodies with these melodic intervals. From the classic masters he took his solidity of design, and from Beethoven his manipulation of themes and logic of development. His was not a dramatic talent, so we do not feel in the developments of Brahms that breathless excitement and cataclysmic tragedy which sometimes characterizes the music of Beethoven; but his music is probably the most compact of all, its logic derived from beautifully calculated development of contrasting musical designs. Every note of Brahms can be explained in terms of music alone. His music always sounds rich in texture, with more emphasis on purely sensuous beauty than is sometimes the case in Beethoven.

If Beethoven is more elemental and tempestuous, Brahms creates a music which is invariably exalted and inspired. Both composers excel in humanity and tenderness. Brahms sounds warmer perhaps than his predecessor because he uses the rich harmonies of the age of romantic music.

The innovations which Brahms brings to the form of the symphony are not many. Chief among them is his treatment of the dance movement which in each of his four symphonies is placed third in the group of four. He uses neither the Beethovenian scherzo, which was not at all sympathetic to his nature, nor the archaic minuet of Haydn. His dance is a slower, sweeter dance with the melodious quality of the folk song. For the form he uses a variant of simple song form.

FRANCK

We have already discussed the great emphasis laid upon cyclic treatment of themes by César Franck (1822-1890) and his school. Franck, like Brahms, was a master of form and entirely independent of his contemporaries. Although he wrote only one symphony, his sonata for violin and piano, quintet for piano and strings, and string quartet are very fine examples of symphonic writing. Aside from the tendency to theme unification, we notice that he is quite polyphonic in style, being especially fond of canon and fugue and of theme combination. The logic of his developments is excellent,* although less dramatic than Beethoven and less lyric than Brahms. He has a genius for symphonic themes which are both melodious and suitable for development.

If there is a serious weakness in the music of Franck it is his overfondness for the chromatic scale and too frequent modulation. This sometimes gives his works a tonal instability, the modulation also leading him into sequences which somewhat lessen the musical interest.

TCHAIKOVSKY

Other frequently heard symphonies are the Fourth, Fifth, and Sixth of Tchaikovsky. Tchaikovsky (1840-1893) like Schubert is not a master of symphonic development but wins his popularity by wealth of melody. To this is added a reflection of his intense emotional nature and a dash of the fresh color of the Russian folk song to make his work interesting. His first movements are generally very long and rather loosely made. However, they are magnificently scored and sound as well, orchestrally speaking, as any symphonies in the literature.

* Mr. Moore's estimate of Franck's developments is by no means universally accepted. To me many of his developments seem obvious and tiresome.—E. S.

The Modern Symphony

Abridged from the chapter "Sonata Form" in "What to Listen for in Music"

By Aaron Copland

UP TO a few years ago, the impression was current that modern composers had abandoned the form of the symphony. No doubt there was a lull in interest on the part of leading men of the first twenty years of the present century. Debussy, Ravel, Schönberg, and Stravinsky in their mature years did not write symphonies. But more recently that has changed.* Symphonies are being written again, if we can judge by the works of Frenchmen like Roussel and Honegger; Russians like Miaskovsky (with fifteen to his credit †), Prokofiev, and Shostakovich; Englishmen like Bax, Vaughan Williams, and Walton; Americans like Harris, Sessions, and Piston. We should not forget the further fact that, even during the period of its supposed decline, the symphonic form was being practised by stalwarts such as Mahler and Sibelius. Perhaps it is indicative of a renewed interest in the form that only in the present day have their works begun to find a place in the regular repertoire of symphonic organizations.

MAHLER

Mahler and Sibelius have been more adventurous in their treatment of the form than some of the later men. Mahler wanted desperately to make the symphony *bigger* than it was. He enlarged the size of the orchestra to gargantuan proportions, increased the number of movements, introduced the choral body in the Second and Eighth, and in general took it upon himself to carry on the traditions of the Beethoven symphony. Mahler has been bitterly attacked as a poseur, as having been hopelessly misled in his pretensions. But if one can pick and choose among the separate movements of his nine symphonies, I for one am certain that his eventual position will be equivalent to that of Berlioz. At any rate, we can find the derivation of new contrapuntal

* Even Stravinsky has recently written a symphony—his second in thirty-five years.—E. S.

† Correction as of early 1943: there are now twenty-three Miaskovsky symphonies!—E. S.

textures and new orchestral colors in his work, without which the modern symphony would be inconceivable.

SIBELIUS

Sibelius has handled the form freely, especially in his Fourth and Seventh symphonies. The latter belongs with the rather rare species of one-movement symphonies. Much has been written of Sibelius's masterly development of symphonic form. But it is a question whether his departures from the usual norm have not been so great as to be almost disconnected from the nineteenth-century model. My own guess is that the Seventh is closer in form, despite its name, to the symphonic poem than it is to the symphony. At any rate, from the lay listener's point of view, it must be remembered that Sibelius's movements are not conventionally constructed and depend on the gradual organic growth of one theme evolving into another rather than on the contrast of one theme with another. At its best, the music seems to flower, often from unpromising beginnings.

If any generalizations may be made as to the handling of the form by more recent composers, one can safely say that the symphony as a collection of three or more separate movements is still as firmly established as ever. There is still nothing puny or casual about the form. It is still the form in which the composer tries to come to grips with big emotions. If any fundamental changes may be discerned, they are likely to be changes of the inner structural setup of an individual movement. In that restricted sense, the form is freer—the materials are introduced in a more relaxed way—the divisions into first, second, and closing groups are much less clear if they are present at all; no one can predict the nature of the development section or the extent of the recapitulation, if any. That's why the modern symphony is more difficult to listen to than the older, to us more fully digested, examples of the form.

Clearly, the symphony, and with it the Sonata Allegro form, is not finished yet. Unless all signs are misleading, they both will have a healthy progeny.

The Symphonic Poem and the Symphonic Suite

Adapted from "Listening to Music"

By Douglas Moore

THE great change which came about in the composer's attitude toward his art at the beginning of the nineteenth century is well illustrated by Beethoven. Instead of conceiving music as objective design, as the classic masters did, composers of the romantic period became increasingly interested in its possibilities as a vehicle for the expression of ideas and emotions.

Not that the greatest composers of the nineteenth century advocated the abandonment of form for program, since each one of them insisted upon the limitations of music in pictorial descriptions. In speaking of his *Pastoral* Symphony Beethoven expressed the general attitude toward program music: "More the expression of inner feeling than picturing." The *Pastoral* Symphony itself shows little deviation from standard shape, the principal innovation being the inclusion of a fifth movement, portraying a storm in the country, between the scherzo and the finale.

Although the importance of design was always admitted, it was perfectly natural that a slight weakening of formal texture should ensue. Beethoven, himself master of form, permitted his interest in the expressive side of music to alter forms; but, as we have seen, the resulting new forms suffered no loss of logic or of musical character.

Beethoven's successors and contemporaries, with the exception of Brahms and Wagner, had less genius than he for the conception and execution of new forms. Deviation from accepted designs generally brought with it a certain weakness and ambiguity. We find that up to the time of Brahms the symphony suffered a decline. When composers such as Schubert, Schumann, and Chopin wrote in Sonata form, it proved to be a less effective medium than others for their melodic and expressive gifts, with the result that they inclined to designs which imposed less formal obligations upon them. In writing for the piano, song form and the single piece became the vogue instead of the sonata. These compositions of Schubert, Schumann, and Chopin, so familiar on recital programs, should offer little difficulty to the listener.

BERLIOZ

In orchestral music, however, the short or extended song form did not seem to provide a sufficiently large canvas. Accordingly, before Liszt, we find the romantic composers still writing overtures and symphonies, compositions of somewhat weakened design which gave an increasing importance to descriptive titles and emotional content. However, even Berlioz (1805-1869), who is generally regarded as the greatest enemy of absolute music, used the forms of the symphony more or less as employed by Beethoven in his orchestral compositions. The *Fantastic* Symphony for all its weird program is entirely explicable in terms of design alone. The reason why this symphony is less great than the symphonies of Beethoven is not that it is revolutionary in form, or relies too much upon poetical ideas; it is simply that the music is inferior to Beethoven's.

LISZT

It was Liszt (1811-1886), master pianist and generous friend to everything that was new in the art, who hit upon the form which came to be known as the *symphonic poem*. He said in explaining his work: "In program music, the return, change, modification and modulation of the motives are conditioned by their relation to a poetic idea. All exclusively musical considerations, though they should not be neglected, have to be subordinated to the action of a given subject."

The symphonic poem, as exemplified in the works of Liszt, consists of one long movement easily divisible into sections. There may occur any number of changes of time and of key, and the composition may be based upon a number of themes. Unity is secured by plan of tonality (always well calculated in Liszt's works), repetition, and development of themes. One feature of this development is called *theme metamorphosis*. It consists in presenting a theme in successively different shapes, bearing always a recognizable relationship to its original state but undergoing changes of rhythm, melody, and harmony which give it an entirely different aspect. This theme metamorphosis is not unlike Beethoven's theme amplification. We find it not only in the symphonic poems of composers who come after Liszt, but even in the symphonies of Brahms.

It would seem that this somewhat loose form would be difficult to follow. It does not permit of standardization as we find it in other symphonic forms. Apart from the program there is no way of predicting what will occur in the composition. For this reason, in listening to a symphonic poem, our enjoyment is always enhanced by a previous understanding of the program, which generally suggests the division of the music into sections and even the disposition of themes.

RICHARD STRAUSS

The most interesting figure in the symphonic poem after Liszt, and the composer who has done most to popularize the form, is Richard Strauss. Born in 1864, Strauss is still living and still writing. Of late years, however, he has been more interested in opera than in orchestral music, and his compositions which are most often played were written at the end of the nineteenth century.

Strauss based his symphonic poems upon the Liszt model, but brought to it a thorough knowledge of symphonic structure and an almost perfect technical equipment. In fact Strauss is so much a master of the orchestra, of polyphonic writing and theme manipulation, that he blinds us to the mediocrity sometimes lurking beneath his complicated musical surfaces. Some of his symphonic poems, however, such as *Till Eulenspiegel, Don Juan, Death and Transfiguration, Ein Heldenleben,* and *Don Quixote,* have taken their place in the standard repertory of the orchestra of today.

Strauss is less dependent upon his program than Liszt. The music often takes shapes which are readily explicable in forms as employed by Beethoven. Strauss has said himself, "The program is a poetical help in creating new shapes." These new shapes are, for the most part, not especially revolutionary developments of such familiar forms as theme and variations, rondo or even Sonata form.

THE MODERNS

Other more or less popular composers of symphonic poems are Tchaikovsky (1840-1893) who was admittedly programmatic even in his symphonies, but who wrote several symphonic poems, among them *Francesca da Rimini;* Scriabin, the Russian composer of the early twentieth century, whose symphonies are really symphonic poems in one movement; Debussy (1862-1918) whose *Afternoon of a Faun* is a masterpiece of design as well as an excellent bit of tone-painting; and Sibelius with the popular *Finlandia,* Ravel with *La Valse,* Dukas with *The Sorcerer's Apprentice,* and Honegger with *Pacific 231.*

The tendency among contemporary composers of the symphonic poem is toward less program and more independence of design. Debussy, Ravel, and Honegger have no story attached to their compositions; the title alone indicates that the material is influenced by a poetic idea. Among American composers of the symphonic poem are to be noted Ernest Schelling with *A Victory Ball,* Gershwin with *An American in Paris,* Hanson with *Pan and the Priest,* and Sowerby with *Prairie.* The symphonic poem as conceived by Liszt is not in accord with the tendency of this age, being rather too diffuse and pretentious, but the idea of a symphonic composition in a single movement with descriptive title continues to be popular with both composers and audiences.

THE SYMPHONIC SUITE

The orchestral suite, so frequently played at symphony concerts, is of two varieties. Neither one is to be confused with the eighteenth-century suite of Bach, Handel and their contemporaries. The old form of the suite has completely failed to interest composers since the time of Haydn. Examples of it in modern times might be found, but not among the works most familiar to audiences.

The first type consists of an arrangement of excerpts from incidental dramatic music or ballet. Although these excerpts may be in any form, they are generally in the simple design of the three-part song form. The usual explanation of their collection and performance as a group of pieces apart from the stage work for which they were composed is that in this way successful dramatic music may be made available for the large concert-going public. Familiar examples of this type of suite are to be found in the *Nutcracker Suite* from a ballet of Tchaikovsky; the suite from *Peer Gynt* of Grieg, consisting of incidental music written for a performance of the Ibsen play; two suites from *L'Arlésienne* of Bizet, originally intended to accompany the action of a play of Daudet; and a suite made by Stravinsky from his ballet *Petroushka.*

The other type of suite is more interesting, symphonically speaking, for instead of being an arbitrary arrangement of musical excerpts for concert performance, it is conceived as a suite entirely apart from dramatic representation. Usually it has a descriptive title like the symphonic poem, but differs from it in that it consists of a number of short movements. As in the symphonic poem, no definite form is prescribed, but simple song form is generally employed.

One of the best compositions of this type is the popular symphonic suite, *Scheherazade* of Rimsky-Korsakov (1844-1909). This suite deals with four Arabian Nights stories and uses the background of the situation for an interesting cyclic treatment of themes.

This scheme of Rimsky-Korsakov really does what Strauss recommended: allowing the program to suggest new forms. This suite is compactly and symphonically made. It creates forms for itself, but forms which are perfectly understandable as design alone. It also serves as a very ingenious illustration of the Arabian Nights story.

There are three symphonic suites of Tchaikovsky without descriptive titles, but they are not played so often as his more programmatic works and his symphonies. Other symphonic suites frequently heard in addition to *Scheherazade* are *Caucasian Sketches* of Ippolitov-Ivanov, and the *Mother Goose Suite* of Ravel, originally written for piano duet but scored for orchestra by the composer.

DEBUSSY

Debussy (1862-1918), the great French composer, has three orchestral works of considerable popularity which might be classed as symphonic suites: *La Mer,* which he calls "symphonic sketches," *Iberia,* classified as "images," and the three *Nocturnes.* All of these consist of three separate movements, but particularly in the first two you will notice that the style is symphonic, a continuous development of thematic fragments against a changing background of orchestral color. Debussy's popularity today seems destined to last. His compositions are the work of a skilled and subtle artist, and the poetical ideas which he so beautifully incorporates in them are never permitted to interfere with the solidity of the musical design.

American composers have written a number of compositions in this style, several of them attaining considerable success. The *Indian Suite* of MacDowell, *Through the Looking Glass* of Deems Taylor, and *Adventures in a Perambulator* by John Alden Carpenter are familiar to wide audiences. Arthur Shepherd has written a suite, *Horizons,* which in addition to the use in one of the movements of American cowboy tunes has a native flavor to recommend it. Jazz has been effectively employed by Gruenberg in his *Jazz Suite* and by Copland in his *Music for the Theatre.**

* Other modern suites of this type include: Milhaud's *Creation of the World;* Hindemith's *Mathis der Maler;* Prokofiev's *Lieutenant Kije;* Charles Ives's *Three Places in New England;* Henry Cowell's *Tales of Our Countryside;* and Herbert Haufrecht's *Square Set.*—E. S.

Oratorio, Cantata, and Mass

Abridged from "Listening to Music"

By Douglas Moore

ORATORIO is really opera with a sacred text presented in concert form. Since the eye is not distracted by action, nor the singers by costumes and scenery, the attention is more concentrated upon musical values. The words still exert upon the music a powerful and by no means friendly influence, but if they are distorted by long figures of melody upon a single syllable, no one much cares, for here music is distinctly the thing. Accordingly we find that the oratorio generally consists of music of more symphonic design. Choruses are more polyphonic than in the opera, the aria is allowed to follow its natural desire for the ABA form. The nature of the text permits of music of a greater degree of seriousness and tragedy of a more moving nature.

The oratorio was made popular by Handel who, as manager of an opera house, hit upon it as a device to keep his company and theater employed during Lent, at which time people were not inclined to visit the theater. Its form has not changed to any degree since its origin. Many of the greatest composers have written in this category, among them Handel, Bach, Haydn, Mendelssohn, and Franck. More recently successful oratorios have been written by Elgar, the American composer Horatio Parker, and Stravinsky. The oratorios of Bach—the *St. Matthew* and the *St. John* Passions—are among his greatest works. In the *St. Matthew* Passion, which deals with the story of the trial and crucifixion of Jesus, Bach uses his chorus with striking dramatic effect. The characters of the drama are represented in recitative, there are frequent arias descriptive of exalted states of feeling, but the chorus represents the mob and the part it played in the story. It shouts for the release of Barabbas and for the execution of Jesus, and again it weeps at his tomb. It also is used for simple four-part chorals which are interspersed throughout the action, but which are really intended to be sung by the audience.

THE CANTATA

The *cantata* is a choral form. It originally consisted of a short drama in recitative without dramatic action, and as such was written by many of the early Italian composers, among them Carissimi, Alessandro Scarlatti, and Pergolesi.

Bach employed the form as a short religious service in his church at Leipzig. One type of the cantata is based upon a familiar German chorale from which it takes its name. A polyphonic chorus begins the work, there are recitatives and arias, and for the end a simple four-part harmonization of the chorale. A beautiful example of the chorale cantata is *Christ lag in Todesbanden*. Bach wrote five complete sets of cantatas, one for every Sunday and holiday of the year; but, as in the case of his other choral works, many of them have been lost. In those that remain to us we find some of his greatest music.

In modern times the cantata is usually a work for chorus set to a sacred text * which is too short to be called an oratorio. A good example of modern cantata is Debussy's *Prodigal Son,* with which he won the Prix de Rome.

THE MASS

The other great branch of choral music concerns itself directly with the Roman Catholic service, the *mass*. From earliest times of Christianity the service has included five musical parts each serving its particular function, the Kyrie, Gloria, Credo, Sanctus, Benedictus, and Agnus Dei. During the Middle Ages when unaccompanied monophonic † music of the type known as Gregorian chant was used, many masses were composed and sung. Later, when the great polyphonic school of Palestrina appeared, the mass was the principal form of composition. In Gregorian chant, design was little organized, the music following the lead of the words. In the Palestrinian mass, the form found in the motet was ordinarily the rule. Masses were usually based upon traditional Gregorian themes.

In the time of Bach, composers again became interested in the mass, although the type of composition produced was rather too long for inclusion in the service. Bach's great B minor Mass, written to the Catholic order of service although he himself was a devoted Protestant, is probably his greatest composition. It falls into the traditional parts, but each section of the words is made to contain a number of separate pieces. Some of these are for chorus and some are arias or duets as the language of the particular part seems to suggest. The Kyrie consists of

---

* Many American cantatas have recently been written to secular, patriotic texts. Noteworthy are Earl Robinson's *Ballad for Americans* and George Kleinsinger's *I Hear America Singing*. Most distinctive among Soviet patriotic cantatas is Prokofiev's *Alexander Nevsky.*—E. S.

† Monophonic: Music consisting of one line of melody, unaccompanied.—E. S.

three parts, the Gloria and the Credo of eight, the Sanctus and the Agnus Dei of two, and the Benedictus of one.

One of the great advantages of the use of the text of the mass is that its words may be indefinitely divided and only one phrase used for a musical piece. The repetition of this phrase corresponds with the natural inclination of musical phrases to repeat themselves. In the Bach mass the choruses are polyphonic, some of them strict fugues and others using imitation in a somewhat freer form like the old motet. The arias contain lovely melodies and beautiful imitation between voice and instrumental accompaniment. There are no recitatives—another advantage of the mass, musically speaking.

Since Bach many fine concert masses have been written, some of them as a special form (*e.g.,* the Requiem mass for the dead), and others of the ordinary variety. Many musicians consider Mozart's Requiem Mass his finest work, as well as in the case of Beethoven, his *Missa Solemnis.* Both compositions were among the last works of their composers.

Among other composers of the mass there are Berlioz with his tremendous Requiem; Brahms with his *German Requiem,* in which instead of the usual words he employs a biblical text to produce one of his greatest works; and the French composer Fauré, who has written a very lovely Requiem Mass.

PART THREE

In the Concert Hall

III. In the Concert Hall

I SHALL never forget the first time I heard a symphony orchestra. I was twelve, and the program was of the "standard" type that visiting orchestras reserved for Brooklyn concerts, consisting (as I remember it) of *Scheherazade, Les Préludes,* Tchaikovsky's *Pathétique,* and one or two other war-horses. The conductor was apparently bored—I can see him now, pulling out his watch every once in a while, as if wondering how much longer he must wait for his dinner.

As for me, however, I was in seventh heaven. The huge masses of tone penetrated my every muscle and fiber; the newly discovered sounds and combinations of brass, timpani, winds, and strings were intoxicating, at times frightening; and the Tchaikovsky *tuttis* with the whole orchestra sizzling up to the inevitable cymbal-bass-drum crash left me trembling and pounding with enthusiasm. That night I sat up late to write my first "poem": "O, swelling tones on high. . . ."

Probably everyone has had his or her "first" and reacted accordingly. Nowadays the thrill of discovering symphonic music must be chiefly the privilege of infants in their cradles, for many radio-conscious youngsters seem able to recognize half a dozen different instruments at the age of three or four. With the tones of broadcast orchestral music sounding about us almost hourly—on bathing beaches, in taxis, waiting rooms, war factories, hospital wards, and movie houses—Americans are today growing up to an easy familiarity with oboes, bassoons, trombones, harps, and glockenspiels and with the standard orchestral literature, even though many have never heard or seen a symphony orchestra in the flesh.

The simplicity and convenience of radio listening, and the wider range of the radio orchestra's repertory have made many feel that the concert is a thing of the past. Certainly radio has become an indispensable instrument of our musical life.

But radio listening lacks a definite something that you get from a fine concert. No matter how much you enjoy radio music, it is essentially a one-man affair, and sometimes rather casual—you don't hesitate to turn off the symphony even in the middle of a bar, if Cousin Dick or Uncle John drops in for a visit.

The concert, on the other hand, has an almost ceremonial quality. Several hundred or thousand people listening together to a great work of music derive something from each other—a sense of mass sympathy, of mass excitement, of heightened participation in a significant communal event. A distinguished concert—Koussevitzky conducting *La Mer*, or Toscanini conducting Beethoven's *Missa Solemnis* or Shostakovich's Seventh—is perhaps the closest modern approach to that social and spiritual exaltation that the Athenians must have felt when listening to their Tragedy, or the builders of Gothic cathedrals when their building was completed and the first Mass celebrated in it.

Many of those who experience this quality of pleasure, however, are not consciously aware of how modern a form the symphony orchestra is, or of how closely its beginnings are bound up with the rise of democracy. The earliest public concert halls and independent symphony orchestras are barely two hundred years old, most of them much younger than that. Before the American and the French Revolutions the music-lover who wished to hear a symphonic concert was out of luck, unless he happened to be registered in the Almanach de Gotha; for, with few exceptions, all orchestras were privately owned by the aristocratic class. Performances took place in small court or Residenz theaters (usually seating 200-300 persons) and admission was by invitation—for blue-blooded ears only! Even the compositions written to order for such concerts remained the property of the noble patrons, who jealously guarded them under lock and key.*

In such court concerts and in most other important musical performances (mostly religious) of the pre-democratic age, both performer and composer were liveried servants—mere hired help; their job was to provide pleasure and entertainment for the taste of their socially superior listeners.

Not until the democratic spirit flowered and the *public* symphony concert was established, could the musician emancipate himself, act as a free and independent individual. Music left off being merely enter-

---

* Bach's *Brandenburg* Concertos, many of Haydn's symphonies, and countless other compositions of the period were usually performed once, and then buried in private court libraries. To make sure the composer would not give them out to the public, he was generally bound, in his contract with his employer, not to make more than one copy of each work.

tainment and became now and henceforth a communication between the artist and his fellow men. Speaking as an equal to equals, the artist was for the first time free to be fully himself, to unleash all the ideas, impulses, and emotions that stirred him as a human being. The listener, too—the common, unpedigreed man—was now able, in the free atmosphere of the concert hall, to identify himself completely with the surge and movement of orchestral music, to experience the grandeur, terror, heroism, aspiration, or despair of the great symphonic master-pieces. *Vom Herzen, mag es am Herzen gehen* (from the heart, may it go to the heart), wrote Beethoven at the head of one of his works, and this has applied to the best concert music ever since.

Whereas the court concert, designed for a very narrow circle of listeners, was necessarily limited to a rather conventional program range, the public concert, depending for its support on a paying—and constantly fluctuating—audience, had to provide a variety of attractions appealing to all tastes. True, the first public orchestral programs offered a mixture of musical styles that would strike us today as being far from catholic. Thus, a sample program of the 1780's might include a symphony, a concerto, several operatic arias, a "battle piece," a composition describing a storm at sea or a fire (complete with clanging bells, "crowd noises," etc.), some improvised variations on a popular tune, a sonata improvised on a theme submitted by a member of the audience —and finally, another symphony or concerto to close with. Certainly your money's worth!

It must be remembered, moreover, that at those early concerts almost all the music was new music, much of it written specially for each performance. Audiences of those days relished the excitement of continually hearing new works, and would no more have tolerated the frequent repetitions that characterize our modern concert fare than a movie audience of today would put up with a series of double bills consisting 90% of year-old or ten-year-old pictures, with a new release provided every six or eight weeks only.

The tradition of the varied type of program still persists in the modern concert hall, if in slightly more restrained form. A typical program today may open with a classical overture or symphony, followed by a romantic concerto, an impressionist or modern tone poem or ballet suite (or even a short American work—usually as short as possible!), and ending with some sure-fire piece: Strauss' *Don Juan,* the Polovtsian Dances from *Prince Igor,* or *The Sorcerer's Apprentice.* Of course, the conductor may follow roughly the reverse order, starting with a series of short compositions and leading up to the Brahms, Tchaikovsky, or Beethoven symphony as *pièce de résistance.*

There are other ways of building a program: the one-composer type—all-Wagner, all-Tchaikovsky, or even all-Sibelius; the big-work-prefaced-by-something-charming type for special occasions—Beethoven's Ninth introduced by the delightful First; or an hour-long Bruckner or Mahler or the Shostakovich Seventh with a Handel suite as *hors d'oeuvre.*

Haphazard though programs may sometimes seem,* they are usually the result of many hours of careful thought and planning on the part of the maestros. Conductors have to bear in mind such matters as the pace, texture, type of orchestration, and lyric or dramatic quality of the various works being considered. If one composition is full of big climaxes, all *Sturm und Drang,* it will be well to follow it with something quieter and more lyrical; if one work calls for extensive and prominent use of the percussion and brass instruments, common sense will dictate that the next will lean heavily on string or wood-wind tone.

These are some of the problems of the conductor. What of the listener? Though enjoying the musical contrasts provided by a skillful program-builder, he may sometimes find himself confused by the succession of totally different styles presented. This is especially true of the listener who is concerned with the "meaning" of the music he hears.

The whole question of understanding the "meaning" of orchestral music originated in Romantic days, about the time of Beethoven, when composers began putting a definite "content"—emotional, dramatic, or pictorial—into their instrumental works.† In line with his gradually evolving conception of music as a communication between man and man, Beethoven wrote into the score of his *Pastoral* Symphony various annotations ("Scene by the Brook," "Lively Peasant Gathering," "Thunder Storm") suggesting certain specific images associated with the various movements. Berlioz went a step farther, specifying that a detailed narrative program be printed and distributed to the public as

---

* It must be admitted that programs are not infrequently planned from other than strictly artistic motives—*e.g.,* the desire of a guest conductor to show his versatility; the impulse to play a tricky piece as well as Stokowski plays it; or the need of finding a vehicle for a special soloist.

† Of course almost all choral, operatic, and ballet compositions, both before and since Beethoven, have been based on a definite subject or story—made clear to the listener by the words that were sung and/or by stage action. As for orchestral music of the aristocratic era, there was nothing to "understand," since the purpose of the music, as stated above, was not to communicate but to entertain.

they entered the hall, so that they might clearly follow the "story" of his *Fantastic* Symphony.

Berlioz and his colleagues inaugurated the era of "tone poems," "symphonic narratives," "tone pictures," "images," and even "musical portraits"; and these invited an avalanche of rhapsodic "interpretations," "commentaries," and "analyses" of every work in the orchestral repertory—whether or not it had been intended by its composer to have any "story." Enthusiastic commentators bestowed flowery and sometimes fantastic programs on simple and unpretentious works, seeing exotic caravans, village weddings, Dionysian revels, and Titan combats in music that had originally been produced as a perfectly plain sequence of melodies, themes, and counterpoints. At the height of this romantic craze, some well-meaning listeners devoted more time and energy to reading their programs than to listening to the actual music itself. "Down with programs!" shouted Gustav Mahler when confronted with one of the more lyrical specimens of the program commentator's art as applied to his First Symphony; and many another composer would enthusiastically agree with Mahler that "the audience should be left to its own thoughts about the work that is being played—it should not be forced to read during the performance." (Though this sentiment did not, apparently, deter Mahler himself and many other denouncers of "programs" from writing out *strictly private* but very elaborate analyses of their own compositions—which usually had a mysterious way of leaking out and being printed in the program booklets after all!)

As an auxiliary to sensitive listening, but never a substitute for it, simply written factual material about the nature and background of an orchestral composition often adds to the pleasure of going to concerts or listening to the radio. Whether Beethoven did or did not intend his Fifth Symphony to depict Fate knocking on the door is unimportant; but it does help us to know that this is a symphony of struggle and victory—that in many ways its form and content were revolutionary for its time.

Each work of a true composer has, of course, its own unique quality and personality, revealed only through the music itself. But no single composition is ever totally unrelated to the rest of a musician's creation or to other music of its time. A sensitive commentator should reveal such relationships, point out the composer's general objectives and style, and then—let us hope—discreetly leave the concert-goer to his inviolable right to enjoy the music in his own private fashion—to beat time, purr, grunt, sway violently, hold his head in his hands, mutter imprecations, drop into a stupor, dream about charming females, worry about sonata form—or consign the whole thing to the devil and go to sleep. If we Americans have one inalienable right, it is the right to say: "I don't know anything about music, but I'm going to listen to it in any way I darn please!"

Johann Sebastian Bach: Orchestral Works

Abridged from "Symphonic Masterpieces"

By Olin Downes

BACH's small orchestra, which would be called today not a "symphony" but a "chamber" orchestra, was not nearly equal in sonority or variety of tone-tint to our modern body of instruments, but it was more than sufficient for his expressive purposes in the concert-room. This orchestra consisted predominantly of "strings"—instruments, large and small, of the violin family; with flutes, oboes, and sometimes a bassoon, for the "wood-wind" choir; high trumpets and sometimes a horn or two for the "brass" of the fuller scores; sometimes kettledrums, and in most cases a harpsichord to fill out the harmony.

In those days the art of the modern conductor was unknown. The leader of the orchestra, who was often the composer himself, sat at the harpsichord (a keyed instrument, and one of the precursors of the piano), or in the seat of the first violinist, established the tempo, and occasionally by a gesture indicated a change of pace or some other salient feature of the interpretation. But the fine shadings, the blazing rhetoric and tremendous climaxes of which the modern orchestra is capable, and which form so much of the stock in trade of the conductor of today, were absent. Nor had the Bach orchestra great flexibility. It afforded planes, rather than shadings of instrumental tone. One passage would be played softly "piano" and the next loudly—"forte"; perhaps only relatively soft or loud, but without modern mezzo-tints. Contrasts rather than gradations of "piano" and "forte" were the style. The beauty and significance of the music lay in its melody, rhythm, and structure. It was a less nervous age than ours. The composition, without, as it were, raising its voice to a dramatic pitch, spoke for itself and with no ulterior meaning. Thus Bach's chamber orchestra was not intended for dramatic effect. It was intended to weave wonderful patterns of pure music.

Bach had a strong sense of the fitness of things. Frequently in pages of his Cantatas and Passions he uses his orchestra for purposes of tone-painting, in accordance with situations suggested by the text. But when he sits down to write for a few instruments ordered music in which purely melodic and rhythmical ideas bud and foliate, as a tree grows from the ground and puts out branches and leaves; when the plenteous-ness of his invention, the exuberance of his workmanship, and his own abounding vitality seize you and make your blood dance in your veins as his motives dance in the orchestra—he communicates an incompa-rable feeling of health, logic, and beauty. You listen and are musically complete. In Bach's music is something profoundly nourishing and lifegiving—something which seems to be in league with basically simple rhythms of the universe, and the pulse and growths of nature.

When Bach wrote in the orchestral forms of his time he was con-tent to use accepted forms and fill the old bottles with the new wine of his genius. The forms in which he wrought so masterfully were prin-cipally the suite, or overture—the terms being at the time synony-mous—and the concerto. The symphony as we know it today had not yet appeared. The suite was a collection of dance forms based on rhythms which had in previous ages accompanied the actual perform-ances of dancers, or other festivities. The elementary dance forms were then taken by composers of learning and genius as a basis for richer and more varied designs, carried far beyond the point of their origin.

The various dances that made the suite came from different parts of the world and different ranks of society. Nationalism was not yet the influence in music that it became in a later century, and the forms of the suite were of international derivation. Thus the Allemande, a flowing movement in a duple rhythm, purported to come from South-ern Germany. The lively Courantes were of two sorts, the one of the French, the other of the Italian persuasion. The grave Sarabande was an old Spanish dance; the Gigue was supposed to be of British origin.

The suite was often preceded by a free preluding movement, and the composer, if he chose, could write in other dance measures than those already mentioned—the Gavotte, Bourée, Passepied, Menuet, Polacca or Polonaise—this last a Polish title, though the Polonaise of Bach's B minor suite for flute and strings is far from the form as con-

ceived by Chopin. And there were movements of less exact identification, such as the Air (originally a dance movement in spite of its title
and melodic character), and fanciful titles such as "Badinerie," or
"Rejouissance"—movements in lighter vein, possibly suggested by the
grace and playfulness of certain French compositions of the period.
There were different variation-forms. Some were called "doubles." A
Sarabande or other dance would be played first in simple outline; the
"double" which followed would be the same melody elaborately
varied. Grander variation-forms were the Chaconne, or its close relative, the Passacaglia. Of these Bach has left the world two incomparable examples: the Chaconne from the D minor suite, or "partita," for
violin alone, and the colossal C minor organ Passacaglia. It can be seen
from the foregoing that if the amazing effects of the modern orchestra
were not yet possible; if Bach reserved his greatest instrumental conceptions for the organ, nevertheless a very considerable variety of musical
expression was attainable with a few instruments and in the forms of
the old suite—particularly as these forms were developed and sublimated at the hands of the master.

Lastly, to conclude this phase of the subject, we come to those
forms of larger dimensions and fewer divisions than the suite, which
were ancestors of both the concerto and the symphony of the later
period: the concerto for a solo instrument or instruments with orchestra, and—the biggest orchestral form of the day—the concerto grosso.
A characteristic of this noble form was the division of the orchestra in
two principal parts: a small group of solo players called the "concertino," and the larger ensemble group known variously as the "ripieno"
or "tutti" (or, in earlier days—the very title later bestowed upon the
forms as a whole—the "concerto grosso"). The splendid possibilities
of the concerto grosso lay in the opportunities not only for the development of melodic motives, but also for the play of both solo and ensemble elements, the march and countermarch of division against division,
part against part.

THE SUITES

Bach left four orchestral suites, for different instrumental combinations. The first one, in C major, is for two oboes, a bassoon, and
strings. The second one is in B minor, for flute and strings. The third
is the suite in D major, with the justly famous Air—that noble and
tender melody that the violinist Wilhelmj made popular in his arrangement for the G string. The last suite is in the same key, and, like the

third, more heavily scored than the earlier ones. It would be superfluous to describe these suites in detail, while it is not exaggeration to say that each one of them is a mine of strong and beautiful music. The two most frequently played are the delicious second suite, for the flute and strings, and the third, with the celebrated Air already referred to, and other pieces also famous.

THE BRANDENBURG CONCERTOS

These suites and the *Brandenburg* Concertos belong to the time when Bach was concertmaster for the Prince of Cöthen. There he had an orchestra to experiment with, and an employer who was an uncommonly intelligent patron of music. Wherever he went in the course of his hard-working life, Bach took what musical means came to his hand, exploiting to the utmost their possibilities. The *Brandenburg* Concertos are his first attempts at instrumental composition on a big scale. They constitute superb examples of his power of synthesis and origination. In them Bach exemplifies all the resources and possibilities of the concerto of his day, while his audacious employment of wind instruments was beyond anything previously attempted.

The opening allegro of the first *Brandenburg* Concerto, in F,

is a prototype of many of Bach's fast movements in the pulse and vigor of the music, the glints and contrasts of instrumental color, and the almost cellular development of the ideas. The slow movement, as customary in this form, is the melodic one. It consists largely in a duet of the first oboe and the small, high-pitched violin that Bach selects for his string solo, over the quiet accompaniment and the occasional rejoinder of the lower stringed instruments. The finale, again in a fast tempo, dismisses the more poetical mood of the preceding section by passages of the gayest and most rollicking humor. The rhythms and motives are almost those of the folk dance. This concerto is quite fully scored for horns, oboes, high violin, and the customary other strings.

The first and second *Brandenburg* Concertos are closely related as regards form and in key. Very different from the first, however, and highly ingenious is the color scheme in the second, achieved by combinations between the solo trumpet, solo flute, solo oboe, and solo violin, set against the "ripieno" of the other strings. This, figuratively speaking, is Bach with his coat off, in the open air, leading the measure. A rapid florid figure is usually set against a stockier and more energetic movement in another part. Flying passages contrast delightfully with the sustained singing tones of other voices. The sonorous "tuttis" crash in after exhilarating solo displays, as if to say "bravo!" With four measures of this music, or even two—such is the divinity of its arithmetic— the listener feels instinctively aware of all that is to come, while, on the other hand, there is such constant germination of the motives that it is certain Bach could have continued for many more pages without exhausting his ideas or our interest. For the slow movement, flute, oboe, and violin converse together over a steady moving bass. The finale is a lively and audacious combination of rhythmic figures and the strongly contrasted colors of trumpet, flute, oboe, and string tone.

The third *Brandenburg* Concerto has quite a different plan. It uses only strings, and divides the orchestra not in solo and ensemble parts, but in three groups, of equal size, each comprising three violins, violas, and 'cellos. Those players, virtually soloists all, must be stout fellows; the sturdy two-fisted opening movement asks not only a substantial tone but the hearts of men.

In modern performance the number of players in each choir is proportionately multiplied. The first movement is followed by the shortest slow movement in orchestral music—two measures! Measures which are really only sustained chords to separate the two quick-moving divisions of the work from each other. In the last section there is more display of individual part-writing than in the first, two themes flying with nimbleness and legerdemain from group to group of instruments.

The fourth *Brandenburg* Concerto has a first movement scored piquantly for a solo violin, two solo flutes, and the "ripieno" strings. At first the strings mark by a sharp stroke the beat, while the flutes carry the lilting tune. Later on come some whirling passages of great velocity for the solo violinist—who must have been a good man, possibly Spiess of the Prince's band, or even Bach himself, for he in his youth was no indifferent executant on the violin as on other instruments. The slow movement is an excellent illustration of the contrasts in planes of sonorities which Bach's instrumental music often affords, and to which reference has already been made. It juxtaposes soft and loud passages which answer each other. Stocky counterpoint, at a vigorous pace, and rapid scale passages that relieve it, make the stuff of the finale.

The fifth *Brandenburg* Concerto, in D major, for performance by solo flute, solo violin and solo harpsichord, is the one which gives prominent display to the keyed instrument. The festive figure that opens the movement

is carried along vigorously by the harpsichord (or usually, when it is played in these days, by the piano). There follow various combinations of concertante and "ripieno," with special bravura passages for the harpsichord player, and finally a long and unaccompanied cadenza for that executant which is a masterly summing up of what has preceded, extending almost to the end of the movement. The slow movement is for the polyphonic ensemble. In the finale the harpsichord again takes a prominent part.

The sixth *Brandenburg* Concerto, in B flat, is for solo violas and 'cello, with the strings "ripieno." It begins with a swinging "canon in the unison," one part imitating at the distance of a single beat the motive just played by another part, and so continuing throughout the movement, which, following this precise method, provides the most exhilarating music. The slow movement is the one that is deepest in meaning and the most elaborate in the part-writing of any slow movement of the *Brandenburg* set. There are four separate and eloquent melodic lines. There is a noble severity of design, profound beauty and feeling. And again, in the finale, Bach's laughter echoes through the world.

Such are a few of the surface characteristics of the *Brandenburg* Concertos. Bach wrote other concertos for solo instruments and orchestra—two concertos for solo violin, and the concerto for two violins; concertos for solo harpsichord, two concertos for two harpsichords and two for three harpsichords, and the quadruple concerto, which is a transcription by Bach of the Vivaldi concerto for four violins with orchestra. Most of these concertos, however, are transcriptions by Bach of concertos for solo violin or for other instruments by other composers. He was all the time absorbing music, any and all music that he deemed worthy of study, and transcribing it. He transcribed for different instruments a great many of his own works. When he transcribed he often developed. When the concertos come from an outside source they are more than copies of other men's music, in many cases constituting improvements on the original which have caused otherwise perishable material to survive and come down to us.

Georg Friedrich Handel: Water Music

From "Everybody's Music"

By Schima Kaufman

AT A time when kings could take their pleasures seriously and affairs of state with grace, the beefy Handel was called upon to write a serenade for an elaborate water party on the Thames, in honor of George I and his lovely ladies. The evening (July 17, 1717) was a gay success, according to the details given in Newman Flower's excellent life of Handel, especially as George bowed himself out of the indignity of assuming the cost.

"Baron Kilmanseck," reads a contemporary report, "seeing that H.M. was vexed about these difficulties [the expenses], resolved to give the concert on the river at his own expense, and so this concert took place the day before yesterday. The King entered his barge about eight o'clock with the Duchess of Bolton, the Countess of Godolphin, Mad. de Kilmanseck, Mad. Were, and the Earl of Orkney, gentleman of the king's bedchamber, who was on guard. By the side of the royal barge was that of the musicians to the number of fifty, who played all kinds of instruments, viz, trumpets, hunting horns, oboes, bassoons, German flutes, French flutes à bec, violins and basses, but without voices. The concert was composed expressly for the occasion by the famous Handel, native of Halle, and first composer of the king's music. It was so strongly approved by H.M. that he commanded it to be repeated, once before and once after supper, although it took an hour for each performance."

Franz Josef Haydn: Symphony in E flat Major

From "Symphonic Masterpieces"

By Olin Downes

IN HIS later years Haydn traveled twice to London, where he was lionized and rewarded munificently. Students of his works find the symphonies which he wrote for the London impresario Salomon richer in their content than other compositions that Haydn cast in the same form. This special importance is attributed by them not only to Haydn's maturity as a composer, but to the effect of the new experiences and impressions of his journey, and, very possibly, the fertilizing influence of his contact with the younger Mozart.

The twelve Salomon symphonies were published in two sets of six each. The one here discussed is No. 3 of the second set. It is the so-called "symphony with the kettledrum-roll." In its pages Haydn conducts several experiments, some of them looking to the future of symphonic music. One of these is the reappearance of a theme heard in the introduction in the main movement which follows.

Ordinarily, in Haydn's day, the slow introduction of the first movement of a symphony was a mere ceremonious prelude to what followed. It established atmosphere and gained the attention of the audience. But in this symphony the portentous theme,—

preceded by a drum-roll, which stalks about in the opening measures of the introduction, returns, like a specter at the feast, in the midst of quick and gay music that follows. This occurs towards the end of the movement, after a brilliant passage and a pause, or "fermata." There, again, we hear the drum-roll, followed by the theme in its original form. But Haydn has done subtler things than that. In a later place he gives a fragment of the introductory theme to his violas and 'cellos—following another "fermata"; and the coda, or concluding part of the movement, begins with a phrase of the same introductory theme, so altered in rhythm and form that one must look twice to realize its origin.

The second movement is a theme with variations. The theme has among other distinguishing characteristics the fact that it is half in the major key and half in the minor. The first section is C minor, the second C major. The variations hold to this harmonic scheme. It is not until the coda that Haydn allows his fancy to wander freely through distant keys and tonal vistas that freshly enchant us. Croatian melodies are in this symphony, including the first theme of the first movement proper; the theme on which the variations of the slow movement are built;

and the chief theme of the last movement.

Franz Josef Haydn: Symphony in G Major (Military)

From Philharmonic-Symphony Program Notes

By Louis Biancolli

COMPOSED in 1794, the *Military* Symphony was one of the second set of six commissioned by the English impresario Johann Peter Salomon for a London subscription series. Haydn's manuscript carries the date 1794. Since the Austrian composer had arrived in London early that year and taken lodgings at No. 1, Bury Street, St. James's, it may be assumed he wrote the symphony there. It was apparently first played in the Hanover Square Rooms on May 2, 1794.

The Symphony in G major gets its title largely from the allegretto, which replaces the usual andante as second movement. There the bass drum, cymbals, and triangle combine in what the eighteenth century termed "Turkish Music." A martial note is also struck by the trumpet call occurring in the closing pages of the allegretto. "The trumpets sound the signal for falling into the line," says one analyst, taking the "Military" title literally. The oft-repeated theme of the movement—a simple and amiable march motif first stated by violins and flute—derives from a French romanza, *La gentille et jeune Lisette.*

Haydn found earlier use for this song in his *La Reine* Symphony and in a lute concerto written for the King of Naples. The so-called "Turkish Music" can also be heard in the accompaniment to the G major second theme of the Presto finale.

Of the twelve "London" symphonies Haydn wrote that they were music "suffused with the sense of mellowness and maturity, of long experience and an old age honorably won; too serene for passion, too wise for sadness, too single-hearted for regret, it has learned the lesson of life and will question its fate no farther."

Wolfgang Amadeus Mozart: Haffner Symphony

From "Symphonic Broadcasts"

By Olin Downes

MOZART wrote more than one symphony in D major. This one is the so-called *Haffner* Symphony, composed in furious haste, for it had to be completed within a fortnight. This was in 1782. The Haffner family of Salzburg were good friends of Mozart. For the marriage of the Haffner daughter Elise in 1776 Mozart had been commissioned to write a Serenade. His father wrote him six years later that there were further festivities in the Haffner mansion and need of a new work. Mozart planned at first another Serenade, but the Serenade became a symphony. Other tasks were crowding poor Mozart at the same time. He sent the music to his father piecemeal, and then forgot about it. When the father returned the score to Wolfgang six months later the son remarked: "The new 'Haffner' symphony has quite astonished me, for I did not remember a note of it. It must be very effective." It *is* very effective, and more, for it is one of the most charming of all the Mozart symphonies. It is without a trace of haste or friction. The symphony is in the customary four movements. The middle part of the minuet is based upon an air from an operetta Mozart had composed for the Munich Carnival of 1775, although the air is altered in this place. The music is of an adorable simplicity, the instrumentation of a special transparency and radiance, even for Mozart.

Wolfgang Amadeus Mozart: Jupiter Symphony

From "Standard Concert Guide"

By George P. Upton and Felix Borowski

AMONG all the symphonies of Mozart not one can equal the dignity, loftiness, and skill of the Symphony in C, the last from his pen, which by common consent, as it were, has been christened the *Jupiter,* both as compared with his other symphonies and with the symphonic works of other composers before Beethoven appeared with his wonderful series. It was composed within a period of fifteen days, and completed August 10, 1788.

It has no introduction, but begins at once with the principal theme of the Allegro, which is constructed upon two subjects—the first strong and bold in character at times, and again restful; and the second gay, even to verge of hilarity. The first theme is as follows:

The second theme is given out by the strings, and its hilarity is intensified by the following episode, which dominates the whole movement, so far as its expression is concerned:

The Andante is highly expressive. The materials which compose it are exquisite melodies whose beauty, especially that of the first, with muted violins, must appeal even to the dullest ear. The opening theme is as follows:

After a repetition of four bars by the basses a new melody appears in the bassoons, which leads up to the second theme,

given out by the oboes and full of rest and contentment. A charming Coda brings the beautiful first part of the movement to its close. The second is devoted to the contrapuntal development of all this melodious material, which is accomplished with marvelous skill, and at the close returns to the original key and melody.

The Minuet is one of the happiest and most charming of all his numbers in this rhythm. There is a swing, an elasticity of movement, at once light and free, and a gaiety and freshness which belong almost exclusively to Mozart.

The Finale is the masterpiece of the symphony. In combinations of the most astonishing contrapuntal skill with freedom of movement it will always remain a monument to the genius and knowledge of the composer. It is built up on four themes developed in fugal treatment. Colossal figures of counterpoint are combined with the most graceful motives, each thoroughly individual in character and all fitted together in every variety of union, but never at the sacrifice of that grace and fancy for which Mozart is so conspicuous.

Ludwig van Beethoven: Symphony No. 3 (Eroica)

From "Symphonic Masterpieces"

By Olin Downes

THE inspiration of the *Eroica* Symphony, and the manner in which Beethoven changed its dedication, are strangely symbolic of the nature of the composition and the place that it occupies in art. We know that when Beethoven began his symphony he had in mind Napoleon Bonaparte. There is no question about this. The erased dedication on the manuscript title-page of the symphony is the evidence. But when Beethoven thought of Napoleon he thought of the First Consul of the new French Republic, the liberator of humanity, the destroyer of king-craft and all that that estate implied. Then Beethoven received the news that Napoleon had had himself declared Emperor. He tore up the dedication page in fury, crying out that Napoleon had become nothing but an ordinary man, "and now he will turn tyrant." And the symphony was described on the title-page as "composed to celebrate the memory of a great man." The work, in other words, was rededicated, not to Napoleon, the cracked statue of a hero, but to the heroic spirit in man. *That* became Beethoven's theme. *That* was what Bonaparte stood for in Beethoven's mind when he composed the symphony. And so we have a score cleansed, as it were, of any literal or programmatic associations, which treats not of an individual but of an ideal, in terms of the greatest music. There is no attempt here to give us a portrait of the dress and the buttons of a hero, or the deeds of an egotistical individual —anything but such an attempt as Richard Strauss made when he celebrated himself in his tone-poem *Ein Heldenleben* (*A Hero's Life*). The *Eroica,* or "heroic," symphony is impersonal as the tomb of the Unknown Soldier, a monument to the deathless spirit of man. It is as if a mysterious destiny, in causing Beethoven agony by tearing down an idol before his eyes, had taken the ultimate pains to insure the greatest destiny for his creation. We have in this work not a personal outpouring so much as a masterpiece which balances form and profound feeling, and looks down from its height on the music of two centuries.

Therefore, there is no program for this symphony such as Beethoven gave us for the *Pastoral*. But the thought back of the work is obvious in the musical material. The gap in style between this symphony of Beethoven—his Third—and the Second Symphony, which it followed by an interval of only one year, is deep and wide. There is perhaps no greater leap in the symphonic evolution of any composer. The distance between the works has been explained as due to development in other scores, not symphonies, which came from Beethoven's pen in the intervening period. But I cannot find in those other scores any real approach to the *Eroica*. The real cause of the change is the impregnation of Beethoven's thought by a new intellectual conception.

The first movement of the symphony is surely to be construed as the picture, in broadest and most impersonal terms, of heroic character, in which resolve and tenderness, faith and the tragic consciousness, have equal representation. There is no formal introduction, as there was in the earlier symphonies of Beethoven—merely two brusque major chords and the immediate announcement of the hero theme. It is a theme bare to starkness, very plain, and based on intervals of the commonest chord.

It is announced and expanded by the orchestra. Between this theme and the second are long connecting passages which are no longer episodes or mere connecting passage works, but significant musical ideas, closely related to and expansive of the import of the main themes. The architecture of the movement is on the grandest lines. The second theme is less a melody than a succession of chords—in other words, a *harmonic* rather than a *melodic* theme, tender and lofty in sentiment. It is noticeable that in this symphony, unlike the works of Beethoven's predecessors, there is not the sharp demarcation and partitioning off of first from second and subsidiary themes. The movement is much more plastic and connected in its parts—more so than any earlier symphony Beethoven had written. The treatment of the ideas is lengthy, and very rich and bold. The hero theme is endlessly manipulated, and always with fresh resource. In one place, after the exposition of his material, Beethoven drives home repeated sharp dissonances—chords in which an E-natural rasps against an F—with the most startling and dramatic effect. The place is thrown into high relief by the suave harmonies which immediately follow.

All this and much more takes place in the first two-thirds of the first movement of the symphony, which comprises the Exposition of the themes and their free development. The return to the Recapitulation of the material of the Exposition is accomplished in such an individual manner as to have disconcerted Beethoven's contemporaries. In fact, Beethoven's pupil Ries, at the first rehearsal, thought that this intentionally dissonant passage was a mistake in the score, and nearly got his ears boxed for calling the composer's attention to it. The passage is the one in which the solo horn, playing the first notes of the hero themes, appears to come in too soon, against a harmony that does not belong to it. Two measures later the horn repeats its motive, now with the right harmony, and we have the long and splendid repetition of the Exposition and the coda, or peroration of the movement. This movement in itself is almost a symphony.

Its antithesis is the epic lamentation of the second movement, the incommensurable Funeral March. It is said that after he had eradicated Napoleon's name from his score, Beethoven never again referred to him, until he was told, seventeen years later, of Napoleon's death at St. Helena. He is reported to have said, "I have already composed the proper music for the catastrophe." If he said that, he underestimated his dirge, which is for all humanity. The march begins heavily, tragically, in the minor key.

Later, in the middle part, it changes to major, with a more sustained and consoling song. But the emotional climax is reached by means of a fugal development (Measure 114) followed by the awful proclamations of the trombones which made Theodore Thomas think of the Resurrection Day—and that does not exaggerate the tragic grandeur of the passage. You will notice the touch of drama and spectacle at the end of the march—the broken, disjointed fragments of the march, played softly, with pauses of silence between the fragments, as if the last words of leave-taking and homage had been choked by sobs.

Many, Thomas among them, find in these first two movements of the symphony the real *Eroica,* rating them as distinct, apart from and superior to the movements which follow. Others, making no unfavorable comparisons, are puzzled to discover the relation between the two first and the two last themes, especially as the movements which make the second half of the symphony are joyous in tone. How are they to be construed? The scherzo is music of joyous rustlings and horn-calls; it has the tang of the Autumn forest, and the promise of Nature's eternal cycle of deaths and resurrections. The finale, the capstone of the gigantic creation, is a set of variations on a simple, stark theme.

Each listener will have his own explanation of these movements. For some the scherzo will be the voice of what we know as life, murmuring strangely and joyously of the glory of death. The choice, for the finale, of the theme with the enigmatic repeated B flats, is the highest wisdom, a theme that grew for years in Beethoven's consciousness. He had used it first, in a comparatively superficial way, in his *Prometheus* ballet; then as a basis for the fifteen piano variations, Op. 35.* But still he had not plumbed all the secrets of that simple motive. He expands it now on lines that stretch out into infinity. It is not romantic feeling that Beethoven seeks here, but something more vast and eternal. He has done with transient emotions, profound as they may be, and immortalized by him in the first part of the symphony. That first part was life; this is beyond life. We have a protean set of variations, pure music, symbol of order, power, spirit; play of invisible tones about a certain central point; sovereign evocation of form and rhythm. Their development includes the return of the first theme of the symphony, which has already reappeared, in different disguises, in the Funeral March and the scherzo. Perhaps this finale is the most "absolute" tonal design to be found in the nine symphonies. Perhaps, because of its balance and

* Also, as the melody of a Contradanse.—E. S.

emotion and thought, feeling and form, and all-surpassing grandeur of design, the *Eroica* will one day stand forth as the greatest of all symphonies.

Ludwig van Beethoven: Symphony No. 5

From "Symphonic Masterpieces"

By Olin Downes

IT WAS Robert Schumann who said that revolution might be confined within the four walls of a symphony and the police be none the wiser. Beethoven's revolution is inaugurated with the famous motive of four notes, of which he is supposed to have said, "Thus fate knocks at the door." It has never been proved that Beethoven originated this phrase, but it expresses the music. Those four notes, those imperious knocks of destiny on the door, proclaim a new spirit and a new day. Nothing could be simpler, and more blunt, imperious, unsafe for the established order. With that roar of rage Beethoven strides upon the scene, and his mien is terrible.

Observe what happens after those four notes, loaded with dynamite, have been twice sounded:

How these same notes, with their savage and implacable force, invest the orchestra! Observe this too: Beethoven's practical abnegation of melodic forms, phrases, or periods, in favor of rhythm. Here is almost nothing but the onslaught of rhythm which sweeps everything before it. There is a moment of brief melody—the second theme, introduced by a powerful variant of the first—melody which hangs like a flower over the abyss, while the obstinate rhythm threatens underneath— melody which is swept away like everything else so unfortunate as to be in the path of this Vesuvian eruption! All is shattered, reassembled, and shattered again by the driving power of the rhythm. Perhaps you will notice a place about two-thirds through the first movement, when chords are exchanged softly by different instruments—strings and wood wind—like the sighs of one utterly spent by the conflict, only to be answered with redoubled fury by the whole orchestra. Thus the first movement of Beethoven's Fifth Symphony, one of the shortest and the most dramatic he ever composed, is made from the four notes which, if you heard them apart from their context, you would imagine could be invented by any child with one finger on the piano. The structure reared on those four basic tones is one of the proudest that Beethoven achieved.

The second movement of the symphony is in the form of a noble theme, with simple but most eloquent variations. The next two movements are joined, and their dramatic significance is plain from the re-entrance, in varied form, of the Fate theme. Nothing that Beethoven did is more indicative of his manner of turning a classic form to individual purpose than his procedure in the third movement of the Fifth Symphony. It is much less a dance than it is a mysterious and catastrophic preparation for the finale, and this preparation hinges on the Fate theme. The opening measures are charged with suspense.

Basses and 'celli grope about, as if in a troubled dream. When will the sleeper awake? Suddenly a horn raps out the Fate motive in an altered guise, but unmistakable in its derivation from the four-note motive of the first movement. Replying to the horn, other instruments take up the theme, chanting it in different choirs. The double-basses, with a rough and energetic motive, gambol clumsily about like the rumblings of an earthquake in the orchestra. Signs and portents accumulate. The first part of the scherzo returns in a way which enhances the mystery— almost inaudible pluckings of the strings, whispers of the Fate theme, as of something impending, something immense and awful gestating.

The orchestra becomes more vague and uncertain—this orchestra of Beethoven's, which has been dealing its sledge-hammer blows at fate. At last it lies supine, like a monster asleep. A single opaque chord is suspended in the atmosphere. Everything is in a mist. Then the drum begins to beat, at first very softly, then with an immense crescendo which launches into the triumphant finale.

Ludwig van Beethoven: Symphony No. 6 (Pastoral)

From "Symphonic Masterpieces"

By Olin Downes

THERE is often occasion to marvel at the fidelity and sensitiveness with which music, mirror of the human spirit, is affected by the slightest breath of feeling or sensation that passes over its surface, and records with a truthfulness beyond the composer's control the deepest secrets of his being. Beethoven calls his Sixth Symphony *Pastoral*, which, indeed, it is.

Beethoven listened to the monotonous sounds that rose from the fields, the murmur of the brook, the voices of birds and insects, and worshiped. He heard the voice of God in the thunder; he was drunk with the perfume exhaled from drenched earth, plant and flower. The *Pastoral* Symphony is a hymn to Nature. It is also program music, arrant program music, although purists and opponents of this method of musical composition attempt to make light of the fact, and to palliate Beethoven's incidental approaches to realism by repeating his oft-quoted words, "More an expression of feeling than portraiture." The fact of a program, as Beethoven showed, is not the least guarantee for or against great music.

Beethoven's descriptive notes for this symphony, published in the program of the first performance in Vienna, December 22, 1808, are fuller than those now printed in the published score. There are actually five movements in this work, but the last three are joined together, making only three separate movements. The first movement is intended to portray the "Pleasant feelings which awake in man on arriving in the country." The second is the "Scene by the brook." The third movement, or its component—in Beethoven's word, "Piece"—depicts the "Jovial assemblage of country-folk; interrupted by Fourth Piece—Thunder and Storm; to which succeeds Fifth Piece—Beneficent feelings, associated with gratitude to the God-head after the Storm."

It is said that Beethoven drew to a certain extent upon folk songs of the countryside for this symphony, but it is easier to make the claim than to prove it, although had he done so he would not have lessened the originality of the works.* For it is not only the original theme that counts, but the shaping of the theme, the manner in which the mighty blacksmith, Beethoven, pounds and welds his stubborn material into the proper shape to make the framework of the symphony. And it is not only the shaping but the development of the germinal phrases that makes the strength and glory of the great structure. The method adopted by Beethoven in his first movement, designed to portray the happy man's impressions of the countryside, is a special one, bordering on impressionism. He is deliberately monotonous. There are the stirrings of the idle breeze, the sounds of birds and insects, vague distant calls, absence of emotions or introspections of an individual. In the first movement one little pastoral motive is repeated for fifty-two measures, and it fascinates us. In the second movement the quiet and meaningless murmur of the brook gives us the respiration felt through all the themes and harmonies built upon it. These include the passages in which a flute impersonates the nightingale, an oboe the quail, a clarinet the cuckoo—quasi-humorous details of the tonal picture. In the next part there is typical Beethoven humor in the dance played for the country-folk by some third-rate village band, which strikes the measure, while a bassoonist, who evidently is able to produce only four notes on his antique instrument, brings them in when he can, with an inspired lumpishness which jibes with the other parts! The dance has its middle part, more rude, vigorous, wooden-shoed—the dances in the wood were ruder than those at the inn of the "Zwei Raben," frequented by Beethoven. When the first part of this scherzo returns

---

* Compare the discussion by Béla Bartók on p. 45.—E. S.

it is interrupted by the patter of raindrops, and presently the thunder-storm bursts in its fury. M. d'Indy calls attention to Beethoven's scheme of tonality in this symphony. All the movements except this one are in the major. The darker tonality of F minor is reserved for the storm. One hears the thunder and of course the wind. One almost *sees*, with sudden sharp chords of the orchestra, flashes of lightning. The storm departs in the distance, the pipes of shepherds and thankful songs echo through the orchestra.

The strings weave beautiful elaborations on these motives, and so the *Pastoral* Symphony comes to an end.

Ludwig van Beethoven: Symphony No. 7

From "Symphonic Masterpieces"

By Olin Downes

IN CONTRADISTINCTION to the Sixth or *Pastoral* Symphony, Beethoven's Seventh has no "program" or dramatic idea back of it. It is purest beauty, and in its impersonality is a hasty retreat from the programmatic indications of the former work. Unfortunately for the effect on lesser minds, Richard Wagner, in writing of the Seventh Symphony, called it "the apotheosis of the dance," and his remark, wholly justified in spirit and never intended literally, had dire consequences. The day came when Isadora Duncan "danced" the Seventh Symphony. But the work has survived this *bourgeoiserie* and even the gratuitous explanations of commentators who have sought to provide clues to its meaning.

There are none. The Seventh Symphony is beyond explanation. The listener is thrilled by the beauty and glory of the music. As he gains familiarity with the work, its details become always more distinct and impressive. But see ever so far, the mystery of the music is farther than that. The product of the genius of a man, it becomes mirror of the genius of the universe.

It happens that four of Beethoven's nine symphonies have introductions: the First, Second, Fourth, and Seventh. Of these the introduction to the Seventh Symphony is the freest in its fantasy, the noblest and most imposing: a majestic chord of the orchestra, a broad, swinging phrase, heard first from the oboe, then strengthened by other instruments as stronger sonorities are needed to chant it against an upward dancing procession of the strings. Other contributory ideas and surprising modulations lead with inevitability to the rhythm of the main body of the movement, established by an oft-repeated E that rings through the air.

On the basis of this rhythm, and the theme that it generates,

Beethoven creates virtually his entire main movement. Phrases which are actually parts of the principal idea could be detached and called "second theme" and "sub-theme" to satisfy the analysts; actually there is one theme, one intoxicating idea which Beethoven refuses to leave, and with which he makes marvelous diversion. Certain novelists have told us that when they created a real character, that character seemed to get out of hand, to act of its own initiative, and do things that its creator had not intended. Beethoven's motive appears to have a like individuality and dynamism. Actually it is never beyond control. The composer remains the unquestioned master of his inspiration. The exuberance and abundance of the music show that he could have continued his movement for many more pages than he does, but his sense of proportion is inexorable. There is not a superfluous note in all this plenty. Near the end of the movement comes a celebrated passage which caused another composer—the youthful Weber, whose years had not bestowed enough insight to save him from ridicule for the statement by posterity —to remark that Beethoven was now "quite ripe for the madhouse." It is the great place toward the end where the violoncellos and double-basses, deep down in the orchestra, concern themselves with a powerful, chained bass of five notes which they keep repeating, while overhead a tremendous climax accumulates.

The second movement is the famous "Allegretto." Beethoven originally marked this movement "andante"—slow. He later, and properly, designated more accurately the tempo he wanted as "allegretto"—somewhat fast, or less than fast. The Seventh Symphony is without a slow movement. Its mood is too exuberant. It is too free of our planet! Shall this symphony only walk? The main motive of the allegretto is a hymn-like melody—less a melody, perhaps, than a pulse which beats joyfully and persistently in one or another part of the orchestra. The motive is hymned by lower strings. Then it is heard combined with a yearning phrase of violas and 'celli. These two figures interweave. Later there is a change from minor to major, and a new melody, in a different rhythm, for clarinets and bassoons. (But even here can be felt in the depths of the orchestra, as if at the base of creation, the unchanging pulse.) When the first subject returns it is treated in a new way, in the fugal manner. A counter-subject in short notes is set against the initial motive. What the composer is driving at is not at first clear, until the hymning theme, with brilliant counterpoint twining about it, is proclaimed by the full orchestra. For a conclusion, fragments of the motive are tossed from instrument to instrument, and the orchestra sounds the same chord which opened the movement, and a rapturous sigh of the violins brings an end.

The third movement, the scherzo, is energized Haydn. This, at least, is true of the first part, a peasant strain. The contrasting passage is one of the supreme moments in Beethoven. The melody here given the strings is said to be that of a pilgrim hymn heard by the master at Teplitz. What gives the passage its singular and haunting beauty is the A, preceded by its auxiliary G-sharp, and sustained by horns and later by trumpets and other instruments. Sometimes the magical tone sounds from afar, sometimes it is flung out a mighty paean of praise, with all the instruments' power and glory.

For the finale, Beethoven makes Homeric horseplay with a melody in the character of an Irish folk tune.

The finale takes on the character of a cosmic reel. Jocose ditties stagger through the orchestra and cavort into space—the cat and the fiddle, the cow that jumped over the moon! Toward the end Beethoven resorts again to the device of a persistent bass such as he used so magnificently in the first movement.

"The Grand Symphony in A, one of my very best," said Beethoven.

Ludwig van Beethoven: Symphony No. 9 (Choral)

From "Symphonic Masterpieces"

By Olin Downes

THE imposing proportions of the Ninth Symphony, with its choral finale which chants the brotherhood of man, give the work a special place among Beethoven's creations and a special consideration on the part of the public. But the colossal work has other claims to greatness.

None of Beethoven's compositions came readily from his pen; this one represented a long and tortuous gestation. It seems that the composer's plan was not completely clear to himself until three-quarters of the symphony had been created. He was in doubt particularly as to the form which the finale should take. This is not surprising, since the Ninth Symphony is partly symphony and partly cantata, and the combining of the two styles was a problem even more perplexing in Beethoven's day than it would be in ours. In fact, Wagner found here the tacit acknowledgment on Beethoven's part that the symphony had gone as far as it could without the addition of song and dramatic idea to the instrumental scheme, and this conclusion influenced Wagner profoundly in his course as a composer of opera.

The Ninth Symphony appears as a magnificently imperfect creation; * as imperfect, let us say, as some tremendous torso of a Michelangelo which implies more by its very pathos and imperfection than a composition neatly and successfully perfected could do. Certainly this is the most profoundly subjective of Beethoven's symphonic utterances. In the pages of his symphonies he is universal rather than personal. His most introspective musings he reserved for the last piano sonatas and string quartets. But here in the Ninth Symphony—at least in its first and third movements—is Beethoven himself peering through chaos in loneliness and need seeking a path. No circumstance could have been more symbolic of the master's situation in life and in art than the occasion of the first performance and the tableau presented to the audience: Beethoven standing on the stage, his head sunk on his breast, beating time for the orchestra (which had been warned to

---

* This view is widely held by a number of musicians, but I must dissent. The Ninth Symphony has always seemed the most magnificent and perfectly balanced of all.—E. S.

disregard his motions); surrounded by silence; unaware that the music had ceased, when he was turned about by one of the singers, Fräulein Unger, to perceive the multitude shouting and with many persons in tears.

The symphony opens with vagueness and suspense, the famous "empty fifths" vibrating softly from the strings. Fragments of the great stark theme that is to come flash across the darkness, and suddenly the orchestra, in gigantic bare unisons, hurls it forth—the Word!

One can think of Genesis: "And the earth was without form and void. And God said, 'Let there be light.'" Immense enfoldments follow. The musical material is now grim and tremendous, now singing and tender. It is developed in great detail, yet without the obscuring of vast lines. The return after Exposition and Development to the Recapitulation is especially tremendous, when, over roaring drums, fragments of the great theme hurtle together and flash and splinter, as lightning might strike in a mountain gorge. The ending is pathetic, with the notes of the heroic theme flung out over sullen basses which roll like an ocean after the storm.

The second movement sets a powerful rhythm a-working. It has a gigantic simplicity and dynamic force. The universe dances. Imitations, foreshortenings, extensions of the dance figure, are in Beethoven's most concentrated style. The trio, a passage of starry serenity, was composed before the rest of the movement. When the earlier part of the scherzo returns, there are further rhythmic transformations. Blows of the kettledrums, solo, fortissimo, interrupt the rhythm with characteristic energy and brusquerie, an effect which caused the audience at the first performance to applaud in the midst of the movement.

In the slow movement Beethoven dispenses with strict form. The movement has two lyrical themes, which are heard in alternation, with variants of one of them.* "As to the beauty of these melodies," wrote Hector Berlioz, "the infinite grace of the ornaments applied to them,

* This is the second:

the sentiments of melancholy, tenderness and passionate sadness and of religious meditation which they express—if my prose could give [of] all this even an approximate idea, music would have found in the written word such a competitor as even the greatest of all poets was never able to oppose to it. It is an immense work; and, when once its powerful charm has been experienced, the only answer for the critic who reproaches the composer for having violated the law of unity is 'So much the worse for the law.' "

The conception of a symphony with a chorale finale had long been forming in the master's consciousness. As a youth of twenty-three he had attempted a setting of Schiller's "Ode," but the theme he then created had nothing to do with that of the Ninth Symphony. Nor was the theme of the finale the only problem which confronted him. How connect in a natural and logical manner the choral conclusion with the preceding movements? That was the crux of the problem. Beethoven's sketch-books, extraordinary documents of his creative life, tell us of his struggle. He seems to have decided that some preliminary words must introduce the passages for chorus and quartet. What words were they to be? The sketch-books are littered with fragmentary musical motives and phrases of text.

Thus, over the notation of a musical phrase of recitative: "No, these . . . remind of our despair." And later, "My fri . . . let it be celebrated with . . ." and more musical notation. Farther on, "Oh not this . . . something . . . but only a little merrier . . . (nor this either it is but sport, or no better) . . . (nor this it is too tender) . . . (for something animated we must seek) . . . (I shall see to it that I myself intone something then do you sing after me) . . . This it is ha now it is found I myself will intone it. . . . Ha this is it now is discovered . . . Freu . . . meilleur." And later the memorandum, words and notes, with which Beethoven rushed into a room one day crying out to Schindler (according to that gentleman's recollection), "I have it! I have it! Let us sing the song of the immortal Schiller *Freude!*" He had been, in these days, more than ever preoccupied, suspicious, a lone wolf among his kind. But he had found what he was seeking. The remaining months of 1823 saw the completion of the symphony, which was first performed in Vienna, March 7, 1824.

The finale, close upon the mystery and exaltation of the preceding movement, opens with a terrific hullabaloo of the instruments, highly discordant, which is answered by an admonishing recitative of 'cellos and basses. But these instruments are helpless in their attempt at pacification. The racket bursts out again. A shorter conciliating phrase of the recitative proposes, as a solution, some measures of the introduction. These too are furiously dismissed. Then, in answer to persistent summons, a fragment of the scherzo is heard. It is rejected, but more gently, and now there is anticipation of the theme of the "Ode to Joy." After one more gesture of recitative, it is given extended statement by the orchestra.

Observe how Beethoven, whose ideas came to him in symphonic and not in vocal guise, clings to his instruments. No sooner, however, has the choral subject received its symphonic endorsement than the orchestra is seized with fresh rebellion. It howls more loudly and terribly than ever; two opposed chords, shrieking to high heaven, sound at once all the notes of the harmonic minor scale!

This clears the air. Now the solo baritone propounds a sentiment to the melody of the recitative earlier sounded by instruments: "O brothers, let us have no more of these sad tones. Let us rejoice together." The basses of the chorus, the solo quartet, the full chorus, expand the theme. Thereafter come sundry variations and interludes for solo voices, for quartet, for chorus. The solo tenor, with the chorus, sings a march movement, inspired by the thoughts of "heroes" and "victory" in Schiller's text. A passage for full chorus apostrophizes the united, advancing millions, and the stars that form the canopy of the Father's dwelling in the heavens. The mood becomes more jubilant, with brilliant passages for the vocal ensemble against rushing instrumental figures. The pace quickens. There are shouts, "Hail thee, Joy, from heaven descending," and so ends the Ninth Symphony and Beethoven's dream of an advancing liberated mankind.

Franz Peter Schubert: Unfinished Symphony

From "Symphonic Masterpieces"

By Olin Downes

SCHUBERT composed his *Unfinished* Symphony when he was twenty-five, when the tragedy of his short, humble and poverty-stricken life was eating into his soul. There is the story that he composed the two movements in gratitude for having been elected an honorary member of a music society of Linz. Only a little time before he had been hurt and bitterly discomfited by the refusal of the Society of the Friends of Music [Gesellschaft der Musikfreunde] of Vienna, based on a technicality, to admit him to membership. We know this latter thing to be true, and we know of poor Schubert's gratification when the smaller and less important society accepted him. As for the question of his purpose in composing the fragments of the *Unfinished,* the facts, as modern research has proved, disagree with the legend; but the principle involved in the legend holds true as a revelation of Schubert's character. He could have done just that. He could also have written these incomparable movements for no purpose whatever save relieving his mind of the pressure of inspiration. He could have tucked them in a drawer and forgotten them because of the importunities of new ideas always thronging through the mind of a man whose creative fertility has become proverbial, who thought nothing of composing eight songs in a day, and whose creative fever burnt him up in his thirty-first year. Also—what remains perfectly possible—there might be in existence, in some hiding-place, the two missing movements of the *Unfinished* symphony. They might still turn up, as new Schubert manuscripts often turn up, for his productivity was incredible.

Whatever the explanation, the two movements that exist are among the highest creative flights Schubert ever took, and are the most concise and concentrated in their workmanship of all his symphonic writings. They show what might have happened if Schubert could have lived the allotted span of mortal years and received a tithe of the attention and encouragement given to his contemporary Beethoven.

It was given to Schubert to answer human experience with music of a beauty that gives us ineffable consolation and surcease from pain. The somber and purely Schubertian phrase for the 'cellos and basses which makes the introduction is a confounding stroke of genius, establishing, in ten measures, mood and a thematic cornerstone of the movement. Then we hear the murmuring accompaniment of the strings that reminded Schubert's admirable biographer, Edmonstoune Duncan, of the sea. Over the tossing figure the oboe sings its haunting complaint.

The same astonishing conciseness noted in the introduction is observed by the preparation for the second theme with a few chords of the strings and the sustained tone of the horn. Everything in the symphony is the essence of Schubert, and the second theme for the 'cellos is one of his sheer inspirations.

Passages of its development are wildly dramatic and at the end the phrase of the introduction returns with a stripped tragic power worthy of Beethoven.

It would be a pleasure, and useful as a background for this symphony, to say much of Schubert himself, his simplicity, his loving-kindness, his essential solitude, in the midst of unceremonious friends and boon companions that he loved; his pathetic need; his bitter griefs, of which he complained only in terms of song; the singular purity of his soul. Also his pranks and impromptu performances as pianist, when he would improvise waltzes and country-dances for good company at an inn in the mountains; his good-natured fury because he could not play the difficult finale of his own *Wanderer* Fantasy; the dismal lodgings with the poet Mayrhofer; the days when Schubert wore his spectacles to bed in order that he might be ready to go on with his composing the instant he awakened; the clothes he shared in common with companions as poverty-stricken as himself; his happy escapes from the society of aristocrats to that of peasants and housemaids; his performances of his song "The Erl-king" on a hair-comb. There never was so lovable and improvident a man, unless it was Mozart, and even Mozart knew more of the world and the ways of great society. Schubert, after the funeral of Beethoven, whom he adored, drank a toast to the one of his group who should be the next to go. That one was Schubert himself, and a few days before his death a friend rushed out and sold a number of his greatest songs for a few cents apiece. Schubert once said, "My music is the product of my genius and my misery, and that which I have written in my greatest distress is that which seems best to the world." But the epitaph, more poignant than any other could possibly be, of this life cut short, is the *Unfinished* Symphony.

Franz Peter Schubert: Symphony in C Major

From "Symphonic Masterpieces"

By Olin Downes

THE *Unfinished* and the C major Symphonies are the ones of the eight that Schubert composed which survive him. The other symphonies, in greater or lesser degree, are formative. These two are without a parallel in symphonic literature. In a way they supplement each other. The one is a song of which humanity can know the beginning, but never the end; the other is one of the most sublime outpourings of joy in the literature of music.

The great Schubert C major Symphony lasts for nearly an hour of wonderful sound. The composer's inspiration does not flag for a moment. The solo horn that opens the work sings its way straight into the blue.

This melody, characterized at first by an Olympic serenity, winds through different registers and choirs of the orchestra. As the mood becomes more exultant, counter-figures are wreathed about it. It is flung out mightily by instruments in unison. Calls from afar echo thunderously down corridors of space and time.

The tempo quickens, to usher in the main body of the movement, which, above all, and like the rest of the symphony, is a play of rhythms. For this is the symphony which, more than any other, merits the title Wagner gave Beethoven's Seventh—"The Apotheosis of the Dance."

The opening theme combines within itself two rhythms, a decisive beat in "two" time, and a triplet figure that leaves the earth with a rapturous flutter of wings. The two rhythms sound sometimes in succession and sometimes simultaneously, until preparation is made for the second theme. This is a dance measure, the melody given to wind instruments, with whirling accompaniment figures for the strings—an orchestral device often found in this symphony. And thereafter songs pour from the instruments in such profusion that there is scarcely time for the development of one idea before another crowds swiftly upon it. The movement ends with the orchestra intoning in great unison the theme of the introduction.

In the slow movement there is the tinge of Hungarian melancholy which affected every great composer who lived in Vienna, saving only the deaf Beethoven, who could not hear the gypsies. The oboe, after some introductory passages by plucked strings, intones a melody in the minor key which oboes and clarinets repeat in thirds.

The strings respond with a more flowing phrase. Full chords of the orchestra, in march rhythm, are echoed by the wood winds. A new and dreaming phrase for the strings is heard, followed by the horn, of which Schumann spoke when he said, probably referring to this place, that it "seems to come from another sphere, while everything listens, as though some heavenly messenger were hovering around the orchestra." When the march is resumed the motion is augmented by extra rhythmical figures played by trumpets, horns and other accompanying instruments. And now comes the one place in the symphony where tragedy lifts its head and utters a sharp cry of pain. It is a passage of shattering drama, a cry of agony, suddenly broken off, and followed by a pause of silence. Then the solo 'cello is heard, an answer of infinite tenderness. The music modulates into the major tonality. In due course the minor key returns and the march theme files off in the distance.

The scherzo, grandly designed like all the rest of the symphony, begins with a vigorous peasant step, and exuberant gayety. The contrasting middle part, the trio, is a melody which epitomizes all that is poetical, sentimental, nostalgic, in the nature of the Viennese, of whom Schubert was one. The starry evening! The swaying dance! Or, let us say, the purpling hills and the wistful thoughts of the little man who, so far as we know, never experienced woman's love, though he dreamed and sang of it in unforgettable strains.

What could be done after all this? What only Schubert could do! His finale is Dionysiac. The orchestra is possessed of an intoxication only matched by the potency of the ideas. It is a vertiginous whirl of inspiration—the dance-apotheosis. Toward the end four great C's, an intensive rhythmical development of the accompaniment figure of the second theme, earlier announced, are sounded in earth-shaking unison by massed instruments, as if winged Pegasus, poised for his flight, stamped the world in his impatience and joy. Shouts of the entire orchestra answer him; the symphony sweeps tumultuously to its close. It is all prodigious past the telling.

No more than the *Unfinished* was Schubert to hear this last of his symphonies. He is said to have intended it for the Musikverein of Vienna, which found the composition too difficult to play. It was performed by the Gesellschaft der Musikfreunde, December 14, 1828, a few weeks after Schubert's death. It was repeated by the same body a year later, and then lay forgotten until Schumann visited Schubert's brother Ferdinand in 1838 and sent a copy of the symphony to Mendelssohn in Leipzig. He, making some cuts in it, gave it repeated and successful interpretations.

This music is so simple and so frank that at first you may take it for granted. The better you know it, the more impressive it becomes. Though it follows generally classical precedent, it is not a work of the Beethoven tradition. That was left for Brahms to carry on. Because of its completeness as well as its prodigious inspiration this symphony of Schubert's is perhaps the only work of sufficient greatness before Brahms to take a commanding position in the wake of the immortal Nine.

Robert Schumann: Symphony in B flat (Spring)

From "Symphonic Masterpieces"

By Olin Downes

THE most romantic and personal of symphonies are the four by Robert Schumann. They are the outpourings of a young poet's heart, who molds the classic form to his heart's desire.

The ten years of Schumann's career as symphonist were from 1841 to 1851; 1840 was the year of his marriage to Clara Wieck, a happiness which colored all his art. He had waited long for his bride, and had known bitter hours of discouragement and frustration. For once in history a happily consummated romance did inspire a composer. Up to the time of his marriage Schumann had written entirely for the piano. He now literally burst into song, producing by the score a unique series of Lieder, and then turned to the symphony. One day he read a poem by Adolph Boettger—a minor German poet, a poem of gloomy cast. Observe how we make our world in accordance with our image of it! The poem begins with a melancholy apostrophe to the "dark storm cloud" and an entreaty that it change its course. It concludes with the line that set Schumann's soul vibrating: "In the valley blooms the Spring."

The best index to the nature of this work is provided in a letter Schumann wrote Wilhelm Tauber who was to conduct a performance of it in Berlin. "Could you infuse," says our tone-poet, "into your orchestra . . . a sort of longing for Spring? . . . The first entrance of the trumpets, this I should like to have sounded as though it were from above, like unto a call to awakening; and then I should like reading between the lines, in the rest of the introduction, how everywhere it begins to grow green, how a butterfly takes wing and, in the allegro, how little by little all things come that in any way belong to Spring. True, these are fantastic thoughts, which only came to me after the work was finished; only, I tell you this about the Finale, that I thought of it as the good-by of Spring."

A trumpet call, as from on high, is answered by a shout from the full orchestra. There is then a growing agitation among the instruments. The joyous tumult leads into the exultant main movement. This opens with a lively version of the initial trumpet motive, of which the rhythm dominates the movement.

A marchlike rhythm leads to the second theme, a lovely, plaintive phrase given to the clarinets. In the development of the material some subsidiary matter is added, but everything moves to the propulsive energy of the first theme, and it is impossible not to think of mounting sap and universal stir of life.

The return from free development to the first theme is preceded by the proclamation of the introductory trumpet call and the orchestral response. At the end of the recapitulation comes a long-breathed concluding subject, a hymn of thanksgiving for the new life that has come to the earth with the Spring; and again the victorious fanfare sounds from the skies.

Lovers of Schumann have special treasures, and surely a particular place must be given to the dreamily passionate song that makes the burden of the first movement. The melody of the slow movement, possessed of the fervor and languor of Spring, floats like a water-lily on the surface of the orchestral accompaniment; later it is played by the violoncellos with ornamentations of the violins. The movement ends with soft chorale-like harmonies for the trombones, and a gently interrogatory phrase of the clarinet, which is not a conclusion.

For the answer comes, after a short pause, with the virile attack of the scherzo. Scherzo movements in all the Schumann symphonies have a special character, not fantastic or demoniac, like Beethoven's, but rather poetical transfigurations of German folk dances. Some of the dance rhythms are heavy-footed and redolent of the good soil. Others, less physical, evoke thoughts tender, mocking, gay. Schumann extends these movements beyond the customary proportions of the three-part scherzo form, which has earlier been described. And so in the scherzo of this "Spring" symphony there are two "Trios," or middle parts, with piquant alternations of rhythms and of tempi. Just at the end is a little, unique coda, a teasing afterthought, of the greatest charm.

Schumann has told us his conception of the last movement—the thought of Spring's farewell as she trips onward over the countryside. This is the lightest and perhaps the least of the four movements, but it is delicious. The introductory theme has the inflection of a light-hearted serenade. Now the music hurries, now it dallies. Shouts of horns and wind instruments, over rushing strings, signalize the gay flight.

Hector Berlioz: Fantastic Symphony

The chapter "Landmark" in "The Well-Tempered Listener"

By Deems Taylor

THE *Fantastic* Symphony is a phenomenon, first, by reason of its instrumentation. Besides the instruments of the customary symphony orchestra, the score calls for an E-flat clarinet, four bassoons (instead of the ordinary two), two cornets (as well as two trumpets), two tubas, four kettledrums, two harps, and church bells. Berlioz also stipulates that there be at least sixty players in the string section, and, if possible, four harp players. This means an orchestra of not less than ninety men. Reasonable enough, to our modern ears; but if you will remember that the first performance of Beethoven's Ninth Symphony, only six years before the première of the Berlioz work, was given by what was then considered a gigantic orchestra of about seventy-five players, you can imagine what a sensation this *Fantastic* Symphony must have caused when Paris first heard it in December of the year 1830.

Not only did the piece make unheard-of demands as to the size of the orchestra that was to play it, but it was equally revolutionary in its treatment of the instruments. Berlioz dared to look the orchestra in the face as a single gigantic instrument, a variety of human pipe organ upon which the composer could play as he chose, pulling out any combination of stops that his imagination could conceive. Since his time there have been only six composers, I should say, who can stand beside him as masters of the art of orchestration: Wagner, Rimsky-Korsakov, Strauss, Debussy, Ravel, and Stravinsky. That's a rather impressive achievement for a man who has been dead nearly seventy years. His treatise on orchestration is still a standard work of its class, one that can still be studied with profit by any composer. This *Fantastic* Symphony of his is still remarkable for the extremely *modern* sound —not of the music, but of the orchestra. It is hard to realize that its instrumentation was finished only two years after that of Schubert's C major Symphony.

But there is another, equally important, way in which the Berlioz *Fantastic* Symphony is a landmark. It is one of the earliest true symphonic poems. While it is, technically speaking, a symphony (in five movements, to be sure, but so is Beethoven's *Pastoral*), and develops its themes in the symphonic manner, it is essentially descriptive music, and follows a specific and elaborate dramatic program.

There is no difference in the composer's *intent* between this work and Liszt's *Les Préludes,* for example. The only difference in form is that Liszt writes his tone poem in one movement, while Berlioz writes his in five, and calls it a symphony. As a matter of fact, he calls it that only in the subtitle. The full title is *Episode from the Life of an Artist; Fantastic Symphony in Five Parts, by Hector Berlioz.* On the programs for the first performance appeared a foreword written by Berlioz himself, followed by his general program note for the work as a whole:

"Program of the symphony. A young musician, morbidly sensitive and endowed with a vivid imagination, drugs himself with opium, during an access of lovesick despair. The dose of narcotic, too weak to prove fatal, plunges him into a heavy sleep, accompanied by the most fantastic visions, during which his sensations, his feelings, and his memories, translate themselves, in his sick brain, into musical thoughts and images. Even the woman whom he loves has been transformed into a melody, has become, as it were, an *idée fixe*—a fixed idea that keeps recurring and which he hears throughout the music."

Now this, of course, is not only the general program, but a general apology for *having* a program. Where a modern composer would simply say, "a young man drugs himself and sees strange visions, and here they are," Berlioz is quick to explain that the visions have accommodatingly turned themselves into music—a concession, I should say, to the prejudices of his generation, which wasn't used to such outlandish things as tone poems.

The first movement is called "Dreams—Passions." Berlioz's note is as follows:

"He recalls at first the soul-sickness, the waves of passion and of melancholy, of reasonless happiness, that used to sweep over him before he first saw the Beloved One; then he recalls the volcanic love that she inspired in him, his moments of delirious anguish, his jealous rages, his moments of returning tenderness, and of religious consolation."

As you see, this is not particularly definite, and the music for it has none of the detailed, literal pictorial quality of the score of one of Richard Strauss's tone poems. Its most noteworthy feature is that the melody representing the Beloved One, who is the cause of all the trouble,

occurs right at the outset, played very slowly and softly by the muted violins. This is the Fixed Idea the artist cannot escape: one can find it somewhere, easily identifiable, in every movement of the symphony.

The second movement is entitled "A Ball." In it the artist, in the words of the composer, "finds his Beloved at a ball, in the midst of the tumult of a brilliant fête." Nothing complicated here, simply a brilliant dance movement, interrupted by quieter sections wherein one hears again, in unmistakable terms, the theme of the Fixed Idea.

Third movement: "A Scene in the Fields." Berlioz describes it as follows:

"A summer evening in the country. He hears two shepherds who play, back and forth, a pastoral tune, the *ranz des vaches*. This rural duet, the setting, the soft murmuring of the trees, lightly swayed by the breeze, some glimmerings of hope that he has lately perceived, all unite to bring an unaccustomed peace to his heart, and to lend a more smiling tint to his thoughts. But She appears again; his heart contracts, painful forebodings oppress him. What if She should be false! One of the shepherds resumes his naïve tune. The other fails to answer. The sun slowly sets . . . distant thunder . . . solitude . . . silence."

Next, the fourth movement: "The March to the Scaffold."

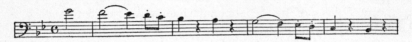

This is perhaps the most famous single movement of the entire symphony. Berlioz describes it as follows:

"He dreams that he has killed the one he loves, that he has been condemned to death, and is on his way to the gallows. The procession advances to the sound of a march, sometimes somber and threatening, sometimes brilliant and yet solemn, in which the heavy sound of slow footsteps succeeds, without transition, the wildest outbursts. At the end, the Fixed Idea reappears for an instant, a last thought of love, as it were, cut short by the death-blow."

Now comes the finale. It is called "Dream of a Witches' Sabbath." Berlioz's note reads:

"He sees himself at the Witches' Sabbath, in the midst of a company of fearful ghosts, sorcerers, monsters of all sorts, united for his funeral. Strange sounds, groans, bursts of laughter, distant cries, to which other cries seem to answer. The melody of the Beloved reappears, but it has lost its characteristic nobility and timidity. It is nothing but a vulgar, trivial, grotesque dance tune. She, too, has come to the revel. Yells of joy greet her arrival; she plunges into the diabolic orgy. Funeral bells . . . burlesque of the *Dies Irae* . . . round dance of the witches. The round dance and the *Dies Irae* are heard together."

Now this movement is in several distinct sections. First come the "ghosts and monsters," then a sort of jig version of the Fixed Idea theme, played shrilly on the E-flat clarinet. Next we hear the sound of chimes, followed by the medieval hymn, *Dies Irae,* played first by the tubas. When the bells stop tolling, we find ourselves at the round dance of the witches, the fourth section. The revelry grows wilder and wilder, the *Dies Irae* re-enters, in combination with the witches' dance, and the symphony comes to its end on a terrific sustained C major chord.

Felix Mendelssohn: Midsummer Night's Dream Overture

From "Everybody's Music"

By Schima Kaufman

MENDELSSOHN, the Peter Pan turned upside down, the never-young boy of music, composed his magnificent Overture to *A Midsummer Night's Dream* at the age of seventeen. He showed the first draft of the score to his "mentor," Adolph Bernhard Marx (who was later to become one of his bitterest critics), and for once was prevailed upon to accept criticism from an outsider.

Concerning this overture, the book *Mendelssohn: a Second Elijah* [by Schima Kaufman] contains the following information:

"In a few weeks the portion of the overture Felix had shown Marx was rewritten and completed. It was dated August 6, 1826, and, like his other compositions of the past six years, bore the puzzling initials L.v.g.G., known only to himself. It astonished everyone, even Marx, who could condemn the sky for being blue, was immensely pleased, and prided himself on his 'share' in it. An arrangement was made for piano duet, and frequently the elated composer played it with his aide-de-camp, Fanny [his sister]. Despite this unsatisfactory garb, with all the subtle symphonic tints missing, the work glowed with a poetic humorous beauty and Shakespearean charm that surpassed the elf-touched Octet. As an orchestral piece it was bewitching.

"At the beginning, a few wind-blown notes sounded the Open Sesame of a deep-buried fairyland.

"The realistic braying of Bottom on the bassoon

added confusion to the proceedings, and Oberon's repeated song, strewing blessings through the Palace of Theseus, now sung with distant stillness, returned the overture to the brink of the spirit-infested wood. From there the same wind-blown notes heard at the beginning ushered back the world of reality, and the dream was over!"

Johannes Brahms: Symphony No. 1

From "Symphonic Masterpieces"

By Olin Downes

BRAHMS waited ten years longer than Beethoven did to issue a first symphony, and was undoubtedly hesitant because of his awe of the composer of the Nine. In the interval of the seventy-six years that elapsed between the two works, Brahms had opportunity to benefit by the colossal strides of Beethoven himself and by immense technical advances in composition and orchestration. Another thing: to write a symphony in 1876 was considerably more of a responsibility than to undertake one in 1800. In 1800 the symphony was a comparatively modest affair. But with the appearance of the *Eroica* Symphony of Beethoven in 1804 all that was changed. The symphonic form was now the repository of the grandest musical and emotional conceptions. When Schumann, as a critic, discovered Brahms, and revealed him to the world in a famous article, he spoke of him as a creative artist who sprang forth fully armed, like Minerva from the head of Jove; and that, thanks to Brahms's patience, structural power, and depth of meaning, holds true of the C minor Symphony. It is monumental in proportions and epical in spirit, complex in structure, essentially dramatic as Beethoven's Fifth Symphony is dramatic, and, incidentally, concerned with the same theme.

The first movement is storm and stress; everything in it is tremendous, concentrated, richly developed, and packed together with great strength and a bardic power of utterance. The opening is one of the greatest pages of modern orchestral music, born of mist and storm and towering heights. The striving phrase heard over the pounding drums is the basic motive of the symphony, reappearing in many different guises in the following movements. It recurs like a question in measures of the slow movement. It ponders, dark-visaged and Faustlike, in the opening measures of the introduction of the finale, before the orchestral sky clears and Brahms's horn brings promise of salvation. There are pages in the first movement when it is as if the earth were in travail.

From all this turmoil the slow movement is remote, although its exaltations are haunted by questionings and agitations of the spirit. The third movement is not a minuet or a scherzo, but an allegretto—not a dance but a walk through nature; not laughter but a smile tinged with melancholy, and a departure, original with Brahms, from the customary symphonic form.

In this symphony the last movement as well as the first has an introduction, and the second introduction is perhaps Brahms's boldest imaginative flight. It begins in a vein of somber reverie. Curious pizzicato passages of the strings and savage outbursts of the full orchestra prelude the passage where the strings *tremolo* shimmer out like the opening of the heavens, and the horn calls as from above.

There have been various explanations of this dramatic passage, of the origin of the horn motive, and its meaning. The prophetic motto, following after dark mystery and brooding, precedes a chorale played softly by the trombones. Thereafter the horn-call, repeated, is answered by flute and trumpet, and this leads to the finale. Some have found in the theme that opens the last movement proper

an imitation of Beethoven's theme in the finale of the Ninth Symphony, and Brahms was pardonably irritated by the reminiscence hunters. The resemblance is one of only two measures and the analogy is far-fetched. The broad-arched theme chanted by the strings is the beginning of a movement that proceeds with a power and drama which are irresistible. A criticism of this victorious movement could be that it contained too many ideas and too rich development. But what could be omitted? It is a special test of a conductor's powers of synthesis.

Johannes Brahms: Symphony No. 2

From "Symphonic Masterpieces"

By Olin Downes

THE lyrical beauty of Brahms's Second Symphony makes it perhaps the most popular of the four works he composed in this form. The contrast between this symphony and the heroic First is complete, and it is strikingly analogous to the differences between Beethoven's Fifth and Sixth Symphonies. Brahms's First and Beethoven's Fifth are both in the same key and in a heroic vein. Both composers took considerable time with these works, although Brahms, who was forty years old before his first symphony saw the light, was by far the more deliberate. Then, after the two C minor symphonies of storm and stress, each man produced, in a short time, a work which offered ingratiating contrast to previous epic utterances. Each of these works, furthermore, implies a "return to nature." Beethoven's symphony in F is avowedly so. The title *Pastoral*, as well as the music, proves it. Brahms's D major symphony has no title; it is less impressionistic, closer knit, and stronger in its fabric than the corresponding work of Beethoven; but it, too, is surely of nature, and its vernal loveliness is like unto that of the Spring.

The opening, with the four notes of the 'cellos and basses and the reply of the dusky horn,

is the emotional as well as the musical key of the composition. The melodies that stream and intermingle in the orchestra, the lusty power of certain contrasting passages, and the coda, in which the magical horn is heard again, haunting forever the memory—all this is Spring herself. The second movement, grave and poetic, is Brahms in a brown study. For his contemporaries the movement was "a hard nut to crack." For us it is not so formidable. We know Brahms better, and admire him the more for his complete originality and fearlessness in self-expression. Here he thinks aloud. In his own way, and sometimes in long sentences, he formulates his thought, and the movement has the rich chromaticism, depth of shadow and significance of detail that characterize a Rembrandt portrait. It is also the admirable foil to the virility and élan of other movements. The third movement, with its delicious modulations and capricious changes of rhythms, is all built on the pastoral melody that the oboe sings over the strings pizzicato. The finale begins with a kind of theme that is a hallmark of Brahms's style—a motive played in unison by many instruments, which creeps mysteriously through the low registers of the orchestra before its brilliant proclamation by the full band. There are also rhythmical effects for which this composer has a fondness—alternating two and three rhythms, or groups of notes in these two rhythms, opposed to each other, and sudden explosive accents remindful of Beethoven. Later the violins take up a new song, having for its bass a motive from the opening theme of the movement, which later, flung out by the trumpets, brings the glorious conclusion. When Brahms had finished this symphony he wrote his friend, Dr. Billroth, saying, "I don't know whether I have a pretty symphony. I must inquire of learned persons!"

Johannes Brahms: Symphony No. 3

From "Symphonic Masterpieces"

By Olin Downes

DID Brahms ever write a more thrilling theme than the one which leaps from the orchestra like a bolt from Jove at the beginning of the Third Symphony?

And what is more poetical than the end of the symphony, when that same fury theme, or a fragment of it, is heard again in terms of sunset splendor? The symphony is a further development of Brahms's mastery of material, and variety of rhythms, and its nature is very romantic.

The first and last movements of the Third Symphony are closely connected by theme and mood. These movements are heard, as it were, against a background of mountain, sky, and singing winds. The two inner movements are in a different category. They are in fact less symphonic in character than the corresponding parts in any of the other Brahms symphonies. These inner parts of the Third Symphony are smaller and more intimate in conception. Carefully as they are worked out, they have nevertheless such unity and mood that they sound almost as improvisations. Some feel that these movements are rather expansions of Brahms's chamber-music style, or even of the structures of his shorter piano pieces, than appropriate for a great symphony. The more fanatical of the "Brahmins," who are content with nothing but the most extravagant praises of "the master," will probably dispute this. For me the special effect of these movements lies precisely in their intimate and personal nature. They are cradled between the Jovian beginning and the towering finale as valleys lie between towering heights.

The second movement grows from a melody which has the char-acter of a German folk song or lullaby.

Its melodic offshoots cluster about the principal theme, with a brief passage of necessary contrast. The third movement is one of a compassionate melancholy and introspection, the principal theme given a special color by the combined tone of 'cello and clarinet. The "color" of this movement is not less original and unprecedented in orchestral music than the peculiar technic and poetical coloring, in another field, of Brahms's representative piano pieces. Schumann was not more personal. The finale is energetic and magnificent, and the last pages have the glory and serenity of the afterglow.

Johannes Brahms: Symphony No. 4
From "Symphonic Masterpieces"

By Olin Downes

IT IS very interesting to examine Brahms's progress as a symphonist. He appeared in the time of so-called romanticism in music, when considerations of form were largely subordinated to subjective expression. Liszt was then creating his symphonic poems and Wagner his tremendous music-dramas—all works strongly colored by literary and poetic ideas, and by a very personal attitude on the part of the composer. Brahms, in his First Symphony, if not an outright romanticist, is yet "romantic" in his attitude, just as Beethoven in his Fifth. Later on we are witness to Brahms's progression backward— or forward—from the "romantic" to the "classic" persuasion. The Fourth Symphony is a pure classic masterpiece. From this, however, it is not to be assumed that the symphony is only a work of design, without subjective undercurrent. Quite the contrary! While Brahms has long since parted company with the storm and stress of the First Symphony, the accents of the Fourth are in the highest degree charged with the resignation and the profound understanding that his own earnest nature and the passage of the years had brought him, and the nobility that existed under his crusty exterior. The romanticist has been purged of his passion. The fury and strife are gone. With them has gone the quality of action and drama which inspired earlier pages. But in the Fourth Symphony something has replaced these things, something even more precious, and wiser.

It is perhaps significant that Brahms, ordinarily certain of himself and his work, had misgivings and questionings about this symphony. Did it touch more distant horizons than any to which he yet had raised his eyes? Or was he merely suffering from failing strength and ill-health? Or was he, as some might claim, affected by the spirit of a period which had seeds of decadence? Some find the symphony an expression of rank pessimism. They say that it is bitter, that it drips melancholy like the yew tree, that its thoughts are of death. But pessimism is not despair, nor need it be in any sense ignoble. If Brahms's thoughts at the time he wrote this symphony were turning toward his own end, which was near, death must have appeared as it should appear to all of us, as a tender friend and a supreme consoler. It is a far cry from such a spirit and art as that of Brahms to the art of a Whitman. And yet there is something in this Fourth Symphony which may well turn the memory to the words of the great American poet in "Out of the Cradle Endlessly Rocking," when he writes of the secret word that the waves kept whispering to the boy who watched the lonely nightbird from among the reeds on the shore. Here, in this symphony, are perhaps premonitions of the other side of life, vistas of a beauty linked with eternity, beauty as mysterious and inexplicable as the design of a pine tree against a flaming autumn sky.

The first movement begins with the lovely theme with which the orchestra is soon weaving arabesques.

It continues with motives that supply the necessary energy and masculinity to balance the more delicate traceries; and all this is murmurous of some legendary land, autumnal and infinitely beautiful. The second movement is an exquisite play of ancient and modern tonalities, hauntingly poetical and suggestive of distance. The motive of the solo horn is cast in the so-called "Phrygian" mode (when the F-sharp and D-sharp of E minor become F and D-natural). Later on this "modal" treatment gives place to a version of the theme in the major key, with enchanting effect. But in the third movement Brahms is again old bear's-paws, with his feet on the good earth, rapping out his rhythm in music that tingles with force, laughter and joy.

The final movement is the great Passacaglia, capstone to the whole edifice. Some may find in it the same esthetic significance as in the finale of Beethoven's *Eroica.* On a theme eight measures long are built masterly variations and a coda.

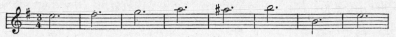

The pervading motive is always present, in one or another form, and with different orchestrations. It is variously altered and disguised, but if examined shows how closely Brahms is sticking to his text. After each one of the variants it would be fair to applaud, save that some of them go too deep for applause and can only be rendered silent homage. One of these is the twelfth variation for the solo flute, over soft chords of horns and violins; others are the fourteenth, with its chorale for the trombones; the passionate seventeenth and eighteenth; the song of the wind instruments in variation 28. But it is inadvisable and superfluous to confuse the listener by reference to details in this movement. Indeed, nothing is more striking than the manner in which the variations are put together. Thus the movement is not a series of episodes, but rather of linked evolutions of a single thought, with a final great sweep from the sixteenth variation, when the theme is uttered with such magnificent energy by the brass choir, to the end. It could be said that Brahms had been unconsciously preparing himself for the composition of this Passacaglia through many years of gradually acquired mastery of the variation form. The movement is his last symphonic will and testament. Some consider that the Fourth Symphony represents the end of a long musical epoch, and they explain its pervading spirit as the farewell of a master whose thoughts turned away from the present and back to the faith of his great forebears— Bach, Handel, Beethoven, Schubert. But this noble and reflective work appears more secure, and more rather than less in touch with living musical thought, as the years pass. If this be resignation it is the resignation of strength, faith, awareness of the indestructibility of thought and beauty.

Johannes Brahms: Concerto for Violin and Orchestra

From "Everybody's Music"

By Schima Kaufman

BEETHOVEN, Mendelssohn, and Brahms delivered themselves of one violin concerto apiece. Other composers were more generous to their long-haired brethren, but none reached so high a plane of exalted beauty as these three. For Brahms the great violinist Joseph Joachim acted as midwife and godfather, helping his violinistic offspring into the world and then standing by for the official baptism. The child of Brahms's brain turned into an enfant terrible, upsetting many a good fiddler's composure and practising habits. Indeed, its technical difficulties were so prodigious that a witticism soon went forth to this effect: "The Brahms Concerto is not *for* the violin, but *against* it." But Brahms never wrote for lazy musicians! Even Joachim could not persuade him to change his mind. We have it on good authority that Brahms turned a deaf ear to all his friends' hints and would accept nothing but bow markings, fingerings, and a noble cadenza which has become a part of the work.

The Concerto was written in 1878, a year after the Second Symphony, which is in the same key of D Major. Originally it consisted of four movements. A Scherzo was thrown out, and the Adagio so thoroughly revised as to be virtually new. "The middle movements have gone," the composer lamented, "and of course they were the best!" Little has posterity shared his gloom. The Adagio is a meditative, idyllic interlude with elaborate violin figuration over the themes in the orchestra. The magnificent first movement opens with a long *tutti* introduction.

followed by the solo instrument in "an imaginative and eloquent discourse upon what has been previously heard." The finale is a rondo of strongly marked Hungarian character.

Like the piano concertos, this work may be regarded as a symphony with a part for solo instrument.

Antonin Dvořák: New World Symphony

From "Everybody's Music"

By Schima Kaufman

IN 1900 Dvořák himself suppressed as a lie that portion of Kretzschmar's analysis which asserts that the composer made use of "Indian" and "American" motives. "I tried to write only in the spirit of those national American melodies," he insisted.

Partisans of Edward MacDowell had previously thought the good doctor was wrong in touching the Negro spirit at all—it should have been Indian—and Mr. MacDowell wrote an "Indian" suite to show him how. Later the biographer of Smetana "proved" that the themes of the E minor Symphony were not even Negro, but indigenous Czech tunes! Still another traced the spiritual to Ireland and Scotland. Thus, over the body of the composer, so to speak, raged a merry war of scholars, not unlike the case of Ibsen, who was informed by his critics that he had written "modern allegories," not problem plays.

Fortunately the symphony has survived the discussions upon it. In four movements, each with its brief introduction, it is in the conventional symphonic form. The tonal canvas upon which Dvořák paints is broad and rich, exquisite and full-bodied, filled with the awed wonder of a new land and, perhaps, an awakened nostalgia for his own.

(1) Adagio: The lower strings, answered by flutes and oboes, softly announce the first glimpsing theme; Allegro molto: coming

farther inland, horns sound a strongly rhythmic melody based on the five-tone scale;

the flute solo, reminiscent of "Swing Low, Sweet Chariot," is taken up by the various choirs in the "working-out" section.

(2) Largo: The romantic English-horn theme—the spurious "Going Home"—was inspired by Longfellow's poem *Hiawatha's Wooing*.

(3) Scherzo: "Eager, impetuous, aggressive—sportive in the trio."

(4) Allegro con fuoco: A broad and fiery theme for brass, repeated by strings; a second theme given out by clarinets, after which is a summary of the main themes of the preceding movements.

Richard Wagner: Meistersinger Prelude

From "Symphonic Masterpieces"

By Olin Downes

A RECITAL of Wagner's deeds in music becomes an unending tale of marvel. Wagner had conceived the plan of *Die Meistersinger* (completed in 1867, produced 1868) very early, as early as or even earlier than *Lohengrin*. But, though some have claimed that he made early sketches for the quintet from the last act of *Die Meistersinger*, he apparently did not set himself definitely to its composition till the middle of March, 1862. He was, as usual, terrifically in debt, but had settled himself comfortably in Biebrich, in rooms that looked out upon a garden and a flowing river, and the creative mood, as he had hoped it would, descended upon him. In his autobiography he tells us that "As from the balcony of my flat, in a sunset of great splendor, I gazed upon the magnificent spectacle of 'golden' Mayence, with the majestic Rhine flooding its outskirts in a glory of light, the Prelude to my *Meistersinger* again suddenly made its presence closely and distinctly felt in my soul. Once before had I seen it rise before me out of a lake of sorrow, like some distant mirage. I wrote down the prelude exactly as it appears today in the score, containing the clear outlines of the leading themes of the whole drama. I proceeded at once to continue the composition, intending to allow the remaining scenes to follow in due succession."

We must consider for a moment the basic dramatic motives of the opera if we are to grasp fully the meaning of this Prelude. The principal characters in the plot are Walther von Stolzing, poet and knight; Eva, daughter of a rich burgher of old-time Nuremberg, whom Walther loves, but whose hand he can win only by proving his genius in song; Hans Sachs, the famous cobbler and Mastersinger, who personifies the wisdom of experience and sacrifice, and the great-heartedness of the people; and Beckmesser, the crabbed clerk, pedant, and theoretician, who expects by virtue of his hollow learning and pretense to win Eva for himself. At last Beckmesser and Walther are pitted against each other in a contest of song, when Walther's genius, youth, and love put the now ridiculous Beckmesser to flight. Walther is acclaimed a Mastersinger; Eva is given to him as his bride; the populace enthusiastically salute the poet and the noble Sachs.

Walther, of course, is Wagner himself. Beckmesser is prototype of Wagner's antagonists among the critics. Hans Sachs is the virtue and wisdom of the people, prompt to recognize the creative artist and find expression in him. The final moral is that the greatest genius must have its roots deep down in the soil of the race that gave it birth, and that the aristocracy of genius can in turn raise the people to new levels of beauty and understanding.

The Prelude begins with the first of the two *Meistersinger* themes,

a splendid pompous march emblematic of that famous sixteenth-century guild of musician-tradesmen and merchants who practised art industriously, even though they tended to conventionalize it, and gave poetry and music official importance in the lives of the people. The march theme is followed by phrases that relate to Walther's Prize Song and his love for Eva. This leads to the second *Meistersinger* theme, also in march rhythm, and, if anything, more weighty than the first. You are to see them, these Mastersingers, as they wend their way to the banks of the river to hold the contest of song—the noble Sachs, the majestical Pogner, the mincing Beckmesser, clad in rich fabrics and colors, mighty in the consciousness of their own pith and prosperity and worth. Banners fly, the people dance and cheer and crane their necks as the leading citizens of the free and imperial city of the olden time pass by. This second march theme, which Wagner is said to have taken from the "Crowned tone" of Heinrich Mügling, is extended with music heard in the festive concluding scenes, the music of the crowd and the holiday. A short, impetuous phrase given the strings speaks of the love of Walther and Eva, and the basic motive of Walther's Prize Song is developed by the orchestra.

This is the substance of the first part of the Prelude, which propounds all its musical material. The second part comes with the fugal caricature of the *Meistersinger* theme, combined with a motive heard when the populace makes fun of Beckmesser in the last act. The fugue is cackled by the wind instruments, with humorous asides by trilling strings and other similar effects. Thus Wagner makes fun of the pedantry of the Beckmessers. The progress of the fugue is hotly contested, from time to time, by the warm and impetuous motive of Walther and Eva. The two motives oppose each other with increasing obstinacy, which brings the fugue to a climax.

The third part of the Prelude begins when the brasses thunder out in its full grandeur the first *Meistersinger* theme, which disperses the fussy counterpoint, while an exultant phrase wreathes the motive of the sturdy march. Now occurs that sheer explosion of genius, the peroration of the *Meistersinger* Prelude. Three themes and a fragment of a fourth are heard at the same time, as though it were impossible to keep them apart and oblige each one to wait its turn. Softly, in the basses, walks along the theme of the Mastersingers. Above sings the Prize Song of Walther. In between may be heard the fanfares of the second *Meistersinger* motive, and across the strings flits a motive associated with Beckmesser. The glorious hubbub grows, the music swells with lustiness and festivity to the final proclamation, with all possible orchestral brilliancy, of the *Meistersinger* music.

Richard Wagner: Tristan Prelude and Love-Death

From Philharmonic-Symphony Program Notes

By Robert Bagar

IN 1854, when Wagner was in the midst of composing the *Ring*, the idea for an opera on the Tristan theme came to him. Not till three years later, however, did he begin actual work on it, and the music drama was finished in August, 1859. Complications of various kinds interfered with the production of the opera, but it finally obtained its première at the Royal Court Theater in Munich, on June 10, 1865, under the direction of Hans von Bülow.

Wagner's version of the tale combines features from numerous legends. Very likely of Celtic origin, the story, as the German composer utilized it, makes room for myriad delvings into psychology and metaphysics, some of which are not easy to follow. We must assume, as Ernest Newman suggests, that the characters and their motivations were perfectly clear to the composer, if they seem not to be altogether to the listener.

The Prelude, A minor, 6/8, makes a very gradual and long crescendo to a mighty fortissimo, followed by a briefer decrescendo, which leads to a whispered pianissimo. Free as to form, and ever widening in scope of development, it offers two chief themes, a phrase, uttered by the 'cellos, is united to another, given to the oboes, to form a subject called the "Love Potion" theme, or the theme of "Longing."

Another theme, again announced by the 'cellos, "Tristan's Love Glance," is sensuous, even voluptuous in character.

After the Prelude, the orchestra enters into the "Liebestod" or "Love-Death," that passionate flow of phrases, taken mostly from the material in the second act Love-Duet. Isolde (in the opera) sings her

song of sublimated desire. Franz Liszt is responsible for the application of the term *Liebestod* to that part of the music which originally had been named *Verklärung* by Wagner himself.

Richard Wagner: Ride of the Valkyries

From "Everybody's Music"

By Schima Kaufman

IN *Die Walküre,* the second opera of Wagner's gigantic *Ring* (which took him twenty-six years to complete), the nine Amazonian daughters of Wotan and Erda are the Choosers of the Slain (*Walküren*), who wait upon the heroes in Valhalla, mark them for death in combat, and bear away the bravest to be restored as the protectors of the Gods.

The Ride is based upon the opening scene of the third act.

The Maiden Warriors have a meeting place in a wild rocky gorge, high up in the mountains. Thunder and lightning rend the sky. The Valkyries, a slain hero across each saddle bow, are discerned riding through the air, pausing only to alight on some jutting crag. "Hoyotoho!" sounds their harsh battle-cry, blending with the whinnying and stamping of their restless steeds and the shriek of the gathering storm. The music, which Wagner thought of arranging himself for concert performance, terminates with a coruscating downward sweep, the Valkyries having disappeared into thin air.

Nicolas Rimsky-Korsakov: Scheherazade

From "Stories of Symphonic Music"

By Lawrence Gilman

PREFIXED to the score of this suite (published in 1889) is the following program, printed in French and Russian:

The Sultan Schahriar, convinced of the faithlessness of women, had sworn to put to death each of his wives after the first night. But the Sultana Scheherazade saved her own life by diverting him with stories which she told him during a thousand and one nights. The Sultan, conquered by his curiosity, put off from day to day the execution of his wife, and at last renounced his bloody vow entirely.

Many wonders were narrated to Schahriar by the Sultana Scheherazade. For her stories the Sultana borrowed the verses of poets and the words of folk songs, and fitted together tales and adventures.

1. The Sea and Sindbad's Ship.
2. The Tale of the Kalendar-Prince.
3. The Young Prince and the Young Princess.
4. Festival at Bagdad. The Sea. The Ship is Wrecked on a Rock Surmounted by a Bronze Warrior. Conclusion.

There is doubt as to Rimsky-Korsakov's precise intention in the program of this suite. Which one of Sindbad's voyages is described, which of the three Kalendars is referred to, and what adventure of what young prince and princess, the composer leaves to his hearers to decide. Moreover, the event mentioned in the last number of the suite—the wrecking of the ship upon a rock surmounted by a warrior of brass (not "bronze")—occurs in the story of the third Kalendar, while the wreck of Sindbad's ship occurred under different circumstances. The truth seems to be that Rimsky-Korsakov has aimed at translating into music the spirit and atmosphere which unifies the various stories, and has not troubled himself about the accuracy or the consistency of his paraphrase. Like Scheherazade herself, he has strung together, without regard for continuity or coherence, whatever incidents and fragments suited his purpose. Thus his music is to be taken as a gloss on the tales as a whole—on their general and underlying mood, their color, their imaginative essence.

I. THE SEA AND SINDBAD'S SHIP

The first theme of this movement, heard at the opening,

has been identified both as the motive of the Sea and as that of Sindbad. Later we hear (solo violin, with harp chords) the motive of Scheherazade

An undulating *arpeggio* figure has been called the Wave motive, and a theme first sung by the solo flute that of the Ship. The Sea motive forms a climax of the full orchestra. There is a tranquil close.

II. THE TALE OF THE KALENDAR-PRINCE

After an introductory passage, we hear the Scheherazade theme on a solo violin with harp accompaniments, followed by a theme, *quasi recitando,* for solo bassoon, which seems here to have the role of narrator.

There is an intermezzo of Oriental character. The end is spirited.

III. THE YOUNG PRINCE AND THE YOUNG PRINCESS

Some think, from the similarity of the two themes typical of prince and princess, that the composer had in mind the adventures of Kamar al-Zaman (Moon of the age) and the Princess Budur (Full moon). This movement is idyllic, a romanza evolved out of two themes of folk-song character.

IV. FESTIVAL AT BAGDAD. THE SEA. THE SHIP IS WRECKED ON A ROCK SURMOUNTED BY A BRONZE WARRIOR. CONCLUSION.

The motive of the Sea begins the movement; the Scheherazade theme follows; then (*Allegro molto e frenetico*) begins a brilliant depiction of the revels at Bagdad. Then, abruptly, we are transferred to a scene on shipboard. "We seem to plunge into the broad movement of the surging sea, straight on to the fateful event." While the jollification is at its height the ship strikes the dreadful rock. "The trombones roar out the Sea motive against the billowy Wave motive in the strings. . . . The storm dies. . . . There is a quiet ending with development on the Sea and Wave motives. The tales are told. Scheherazade, the narrator, who lived with Shahriar 'in all pleasance and solace of life and its delights till there took them the Destroyer of delights and the Severer of societies, the Desolater of dwelling-places and the Garnerer of graveyards, and they were translated to the ruth of Almighty Allah,' fades away with the vision and the final note of her violin."

Modeste Mussorgsky: Pictures at an Exhibition
From Philharmonic-Symphony Program Notes

By Robert Bagar

VICTOR HARTMANN, prominent Russian painter and architect who was an intimate friend of Mussorgsky's, died in 1873 at the age of thirty-nine. The composer visited an exhibition of the artist's water-colors and drawings, held at the Academy of Arts, St. Petersburg, shortly after Hartmann's death. From that visit grew a resolve to set to music, as it were, ten of the pictures in the form of a piano suite, as a memorial tribute to his friend.

Mussorgsky, not the type to wax enthusiastic over his own labors, yet bubbled and brimmed with excitement in the creating of this composition, and it is not difficult to understand why. In the first place, he was deeply affected by the demise of the painter, a fact which would of itself call the sum total of his resources into play. Then, Mussorgsky could do surprisingly good work under pressure, particularly when not fettered, so to speak, by matters of development, orchestration, and so on.

In a lengthy letter to his friend Stassov, Mussorgsky wrote:

My very dear friend, what a terrible blow! "Why should a dog, a horse, a rat have life"—and creatures like Hartmann must die! . . . This is how the wise usually console us blockheads in such cases: "He is no more, but what he has done lives and will live!" True—but how many men have the luck to be remembered? That is just another way of serving up our complacency (with a dash of onion, to bring out the tears). Away with such wisdom! When "he" has not lived in vain, but has created—one must be a rascal to revel in the thought that "he" can create no more. No, one cannot and must not be comforted, there can be and must be no consolation—it is a rotten mortality! If Nature is only coquetting with men, I shall have the honor of treating her like a coquette—that is, trusting her as little as possible, keeping all my sense about me, when she tries to cheat me into taking the sky for a fiddlestick—or ought one, rather like a brave soldier, to charge into the thick of life, have one's fling, and go under? What does it all mean? In any case the dull old earth is no coquette, but takes every "King of Nature" straight into her loathsome embrace, whoever he is—like an old worn-out hag, for anyone is good enough, since she has no choice.

There again—what a fool I am! Why be angry when you cannot change anything? Enough then—the rest is silence.

Mussorgsky's original score of the *Pictures at an Exhibition* comprised ten actual program pieces, each connoting a different subject. For preface there is Promenade, which is also repeated several times between sections as a connecting link. The work was composed in June, 1874.

Promenade. "The composer here portrays himself walking now right, now left, now as an idle person, now urged to go near a picture; at times his joyous appearance is dampened, he thinks in sadness of his dead friend," according to Stassov, to whom the suite is dedicated. The Promenade appears between sections up to the fifth.*

The Gnome. Stassov's interpretation of this subject conceives of it as "a child's plaything, fashioned, after Hartmann's design in wood, for the Christmas tree at the Artists' Club (1869). It is something in the style of the fabled Nutcracker, the nuts being inserted in the gnome's mouth. The gnome accompanies his droll movements with savage shrieks." Riesemann describes it as "the drawing of a dwarf

* The melody is given on page 543.

who waddles with awkward steps on his short, bandy legs; the grotesque jumps of the music, and the clumsy, crawling movements with which these are interspersed, are forcibly suggestive." Authority, however, would seem to rest with Stassov.

Old Castle. A medieval castle, before whose ancient tower a troubadour lifts a doleful song. The length of this section reflects Mussorgsky's admiration of the picture.

Tuileries. The picture shows an alley in the Tuileries Gardens where a group of children are having a dispute after their play. Ravel makes interesting use of the high wood wind here, aiming at a kind of imitation of the children's voices.

Bydlo—Polish Oxcart. In Polish *bydlo* means "cattle." Here a Polish oxcart, lumbering on giant wheels, draws near, the driver singing a "folksong in the Aeolian mode."

Ballet of Chicks in Their Shells. With reference to this section Stassov says: "In 1870, Hartmann designed the costumes for the staging of the ballet *Trilby* at the Maryinsky Theater, St. Petersburg. In the cast were a number of boy and girl pupils of the theater school, arrayed as canaries. Others were dressed up as eggs."

Samuel Goldenberg and Schmuyle. A picture of two Polish Jews, one rich, one poor, drawn from life (1868) by Hartmann. Mussorgsky liked it so well that the artist made him a present of it. Riesemann considers this "one of the most amusing caricatures in all music. . . . These two types of the Warsaw Ghetto stand plainly before you— you seem to hear the caftan of one of them blown out by the wind, and the flap of the other's ragged fur coat. Mussorgsky's musical power of observation scores a triumph with this unique musical joke; he proves that he can reproduce the 'intonations of human speech' not only for the voice, but also on the piano."

Limoges: The Market-place. Another dispute, this time among market women. In order to give an account of his intentions in this section, Mussorgsky wrote the following words in the margin of his score, "Great news! Monsieur de Puissangeout has just recovered his cow, The Fugitive. But the good gossips of Limoges are not totally agreed about this, because Mme. de Remboursac has just acquired a beautiful new set of teeth, whereas Monsieur de Panta-Pantaléon's nose, which is in the way, remains the color of a peony." All this, of course, is meant to be peasant chit-chat.

Catacombs (*Con mortuis in lingua mortua*). The drawing portrays Hartmann studying the Paris Catacombs by lantern light.

The Hut on Fowls' Legs (*Baba-Jaga*)—Witches' Revelry. A clock appearing in the fantastic guise of the hut of the witch Baba-Jaga. It stands on the legs of fowls.

The Great Gate at Kiev.

Hartmann's drawing of a proposed gate for the city of Kiev. The design, "conceived in the massive old Russian style, had a cupola in the shape of a Slavonic helmet."

Ravel orchestrated the *Pictures at an Exhibition* early in 1923. The work was first performed in this new setting in Paris on May 3, 1923.

Peter Ilyich Tchaikovsky: Symphony No. 4

From "Symphonic Masterpieces"

By Olin Downes

PETER ILYICH TCHAIKOVSKY was a child of the earth, and of the nation of Pushkin and Dostoevsky. Musical purists look down upon him. He was not a classicist. He had not the heroic strength and will of a Beethoven. He spoke in music as one of the insulted and injured. He was all feeling. In his scores he cries out, shakes his fist at the skies, remembers the agony of thwarted love, and the end of every man's desire. Admire such a man, such a neurotic, such a pessimist? I profoundly esteem and rate him a thousand times higher than those who have never known Tchaikovsky's weakness and terror, who shudder at such emotional indecencies, and pull their skirts together at the sound of them. How can *they* know what Tchaikovsky is saying?

The F minor Symphony has four movements. The first is introduced by the Fate theme.

The music pursues a restless and fitful course. The motive of destiny
twice intervenes. "So is all life," wrote Tchaikovsky to his patroness,
"but a continual alternation between grim truth and fleeting dreams
of happiness. There is no haven. The waves drive us hither and thither
until the sea engulfs us. This is approximately the program of the first
movement."

He says that "The second movement shows another phase of
sadness.

Here is that melancholy feeling which enwraps one when he sits alone
in the house at night, exhausted by work; the book which he has taken
to read slips from his hand; a swarm of reminiscences has risen. How
sad it is that so much has already been and gone, and yet it is a pleasure to think of the early years. One mourns the past and has neither
the courage nor the will to begin a new life. . . . And all that is now
so far away, so far away."

Of the third movement Tchaikovsky wrote in an earlier letter
that it would have "quite a new orchestral effect, from which I expect
great things." It is the movement in which the three principal divisions
of the orchestra—strings, wood wind, and brass—are used in succession. This popular movement, the Scherzo, begins with the *pizzicato
ostinato,* in which the players pluck the strings instead of using the
bow. The device has a fantastical effect, not unsuggestive of Autumn
wind and whirling leaves. The wind instruments play a skirling tune.
A marchlike passage for brass and kettledrums ensues. Finally fragments of all these three sections are tossed back and forth by the instruments. "Here," wrote Tchaikovsky, "are capricious arabesques, vague
figures which slip into the imagination when one has taken wine and is
slightly intoxicated. The mood is now gay, now mournful. One thinks
about nothing; one gives the fancy loose rein, and there is pleasure in
drawings of marvelous lines. Suddenly rushes into the imagination

the picture of a drunken peasant and a gutter-song. Military music is heard passing in the distance. These are disconnected pictures, which come and go in the brain of the sleeper. They have nothing to do with reality; they are unintelligible, bizarre, out at the elbows."

"Go to the people," he writes, in explanation of his vodka-ridden finale. There is heard, soon after, a crash of cymbals and whirling descent of strings, a Russian folk song, "In the Fields There Stood a Birch-tree," played by the wood winds.

This movement is "the picture of a folk-holiday. Scarcely have you forgotten yourself, scarcely have you had time to be absorbed in the happiness of others, before untiring Fate again announces its approach. The other children of men are not concerned with you. They neither see nor feel that you are lonely or sad. . . . Rejoice in the happiness of others—and you can still live." But the rejoicing is hectic. It is interrupted again by the sardonic proclamation of Fate. The reckless conclusion is brilliant, yet akin to despair.

Peter Ilyich Tchaikovsky: Symphony No. 6

From "Symphonic Masterpieces"

By Olin Downes

BUT there is no question: the *Symphonie pathétique,* Tchaikovsky's Sixth and last, is his masterpiece, one which will endure as long as any of his music is known. Nowhere else has he approached the burning intensity and the sable splendor of this score. In no other place has he revealed himself with equal completeness and mastery of expression. The *Symphonie pathétique* made such an impression upon the public that for a time it was overplayed. Thereafter it was underpraised. It remains a human document of immense pathos and tragedy. Some are repelled by the hysteria and self-laceration of pages of the music. To this it can only be replied that each of us has a right to the music we like, and vice versa; and that so far as Tchaikovsky was concerned, he never could compose from a safe place. He had a profound humanity and a native sweetness and tenderness, with a tortured sensibility. And he was a very gifted composer. Suffering and knowledge overwhelmed him. The eyes of his spirit saw things they would fain not have seen. He tells us what they saw in a voice that often chokes with rage and pity.

This symphony was Tchaikovsky's swan song. Nine days after its first performance, which he conducted, he died of cholera, and the circumstances of his taking off were so sudden as to give rise to the theory, still widely believed, that following his tonal deposition he committed suicide. There is, however, no reason to doubt Modeste Tchaikovsky's account of his brother's end, told in one of the most fascinating of musical biographies. Tchaikovsky drank a glass of unboiled water and contracted the disease that sent him quickly to his grave. Some curious coincidences gave added color to the suicide theory, such as the fact that the composer had busied himself in the months preceding with the clearing up of documents, revisions of scores, and the destruction of personal records. These, however, appear only as the actions of a methodical worker. Existence had been cruel enough to furnish Tchaikovsky with more than material for a tragic symphony. His essentially noble and compassionate nature, his strange and frustrated relations with life, were sufficient to darken any spirit. The man's inordinate craving for affection had been cruelly wounded by the estrangement of Nadejda von Meck, whose name Tchaikovsky uttered reproachfully in his dying delirium. He did not know that his former benefactress and dearest friend had become the victim of mental derangement, nor was he the man to believe that on the other side of the grave the needful word of understanding could be uttered.

Nevertheless, Tchaikovsky was happy in the creation of this symphony. He knew that he had achieved *his* truth, and produced a great work, despite its cold reception at the first performance. Some historians, Modeste among them, say that the coldness of the audience was due to the fact that Tchaikovsky conducted. He was not an effective leader or interpreter even of his own music. He could not face an orchestra with confidence, still less force it to do his exact bidding. A musician who played under him has told us of a rehearsal with the composer on the conductor's stand—frightened, apologetic, and ever and anon furtively reaching to his back pocket for a flask of courage. But Rimsky-Korsakov heard the first performance of the *Pathétique;* he says that the only fault was the public's slowness to appreciate such an original score. Be all that as it may, Tchaikovsky was well aware that his Sixth

Symphony was "the best, especially the *most open-hearted* [ours the italics] of all my works." To his colleague Ippolitov-Ivanov he wrote: "I told you I had completed a symphony which suddenly displeased me, and I tore it up. Now I have composed a symphony *which I certainly shall not tear up.*" He sends a similar message to Jurgenson, the publisher: "I give you my word that never in my life have I been so contented, so proud, so happy, in the knowledge that I have written a good piece." It is hard to dismiss regretful thoughts of what Tchaikovsky might have accomplished, now that he had fully discovered himself as an artist, if he had lived beyond fifty-three.

Tchaikovsky let it be known that this symphony had a story, but he did not tell what that story was, which is fortunate, since the work is so much greater than any plot could be. But there was the question of naming the symphony—which, by the way, he had sketched on the ocean during his return to Russia from America in 1891. The morning after the first performance of the work from manuscript in what was then St. Petersburg, October 28, 1893, Modeste Tchaikovsky found his brother at a tea-table with the music in his hand. The composer wanted to bestow some title more definite than "Symphony No. 6" before sending the score to the publisher. What should it be? Should it be, for example, "Program Symphony"? But what did that signify if the symphony was given no program? Modeste suggested "Tragic," but Tchaikovsky was not satisfied. Modeste left the room; when on the other side of the door the word "Pathetic" came to him, and he returned. Tchaikovsky was delighted. "Splendid, Modi, bravo! 'Pathetic' "—"And he wrote in my presence," says Modeste, "the title that will always remain."

The symphony has an unusual succession of movements and peculiarities of form. The last movement, for example, is not a brilliant ending, but a dirge. The most exciting movement is the one before the last—the terrible march. There is no slow movement, but instead, for the second part, a dance in the strange and perturbing rhythm of five-four. It will be seen that the symphonic structure is here wholly subordinate to the subjective idea.

The first movement exposes immediately a principal theme, clad in the blackest colors of the orchestra.

Yes! it is pitch-black, and brother to the worm. With the quick tempo
of the major part of the movement, fragments of this theme are tossed
from instrument to instrument. Now it is picked to pieces by wind or
strings; now it is shrieked hysterically by the trumpet. In spite of the
length and diversity of the movement, with its many dramatic episodes,
the composer paints his picture with extraordinary concentration and
with passionate distinctness. He obtains from his instruments extraordinary effects of blackness contrasted with flaring light, as when, early
in the movement, the despairing cry of the trumpet cuts through the
whizzing strings; or when, over yawning depths, the trombones sound
a spectral chant, taken, according to Edwin Evans, from the Russian
Requiem. At one moment the orchestra sings passionately. At another
it lashes itself to frantic pitches of excitement, or falls to yet deeper
levels of lassitude. It is a striking fact that the main theme, so prevalent
throughout the movement, never returns in its complete original form.
It is the haunting second theme which retains its exact shape and most
appealing melodic curve.

That theme is as strongly distinguished by its instrumentation as by
its melody. It is given to the violins with an effect of torturing and undis-
missible remembrance. It is thrown into the greater prominence, on
repetition, by the richness of its orchestral dress.

A climax, very originally conceived, precedes the return of this
second theme. It follows an eruption of tone, after which the orchestra
hurtles downward to depths which shudder and roar with rage—a
passage made from the introductory theme. This detail of structure is
cited as further testimony to the manner in which a composer of genius
makes form and feeling one. The movement, for Tchaikovsky, is one
of unprecedented richness of ideas, development and orchestration.
Compared with his writing in this symphony, the best pages of preceding works are thin. And note the pizzicato scale which persistently
descends, like inexorable destiny, as epilogue of the first movement.

The second movement is in the famous "five-four" rhythm, and
a rare example of the rhythmic problem of five beats solved with entire
naturalness.

If the reader will reflect and experiment a little with the music he knows, he will quickly perceive that most melodies fall into patterns of either two beats or three beats or their multiples. The five-beat pattern is not symmetrical. It is instinctive, ordinarily, to make the five a design of either four or six. The conventional number of beats would here be six. But the music flows with astonishing naturalness, while the restlessness of the essentially asymmetrical arrangement is psychologically the truth of his unrest. It is in the alternative section of this five-four movement that Tchaikovsky makes unforgettable use of the drum. The drum relentlessly pounds the measure, its note rising and falling, while the strings wail over the dull thudding beat.

This is original, but the third movement is more astounding. Its desperate festivity is false, brutal, and sardonic. Its psychological explanation is perhaps that of a neurotic and hysterical nature which keys itself up, for the moment, to a pitch of unconditional defiance and unnatural power. The wild and fantastic music passes like a nightmare. The beginning, with its whirling tonal will-o'-the-wisps and evil exhilaration as of something unholy a-brewing, could accompany the scene of the witches on the heath in *Macbeth*. And now the solo oboe snarls a first intimation of the march.

From over the other side of the world a trombone and then a horn reply, and one remembers De Quincey's opium dream in which he heard music of preparation and suspense, and the sound of cavalcades filing off in the distance to the battlefield where an issue of undecipherable vastness was to be decided—an issue involving all human fate. There is indeed dreadful portent in this march of Tchaikovsky's, for which Mr. [Philip] Hale, whom it is difficult not to quote, coined the one word—"battle-drunk."

In spite of all the stirrings and anticipations, it is some time before the entire march theme is heard. The composer holds back his forces with an astonishing grip and control in preparation. There is here no going off half-loaded, as in other of Tchaikovsky's works. He stares you in the eye, an unswerving stare. The music gathers at his imperious command. The hordes of Russia and the battalions of mankind file by. Their tread shakes the earth, while the trumpets scream salute, and banners are flung to the sky. Hail Cæsar! The unearthly cavalcade draws nearer. The march theme, heard first in fragments, has bit by bit pulled itself out like a lengthening telescope. The movement is a quarter completed when the clarinets, with various orchestral rejoinders, round out the theme. And the fury of the march accumulates. It sees red, it chokes with choler. Drums and brass instruments go into an incoherent fury. Perhaps you did not know that a scale could become delirium? Listen to the sizzling scales of the string and wind sections that answer each other in Tchaikovsky's orchestra. At the last, quite suddenly, this orchestra subsides; it crouches like a beast, and then advances; it boils up over everything; it crashes down to destruction.

And this is the prelude to the inevitable end. In the finale the strings make requiem. Repeating the opening phrase, they sweep upward in a great sigh for poor vanquished life and the eternal farewell to warm and beautiful things. Over a pulsation of the horns a new threnody is sung. The orchestra rises and falls over a vibrating organ point, following which muted horns evilly mutter, and the gong tolls, and trombones intone a solemn chant. Then the melody that the horns accompanied is given the strings, which mournfully discourse together, until the phrase gradually disappears in the shadows. But a note of the double-basses persists a long time, like a throbbing pulse that will not be still.

This symphony is the last utterance of a great artist and an unfortunate man.

Peter Ilyich Tchaikovsky: Nutcracker Suite

From "Everybody's Music"

By Schima Kaufman

TCHAIKOVSKY's peculiar capacity for writing his gayest music during times of deepest stress has more than once been commented upon. Shortly after Mme. von Meck, his unseen benefactress, informed him that she was no longer able to continue the financial arrangement by which the composer received six thousand rubles annually, he was in Paris, preparatory to departing for his American tour (April 1891). There, in a reading room, he picked up a Russian newspaper and learned of the death of his sister, to whom he was deeply attached. The fact that he had started a ballet based on Hoffmann's tale "The Nutcracker and the Mouse-King" made his loss seem doubly keen. For in his last letter from Le Havre, he wrote: "For God's sake, send all details to New York. Today, even more than yesterday, I feel the absolute impossibility of depicting in music the Sugar-Plum Fairy."

He kept a bright journal of his American experiences, was pleased with his successes, and, on his return to Russia in June, was in such good spirits that he was able to throw off an enormous quantity of music. A new instrument, the celesta, which he had heard in Paris, was intended as a novelty in the instrumentation of the ballet, from which the present suite was arranged for concert performance.

The Miniature Overture,

as delicately tinted in its orchestral coloring as a piece of Dresden china, is without 'cellos or basses, the violas taking the place of the grave strings. Six characteristic dances follow. (1) March—the assembling of the wedding guests. (2) Dance of the Sugar-Plum Fairy—the celesta takes the melody "and seems to drop note by note like the tinkle of dewdrops falling from a rose leaf." (3) Trepak—a wild Russian peasant dance. (4) Arabian Dance. (5) Chinese Dance—"The movement breaks off with an abruptness which suggests that someone's boot accelerated the departure of the Chinese musicians." (6) Reed-pipe Dance—appropriately started by three flutes. And, finally, the Flower Waltz in which the poppies and marguerites sway gracefully to several charming melodies, after an elaborate cadenza from the harp.

Alexander Borodin: Polovtsian Dances

From "Everybody's Music"

By Schima Kaufman

BETWEEN writing brilliant treatises on chemistry and lecturing on medicine in a school which he helped found, Borodin wrote music. He was seventeen years composing his national opera, "interesting only to us Russians," and when he died it was still unfinished. The opera was based on an old epic dealing with the Tatar Khan Konchak's capture of Prince Igor and his son in the eleventh century. In the wild, barbaric orgy in the Polovtsi camp, Borodin the man of science reverted to Borodin the natural son of an Imeretian Prince.

The prisoners form a procession (Prelude), followed by Konchak's retainers. A flute and oboe melody is the eastern warrior's homage to his royal captives. Then starts the Dance of the Savage Men (Allegro vivo), a frenzied, whirling clarinet theme to a brutal, syncopated accompaniment of violas, ever faster and faster until the whole company join in the dance. Now (Presto) comes a dance of boys, flashing exhibitions of bareback riding, spear-throwing, and pursuit of the enemy, which the older men cannot restrain themselves from entering.

For the moment, the war games are over (Moderato), and the sinuous maidens, their bare, ankleted feet scarcely touching the hard ground, move to a graceful oriental theme given out by the oboe and viola,

which soon calls to the boys, and for a while both motifs are heard simultaneously. The earlier melodies recur and there is a last wild burst of energy ending with the dancers saluting their leader: "Our Khan Konchak!"

César Franck: Symphony in D Minor

From "Everybody's Music"

By Schima Kaufman

"THE central character of Franck's music may be described by the single word 'mysticism,'" says an analyst of the regenerator of the musical life of France. "This was a region unexplored in music before his time. Before him, music was scholastic, naive, graceful, dramatic, emotional, passionate, descriptive or picturesque, but this new quality had been unrevealed. The mature César Franck, who passed so much of his time in divine contemplation, under whose fingers the organ of Ste. Clotilde conversed rather with angels than with men, led him towards this new development of his beloved art; well was he called the 'Angelic Doctor' or the 'Pater Seraphicus' of music, for his life and his art were closely allied. In seeking for an analogy from the history of painting, the names of Fra Angelico among the ancients, and Puvis de Chavannes among moderns, occur to the mind."

The score of the D minor Symphony was completed in August 1888, and given its first performance in Paris, at a concert of the Conservatoire, on the following February 17th. "The performance," wrote his pupil and biographer, Vincent d'Indy, "was against the wish of most members of the famous orchestra, and was accomplished only through the benevolent obstinacy of the conductor, Jules Garcin. The subscribers could make neither head nor tail of the symphony, and the musical authorities were much in the same position. I inquired of one of them—a professor at the Conservatoire and a kind of factotum on the Committee—what he thought of the work. 'That a symphony?' he replied in contemptuous tones. 'But, my dear sir, who ever heard of writing for the English horn in a symphony? Just mention a single symphony by Haydn or Beethoven introducing the English horn!' "

This condemnation of an entire work because of a novel effect in one of the movements (which, by the way, has long been accepted as one of its most beautiful features) reveals less the ignorance of a standstill minimizer than it does the development of musical Paris of that time. For symphonic composition had not yet forced its way into the curriculum of the sacred Conservatoire, where the popular operatic style was the all-high consideration. Indeed, had it not been for the ignored Franck, who gathered them to him, such composers as Duparc, Chausson, d'Indy, Ropartz, Lekeu, Pierné, and (indirectly) Fauré, Guilmant, Chabrier, and Dukas might have had to go outside of Paris for their instruction.

The D minor Symphony, far from deflecting from the traditions of the great Beethoven, is quite obviously modeled after the Bonn master's most advanced work. In the first movement the twice-reiterated introduction, alternating with the Allegro, shows the direct influence of Beethoven's B flat Quartet, Op. 130! The form may not be the usual sonata form, but then neither was Beethoven's. This eternal harping upon so-called deviation, this pedantic cry that the conception of a vast canvas is entirely askew because the beholder suffers from a bad case of astigmatism, was many times hurled at the head of Beethoven and his predecessors, and will be heard as long as men of genius continue to create masterpieces that are far ahead of their time.

Claude-Achille Debussy: Nocturnes

From "Stories of Symphonic Music"

By Lawrence Gilman

THIS suite was written in 1897-99. In date of composition it stands, so far as Debussy's more important works are concerned, between the opera *Pelléas et Mélisande* (1893-95) and the "symphonic sketches" *La Mer* (1903-05). The score bears no explanatory note or elucidation; but the following "program" (which, it has been remarked, would itself seem to require elucidation) is said to have been supplied by the composer:

"The title *Nocturnes* is intended to have here a more general and, above all, a more decorative meaning. We are not, then, concerned with the *form* of the nocturne, but with everything that this word includes in the way of impressions and special lights.

"*Clouds:* The unchangeable appearance of the sky, with the slow and melancholy march of clouds ending in a gray agony tinted with white.

"*Festivals:* Movement, rhythm dancing in the atmosphere, with bursts of brusque light. Here, also, the episode is of a procession (a wholly impalpable and visionary pageant) passing through the festival and blended with it; but the main idea and substance obstinately remain —always the festival and its blended music—luminous dust participating in tonal rhythm.

"*Sirens:* The sea and its innumerable rhythm. Then, amid the billows silvered by the moon, the mysterious song of the Sirens is heard; it laughs and passes."

These "Nocturnes" may be sympathetically approached only when it is understood that they are dream-pictures, fantasies, rather than mere picturesque transcripts of reality. The brief characterization of them by Debussy's colleague, Alfred Bruneau, is more suggestive than many an elaborate commentary: "Here, with the aid of a magic orchestra, he has lent to clouds traversing the somber sky the various forms created by his imagination; he has set to running and dancing the chimerical beings perceived by him in the silvery dust scintillating in the moonbeams; he has changed the white foam of the restless sea into tuneful Sirens."

Claude-Achille Debussy: Iberia

From "Symphonic Masterpieces"

By Olin Downes

  I. "Par les rues et par les chemins" ("In the Streets and Byways")
 II. "Les Parfums de la nuit" ("The Fragrance of the Night")
III. "Le Matin d'un jour de fête" ("The Morning of the Festival Day")

IT WAS for years the custom of critics to designate Debussy as a tonal impressionist and harmonist of peculiar sensitivity, and, having thus pigeonholed his style, turn complacently to other matters. They had not learned, or they had chosen to forget, that this most fastidious of workmen was deeply averse to saying the same thing twice, and that he was always seeking new aspects of beauty.

In *La Mer* (1905) Debussy had attempted and succeeded in an expression which marked the possible limits of impressionism. Composing *Iberia* (1909), he turned from this method to a harder and more precise style. He remains the tone-painter and worshiper of nature, but his manner of coloring is now that of the "pointillistes," who painted with a multitude of fine points rather than with free brush strokes and manipulations of color. The score of *Iberia* is very detailed and exact if examined closely, and in its development it is the most symphonically conceived of all Debussy's orchestral pieces.

But stand off a little from this tone-picture. Listen from a distance: the sum of its details will be atmosphere and color planes of vivid and exotic hue.

The work is also a triumphant vindication of Debussy's purposes in that, despite the employment of symphonic devices, it is admirably free of conventions of the German school. Nowhere did he more conclusively than in *Iberia* expound a doctrine of development which liberated and followed the inner urge of the musical idea itself, instead of forcing that idea into a preordained channel. And never had he been more close-knit in the exposition of his thought.

How much happens in these three pieces! How logical their sequence and melodic relations to each other! The poetical scheme is the thought of the day, with its light and movement giving place to the perfumed and mysterious night, and the night leading, in turn, to the break of dawn, the stirrings of life, and the brilliancy and commotion of the Fair. In the first movement basic motives are laid down with the finest coördination and craftsmanship. The piece opens with a flourish of pulsatile instruments and pizzicato strings, with certain scintillating accompaniment figures, and a shrill ditty played in the reedy register of the clarinets. This scrap of melody might sound from any corner or roadside of the Spanish land. It returns in many and astonishing transformations in later pages. So, for that matter, does other thematic material laid down as part of the ground plan of the score. Confused calls and sounds are borne forward on robust rhythms, and seem to ring and intermingle in the clear air. The end of this movement is especially poetical. It is shadowed and vague like the falling evening and the melancholy distances of the sky.

The second movement is the apostrophe to the summer night of the exhaling flowers, the soughing breezes, and the "large few stars." Free preluding introduces a habanera figure whose derivation can be traced back to the first movement. The motive pervades the orchestra. The instruments create a moonlit haze of tone and from far away sounds a horn with the melody of a tender song which is but another transformation of the clarinet motive of the opening. A recurring harmonic suspension is aquiver with the night's magic. There are effects of an unprecedented and inexplicable beauty. Who, for example, would suppose that the intermittent cluck of a xylophone would have anything to do with the spell and the passion of a summer night? It has precisely this potency at the hands of Debussy. He uses different scale formations, and there is a passage as chromatic as Wagner. The transporting song of the horn now sweeps passionately in muted strings. A hush falls upon the orchestra, and from far away sounds the faint tolling of bells. . . . The morning breaks. The orchestra flashes color, and one hears the plunking of guitars. Shrill wind-instruments add their notes. An amusing episode comes when, with another thematic transformation, the first violin, solo, saws extravagantly, for all the world as some fakir or mountebank might fiddle and clown it for a group that hailed the performance with shouts of laughter. All is song, rhythm, sun. A master holds out both hands to life.

Maurice Ravel: Daphnis and Chloe

From Philharmonic-Symphony Program Notes

By Pitts Sanborn

COMPOSED for the Diaghilev Ballets Russes, *Daphnis et Chloe* was produced at the Théâtre du Châtelet, Paris, on June 8, 1912. Ravel's score had been published, however, in 1911, and two concert suites had been derived from it. The argument as printed in Ravel's score has been translated by Philip Hale:

First Suite: "A little flame suddenly burns on the head of one of the statues. The nymph comes to life and leaves her pedestal. Others descend, come together, and begin a slow and mysterious dance. They see Daphnis, bend over him and dry his tears. Reanimating him and leading him to the rock, they invoke the god Pan. Little by little the form of the god assumes definite shape. Daphnis kneels in supplication. All is dark. Behind the scenes voices are heard, far off at first. And now there is a dim light. The pirates' camp is disclosed. There is a bold coast; the sea is in the background, with rocks to the right and left. A trireme is near the shore. Cypresses are here and there. The pirates, laden with booty, run to and fro. Torches are brought, which at last throw a strong light on the stage."

Second Suite: "No sound but the murmur of rivulets fed by the dew that trickles from the rocks. Daphnis lies stretched before the grotto of the nymphs. Little by little the day dawns. The songs of birds are heard. Afar off a shepherd leads his flock. Another shepherd crosses the back of the stage. Herdsmen enter, seeking Daphnis and Chloe. They find Daphnis and awaken him. In anguish he looks about for Chloe. She at last appears, encircled by shepherdesses. The two rush into each other's arms. Daphnis observes Chloe's crown. His dream was a prophetic vision: the intervention of Pan is manifest. The old shepherd Lammon explains that Pan saved Chloe in remembrance of the nymph Syrinx, whom the god loved.

"Daphnis and Chloe mime the story of Pan and Syrinx. Chloe impersonates the young nymph wandering over the meadow. Daphnis as Pan appears and declares his love for her. The nymph repulses him; the god becomes more insistent. She disappears among the reeds. In desperation he plucks some stalks, fashions a flute, and on it plays a melancholy tune. Chloe comes out and imitates by her dance the accents of the flute.

"The dance grows more and more animated. In mad whirlings, Chloe falls into the arms of Daphnis. Before the altar of the nymphs he swears on two sheep his fidelity. Young girls enter; they are dressed as Bacchantes and shake their tambourines. Daphnis and Chloe embrace tenderly. A group of young men come on the stage.

"Joyous tumult. A general dance."

Paul Dukas: The Sorcerer's Apprentice

From "Approach to Music"

By Lawrence Abbott

WITHOUT going to extremes of musical realism, this work quite delightfully paraphrases the story of the magician's young assistant who comes to grief by trying his hand at sorcery in his master's absence. The various episodes are discreetly yet imaginatively suggested in the music. For instance, the tale begins with the apprentice murmuring the magic words which he has heard the sorcerer use to animate his broom. (These are represented in the music by weird, mysterious chords.) The broom slowly comes to life, first giving a few convulsive twitches, and then, in obedience to the apprentice's commands, trotting off to fetch water for his bath. (This is suggested by a fragmentary phrase which is twice haltingly repeated, but soon gets going as a rhythmic little tune.)

The story goes on to tell how the broom continues its work until the bath is filled to overflowing. (The music becomes more and more excited as it works up towards a climax.) The apprentice tries to call a halt, but discovers to his horror that he doesn't know the magic formula which is necessary to reverse the proceedings. In his desperation he seizes an ax, and chops the broom in two. To his dismay, both halves of the broom start fetching water, so that it floods in twice as fast as before. (In the music, the blows of the ax are represented by two harsh chords; there is a momentary silence, and then the little theme representing the broom reappears, this time in double form.) The story ends with the return of the sorcerer, who utters the magic words necessary to restore order. (We now hear again the weird, mysterious chords which were played at the beginning to suggest the incantation.)

Richard Strauss: Don Juan

From "Symphonic Masterpieces"

By Olin Downes

CONTEMPORANEOUS with Debussy was his complete antithesis, Richard Strauss. He is descended of Berlioz of the program symphony, Liszt of the symphonic poems, Wagner of the music dramas. He was not so much a revolutionist in his methods and idioms as he was a flaming temperament, a modern intellect, and an astonishing development of his age. He is a symphonist, a realist, and dramatist in one. He was late in turning to the stage, but was expressing drama and psychology before that time in a series of symphonic poems that shook the world.

After years which have made the music thrice familiar and exposed certain banalities, I am taken aback, whenever I hear it properly performed, by the fierce onslaught of the opening measures of his *Don Juan,* the first of the tone poems in which Strauss unmistakably revealed his genius. Before this there was no such intrepid and sensual music, or music of such torrid, and lush, and violent orchestration. *Don Juan* was composed in 1889. It has had its fiftieth anniversary, which is a long time in the modern tonal art. In that time purists and pundits have been telling us that the works of the vulgar and sensational Strauss could not live. Every decade they have been critically buried. But while critics were advancing excellent reasons for Strauss's artistic demise, and declaring the esthetic unsoundness of his program music, Strauss was creating an art of an astonishing and irresistible power. Before *Don Juan* he had composed copiously in various traditional styles, and learned the technics of his business. He had produced one tone poem on the subject of Macbeth, a combination of Brahms and certain fragmentary prophecies of the Strauss to come. But the real release occurred when Strauss's nature had ripened, when contact with literature quickened his creative consciousness, and he had found the courage uncompromisingly to take his own path. The subject of Lenau's *Don Juan* seems to have made a powerful appeal to his imagination. With this symphonic poem a long-pent-up force broke loose—erupted like Vesuvius. What came out was not all pure flame: there were rocks and mud. But Don Juan himself did not set out on his adventures with more defiance and lust of conquest than the youthful Strauss who portrayed him.

To gain all that can be gained from this music it is necessary to take into account Strauss's conception. This Don Juan is not the mere rakehell sensualist of the Spanish fable. He is, after all, an intellectual hero. He is the dreamer as well as the voluptuary, the adventurer who seeks in all women the ideal. The quest is fruitless; disgust and contempt for life grow upon him until existence is intolerable, and in despair he allows himself to be stabbed in a duel. This is the character projected by the Austrian poet, Nicolaus Lenau, and it is this conception which provoked the proud, delirious, and bitter music of Strauss.

In the opening passage the knight is before us, imperious, defiant, aflame with the lusts of life. There are two episodes of love music. Officious commentators, whom Strauss has not taken the trouble to contradict, find in these episodes the figures of legendary ladies— Donna Anna, Donna Elvira. Or what would you? No matter. The headlong music changes its course. With sweeps of the harp, some bell-like tones of the celesta and a phrase of the solo violin, the music becomes nocturnal; the Don woos impetuously. His passion smolders and flames. The amorous song mounts to a palpitating climax, but the mood soon passes. "I flee from surfeit and from rapture's cloy." New fires begin to flare in the music; and now, over a deep murmuring accompaniment of strings and horns the oboe sings a song of the world well lost. An effect of suspended harmonies holds the spell to the last possible moment, when it is dispersed by Don Juan's second theme,

a lordly phrase, one of the most magnificent Strauss ever conceived, given to six horns in unison. To this motive of the horns other instruments make agitated rejoinder. But the redoubtable theme rings out again with knightly scorn. Now Strauss flings his colors like a pot of paint on the orchestral canvas. In one place the Don's horn theme is caricatured in silly fashion by the glockenspiel. This is the place, according to self-appointed elucidators, where, after riotous misbehavior, Don Juan falls intoxicated to the ground, and there pass in his confused brain vague images of earlier experiences and the fleshly phantoms he pursued. The moment when the commentators fancy the knight unconscious is the passage in the orchestra when fragments of the love themes are heard over long-sustained tones of the low instruments. This is the moment that precedes the true climax of the tone poem. Once more the orchestra lashes itself to a frenzy, when suddenly, just as it seems that the tidal wave of tone must crash and overwhelm us, it is transfixed and frozen into silence. There is a catastrophic pause. A veil seems to fall over the instruments. Through this veil of tone cuts a dissonant trumpet note—the mortal thrust, the death of the dream, the end of every man's desire. Perhaps this is the most remarkable page of the whole tone poem. The conclusion is laconic, tight-lipped. There is no wild complaint, no hysterical wailing. Only abandonment of life.

It is strange music from a young man of twenty-four. The energy and color of the score could be explained by the fire of the youthful revolutionist Strauss was when he composed this work. But the ending, with its striking negation of feeling, was a new note in music of the modern German school, and perhaps harbinger of the negativity that has characterized the later period.

Richard Strauss: Till Eulenspiegel

From "Symphonic Masterpieces"

By Olin Downes

WHO was Till Eulenspiegel—or Ulenspiegel, as the Flemings called him? He is a figure of the ages which created a Faust and a Don Juan and other half-mythical characters which symbolize aspects of the soul of man. He is the imp of fantasy and the perverse.

How did Till get his name and reputation? Perhaps because of his malicious jesting at the expense of his fellow-man. For there is a German proverb which says: "Man is as little conscious of his own faults as an owl or an ape, looking into a mirror, is conscious of his ugliness." Till, they say, was a wandering mechanic who lived by his wits, turning up in every town and city. He made himself out to be whatever the situation required—butcher, baker, wheelwright, joiner, monk, or learned metaphysician. He was a lord of misrule, a liar and villain, whose joy it was to plague honest folk and play foul jests upon them. He pillaged the rich, but often helped the poor. If the tone poem means anything but beautiful music, it means that Till is immortal, that his spirit eternally triumphs, though bourgeois and Philistines rage never so furiously together. For Till is freedom and fantasy; his is the gallant, mocking warfare of the One against the Many and the tyranny of accepted things. He is Puck and Rabelais, and there's quicksilver in the music.

The piece begins with a theme worthy of Mozart,

an introductory phrase which is as the beginning of a fairy tale—Strauss's "once upon a time." Then Till's horn theme scampers through the orchestra.

219

Some sharp chords and the rogue's off on his deviltry. What is it all about? When the piece was first performed at Cologne in 1895 Strauss said that if he were to utter the thoughts that certain passages suggested to him, "they would seldom suffice and might even give rise to offense." And in the music there are bursts of coarse and outrageous laughter. But, regarding this work as others, Strauss has permitted certain commentators, more or less self-appointed, to act as Official Spokesmen for him. These gentlemen have furnished a "program" generally accepted as casting light upon the music. According to this, the rogue rides his horse full tilt into the market-place. He upsets the stalls, and the market women yell at him. You hear the clatter in the orchestra— Strauss uses a rattle. Till disguises himself as a monk. He makes love to a fine lady and is furious at his rebuff—a transformation in the minor of his horn theme. He rages at those who mock him. Once he is nearly caught, and badly frightened—you hear his choking cries. But in a moment he's away, his terrors forgotten, his joyous sing-song echoing from far off in the ears of his pursuers.

Till's adventures multiply; his impudence knows no bounds.

Finally he is brought to justice. Sentence is pronounced with pontifical majesty and gloom. The knave grimaces and whines his innocence. "No mercy," thunder horns and trombones and drums, and up he goes, to eccentric skyward leaps of the clarinet and gurglings of wind instruments. And he's done. His adventures are over! But was it Till who died? Strauss's epilogue reassures us. The magistrates destroyed the effigy, not the living soul, and the lovely theme of the introduction returns, opening like the petals of a flower in the orchestra. Till, acknowledging no master but the beauty that beckons from over the horizon, lives still in the hearts of men—once upon a time and forever.

Are we justified in reading into Strauss's music anything of an ulterior or philosophic meaning? There is that in the score which implies more than a purely musical or decorative intent. Till runs amok in the old tales and in Strauss's orchestra, which echoes laughter but also pathos, and sarcasm, and even savage revolt. I think we have here something of a commentary upon life, its ironies and tears, and homage to the triumphant and uncapturable thing that soars and sings high up and beyond prison bars, or scaffolds, or even the excellent rulings of worthy people.

Not a note could be added to or taken from this score without impairing its proportions. It is the expression, not merely of individual genius, but of the soul of a people. Their humor, their homely wisdom and deep and unconscious poetry are in it. And there is the good laughter of Master Rabelais, and the good savor of the earth from which oak and violet grow.

Jean Sibelius: En Saga

From *"Symphonic Masterpieces"*

By Olin Downes

THE *Saga* of Sibelius might well be associated in the mind of the listener with some ancient Scandinavian epic. It is dark, fantastical, fate-ridden in character. Every page carries the impress of the North. Notice the curious orchestral colors. The customary kettledrums are absent. A distant roll of the bass drum and flickering figures of the violins, divided and subdivided among themselves, cast a mist over everything, a mist pierced momentarily by a flute and a flaring trumpet. A huge heavy theme lurches upward through the gloom. The music quickens, the orchestra shrieks and skirls. Later, accompanied by curious sighs of other instruments, the violins intone a monotonous barbaric dance theme. The instruments brood over these things. They rumble and growl, prophesying war. Before the final climax there is an eerie, wailing lament of the muted strings, a passage once heard, never forgotten. Then the orchestra gathers itself, girds up its loins, and leaps into a dance with knives drawn—lust of battle, glory of death. It is a return in spirit to great days forever gone—when we were greater men. Yes! When I hear this music I avow a carnal desire to discard the soft fat ways of life; to set out in oilskins, or something, for somewhere, to discover at least a desperate polar bear bent on conflict! But seriously —who else writes such music today? In these pages Sibelius is the last of the heroes. The music rises to furious defiance. The end of it all is ghostly lament. A gong is used with extraordinary effect under pianissimo chords, remote from the key in which the piece opened.

There is Styxlike blackness and cold; a last flicker of life in the ashes of a fire that flared for a moment in the world's Arctic night, and the indomitable rhythm of the war-dance.

Ernest Bloch: Schelomo

From "Symphonic Masterpieces"

By Olin Downes

A VISITOR, one morning in 1916, to a small ill-furnished room on Lexington Avenue, New York City, was confronted by a man of less than medium height, with eyes that blazed beneath a fine forehead, and a mouth which was a crease of agony. The man was Ernest Bloch. After endless misfortunes he had come to America to conduct an orchestra for Maud Allan. The tour failed. He, fortunately, was left here stranded. It happened that the score he played me, shouting raucously as he assaulted a helpless and tinny upright piano, was that of *Schelomo*. Yelling and pounding, he projected, composer fashion, his music.

No wonder the piano suffered, for this music is wholly orchestral in conception, and nothing less than many instruments could give it vent. The purple and gold of the instrumentation is setting of the somber reveries, the bitter complaints, and prophetic denunciations of the solo violoncello. This solo instrument, with its rhapsodic song, is the voice of Schelomo. Schelomo is the Hebrew form of the name Solomon, and it is of Solomon in his glory, his wisdom and his disillusionments that Bloch sings. In so doing he is expressing the dreams of his own Hebrew race, and is the first great Jewish composer to do so. There have been other Jewish composers—many of them. Some were minor figures, or at least figures historically unknown, who contributed to the lore of Jewish religious or folk music. Others were famous men like Mendelssohn or Rubinstein, whose music, which might have been grandly racial, was so tinctured and weakened by conventionalizing European traditions that it lost its spiritual identity, and was by so much lessened in force and authenticity. Bloch's purpose is otherwise. It is his desire to express not only himself but his race, and he has done this in a manner which places him in the front rank of living composers.

Only a few months before Bloch came to America he had met in Switzerland the 'cellist Alexander Barjansky, to whom the score of *Schelomo* is dedicated, and had seen a wax sculpture by the 'cellist's wife, Catherine Barjanska, of Schelomo. A long-bearded figure sits on the throne clad in royal robes that cover the lower part of the body. The face is very old and weary, with deep sunken eyes, hollow cheeks and protruding temples. It is the King, weary of life, weary of riches, weary of power. Inspired by this sculpture, Bloch composed in a few weeks his orchestral rhapsody, in which, in the words of the Italian critic and musicologist Guido Gatti, "The violoncello, with its ample breadth of phrasing, now melodic and with moments of superb lyricism, now declamatory and with robustly dramatic lights and shades, lends itself to a reincarnation of Solomon in all his glory, surrounded by his thousand wives and concubines, with his multitude of slaves and warriors behind him. His voice resounds in the devotional silence, and the sentences of his wisdom sink into the heart as the seed into a fertile soil; 'Vanity of vanities, saith the Preacher, all is vanity. . . . One generation passeth away, and another generation cometh: but the earth abideth forever. . . . He that increaseth knowledge increaseth sorrow.' " Notice the strange instrumental coloring, the wild outcries, alternating with deep black shadows in the orchestra, from which, as from utter solitude and darkness, there sounds the last soliloquy of the 'cello. This rich, blazing music is fairly flung from the orchestra, and with what fury! At last the passion is spent. The end makes one think of Renan's speech at the funeral of Turgeniev, when he spoke of those reveries which, through centuries, had amassed themselves about that heart.

Bloch says of his music: "I am not an archeologist. It is not my purpose to attempt a reconstruction of Jewish music, or to base my work on melodies more or less authentic. I hold it of the first importance to write good genuine music, my music. It is the Jewish soul that interests me, the complex, glowing, agitated soul that I feel vibrating throughout the Bible: the freshness and naïveté of the Patriarchs; the violence that is evident in the prophetic books; the Jew's savage love of justice; the despair of the Preacher in Jerusalem; the sorrow and immensity of the book of Job, the sensuality of the Song of Songs.

"All this is in us; it is in me, and it is the better part of me. It is all this that I endeavor to hear in myself and to transcribe in my music: the venerable emotion of the race that slumbers 'way down in our soul." And he said also that his setting of certain Psalms, his symphony *Israel,* and his *Schelomo* for 'cello and orchestra, were highly representative of him, "because they come from the passion and violence which I believe to be the characteristics of my nature."

Gustav Mahler: Symphony No. 1
Adapted from Philharmonic-Symphony Program Notes

By Pitts Sanborn

As EARLY as 1883 or 1884 Mahler, then second conductor at Cassel, began work on his First Symphony. It was not performed, however, till after he had become conductor of the Royal Opera at Budapest (1888), where he greatly enhanced his reputation through the brilliance of the productions he directed. Budapest was thus the first city to hear the earliest of the ten symphonies by Mahler, at a Philharmonic Concert, the composer conducting, on November 20, 1889.

On that occasion the program classified it as a "Symphonic Poem in two parts." When it was played at Weimar on June 3, 1894, it was called "Titan," after the novel by Jean Paul Richter. There were also mottoes for the divisions—"From the Days of Youth" for the first part, "Commedia umana" for the second.

The program went on to describe the different movements. The first it termed "Spring and no end. The introduction represents the awakening of nature in the early morning." The second movement, called "Mosaic" or "A Chapter of Flowers," an Andante, was omitted after the Weimar performance. The third, a Scherzo, was denominated "Under Full Sail." It has for its principal theme a gayly dancing Ländler-like melody, which inevitably calls to mind those other composers who knew and loved the Austrian Ländler, Schubert and Bruckner. Beginning the "Commedia umana" division, the fourth movement came in for more elaborate characterization:

"The hunter's funeral procession; a dead march in the manner of Callot [Jacques Callot, a French engraver of the seventeenth century]. The composer found the external source of inspiration in the burlesque picture of the hunter's funeral procession in an old book of fairy tales known to all children in South Germany. The animals of the forest escort the dead forester's coffin to the grave. Hares carry flags; a band of gypsy musicians, accompanied by cats, frogs, crows, all making music, and deer, foxes, and other four-footed and feathered creatures of the woods, leads the procession in farcical postures." The main theme, heard from a muted double-bass, is nothing else than the old French canon "Frère Jacques," absurdly slow and grave as presented here and in the minor mode.

"This movement, expressing moods now ironically merry, now gloomily meditative, is followed immediately by [the fifth] 'Dall' Inferno al Paradiso' (allegro furioso), the abrupt outburst of doubt from a deeply wounded heart."

Mahler notoriously detested all program books for use at concerts, and apropos Ludwig Schiedermair in his biographical and critical "estimate" of the composer tells an amusing story.

Mahler had conducted his Second Symphony in Munich at a concert of the Hugo Wolf Society. In the course of a supper after the concert somebody brought up the subject of program books: "Then it was," says Schiedermair, "as though lightning flashed in a joyous, sunny landscape. Mahler's eyes were more brilliant than ever, his brows knitted, he jumped up from the table in excitement, exclaiming in passionate tones: 'Down with program books! They propagate false ideas! The audience should be left to its own thoughts about the work that is being played; it should not be forced to read during the performance; it should not be prejudiced in any manner. If a composer by his music forces on his hearers the sensations which streamed through his mind, then he reaches his goal. The speech of tones has then approached the language of words, but it is far more capable of expression and illumination.' Whereupon Mahler lifted his glass and drained it, ejaculating, 'Pereant die Programme!' "

Igor Stravinsky: L'Oiseau de feu (The Fire-Bird)

From "Symphonic Masterpieces"

By Olin Downes

ONE of the large number of scores called into being by Serge Diaghilev and his Ballet Russe, a score which introduced a new genius to the modern musical world, was Igor Stravinsky's ballet *L'Oiseau de feu* (*The Fire-Bird*), the scenario based upon a tale of Russian folk lore. This ballet was first performed in Paris in 1910. It is the first of the astonishing trio of compositions which placed Stravinsky, within a period of five years, in the position of the leading composer of his day. The other two were *Petroushka* and *Sacre du printemps.*

Two suites have been made from the music of *L'Oiseau de feu.* The one mentioned here, the first, has six parts, but only three separate movements. The music in its original form accompanies dance and pantomime on the stage. Prince Ivan, hunting, and wandering far, comes into the domain of an enchanter. The introductory measures of the suite consist in sinuous passages for the lower strings, chortlings of clarinets and bassoons, whispering arpeggios of harmonics by the violins, silver notes of the celesta scattered like delicate spray over the harmonies of the orchestra. Such is the musical depicting of the enchanted domain. The pace quickens, with capricious rhythms and curious instrumental effects, as the astonished prince observes from his hiding-place a marvelous bird, with wings of flame, which enters the garden and begins to peck at golden apples that grow on a silver tree. In sport the prince captures the bird, but, heeding its entreaties, releases it, retaining only a feather, which later proves a talisman in time of greatest need.

In the garden of the enchanted dwell captive princesses. The prince watches them dance. The dance of the princesses is gentle and grave. It is a "Korovode," or Russian round dance, preluded by a naïve little phrase on the flutes. The dance begins to the melody of an oboe accompanied by sweeps of the harp. Later the strings enter, warmly, tenderly—an adorable piece, made of the material of Russian peasant song. That is the second movement of the suite.

The sinister magician, Kastcheï the Deathless, who captured the princesses and turned rescuing knights to stone, appears on the scene. Warned by his diabolical instincts of the presence of an intruder, surrounded by his evil crew of monsters, freaks, Bobolochki, Kikimoras, and what not, he instigates a nightmare dance. I can say that I saw that dance, done by Diaghilev's superb interpreters: I saw it! I was there! You will infer the antics of the monsters by the wild shriek of the orchestra, and the savage, grotesque measures of the dance. In time, the Fire-Bird returns, to cast her spell of slumber on Kastcheï and his hosts, and rescue Ivan and his beloved. Thereafter veillike harmonies descend upon the instruments. The harp commences a rhyth-

mic accompaniment. The bassoon—an inspired tone color in this place
—sings the magic lullaby, a hypnotic song, enveloped in weaving harmonies of the upper voices of the orchestra.

The lullaby leads into the final movement of the suite. It is a
transition of exquisite device. This finale celebrates the breaking of
the magician's evil power, and the nuptials of the royal pair. The
knights' images come to life, the princesses are free. Ivan and his
beloved gaze into each other's eyes. A horn winds from far off over
hills of dream. Its burden is an ancient Russian folk tune.

On the stage there are solemn preparations for the nuptials. The horn
melody, repeated and variously transformed, takes on more splendor,
the orchestra piling sonority upon sonority. The glorification of the
song occurs when Ivan and his Princess, her white ermine robes extending the depth of the stage behind her, advance side by side to their
happiness. The folk melody is heard now in an odd rhythm and with
clashing harmonies of the brass which suggest archaic pomp and the
ringing of bells. There stand the pair, as beautiful as the dawn. The
final chords are like gates that swing open to receive and protect them
from evil.

Igor Stravinsky: Petroushka

From "Symphonic Masterpieces"

By Olin Downes

THE exquisite and tender music of *The Fire-Bird* is that of Stravinsky's
age of innocence. He quickly progressed to something quite different,
a curious blend of Russian humanitarianism and the most sophisticated
objectivity—the score of *Petroushka*.

Petroushka is a doll, a puppetlike man. He is the superfluous one,
and the helpless victim of a brutality he cannot combat.

The scene is the Admiralty Square in old St. Petersburg, at the
time of "Butter Week" in the eighteen-thirties. The rising curtain

shows a crowd milling around the show-booths. There is dancing, laughter, horse-play. Two organ-grinders compete with each other, and are capitally taken off by the orchestra. The old showman, with his flute, comes before the people, assuring them by his gestures of an important spectacle. The curtains of the booths are yanked aside, and they reveal three life-sized dolls, figures which prance and cavort in a quick, mechanical way to the music. These dolls are Petroushka, the poor foolish hero of the farce; the Dancer; and the Moor. Petroushka loves the Dancer, but she is insensible to his advances, and, on the other hand, is much taken by the swaggering, coarse, sensual Moor. And so the puppets are set spinning, and one of life's little ironies, in effigy, passes before us.

A roll of the drums and the scene changes to the room of Petroushka. He enters, distracted, consumed with his desires and despairs. He rehearses steps and gestures with which he hopes to impress the Dancer. She enters, but is frightened by Petroushka's eagerness, and soon leaves. The drum rolls again. We see the room of the apish Moor. He is toying with a coconut before which, since he can neither open nor understand it, he soon prostrates himself in worship. Clad in his gorgeous uniform, he is lolling recumbent, when the Dancer enters with her pirouette and her toy trumpet, to coquette with him. The Moor watches her, first with indifference, then complacently, finally with greed. Petroushka bursts in, to the annoyance of the pair, and the Moor kicks him out for his pains. The Dancer, with feigned reluctance, falls into the arms of the Moor as the curtain falls.

Again the scene of the fair. The crowd becomes more uproarious as evening gathers, and snow falls. Dances by grooms and nurses. A lumbering bear is depicted by the tuba in the orchestra. Drunken merchants reel in with gypsy girls on their arms; they scatter ruble notes to the multitude. Suddenly there are cries of consternation. From the booth, before the alarmed crowd, runs Petroushka, terrified and unarmed, pursued by the Moor. The Moor quickly overtakes and cuts him down. The puppet falls with an agonized squeak. The people do not understand. What has happened? The venerable showman steps forward. He reassures them. See! He picks up Petroushka; sawdust falls out. This is not a living man, nor a human heart. Only a mechanism, with sawdust for a soul. Sometimes these mechanisms go wrong, and this one is in need of repair.

The show is over. Gradually the Square is emptied. The showman prepares to shut up shop and retire. But suddenly, over the roof of the booth, is seen Petroushka's ghost, white-faced, with arms that wave in protest, like a crazy semaphore. Ghostly, too, is the commentary of Stravinsky's music.

Several interpretations of *Petroushka* have been quoted; to any of them, or to some other one of his own, the reader is entitled. Its tragedy is the more gripping for its laconism. Let us admit nothing, lest we weep. The scenario of *Petroushka: Scènes burlesques en quatre tableaux,* is by Alexandre Benois. Subject and music appear to reflect the Russian nature. Gogol and Mussorgsky are there. Everything is reflected in the score with a sure and reckless mastery—the movement and tumult of the crowd; the gait and aspect of each leading figure; and the grotesque agonies of the helpless one. A shriek of two trumpets in different keys is the motto of Petroushka's protest. The composition is permeated with Russian folk melodies and also street songs marvelously treated. The technical virtuosity, in the combinations of rhythms and keys, is already breath-taking—I say "already," with thought in mind of the epochal *Sacre du printemps,* still to come. The instrumentation has a new, acrid, and kaleidoscopic glint. One would be tempted to say that the composer who could achieve two such manifestations within a period of two years as *The Fire-Bird* and *Petroushka* could expect an unlimited future.

Igor Stravinsky: Le Sacre du printemps
(The Rite of Spring)

From "Symphonic Masterpieces"

By Olin Downes

Sacre du printemps was an explosion, violent and terrifying and ominous, in the midst of an exhausted society. It was not only a sensation such as Paris (Théâtre des Champs Elysées, May 29, 1913) had not experienced for many years; it appears now almost as a pre-war token of catastrophe, and it was so potent and unshackled that it provided ideas for European music of the next two decades. This latter fact was amusingly evident in America, which was much longer than is usually the case in hearing a novelty by a European composer. The reason for the delay was the literal riot that occurred at the première of the *Sacre,* which frightened our visiting conductors. In Paris the piece was greeted with hisses, cheers, and physical violence in the audience. Pierre Monteux, who conducted, though he became conductor of the Boston Symphony Orchestra in the season of 1919-1922, waited until 1924 to present it to audiences of Boston and New York. The event proved that he need not have waited. The music, which he presented magnificently, was received with immense acclaim.

In the meantime, between 1913 and 1924, all sorts of new music had come over from Europe. Experiments with polyharmony, polytonality, and new rhythmic combinations astonished and captivated us. And then we heard the *Sacre du printemps* and knew at once that this was the treasure house from which Stravinsky's contemporaries, to the enrichment of their art, if not to the impoverishment of his, had helped themselves with both hands—and this with the air of those giving birth to new ideas. With *L'Oiseau de feu* and *Petroushka* our young Russian had shown himself first a youthful promise and then a commanding talent; with *Sacre du printemps* he became the leading figure among the creative musicians of his epoch.

Sir Oliver Lodge said that there was sufficient energy in an atom, if released, to blow a battleship from its place in the ocean to a mountain-top. A portion of this dynamite seems to inhabit Stravinsky's score. Despite which, one can feel desolate in the presence of this sterile force, which is without the shadow of humanity or the remotest suggestion of sentiment, and which, for lack of such fertilizing emotion, becomes perverse, exasperated, sadistic. The music then appears as the vicious outburst of an overstrained civilization. "The primitive man? The super-ape!" cried one of Stravinsky's colleagues. It is too soon to appraise this music, or even try to. It is also worth remembering that Stravinsky's emotion is not of the sentimental or romantic description, and that there is one passage, at least, in *Sacre du printemps* which grips us because of its half-articulate sadness and mystery. That is the introduction to the second part. There, in a strange iron twilight, the earth, helpless in its fertility, seems itself to fear and to lament the endless cycle of deaths and resurrections to come. Elsewhere is a super-dynamism, and a force, so to speak, partly chemical, partly physical, with very little suggestion of feeling, of which Stravinsky, anyhow, is intolerant (at least in the "romantic" sense of the word). The drums of the final pages, with their brutal and terrific impact, strike ears and nerves like bullets.

This is an interesting characteristic of the *Sacre:* that whereas all the other ballet music that Stravinsky wrote is heard to the best advantage with the stage spectacle, the *Sacre du printemps,* so far as any choreography thus far presented is concerned, is at its best in purely symphonic performance. Such an impression squares with remarks of Stravinsky himself. He told Michel George-Michel that the theme which made the basis of the composition came to him as a purely musical conception while he was writing *The Fire-Bird.* (As a matter of fact, the precise notes of the initial theme are contained in Mussorgsky's opera, *The Fair at Sorochintzy.* Stravinsky continued: "As this theme, with that which followed, was conceived in a strong, brutal manner, I took as a pretext for developments, for the evocation of this music, the Russian prehistoric epoch, since I am a Russian. But note well that this idea came from the music; the music did not come from the idea. My work is architectonic, not anecdotal; objective, not descriptive construction." *

According to this, then, story and choreography of the ballet were superimposed, after the conception of the music.

The Rite of Spring, in its official capacity, is concerned with prehistoric ceremonies held by ancient man to make the earth fertile by the sacrifice of a human victim. The first part of the work is called "The Earth's Fertility," and the second part "The Sacrifice."

The slow introduction is supposed to imply "the mystery of the physical world in Spring." The tone color of solo bassoon, later combined with horn and clarinets, has itself a hieratic quality. Wind instruments predominate, a prophecy of Stravinsky's growing devotion to wood and brass, and in place of the more pliant and illusory strings. The curtain rises, and the rhythmic incantation begins. This is called in the score "The Dance of the Adolescents." The accents are vigorous and irregular. Youths and maidens stamp the earth. The dance becomes more violent, and a part of this ritual is a mock abduction of a maiden. "Ronde du printemps"—"Spring Round": There is a pause, a breathing place, while a quaint theme sung in unison by clarinets and bass clarinets is accompanied by trills of the flutes. A solemn new rhythm, with strong and bitter harmonies, introduces another dance. The trumpets, with sharp, grinding harmonies, or polyharmonies, chant a version of a theme already heard, a sort of primitive song of homage. Then come "The Game of Rival Towns" and

* See Stravinsky's own discussion of his experiences while writing the *Sacre,* page 575.

"The Procession of the Sage," when an old white-haired, white-bearded man prostrates himself, and all kiss the ground and rise and dance to music of frenetic power.

The second part of the ballet begins with the music of groping mystery to which reference has been made. "Mystic Circle of the Adolescents": Girls dance, and one of them is chosen for the sacrifice. There are passages of "Glorification," "Evocation of Ancestors," "Ritual Performances of the Ancestors." Then a circle forms about her, the victim lashes herself to the final frenzy. The rhythms become convulsive, disintegrating. She falls, to the beatings and shriekings of Stravinsky's orchestra. The score is a marvelous study in rhythmical and harmonic developments. While the music sounds, no one at all sensible to its force can doubt it. When it was heard in New York for the first time in 1924, there were reviewers who confidently and rapturously announced a new masterpiece for the ages, and few were the pens that restrained their praise.

Since that time Stravinsky has diverged almost completely from the tendencies that the *Sacre* represented. Is this an advance or a retrogression? The time has not come to attempt to answer that question, or, indeed, to put into the pages of a book gratuitous prophecy of the future that lies concealed in our period.

Arthur Honegger: Pacific 231

From "Symphonic Broadcasts"

By Olin Downes

ARTHUR HONEGGER's *Pacific 231* was inspired by the thought of a locomotive. Some find in this music nothing but noisy realism. My impression is of a composer who conceives of the great locomotive in terms of power and glory of motion. I find laughter in this music, too, and youth. When I hear it I think of Honegger himself. I happened to meet him in Paris one night in 1924, when he was thirty-two years old and had just written this particular piece. He was very gay. It was midnight on a street corner, and several of us talked for some time, congratulating Honegger on the success of his locomotive fantasy, which had been brought out in Paris by Koussevitzky a few days before. Honegger is a well-set-up young chap,* with a deep-chested laugh, not the laugh of a European sophisticate. I hear that laugh in his music. I also hear the decidedly Gallic witticisms of that young man—although Honegger is Swiss by birth—and recall the explanatory sentences printed in the fly-leaf of the score of *Pacific 231:* "I have always had a passionate love of locomotives. They are for me like living creatures, and I love them as others love women or horses." And that is truth spoken in jest. Honegger adores the roaring giant of power and speed, which is to him an expression of a phase of modern life and a certain kind of beauty, not a soft or a pretty beauty, but one born of sky-scrapers and machines, and the kinetic energy of this age. You will notice the deliberate suggestions in the music, first of the three-hundred-tonner in repose, its soft breathing of hissing steam, then the slow grinding of the big wheels as it begins to move, and the quicker revolutions of the little wheels within the rhythm of the big wheels; and the accelerating movement, which seems to fling off at the height of velocity a joyous song of the road. Then—a feat which I understand is as crucial a test for the engineer in his cab as it is for the composer at his score-paper—the slowing up of the great mass that has gone hurtling through the darkness, and the stop, with the harsh, grinding harmonies of the last measures. It is amusing, by the way, to observe that it was a European composer and not an American who was the first to perceive a source of inspiration in the *Pacific,* one of our special types of loco-motives.

Aaron Copland: Music for Radio

From "Everybody's Music"

By Schima Kaufman

DESIGNED especially for performance on the air,† *Music for Radio* was completed in Tlaxcala, Mexico, in July, 1937.

"The composer's idea in writing the work," says Mr. Copland,

* Not so young any more. He was born in 1892.—E. S.
† It was written on commission for the Columbia Broadcasting System.—E. S.

"was to seek a musical style and form which would be understandable to a broader audience than that of the concert hall. It was not his intention to mechanically adopt a simple style, but rather to write what was natural to him, confining himself to a musical language that was easily grasped, and avoiding wherever possible the clichés of the usual concert piece. For that reason the themes chosen were straightforward, the harmonies and the rhythms not complex, and the form tended to be sectionally built so as to avoid the more involved development passages.

"The second theme, which has an American folk-song quality, is as good an example as any of this attempted fusion of the composer's manner with a simple style. The general tendency of the work was in the direction of the composition *The Second Hurricane,* an opera for high school performance. Both works are indicative of a desire on the part of many so-called modern composers to bridge the gap between themselves and a wider public through a simplification of style.

"The general outline of the form is a four-part sectional structure indicated: fast—slow—fast—slow. The principally recurring mood, besides that of the folk-song-like second theme, is an energetically rhythmed unison theme at the beginning, and a marchlike, fateful-sounding idea nearer the middle."

The score was subtitled by a letter-writer *Saga of the Prairie.* This title, agreed the composer, emphasized a certain frontier atmosphere derived from the nature of the themes themselves.

Morton Gould: Spirituals for Orchestra

From Philharmonic-Symphony Program Notes

By Robert Bagar and Louis Biancolli

COMPLETED late in 1941, *Spirituals for String Choir and Orchestra* was soon afterward premièred by Artur Rodzinski and the Cleveland Symphony. In writing the suite Mr. Gould sought to convey the mood and idiom of White and Negro Spirituals, without resorting to literal exposition of specific tunes. Admittedly, fragments of actual Spirituals were woven into certain passages. As a rule, Mr. Gould's aim was to "utilize the idiomatic elements in conjunction with much original material."

"I have tried to write music the way one speaks," Mr. Gould told the annotators. "I tried to make it as direct and simple as possible. Part of the 'Jubilee' section is in boogie-woogie pattern. Of course, many contemporary jazz effects coincide with certain rhythmic patterns in our Spirituals. The White and Negro Spirituals make a tremendous body of folk material. One group ties into the other. That is, our White songs are influenced by our Negro songs, and the other way around. What I tried to do was to synthesize some of these features.

"My starting premise was that our Spirituals develop a wide gamut of emotions, musically. These emotions are specifically American. The songs range from strictly spiritual ones that are escapist in feeling, or light and gay, to those having tremendous depth and tragic impact.

"My idea was to get five moods, widely contrasted in feeling. Although most of the work is original as far as thematic material goes, I have used fragments of folk tunes here and there."

Sergei Prokofiev: Peter and the Wolf

By Sergei Prokofiev

(*Though subtitled "An orchestral fairy-tale for children," this composition, written in 1936, has become a favorite with audiences of all ages. The delightful text—the composer's own—is deftly interwoven with a score that is one of the most tuneful and ingratiating in all contemporary music. At the head of the score appears the narrative printed below—E. S.*)

EACH character of this tale is represented by a corresponding instrument in the orchestra: the bird by a flute, the duck by an oboe, the cat by a clarinet in a low register, the grandfather by a bassoon, the wolf by three horns, Peter by the string quartet, the shooting of the hunters by the kettledrums and the bass drum. Before an orchestral performance it is desirable to show these instruments to the children and to play on them the corresponding *leitmotifs.* Thereby the children learn to distinguish the sonorities of the instruments during the performance of the table.

[The text spoken by the narrator follows.]

Early one morning Peter opened the gate and went out on a big green meadow.

On the branch of a big tree sat a little bird, Peter's friend. "All is quiet," chirped the bird gaily. Soon a duck came waddling around. She was glad that Peter had not closed the gate, and decided to take a nice swim in the deep pond in the meadow.

Seeing the duck, the little bird flew down upon the grass, settled next to the duck, and shrugged her shoulders. "What kind of bird are you, if you can't fly?" said she. To this the duck replied: "What kind of bird are you, if you can't swim?" and dived into the pond. They argued and argued—the duck swimming in the pond, the little bird hopping along the shore.

Suddenly something caught Peter's attention. He noticed a cat crawling through the grass.

The cat thought: "The bird is busy arguing. I'll just grab her." Stealthily she crept toward her on velvet paws.

"Look out!" shouted Peter, and the bird immediately flew up into the tree, while the duck quacked angrily at the cat from the middle of the pond.

The cat crawled around the tree and thought: "Is it worth climbing up so high? By the time I get there the bird will have flown away."

Grandpa came out. He was angry because Peter had gone to the meadow. "It is a dangerous place. If a wolf should come out of the forest, then what would you do?" Peter paid no attention to Grandfather's words. Boys such as he are not afraid of wolves. But Grandfather took Peter by the hand, led him home, and locked the gate.

No sooner had Peter gone than a big gray wolf came out of the forest. In a twinkling, the cat climbed up the tree. The duck quacked, and in her excitement jumped out of the pond. But no matter how hard the duck tried to run, she couldn't escape the wolf. He was getting nearer—nearer—catching up with her—and then he's got her, and with one gulp swallowed her.

And now, this is how things stood: the cat was sitting on one branch, the bird on another—not too close to the cat. And the wolf walked around and around the tree looking at them with greedy eyes.

In the meantime, Peter, without the slightest fear, stood behind the closed gate watching all that was going on. He ran home, took a strong rope, and climbed up the high stone wall. One of the branches of the tree around which the wolf was walking stretched out over the wall.

Grabbing hold of the branch, Peter lightly climbed over onto the tree. Peter said to the bird: "Fly down and circle around the wolf's head, only take care that he doesn't catch you."

The bird almost touched the wolf's head with her wings, while the wolf snapped angrily at her from this side and that. How the bird did worry the wolf! How he wanted to catch her! But the bird was cleverer, and the wolf simply couldn't do anything about it.

Meanwhile Peter made a lasso and, carefully letting it down, caught the wolf by the tail, and pulled with all his might. Feeling himself caught, the wolf began to jump wildly, trying to get loose. But Peter tied the other end of the rope to the tree, and the wolf's jumping only made the rope around his tail tighter.

Just then the hunters came out of the woods, following the wolf's trail and shooting as they went. But Peter, sitting in the tree, said: "Don't shoot! Birdie and I have already caught the wolf. Now help us take him to the zoo."

Imagine the triumphant procession:

Peter at the head.

After him the hunters leading the wolf.

And winding up the procession, Grandfather and the cat. Grandfather tossed his head, discontentedly: "Well, and if Peter hadn't caught the wolf? What then?"

Above them flew Birdie chirping merrily: "My, what fine ones we are, Peter and I! Look, what we have caught!"

And if one would listen very carefully, he could hear the duck quacking in the wolf's belly, because the wolf in his hurry had swallowed her alive!

Sergei Prokofiev: Lieutenant Kije
From Boston Symphony Program Notes
By John N. Burk

THE film *Lieutenant Kije* is not known in this country, but description of its subject kindly supplied by Nicolas Slonimsky will help toward an understanding of the spirit of the music: "The subject of the film is based on an anecdote about the Czar Nicolas I who misread the report of his military aide, so that the last syllable of the name of a Russian officer which ended with 'ki' and the Russian intensive expletive 'je' (untranslatable by any English word, but similar in position and meaning to the Latin *quidem*) formed a non-existent name, Kije. The obsequious courtiers, fearful of pointing out to the Czar the mistake he had made, decided to invent an officer by that name (as misread by the Czar). Hence, all kinds of comical adventures and quid-pro-quo's."

I. *The Birth of Kije* (allegro). As befits one who is born in full regimentals in the brain of a Czar, Lieutenant Kije is introduced by a cornet fanfare off stage, followed by the tattoo of a military drum and the shrill of the fife. As the other instruments fall in line, the music keeps its paradelike strut. There is a short andante (still in character), a return of the fife, drum, and cornet.

II. *Romance* (andante). This movement and the fourth are written with a part for baritone solo, alternative versions following in which this part is given to the tenor saxophone, and occasionally other instruments.

III. *Kije's Wedding* (allegro Fastoso). The melodic character of this movement suggests that Kije was subject to sentiment in his nuptials as well as his wooing, while never forgetting that he was a soldier.

IV. *Troika* (moderato). Again a tavern song is introduced to an accompaniment suggestive of the motion of the Russian three-horse sleigh.

V. *Burial of Kije* (andante assai). The description of the film explains the entire cheerfulness which attended the laying away of the imaginary lieutenant. His brief career is summed up in the movement. A cornet fanfare off stage introduces him again, and the themes of his romance and his wedding are invoked. The piece ends with the voice of the muted cornet vanishing in the distance.

Dmitri Shostakovich: Symphony No. 1

From "Everybody's Music"

By Schima Kaufman

THE Symphony No. 1, without nominal key signature, was composed when Shostakovich was still in his teens. It was premièred in Leningrad just before its publication by the government in 1927. Under Leopold Stokowski, the Philadelphia Orchestra played it for the first time in America in Philadelphia on November 2, 1928, establishing it as an instantaneous and overwhelming success. In this work the boyish composer displays an amazing mastery of symphonic development, a rare ear for instrumental timbres, and a mature, artistic, restrained hand over his unusual materials. He does not hesitate to begin his symphony *in medias res,* coming to the point without circumlocutory preamble and achieving a maximum of effect with the slenderest means. His orchestration is so bare at times that a soft pizzicato in the violins sounds like an explosion. His crescendos are built up in the space of a few bars, but seem to cover the distance of a much longer drive. He has a keen editorial eye for condensation and compactness, saying only what is absolutely essential and what is of greatest interest. There are no "stretched out" or padded sections. Everything is relevant and stems from sound organization. The themes are simple yet fresh, with curious astringent twists of humor that etch themselves in the listener's memory.

The first movement starts with a muted trumpet announcing the piquantly reflective main theme, which is soon accompanied by a counter-melody (some consider this a portion of the main theme) by bassoon,

and joined by oboes on a thin plucked chord from the violins. The clarinet now offers a ramification of the trumpet theme with pizzicato background in the 'cellos bringing in other strings and upper winds. A few frowning notes from the horn lead to an inquiry, repeated faintly in the trumpets, which obtains a seemingly irresolute answer in a long-drawn, eerie chord. The strings now play with the main subject, the first violins climbing with rigidly grotesque notes only to make way for the modified theme in seconds. We now come to the movement proper (allegro non troppo) with a gingerly marching theme in the clarinet which is suggestive of the "counter-melody" heard in the beginning.

A new theme from the flute is heard, sounding quite Stravinskyish and seeming to dance off into unashamed Grieg. This is repeated in the oboe and bassoon until it plays itself out, and we return to the grotesque staccato passage of the violins, but this time divided between two solo instruments. The feeling becomes tense and full-bodied. We listen to previously heard material in various transformations, and the movement closes with the clarinet carrying the main theme into inaudibility.

The second movement is a jocose, somewhat angular Scherzo: martial, bright, and highly rhythmic. It ends in an unexpectedly subdued manner.

Lento, the slow movement, begins with a soliloquy from the oboe. Muted violins are answered by the 'cello, then flute and other instruments. It develops a songlike character, yet moves with measured rhythm. The mood is melancholy and reflective, and the movement seems to spend itself in a thin groan. But in a few seconds we are aroused by an increasingly loud roll on the snare drum, and we are ready for the Finale, which is ushered in with a false spurt of energy (one bar allegro molto) followed by a moody Lento. Then begins the movement proper, Allegro Molto, a Finale full of vigorous thrusts, tricky changes, and spirited proclamations as if the composer were even then reliving the triumphant conclusion of the October Revolution.

Dmitri Shostakovich: Symphony No. 5

By Grigori Shneerson

From "Everybody's Music" by Schima Kaufman

IN THE Western World, the object of the *avant-garde* is presumably the overthrow of old artistic foundations, the breaking-out in "new paths," however meaningless and at any cost. For us in the Soviet, however, the *avant-garde* is held to express progressive ideas only when it talks to the people in a new, powerful, and intelligible language. The demands of the wide masses of people, their artistic tastes, grow from day to day. The "advanced" composer is therefore one who plunges into the social currents swirling around him, and with his creative work serves the progress of humankind.

    • Just what is the nature of a truly advanced musical language, it is difficult to say. Only the musically creative act itself may answer this question. Shostakovich, however, has given us a clue with his new work. True, many excellent pages were written by him before; they can be found in his First Symphony, his Piano Concerto, and much of the music for the films. Nevertheless, it seems to me that in this Fifth Symphony, completed in 1937, Shostakovich for the first time appears as a mature artist, a universal composer of magnitude, destined to say something new in music. Each movement gives us a world of passion and experience profoundly felt and expressed. Outstanding are a marvelous richness, a seriousness of thought, which command one's attention from the opening measures. And despite a number of tragic moments, the general character of the symphony is uplifting and life-affirming.

The first movement, Moderato, unfolds the philosopher's concept of the work, the growth of the artist's personality within the revolutionary events of our time.

Energy, emotional power, concentration are the essential features. The musical language is at the same time complex yet clear. A wide polyphonic development, pungent harmonic combinations, an infinite variety in the orchestration serve admirably to convey the thought.

The second movement, Allegretto, is written in a dance form and unloads, as it were, the intensity of the original musical impulse. Here Shostakovich reveals his brilliant mastery of the orchestral palette.

Most profound of all is the Largo, which is a tribute to the composer's melodic gift and his keen sense of form. This movement is very long, yet its interest is sustained throughout. After a tender and affecting conclusion, the Largo flows into an energetic, bright and joyful march, an Allegro.

Broad in scope and expressive power, the Finale leaves one literally breathless.

My Seventh Symphony

Adapted from broadcasts and articles

By Dmitri Shostakovich

ON THE morning of June 22 (1941), I volunteered for service at the front. I received a reply: "You'll be called when required." So I went back to my duties at the Leningrad Conservatory. We attended recitals by members of the graduating class, gave an evaluation of their performances, and signed their diplomas. In that year many gifted pianists, violinists, and singers graduated from the Leningrad Conservatory.

I joined the Conservatory Fire-Fighting Brigade. We were housed in barracks, and it was here that I began work on my Seventh Symphony. Later I was asked to become musical director of the Popular Guard Theater. Soon this theater became the center of Leningrad's leading playwrights, poets, and writers. We produced several interesting plays, one of them an operetta on how Ribbentrop gathered his celebrated conference of diplomats shortly after the outbreak of the War. One after the other groups of actors from our theater left for the front. And when some of them returned they brought with them the splendid fighting spirit of our army. I visited front-line units on two occasions and witnessed numerous instances of the courage that is typical of our people. Simple people, men you meet every day, turned out to be real heroes.

Meanwhile, in the first hot July days, I started on my Seventh Symphony, conceived as a musical embodiment of the supreme ideal of patriotic war. The work engrossed me completely. Neither the savage air-raids nor the grim atmosphere of a beleaguered city could hinder the flow of musical ideas. . . . I worked with an inhuman intensity. I continued to compose marches, songs, and film music, and attended to my organizational duties as chairman of the Leningrad Composers' Union, and then would return to my symphony as though I had never left it.

The first and longest movement bears a dramatic and (I would say) tragic character. [It] tells of the happy, peaceful life of a people confident in themselves and in their future. It is a simple life, such as was enjoyed by thousands of Leningrad's Popular Guards, by the whole city, by the whole country, before the war broke out. Then comes the War. I have made no attempt at naturalistic interpretation of the War by imitating booms of cannon, shell, explosions, etc. I tried to give an emotional image of the War. The *reprise* is a memorial march, or more correctly a requiem for the War's victims. Plain people pay tribute to the memory of their heroes. The requiem is followed by an even more tragic theme. I don't know how to describe it. Perhaps it is the tears of a mother, or even that feeling which comes when sorrow is so great that there are no more tears. These two lyrical fragments form the conclusion of the first part of the symphony. The closing chords resemble the din of distant battle, a reminder that the war continues.

The next two movements were intended as an intermezzo. They confirm life in opposition to war. I tried to express the thought that art, literature and science must advance in spite of war. It is, if you like, a polemic against the statement that "when the cannons roar the muse is silent."

The fourth movement is dedicated to our victory. It is an immediate continuation of the second and third movements, their logical outcome. It is the victory of light over darkness, wisdom over frenzy, lofty humanism over monstrous tyranny.

While I was working on this music, Leningrad was converted into an impregnable fortress. Fresh Popular Guard detachments were constantly being formed. The entire population learned the art of warfare, and it seemed that war had replaced all other affairs. I found, however, that that was not so, for one of my friends told me that all tickets for the Philharmonic concerts had been sold out. Indeed, at all these concerts I found the audience in high spirits and keenly responsive to our performance. My excitement at these concerts was something new, for I came to understand that music, like every art, is a genuine requirement of man.

On the whole I feel that the Seventh Symphony is an optimistic conception. As a composition it is closer to my Fifth Symphony than to my Sixth; it is a continuation of the emotions and mood of the Fifth Symphony.

PART FOUR

High C's and Pirouettes

IV. High C's and Pirouettes

ALMOST since its very beginnings several centuries ago, opera has been among the most bitterly attacked and passionately defended of all the arts. Attacked because, being in essence a composite of poetry, drama, singing, dancing, instrumental music, and several other arts, it has never managed to satisfy the pure lovers of any of these; and defended because in spite of its numerous and undoubted shortcomings, it has continued to exert a steady fascination on its listeners, stirring them on occasion to a degree rarely equaled in any other field. Nothing is easier than to poke fun at the inanities of opera—its trapdoors, steam valves, fairies, dragons, two-ton females emitting delicate bird notes, mortally wounded heroes who take three arias and a half-dozen high C's to die; its strutting, arm-waving, and all the rest. Almost two hundred years ago, Samuel Johnson's *Dictionary* defined opera as "an exotic and irrational entertainment." Today, we all know people for whom three hours at the opera represent three hours of torture—among these being many fine musicians. On the other hand, there are those who will wait in line for hours and forgo many comforts to buy standing room to their favorite operas.

What is opera, then, that with all its failings and incongruities it retains and even increases its hold over masses of ordinary Americans? In recent years, especially since the inauguration of weekly opera broadcasts, millions have come to follow this "impurest" of arts.

Probably the answer is simple. Opera is a "big show," the richest, most varied, and most attractive of all. Those who do not like its pageantry can shut their eyes and listen to the music—the radio audience *must* hear without seeing. Those who find the music too deep at times (especially in Wagner) are diverted by the spectacle of tempests, rainbows, flying horses, mermaids, and Magic Fire scenes. Then there are the lovers of vocal pyrotechnics and *bel canto*⊛ who do not care what's

---

* "Beautiful singing"—the traditional Italian style familiar to every opera-goer.

247

happening on the stage or in the orchestra pit, as long as their favorite soprano or baritone is hitting the high notes in style. The really successful grand-opera composer is aware of each of these types of opera-goer and provides entertainment for all.

Because this is the one country in the world (besides England) where opera is not sung in the language of its hearers, you will probably have to sit through a good many dull moments (they seem like hours) in any opera—places where the characters go into lengthy and apparently meaningful musical conversations, which ninety percent of the audience unfortunately never understands.* You console yourself with the thought that the plot is probably not very important anyway. And even if you cannot follow the tangled intrigues of Mozart's *Marriage of Figaro* or the arguments between Sachs and Beckmesser in Wagner's *Meistersinger,* you *can* hear some exquisite melodies and moving orchestral music, enjoy the antics of a page-boy hiding in a bedroom closet, or a cobbler beating loudly on his last while someone else sings a serenade; and you can watch the processions, ballets, and scenic and lighting effects that are sure to occur in the course of an evening—all for the price of one ticket.

Yet was this sort of random, disconnected enjoyment what the great composers aimed for when they created their operas? Was it what Wagner had in mind when he wrote that music drama should be an expression of the feelings of the entire people, not mere "social entertainment"? Was it what Mussorgsky intended when he labeled his *Boris Godunov* a "national folk drama"? Even the casual opera-goer, listening to the Hallucination Scene in *Boris* or the last act of *Don Giovanni*—and understanding only about half the composer's intentions—is able to experience the grandeur and power of true musical theater. He glimpses, if only for a moment, the potentialities of the art that all the reformers of opera sought and sometimes achieved—*dramma per musica,* drama through music.

There is a world of difference between grand opera as it is produced today and the true music drama that has been achieved at various moments of history. As we hear it at the Metropolitan or elsewhere in this country, opera is often entertaining, colorful, even very beautiful; but nine times out of ten it is a spectacle with various attractions that are not particularly related to one another. We hear some lovely arias,

---

* It was once the custom in Italy to have a round of cards or to go out for a drink during these dry recitations, called in Italian just that: *recitativo secco.*

watch some brilliant scenes, admire some orchestral interludes, and even feel sorry for the dying heroine; but all these enjoyable moments never add up to one single, all-embracing unity. Like a lavish Cecil de Mille movie, opera is highly successful in many distinct departments; as a whole, it falls apart. I have been to many operas and greatly enjoyed many of them. Yet I cannot truthfully say of any opera in modern production that its three, four, or five hours held my continuous, unrelaxed attention, and that everything I heard and saw was completely bound up into one completely satisfying experience.

What, on the other hand, is the essential nature of music drama? It is the complete fusion of all the means employed—poetry, music, dance, lighting, staging, acting, singing—into one artistic whole. The drama must be one in which the audience can participate in an emotional sense, even to the extent of identifying themselves with the characters; and the music must be so integrated with the words and action that it multiplies the emotional participation in the drama a thousandfold. This was what the greatest theatrical composers (Monteverdi, Gluck, Mozart, Verdi, Wagner, and Mussorgsky) understood— each in his own way, of course; and this is what all achieved in terms of the musical and dramatic values of their own times.

It has often been said by the defenders of the *status quo* in opera that all discussions of the relations of music and drama are irrelevant because in the last analysis it was only the music that interested the masters, and only the music that makes the great operas live. Then why is not opera presented simply in concert form—a much easier and far less expensive procedure?

The fact is that all the great composers *were* deeply concerned with the dramatic qualities of the texts they selected, and (in writing their operas) with achieving the most intimate fusion of music, words, and stage action. Monteverdi chose the greatest Italian poets of his day. Gluck fought vigorously for a new dramatic type of libretto, and suggested that opera music should confine itself to strengthening the play.* Mozart was said to have looked through a hundred opera books before selecting that of *The Marriage of Figaro*. Wagner spent years writing his own texts, and in composing the music sought for the most detailed interaction between the two. (He also wrote the most precise stage and scenic directions into his score, indicating the exact co-ordi-

---

* He wrote in his Preface to *Alceste*: "I sought to confine the music to its true function, that of assisting the poetry, by strengthening both the expression of the sentiments and the interest of the situations."

nation of sound and movement.) Verdi was extremely careful in choosing his plots; he finally ended up with nothing less than Shakespeare. Mussorgsky spent months in research to insure the fidelity of his setting of Pushkin's dramatic *Boris Godunov*.

Besides the complete unity of play and music, music drama depends on another factor—the existence of a common bond among composer, producer, performer, and audience. There can be no complete dramatic communication and catharsis unless subject matter, musical style, and technique of production are familiar to all and emotionally shared by all.

Thus Mozart's *Marriage of Figaro*, for example, dealt with the touchiest human question of the period just before the French Revolution: the amorous relations of aristocrats and their unwilling servants. Audiences composed largely of such employees and other commoners hung on every word and note of the musical play (though the aristocrats didn't like it so much), and Mozart was a veritable hero to the free citizens of Prague. They saw and heard themselves reflected in Mozart's characters and music, just as the adolescent of today sees her ideal image in the Hollywood movie queens. They would have liked to act like Figaro and sing as he sang—and they did. The tunes of *Figaro* were whistled in cafés, sung by street-singers and kitchen maids, danced to in all the ballrooms, much to the composer's delight. Mozart's music drama was meant for the people, and they knew it.

The relation that existed between play, music, producer, and audience in Mozart's time no longer exists. As presented today, in an incomprehensible language, in a huge auditorium where the singers have to bellow to be heard, with actors dressed like Dresden China dolls (in Mozart's time they wore contemporary costume), *Figaro* is made into a pretty costume piece, which the audience enjoys immensely, to be sure, but as one enjoys a picture at a museum. *Figaro* is delightful, charming, yet completely remote from real life—the last thing Mozart intended. It has become, in short, the perfect "grand opera." *

The fact that even in such a disintegrated form musical theater

---

* Much nearer to the spirit of Mozart than any "operatic" production are the productions of the "Nine o'Clock Opera"—a group of young Americans who present the composition *sans* orchestra, chorus, ballet, or elaborate sets. But it is sung in English and in modern dress, with natural acting, a few simple props (things that could be found in any American home), and a narrator who discusses the action as though it were happening today in Peoria or Kankakee.

has an ever-growing audience attests to its magnificent possibilities when it can again emerge on its highest level.

For the present, at least, however, this is mere speculation. There is today no genuine music drama in existence, created for and enjoyed by the audience of living Americans. Nor is there the apparatus for producing such a work, should one be written tomorrow. Certainly the last place it could find a home would be that antiquaries' museum, on whose stage our national language is regarded as an interloper—the New York "Met." Over its portals there should be inscribed, "Abandon hope, all ye living composers who enter here!" Of course, the institution on 39th Street has on rare occasions produced what it called "American grand operas." That was precisely the trouble: it was trying to bring to life that which cannot be. American grand opera indeed! You might as well try to grow American Greek temples on our soil, or American Gothic cathedrals, or American Renaissance paintings.

Now a museum of opera has its important functions, and it must continue to exist and be supported. We need more of such, and need them badly. But not so badly as we need an American music drama, conceived, written, and produced for the people of this land.

What will such a music drama be like? Though one could not safely predict, certain signs are already in the air. There is the trend of Broadway "musicals" toward a subtler and more serious music. There is the higher level of the scores written for certain Hollywood pictures. More specifically, there are such typically American combinations of music and theater as Paul Green and Kurt Weill's *Johnny Johnson,* Marc Connelly's *Green Pastures,* Gershwin's *Porgy and Bess,* and Marc Blitzstein's *The Cradle Will Rock.* In each the question of American music drama was approached in a different way; in each some of the artistic problems were explored. Taken all together, they are a start in the direction of musical theater rooted in our soil and people. Their popularity reveals the existence of a wide audience for a new form that will strike deeper than Broadway, truer than opera, and close to the life around us.

It is useless to discuss here the technical qualities of an American music drama. That is a matter for the composer's desk, the writer's workshop, and the producer's imagination. But one thing is certain: it will build on the experiences of the past, of all those historical periods when music and theater formed an intimate part of the people's life. Its creators will know how the masterpieces of the past were brought into being, will know also the failings of the form we call opera. Its audience, too, should be acquainted with the various forms of musical theater that have existed at one time or another.

Dr. Herbert Graf's study tells how opera came to be what it is, analyzes its various types and styles, and discusses the present and the future of music drama in America. Lincoln Kirstein's essay does much the same for the dance and the ballet.—E. S.

The Growth of Opera
Extracts from "The Opera and Its Future in America"

By Herbert Graf

THE theater has always been a mirror of its time, reflecting social as well as cultural conditions, and perhaps we can understand the opera of various periods better when we understand the peculiar conditions out of which each form has sprung. But it requires keen perception to see, behind the thicket of operatic "traditions" and the pomp and showmanship which attend grand opera, the fundamental principles upon which opera is built, principles that derive from man's simple human emotions. To observe these principles in action, it is necessary to go to the very roots of the musical drama and its beginnings as an expression of the emotions of both the individual and the community.

In the wider sense, opera has always existed. Primitive men expressed their fears and joys in song and dance and masquerade. When this primitive folk opera became refined by a high culture, the artistic forms of the species developed: the music dramas of Aeschylus in ancient Greece, the liturgic dramas of the medieval church, and "opera" proper from 1600 to our own day. The reforms of opera—in the eighteenth century the rise of folk opera as well as the reforms achieved by Gluck, Mozart, and Beethoven, and in the nineteenth century the realist reforms of Wagner and Verdi—were not isolated artistic movements, but part and parcel of the life of their times. Thus we see that opera is not the comparatively young and special art that we often think of it as being, but only a particular form of the eternal musical theater, a form determined by the particular social, political, and cultural surroundings among which it was born and developed, and changing as its audience changes.

THE BIRTH OF OPERA IN ITALY

The plan and style of the first opera house were determined by the social conditions which prevailed in the Italy of its period. Society was dominated by the courts of princes, both secular princes and [those] of the Church. Cultural as well as political life was entirely in the hands of the aristocracy, and it was accordingly among the nobles of Florence that, about 1600, the new form of musical art was born.

To understand the rise of this new art, we must know something of the atmosphere in which it came into being. The stream of the human spirit could no longer be confined within the channels of medieval thought. For centuries men had been schooled by their feudal masters and by the Latin teachings of the Church to renounce the joys of earthly life for the sake of a better world to come. Now the invention of the printing press and the discovery of strange worlds were revealing new and long-obscured horizons. The writings of the Greeks and Romans, forgotten for nearly a thousand years, were being rediscovered, and a wave of "humanism" was bringing to light the ancient philosophy of the beauty of the life and arts of men.

The Medicis made Florence the center of the rebirth of the ancient world and here a group of aristocratic amateurs who had studied the musical theories of Hellas planned a revival of Greek drama, in which music was said to have played an important part. For their plays, which they performed in one another's private palace-theaters, they took the stories of Daphne and Eurydice from Greek mythology and set them to a sort of speechlike chanting. Soon the new art became known as *dramma in musica;* then *opera in musica* (works in music); finally just *opera.* At first the public was admitted only occasionally. Later a theater had to be found which would accommodate them. But, of course, aristocratic society and the general public had to be kept apart. This was accomplished by installing the members of the audience in carefully designated tiers and boxes, according to their social rank. The intention of the aristocratic progenitors of the opera was to revive the idea of the old Greek drama. Let us inquire whether that is what they really did.

At the end of the sixteenth century, in Florence, a group of highly educated men, the *Camerata,* gathered at the house of Count

Bardi and discussed the treatises of the ancients on Greek music, which was supposed to have been a recited, speechlike solo song, following the declamation of the word. This form of recited song, the "recitative," was also thought to have been used in the Greek drama. One of the members of the *Camerata*, Vincenzio Galilei, father of the famous astronomer, had discovered three old Greek hymns of Mesomedes, although he could not decipher them. (They were not successfully deciphered until the nineteenth century.) He wrote a *Dialogue on Ancient and Modern Music* and composed several solo songs, as did others in this circle. Among them were the composers Caccini and Peri, both singers, Count Bardi and Jacopo Corsi, in whose home the group later met when Bardi went to Rome, the great poet Rinuccini, and the composer Cavalieri. It is not necessary to go into the controversies of these men, for all had one ultimate goal, that of opposing the contrapuntal style, which Caccini said was "tearing the poetry to pieces for the sake of the music," and of subordinating the music to the expression of the word: "the word first, then the rhythm, finally the tone—not the reverse." Thus, following the Greek pattern of composition, they composed some solo songs and scenes in the recited style to the accompaniment of chordal instruments. The next step was an attempt to revive Greek drama.

PERI AND CACCINI

The first drama set throughout to music in the new style of recited solo-recitative and chorus scenes was *Dafne* by Peri and Caccini. Peri says the music should pursue a middle course between speech and song, while the harmony accompanying the recited song should change only if the meaning of the words warrants a change. Accordingly, the Italian vocal school of the seventeenth century, which is the classic period of artistic singing, and Caccini in the foreword to his book of vocal compositions, *Nuove Musiche,* published in 1601, teach the art of *bel canto*—song which is not only beautiful but dramatically expressive as well, and in which the object of the *coloratura* is not mere ornamentation but the conveying of ideas and emotions. The orchestra consisted of four chordal instruments—the chitarrone, the grand lyre, the gravicembalo, and the great lute (with three flutes being used simultaneously in one number)—and was placed *behind* the scenes, as usual in this early period. As yet there was no overture, but the word *aria* had already appeared. Liberal use was made of shepherds, nymphs, and spirits of the underworld, recalling the vein of ancient

Greek drama and foreshadowing that of Gluck's *Orfeo*. In many places the fidelity of the dramatic expression of this music is still astonishing.

MONTEVERDI

The Eurydice plot was used by Claudio Monteverdi, the first great genius among opera composers, in his first opera, *Orfeo*, performed in Mantua in 1607. This opera was called *favola in musica*, whereas the first operas had not had any subtitles. It is a masterwork, combining the recitative style with rich expression in harmony. Monteverdi has been called the Father of Dissonance, and he was also a pioneer in the wealth of instrumental accompaniment to which he set his solos. This opera contains the first overture, and orchestral interludes at the beginning, middle, and end of arias as well as during the scene shifting. It includes also new effects in instrumentation and is written for an orchestra of thirty-four instruments. Melodies appear in the course of the work as "motives of reminiscence," a technique elaborated upon in Wagner's operas. When one remembers in addition to all these innovations the musical expressiveness of every dramatic gesture, as seen in his *Combattimento di Tancredi e Clorinda*, the dramatic use of dances in the *Ballo delle Ingrate* (The Dance of the Prudes), and the moving emotion of the lamentation of *Arianna*, it will be seen that Monteverdi was the first great master of the new form of musical drama which came into existence in 1600, and which, under the all-inclusive name of "opera," has endured until the present time.

The inventors of opera had intended to revive Greek musical drama, but their attempts fell short of true fulfillment of the Greek idea. For Greek musical drama had arisen out of folk emotion, whereas opera was born in the private palace-theaters of Renaissance courts and was an expression of the artistic interests of the nobility. Could it, having sprung from such an environment, return to the principles of its true, ancient heritage, or would it become a mere form of social entertainment, as in Imperial Rome?

Born amid very aristocratic surroundings, opera grew up to be a little snobbish and artificial. The plots of *Dafne* and *Orfeo*, the constant singing, the stilted acting, the ostentation of scenery and costume, and the plan of the opera house, mirroring the social stratification of the period—all these contributed to making opera what it became. Opera was a child born with a silver spoon in its mouth. Taken about to the parties of the nobility, it soon became spoiled and precocious. Its patrons used it to show off their wealth and social position. Like any spoiled child, it soon lost control of its qualities. The elements of opera became ungoverned prima donnas, each working for its own aggrandizement rather than for the sake of the whole—the music drama. Opera became a medley of independent attractions: singing for the sake of vocal display, dancing to show off feats of virtuosity in bodily movement, scenery for the sake of mere pomp and color. The composer worked for these separate elements rather than they for him. The art of music drama died. Music, acting, and scenery were resolved into formulas, poses, and show—*da capo* arias, *pas,* and typical sets. Art became entertainment. Music drama became grand opera.

CHANGING FORMS OF OPERA

The history of opera since 1600 shows a continual struggle against this tendency. At three periods the musicodramatic conception has been dominant: at the birth of opera, in the eighteenth-century reform which is usually associated with Gluck, and in the nineteenth-century reform which we sum up under the name of Wagner. In the intervals opera turned into grand opera. What are the reasons for these changes? The most obvious one is the changes in the character of the audience.

Opera is the particular form which the eternal musical theater took in the society of the seventeenth to the twentieth centuries. It has never entirely lost the general character which it derived from the court society which gave it birth. But the curve of its development shows many devia-

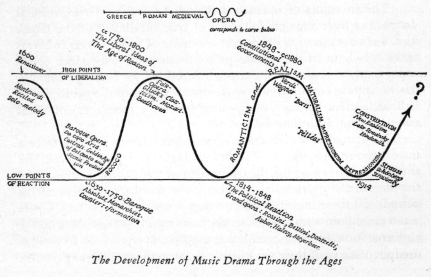

The Development of Music Drama Through the Ages

tions which reflect social changes in the period, particularly the three social movements born of the progress of modern science and education (and reactions to these three movements) : the Renaissance, the liberalism of the Age of Reason, and the revolutions of the mid-nineteenth century. These high points were the eras of individual thinking, as opposed to those of absolute monarchy and Counter Reformation in the Baroque period, of restoration after the French Revolution, and of the Napoleonic Wars and modern imperialism in the machine age leading up to the First World War. The appearance of folk opera and Gluck's reform of grand opera, like Mozart's operas and Beethoven's *Fidelio,* were products of the Age of Reason. Wagner's and Verdi's reforms were the counterparts of nineteenth-century nationalism and the revolutionary movements of 1848.

In the three periods in which opera was pre-eminently folk expression, it was music drama; in the intervals (the Baroque, and the time of Rossini, Donizetti, Meyerbeer, etc.) it was grand opera. But history does not repeat itself. The alternations of innovation and reaction never return opera to its starting point. They are rather subsidiary movements in an essentially ascending line, and opera is ever advancing with society toward new forms.

THE SINGERS

Since the beginning of operatic art, singers had been of great importance, and Gagliano tells us that the composer Peri, who sang the part of Orfeo in his opera *Euridice,* could by his great artistry in song bring the audience to tears or laughter at will. In Rome the cult of singers had now begun to grow. The enthusiasm for singers went so far in the Holy City that the appearance of the singers Costa and Cecci on the same program resulted in a great scandal occasioned by their antagonistic behavior, and following this the performance of female singers was forbidden in Rome. The *genus femininum* was replaced by the *genus neutrum*—the *castrato,* a type of singer completely alien to modern audiences, but one whose influence dominated opera of the seventeenth and eighteenth centuries. The *castrati* appeared in female parts as well as in heroic male parts. At the same time, about the year 1600, these *castrati*—they were also called *musici*—first appeared in Rome, where they often became members of the papal chapel. These men were subjected to an operation in boyhood which resulted in their retaining their high voices. When these high voices were supported by the breathing strength of an adult body, the result was extraordinary vocal virtuosity.

The *castrati* were taught in famous schools, and engaged by courts all over Europe. They achieved enormous fame; the first celebrated *castrato*, Loreto Vittori, was guarded like a jewel by Cardinal Ludovisi.

OPERA IN VENICE

In the republic of Venice, the largest city of Italy in this period, a new light was thrown upon opera. Whereas in Florence and Rome it had been nurtured as a private function of aristocrats, with the public admitted only occasionally, in Venice it became a public institution and took on a more democratic form. Here, in 1637, San Cassiano, the first public opera house at which admission was paid, was opened. It met with such success that the following year a second opera-theater was started, and others soon followed. Between 1637 and 1700 in this city, which had one hundred and forty thousand inhabitants, four opera houses customarily played at the same time; once there were as many as eight. In this period three hundred different operas were given.

The audiences consisted of nobles, merchants, foreign princes and ambassadors who came to the carnival, and the townspeople. The admission of the public resulted in a new form of auditorium, which directly reflects the particular social conditions of the time. It is significant that, in the "free" city, the visiting dignitaries and the rich merchants wished to be sure of maintaining their social distinction. Therefore, the auditorium was divided into tiers, one above the other, and still further separation was provided by the division of the tiers into boxes. Thus the design of the Italian opera-theater assumed a definite form and became a model for all which followed. The boxes were subscribed for by the nobility, as well as by the celebrities to whom operas were often dedicated. The less distinguished citizenry sat in the parterre, paying four lire for admission plus two lire for a comfortable chair.

Musically, the more democratic trend in Venetian opera, which turned it away from the solemnity of ancient drama, had an interesting result: the introduction of popular arias, canzonettas, barcaroles, and similarly well-liked tunes. Many of these arias became extremely popular, were sung as gondolier songs, and became the "hits" of the time. Comic elements, too, grew in importance, and finally comic *intermezzi* independent of the main action were inserted between the acts of an opera; from these, the Italian comic opera of the eighteenth century later developed.

In order to please the public, the most directly melodious parts of the operas—the arias—were featured most prominently. Whereas

Florentine opera had begun as drama set to music, involving recited singing, with the recited and melodious parts of equal importance and both subordinated to the fundamental dramatic idea, the aria now became even more distinctly separated from the "recitative," which was demoted to a secondary function. As opera began to cater increasingly to the desire of the public for mere entertainment rather than the interpretation of true dramatic emotion, these arias froze into stereotyped musical pictures of joy, sorrow, battle, etc., and for them the scheme of the *da capo* aria, consisting of Part A, Part B, and then a repetition of Part A, became the characteristic, accepted formula. Here emotions were typified rather than developed, and the chorus, a remnant of the Greek feeling of community participation in the emotions of the drama, had little value in such an atmosphere.

OPERA AS SPECTACLE

It was in Venice that opera became a spectacle. The French abbé Raguenet says in his report on operas which he saw in Italy: "As far as the machines are concerned, I do not believe that human sagacity can carry invention further than it has progressed in Italy . . . one sees in Venice the appearance of an elephant in the theater; in one moment this voluminous apparition dissolves and an army stands in its place. All the soldiers, solely through the placing of their shields, had formed that elephant, which was as natural and as perfect as though it were a living, breathing beast." The libretti of the Venetian operas are mostly in three acts, each consisting of either three or four scenes.

Jacopo Torelli, famous for his effects of changing scenery, worked in Venice and had instituted his system not only in Italy but in Paris as well. An accurate description by Nicola Sabbatini, which appeared in Ravenna in 1638, tells how settings were painted and describes the use of the curtain backdrops, the mechanism involved in having ships sail across the stage, cloud machines, appearances of ghosts from beneath the stage floor and of gods from above, and the darkening of the stage. Traps played a great part. There is one opera in which six elephants carrying a throne with eighty persons go down on a trap until only the throne remains on the stage floor. Animals were in high favor: lions, bears, monkeys, and birds were popular, and their use, along with machine effects, is still seen in Mozart's *Die Zauberflöte*, and even in the operas of Wagner.

By the end of the seventeenth century, Naples ranked second only to Venice as an opera city, and it soon surpassed it. Here opera became the realm of the virtuoso singer. The libretti were arranged as a chain of *da capo* arias to be embroidered by the singer's technique. The arias were connected by recitatives, which substantiated a pretext of story and action. The effect of this is noteworthy: drama became only an occasion for the arias of the singers, and the aria, not the dramatic content, became the *pièce de résistance*.

The first great composer of this period was the prolific Alessandro Scarlatti, who wrote more than one hundred operas and hundreds of other compositions. He was great in his capacity for vocal expression and for instrumental effects. The rather dry scheme of the stereotyped Neapolitan opera was brought to its artistic climax in the operas of Handel, which represented a turning point in operatic history.*

OPERA FOR MONARCHY

Opera had early been exported from Italy, and along with it had gone composers, librettists, singers, ballet masters, and stage designers to the Catholic courts of Europe, where absolute monarchy was in its prime. The names of the Sun King, Louis XIV, in France and his imitators in Vienna are synonymous with absolute power at its most splendid height. These monarchs reigned supreme, with the nobility, their satellites, and the people having no voice in government. Opera was taken over by these rulers, who found in the worlds of Jupiter and Caesar models for their "divine" might. Tribute was paid to them in the prologues and in hundreds of miracle effects. As may be seen in the paintings of Rubens and Tiepolo, the spirit of the Renaissance *trionfi* continued now in the Baroque pomp of the operas given at court; there were not only indoor performances but outdoor festivities in the royal gardens as well, and music, the ballet, horse tournaments, and fireworks were all used. Or, if Lent forbade these spectacles, religious oratorios and scenes from the Holy Sepulcher were enacted in church. Italian Baroque opera became the festive form of the European court theaters in the seventeenth and early eighteenth centuries.

COURT OPERA IN FRANCE

In no other country had the concentration of absolute power in a monarchy taken stronger or more definite form than in France, where it had been built up by the Cardinals Richelieu and Mazarin and was really personified in Louis XIV. The power of the nobles had been broken; they lived subject to the beck and call of a king who reigned

---

* For a discussion of Handel's operas, see page 349.—E. S.

without parliament and, after Mazarin's death, without a premier. He could rightly say *L'état, c'est moi!* He built the castle of Versailles, after his own plans, in a dry spot where water had to be brought from a considerable distance for the lavish fountains and the main reservoir. The whole burden of the luxury of the court fell on the people, since the nobles were tax-exempt. The court life which went on around the monarch and his satellites was a subject of special protocol. Ingenious were the refinements of system and intrigue. Mastery of form is characteristic of this period of French thought, and it is richly exemplified in the tragedy of Corneille and Racine, with its crystal-clear language and construction. This devotion to form in art and declamation as taught in the academies and the royal theater, the Comédie Française, had a significant part in forming a national style of French opera.

Another characteristic element was the importance of the dance. As in the Italian Renaissance, celebrations with pageantry, music, and dances held a prominent place in sixteenth-century France. From the time of the famous *Ballet Comique de la Royne,* the ballet remained an integral part of all French festivities, whether inserted into the operas or comedies of Molière, or given as a special performance as *opéra* or *comédie* ballets, in which the king himself often took part. The importance of the ballet at that time endures throughout the history of French opera, and even Wagner was forced to acknowledge its traditional place when he added the Bacchanal to his *Tannhäuser* for its performance in Paris.

Italian opera was brought to Paris by Cardinal Mazarin, who as a student at the Jesuit College in Rome had sung in the performance of the opera *St. Ignazio.* When he became premier, after Richelieu's death, he favored the importation of Italian opera, bringing operas from Venice and Rome, with Italian singers and Torelli, the famous stage engineer. The form of the Italian opera-theater was introduced in Paris, but not even two operas by Cavalli, one of which had been performed for the celebration of the marriage of Louis XIV, were successful. The French national style had achieved too clear and definite a character to permit the acceptance of foreign art unchanged.

Finally, the king granted the French poet Perrin and the composer Cambert a monopoly on a public opera house, the so-called *Académie Royale de Musique*—the name which the Grand Opéra of Paris still bears. Soon this franchise fell to Lully, an Italian who had come to Paris originally as a kitchen boy and had later become a violinist and then conductor and composer of the king's string orchestra. In collaboration with Quinault, a poet of the school of Corneille, Lully composed dramas of which the king frequently selected the subjects, and in which the style of the declamation of French tragedy and the dance were combined with priests, shepherds, demons, solemn choirs, and processions. Lully was general manager, stage director, dancer, and actor in one person. Reputed to be a dictator of the stage, who did not even shrink from resorting to violence to gain the results he desired, he carefully supervised the action and grouping on the stage and stressed, above all, clear pronunciation. He is also credited with the endeavor to introduce historically accurate costumes. Lully's operas typify the original French opera style—a style based on the traditions of French tragedy, *tragédie lyrique,* which in contrast to the many scenes of the Italian opera had a form of five acts with one set each. One of these was often of an underworld scene, and in the fifth act a god presented a miraculous solution by means of the mechanical trick of Euripides' *deus ex machina,* as, for example, in Gluck's operas. The ideas of *gloire* and *amour* are always uppermost in French opera.

These early years of the eighteenth century saw the beginning of a political change in France. Moral and economic corruption, and the laying of heavy taxes upon the people with no government representation to protect their interests, were paving the way for open revolt against an all-powerful monarchy. The decadence of the court and its circle was not without its influence on architecture. The massiveness of the Baroque architecture yielded to the thousand-and-one small ornaments of the Rococo style. In opera, the arias were ridiculously ornamented by countless coloraturas in which the singers indulged themselves liberally according to their whims. The dramatic element received little attention. Any obligation to develop a plot was casually discharged by the *secco* recitatives, and the audience often employed the time which these occupied in talking, playing cards in their boxes, or taking refreshment, until it was time for the next *da capo* aria.

SINGER'S OPERA IN ITALY

The technique of singing and staging had never reached such heights. In this period there were four great conservatories in Naples alone, and it was in Naples that Carlo Broschi, called Farinelli, was taught. In Tosi's *Opinioni de cantori antichi e moderni* (1723), the standard book of the *bel canto,* the rules of that classic school of singing in the eighteenth century are laid down. The singer was not only to execute the music, but was to take part in its composition. His liberty to add vocal ornamentations and improvise on the music written—the *cantar al mente*—Tosi termed the *true art of the singer*. He included also the art of employing *passi,* which comprised appoggiature, trills, and passages, the knowledge of the *filar il tuono* (sustaining the tone) and the *messa di voce* (the development of a tone from the softest *pianissimo* to the strongest *forte*). The second and particularly the third parts of the *da capo* aria were rich soil for ornamentation by the singer, for, as Tosi said, "this can either establish his greatness or ruin him." The singers dominated the theater, and it is a well-known story that the giant Handel, constantly fighting against the virtuosi, carried Cuzzoni bodily to the window and threatened to drop her out when she refused to sing a simple canzona and sang, instead, a *da capo* aria.

The most famous of all singers was Farinelli, whose technical skill in executing passages and trills and whose ability to increase and diminish volume of notes were well known. In London the ladies were entranced by his singing, one of his admirers going so far as to exclaim from a box, "One God, one Farinelli." At the age of thirty-two, at the climax of his career in London, where his appearance so seriously endangered the supremacy of Handel's company as to threaten it with bankruptcy, he left to go into seclusion at the Spanish court. Burney writes that he sang the same three arias every evening for ten years for the benefit of two feeble-minded kings, and he was reputed to have cured Philip V of melancholia. Later, a wealthy man, he retired to his palace in Italy.

BAROQUE OPERA

In the Baroque opera the technique of operatic staging was firmly established, and the devices developed in this period, such as wings and borders, backdrops and machines, are still in use today. But by the beginning of the eighteenth century, staging, like singing, had become so much an end in itself that Servandoni could mount whole spectacles as *spectacles de décoration,* with moving scenery and without any people. What must be noted above all, however, is that opera as it developed in the Baroque age became ever more completely the antithesis of the Greek idea. It was sheer social entertainment. Plots were taken from sources entirely foreign to the feelings of the people. Music fell far short of expressing the dramatic import of the text and became purely personal in purpose. As for scenic production, the singing, acting, scenery, and costumes served chiefly one end—their own effectiveness; they were not harnessed to the purpose of the drama. There came a point where Baroque opera had traveled so far from the origins of opera that a reaction was bound to come. And since opera was a function of the court society of the time, the reform of opera was destined to spring from the same sources which were to rise up against the political decadence of the age.

REACTION AGAINST BAROQUE OPERA

It was the progress of science and philosophy which broke the ground for the development of the new sociological ideas which were to overthrow the decadent order of absolute monarchies that had been all-powerful in the Baroque period. In the eighteenth century the foundation of a new democratic society was laid. Montesquieu, Voltaire, the Encyclopedists, and Rousseau with his reflections on the artificiality of culture, the equality of men, and the return to nature, took up the cudgels for freedom and the liberation of the downtrodden.

Traces of this growing sentiment were found in Germany, too. In the north the language and culture of the French were imitated, and Voltaire was a frequent guest at the court of the king in Berlin. In the south the new ideas were reflected in the liberal regime of Emperor Joseph II in Vienna, which witnessed the great period of classic music in the works of Gluck, Haydn, and Mozart.

It was only natural that reforms in courtly society should be mirrored in the art which had become its characteristic expression—the opera. Between the years 1720 and 1740 opposition to Baroque opera mounted, and the literary champions of the Age of Reason became its bitterest critics. In England Swift, Pope, and especially Addison ridiculed the Baroque opera. In Italy Benedetto Marcello wrote his famous pamphlet *Il teatro alla mode* (the theater *à la mode*) in which he poked fun at the egocentric behavior of the various participants in opera: authors, composers, managers, singers, and scenic artists. His booklet sounds like a modern satire on grand opera. He writes: "The subject matter of the opera will include prisons, daggers, poisons, letters, bear-hunts, bull-fights, earthquakes, bows and arrows, sacrifices, and insanities, because by such unheard-of events the public will be more than ordinarily excited." Of the *castrato* he writes, "Singing the aria, he may well decide that he will pause where and when he pleases, in the cadenza improvising such passages and embellishments that the orchestra director lifts his hands from the harpsichord and takes a pinch of snuff while he awaits the pleasure of the *divo*. He will treat the dramatic action according to his own caprice, since the modern artist need not understand the sentiments expressed in his own words, nor trouble himself to co-operate by gestures or movements.

"On singing the *da capo* he will change the whole aria to suit himself even though his changes have no connection whatever with the harmony of the author or the convenience of the orchestra players and though these variations may even include a change of tempo. No one cares, since the composer of the music is resigned to anything."

DEMOCRATIC REFORM OF OPERA

The new liberal ideas that had grown up in the eighteenth century finally led to the revolutionary rearrangement of the existing social order in the direction of the dream of democracy. As one of the by-products of this development, there came about also a democratic reform in the opera. This took the following forms:

1. The creation of folk operas in Italy, France, England, Germany, and, as a carry-over from developments in England, America.
2. The simplification of grand opera by Gluck, who reverted to the classic models of ancient and early Florentine musical dramas.
3. The creation of the masterworks of Mozart and Beethoven, as a result of the important fusion of the fresh source material of folk opera and the elaborate technical perfection of grand opera in the great Viennese school.

ITALIAN FOLK OPERA

While at certain periods the art of the drama has been brought to great heights by outstanding men, the eternal stream of folk drama has flowed continuously through history. The popular and more ephemeral plays of the folk theater have always cast the immortal types of human character—the lover, the clever servant, the stupid master, and the braggart soldier—embodying them in simple plays with improvised dialogue, folk tunes, and dances, on simple stages, from the age of primitive dancing and the ancient mime to the medieval theater and the *commedia dell' arte* of the Renaissance. Southern Italy was fertile ground for the folk play, as it had been the place of ancient folk comedies; and comic operas, including street scenes, dialect, and folk tunes, had thrived in the Neapolitan folk theaters as early as the seventeenth century. Comic elements soon wormed their way into grand opera in Venice and Rome, and became incorporated in separate scenes called *intermezzi*. The Italian *commedia dell' arte* players strolling through Europe had in their repertory parodies on the artificiality of grand opera, of which they made great capital, and as early as the latter part of the seventeenth century an Italian troupe at the court of Louis XIV performed in French travesties of whole Lully operas, with an admixture of original music and street songs. France called this version of the song-play, as distinguished from serious opera, *opéra comique*. Because Italian comedians had dared to criticize Madame de Maintenon, the mistress of the king, they were banned for a time.

THE BEGGAR'S OPERA

By 1716 they were again restored to grace in Paris, and in London they gave performances so successful as to inspire in 1728 an English attempt at song-play, *The Beggar's Opera* by John Gay and Pepusch—a parody on grand opera and its social patronage. The hero is a bandit leader, has six wives, and lives by robbery in collusion with the police. He is caught and sentenced to hanging, but to avoid a gruesome finale which, had it been carried through, might have weighed down an audience which wanted its entertainment light and gay, the hero is pardoned.

Since Baroque opera usually began with a prologue in praise of its august patron, *The Beggar's Opera,* not to be outdone, also had a prologue, represented not by a mythological figure as was customary in opera, but by a beggar, who began by emphasizing his humble descent, saying: "If poverty be a title to poetry, I am sure nobody can dispute mine. I myself am one of the company of beggars." And he goes on to say: "I hope I may be forgiven that I have not made my opera throughout unnatural like those *en vogue;* for I have no recitative." *The Beggar's Opera* had dialogue instead of recitatives, and popular songs, marches, dances, and English ballads instead of *da capo* arias. It was thus known as a "ballad-opera."

The production met with enormous success. Within two months it had already been given thirty-six times. Within the next twelve years more than one hundred ballad-operas were written, and when in its further development the form was extended, it retained its genuine character of opera with dialogue. There has never been any English grand opera which has become part of the international repertoire. But the tradition of English ballad-opera contributed notably to the beginnings of opera in America, which derived from *The Beggar's Opera* through the works of Arne, Bishop, Shield, etc., and on through the light operas of Gilbert and Sullivan and Victor Herbert.

It is interesting to trace the important contributions made by these simple comic operas to the later development of opera. In Italy the *intermezzi* became separate comedies in song, filling the entr'actes of serious opera, and the *opera buffa* originated (in contrast to *opera seria*). Pergolesi's *La Serva padrona* (The Maid Rules the Master, produced in 1733) was the first comic opera to be given all over the world, and it is still performed. The same simple form is preserved in another of Pergolesi's works, *Il Maestro di musica* (The Music Master), a less familiar but no less masterly opera.

FRENCH OPÉRA COMIQUE

With these works as a model, France began to develop folk opera of its own, and it is not strange that in the same year that brought Pergolesi opera to Paris Rousseau wrote the first modern French *opéra comique, Le Devin du village* (The Village Fortune-teller), a very successful work in which he used chansons, romances, and rondeaux in folk style, carrying on the traditions of French musical song-play, which went back to the thirteenth-century play *Robin et Marion*. With his *Devin du village,* Rousseau laid the basis for a French folk opera which would keep pace with the bourgeois drama that Diderot had brought to the middle classes. *Opéra comique,* the realistic musical play with dialogue, was established as a democratic counterpart of the exclusive grand opera.

GERMAN SINGSPIEL

The development of folk opera in Germany followed a similar course in the eighteenth century, and was responsible for the rapid ascendancy of German opera. In 1727 Heinrich Koch performed the German Singspiel *Der Teufel ist los* (The Devil Is Loose), which followed the English ballad-opera *The Devil to Pay* by Coffey. This play was adapted by Weisse and Standfuss, and later by Johann Adam Hiller, the progenitors of German folk opera, which, after the manner of the English and the French, combined simple dialogue stories with songs, the tunes of which were sung at inns and in the streets. These Singspiele belonged to the theater of the spoken word rather than to the musical stage. German folk opera was waging a hard struggle to subdue the dominance of foreign opera and drama, and unlike its competitor it did not enjoy the favor of the courts. The singers were actors, and a contemporary report says that Hiller did not write for singers but for actors who otherwise "would not dream of singing even while drinking their wine." But in spite of its modest and pristine appearance, the Singspiel was a creative fount from which Germany drew much of the vitality that flowed into the masterworks of Mozart, Beethoven, and Weber.

GLUCK AND MUSIC DRAMA

The creation of folk opera given in the vernacular in Italy, France, and England grew out of the liberal ideas of the Age of Reason, and this "back to nature" influence, so strong in folk opera, was not without effect on grand opera itself. Reform attacked the strongholds of grand opera and made it turn back to the simple and classic conceptions of its Florentine founders. This return is inseparably associated with the name of Christoph Willibald von Gluck.

Gluck, having written many operas in Italian style and some French *opéras comiques,* suddenly changed to a different style and wrote his *Orfeo* in Vienna in 1762. This constituted a noteworthy reform in grand opera, a return to the simplicity of pure musical drama molded along classic lines and thus to the ideals of opera's Florentine founders. As such, it paralleled the classicism which appeared in all fields of art in the middle of the eighteenth century—in architecture, painting, literature, and drama. It sprang abruptly from the desire to revert to the true, simple, and natural forms—"back to nature"—in the manner of the classics.

From Vienna Gluck went to Paris, where he became the center of the new French school. For Paris he wrote, in French, the two operas on Iphigénie, *Armide* and *Echo et Narcisse,* and made new versions of *Orfeo* (rewriting the title role for a tenor, while the Viennese version had stuck to the Italian tradition of the *castrato*) and *Alceste.* In these works Gluck returned to the principles of truthful musical drama. His ideas on the reform of opera are expressed in his famous forewords to *Alceste* and *Paride ed Elena.* "I strove," he wrote in the first one, "to lead music back to its true task, which is to support the poem in order to strengthen the expression of the feelings and the interest in the situations without interrupting the action. With regard to the arias and coloraturas, I wanted to ban all those misuses against which healthy common sense and true taste have fought so long."

Characteristically, Gluck, like Lully before him, took care of the direction of the performances himself. With greatest exactness he

rehearsed the orchestral passages again and again, and insisted on careful co-ordination with the scenic designer, ballet master, and stage
mechanics. Influenced by Noverre and the French drama, he laid great
stress on the action, and it is interesting that he chose the soubrette
Bernasconi for the part of Alceste, preferring the natural emotion of
a singer of the *opera buffa* to the artificial prima-donna type.

The reform of Gluck was a result of the Age of Reason, and his
style and ideals were preserved for some time, particularly in France,
by the composers Sacchini, Salieri, Cherubini, and others. Yet gods and
mythical heroes could still have meaning only for the well educated,
that is, the upper class. A significant change had taken place, however.
Opposition to social privilege and corruption was rising; the Third
Estate was demanding an equal place in the social order. The progress
of science, and the new and greater courage of the people to criticize the
social regime, heralded the outbreak of a revolutionary movement which
cried out for equal rights for all.

THE MINGLING OF FOLK AND GRAND OPERA

With the rise of liberal ideas at the end of the Baroque period,
grand opera—*opera seria*—ceased to exist, and even the genius of
Mozart in his opera *La Clemenza di Tito* could not revive it. The use
of Greek subjects disappeared almost completely for a century. The
revolutionary impetus behind folk opera absorbed the more elaborate
apparatus of grand opera, and in the latter half of the eighteenth century folk opera expanded, taking on more comprehensive subjects and
forms than it had known in the days of its simple beginnings. The
depiction of a pristine world gave way to the treatment of national
historical themes and the expression of contemporary emotion. Opera
then became a voice of the people and of their time.

In Germany a similar expansion of the technique of folk opera
and assimilation of that of grand opera were evident in the foundation
of the national opera given in German, beginning with the Singspiele
of Hiller, of which the operas of Mozart, Beethoven, Weber, and
Wagner were all descendants. In the last fifty years of the eighteenth
century German drama and theater were rising to prominence.

FOLK OPERA IN VIENNA

Vienna at this time was the greatest music city. Here the folk
theater was specially important, and the "high" theater never lost touch
with it. From the days of the first folk stages under Stranitzky at the

beginning of the eighteenth century, the tradition continues through the folk theater of Kurz, for which Haydn wrote his Singspiel *Der neue krumme Teufel*, in 1751, and Schikaneder's theater, for which Mozart wrote *Die Zauberflöte*, to the fairy tales and comedies of Raimund and Nestroy, the operettas of Johann Strauss, and modern Viennese operetta.

In the folk theater of Vienna the Arlecchino of Italian *commedia dell' arte* became Kasperle; we know him in Mozart's Leporello and Papageno. The tradition behind the *commedia dell' arte* was combined with the gay and spirited humor of the Viennese, their sentiment, and their love of fairy tales, drama, and opera. Here the folk opera grew until a climax was reached when the Emperor Joseph II (1741-1790), in addition to supporting Italian opera, made his imperial Burgtheater the home for the "National Singspiel."

The encouragement of a liberal emperor, added to the generosity and artistic inclination of society and the interest of the public, produced that great synthesis of tradition and contemporary endeavor which we know as the Viennese "Classic" school of Haydn, Mozart, and Beethoven. This same unification is seen in the marriage of the elaborate technique of Baroque opera to the rising inspiration of folk opera, manifest in the works of Mozart, which symbolizes the true mission of old Austria, Vienna and Salzburg—the fusing of Italian and German cultures.

MOZART

Mozart was acutely aware of the human problems of his own time. He was never the naïve Rococo composer that the weight of Wagner's dramatic personality made him appear to many for a time. Ernst Lert, in his book *Mozart auf dem Theater*, has given valuable insight into Mozart's relation to the theater. Richard Strauss once said: "They blame me for always looking for sensational plots. Look at Mozart! He always picked subjects that pertained to his own time: the rising Third Estate in *Figaro*, the libertine in *Don Giovanni*, the ideas of tolerance and freemasonry in *The Magic Flute!*" The truth is that Mozart's masterworks are not concerned with Greek mythology, but are in close touch with the feeling of his time. The man who could not remain in servitude to the Archbishop of Salzburg had a heartfelt understanding of the political and artistic problems of his day.

Die Entführung aus dem Serail (1782) was the first important German opera. It was produced, in the face of the scheming opposition of the Italian faction in Vienna, by special order of the Emperor. Mozart's next opera, *Le Nozze di Figaro*, in Italian, met with the same opposition. The libretto of this work was a most sensational drama of Beaumarchais, sensational in that it expressed rampant political tension. Here the seething of a downtrodden multitude broke through to the surface in a barely concealed rebellion against aristocratic privilege. In another way, too, this opera was a startling novelty: it was in the modern dress of the period. Mozart took part in the staging of his operas himself; to him singing and acting were a single unit.

Prague gave Mozart and his *Figaro* a reception of the greatest enthusiasm, and the grateful composer wrote his next opera, *Don Giovanni*, for that city. In this *dramma giocoso* the characteristics of the Italian opera, *seria* and *buffa*, were brought together in a play Shakespearean in its variety. *Così fan tutte*, an Italian *opera buffa* very refined in its psychology, followed, and after unsuccessfully attempting to revive *opera seria* with his opera *La Clemenza di Tito*, Mozart set his hand to the composition of *Die Zauberflöte* (The Magic Flute) for the folk theater of Schikaneder. Originally this was to be just another of the fairy tales familiar in the folk theater, frolicsome and full of magic. But Mozart found in it a wonderful opportunity to illustrate the struggle of human beings to better themselves, the fight between good and evil, and the liberal ideas of brotherhood which were current in this period. The opera is in fourteen scenes, from the realm of the Queen of the Night to that of the Sun; it is full of symbols of human sanctity and wisdom. Held together by dialogue, all forms of music were united: simple folk songs for Papageno's naïve joy and sorrow, brilliant Italian coloratura arias for the Queen of the Night, music in the style of Gluck for the priests, and a choral fantasy in the manner of Bach for the mystic trial by fire and water. *Die Zauberflöte* runs the whole gamut of the human soul; it is the true folk opera, and as such it found no small place in the hearts of Beethoven, Goethe, and Wagner.

BEETHOVEN

Mozart's masterworks reflected the emotion of the time, and in their gentleness lay their strength. Beethoven, on the other hand, never subdued the great passion for freedom which pounded in his heart. He symbolized it, in *Fidelio*, in the suffering of the innocent political prisoner, hoping for deliverance through the heroic effort of a loving woman. Beethoven loathed tyrants and all they stood for, and in *Fidelio* Romantic protest burst the bonds of Classic reserve. Based upon

Bouilly's French libretto for Gaveaux's *Léonore, ou L'Amour conjugal,* Beethoven's opera maintained the heritage of the German Singspiel, with spoken dialogue. But, more important, it was a heroic outpouring of the revolutionary feeling that was rife at the time, and the vehemence of its vocal and orchestral expression struck out on a new path that was to lead to Wagner's work.

EFFECTS OF FOLK OPERA

The new folk opera was ultimately an enormously creative force in the development of later opera. It had new blood in its veins; it stemmed from the people. It replaced the stagnant artificiality of aristocratic Baroque opera, which was decaying. The pompousness of antique gods and heroes gave way to realistic portrayals straight from the hearts of a simple people. Powdered wigs were relegated to the cupboards. At first it was only the comic song-play which introduced more dramatic truthfulness into opera. This was given in dialogue form, with music interpolated when directly called for by the emotional situations. The wave of realism swept away the *castrati,* and the virtuoso coloratura roulades of the prima donnas. Singing was now a natural medium of expression in drama, not music for the sole sake of musical effect. The more natural-sounding baritone and bass voices, once used only in minor parts, now achieved equal importance with the tenor and soprano. Mozart gave the title roles of *Don Giovanni* and *Figaro* to the lower voices. The natural interpretation of the dramatic content influenced the musical treatment, enriching the harmony, melody, rhythm, and instrumentation. An endless variety of new musical forms took the place of artificial coloraturas interspersed with realistic *parlando* singing—an imitation of chattering best known in Mozart's *Marriage of Figaro* and Rossini's *Barber of Seville*—and the sedate chain of *da capo* arias gave way to a variety of songs, cavatinas, romances, comic arias, duets, and ensembles of from three to six voices, while the Finale became a climax which in masterworks like Mozart's *Figaro* was notable for its lifelike musical portrayal.

The more true-to-life approach of folk opera called for natural acting, scenery, and costumes. This opera centered around a dramatic idea, of which every element now became the servant—not, as formerly, the master.

The national pride and patriotism of the people of the nineteenth century was preceded and in part brought about by the spiritual movement called Romanticism. Though it appears in different countries in various forms, its traits are substantially the same everywhere. New national schools of literature, music, theater, and operatic art were founded not only in France, Italy, England, and Germany, but also in Russia, Poland, Bohemia, Hungary, and the Nordic countries.

WEBER

Weber (1786–1826) carried on the German Singspiel tradition which had begun with Hiller and which had been continued in Mozart's *Magic Flute* and Beethoven's *Fidelio*. In *Der Freischütz* he composed the true German Romantic opera with dialogue. The huntsmen's choruses voice the spirit of the volunteer huntsmen corps in the War of Liberation, while every strain of the opera shows the deep feeling for nature characteristic of Romanticism in general and of its German branch in particular. The scene in the wolf's glen is remarkable not only for the new orchestral effects which give it its demoniacal character, but also for the fact that the entire scene is composed as a single musical unit. This same principle of composition is even more elaborately worked out in Weber's *Euryanthe,* which was clearly the model for Richard Wagner's musicodramatic technique. According to Weber, *Euryanthe* is a "purely dramatic attempt, which intends its effect to come only from the combination of all the related arts, and which would be futile if stripped of their assistance." It is not a dialogue opera but is composed with recitatives throughout.

OPERA IN PARIS

Paris at this time was the real capital of Europe. Although the Bourbons had been restored to the throne in 1814, the spirit of individual freedom could not be totally repressed. The revolutionary movements of 1830 and 1848 spread from Paris to other European states. From the time when Charles X had been defeated in his attempt to restore absolute monarchy and deposed, Paris had been the meeting place for the free thinkers of Europe. Heine, Liszt, Chopin, Rossini, Meyerbeer, and Offenbach, all made Paris their home. Bellini and Donizetti, Verdi and Wagner, all composed for Paris audiences.

The emotional flare-up of the revolution before and after July, 1830, again charged grand opera with vitality. Romantic historical subjects were given a prominent place, especially by Scribe, an expert librettist, and theatrical and vocal effects were combined in the staging of brilliant spectacles. This was the era of the modern grand opera of

Auber, Rossini, Halévy, and Meyerbeer. Auber's *La Muette de Portici,* written in 1828, created a sensation with its realistic treatment of Italian local color—its fishermen's songs, dances, and chorus scenes. The fact that its title part was a deaf-mute was a courageous departure from operatic routine. But its violent plot, involving the insurrection of an oppressed people against tyranny, was even bolder, and the Brussels performance of this work is said to have set off the Belgian revolution of 1830. No less exciting was Rossini's *William Tell,* which he wrote for the Paris Opéra. The overture, the choruses, and especially the oath taken at Rütli, with its dramatic treatment, are still effective today. Halévy's *La Juive,* a study in dramatic contrasts, confronting Cardinal and ghetto Jew, follows in this same line—a line which is climaxed by the work of Meyerbeer.

MEYERBEER

Meyerbeer was a German-Jewish composer, born in Berlin in 1791. He studied in Germany, worked for a time in Italy, and then went to Paris. Among the grand operas which he wrote for that city are *Robert le Diable, Les Huguenots, Le Prophète,* and *L'Africaine.* In them Meyerbeer combined against a romantically historical background the French sense of the theater with Italian vocal and German orchestral techniques, to produce a striking result. Scenic contrasts, mass effects, ballets—ballets of nuns in *Robert* and of ice-skaters in *Le Prophète*—and brilliant vocal devices for the soloists molded the traditions of Baroque opera to a more democratic conception, reflecting the society which was entering upon an era of industrialism and commerce. The art of grand opera, of achieving theatrical effectiveness in the treatment of plots and of solo and mass scenes, was studied by all the great opera composers of the time. It is inconceivable that either Verdi's *Aïda* or Wagner's works would have been as successful as they were without this technique.

ITALIAN OPERA OF THE 19TH CENTURY

The Italian opera of the nineteenth century likewise mirrored in many ways the ups and downs of Italian politics, and in both fields Romanticism was an active force. Paris was the great center to which Italian composers looked for recognition. The outstanding Italian composers of the Romantic era—Cherubini, Spontini, Rossini, Bellini, Donizetti, and Verdi—all wrote operas for Paris. Politically, too, France influenced Italy strongly. The French revolutions of 1830 and

1848 spurred the Italians into a revolt of their own; their spirited battles for independence from Austrian domination finally won, they founded the United Kingdom of Italy in 1861.

ROSSINI

After Napoleon's downfall the echoes of his triumphs began to die out in Italian opera as in France. The mass scenes and fanfares familiar in the operas of Simon Mayr gave way to Romanticism in the operas of Mercadante and Pacini. But it was the popularity of Rossini's works which best showed the mood of a world now tired of struggle and ready to sit back and enjoy life. His melodious comic operas, of which *L'Italiana in Algeri* and *La Cenerentola* were the most popular, were heard enthusiastically throughout Europe and in America; they still provide excellent musical entertainment. The first performance of his masterpiece, *The Barber of Seville*, in Rome, was a fiasco, but later it made its mark in musical history so successfully that Paisiello's already famous opera of the same name was eclipsed. Of Rossini's serious operas, *Tancredi, Otello, Mosè in Egitto*, and a host of others, only one, *William Tell*, his last stage work, seems fresh today. It is perhaps no accident, but a fact revealing essential traits of his character, that after he composed this work he could go into retirement, at the age of thirty-seven, and in the remaining thirty-nine years composed hardly at all, living only for the companionship of his friends and their witty conversation, and concocting rare and tasty samples of his own cooking.

DONIZETTI AND BELLINI

After Rossini's retirement, Donizetti became his successor, and in the casualness (often even carelessness) with which he wrote melodies he followed faithfully in Rossini's footsteps. His *L'Elisir d'amore* and particularly *Don Pasquale* are among the masterworks of the *opera buffa*. *La Fille du régiment*, still popular, was written for the French Opéra Comique. *Lucia di Lammermoor*, one of his serious works, has long been admired in spite of the fact that its story, based on a novel by Walter Scott, is a grotesque medley of suicide, murder, and madness. However, ghoulish though the story was, it offered opportunities for some brilliant coloraturas. It is interesting to remember that the piano score of Donizetti's *La Favorita*, written for the Paris Opéra, was made for the publisher Schlesinger by none other than Richard Wagner. Bellini, who died when he was only thirty-four, had a fine and poetic musical talent which is best sensed in his opera *Norma*, and Wagner and Chopin were among the admirers of his melodic gift. *La Sonnambula* and *I Puritani* are, like *Lucia,* concerned with madness and renunciation, and in these works Romantic opera finds its *reductio ad absurdum.* But Rossini, Donizetti, and Bellini, in their preoccupation with effects of vocal virtuosity, form a single group.

VERDI

Verdi represents the climax of Italian Romantic opera. His earlier works reflect the excitement of the Italian revolution and their fiery melodies are echoes of the forging of Italian freedom under Cavour and Garibaldi, who fought for the United Kingdom of Italy under Victor Emmanuel. The unison choruses of *Nabucodonosor* and *I Lombardi* were so simple and vigorous in style that the tunes were sung and whistled on the streets. The music and story of the familiar tenor aria *Di quella pira* from *Il Trovatore,* which tells of the fire from which Manrico fights to save his mother, were more to the contemporary audience than just another operatic scene: in them they felt a symbol of their own struggle. The very initials of their political motto, *Viva Emmanuele Re d'Italia,* spelled the name of VERDI.

Verdi's choice of subjects frequently ran afoul of the censors. In *Le Roi s'amuse* (*Rigoletto*) and in *Un Ballo in maschera,* in which Scribe had dramatized the assassination of King Gustav III of Sweden, the composer became embroiled with the censorship and finally had to bow to certain changes in the libretto, which, in the case of *Un Ballo in maschera,* changed the whole sense of the opera and transplanted the locale of the story to Boston! Verdi wrote four operas for Paris—*Jerusalem, Les Vêpres siciliennes,* a new version of *Macbeth,* and *Don Carlos*—and his association with the style of French grand opera is evident in the orchestration and in the spectacular treatment of masses in *Aïda,* which he composed for the opening of the Suez Canal at Cairo in 1871. Then, after an interlude of sixteen years, the seventy-four-year-old master wrote *Otello,* and at eighty he created the unsurpassed comedy of *Falstaff.* In these two works Verdi's great psychological insight and his talent for conveying his meaning in musical terms brought the realistic Italian opera to its musical and dramatic zenith. In this, Verdi's reform ran parallel to Wagner's.

But Verdi approached the problem from a different angle. His greatest resource was the power of true vocal melody. The melodies were never written for musical effect alone, but were clearly conceived to achieve the dramatic intent. In 1848, when Verdi was only thirty-five, he wrote the librettist Cammarano regarding his *Macbeth*: "The part of Lady Macbeth has been assigned to Tadolini, and I am much surprised that she should lend herself to it. You know how much I esteem Tadolini and she knows it herself, but in our common interest I would consider it necessary to think this over a bit. Tadolini has too great qualities for the part! Tadolini's appearance is good and beautiful and I would like to have Lady Macbeth deformed and ugly. Tadolini is a perfectionist in her singing, and I would like to have her not sing at all. Tadolini has a marvelously bright, clear voice, and I should like to have for Lady Macbeth a stifled, hollow, harsh voice. The voice of Tadolini has the quality of an angel; the voice of the Lady needs something of the devil."

Verdi's letters, compositions, and whole manner of life show him to have been the "peasant of Roncole" which he liked to call himself. Like Mozart, he was able to achieve the perfect and complete combination of drama and music, and even though his later works were colored to a degree by the orchestral technique and harmony of Wagner, he remained unalterably Italian and was to the Italian opera what Wagner was to the German.

WAGNER

Richard Wagner was born in the same year as Verdi, 1813, in the year and place (Leipzig) of Napoleon's defeat. The span of Wagner's life saw the rise of German power up to the victory over the French in 1871 and the founding of the German Empire. Wagner, who became the great master of German opera, used the tools that had been evolved from the simplest beginnings through Mozart's *Magic Flute,* Weber's *Freischütz,* and the achievements of German symphonic music. Further, he combined these with the apparatus developed in the operas of all countries, from the early musical drama of Gluck to the French and Italian grand opera of the Spontini-Meyerbeer period. To all these elements Wagner added the rich plot material of Romantic poetry, the influence of Schopenhauer's and Feuerbach's philosophy, the ever-widening range of historical knowledge, and the latest achievements of realistic scenic production on the theater stage. All these elements he put into the caldron of his reform, the goal of which was the return of opera to the ideal of music drama (all the elements of the opera to serve dramatic expression). In pursuit of this idea, he not only wrote both words and music but with incredible perseverance and energy organized the actual performance of his works, conscripting the aid of his friends and every available means, and even supervising the building of his own opera house, the Festspielhaus in Bayreuth.

Wagner's participation in the May revolution of 1849 made him a political outcast, and he was forced to flee Germany and to spend twelve years in exile. It was during this time that he worked out his revolutionary theories. The fundamental demand of his essay "Art and Revolution" was that art should be recognized as a social document of folk expression, as it had been in Greece, and not as mere social entertainment. In another article, "Opera and Drama," he reiterated his belief that music and scenic art should be subordinated to the drama.

He early conceived the idea of a festival theater to give model performances, but it was years before he could realize this dream. Meanwhile he produced a new version of *Tannhäuser* for the Paris Opéra, but it was withdrawn after three performances, as the result of too great opposition and intrigue. In Munich, where he had found an enthusiastic patron in Ludwig II, he performed his new *Tristan und Isolde* and *Die Meistersinger von Nürnberg* with Hans von Bülow conducting. Plans for a festival theater here had to be given up again because of strong opposition. But finally, in 1876, he did succeed in opening his private Festspielhaus on a hill in Bayreuth with the *Bühnenfestspiel* (festival play) *Der Ring des Nibelungen*. His last work, *Parsifal*, followed in 1882, originally intended as a sacred festival play to be given only in Bayreuth. It was but a year later that Wagner died, having accomplished, through his tremendous driving determination, nearly all he had set out to do.

Wagner's main goal was the reform of opera into drama based on the "simple human" element. Although the Florentine founders of opera and later Gluck had had the same purpose, they used plots from antiquity whereas Wagner used the saga and history of his own people. Setting out from the one basic principle that drama should be the basis of opera, Wagner waged his battle for reform with impressive consequences, the story of which is told in the systematic inclusion of all the elements of music and scenic production—voice, words, orchestration, acting, scenery, costumes, lighting, and finally the theater building itself.

Wagner tolerated no indulgence in song for the sake of song or music for the sake of music, and consequently never wanted the dialogue or recitative separated from the aria, but rather united with it as "dramatic melody." He said: "In my opera there is no difference between the recited and sung phrases; my declamation is song and my song, declamation." This uninterrupted dramatic melody, which led to the dissolution of "absolute" musical forms, is supported by an orchestra developed from that of Beethoven and Weber. In Wagner this orchestra had the role of the ancient chorus: it was the commentator on the development of the drama. The freedom of the singer to ornament his songs at will (the *cantar al mente*) was abolished, and every note in the recitative became precisely measured. Great importance was laid on good diction. Wagner wrote Julius Hey, who as "technical voice adviser" assisted him at the Bayreuth rehearsals: "The indisputable fact that an exhaustive study of language is a fundamental of the German art-song must be recognized." Hey, in his book *Deutscher Gesangsunterricht* (German Singing Method), declares that German song, in contrast to Italian method, should develop the tone from the word. Wagner, considering the drama as the essence of opera, once went so far as to demand that opera and drama should be played by a single company, and requested that parts be read at rehearsals, saying: "The singer ought first to recite his part correctly before attempting to sing it." Wagner's great plea before the opening performance of the *Ring* in Bayreuth was imparted in a bulletin board notice to his singers which read: "LAST REQUEST of my dear colleagues. Enunciation! The long notes will take care of themselves; the small notes and their meaning are what matter."

Wagner was extremely exacting in his requirements of acting. During his time the famous German theater group sponsored by the Duke of Meiningen achieved sensational success, owing to the careful preparation of their realistic acting and their authentic historical costumes and scenery. Wagner introduced the same attitude into opera, giving it true-to-life acting and banishing the humbug of stereotyped operatic gestures. Since his music followed the drama without the stops imposed by the old "closed" forms, the action could be developed with ease and naturalness. However, the gestures were still grandiloquent, like the speeches of the bearded patriots of the time haranguing their parliaments. Photographs of the period show such famous Wagnerian singers as Albert Niemann and Schnorr von Carolsfeld in the roles of Lohengrin and Tristan as imposing figures with luxurious beards, while the Brünnhildes and the Isoldes resembled the Germania of countless heavy German sculptures.

In order to assure coherence of acting and music, Wagner gave exact directions as to how he wanted this unity to be brought about, frequently tying certain gestures and movements to the corresponding musical phrases. He applied the rule of realistic acting to the chorus as well. He called the old opera chorus "scenic machinery made to walk and sing, and the mute splendor of scenery transformed to moving noise." He changed all this and, like the Meiningen group in their famous mass scenes, made the chorus a living part of the drama, as in *Lohengrin* and particularly in the very realistic flogging scene at the end of Act II in *Die Meistersinger*. For the ballet, too, he found a dramatic function in the Bacchanal of *Tannhäuser*.

As early as 1851, Wagner wrote: "Our theatrical institutions have in general no greater purpose than the proffering of entertainment, repeated night after night, uninspired and responding to no intense desire, but forced on the public as a business speculation, and accepted perfunctorily by the bored society of our large cities. Everything which, from a purely artistic standpoint, has been at odds with this conception of the theater, has always been in vain." From this time on, the idea of a theater developed rapidly in his mind and, with the will power and tireless effort which he applied to everything he did, he finally achieved the Festspielhaus in Bayreuth. The very design of the theater was certainly the creation of a genius.

With a single blow, Wagner smashed the tradition of the Italian court opera-box theater, the style of which had been almost universal since the building of San Cassiano in Venice in 1637. The old opera house in Bayreuth, built by Giuseppe Galli-Bibbiena in 1748, offers the most striking contrast to the Wagner theater on the hill above the city. The old building is a resplendent example of the old-style court theater. Around the center box, where sat the reigning prince, were situated the seats reserved for local aristocrats, divided into tiers and boxes corresponding to the rank of their occupants. The center box is actually the only one which allows the stage to be seen from the proper angle, and the lower the spectator in the social scale, the farther from the ruler he sat and the more distorted the stage picture became. This system and the splendor of the auditorium itself point to the importance of the audience rather than the stage. How different from the Wagner theater! In 1849 Wagner wrote with regard to the form of modern theater buildings that there were "traditional conventions which have nothing to do with the requirements of pure art." In 1862 he published his plan for a temporary theater, with an amphitheatrical auditorium and invisible orchestra. The cornerstone of the Festspielhaus was laid in 1872 and the theater opened in 1876.

In the construction of this theater there was one guiding thought—

an unrestricted view of the stage from every seat in the house. To this end the auditorium was kept within unpretentious bounds, and the floor raised in amphitheatrical rows. There were no side boxes, and the view of the stage was unobstructed by the lowered and now invisible orchestra, in accordance with an idea suggested by the architect Schinkel in 1841. Since one seat was no better than another, all were sold at the same price. Derived from the Greek theater, this auditorium belonged to no one class of society, but to all classes. The auditorium was no longer the most important part of the theater; instead, attention was centered on the stage. Great pains were taken to make the stage function as adequately as possible, and it was equipped with every means to facilitate the technical side of production. This whole theater was far ahead of its time—an artistic and democratic solution of the theater problem, which had hitherto scarcely been touched. Yet for more than fifty years afterward, in great capitals, opera-theaters continued to be built in the old style, just as though there had been no social change to warrant a new conception of the theater.

CZECH OPERA

In countries where the national idea was suppressed by the domination of a foreign government opera was one of the means of expression by the people. The Czechs, throttled by Austrian rule, spoke through the operas of Smetana. The spirit of this musical country, whose people are sentimental and at the same time exuberant in their dances, is well portrayed not only in the melodious *Bartered Bride,* which has become the Czech national opera, but also in other operas not so well known. In the twentieth century, Jaromir Weinberger's melodious *Schwanda, the Bagpiper* follows the tradition of Czech folk opera, and the Moravian Janaček composed the vigorous peasant operas *Jenufa, Kata Kabanova,* the *Memoirs of a Dead-House,* based on Dostoevski's novel, and the poetic and altogether lovable animal-story opera, *The Crafty Little Fox.*

RUSSIAN OPERA

The Romantic period in Russia is connected with the literary field, particularly with the poet Pushkin. It was in this era that revolt began to stir, as the people strove for freedom from the powers which repressed them, and kept Russia separate from the countries of western Europe. The growing national feeling is clearly expressed in Glinka's *Life for the Czar,* in which he used folk melodies freely. This opera and his *Russlan and Ludmilla* are still popular works in the Russian repertory. Dargomijsky's *Rusalka* (Watersprite), another Romantic opera, was followed by many which are well known in America— Tchaikovsky's *Eugen Onegin* and *Pique Dame*, Borodin's *Prince Igor*, Rimsky-Korsakov's *Sadko*, *Le Coq d'or*, and *The Czar's Bride*, and Prokofiev's *Love for Three Oranges*. Mussorgsky's *Khovantchina* and *The Fair at Sorochintzy* are both interesting works which would be valuable adjuncts to a modern repertory, and *Boris Godunov* is among the most important works of the century. As folk drama it speaks naturally for the hearts and souls of the Russian people, using new, bold harmonies and rhythms. Except in Leningrad, *Boris* is unknown in the original form on the stage, as it is always given in the Rimsky-Korsakov version, which was written to remedy certain alleged weaknesses in the original. It is, nevertheless, an unfortunate distortion of the naturalness of this great work. The Soviet composer Shostakovitch, who himself has composed the vigorous *Lady Macbeth of Mzensk*, influenced by *Boris*, is said to have made a new version of Mussorgsky's masterwork. *Boris*, although now some seventy years old, pointed far into the future, both in its realistic expression of folk life and in its musical idiom.

NATURALISM IN OPERA

Bizet's *Carmen* was the first French opera to manifest naturalistic traits. This opera as it is usually given, as grand opera with recitatives, does not follow Bizet's original intention, for he composed it as *opéra comique* with dialogue, and it was the beautiful southern *limpidezza* of this form which Nietzsche so admired and which made *Carmen* for him the antithesis of Wagner's musical drama. But whereas the naturalistic details of *Carmen* are set in a Romantic background, the *verismo* of Mascagni's *Cavalleria rusticana* and Leoncavallo's *Pagliacci* are naturalistic in a brutal and theatrical manner which never fails to affect an audience. Giordano used this naturalistic technique in the operas *Mala vita* and *Fedora*, and it was excellently mastered by Puccini. In *Manon Lescaut*, in the moving and poetic *Bohème*, and in the sentimental *Madame Butterfly*, this composer's theatrical sense and melodic invention are no less effective than in the brutal *Tosca*, which was inspired by Sarah Bernhardt's performance of Sardou's drama, and in the movielike naturalism of *The Girl of the Golden West*, based on Belasco's production. Puccini wrote a masterpiece of comic opera in the one-act *Gianni Schicchi*, which with the realistic *Tabarro* and bitter-sweet *Suor Angelica* formed a triptych. Similar in style are the German-Italian composer Wolf-Ferrari's charming operas, *The Secret of Suzanne* and the *Quattro Rusteghi,* which belong among the best comic operas of modern repertoire and which follow Verdi's *Falstaff.* Puccini's *Turandot,* completed after the composer's death, by Alfano, was the last true grand opera.

IMPRESSIONISM

The attempt to convey to the mind of the spectator an impression and its psychological effect, rather than an actual picture, is called in painting Impressionism. In much the same spirit, Wagner in his *Tristan* expressed moods rather than details of dramatic development. There was very little action, but a rich symphonic palette of harmony and rhythm by which all the nuances of the psychological development of the characters could be subtly painted.

Debussy, in his *Pelléas et Mélisande,* carried on the precepts of Wagner's *Tristan* in a recitative style which recalled the first days of Florentine opera, though in a modern adaptation. He adhered closely to Maeterlinck's words, and expressed the finest shadings of mood by even greater and subtler subdivision of the harmonic material.

Pelléas was followed in France by Dukas' *Ariane et Barbe-Bleue,* and later by the more realistic approach of Ravel in his delightful *L'Heure espagnole.* The Hungarian Bartók (*The Castle of the Knight Bluebeard*), the Spaniard Falla (*La Vida breve*), and the Italians Respighi, Pizzetti, and Malipiero also wrote in the Impressionist style.

RICHARD STRAUSS

Generally speaking, the theater of the early twentieth century clung tenaciously to the old ways, as did the world of politics. Every conceivable method which had been developed for the Romantic and realistic stage was developed to the point of exhaustion, and the idea of Baroque opera was revived in the service of a new flourishing society, especially in Berlin, which blossomed with prosperity and well-being in the political ascendancy of the German Empire. The brilliancy of the Richard Strauss orchestra caught this spirit. Strauss brought the Wagnerian music drama to the extreme limits of intensity and realistic orchestration. In his operas *Salome* and *Elektra* the action is condensed into a one-act drama lasting only about an hour and forty minutes. The orchestration of *Salome* is exceptionally rich and colorful: it can illustrate everything from soft moonlight to the decapitation of John the Baptist. The stark realism of this giant orchestra was even surpassed in *Elektra,* composed in the same year in which Sigmund Freud published, in Vienna, his *Method of Psychoanalysis* and the poet Hofmannsthal applied the characterization of modern psychopathology to the drama of Sophocles.

Elektra represented a turning point in modern opera. There was hardly any way in which the human voice and the orchestra could be employed more realistically, just as it was impossible to outstrip the realistic effects of Max Reinhardt's scintillating Berlin productions: the real forest in *A Midsummer Night's Dream,* the real church in *The Miracle,* the mass scenes in *Oedipus.*

TWENTIETH-CENTURY TRENDS

The repercussions of *Elektra* presaged a new movement which was about to arise before the first World War, a movement representing the desire of individuals to indulge in the expression of their own sensitivities in order to create new forms. The fire of this new expressionism is seen in the music of Stravinsky's ballets (especially *Le Sacre du printemps*) written for Diaghilev's Russian ballet. The chaotic dream world of the Futurists and the paintings of Picasso are no less characteristic than Schönberg's music of a time when Einstein was questioning the fundamental concepts of physics, and the composer himself began to question the bases of the tonal system. The prescience of artists and scientists foretold the destruction of the Old World.

EXPRESSIONISM

In Vienna another group tried to make opera interpretative of its time by abandoning old methods and offering a completely new one, expressionistic in dramatic technique and atonal in music. This movement is exemplified in Schönberg's monodrama *Erwartung* (Expectation) and *Die glückliche Hand* (The Lucky Hand), which is like the slow-motion analysis of the psychological effect of an instant, in the form of a musical drama, and in the first opera written by his pupil Alban Berg, *Wozzeck.* These works represent the exhaustion and dissolution of *Tristan* harmony, though Berg tried to introduce a constructive element in the shape of musical forms like the fugue, passacaglia, etc., in each scene, and had much the same purpose in mind when he used Schönberg's twelve-tone technique. The success of these methods, however, is debatable, and I believe that the extraordinary effectiveness of Berg's music lies in his very subtle underscoring of the drama. Hindemith and Křenek in their earlier works subscribed to the theories of expressionism, although Hindemith in his opera *Cardillac* resorted to the medium of the polyphonic style.

NEOCLASSICISM

Even more important than this was an intellectualist trend to return to ancient models, among the young French artists led by the poet Jean Cocteau and the painter Picasso, who thought in terms of an emotionless mechanical world, and this movement became Neoclassicism. Its foremost example in the operatic field is seen in the Cocteau-Stravinsky "oratorio opera" *Oedipus Rex.* The basic idea of the theater, beginning with primitive dances and continuing until the theater of our own day, was that the spectator should identify himself more or less with the dramatic illusion, and be deeply engrossed in it. The Parisian *salon*-rebels opposed what they called this "passive" emotional enjoyment, and wished to replace it by a more "active" and detached attitude. They held that the drama and all that went into its production should be presented to the audience as an "objective" picture—distinctly separate from the audience, so that the spectator would not become emotionally involved in the subject, but could simply consider the ideas presented. Drama and listener being thus separated, a speaker was introduced as an intermediary between the two. To preclude any chance of the auditor's succumbing to the dramatic import, a Latin text was used, the content of which was summarized by the speaker, in the vernacular. Thus the "complete objectivity" of modern musical drama was perfected. In *Christophe Colomb,* by Paul Claudel and Darius Milhaud, the drama was performed by a combination of stage action and movie projection and was commented upon by a speaker to a neutral chorus which represented the audience. Milhaud's "minute operas" were based on a similar principle of "objective" music.

THE LEHRSTUCK

Bert Brecht used the idea of including the audience as participants in *Lehrstücke* (Lesson Pieces), one of which was set to music by Kurt Weill in *Der Jasager* (The Yes-Man) and another by Hindemith in his composition on the story of Lindbergh's New York-to-Paris flight. Hindemith uses the same idea in his school opera *We Build a City.* Kurt Weill made effective use of song-play and jazz in his modern version of *The Beggar's Opera* and his *Rise and Fall of the City of Mahagonny,* in which American folk tunes occur. Weill has carried on the same form of composition in the music he has written for Broadway musical productions.

MECHANICAL REALISM

Realistic subjects made their entrance into operatic plots in Křenek's *Jonny spielt auf,* in which there is a modern hotel, a railroad station, and a Negro jazz musician, and in Max Brand's opera *Maschinist Hopkins,* the story revolving around a machinist who kills his friend in a fit of jealousy and disposes of the corpse by throwing it into the wheels of a machine in a modern factory. In the night his guilt drives him back to the machine room, and a speaking chorus of machines chants his remorse. Hindemith's *Neues vom Tage* is similarly modern in theme. Two artists, man and wife, arrange for publicity purposes a scandal of adultery, with the help of a matrimonial agency, and the scenes are laid in a museum, a business office, etc., even including the discovery of a lady in a bathtub. One of his humorous sketches, *Hin und zurück* (Return Trip), involves the petty jealousy which besets a modern home. Even the serious Schönberg wrote a one-act modern opera, at the end of which a child asks: "Mother, what are 'modern people'?"

When the tension of political and social developments drove such men as Hindemith, Schönberg, Stravinsky, Korngold, Weill, Milhaud, Křenek, Weinberger, and many others to America, it seemed clear that the development of opera was at least temporarily ended in the Old World, and that its immediate future lay in the New.

SOCIAL BASIS OF EUROPEAN OPERA

Throughout its history opera in Europe has been an organic part of the political and social worlds which surrounded it. Since we have now brought this historical survey up to the present, or the immediate past, it may be well to review briefly the path it has followed.

Opera in its earliest years belonged to the aristocrats and nobility and was maintained by them in their courts, as we have seen. Later, when republics superseded monarchies, the states took over the opera houses and gave them the necessary financial support. Throughout Europe opera houses were maintained by government appropriations and were often administered by the Ministries of Education. In German-speaking countries the subsidies were very liberal. In 1931 in Germany there were eighty government-supported opera houses, twenty-one of which gave opera exclusively in daily performances, the remaining fifty-nine giving operettas and drama as well. Government interest and support had reached its peak in 1928. In that year Berlin, which already had the newly reconstructed State Opera House and City Opera House, opened its *third,* the Krolloper, under the direction of Otto Klemperer. That season in Germany broke all records. Sixty world premières were given. The government appropriation for opera was 60,000,000 marks, at that time some $15,000,000. The city of Frankfurt-am-Main, with some 450,000 inhabitants, spent 2,800,000 marks for its two theaters, one for opera, one for drama—and the greater portion of this sum went to the opera house. After 1929, when budgets were drastically reduced, the appropriation for opera was also cut. But, even after this, Frankfurt had in the year the author went there as stage director an annual allotment of 2,700,000 marks—about $700,000. And in the year 1931, when finances were at a low ebb, the total appropriation in Germany was over 40,000,000 marks—some $10,000,000. Austria, which was far from rich, allowed nearly a million dollars for the two Viennese state theaters in 1932, and even then the state had to make up an additional deficit. Basel, Switzerland, with no more than 150,000 inhabitants, managed to maintain a municipal theater which required about $150,000 a year. In Russia and Italy, too, opera was generously subsidized; even in France the subsidies, while much lower, were still considerable.

By virtue of an assured government allowance, opera organization was guaranteed. The season was long, lasting in many countries from nine to eleven months, and artists were engaged for several years at a time. The manager was able to plan ahead in building up the repertory and in providing for new productions. The stage equipment was thoroughly modern. Traditionally, opera in Europe has been an integral part of the cultural life of states and cities, recognized as such, and accordingly well supported.

REPERTORY AND THE AUDIENCE

Opera repertory, its plots and music, bore a relation to the particular European audience for which it was given. The world of Orpheus and Daphne was appropriate to the aristocratic Florentine Renaissance audience, that of Caesar and Jupiter to the absolute monarchs. The realistic folk opera of the eighteenth century with song and dialogue was an expression of the liberal spirit of the time, just as Wagner's *Siegfried* represented the German trend of thought in 1871. French grand opera of the nineteenth century suited its tone to the patronage of the first rich modern industrialists, and Stravinsky's *L'Histoire du soldat* reflects the atmosphere of 1918. Generally speaking, tradition still is strong enough to make the standard repertory a living art to a large group of people. In addition to new productions of the standard repertory, European managers whose subsidies were guaranteed were enabled to devote some part of their programs to untried contemporary works, without having to worry about the consequence of poor box-office returns, which otherwise would have hung over their heads like a sword of Damocles. A manager thus protected could give new operas which dealt with present-day problems, and by these experiments encourage the further development of opera.

Although there will always be some who go to the opera solely for its stars, its splendor, and its effectiveness of the more sensational kind, opera in Europe after the first World War was generally considered from a musicodramatic point of view, as is evident from the fact that it was nearly always given in the vernacular. Despite whatever loss of esthetic subtleties may be involved, Viennese audiences have heard *Aïda* sung in German, Paris *Die Meistersinger* in French, and Stockholm *Carmen* in Swedish. *Lohengrin* in Czech may seem to Americans far-fetched, but the Czechs will not have it otherwise. Budapest hears *Louise* in Hungarian. Toscanini, conducting a work as difficult to translate as Debussy's *Pelléas,* had to do it in Italian in Milan, and the practice is universal, despite the fact that translations usually leave much to be desired. This is lamentably true of the German translations of the standard French and Italian works, and vice versa. Yet the fact remains that the understanding by the audience of what is sung is given preference over every other consideration.

Although European opera in some respects has come very close to realizing the idea of music drama, and opera productions are often presented in up-to-date style, with modern equipment and as unified presentations which appeal to the taste and intelligence of the audience as well as to its ears, it is questionable that even in Europe opera has generally become a popular art. In no sense can it be said that opera has approached the community-theater idea of the Greeks, which it originally set out to imitate. Its failure to do so was also seen in the character of the European festivals—Bayreuth, Salzburg, Munich, Florence, Glyndebourne, and others—where opera performances have been given which were models of artistic craftsmanship, but where high prices restricted them entirely to well-to-do society. The Salzburg Festival of 1937, under Max Reinhardt, Arturo Toscanini, and Bruno

Walter, represented the final expression and the apotheosis of the Baroque tradition of European opera.

Like the social and cultural structure of which it is a part, opera in Europe has changed with each new political reform. But, like political organization, it has ultimately clung to tradition and has strenuously resisted any attempts at fundamental changes imposed by new conditions in the lives of the people. Contemporary history is witness to this deadly struggle.

OPERA IN AMERICA

While the kings of seventeenth-century Europe were trying to quench the kindling fire of progressive thinking in their subjects, and had set up absolute monarchies of concentrated power, the glorification of which was one of the principal functions of grand opera, political and religious pilgrims were making their adventurous way to the newly discovered continent of North America. Here they sought to build a new world, dedicated to the ideals of liberty and social justice.

Amid the bitter hardships and toil of pioneering, artistic expression was limited to religious song and service, and not until the cities which had been established on the Eastern seaboard were linked by relatively easy means of intercommunication were theaters built. These first theaters, simply designed, were constructed along the lines of those in England, for London set the pace for life and art in colonial America. Now, it was natural that grand opera, concerned with Daphne, Orpheus, Jupiter, and Caesar, the splendor of kings and the ritualism of the Catholic Church, in luxurious productions of panoramic display, employing *castrati,* could hold no place in the lives of the North American colonists. The breach between court life in Europe and the stark struggle for a bare living in the New World was too great. These builders were too realistic; moreover, they had no means at hand for copying the elaborate European models, even if they had wanted to do so.

EARLY BALLAD-OPERA

The first opera performance on record was *Flora, or Hob in the Well,* given on February 18, 1735, in Charleston, South Carolina. In the fifty years which followed, simple English ballad-operas were given, of the kind that had reached the heights of popularity in England after the success of *The Beggar's Opera,* performed in London in 1728. This type of opera had been readily adopted by American cities, and there are records of performances in New York, Charleston, Baltimore, Williamsburg, Philadelphia, which was the largest city of that time, and at a later time in Boston.

The ballad-operas given in these early theaters were simple plays which drew their themes from everyday life. Dialogue was, of course, in English, and simple folk tunes were employed after the manner of *The Beggar's Opera,* which had had its New York première in the first Nassau Street Theater, in 1750. One of these ballad-operas, advertised as "a new American comic opera, of two acts, called *The Disappointment; or, the Force of Credulity,"* was given in Philadelphia in 1767. It is interesting to note that among its eighteen songs was "Yankee Doodle."

After the War of Independence had been won and the Federal Union established, opera began to extend itself, and the plots, which had hitherto confined themselves to the life of small towns and everyday incidents, took on a more pretentious tone. An "allegorical-political opera or dramatic cantata" called *The Temple of Minerva,* by Francis Hopkinson, was performed at the hotel of the Minister of France in Philadelphia, in 1781. It has been called the first American attempt at grand opera, and others soon followed. A surge of patriotism is reflected in operatic titles of the day: *Columbus; The Launch, or Huzza for the Constitution;* and *The Fourth of July, or Temple of American Independence.* The latter was performed in New York on July 4, 1799.

Thus we see that the operas of the colonial and Revolutionary period, which embraces roughly the second half of the eighteenth century, were simple English or American folk operas.

DOMINANCE OF FOREIGN OPERA

With the invention of the steamship, America's contact with Europe grew closer, and, with the expansion of industry in the North, people began to enjoy a new prosperity. Ambition born of new wealth fired society to adopt the culture it knew as European. Original opera companies were imported from Europe. It was in 1825, the year of John Quincy Adams's inauguration, that New York saw its first real season of grand opera. Manuel García's Italian Opera Company, which included his daughter Marie Malibran, came to New York, and enjoyed the patronage of what was known as the "high kick of society." García presented nine Italian operas in the original language, the first work performed being Rossini's *Barber of Seville,* and this is said to be the first opera ever heard in Italian in this country.

Attempts to establish opera in English, or even an American opera, could not stem the advancing tide of foreign opera. The revolution of 1848 in Europe had driven many musicians to this country. Their activity stimulated interest in opera. German operas moved up to a position of ranking importance. In 1855, at Niblo's Garden, twelve nights were given over to the performance of German opera, and this was repeated in the years which followed, the singers being accused of "inexorable shrieking." *Der Freischütz* and *Fidelio* were given in German, and in 1859 the first Wagnerian opera, *Tannhäuser,* was presented. Four years later a season of German opera was given at Wallack's Theater, and this became the German opera house. German opera had now taken its place beside Italian and French opera.

With the growth of trade and industry, and the expansion of the country to the West which followed the building of the railroads, opera established itself in Chicago, and, after the Gold Rush years, in San Francisco. New opera houses were built. In New York the newly built Astor Place Opera House was followed in 1854 by the opening of the Academy of Music at Fourteenth Street and Irving Place, which for many years was *the* opera house of New York society. In the year 1857 Philadelphia built its opera house, also called the Academy of Music. New Orleans soon erected an opera house, as did Chicago and San Francisco. Opera in foreign languages became firmly rooted as a part of society life, and with it came all the array of grand opera—social splendor, the cultivation of virtuoso effects for their own sake, and the star system. The famous singers of the day, Malibran, Jenny Lind, Patti, Lucca, Sontag, and many more who were to become great names in the history of opera, were triumphantly received. From the middle of the century on, opera in English lost favor with society, and the foothold gained by opera in foreign tongues was one which it has not yet relinquished.

AMERICAN FOLK OPERA IN THE THEATER

So great was the prosperity of foreign grand opera during all this period that it is easy to overlook the fact that a native American opera never ceased to exist. In fact, from the date of the very first performance to the present day there runs a clear line of American folk opera. Its development begins with the earliest ballad-operas with dialogue and songs, in the colonial period, and it continues through the minstrel shows in which Stephen Foster's songs were used, Victor Herbert's forty-odd light operas, and DeKoven's classic *Robin Hood*. All of these folk operas were written for the theater rather than for the opera house.

OPERETTA AND MUSICAL THEATER

In our own time the popularity of operettas—*The Merry Widow, The Chocolate Soldier, Naughty Marietta, Mlle. Modiste, The Student Prince, Katinka,* and *The Firefly*—was followed by that of musical comedies and shows like *Sally, Oh Kay,* the *Ziegfeld Follies,* and the *Music Box Revues.* While the elaborate and spectacular quality of the musical shows was more in its element in the atmosphere of the movies and the movie theaters, the simple emotions of the musical folk play have remained on Broadway, in such original native works as Jerome Kern's and Edna Ferber's *Showboat,* with lyrics by Oscar Hammerstein, and the Negro play *Green Pastures,* which can be called American folk operas. Their tradition was continued by Paul Green in his symphonic drama *The Lost Colony,* which uses English madrigal music and has for its subject the tragedy of the first English settlement in America, and his *Johnny Johnson,* for which Kurt Weill wrote the music. While still in Germany, Weill worked toward the idea of the musical theater, and he has continued this work here with music to Franz Werfel's *Eternal Road* and Maxwell Anderson's musical play *Knickerbocker Holiday* and Moss Hart's *Lady in the Dark.*

The efforts of American opera composers have been directed toward leading opera back to the theater. In 1934 *Four Saints in Three Acts* by Gertrude Stein and Virgil Thomson, performed with an all-Negro cast, created a sensation with its witty cynicism, which seemed to prick the bubble of operatic illusion. George Gershwin's *Porgy and Bess,* performed in 1935 by the Theatre Guild, again with an all-Negro cast, is at the opposite end of the operatic world. Its action takes place in Catfish Row, a section of Charleston, South Carolina, where the aristocrats had once lived, but in the time of the story the site of a Negro tenement. In music and plot this work is perhaps closest of all to the idea of a modern American folk opera. In 1939 a short season of the American Lyric Theater under Robert Edmond Jones was given in New York, during which Fritz Reiner conducted Douglas Moore's folk opera *The Devil and Daniel Webster.* Marc Blitzstein's play with music, *The Cradle Will Rock,* had a run of several months at the Mercury Theater.

NEW MEDIA FOR OPERA—RADIO

The tremendous growth of musical interest and technical development has opened new doors to opera. Radio has been the real popularizer. In spite of the fact that there have been very few original ideas for adapting opera to this medium—of which the chief one is the explanation of the dramatic content by a commentator before each act, as the language is usually foreign and there are as yet no other accepted substitutes for visual effects—the radio has had an exhilarating effect on the people's enjoyment of opera. Actually, only one part of the composer's work reaches this audience—the music. But some composers have been commissioned to write operas for the particular requirements of radio. *The Old Maid and the Thief* by Menotti was written especially for radio. It was given in English, and the visual elements were replaced by reportage and sound effects.

TELEVISION

Television is still too new to have had a pronounced influence on opera. However, those who saw the first televised opera, *Pagliacci,* given by the N.B.C. on March 10, 1940, will not have forgotten the close-up of Tonio's face in the Prologue. To see the comedian's tear-filled eyes gave the musical expression greater intensity than would have been possible in the theater. Television offers the same advantages as the motion picture for conveying minute details of facial expression and gesture more intimately than can be done from the opera stage. The day soon will come when this new door will be opened wide to receive opera.

FILMS

Another medium for opera lies in the films. Thus far, producers have offered only operettas or musical revues, but these have had extraordinary success. In some cases films have been made into vehicles for such operatic stars as Lawrence Tibbett (*The Rogue Song*), Grace Moore (*One Night of Love*), Lily Pons (*Paris in the Spring*), and Kirsten Flagstad (*Big Broadcast of 1940*), with the use of single arias or operatic scenes. Although a great many opera composers are now living in Hollywood, producers have hesitated to film an entire opera, deterred by their feeling that the "unnaturalness" of opera would not be convincing in so naturalistic a medium, and that an opera could not be taken "as is" and be made into a good movie. Obviously, there is much truth in these assumptions, but scenes from Max Reinhardt's *Midsummer Night's Dream,* with the Mendelssohn music adapted by Korngold, have already shown what wonderful operatic effects can be achieved in films—the apparition of the fairies coming out of the fog, for example, and the coming of night. The genius of Walt Disney has unfolded a hundred new possibilities for creating visible forms out of music. In his films there is a close co-ordination of optical and auditory effects; *Fantasia* is a great step forward in employing the movies to convey musicodramatic expression.

AMERICAN OPERA

If the past is any guide to the future, it would seem that the present situation of grand opera here makes the time nearly ripe for the development of native American opera which, combining the technique of European grand opera with a content and a style truly expressive of the American people of the present day, will become a rich and complete art form. It is not for any chauvinistic reasons that we must work toward an American opera, but only because opera, like any other theater form, has no reason for being if it is just an exhibition. In all great periods of opera—or of any other art, for that matter—it has had its roots in the hearts of its audience, and has crystallized their innermost, inarticulate feelings.

Opera is going forward to meet the new audience. In order to reach them opera is changing. In spite of the obstacles of economy and convention, methods and standards for the future of opera in America are being prepared. Along what lines shall these new methods and standards be developed? [The answer hinges on three important points.]

FINANCIAL SUPPORT

1. Opera must be folk theater—expressing the emotions of the people in musical drama—not the mere entertainment form. In return, it should be given an official place in the cultural life of the city and state.

Opera has never been a money-making enterprise. Business organizations cannot be expected to assume the financial risk of backing opera. But why should not opera be as worthy of public support as symphony orchestras are? Whether the maintenance of opera will be taken over by private foundations or by municipal or state governments will doubtless depend largely on political developments. If circumstances will not permit it to be supported by local government, it will at least have to benefit by tax exemptions. The levying of a "cultural" tax averaging no more than ten cents per person per year in New York City would provide a revenue of about $750,000—an adequate sum to establish opera, with orchestra, chorus, and ballet, on a sound basis.

The building of a modern opera house would also do much to solve the financial problem, for it would make opera much more nearly self-supporting. The present form of box-theater is a relic of the aristocratic court-theater, which has no place in present-day life. If this form with its tiers and boxes were abandoned, a theater could be built which would have a vastly increased seating capacity, and in which every seat would have an undisturbed view of the stage. In such a theater, prices could be lower than they are today.

COMMISSIONS

2. Performance of new works. These are important, as they represent the feelings of their own time and without new compositions opera cannot continue as a living art.

But a modern composer cannot afford to spend months writing an opera without having at least a reasonable assurance that it will be performed. This difficulty would be overcome if operas were either commissioned in advance by the theater—many masterworks, particularly until Mozart's time, were commissioned beforehand—or were at least written with the collaboration and advice of the theater. Many of the old operas were written for the particular requirements of individual companies and singers. Co-operation between composer and theater would assure a practicable theater technique. In earlier times composers started out with this knowledge, since most had been opera conductors, and Lully, Gluck, Mozart, Weber, and Wagner were their own stage directors as well. Lacking some such experience, how shall a composer master the art of the musical theater?

As for plots and music, they need not be based on Apollo, Osiris, or Brahma. There is much good plot material to be found in the problems of modern life and history, if they are sufficiently moving and can be expressed by music. Mozart and Verdi used also contemporary problems in *Figaro* and *Traviata,* and the costumes were as modern in their times as those that are worn in *The Man Who Came to Dinner* are today.

It is debatable whether the recitative and symphonic treatment used by Wagner would be best suited to the American form, or whether it would not be better to keep to the form of dialogue and musical numbers—the form with which America started—as a basis for the new compositions. The desire and necessity of reaching their audience and projecting their drama could free composers from the inhibitions which in recent years have often kept them from writing real, singable melodies, for fear of not being "modern."

MODERN PRODUCTION

3. The new audience has an attitude toward opera which differs from that of the audience of twenty-five years ago. Present-day operagoers are not interested just in entertainment; they are concerned with drama and with music. The most significant indication of this change is the great growth in the interest in Wagner's musical dramas in recent years, and the present growing popularity of Mozart's operas, none of which can be really appreciated from a purely musical aspect alone.

The increasing interest in the opera as drama has made new demands upon the visual side of production. The present audience is not made up either of dilatory and sentimental dreamers or of people full of memories of past operatic manners. Our contemporary operagoers have been trained by the movies to expect reality in a production. They demand that dramatic credibility—accepted as a necessity in spoken drama—be present in opera as well.

In this day and age it is not enough for a singer to have a great voice, if his appearance and acting are not in character with his role. Gradually, heroic proportions of voice and body seem to be disappearing from the operatic stage, and singers present a more pleasing appearance and one more appropriate to most roles. These new singers often have smaller voices than the older type of opera star, but this fact is to a certain extent compensated for by the development of the microphone.

Gestures and movements must ring true. The old stock operatic gestures—hand-to-heart and arm outstretched—are rapidly becoming ridiculous. Formerly they often merely accompanied the singer's breathing: he had nothing more to emphasize than his vocal ability. But, with the shift of emphasis to the dramatic content of a work, gesture is an important means of expression. If, however, good acting in opera depends on dramatic interpretation, and dramatic interpretation, in turn, depends on language, then we must go a step further and say that acting must directly follow the meaning of the words spoken.

A singer who is able to recite his lines with attentiveness to the detailed implication of all words is already a good actor. Besides vocal ability, then, clear diction and skill and grace in bodily movement are also essential. For the latter, modern dance methods offer valuable help. The new generation of singers—Lawrence Tibbett, Lily Pons, Grace Moore, Gladys Swarthout, Risë Stevens, and many others—have proven in creditable performances that it is possible to be both a good singer and a good actor, and their ability is also shown in the motion pictures they have made.

It is equally important for the chorus and ballet to become integral parts of the dramatic conception. There is nothing less convincing than a chorus which stands stolidly by during an exciting scene, nonchalantly singing measure after measure, oblivious of what goes on around it, or a dancer who executes artificial and meaningless steps which have nothing to do with the drama.

Audiences today are more critical of scenery than they used to be. They are no longer willing to accept a rock which flutters and waves as the least breeze moves the canvas upon which it is painted. Nor do they find overstuffed prima donnas and chorus ladies bedecked with more jewels than an Indian maharaja to their taste. This useless accumulation of separate effects must be replaced by well-chosen forms, colors, and lighting, correlated with the music, all the elements embodied in a scenic unity.

OPERA OF THE PEOPLE

Today opera is no less a reflection of the changing society of its time than it has been in the past. The crisis of the old form and the rise of new forces are the expression of the political developments of our age, which with terrible strife are changing the social structure and frustrating art in most parts of the world. While the political upheaval at the moment endangers opera in Europe, America is in the unique position of being able to preserve this art and even develop it. With its new and keenly interested audience, its unsurpassed native talents and, at the same time, its inheritance of the techniques, the traditions, and many of the greatest talents of European culture, it will not waste the great opportunity that is offered, but will combine these forces of the Old and New Worlds to bring about a new, creative reform of this eternal art. Thus we may expect that the next chapter in the history of opera will be written in America and that its title will be *Opera of the People*.

Ballet and Music

By Lincoln Kirstein

Article in *The International Cyclopedia of Music and Musicians*

MUSIC written for theater, that is, to accompany danced or sung action, has certain limitations not shared by other music. While in one sense music is the most important initial feature of dance, inasmuch as it serves as root-rhythmic base, it cannot exceed a certain point of importance without competing with the action for which it is composed. Theater-music is intended to order and emphasize the activity in spectacle. It is music with a "program"; it indicates and describes for the ear what the eye sees. Its description is frequently far from literal. There is visual as well as aural counterpoint. At moments of intensity or stress certain composers have supplied the contrast of calm or silence, which may be only a more subtle indication of movement, as in Stravinsky's scene of the rape in his *Persephone* (1933). Theater-music is "impure" and dependent on many extra-musical or arbitrary features of style, mood, and expression. It is "occasional" music inasmuch as in the greater part it is created for specific theatrical occasions; it is illustrative inasmuch as it accentuates or clarifies specific dramatic or visual activities. Dance-music draws from a combination of vocal and instrumental sources. The primitive danced song with stamped accompaniment soon turns into a dance accompanied by singers with percussive apparatus, drums, gongs, clappers. Sometimes the vocal lineage is dominant, frequently the instrumental. The great division between dance or theater-music and music's other forms is in the nature of its impulse. Dance-music specifically impels toward physical movement. The other forms of music may do so, though not necessarily.

PRIMITIVE DANCE-SONG

The development of the arts of music, dance, and theater is almost inextricable from their origin. The history of one immediately involves the others. The very instruments of their production are shared by each, and while in an ultimate development each art will be seen to have its purified expression, we find that the perfection of their uses

298

will involve a synthesis, however unlike in character and style, nevertheless very similar to their original spontaneous employment.

If we search for the basic art of the three, it is probably dance. The dancer inhabits his own instrument, his human body. His palms slapped against thighs, his feet pounding on earth are his rhythmic and percussive accompaniment. His voice and his imagination, acting from imitation of birds and animals around him, first dramatize his destiny by descriptive poetry and its framing melody, which will become both tragedy and opera.

In primitive cultures, dance, music, and drama are performed as magic, ritual acts by the whole tribe to achieve specific results: relief from drought, thanksgiving for harvest, victory in battle, and to accompany the climactic acts of the individual in tribal life, birth, coming of age, marriage, and death. Danced song and acted drama involved the whole community. At this stage there is no separation between actor and audience. But there is soon a difference between dance-leader and his chorus. To make the rite more efficient, a leader orders the forms and ceremonies. He may represent god, priest, or king, but he is chief mover and in him is resident the motivating power. Chorus becomes an audience, and increasingly passive, to develop into a choral and finally specifically orchestral accompaniment. The priest-dancer finds opponents or co-actors who make his acts more real to his watchers. The solo-dancer is joined by partner singers, and both their voices and movement characterize their separate functions.

Primitive cultures offer us fascinating and highly developed formal solutions for their functional dramas. Recently, owing to anthropological musical research and its popularization through phonographic recording, we have been able to understand as never before the interrelationship of basic music and dance in different countries and cultures, its striking similarities and differences.

THE GREEKS

In the Bible we have continual reference to accompanied dances of victory and praise. Blown tubes, plucked guts, and struck skins underwrote the sung verse of the Semite tribes on their passage from Mesopotamia to the Nile. In Egypt considerable refinement was achieved in ritual activities of the priest class. Dance and song were still functions of state religion, not recreation or entertainment, although there are records of imported captives who gave acrobatic or juggling shows to musical accompaniment. The Greeks borrowed heavily from Egypt in sculpture and architecture, probably in music and verse, and in Greece there was the first flowering of music-drama as spectacle, such as we recognize today.

The early Greek tribes, in their kinship with others all over the world, had song and dance. With the developing cult of Dionysos, a deity who has counterparts in Syria, India, and Egypt, choral-dances received concentrated impetus. Out of early choral hymns emerged the dithyrambs, sung and danced myths on occasions of harvest and planting. Sung statement and comment, chanted question and answer, were framed with mimetic gestures and danced interludes. The aulos, a simple reed pipe blown by priests of Apollo, gave pitch and background to their song. The fragments of Greek music surviving are the subject of so much controversy that one can hardly generalize over their special properties for dancing. But the mature Greek drama, with its architectural system of metrical accent, provides ample evidence of the complexity and variety of the attendant dances. The "orchestreia" was originally the place for the dancing, a ground set in front of "skéne" or stage-scene where the chorus executed their dramatically necessary evolutions. The choir-leader or "choregos" not only led the movement, but directed singing, probably indicating tempi and cadence. We have now in essential origin the orchestra and its conductor; only here, the conductor is also composer, first dancer, and probably choreographer as well, with the orchestra as corps de ballet and singing comment. The vocal accompaniment supporting the verse-meter was accented by flute, drums, cymbals, and possibly shell or bone castanets. The dance patterns were prearranged as far as floor-pattern went, but since the vocabulary of gesture and movement itself was not greatly developed, there was a great element of improvisation in the danced details. This was also perhaps true of the music.

THE ROMANS

The Roman stage degenerated from the Greek synthesis of music-dance-drama. Theater in Greece always retained its religious connections and even after it ceased having a strict connection with priest-governed rite, its ethical atmosphere was evident. Plato and Aristotle testify to the moral use of music and dance. The Romans took over from Greece the entertaining element of their comedy and rendered it farcical. Tragedy in Rome developed into circus-spectacle. The chief contribution was the invention of mimetic drama, an elaborate dumb show not close to dance. Dancing was relegated to incidental divertissement. Actors, singers, and dancers were all now purely professional entertainers, in the same general category as courtesans. This professionalism of theater-artists under the Caesars destroyed the stage as an institution for a thousand years, for on account of their association with the corrupt public-games as a class of entertainers, the ascendant Christian Church struck particularly at players, singers, and dancers.

THE CHRISTIAN MASS

Although the triumph of the Christian Church over the Roman Empires of East and West was complete, and stage as entertainment was banished, Christianity recognized the inherent popular love of spectacles to which the prodigality of the Emperors had pandered. Just as the Christian Church appropriated pagan myths to its own saints, it also assimilated pagan ritual to its own rites. Within two or three centuries the ceremony of the Mass became a highly developed religious drama. Elements of poetry and song were dominant. Dancing had received the worst name possible in its association with obscene late Roman shows. But even in the Mass, the element of movement dictated by words and music was not absent. Gestures of genuflexion, elevation, prostration, besides manual movements indicating the Cross itself, were highly accentuated to be visible to the congregation. The officiating priest was choregos, first singer, actor, and in this sense dancer. From this, in the original tribal sense, he was a representative of God. He would have his own special chorus later, but even at the first there was the congregation, at once audience and accompaniment. Church architecture provided a separated and raised platform for the performance of the Mystery itself. The Romanesque and Gothic builders developed shelter and monument in one fabric, on an increasingly efficient frame. Acoustics, sight-lines, and noble atmosphere through glass, cut-stone, and brilliant clothes robed the Ordinary of the Mass in operatic magnificence. No stages for entertainment were built for nearly a thousand years. But the cathedrals improved on their own spectacular needs in every new church they built.

Religious processions with marching choirs included dances, and particularly in the early Christian Church among near-Eastern sects later declared heretical, dancing was by no means absent. But excessive movement recalled the whoredoms of Rome and was always an excuse for ecclesiastical purge. Native secular dancing-songs were employed by early Christian musicians. Melodies, already popular among the congregations, served as basis for hymn-tunes. The Church had studied the traditional Greek modes and discarded the Ionian and Aeolian (from which our major and minor scales evolved) for their worldly connotations and because they were thought to be particularly applicable to dancing. Gregorian chant, the dominant contribution of Church music, with its irregular rhythm and cool austerity, produced a thin atmosphere of almost static tension in which physical movement was a practical impossibility.

MEDIEVAL DRAMA-DANCE

Although the Church destroyed the stage as an institution it encouraged poetry and music for its own ends. While it did not foster dancing and suppressed any professional manifestations, it winked at popular folk customs in which dancing was a perennial feature. The persistent customs of place or season cannot be separated from dance, and rude dances became bolder and more expressive as the Middle Ages waxed into early Renaissance. Folk custom fostered folk song and folk dance in Central Europe as well as in Germany, Italy and the south of France. The Minnesingers sang to their capering *Springtanz.* The English Morris, with hobbyhorse and ankle bells, has its stray connections with Spain and the Moors. The troubadours of Provence continued, in spite of active Church prosecution, traditions of the professional entertainer, and continued the possibility of song, drama, and movement when it would produce Adam de la Hale (*c.* 1230–*c.* 1286), and his "Jeu" of *Robin et Marion,* a primitive pastoral comedy interspersed with songs, probably accompanied by dances.

With the release from Church domination and the rise of feudal aristocracy, a new impetus was given to the dramatic arts. There were still no theaters, but ballrooms or courtyards did instead. Professional musicians were few, but they were beginning to be honored for their usefulness. The prestige of painters was already protected by joining guilds of druggists and color makers. The society of dancing masters was yet to come.

RENAISSANCE FLOWERING

The opening of new possibilities by the rediscovery of the artistic principles of Greece and Rome was reflected in music, as well as in architecture, upon the dance. Gregorian chant and plain-song took over the Greek modal system, through the agency of Byzantine culture, but the modes did not permit very strong rhythmic usages. The subtle irregularity of Gregorian music which fitted the austerity of sung Latin prose came into direct conflict with Renaissance ideas of a freer form. The Italians now began to develop a sustained melodic line with rhythmic accents infinitely more adapted to physical movement than anything else then extant. The perpendicular or dominantly horizontal style of the Italians replaced the flat linear attitude of the Middle Ages. Through Provence, Sicily, and North Italy there emerged with the Carnival Songs of Heinrich Isaak (*c.* 1500) also the Ballo, a dance performed in a ballroom or the open air to sung and instrumental accompaniment. The dancers sang their own words. The diminutive of the term, *balleti,* has come down to us as "ballet," which specifically refers not to social but to theatrical dancing. The English metrical forms of "ballet" and "ballad" are cognates. In between the styles of dramatic and lyric chamber music emerged the form which Monteverdi (1567–1643) called *Ballo* and which we can roughly translate as "ballet."

In the princely shows of Renaissance Italy and France many advances were shown over the medieval "mascarades." What had previously been rude, unorganized, fantastic, and "Gothic," now based on the revived learning, became sophisticated, logical, full of allegorical and literary allusion, and "Classic." The Renaissance theater at first employed aristocratic amateurs as singers, actors, and dancers, but soon the competitive demands of various courts created a professional caste. In 1489, at the Milanese court of Gian Galeazzo, was held a famous entertainment utilizing instrumental music as specific and theatricalized accompaniment for a suite of dances, which was at once the immediate precursor of ballet and opera. In the fifteenth and sixteenth centuries social dancing on a conscious and artificed basis received an enormous European impetus. And music, which had been fertilized by French and Italian madrigalists, Flemish instrumentalists, and the revived interest in antique musical ideas, was ready to work with the dancing masters.

THE DANCE SUITE

All through the Middle Ages there was the double stream of rude and lusty peasant dance, mingling with dignified and elegant court dance. The peasant's feet leaped high, and left the earth. The courtier's stayed flat to the marble floors. Music began to play more and more an important role. It became almost the director of the steps, because even in spite of sung words, rhythmic periods had to be clearly defined to indicate contrast or variety in the change of floor-plan figuration, the movement and direction of dancers' bodies. Cadence had to be marked clearly and thus began one of the first lines to contemporary harmonies. The English folk dance, for example, originated the two-part and three-part form, with its series of contrasts, repetitions, and variations. A combination of the forms resulted in the rondo or round dance. Court dances intended more for deliberate display and subtle flirtation than for hearty fun received vigor and formal strength from the dances of the people, whether Italian, German, or English. The dancers in the castle began to use more movement with lifts and kicks, imitating rustic pleasures. The *haute danse* and the *basse danse* fused for theatrical use.

When the Medici court crossed to France (1565), Italian opera had already produced the first quavering prototype of lyric drama which one day was to result in Rossini and Verdi. What had seemed a classic revival turned out a baroque invention. The Milanese dancing masters of the Renaissance, the Flemish instrumentalists working in Florence, now combining their innovations with the choral composers of Paris and Fontainebleau, gradually evolved an order of formal dances which became the "Suite." Couperin would indeed call his suites "Ordres"; in Germany they were "Partitas." Mainly through the *Orchesography* of the monk Jehan Tabourot, first published in 1588, we can reconstruct dance steps which made up these suites. From the social dances were born the theatrical dances. From the dance suites evolved the sonata, the symphony, and the tone poem, all of whose forms have been used in the developing history of musical accompaniment for dancing.

At first the dances at court balls were given in any desired order, the caprice of a lady or of the master of ceremonies; but gradually from habit and a certain logical evolution of preference a sequence arranged itself. The grave pavane, an ostentatious, sober march-dance, was followed by the gaiety of contrasting galliard in 3/4 time. The allemande, dominantly a French dance of German origin, supplanted the pavane as the first form of the purely classic suites of Bach's epoch. The courante was popular under three forms from about 1550 to 1750. Of Franco-Italian origin, it was characterized by running passages of eighth notes in 3/4 time. The sarabande holds among the dances of 3/4 time the same grave position as pavane in 4/4. It has Mozarabic roots traceable to the twelfth century. It often used castanets or bells, and was associated with the deliberate languor of the courtesan. The gigue was, as Shakespeare wrote, "hot and hasty," in 6/8, 9/8, or 12/8 time. French and Italian jig forms are old, but the English model is conceded generally to be its archetype. The basic members of the suite were allemande, courante, sarabande and gigue. Some time later composers began inserting between the third and fourth either one or two other dances, not only the minuet but also the gavotte, bourrée, rigaudon, or passepied. The minuet, the most characteristic dance of the eighteenth century, was originally a *branle* of the province of Poitou. But after its introduction into the French Court around 1650, its tempo and style were moderated. The small or *menus* steps were retained with the name, although, as in the case of other dances, the same term categorized a number of variants developed over the two centuries of their popularity.

The complex forms of chaconne and passacaglia concluded the suites. The chaconne, perhaps of Spanish origin, became the concluding dance of a ball; the dancers forming two lines, ladies on one side with their partners on the other. Everyone danced for eight bars; then a couple or a small group performed different figures between the ranks. Then everyone danced the first figure, after which a second couple or group performed another, to be followed again by the opening. This continued until everyone had danced and there was a general finale. However simple this may sound, many very serious musical ideas arose from the chaconne. A more extended composition, extending to five or six parts, covering four or five engraved pages, and a rich exposition of the rondo were the more or less immediate results. From Couperin to Pachelbel, Handel, and Bach, we have a purely musical exposition of the passacaglia which was at first only a final dance.

All these dance forms and many lesser mutations and alternates of them were taken over from social dancing proper to be used by theatrical dancing masters in forms which were far more complex and dramatic than those practised simply in the ballroom. Certain kinds of action seemed to call for certain dance patterns. Dancing masters were also professional musicians. Their musical ingenuity in collaboration with the lyric poets controlled their choreographic creations.

THE ACADEMIES OF MUSIC AND DANCING

French court entertainments toward the end of the sixteenth and the beginning of the seventeenth century increasingly featured interludes which called for masked and fancy-costumed parties of dancing courtiers. These *entrées,* at first arranged on an accidental plan, tended to become more elaborate. Dance-music which they caused to be written was more extended than for social dancing, and dramatic and mimetic action was introduced in the dances beyond the strict steps and gestures of ordinary dance measures. In 1581 was given the *Ballet Comique de la Reine Louise,* generally accepted as the first ballet to be performed in a form which was crystallized enough to dominate its successors in traditional stage dancing. It was full of Italian influences from opera, oratorio, and dance, but was sung in French and founded the school of French ballet-opera which was to dominate European theater for two centuries.

Not until 1643 did Paris hear Rossi's *Orfeo,* its first Italian opera. In 1645, Cardinal Mazarin imported an Italian singing troupe. For years a minor poet, Perrin, and the musician Cambert had tried to back French opera against the southerners and not until 1669 were they granted a charter for founding an academy with state sanction. The aid of Louis XIV was indispensable. The patronage of great nobles had paled in the light of the Sun King, and only state support insured any permanent security for work. But an Italian was to have the final victory, for it was not Perrin but J. B. Lully, a Florentine menial in the household of the King's cousin, who became the first real head of the Académie Royale de Musique et de Danse. His ballet music had made his first success, and the King had liked him from their early association in the preparation of court shows. Lully had written incidental music for Molière's comedies, and we have here the crossing of the tradition of the popular Italian improvised comedy, the Commedia dell' arte, with French court dancing. Lully composed numerous operas from 1673 to his death in 1687, in which danced action played an important and more or less integrated part.

FRANCO-ITALIAN MUSIC

The Academy of Lully was imitated all over Europe and gave music and dance a professional dignity apart from its rather servile court affiliation. The Russian Academy was founded in 1673. Vienna, Milan, later Copenhagen, Berlin, Warsaw, and numerous provincial towns followed suit. The theater left the ballroom and built its own stage where larger audiences than the restricted aristocracy could enjoy music and dance. "Danse de la cour" becomes "Danse pour la scène." In ballrooms small gestures were all that were needed or seemly. On the stage, exaggeration is a necessity to make plain to people seated at a distance what actually is intended beyond the footlights. A scientific attitude toward music, dance, and their relationship to the stage was the natural result of the foundation of the Academies.

On a basis of five absolute positions, indicated by Arbeau (1588), and reillustrated in Rameau's *Dancing Master* (c. 1725), theatrical dancing based on social dance found its own direction. A series of exercises for suppleness, precision, and brilliance which gave the dancer's body what finger exercise did for the pianist's fingers, was developed on an efficient anatomical basis from John Rich's famous Manual (1712). English dancing masters had the tradition of the court masque under the Elizabethan and Jacobean dispensations on which to work. The French were always crossing the Channel. Purcell's *Dido and Aeneas* (1689) was written for the pupils of Josias Priest's Singing and Dancing Academy. Purcell's ballet music was remarkably effective and suitable for stage presentation. The English also were active in dance notation and dance music.

On the Elizabethan stage there was a considerable use of stage music to accompany the spoken words, or as the Dumb-Show in *Hamlet* to provide atmosphere for movement which might not be far from dancing. The casket scene in *The Merchant of Venice*, the coming to life of the statue in *A Winter's Tale*, called for music. In Webster's *Duchess of Malfi* there is music needed for an elaborate ecclesiastical ceremony dramatically important to the plot; and in *The Revenger's Tragedy*, the tragedy occurs to gay revel music which points the catastrophe.

LA DANSE D'ÉCOLE

The "Danse d'école," which is "Classic Ballet" or the traditional theatrical dance, developed an extensive vocabulary of terms referring to movements, gestures, and steps in the several state-endowed schools. Its "lingua franca" was and is French, as that of music is Italian, whether other directions are given in Russian, English, German, or Danish. Succeeding dancers and choreographers add their research and invention to the body of theatrical information which is exact, legible, and capable of sensible repetition. Classic ballet in every one of its mutations has musical parallels. It was conditioned by the modes of civil dress used as theater costumes of each decade, by increasing technical facility in architecture, by literary taste and by economic patronage and pressure. Classic ballet is a *materia coreografica*, as practically complex and useful to the dancer as materia medica to the doctor. It permits no improvisation and is an exact science.

THEATER DANCE IN THE 18TH CENTURY

Just as the sonata replaced the dance suite, so, with the benefits of sonata form and its more symphonic extension, the diverting opera-ballets of J. P. Rameau (1683-1764) replaced the heroic antiquity of Lully's ideal. In one sense it was a step back rather than forward. In Lully's operas the dances may have slowed the action but they were never separate from it. In Rameau's, the danced parts, however elaborate, are little more than divertissements, parallel to the late Renaissance entrées and ballet mascarades. As far as music and dance are concerned, they were as technically progressive as they were dramatically retardative. The old-fashioned dance patterns, which held flat to the ballroom floor, were released on the new raised stages into aerial virtuosity, and the tradition of male virtuosity in *la danse d'éléva-tion* was born. Rameau's operas, with their weak libretti, turned their backs on the subjects of Lully's mythological and heroic poems drawn from Tasso and Ariosto. Now Mexico, Persia, or China was used, transformed into French taste as dominant background for music and dance. The exotic element, imaginatively conceived, the idea of far places brought near, replaced the earlier infusion of actual folk dance.

At first it was the conservative Lullists opposing the defenders of Rameau. Later in the century it was the followers of Piccinni and conservative Franco-Italian taste against the innovations of Gluck and a return to the heroic style. After Rameau, who was essentially no innovator himself, the opera-ballet became fixed in a cold, formalized pattern. Certain musical forms became arbitrarily, through habit, attached to certain dances, which in turn characterized actions only varied as the costumes and scenery happened to represent a Parisian Persia instead of a Parisian Peru. The dancing costumes, shoes, masks, stiff wide skirts for men and women alike limited any free development of movement or expressive action. The great ballet master J. G. Noverre (1727-1809) joined with C. W. Gluck (1714-1787) in a reform of the situation.

In a composite art form like ballet-opera, component parts are not to be judged away from their whole, yet there is always professional competition among the collaborators, sometimes only philosophical, but frequently practical, to render either music, decoration, or dance the most important. And in each field there are at least two points of view. In the dance, for example, the conservative French opera-house amateur, whether in the eighteenth, nineteenth, or twentieth century, has always held that the dance is enough if it is an agreeable display of pretty girls in pretty clothes to pretty music, a divertissement which at its most dignified can be considered as art for art's sake, dance for the sake of dance. But in every generation there is the opposite view, based on the moral and ethical attitude of Aristotle. Dance, music, or any art form is no technical display but should express relations and emotional values calculated to affect the audience toward a desired end. Noverre, although he had to fight through his reforms in the opera houses of provincial capitals before he was permitted to create in Paris, did inject a dominant element of pantomimic gesture to replace the meaningless prettiness of previous choreography. In this he was aided by Gluck, who composed *Don Juan* in Vienna (1761), which was the masterpiece of the new heroic ballet style. This ballet was revived by Fokine in 1936. It was originally considered a return to the speechless drama of the Roman dumb-show which was in itself a virtuoso technique and far removed from the free flow of inexpressive if charming theatrical dancing before and since. Gluck's expressive accompaniment paved the way for Wagner, as well as Liszt, Berlioz, Richard Strauss, and the tone poets of our own day whose music is used as the basis for our dance dramas. Noverre tried to restore to the abstract and arbitrary dance a human element, to give back to the human body a display of its intellectual dignity beyond its occupation with acrobatics or plane geometry. He could have found no more perfect collaborator than Gluck.

DANCE-MUSIC IN THE 19TH CENTURY

The French Revolution and the ensuing Napoleonic struggles not only sealed the contributions of the eighteenth century, but—as far as dance music went—marked the dividing line between what we may call "antique" forms and what we understand today as music for our dancing which can still be revived with interest in a state of its original integrity, without too drastic cutting or reinterpretation to fit it for the dictates of contemporary taste.

It is not so much that there were startling innovations in the new century. Its major development, the ascendant romanticism of "program music," had precedents in Gluck's ballet-symphonies, and as far back as the Renaissance madrigalists. But now the theatricalization was more intense, the scope and contrast of orchestral effects were greater.

We have seen that folk dancing was absorbed into social dancing and that the combination vitally affected dance and music in the theater. In the nineteenth century dancing in public and private ballrooms reached an extravagant popularity. The waltz, stemming from such forms as South German and Austrian *Ländler,* the allemande, and as far back as the volta, could have been heard in the last quarter of the eighteenth century in Mozart's "German" dances. It was popularized in a two-act ballet by Gardel called *Danseomanie* (1800), with music by E. N. Méhul (1763-1817). The waltz swept Europe and was censored for its erotic implications, for here for the first time within living memory so-called polite people were seen absorbed in vertiginous movement, and in each other's arms. The waltz experienced numerous mutations. Each decade an acceleration of tempi, a greater freedom of rhythmic and melodic development, rendered each previous form old-fashioned. The instinctive impulse which demanded increasing physical stimulation dictated the music. The great waltz of Weber used (1911) for one of Fokine's most famous *pas de deux, Spectre de la Rose,* was originally a piano piece (1815), later to be given the superb orchestration of Berlioz. The enchanting pieces of Lanner and the elder Strauss culminated in the magnificent rhapsodic waltz poems of Johann Strauss, who, leading his own orchestras, intoxicated Europe and America with dance-music. His direct influence can be felt in the tone poems of Richard Strauss, in almost each of which one hears a haunting waltz melody as a dominant theme. In the *Rosenkavalier,* an opera set in the eighteenth century which by archeological tenets should hold at best a minuet, we have a series of waltzes which mark the peak of the developed form.

The ballroom appropriated folk music to its glittering salons, but instead of taming it as in the Renaissance, the tunes were rendered more complex until on the stage they reached their logical theatrical apotheosis. Waves of popularity for the Central European polka and mazurka swept Europe, rivaling the waltz. The Hungarian dances as expressed by Liszt's pianistic virtuosity were only one facet of the appropriation of exotic folk forms to theatrical music. Just as the dance suites of the days of Bach were constructed on the patterns of pavane and gigue, ballet suites for nineteenth-century opera-house stages included developed forms of the waltz, polka, polonaise, mazurka, and their various mutations of redowa, polka-mazurka, and sicilienne.

The quadrille, or square dance for four couples with figures based on Anglo-French contredanse, was followed by the cotillion and the German ballroom dances with elaborate mimed and danced games set in their musical pattern. The tunes were frequently borrowed from popular operas or musical comedies.

The opera-ballet itself became a characteristic nineteenth-century institution. Ballet-divertissement, on the eighteenth-century plan, began to incorporate itself into the framework of the opera plot. In *Don Giovanni* (1787), for example, Mozart, who had written much court ball music, has his famous minuet serve not as a display in itself but as an atmospheric background for the imminent tragedy, with the sung words coinciding with music and its dance. A formula arose in which there was usually a ballet in the second act, or at least not before the second act. Wagner, forced to insert the Bacchanale in *Tannhäuser* for its Paris debut (1861), owing to the exigent demands for ballet, created a riot because he placed it first of all. The members of the fashionable Jockey Club rarely finished their coffee and cigars before the middle of the second act.

Dances in the repertory of opera as performed today are well known but rarely considered in the frame of their origin. The Kermesse scene in *Faust* uses no Flemish peasant-dance, but is a "valse du salon" of 1859. Similarly the Ball scene in *Roméo et Juliette*. It is true that later in the century a more vigorous flavor of the original locale or epoch was introduced, as in Wagner's festival dance in the last act of *Meistersinger,* and in Smetana's *Bartered Bride;* but the Polonaise in *Boris Godunov,* laid in medieval Russia, was a court entrance dance of the period of 1850; the charming music of Bizet for *L'Arlésienne,* used frequently for *Carmen,* is more French than Spanish. The danced chorus in the gambling scene of *Traviata* is a curious jumble of Spanish, Italian, and Hungarian ballet entrées. There was a strong pseudo-oriental infiltration in such dances from *Aïda* as the ballet of priests to sung accompaniment, but it was Egypt strained through a thick web of Italian orchestration. Similarly the ballet music *à l'Indienne* from Delibes's *Lakmé.* Dance music with choral accompaniment was effectively used by Emanuel Chabrier (1841-94) in the Polish scene of *Le Roi malgré lui,* and in the brilliant Tatar encampment of Borodin's *Prince Igor.* In Auber's *Muette de Portici* (1828), the role of the dumb girl was always taken by a famous dancer. Pavlova appeared in a film of it in 1916.

The Russians by 1800 had their state theaters with a considerable national tradition, as well as the perennial visits of foreign stars. Taglioni, Elssler, and the Italians all came to St. Petersburg, bringing with them their repertory of music by Adam, Cesare, Hertel, and Pugni, the accomplished musical producers for the stage of their time. Minkous, Pugni, and Drigo turned out scores on command of the choreographers to fit the exigencies of the particular work to be mounted: so many bars of march for entrance, so many bars more of waltz for a "pas de guirlandes," and a galop for finale. However, Tchaikovsky (1840-93), in his three great ballets *Swan Lake, Nutcracker,* and *Sleeping Beauty,* elevated what had been previously hack scores into a succession of musical masterpieces. *Swan Lake* was an attempt to create a really symphonic score, but even its wonderful orchestration was a failure at the first performance (1877). It was held to be too "Wagnerian," too cohesive and serious for a pretty ballet. Tchaikovsky, more than any other composer of his period and even to our own day, understood the *danse d'école,* its relation to spectacle and its subtle connection with the popular ballroom dances of his day.

In France, Godard and particularly Delibes turned out good ballet scores. The framework was rather mechanical. A subject of national interest, say Brittany, Hungary, Spain, or Italy, was provided with a tenuous libretto and set numbers were inserted to show off in their arbitrary hierarchy the various members of the corps de ballet, the first classic dancer, or prima ballerina, the first character dancer, a duet for first male dancer and ballerina, a *pas de quatre* for four ranking soloists, etc. The individual technical capacity of the dancers, their personal style or taste frequently dictated music as well as steps.

In light opera, such composers as Offenbach would borrow, from vaudeville or music halls, popular dance forms such as can-can, galop, or the extended Viennese waltz as choral and danced backgrounds for act climaxes and final curtains. When the siege of Paris ruined the lyric theaters in 1871, Offenbach salvaged his magnificent repertory by producing his operas as ballet-pantomime.

There has always been a certain genre of theater-music which is neither specifically ballet nor useful for ballet in opera. This is the dance-music written to enhance stage effects in the specifically dramatic repertory. Purcell's music for Shakespeare's *Tempest* probably had dance accompaniment. At the French State Theatre of the Comédie Française, Racine's tragedy of *Athalie* (1691) had scores written for various new versions by Clérambault in 1756, by Gossec in 1768, by Perne in 1821, and by Mendelssohn (1842). Mendelssohn's music for

A Midsummer Night's Dream (1826-32) and Bizet's for the play of *L'Arlésienne* are standards of their kind. Grieg wrote for Ibsen's *Peer Gynt*. The American composer Roger Sessions's best-known work is a suite drawn from his music for Andreyev's *Black Maskers* (1923).

CONTEMPORARY THEATRICAL DANCE-MUSIC

The Universal Exhibition of 1900 held in Paris showed a number of native dancers sent by the Russian, the Spanish, and Oriental governments. The effect of national dances performed with accurate, untheatricalized accompaniment gave the visitors to this great World's Fair an excellent idea of the roots of folk culture which nineteenth-century opera houses had prettified past recognition. Loie Fuller, an American, experimented with Edison's new illuminating principles, adapted to the stage, casting butterfly-colored lights on huge whirling draperies. Isadora Duncan, by way of the Greek spirit, brought to the dance by force of her remarkable personality a new profundity, a fresh impetus, and a new musical insight. Spurning the cheap music which was normal for her period, she elevated her recitals with works heretofore considered only the property of concert halls. Gluck was her favorite, but she also used Wagner, Beethoven, and Chopin. Her reforms in dancing itself, in costume, and in the philosophy of stage art, were among the most influential of our day.

In Russia, the Imperial theaters in St. Petersburg and Moscow had reached a bureaucratic stagnation inevitable in a monolithic autocracy. Ballet had petrified into a formula for technical display with music providing incidental springboards for acrobatics. Now a young revolutionary dancer, Michel Fokine, proposed around 1905 certain specific reforms independent of, but parallel to, Isadora Duncan. She was working her own free and untraditional line; Fokine in the academic tradition of *la danse d'école*. Native Slav composers like Dargomijsky, Glinka, Borodin, Balakirev, and Mussorgsky had used true folk melodies for fine operatic danced scenes, but the dominant accompaniment for the official two-, three-, and four-act ballet proper was more Italianate, the heritage of the nineteenth-century Franco-Italian European opera-house repertory. Delibes, Pugni, Drigo, Glazunov, Minkous, and Rubinstein were scarcely a stimulating basis for revolutionary choreography. Rimsky-Korsakov was not recognized.

However, Fokine's reforms, as illustrated by his own early masterpieces, were accomplished not in Russia at all, but with the Russians in their tours of Western Europe. Both Serge Diaghilev (1872-1929), the great ballet director, and Fokine, owing to their radical artistic tendencies, were not permitted free use of the Imperial theaters. They turned this restriction into a triumph. Diaghilev, capitalizing on interest stimulated by the Franco-Russian political entente, produced in successive Paris seasons, starting from 1907, concerts, opera, and ballet using the whole apparatus of the combined Moscow-Petersburg theatrical machine. Heretofore, Western Europe had been almost entirely ignorant of the great Russian composers, in spite of Debussy's earlier knowledge of the score of *Boris* (1890). The so-called Russian ballet of Diaghilev from 1909 to 1929 was a continual activity for the best in music, dance, painting, and poetic ideas, and a revelation, first of Russia to the Western World, then of the Western World of art to itself.

Diaghilev more or less accidentally came upon his formula for the one-act ballet when he appropriated for reasons of haste and economy the "ballet-acts" of operas then in the Russian repertory, such as the choral dances from Borodin's *Prince Igor* (1909). The program of three contrasting ballets in an evening, instead of a single long one, made for greater variety and yet relegated what was often a dramatic, sustained form into the genre of light entertainment. Diaghilev was responsible for the discovery and promotion of numerous unsuspected talents in every field of theater. He had started his life with producing opera, and even at the end in Monte Carlo, he tried again with unfamiliar stage works of Gounod and Chabrier.

The first so-called "golden" period of the Diaghilev ballet was essentially Russian. Igor Stravinsky, commencing his ballet work by orchestrating two piano pieces of Chopin for Fokine's *Les Sylphides* (1909), followed with *L'Oiseau de feu* (1909), *Petroushka* (1911), *Le Sacre du printemps* (1913), *Chant du rossignol* (1920), *Pulcinella* (1920), the opera *Mavra* (1922), *Les Noces* (1923), *Apollon Musagètes* (1928). The stylistic development of Stravinsky's consecutive contribution accurately echoes the changing vogues of the Russian ballet. At first the genre of Russian fairy-tale set in a French taste gave way to the violent barbarism of remote Russia. His final eclecticism testified to the international interests of the School of Paris. The later Stravinsky's marvelous reworking of Handel, Delibes, Pergolesi, and Tchaikovsky by his own inimitable touch sets him with his compatriot Tchaikovsky as composer of the most useful ballet music we can find today, if not in specific works still in the repertory, then at least as models.

Debussy's famous *L'Après-midi d'un faune* was used in 1912, and his *Jeux* (1913) was composed for Nijinsky. Maurice Ravel contributed *Daphnis et Chloé* (1912). For Diaghilev, Prokofiev wrote his bouffonade *Chout* (1919), *Le Pas d'acier* (1927), a hymn to the new Soviet Russia, and *Le Fils prodigue* (1929), his masterpiece. But Diaghilev after the War turned from Russian toward French music and specifically to the group of *les Six,* which included Poulenc, Auric, Milhaud, all affected by Erik Satie and *La musique simpliste,* a tender and clever adaptation of popular music with contemporary ideas affected by cubism, functional architecture, and the post-war social scene in Paris. Falla's *Three-Cornered Hat* (1919) was a masterly use of native Spanish melodies with a vocal overture. Diaghilev exploited the younger English, Russian, French, and Italian composers year after year. His was the greatest coherent creative patronage of theater arts since the Renaissance. He was imitated by the munificence of the dance-mime, Ida Rubinstein, originally a member of his troupe. For her annual spectacles the poets Claudel, Valéry, Gide, worked with the musicians Stravinsky, Honegger, Ravel, and Roussel. The d'Annunzio-Debussy *Martyre de Saint-Sébastien* was written for her; likewise the Ravel *Bolero.*

Diaghilev also freely used reworkings of old music, not even specifically composed for dancing, but useful to him for certain productions he wished to present. Rossini, Cimarosa, Scarlatti, Montéclair, Gounod, Handel, Fauré, Liadov, and Mussorgsky were arranged or orchestrated by such able talents as Respighi, Casadesus, and Sir Thomas Beecham. Through the French "Musiquette" aspects of his repertory, social satire and American Negro jazz were mingled. Diaghilev was an artistic monopolist who appropriated whatever he wished, irrespective of its age, previous reputation, or use, to create a contemporary shock, effective for a single season, or, as was often the case, for many seasons.

The use of music such as the Strauss *Till Eulenspiegel* (1916) by the dancer-choreographer Nijinsky showed that the vocabulary of theatrical dancing had expanded enormously in combination with expressive pantomimic movement, so that the setting to dance terms of a tone poem originally intended only for orchestra seemed increasingly less of an anomaly. After Diaghilev's death (1929), the hereditary ballet troupes continued his formulae without change, except for two outstanding differences. In the ten years since his death the so-called Russian ballet has not been responsible for a single composer unknown to Diaghilev. And the choreographer Massine (b. 1897) has discarded the tone poem or dance suite system in favor of the full-sized four-movement symphony. He has used Brahms, Tchaikovsky, Berlioz, and Beethoven. His choreography to their works, all (except for the Berlioz *Fantastique*) without dramatic programs of their composers' devising, is accidental literary illustration in dance tableaux to music which requires none, and indeed repels this gratuitous illustration. Its popularity lies in his choreographic skill, the familiarity of the music, and the scale of production.

In opposition to this musical expropriation, another Diaghilev choreographer, Serge Lifar (b. 1904), ballet master of the Paris Opéra, issued his *Manifesto* (1935) heralding independence of any musical accompaniment save percussion. This was an extension of the attitude of Mary Wigman, the German modernist, who had been in violent rebellion against the *danse d'école*. She had studied with the Swiss musical educator, Jacques-Dalcroze, a profound musical scholar, who showed that dancers of his epoch (*c.* 1914) not only ignored the musical phrase and sequence of basic steps, but also were content never to push their means of movement beyond traditional academic habits. Wigman, however, resenting his overemphasis on music, experimented with percussion, spontaneous improvisation, and later atonal effects. She is the choreographic counterpart of the Viennese musical school of Schönberg and Alban Berg.

In America, as with everything else, our dominant influences have come from abroad, but we soon use them toward specifically national ends. In the nineteenth century, Stephen Foster's popular songs were frequently adaptations of Irish folk-dance tunes. The Minstrel Show by 1850 had laid the basis for Negro song and dance as a theatrical contribution. European opera and ballet music appeared as the material for quadrilles and cotillions. The Creole, Cuban, Mexican, and native American dance melodies appeared not only in Dvořák from his stay here, but also in the older generation of our own home-grown composers, MacDowell, Chadwick, Henry F. Gilbert, John Alden Carpenter, and in the light operas of Victor Herbert and Jerome Kern.

Russian choreographers who were with Diaghilev continually left him to work in America with American material, creating their own schools and companies which bridged the gap between the Russo-American School and what will eventually be American ballet itself; just as Russian ballet was French in the eighteenth century, and the

French was basically Italian in the seventeenth century. Fokine in 1919, Bolm in 1916, Massine in 1931, Balanchine in 1933, Romanoff in 1938, have brought over the working methods of the international Diaghilev school. American composers and choreographers are now hard at work making their choice and use of them.

Marc Blitzstein, Paul Bowles, Elliott Carter, Jr., Aaron Copland, Ray Green, Clair Leonard, Robert McBride, Jerome Moross, Walter Piston, Virgil Thomson, of the younger American generation, have all felt the influence direct or indirect of the musical taste prevailing in Paris from 1925 to 1935, either through study with Nadia Boulanger or by exposure to the Ecole de Paris. All of them returned to America with a new determination to use American material for American dancers. Already a considerable repertory has been built up for the use of local companies touring from bases in Philadelphia, Chicago, San Francisco, and New York.

In the field of the "modern" dance, stemming from the original tutelage of Ruth St. Denis and Ted Shawn, an early exoticism and a borrowing from Oriental sources were replaced first by a violent anti-melodic reaction to parallel the attitude of Wigman, and then an eager study of the Renaissance preclassic dance forms. Under the pianist Louis Horst, and the great American dancer Martha Graham, a special study has been made of the ground bass and the root choreographic forms of the early dance suite. At first rather aimed as a destroyer of the *danse d'école,* this training has developed into a corroboration of the ever-living truths in traditional theatrical choreography. But independently and in creating audiences, the "modern" dance has done much for the growing appreciation of music and dance collaboration in America.

[In addition to Shawn, St. Denis, and Graham, others who have contributed and are contributing to the growth of the American dance are Jane Dudley, Hanya Holm, Doris Humphreys, Eugene Loring, Agnes de Mille, Anna Sokolow, Helen Tamiris, and Charles Weidman. In the years since 1938, when the above article was written, ballet and "modern" dance, formerly quite distinct from each other, have come closer together, and elements of both have fused with technics of popular and folk dance in a characteristically American type of "theater dance" that promises much for the future.—E. S.]

PART FIVE

Meet the Composers

V. Meet the Composers

I T IS pretty generally agreed, by this time, that the facts of a composer's life cannot of themselves give us an understanding of his music. The type of biography that interpreted every composition as a reflection of some particular event in an artist's career was vastly popular in the romantic age; it still serves as the model for most Hollywood music scripts. Today we have abandoned the notion that a given composition is necessarily the record of the composer's experiences, for there have been all too many composers who wrote gay and robust music while in a state of dejection, and vice versa.

This train of thought has led certain commentators to the opposite conclusion: namely, that music has *nothing* to do with a composer's personal life; that it exists entirely in a self-contained world of its own. This view is supported by the evidence of the almost endless series of Cantatas that Bach turned out every week for years, with almost clocklike regularity. Where in all these compositions, we are asked—or in the other works of Bach, for that matter—do we find any reflection of "Bach the man"? Do the *Brandenburg* Concerti or *The Well-Tempered Clavichord* tell us anything of the composer's character, of his disputes with the authorities, the time he was jailed for insubordination, or the joys and sorrows of his family life? Diligent comparison of the great Johann Sebastian's scores with the known facts of his career fails to reveal any psychoanalytical information concerning his "spiritual life." This composer's art, then, would suggest that "biography is irrelevant to music."

The truth of the matter probably lies somewhere between the two extremes. Biography *per se* cannot "explain" a man's music; but when read in connection with a keen knowledge of the music itself, it can be and often is deeply illuminating. Of course, certain musicians seem to put more of their personal lives into music than others. But behind every great art work there is a man and a personality.

There are exhibitionists such as Richard Wagner, for instance, to whom music was always a necessary outlet—a "sublimation" if you will—for an intense, ecstatic and tortured ego. In his case, fortunately for us, all the finest aspects of his personal character were reserved for his composition; the shoddy and repulsive ones being confined to the acts of his daily life.

Then there is the sober, reticent artist such as Brahms, who had a horror of all forms of self-display, and whose music carries a noble reserve. It is the mirror of the man, to be sure, but of a man for whom music was a goal and an ideal, not an appendage of personality.

The relation of a composer's music to his life depends to a large extent on his conception of the function of art. While this varies from person to person, as we have seen, it is also true that certain periods have tended to stimulate self-conscious individualism, while others have led composers to a more objective, functional view of their work.

Thus, in the medieval Church and in the courts of the absolute monarchs of the seventeenth and eighteenth centuries, the musician was considered—and to a large extent considered himself—as simply a craftsman, one engaged to provide music for a given purpose just as a cook was hired to provide food, or a carriage-maker to build coaches. In none of these cases was there question of the artisan expressing *his* private joys or troubles; his job was to meet the requirements of churchman or prince, with the greatest skill and craftsmanship he had in him.

Of course there was such a thing as pride in one's work and a difference between the accomplishments of various individuals. But the modern concept of music as a reflection of personality was almost entirely absent. This was revealed in the common eighteenth-century practice of musical borrowing. A musician of today would be chagrined if it were shown that the main theme of his latest work came note for note from someone else's composition. A favorite indoor sport among a group of young composers I once belonged to consisted in remarking:

"Your first theme sounds like Hindemith; your second is slightly Stravinsky-ish; and those four last chords are nothing but Scriabin's fifth Prelude." This was supposed to annihilate you—but, of course, you retorted that *his* music echoed Schönberg, Debussy, and Henry Cowell.

All these criticisms would have sounded like sheer gibberish in the days of Bach and Handel. If someone had told Bach that the subject of his great G minor organ fugue sounded like that of a certain Hamburg composer (Mattheson) he would probably have remarked (as Brahms once did when accused of being influenced by Beethoven), *"Das weisst jeder Esel!"* (Any ass knows that!) For that theme and many others that Bach used were taken frankly and without apology from other men's music, the idea being, "He's found a good tune— why shouldn't everyone have the use of it?" Composers borrowed melodies, technical devices, even whole movements of compositions from each other as a matter of course; no one thought it in the least reprehensible.

Bach used themes of Corelli, Legrenzi, and Mattheson, and whole compositions by Vivaldi, rewriting them in his own manner. The results are gratifying to our ears today. Handel had this objective attitude towards composition to such an extent that, according to Cecil Gray, he derived no fewer than 16 of the 39 sections of his magnificent *Israel in Egypt* from other composers! Listening to the music now, it is impossible to tell where the others leave off and Handel begins—and who cares? *

The idea of making music a consciously personal art arose with the appearance of individualism as a way of life. The concept of the value and importance of the individual appeared at various historic moments, was crushed, and then rose once more—the whole process being repeated several times and affecting every branch of life. The musician was not immune.

It is hard for modern ears to detect any very personal quality in music before the Renaissance. But with the coming of that era of

---

* The practice of building music on another man's theme is familiar to us today in the work of the jazz performer and arranger. No one thinks less of Benny Goodman's improvisations because they are based on "Dinah," "Sweet Sue," or "Five o'Clock Jump."

passion and violence and the emergence of such giants as Shakespeare and Michelangelo, it is not surprising that individual personalities bloomed in music, too. The makers of the Madrigal and of the first Opera were strong and colorful figures. No longer bound by the restraints of feudalism, they were free to develop personal traits in their work. The age of the Italian city states and Elizabethan England produced such men as the brilliant, versatile Orlando di Lasso, the passionate Monteverdi, the keen, witty Clément Jannequin, and the richly endowed men of England: Byrd, Morley, Weelkes, and Dowland—each of whom stood out as a distinct, fully realized individual.

Individualism and intimate self-expression suffered an eclipse in the epoch of absolute monarchy following the end of the Renaissance. At the court of Louis XIV the only individual who mattered was the Sun God himself; and all throughout Europe from Madrid to St. Petersburg, big and little princelings aped his pompous despotism. Once again the composer became a mere functionary, providing music as a commodity to be used.

Most of this music is stilted, cold, and—for us today—quite meaningless. It was considered extremely bad taste for composers to express simple, natural, warm emotions; those who insisted on doing so found themselves ignored and rejected. Henry Purcell's fame rested on his showy court music, not on his finest and warmest work, *Dido and Aeneas* (which was performed only in a girls' school); while the oblivion in which Bach remained is well known. The most successful composers of this period were those who cultivated pomp and formality—Lully, Rameau, Telemann, for instance. Handel got by only because of his absolutely Herculean drive and the fact that during the greatest years of his career (those in which he wrote *Messiah* and the other oratorios) he was longer dependent on royal patronage. Already he appealed to the common people of England, whose taste for rugged, natural simplicity found an echoing note in his later music.*

The second and definitive rise of individualism in music was associated with those struggles for liberty and human rights which also gave birth to our democracy. The year 1789 marked the end of serfdom

---

* Yet, simple and natural though Handel's style seemed to the English, it appeared strained and artificial to the still plainer American, Benjamin Franklin. See page 668.

in France; the following year terminated Franz Josef Haydn's semi-feudal servitude at Esterház. "On his own" for the first time, Haydn was now able to write exactly as he wished, and the remarkable new blossoming of the sixty-year-old artist under the conditions of personal freedom is one of the most striking phenomena in the history of music. The twelve Salomon Symphonies, which are played more frequently today than all the 90-odd Esterházy symphonies put together, date from this period.

With Haydn and Mozart (especially in their later, free-lance years) we already have the type of the modern composer who writes to express himself rather than any lord or employer. Mozart's last works, especially the G minor Symphony, the G minor Viola Quintet, the C minor Fantasia, and parts of *The Magic Flute* carry the intro-spective, passionate quality of a man aware of the conflicts and frustra-tions of his inner life.

With the rapid spread of the movement toward individualism following the French Revolution, musicians no longer hesitated to make their art an embodiment of personal desires, aspirations, fan-tasies, and actual experiences. Schubert's songs were almost instinc-tively autobiographical. The "wanderer" who could find no joy on earth, the loveless one mocked by the horrible *"Doppelgänger,"* the *"Leiermann"* (organ-grinder) whose tunes found no hearers and brought him no sustenance—all were images of the luckless composer himself.

In Berlioz' music, self-conscious individualism reached its full. The crowds who came to the première of the startling *Fantastic* Sym-phony heard no piece of "absolute" music; they knew that the morbid poet was none other than the composer himself; and that the "eternal beloved," whose theme appeared almost as an obsession in every move-ment, was the lovely Henrietta Smithson. So closely was music inter-woven with personal allusions that after the concert the whole crowd trooped over to the theater where the actress was playing, as if to check on the musical portrait drawn by Berlioz.

It is the Romantic type of stormy, untamed musician that remains in the public mind today as the type of "great composer." Whether or not this picture was entirely true even of the Romantics themselves (it is known that some of them liked to appear much more tempestuous and "impractical" in public than they actually were in private), the fact remains that the details of personal biography bulk much larger in understanding and estimating the work of these men than is the case with composers of an earlier or a later age.

It is for this reason that most of the space in this part is given to the musicians of the nineteenth century. On the whole, they are no greater, and no less great, than the artists of any other epoch. But knowing them as people tells us a great deal more about their music than is the case with their predecessors or successors. And they are interesting to read about.

There Were Great Men Before Bach
Abridged from "Men of Music"

By Wallace Brockway and Herbert Weinstock

THE fierce, blinding sun of the high Renaissance was beating down on papal Rome when Giovanni Pierluigi da Palestrina, the greatest of the old composers, was writing Masses for worldly and splendor-loving pontiffs. Around him flowed the variegated life of sixteenth-century Italy, given its pattern, texture, and color by this phenomenal upsurge of human ambition. Everywhere artists were celebrating the victory of the senses: sculptors were exploring with rediscovered candor the contours of the human body; painters were transforming their peasant mistresses into the Mother of God; architects were masking the harsh Gothic face of the cities with gracious temples and colonnades, and philosophers were dreaming of Plato, that prince of pagan poets whom a blasphemous humanist had actually proposed for sainthood. In the midst of all these busy sensualists ostensibly re-creating the classic past, but in reality creating the modern world, Palestrina was patiently putting the finishing touches to the Gothic edifice of medieval music.

By Palestrina's time music was an exceedingly complicated affair. Like every other art, it had developed slowly and painfully from meager beginnings. From the ritual grunts of savages it had evolved with geologic slowness into an adjunct of the Greek drama. Whether, if we knew how to perform it, Greek music would appeal to us or not we can never know, for, as a wise English critic has said, "All the research in the world will not enable us to understand the Greek musician's mind."

MEDIEVAL CHURCH COMPOSERS

From a strictly pragmatic point of view, music blossoms at that moment in the fourth century when Ambrose, Bishop of Milan, decided to regulate the singing for the services in his diocese. The Ambrosian chant—the first thoroughly recognizable ancestor of music as we hear it—is the leanest and most solemn adaptation of the Greek modes, the ancestors of our modern scales. This somber singing can still be heard in certain Milanese churches, but today we are more familiar with the elaboration of St. Ambrose's system known as the Gregorian chant, which largely superseded the older musical service at about the beginning of the seventh century. Some think that St. Gregory, the greatest Pope of the early Middle Ages, sponsored, or even devised, the innovation; less romantic historians believe that he was too busy with barbarians, heretics, and plague to bother with ideas about music.

For a thousand years the music of the Church was rigidly melodic: that is, it attained its ends without the use of harmony as we conceive it today. The troubadours and minnesingers accepted unquestioningly this purely horizontal tradition of music, and lavished their imagination on the melody and words. But neither these gay itinerant musicians nor the formulators of primitive counterpoint (whoever they were) can be called real composers.*

The Renaissance, which exploited the individual ego, gave birth to the composer with a name. Until then men had been content to submerge their names in anonymous giving of their talents: the musician was as nameless as the altar boy swinging the censer. In the Middle Ages music had no separate identity: it was as much an accessory of the sacred rite as Greek music was of the drama. Definitely, purposely, a part of some greater whole, it was designed to recede. It is no coincidence that the first pieces of self-sufficient music are (with few exceptions) not anonymous: they were still written for the Church, but the composer had begun to think of his music as a living thing he had created.

* Admirers of Troubadour musicians and the Gregorian Chant might enter objections here.—E. S.

DUNSTABLE AND OKEGHEM

Considering the exalted and ancient lineage of the other arts, it comes as a shock to find that the first composer, in the modern sense of the word, was an Englishman who died in 1453. This man, John Dunstable, is an almost mythical figure, a sort of English Orpheus who was even credited with the invention of counterpoint—a feat obviously beyond the abilities of a single individual. Little of Dunstable's music survives, and he might have vanished from history altogether if it had not been for his long and fruitful association with Continental musicians of his age, whose successors—especially the Flemish masters—evidently studied his methods to great advantage.

Dunstable's suave and euphonious style tended temporarily to soften the harsh contours of the music of the Flemings. But Jean de Okeghem reverted to the austerity of earlier Flemish music, while vastly increasing its technical resources. Okeghem has been called the greatest music teacher of all time, and in his relentless pursuit of a new methodology has been likened to the modern experimentalist, Arnold Schönberg. This is by no means a forced comparison, for the purely esthetic results of their efforts are, in both cases, open to question.

JOSQUIN DES PRÉS

Like many another outstanding theoretician, Okeghem was fulfilled in the work of his pupils, the greatest of whom was Josquin Des Prés. Coming upon Josquin after mingling with his still shadowy predecessors is like emerging suddenly into the light of day: he is recognizably a modern man, an erratic genius whose checkered career extended well into the sixteenth century. He was born in the dawn of a new age, when the Turks swarming into Constantinople and Gutenberg devising the printing press helped to liberate forces that would destroy the Middle Ages. Josquin emerges from the mists as a singer at Milan in 1474. He was then about thirty years old, and it seems probable that his sophistication was already such that even the excessive splendor of the court of the Sforzas could not overawe him. For he was no stranger to court life, as he himself testifies: he had studied under Okeghem at the royal chapel of Louis XI. As he left the then cheerless city of Paris with a whole skin, we may be sure that he did not make the sour French monarch the butt of those practical jokes for which he later became notorious.

Within the next decade or so, Josquin made a leisurely progress 'through the burgeoning duchies of northern Italy, where beauty-loving and neurasthenic princes welcomed good musicians with the extravagant warmth of those lush and expansive times. He finally arrived at Rome, which was for two hundred years to be the center of the musical world, and became a singer in the papal chapel, thus choosing a road to fame that became stereotyped with his successors. Perhaps the choristers in the Pope's service lived aloof from the dissolute life of Renaissance Rome, but if they came much into contact with that grand old rake, Innocent VIII, or his even more riotous successor, Alexander VI, they must have witnessed some of the most colorful and improper scenes in the history of even the Eternal City. Here, despite the obvious distractions of Borgian Rome, Josquin worked on his first book of Masses—probably some of them were sung in the Sistine Chapel with the composer himself taking part.

Josquin died in 1521. Later composers, exploiting even further the devices he had used and the styles he had vivified, crowded his music out of the churches with motets and Masses of their own. For almost four hundred years Josquin has been hardly more than a name. Yet the most painstaking musicologists, after piecing together the pitifully sparse details of his life, round out their labors by unanimously acclaiming him a genius. Although rarely performed, a sufficiently large amount of his music survives for us to visualize him three-dimensionally as a composer. He widened the scope of musical art unbelievably: he advanced and subtilized the technical resources of his predecessors; more important still, he discovered that music can be made the vehicle of varying human emotions. Even the most baroque of Josquin's works, though full of higher-mathematical intricacies, are nevertheless expressive—the music of a man who felt deeply and made spacious melodies. What sets him above the earlier masters—and, indeed, above most composers—is precisely this richly varied expressiveness. His music possessed a powerful appeal for his contemporaries, who invariably referred to him as "the wonderful" or "the marvelous" Josquin. Luther, a good judge of music, and himself a composer of sorts, said, probably of Josquin's less intricate style (for this downright reformer had little use for musical monkeyshines), that others were mastered by notes while Josquin did what he pleased with them.

Josquin's effect on music was not wholly salutary: his associates and followers—particularly the Flemings—admired him most as a superb craftsman, and tended to forget the more purely musical excellences of his style. Uncritically digesting his technique, they then began at the point beyond which prudence and taste had prevented Josquin from venturing, and went on to create monstrous complexities, at which, finally, the Pope himself began to shudder.

For almost two hundred years the Holy See had been vaguely disturbed by the growing elaborations and often glaring inappropriateness of the music for the services. The complaints were numerous: secular tunes and even words were used; different sets of words were sung simultaneously, and at times the style was so florid that the words, lost in the mazes of ornamentation, were completely incomprehensible. Imagine a solemn High Mass sung to the tune of *Oh! Susanna,* with the tenors crooning *Kiss Me Again* and the basses growling *Asleep in the Deep!* This is the sort of thing we might still hear if an affronted and conscientious Pope had not moved to reform these evils.

Reform was in the air. The Council of Trent, originally convened to checkmate Luther's criticisms by a general housecleaning, was reconvened in 1562 by Pius IV, after a recess of ten years. Among what they doubtless considered far weightier matters, the fathers of the conclave found the degraded state of church music worthy of their august consideration. Therefore, with the Pope's emphatic approval, two cardinals were appointed in 1564 to see that sacred music was once more made sacred. At first the situation seemed so hopeless that there was talk of restricting the musical services to the traditional body of plainsong. It is possible that this deadening remedy had already been seriously considered when a man was found who could evolve an idiom both artistically mature and ecclesiastically acceptable.

PALESTRINA

Giovanni Pierluigi da Palestrina, the man who saved the art of music,* was thirty-nine years old at this time. Like the magnificent Leonardo, he had taken as his own the name of his native village, where he was born in either 1525 or 1526. Palestrina is, and doubtless was, a drowsy and picturesque little town nestling in the craggy fastnesses of the Sabine Mountains. The composer's parents were people of substance in this obscure place, holding their land in fee of the powerful Colonna family. It is probable that one of the Colonnas took notice of the child, and persuaded his parents to let him enter the papal service. At any rate, we know that as early as his twelfth year Palestrina was

---

* This figure of speech applies, of course, only to Catholic Church music. The writers of Lutheran music, dance music, madrigals, etc., were obviously unaffected by and quite indifferent to the decisions of Pope or Cardinals.—E. S.

living in Rome, and serving as a choirboy in the basilican church of Santa Maria Maggiore.

After seven years in Rome Palestrina returned to his native town with a life appointment as organist and choirmaster of the cathedral, offices carrying the revenues of a canonry. His fortunes were on the upgrade. Three years later, his marriage to a local heiress diverted a fat dowry his way. Shortly afterwards, Giovanni Maria del Monte, Cardinal Bishop of Palestrina, became Pope as Julius III—an event of prime importance in the ascending sequence of Palestrina's fortunes. Almost immediately the new Pope appointed his organist choirmaster of the Julian Chapel, the nursery for future Sistine singers. Palestrina dedicated his first book of Masses to the Pope, who responded by giving him a life appointment as a singer in the papal chapel, thus enabling him to give up his exacting duties at the Julian.

In March, 1555, Julius III died, and the next month Cardinal Cervino was elected to succeed him, assuming the curiously archaic name of Marcellus II. Unfortunate in life—he had enjoyed the papacy but three weeks when he died, probably poisoned—he was singularly fortunate in his post-mortem fame, for Palestrina's greatest Mass was named for him. Giovanni Pietro Caraffa followed the luckless Marcellus, and as Paul IV connected himself inextricably with the most exquisite refinements of the Inquisition, to which, as a Neapolitan, he was peculiarly fitted to lend his inventive genius. One of his first acts was to rescind Palestrina's "life" appointment in the Sistine: the morbidly devout pontiff could not brook the idea of a married man singing in the Vatican.

Palestrina interpreted his dismissal as a personal slight (though two other married members of the choir were let out at the same time), and his health suffered. The niggardly pension that Paul assigned him could scarcely compensate for his loss of prestige, though his injured feelings were somewhat assuaged by his appointment to succeed the renowned Di Lasso as musical director of St. John Lateran, "of all churches in the world the mother and head." However, this position seemed to be better than it actually was: the music was not well endowed, and Palestrina was constantly at loggerheads with his employers, who do not seem to have appreciated him. This impossible situation was terminated by his resignation in 1560, possibly with the intention of devoting himself exclusively to composing. Sorely disturbed though he was by the undignified bickering at the Lateran, he yet composed, in the *Improperia* for the Good Friday service, the work that raised him to a pre-eminence that went almost unchallenged until his death.

The *Improperia* brought Palestrina so much acclaim that he was besieged simultaneously by requests for more compositions and by appeals to re-enter the service of the Church. The compositions were forthcoming in profusion, but he hesitated to return to masters who had treated him so ambiguously. After eight months of unemployment, however, he consented to return to Santa Maria Maggiore, to lead the choir in which he had sung as a child. Here he remained for six years.

The fanatical Paul IV died in 1559, and there ascended the throne of St. Peter one of the most amiable figures of the late Renaissance, Giovanni Angelo de' Medici. This cultured and enlightened philosopher, known as Pius IV, was evidently deeply impressed by Palestrina's music, for he requested that the *Improperia* be copied into the manuscript books of the Sistine Chapel. It is possible that the simplicity and genuine piety of these Good Friday pieces led the Pope's commissioners to turn to Palestrina in solving the crisis created by the ultimatum of the Council of Trent. But it is impossible to verify the old tale that it was the *Missa Papae Marcelli* that won them over. If Pius IV did not really say that the *Missa Papae Marcelli* was comparable to the music heard by St. John the Divine during his vision of the New Jerusalem, he should have said it. After all, it is merely a florid Renaissance way of saying exactly what critics have been saying ever since. But the making of heavenly melodies was not very profitable, and Palestrina welcomed the largess of wealthy clerics and noblemen.

In 1565, Palestrina's friend Pius IV died; he was succeeded the following year by the cantankerous Inquisitor General, Michele Ghislieri, who assumed the name of Pius V. This thoroughly morose monk (the last sainted pope) reappointed Palestrina to the Julian Chapel in 1571, this time as choirmaster. Meanwhile, the composer's creative genius was at flood: Masses, motets, and sacred madrigals flowed from his pen unceasingly, and apparently without effort. Two of the madrigals commemorated the signal victory of the allied Venetian, Spanish, and papal navies over the Turks at Lepanto.

Despite Palestrina's many friends among the powerful and holy of the Renaissance—a list of his dedications reads like a sixteenth-century *Almanach de Gotha*—his life was cheerless and pinched. His wife and two musically promising sons died within a few years of each other, and he was left with one rascally boy who not only plagued him during his life, but also, as his father's musical executor, damaged his musical reputation after his death. His second marriage, at the age of fifty-six, could not well have been a romantically happy one: he needed money and someone to preside over his household. The woman of his choice was a widow in comfortable circumstances, and presumably in need of the same human companionship that Palestrina craved. He took over a fur-and-hide business she had inherited from her first husband, and made a decided go of it, buying much valuable real estate with his profits.

The last seventeen years of Palestrina's life were marked only by domestic vicissitudes; officially, through his honored connections with the Vatican, he had achieved the utmost distinction the Renaissance had to offer a musician. Others might be better rewarded, but the fact remained that Palestrina's offices gave him the tacit dictatorship of the musical world. Only a technical question of seniority of service kept him from the position of master of the papal choir. He issued his works with almost calendar regularity, though not in the sumptuous format that distinguished the publications of certain of his contemporaries who enjoyed the patronage of a mere king or duke—the Popes were not so munificent to their musicians as to their painters and sculptors.

Palestrina was not one of the most prolific composers: he left only ninety-three Masses, five hundred motets, four books of madrigals, hymns, and offertories for the whole Church year, three books of Magnificats, three of litanies, three of lamentations, and two of sacred madrigals—a mere trifle compared to the incredible output of his well-kept contemporary, Orlando di Lasso. But the percentage of excellence is amazingly high: Palestrina seldom fell below his own standards, which were uncompromising.

Sir Donald Tovey has pointed out that Palestrina, like Spinoza, was a God-intoxicated man. His secular compositions are negligible in number, but in his Church music he did not invariably follow the letter of the regulations laid down by the Council of Trent. He frequently used secular tunes for sacred texts: for instance, he used the folk melody *L'Homme armé* as the basis for two Masses. He set another Mass to the tune of a French love song. However, his intense devotional fervor so spiritualized these lay melodies that all trace of their vulgar origin was removed.

In the rather barren controversies that rage perennially over the comparative worth of various compositions by a single master, and which are particularly unprofitable in the case of a composer so rarely performed as Palestrina, the vote is always divided. The *Missa Papae*

Marcelli is by no means unchallenged in its pre-eminence: at least three other Masses compete for highest place. *Assumpta est Maria,* for instance, has been compared (with complimentary intent) to the *Sistine Madonna.*

In the dedication to Gregory XIII of his fourth book of Masses, Palestrina shows a lively sense of his own gifts as a composer. His contemporaries already regarded him as one of the fountainheads of music. One of them, the Spaniard Victoria, so admired him that he not only imitated the Italian master's musical style, but is said to have copied his somber clothes and the cut of his beard. In 1592, a group of accomplished north-Italian composers presented a collection of vesper psalms to Palestrina, with a dedication that reflects the reverence in which he was held during the last years of his life. Its language is extravagant, and would be fulsome if addressed to any lesser personage: "As rivers are naturally borne to the sea as their common parent and lord, and rest in its bosom as the attainment of their own perfection, so all who profess the art of music desire to approach thee as the ocean of musical knowledge to testify their homage and veneration."

During his last years, his responsibilities somewhat lightened, Palestrina continued, as was his oft-expressed intention, to create music for the greater glory of God. Old age did not stem his creativeness, and he was preparing his seventh book of Masses for publication when he died, on February 2, 1594. His intimate friendship with Filippo Neri lends plausibility to a legend that he died in the saint's arms.

Palestrina was buried in the old basilica of St. Peter's, but his tomb was moved during the demolition of the church, and no longer exists. Records preserve the epitaph, its Latin sonorousness aptly saluting the greatness of his achievements:

JOANNES PETRUS ALOYSIUS PRAENESTINUS
MUSICAE PRINCEPS

With the *Missa Papae Marcelli* there began the last phase of purely vocal contrapuntal development, enriched by later works of the Prince of Music himself and his most eminent contemporaries— Orlando di Lasso and Tomás Luis de Victoria.

ORLANDO DI LASSO

Of this peerless constellation, Di Lasso had the most eventful life. His was the first really big success story in music. Noble patrons competed for the honor of employing him: he started out as the favorite of a Gonzaga, and ended up at the court of Munich in the softest musical berth in Europe. The pomp and glitter of his life is rather like Leonardo's. He spent his vacations running pleasant diplomatic errands for his powerful patrons. Everything conspired to produce for him those ideal circumstances for which every composer yearns.

Orlando was born at Mons, in what is now Belgium, about 1530. Even at the age of nine he had progressed so far musically, and had so angelic a voice, that he was thrice abducted, the third time by agents of Ferdinand Gonzaga, Viceroy of Sicily. His lifelong habit of consorting with noblemen was formed early, and after his voice broke he spent several years fancying the high society of Naples and Rome.

Orlando's bent was, from the first, secular. Unlike Palestrina, who passed his entire life in the papal service, Orlando held only one brief church appointment, and that early in his life: the direction of the choir at St. John Lateran. He left this post to resume his wanderings with a highborn friend, and may even have reached England before settling temporarily at Antwerp in 1555. In that year he brought out his first two publications, a book of madrigals, mostly on verses by Petrarch, and a collection of madrigals, chansons, and villanelle, with four motets trailing after.

Orlando cannily dedicated his first book of motets to the future Cardinal de Granvella, and that rising statesman promptly recommended him to the attention of Albert V, Duke of Bavaria. It was at the brilliant court of the Wittelsbachs, at Munich, that Orlando passed most of his life. At first only a court singer (he had to learn German before assuming heavier responsibilities), he already drew a larger salary than the *Kapellmeister*. He married a rich Bavarian girl. Within an amazingly short time after his arrival in Munich he himself was *Kapellmeister* and one of the Duke's most trusted ambassadors. And in 1570 the Emperor Maximilian II ennobled him.

Orlando's fame soon spread throughout Europe, and he was received with great enthusiasm wherever he went. An exuberant love of fun endeared Orlando to a Paris ruled by Valois and Medici. The judicious Abbé de Brantôme spoke of some music he had written at Catherine de' Medici's order as the most melodious he had ever heard, while Charles IX's admiration became so intense that he offered to engage Orlando as a chamber musician at a fabulous salary. He declined the honor, but continued on such friendly terms with the royal family that Henri III, the last of the Valois, gave him a pension and special privileges for publishing his music in France.

The truth is that Orlando needed no favors from foreign potentates. His salary at Munich was more than lavish, and the conditions under which he worked literally have no parallel. His job was simple: to write as much as he wished in whatever style he chose. The only thing the Duke asked for himself was to be on hand when Orlando's works were performed. The many musicians who thronged the court of Albert V were at Orlando's beck and call: in the realm of music he was as absolute as the Duke was in affairs of state. If Orlando wrote a Mass, he could order its immediate performance in the ducal chapel; if he wrote a madrigal, the chances were that it would be sung at a court gathering the same evening. Here the ideal circumstances of demand and immediate performance were realized as they never have been since.

While fortune kept her fixed smile turned on Orlando, he continued to issue Masses, Magnificats, *Deutsche Lieder,* and chansons in bewildering abundance. Albert V died in 1579, and his son, Orlando's close friend, succeeded him as William V. Albert's lavishness left the treasury depleted, but Orlando did not suffer—on the contrary, his salary was doubled within the next few years. Meanwhile, the Jesuits got at the Duke, and their influence slowly seeped into the court, blotting out the old gay life, and making William so unpleasant that history has nicknamed him the Pious. Orlando, as a clever courtier, must have responded to this revivalism, and yet in 1581 his villanelle are still overflowing with the very essence of comic drama—hold, indeed, the germs of *opéra bouffe.* The Duke's bigotry seemingly imposed few restrictions on Orlando, and more than ever he wrote magnificently, with subtlety, expressiveness, freedom, and boundless audacity.

The last decade of Orlando's life was marked by a growing sobriety of attitude. His fifth book of madrigals, published in 1585, revealed this change. Like some of his earlier efforts in this genre, they were settings of Petrarch, but the overdone chromaticism of the early pages now gave way to a purer diatonic style. It was as though he was censuring himself for his youthful extravagances, and subjecting his gifts to more rigorous discipline. But the strength of strength's prodigy began to fail, and 1586 passed ominously without a publication. The Duke noticed Orlando's failing health, and presented him with a country house to which he might retire from the strenuous ritual of court life.

On May 24, he dedicated his *Lagrime di San Pietro* to Clement

VIII. It was his swan song, and before its publication he died, on June 14, 1594, little more than five months after his peer Palestrina.

Orlando is one of the most difficult composers to analyze: not only did he write almost two thousand works, but he wrote them in a bewildering multiplicity of styles. If he were performed as often as Wagner, it would take many months of ceaseless listening merely to hear all of him; as it is, he is performed even less than Palestrina. His works range from ribald, actually bawdy chansons (which blushing editors permit us to see only in bowdlerized versions) to some of the most sublime devotional music ever written. Between these extremes are pieces expressing every subtle shade of emotion.

In surveying the vast and elevated domain carved out by Orlando's genius, critics have espied few of those isolated peaks that crown the Palestrinian landscape. The altitude is consistently very high, but the slopes are gentle: there is no *Missa Papae Marcelli*, no *Assumpta est Maria*. There is, nevertheless, general agreement that Orlando's setting of the seven penitential psalms is his greatest single work. In the musical language of God-directed contrition and sorrow, Orlando has never been excelled by anyone, has been equaled, perhaps, only by the Bach of the *St. Matthew* Passion. In these poignant lamentations, all earthiness and ribaldry have been burned out by searing emotion, and what remains is the very distillation of sublimity.

VICTORIA

Tomás Luis de Victoria is the third of this great trio of sixteenth-century religious composers. He was born at Ávila, probably about 1540. Victoria was a priest. He, rather than Palestrina, was the paragon sought by the reforming fathers of the Council of Trent: he never composed a secular piece or used a secular theme. He inscribed a book of motets and psalms not to a living patron, but "to the Mother of God and to All the Saints." In dedicating a book of Masses to Philip II of Spain, he said that he had been led by instinct and impulse to devote himself exclusively to church music. At the same time, he bade farewell to composing, saying that he was determined to resign himself to the contemplation of divine things, as befitted a priest. He made this vow in 1583, but the urge to create was too strong, and before he died, almost thirty years later, he had published many other volumes.

In forming our judgment of Victoria, we are not embarrassed by the overwhelming output of an Orlando. The Spaniard was not a prolific composer: he left less than two hundred separate compositions.

The most striking characteristic of his music is its hint of Moorish influence: it sometimes uses those harmonic and rhythmic devices which, however metamorphosed and cheapened, are to this day the unmistakable hallmark of Spanish music. Victoria, even in his imitation of Palestrina, retained his special native quality: his Spanishness is as obvious as that of Albéniz or Falla, though it is asserted less blatantly.

No less Spanish is Victoria's pervasive mysticism, which occasionally borders on hysteria. He was very sure of his mission. In the dedication of the *Canticae beatae Virginis,* one of his most ecstatic outpourings, he declared that his aim was to compose music solely as a means for raising men's minds by pleasant stages to the contemplation of divine truth. No music would be more likely to accomplish such a purpose than Victoria's, though cynical ears may hear in its sounds more descriptive of Mohammed's paradise of houris than of a seemly Christian heaven.

The death of Tomás de Victoria in 1611 brought to a close the great age of unaccompanied vocal polyphony. Music had gone far since that almost mythical past when St. Ambrose devised his chants, but even in its complex development it had kept to substantially the same road. The great musical trinity who lifted their art to equality with painting and sculpture, and added to the splendor of the dying Renaissance, were better composers than Okeghem and Josquin. They handled richer materials with more freedom, with more sweep and emotional depth, than the old Flemish masters. With all their multifarious gifts, they had summed up twelve hundred years of technical progress, and had set up enduring monuments to the past. The sound of their own mighty cadences, as well as their very position in history as the inheritors and fulfillers of the great tradition of ecclesiastical music, deafened them to the feeble murmurs of the new music coming to life around them. The first opera—a puny infant—was performed while two of them were still alive.

From Monteverdi to Rameau

Extracts from "Music, Classical, Romantic, and Modern"

By A. Eaglefield Hull

THE outstanding musical figure of the Italian Renaissance, Claudio Monteverdi, is too often vaguely considered as the composer of the first grand opera, *Orfeo;* but his other musical activities are equally important. Like Bach in later times, he faced both ways. He wrote madrigals and church music in the antique contrapuntal style, and when doing so, he indulged his taste for musical figures of a pictorial intention, as did the other masters of these severe styles. Yet the madrigal had sprung originally from the Italian pastoral folk song, the *frottola;* and we see in Monteverdi, as in other early masters, a distinct leaning towards a more harmonic style through the greater use of block chords. His music becomes more and more a homophonic and syllabic commentary on the words, and increasingly pictorial in intention. In his *Catene del Amore* (Love-Chains) we find long festoons of thirds used to suggest the weaving of garlands. Sighs are translated into music by pauses. The voices rise on the words *heaven, heights, ascension;* and fall on such words as *earth, abyss.* Broad undulating thirds represent the waves of the sea. The most daring discords and unexpected modulations are used to express martyrdom, sadness, pain, and tears. This preoccupation with a literal translation is heard also in his opera *Orfeo.* There the voices ascend on the word *cielo* (heaven), scatter into rapid notes on *fugge* (flees), drop a sixth on *il precipizio* (precipice); on *zoppo* (lame) go in long notes, and on *ali* (wings) rise in runs of semiquavers [sixteenth notes]. In his *Combattimento* and Warrior-madrigals (he had to accompany the princely patron on military campaigns) he is frankly realistic. He finds the right vocal rhythms for the stamp of the horses, the impetuosity of the charge, and the terror of the vanquished. His *Scherzi Musicali* are more lyrical.

In Monteverdi's time (he was born in 1567) few professions were more honourable and remunerative than the musician's. He was expected to live in a certain style. Monteverdi occupied an expensive house, kept a carriage and horses, men and women servants. His patron, Vincenzo Gonzaga, the Duke of Mantua, was the type incarnate of the

Italian Renaissance princes. Devoted to display, fêtes, plays, balls and ballets, he was both generous and harsh, assassinating any artists who failed him, overwhelming with gifts (rarely money) those who served him well. He pursued pleasure tirelessly; love and music, painting and alchemy, absorbed him. He brought as much care to the engagement of a new singer, or the purchase of a famous picture, as to the acquisition of a new province. Yet for all this, the prince had no consideration for his artists, and with his sudden requests for new operas and cantatas at short notice for state visits, royal weddings, and other court ceremonies, he overworked Monteverdi cruelly. "I do most humbly beseech your most Serene Highness," Monteverdi wrote to his patron, "for the love of God, no longer to put so much work upon me; and to give me more time; for my chief desire is to serve you, and this excess of fatigue will not fail to shorten my life." Monteverdi was no time-server, and his artistic conscience rebelled at doing things to order at such short notice. He was much happier when finally released from such high-handed treatment, by accepting a post in the free city of Venice, where he spent the last thirty years of his life, writing many operas for the first public opera houses there. He died in Venice in 1643 at the ripe age of seventy-five, his mind fresh and young to the last.

THE SCARLATTIS

Of the two Scarlattis, Alessandro and Domenico, father and son, it is hard to say which had the more genius. Domenico, the wonderful harpsichord player, had the greater inventive powers. His father (1660-1725) wrote chiefly for the voice and kept to the classical opera-forms; he was the chief user and abuser of the "ABA" form (first air—middle contrasted air—first air repeated), which he used for all his solos: and his admirer and follower, Handel, was not much more inventive in this respect. The leisurely chamber-cantata, with its formal set airs and duets, was immensely popular in the Italy of the seventeenth century, and Alessandro Scarlatti was at once its greatest and most fertile exponent. He wrote no fewer than seventy operas, besides hundreds of other works, and spent all his time between Naples, Rome, Florence, and Venice producing them. More than half of his works are now lost, but the amount that remains is still enormous and bewildering in its variety. Very little of his pedantic chamber music or of the fine tunes of his operas is heard nowadays, but he is a big figure for the musical historian. He means more to us when we acknowledge that his best pupil was Mozart.

Far more significant is the music of his son Domenico (1685-1757), one of the first of the virtuoso clavier-players, whose technique was so amazing that the Italians were wont to say, "He is possessed of the devil." He spent a quarter of a century in Spain, as cembalist to the Court at Madrid, and there is no question of the excellent effect of the Spanish environment on his works.· His complete keyboard pieces (over 300) have been published in twelve volumes, and they are as vital on the piano of today as they were on the harpsichords of Madrid and Naples in his own time. These joyous pieces are typical of the pleasure-loving courts of Italy, where his taste was formed, and of Spain, where his art was most fully exercised and developed. The recent reaction against the Romantics has had the two-fold effect of sending people of taste back to these early classical keyboard pieces, as well as forward to the Impressionist and Post-Impressionist music.

LULLI

What Alessandro Scarlatti, the opera-composer, was to Italy, Jean Baptiste Lulli * was to France. If Louis XIV was the arch type of the aristocratic and fashionable European courts of the seventeenth century, Lulli was the typical classical musician of this period. Born in Italy (1632), sent as a page to a great lady of the French Court, Mlle. de Montpensier, he was quickly promoted to be leader of the King's Band. A graceful dancer, an able composer, an expert stage-manager, an alert and astute man, able to use even his misfortunes so as to rise higher—he was just the man to realise the ideas of the Grand Monarch.

The fêtes at Versailles were carried out with the utmost sumptuousness. In the Tuileries, balls, serenades, concerts, masques, ballets, succeeded each other all the year round. Pleasures and vices were everywhere, but all were clothed in the robes of ceremony and dignity. Life itself was a stately ballet moving to a dignified measure. Courtiers monstrously bewigged and peruked, courtesans with the grand manner, dances, majestic as a peacock, slow enough for the whispered intrigues of love, architecture itself befrilled in exuberant ornament—everything was to the taste of this young and wily Italian, who added to the impulsiveness of his Southern blood and habit of audacious scheming, a love of pomposity as great as that of the monarch himself. This organiser of royal pomps, of scenes of pleasure, did more for

* The original Italian form of Lully's name.—E. S.

the ballet than he did for music. In his day it was a dance, a masque and an opera all in one—a series of pictures or slight incidents, strung together with the lightest of links, crystallising into rigid operatic conventions. Mythological subjects alone were favoured; for nearly two hundred years, the court and public never seem to have wearied of the loves of gods and goddesses, shepherds, nymphs and fauns, framed in classical landscapes and decked out in French court dress. The resources of Versailles seemed endless. The staging was sumptuous. One of these productions alone, the *Cérémonie turque* in the *Bourgeois Gentilhomme,* cost 2,600 pounds to produce.

Lulli's triumphal career was cut short by a curious accident—in 1687 he was conducting his *Te Deum* for the recovery of the king from illness, when he struck his foot with his long, heavy-mounted baton. Blood poisoning set in, and he died in his large canopied bed at Ville l'Evêque; and a sumptuous monument was erected to his memory in the chapel of his patron-saint, St. Jean Baptiste.

In music, Lulli was no initiator; he merely used other people's materials. His pomposity, majesty and grandeur arise from his sober and dignified harmonic style (one devoid of complexity and chromaticism) rather than from any elevation of mind. His firmly strutting bass and the absence of any rhythmical surprise give his music a perfect assurance. Like Handel and most of the Italian composers, he is prone to stereotyped cadences. First and foremost he was a formalist, a co-ordinator. If he did not invent the so-called "French Overture" form * he certainly established it. His form was adopted by Bach, Handel, Purcell and others. He also helped to establish the general type of lyrical tragedy, ballet-opera, and heroic pastorale. More than any other composer he understood the music of pleasure, that art to which the royal aesthete Louis XIV always gave first place in his "Earthly Paradise" in which he tried to forget all earthly cares.

The France of Lulli's time was a France given over entirely to the Italian in music. As M. Denéréaz says, Lulli's music was a magnificent, though somewhat cold, morning light; his successor Rameau announced the rubicund day.

COUPERIN

François Couperin was the second leading music figure of Louis XIV's time. The Couperin family affords the most striking example

---

* A slow, majestic movement in 4/4 time with dotted notes, followed by a lively movement of dancelike nature in triple time.—E. S.

of a French musical dynasty. For two centuries this family was illustrious in furnishing remarkable artists to the musical establishments of the French courts and eminent organists for the principal Paris churches. From the early part of the seventeenth century up to the beginning of the nineteenth, Couperin fathers, mothers, uncles, nephews, aunts, nieces and cousins, were court composers—clavecinists, violinists, singers, or organists—whose outstanding talents were widely recognized. But the chief was François (1668-1733), called "Couperin le Grand" by reason of his pre-eminence as composer and player. He was organist of St. Gervais's Church in Paris for forty-four years, Superintendent of the Court Chamber-Music and Royal Instructor to both Louis XIV and Louis XV. He is deservedly famous for his many keyboard suites, originally written for the "clavecin" and now frequently played on the pianoforte.

These suites, all known and loved by Bach, who modelled many of his own on them, had also a great influence on two other classical composers, Handel and his friend Domenico Scarlatti. They were published by the composer in four books at various times, 1713, 1717, 1722, 1720. Departing from the practice of the composers of his time, he strings his pieces together into larger groups, not called suites but *ordres*. The four books contain twenty-seven of these *ordres*, comprising in all nearly 200 pieces. These consist of dance-measures, rondeaux, and pieces with all kinds of fanciful titles; others are inscribed with the names of well-known dancers in the royal masques and ballets. The dance-pieces include allemands, passepieds (canaries), courantes, sarabands, minuets, gavottes and jigs. We find titled pieces which call to mind the subjects of Watteau's quasi-classical and pastoral pictures: *Fanfare for Diana's Procession, The Foresters, The Bees, The Pastimes at St. Germain-en-Laye, The Carillon of Cytherea, L'Himen-Amour, Les Graces incomparables,* etc. Such pieces as *La Florentine, La Nanette, L'Amazone, La Mimi, La Gabrièle, L'Angélique, Olimpique, La Flore, The Little Nuns, The Lady with the Waving Plumes, La Drôle,* all refer either to favourites of the stage, or to Couperin's fashionable pupils. And one likes to think that Couperin has indicated their varied dispositions. Nor did he refrain from the portraiture of his own family and friends. *La Soeur Monique* is his own daughter who entered a nunnery under this name.

Couperin is equally adept in depicting various moods: *Happy Thoughts, The Lugubrious One, Tender Languors, The Wandering Shades* (spectres), *A Soul in Trouble,* etc. Even his romantic subjects are all treated with a classical finish and a courtly lightness of touch. He has humour too, flippancy, and even a touch of irony: *Slight Mourning*, or *The Three Widows*, etc. There are also Sphinxes, such as the piece *Les Culbutes Ixcxbxnxs*, and little jokes such as *Le Tic-Toc-Choc*, *The Crossed Legs*, and the sly little *Pince-sans-rire*.

There is no doubt that in order to get the full flavour of all these pieces, they should be played on the harpsichord, as the elaborate system of ornamentation is best suited to that kind of precise and penetrating tone; but they come out well on the modern piano-forte and easily evoke visions and pictures of the gay life of the age of Louis XIV, that voluptuous yet most tasteful First Gentleman in the Europe of the seventeenth century. Couperin's high qualities of grace, elegance, sensibility, tenderness, irony and discretion, added to the perfect mastery of his particular art—the art of the miniature, by the way—made him one of the greatest of all masters of French musical style. No wonder the twentieth-century musicians Debussy and Ravel acknowledge him as their true master.

RAMEAU

Three years before Lulli's death, was born one destined to replace the Lulli tradition which was still powerful for fifty years after his death. Lulli's music was never genuinely French; it was Italian melody grafted on to the French taste for external magnificence. Rameau's music on the other hand is typically French—the perfection of taste. It is full of grace, devoid of force (for force is brutal), and without emphasis (for emphasis is vulgar). His Latin sentiment without sentimentality sometimes becomes nearly as profound in feeling as Bach or Beethoven; but he is inhibited by his superficial mask of elegance.

Unlike most of the composers of his century, Jean Baptiste Rameau arrived at his art through a profound study of musical theory. Born in 1683 and dying in 1764, he was contemporary with J. S. Bach, Handel, and Domenico Scarlatti. His first opera, *Hippolyte et Aricie* (first performed when the composer was fifty years old), was immediately attacked by the Lulli-worshippers. Disappointed, he simply said, "I was mistaken; I thought my taste would be successful. I have no other; and shall compose no more." But during the next twenty-one years he wrote twenty-one operas. *Castor et Pollux* (1737), with a more logical libretto, established his fame as France's greatest composer. Opposition, however, still continued; people complained of the number of semiquavers [sixteenth notes] in his music, and the hard-worked orchestra said they "hadn't time to sneeze." The famous Rousseau pursued him implacably with his eternal cry of "Back to Nature"; Voltaire retorted that it takes a whole generation for the human ear to grow familiar with a new musical style. The Encyclopædists, the "moderns" of the day, asked for real human interest instead of ballets with Apollo or Hercules as figureheads. In their zeal, they declared duets "unnatural," condemned fugues as "the remains of the Gothic spirit," and clamoured for the supremacy of the vocal art with simple accompaniments. Harmony for them was only important in its relation to melody. Rousseau certainly had a keen feeling for music, but this did not make him a musician. D'Alembert disliked sonatas; Fontenelle put his famous query, *"Sonate, que me veux-tu?"* As a matter of fact, Rameau was no innovator; he at first rebelled against the conventional operatic routine, but he clung to the old classical subjects with spectacular display. Fond of mechanical stage-devices such as tempests, earthquakes, fires, he leaned to the descriptive side of music, making great efforts with simple means—the assault of Titans in *Naïs* done by syncopated notes, the ending of Chaos and the Sunrise in *Zaïs,* the monster rising from the waves in *Dardanus.* For storms he uses scales in contrary motion, and, Wagner-like, he suggests fire in *Zoroastre* by brilliant trills and sparkling grace-notes.

In his keyboard music Rameau is the continuation and the complement of Couperin le Grand; but Couperin reflects the taste of an amiable society devoted to pleasure, whereas Rameau is the French rationalist. Like Couperin, he puts special titles to his dance pieces, minuets, musettes, chaconnès, *contre-danses,* etc., showing that he aimed at "character-pieces"; and he uses the dance forms to convey feelings quite apart from the associations of the actual dance. His three little collections of harpsichord pieces (1706, 1724, 1731) follow the fashion of the times with their descriptive titles, *Rappel des oiseaux, La Poule,* etc. In *Les Tourbillons* (gusts of wind stirring up dust) he anticipates Debussy; and in the piece entitled *L'Enharmonique* he shows himself as greatly daring. He carries French keyboard music in his *Gavotte with Variations,* and other pieces, to the highest point ever reached before the appearance of Debussy and Ravel.

PURCELL

Henry Purcell (1659?–1695) was a prodigy composer, writing trios and anthems at the age of nine. His anthems contain much fine music, although his true greatness is not found in them. When he takes himself seriously, he reaches a noble expression, with deep pathos, powerful declamatory passages and massive choral effects.

It is in his music for the stage that Purcell is at his greatest. There his magnificent gift of melody places him with the two greatest melodists the world has ever known, Mozart and Schubert; and his marvellous "sense of the theatre" has only been equalled in music by Wagner's. He had also a peculiar genius for expressing "English undefiled," recognizing the full importance of the words at a time when few composers gave them a second thought. His literary sensitiveness was doubtless developed by his close friendship with Dryden and other poets. But, as a rule, his works are deficient in that unity so essential to all works of art. One can transplant his songs and choruses from one work to another without damaging the unity of aim, for which he never sought. Of all musicians, he takes the shortest views; he is always concerned only with the immediate moment. Yet he achieved one perfect opera, *Dido and Aeneas,* the only one of his set to music *throughout.* Some authorities, indeed, have called it the *only* perfect English opera. The librettist, Nahum Tate, fortunately had the power here of producing a superb climax and then desisting.

But Purcell's art is first and foremost a really English art; no music is more English than his. His love of good broad tunes, swinging lilts, direct expression, special English forms such as military marches and quick-steps, the masks, national subjects, the pomp and circumstance of war, are all part of his Englishry, which is seen as clearly in his numerous short harpsichord pieces as anywhere. Purcell was a real genius, a serious and true artist, and his death at the early age of thirty-seven seems to have prevented his revealing his full measure. As it was, he left enough works of a superfine quality behind him to fill twenty-two volumes of the edition of the Purcell Society, which started its labours in 1876 and finished them in 1926. These works include anthems with orchestral accompaniment, cantatas, operas, plays with songs, royal odes, masques, chamber-music, harpsichord and organ pieces, duets, trios and catches. Every music lover should feel it to be his proud and pleasing duty to become acquainted with as much of Purcell's music as possible.

Georg Friedrich Handel

Adapted from "Handel"

By Romain Rolland

No GREAT musician is more impossible to include in the limits of one definition, or even of several, than Handel. He reached the complete mastery of his style very early (much earlier than J. S. Bach), although it was never really fixed and he never devoted himself to any one form of art. It is even difficult to see a conscious and a logical evolution in him. His genius is not of the kind which follows a single path and forges right ahead until it reaches its object. For his aim is to do well whatever he undertakes. This capacious mind looks out on the whole universe, and on the way the universe depicts itself, as a picture is reflected in calm and clear water. He owes much of this objectivism to Italy, where he spent many years, and the fascination of which never effaced itself from his mind; and he owes even more to that sturdy England which guards its emotions and eschews sentimental effusions. But that he had all the germs of his art in himself is already shown in his early works at Hamburg.

From his infancy at Halle [where he was born on February 23, 1685], Zachau had trained him not in one style, but in all the styles of the different nations, leading him to understand not only the spirit of each great composer, but to assimilate the styles by writing in various manners. This essentially cosmopolitan education was completed by his three tours in Italy and his sojourn of half a century in England. He never ceased to follow up the lessons learnt at Halle, always appropriating to himself the best from all artists and their works. Wherever he passed, he gathered some musical souvenir, buying and collecting foreign works, copying them—or, rather, copying down in hasty and often inexact expressions any idea which struck him in the course of reading. This vast collection of European thoughts, which only remains in remnants at the Fitzwilliam Museum at Cambridge, was the reservoir, so to speak, from which his creative genius continually fed itself. Profoundly German in race and character, he had become a world citizen, a European with a taste for Latin culture.

He drew not only from learned and refined music—the music of musicians—but also from the founts of popular music, that of simple, rustic folk. He noted down in his manuscripts the street cries of London, and he once told a friend that he received many inspirations for his best airs from them. Certain of his oratorios, like *L'Allegro ed il Penseroso,* are threaded with remembrances of his walks in the English country; and who can ignore the *pifferari* (Italian peasant's pipe) in *Messiah,* the Flemish carillon in *Saul,* the joyous popular Italian songs in *Hercules* and *Alexander Balus?* Handel was not an artist lost in introspection. He watched all around him, he listened, and observed. Sight was for him a source of inspiration, of hardly less importance than hearing. His blindness (which should have rendered his hearing still more sensitive) soon paralyzed his hearing when its principal source of renewal was withdrawn.

Thus, saturated in all the European music of his time, impregnated with the music of musicians, and the still richer music which flows in Nature, he wrote as one speaks, he composed as one breathes. He never sketched out on paper [but] wrote straight off as he improvised, and in truth he seems to have been the greatest improviser that ever was. He wrote his music with such an impetuosity of feeling and such a wealth of ideas that his hand was constantly lagging behind his thoughts, and in order to keep pace with them at all he had to note them down in abbreviated manner. But he had at the same time an exquisite sense of form. No German surpassed him in the part of writing beautiful melodic lines; Mozart and Hasse alone were his equals in this. It was to this love of perfection that we attribute that habit which, despite his fertility of invention, causes him to use time after time the same phrases, each time introducing an imperceptible change, a light stroke of the pencil, which renders them more perfect.

Handel worked no less with the music of other composers than with his own. If one had the time to study here what superficial readers have called his plagiarisms—particularly [in] *Israel in Egypt,* where the most barefaced of these cases occur—one would see with what genius and insight Handel has evoked their secret soul from the depths of these musical phrases. This evocatory character of Handel's genius should never be forgotten. He who is satisfied with listening to this music without seeing what it expresses, who judges this as a purely formal art, and who does not feel his expressive and suggestive power, will never understand it. It is music which paints emotions, souls, and situations, the epochs and the places which are the framework of the emotions and which tint them with their own peculiar moral tone. In a word, his is an art essentially picturesque and dramatic.

The inner meaning of his works was falsified in the century which followed his death by the English interpretations, [which were] strengthened further in Germany by those of Mendelssohn and his numerous following. By the exclusion of and systematic contempt for all the Handel operas; by eliminating nearly all the dramatic oratorios and even here giving an exaggerated supremacy to *Messiah;* by the interpretation of these works, in a pompous, rigid and stolid manner, with orchestra and choir far too numerous and badly balanced—there has been established the tradition which makes Handel a church musician after the style of Louis XIV—all decoration, columns, statues, and pictures by Le Brun.

Handel was never a church musician; he hardly ever wrote for the church. Apart from his *Psalms* and his *Te Deum,* composed for the private chapels and for exceptional events, he only wrote instrumental music for concerts and for open-air fêtes, for operas, and for those so-called oratorios which were really written for the theater. The first oratorios he composed were acted. And if Handel resolutely abstained from theatrical representation—which alone gives the full value to scenes such as the orgy and the dream of Belshazzar, expressly conceived for acting—on the other hand he stood out firmly for having his oratorios [produced] in the theater and not in the church. There were not wanting churches in which he could give his works, and by not doing so he turned against him the opinion of religious people who considered it sacrilegious to carry pious subjects on the stage; but he continued to affirm that he did not write compositions for the church, but worked for the theater—a free theater.

It is difficult to speak of "the opera" or "the oratorio" of Handel, for we do not find any single type. All the European tendencies of that time are reflected in his operas: the model of Keiser in his early works; the Venetian model in his *Agrippina;* the model of Scarlatti and Steffani in his first early operas. In the London works he soon introduces English influences, particularly in the rhythms. Again, those great attempts of genius to create a new musical drama: *Giulio Cesare, Tamerlano, Orlando;* later on, those charming ballet-operas inspired by France: *Ariodante, Alcina;* later still, those operas which point towards the *opéra comique* and the light style of the second half of the century: *Serse* and *Deidamia.*

Handel was too universal and too objective to believe that [but] one kind of art was the true one. He believed in two kinds of music only, the good and the bad. Apart from that he appreciated all styles. Thus he has left masterpieces in every style, but he did not open any new way in opera for the simple reason that he went a long way in nearly all paths already opened up. Constantly he experimented, invented, and always with his singularly sure touch. He seemed to have an extraordinary penetrating knowledge in invention, and consequently few artistic regions remained for him to conquer. There were new forms: the dramatic duet or quartet, the descriptive symphony opening the opera, refined orchestration, choruses and dances..

His operas were continually adapted to the changing tastes of the theater public of his age, and of the singers he had at his disposal; but when he left the opera for the oratorio he varied no less. It was a perpetual experimenting with new forms in the vast framework of the concert drama; and the instinctive ebb and flow in creation seems to have caused his works to succeed one another in nearly opposite styles of feeling and form. In each one Handel indulged momentarily a certain side of his feelings, and when that was finished he found himself in the possession of other feelings which had been accumulating while he was drawing on the first. He thus kept up a perpetual balance, which is like the pulsation of life itself. After the realistic *Saul* comes the impersonal epic of *Israel in Egypt*. After this colossal monument appear the two *genre* pictures, *The Ode for St. Cecilia's Day* and *L'Allegro ed il Penseroso*. After the Herculean *Samson*, a heroic and popular tragicomedy, sprang forth the charming *Semele*, an opera of romanticism and gallantry.

But if the oratorios are so wonderfully varied they have one characteristic in common even more than the operas: they are musical dramas. It was not that religious thought turned Handel to this choice of Biblical subjects, but [that] the stories of the Bible heroes [were] part of the very lifeblood of the people whom he addressed.

Without doubt, these oratorios were not made for stage performance, did not seek scenic effects, with rare exceptions—as for instance the orgy of *Belshazzar*. But passions and personalities were represented always in a dramatic fashion. Handel is a great painter of character, and the Delilah in *Samson*, the Nitocris in *Belshazzar*, the Cleopatra in *Alexander Balus*, the mother in *Solomon*, the Dejanira in *Hercules*, the beautiful Theodora, all bear witness to the suppleness and the profundity of his psychological genius. If in the course of the action he abandoned himself freely to the flow of pure music, in the moments of passionate crisis he is the equal of the greatest masters in musical drama. Is it necessary to mention the terrible scenes in the third act of *Hercules*, the beautiful scenes of *Alexander Balus*, the Dream in *Belshazzar*, the prison scenes in *Theodora* or in the first act of *Saul*, and—dominating all—certain of the choruses of *Israel in Egypt*, *Esther*, and *Joshua*, and in the *Chandos* Anthems, which seem veritable tempests of passion?

It is by these choruses that the oratorio is essentially distinguished from the opera. It is in the first place a choral tragedy. These choruses held a very important place in French opera, but their rôle was limited to that of commentator or else merely decorative. In the Handel oratorio they became the very life and soul of the work. Sometimes they took the part of the ancient classical chorus, which explained the drama, as in *Saul, Hercules, Alexander Balus, Susannah*. Sometimes they added to the shock of the human passions the powerful appeal of religion, and crowned the human drama with a supernatural aureole, as in *Theodora* and *Jephtha*. Or finally the chorus became the actors themselves, or the enemy-people and the God who guided them. It is remarkable that in his very first oratorio, *Esther*, Handel had this stroke of genius: in the choruses there we see, superbly depicted, the drama of an oppressed people and their God who led them by his voice.

The oratorio being a "free theater," it becomes necessary for the music to supply the place of the scenery. Thus its picturesque and descriptive rôle is strongly developed and it was by this above all that Handel's genius so struck the English public. Saint-Saëns wrote: "I have come to the conclusion that it is the picturesque and descriptive side, until then novel and unreached, whereby Handel achieved the astonishing favor which he enjoyed. This masterly way of writing choruses, of treating the fugue, had been done by others. What really counts with him is the color—that modern element which we no longer hear in him. . . . He knew nothing of exoticism. But look at *Alexander's Feast, Israel in Egypt,* and especially *L'Allegro ed il Penseroso,* and try to forget all that has been done since. You find at every turn a striving for the picturesque, for an imitative effect. It is real and very intense for the medium in which it is produced, and it seems to have been unknown hitherto."

Perhaps Saint-Saëns accentuates too much these descriptive tendencies of Handel as exceptional in his time. A great breath of nature was passing over German music, and pushed it towards tone-painting.

Telemann was, even more than Handel, a painter in music, and was more celebrated than Handel for his realistic effects. But the England of the eighteenth century had remained very conservative in music, and had devoted itself to cultivating the masters of the past. Handel's art was then more striking to the English on account of its "color" and its "imitative effects." I will not say with Saint-Saëns that there was no exoticism, for Handel seems to have sought this very thing more than once, notably in the orchestration of certain scenes for the two Cleopatras—*Giulio Cesare* and of *Alexander Balus*. But what was constantly with him was tone-painting, the reproduction through music of natural impressions—a poetic evocation of the raging tempests, the tranquil sea, the dark shades of night, the twilight which envelops the English country, the parks by moonlight, the sunrise in springtime, and the awakening of birds. *Acis and Galatea, Israel in Egypt, Allegro, Messiah, Solomon,* all offer a wondrous picture gallery of nature, carefully noted by Handel with the sure stroke of a Flemish painter, and of a romantic poet at the same time.

This romanticism drew upon him both admiration and violent criticism. "He cannot give people pleasure after the proper fashion," writes the anonymous author [of a letter of 1751], "and his evil genius will not allow him to do this. He imagines a new *grandioso* kind of music, and in order to make more noise he has it performed by the greatest number of voices and instruments ever heard in a theater. He thinks thus to rival not only the god of musicians, but even all the other gods; for I expected that the house would be brought down by his tempest, or that the sea would engulf the whole. But more unbearable still was his thunder. Never have such terrible rumblings fallen on my head." Similarly, Goethe said, after having heard the first movement of the Beethoven C minor Symphony: "One expected the house to fall about one's ears."

It is not by chance that I couple the names of Handel and Beethoven. Handel is a kind of Beethoven in chains. He had the unapproachable manner, like the great Italian artists who surrounded him—the Porporas, the Hasses; and between him and them there was a whole world. Beneath the classic ideal burned a romantic genius, precursor of the *Sturm und Drang* period; and sometimes this hidden demon broke out in brusque fits of passion—perhaps despite itself.

The orchestral music of Handel comprises twelve Concerti Grossi (1740); six Oboe Concertos (1734); the Sinfonias from his operas and oratorios; his open-air music—*Water Music* (1715 or 1717), *Firework Music* (1749); and Concerti for two horns.

Although Handel was a visualist, and though his music had a highly descriptive and evocatory power, he made only a very restrained use of instrumental tone-color. However, he showed on occasion a refined intelligence in its use. The two oratorios written at Rome, and his great virtuoso works *The Triumph of Time* and *The Resurrection* (1708) have a fine and well-varied orchestration. In London he was one of the first to introduce the horn into the opera orchestra. "He was the first," says Volbach, "to assert the expressive personality of the violoncello." From the viola he knew how to secure many curious effects; he gave to the bassoons a lugubrious and fantastic character; he experimented with new instruments, small and great; he used the drum solo in a dramatic fashion for Jupiter's oath in *Semele*. For special situations, by instrumental tone-colors, he secured effects not only of dramatic expression, but also of exoticism and local color.

But great painter as Handel was, he did not work so much through the brilliancy, variety, and novelty of his tone-colors as by the beauty of his designs and his effects of light and shade. With a voluntarily restrained palette, with the sober colors of the strings, he yet was able to produce surprising and thrilling effects. He had less recourse to the contrast and mixing of instruments than to the division of the same family of instruments into different groups. On the other hand, when he considered it advisable he reduced his instrumental forces by suppressing the viola and the second violin, whose places were taken by the harpsichord. All his orchestral art lies in true balance and economy, which, with a few colors, yet knows how to produce as powerful impressions as our musicians of today with their crowded palette. Nothing, then, is more important, if we wish to render this music truly, than to avoid upsetting the equilibrium of the various sections of the orchestra under the pretext of enriching it and bringing it up to date. The worse fault is to deprive it, by a useless surplus of tone-colors, of that suppleness and subtlety of nuance which is its principal charm.

Let us consider his Concerti Grossi. None of his works is more celebrated and less understood. Handel attached to them a particular value, for he published them by subscription, a means which was usual in his day but which he himself never adopted except under exceptional circumstances.

The kind of Concerto Grosso which consists chiefly in a dialogue between a group of solo instrumentalists (the *Concertino*) and the full body of instruments (*Concerto Grosso*), to which is added the cembalo, was, if not invented, at least carried out to its perfection and rendered classical by Corelli. The works of Corelli, aided by the efforts of his followers, had become widely known in Europe. Geminiani introduced them into England, and without doubt Handel did not hesitate to profit by the example of Geminiani, who was his friend; but it is much more natural to think that he learnt the Concerto Grosso at its source at Rome, from Corelli himself during his sojourn there in 1708.

After Corelli came Locatelli, and especially Vivaldi, who transformed the Concerto Grosso by giving it the free character of program music. But when the works of Vivaldi were played in London in 1723 and became thoroughly known to Handel it was always to Corelli that he gave the preference, and he was very conservative in certain ways even about him. The form of his concerto, of which the principal movements varied from four to six, oscillated between the suite and the sonata, and even glanced towards the symphonic overture. It is this for which the theorists blame him, and it is this for which I praise him. For he does not seek to impose a uniform cast on his thoughts, but leaves it open to himself to fashion the form as he requires, so that the framework varies accordingly, following his inclinations from day to day.

The spontaneity of his thought, shown by the extreme rapidity with which the Concerti were composed—each in a single day at a single sitting—constitutes the great charm of these works. They are not all of equal value; their conception itself, which depended in a way on mere momentary inspiration, is the explanation. The Seventh Concerto, for example (the one in B-flat major), and the last three have but a moderate interest; they are among those least played. But to be quite just we must pay homage to the Second Concerto in F major, which is like a Beethoven concerto, for we find there some of the spirit of the Bonn master.

Let us now come to that class of Handel's instrumental music to which historians have given far too little attention, and in which Handel shows himself a precursor and at the same time a model. I refer to his open-air music. This type took a prominent place in English life. The environs of London were full of gardens, where, Pepys tells us, "vocal and instrumental concerts vied with the voices of the birds." Handel wrote pieces especially intended for these garden concerts.

Generally speaking, he attached very little importance to them; they were little sinfonias, or unpretentious dances like the Hornpipe, written for the concert at Vauxhall in 1740.

But he composed some open-air works on a larger scale: from 1715 or 1717 the famous *Water Music,* written for the royal procession of barges on the Thames, and the *Firework Music* composed for the firework display given in Green Park on April 27, 1749, in celebration of the Peace of Aix-la-Chapelle.

The *Water Music* has a grand serenade in the form of a suite comprising more than twenty movements. It opens with a pompous opera overture; then come dialogues, with echoes of horns and drums, where the brass and the rest of the orchestra, which are arranged in two sections, respond. Then follow happy and soothing songs, dances, a bourrée, a hornpipe, minuets, popular songs, which alternate and contrast with the joyful and powerful fanfares. The orchestra is very nearly the same as in his usual symphonies, except that considerable importance is given to the brass. One even finds in this work certain pieces written in the chamber-music style, or in the theatrical manner.

With the *Firework Music* the character of open-air music is even more definitely asserted, quite as much by the broad style of the piece as by the orchestration, which is confined entirely to the wind instruments. The composition is divided into two parts: an overture which was to be played before the grand firework display, and a number of little pieces to be played during the display. The overture is a sort of stately march, has some resemblance to the overture of the *Ritterballet* of Beethoven, and is, like it, joyful and sonorous. The shorter movements comprise a bourrée; a *Largo alla Siciliana* entitled *Peace,* of a beautiful, heroic grace, which lulls itself to sleep; a sprightly allegro entitled *The Rejoicing;* and two minuets for conclusion. After 1740 Handel wrote hardly any other instrumental music than the *Firework Music* and the two monumental concertos for two horns.

The final evolution of his thought led him in the direction of music for the masses—for wide spaces and huge audiences. He had always in him a popular vein of thought. His art, which renewed itself perpetually at this rustic source, had in his time an astonishing popularity. Certain airs from his operas were circulated and popularized not only in England, but abroad. It is only a stupid pride and a small heart that denies value to the art which pleases humble people. What I wish to point out chiefly in the popular character of Handel's music is that it is always truly conceived for the people, and not for an élite, as was the French opera between Lully and Gluck. Without ever departing from his sovereign ideas of beautiful form, in which he made no concessions to the crowd, he reproduced in a language immediately "understanded of the people" those feelings in which all could share. This genial improviser, compelled during the whole of his life (a half-century of creative power) * to address a mixed public, was like the orators of old, who had the cult of style and the instinct for immediate and vital effect. Our epoch has lost the feeling of this type of art and men: pure artists who speak to the people and for the people, not for themselves or for their confrères. Today the pure artists lock themselves within themselves, and those who speak to the people are often mountebanks. The free England of the eighteenth century was somewhat like the Roman republic, and indeed Handel's eloquence was not without resemblance to that of the epic orators, who left their mark on the shuddering crowd. Sometimes his eloquence actually incarnated the national spirit, as in the case of *Judas Maccabaeus* immediately after the Jacobite rebellion. At the first performances of *Israel in Egypt* some of the auditors praised the heroic virtues of this music, which could raise up the populace and lead armies to victory.

By this power of popular appeal, as by all the other aspects of his genius, Handel was in the robust line of Cavalli and Gluck, but he surpassed them. Alone, Beethoven has walked in these broader paths, and followed along the road which Handel opened.

John Sebastian Bach

Abridged from "Studies of Great Composers"

By C. Hubert H. Parry

THE family of John † Sebastian Bach traced back their pedigree for many generations, which spread over more than a hundred years. And they not only knew their pedigree, but they knew a good deal about each individual member of it; and what his character was, and what

---

* He died in London on April 14, 1759.—E. S.

† The use of "John" instead of "Johann" was habitual with this author in writing of the Bach family. Indeed, it was common among his generation of British writers on music.—E. S.

were his occupations. Moreover, the quality which connects them all together most remarkably is their constant devotion to music. This was so great as to force itself upon the attention of the public; and in Erfurt, one of the towns where they filled prominent musical positions, it even came to pass that the town musicians were generally called "Bachs" from habit, whether there was a member of the family among them or no. They made Thuringia their home, and their affection for their native country was almost as great as their invariable devotion to their art. As generation succeeded generation, their fame as musicians increased and spread abroad, till the time of the great John Sebastian [1685-1750], when it arrived at its culmination; and is still survived to a considerable extent in his sons, and then abruptly came to an end.

The earliest member of the family of whom much is known that is worth knowing, was Veit Bach, who was born somewhere about 1550. He was not by profession a musician, but a miller and baker. He had decided tastes for music; and is said to have spent the spare time he could find from attending to his mill, in playing on some instrument like the zither. He had a son called Hans, who was a carpet weaver by profession, and a merry man by nature, and played upon a fiddle of some sort. Hans travelled much from town to town, and amused people with his fun, and pleased them with his playing; and he became a well-known and popular character throughout all Thuringia. He had several sons, all of whom had musical tastes, but the most important of them was Heinrich, who had the same cheerful bright disposition as his father, and better developed musical abilities. He became organist at Arnstadt, and lived on even after John Sebastian was born, till 1692, by which time he had officiated in that capacity for more than fifty years. He was not only important for his own abilities, but as the father of the two most distinguished members of the family before John Sebastian, both of whom he educated himself. These were John Christoph and John Michael. The former was court organist at Eisenach, and famous as one of the greatest performers of his day, and as a masterly and noble composer. The latter, who was the younger brother, was organist at Gehren, a place near Arnstadt, and was also distinguished as a composer; and he is also memorable as the father of John Sebastian's first wife, Maria Barbara. Besides these there were a great many more who were notable musicians, and sterling, healthy, true-hearted men; so that all things tended naturally to the culmination in John Sebastian.

He too was directly descended from Veit and Hans Bach, but not in the same line as John Christoph and John Michael. His father, John

Ambrosius, was their cousin, and in the earlier part of his life had lived at Erfurt, where he gained distinction as a musician, and married the daughter of a furrier, named Lämmerhirt. In 1671 he moved, and settled in Eisenach, where John Sebastian was born in 1685, probably on March 21, as is guessed from the day of his baptismal register, for there is no actual register of the day of his birth. He thus came into life surrounded by family traditions, which besides their musical aspect always had a very strong German character about them. He had too all the strongest and deepest influences of German Protestantism around him; and these things had so much effect upon his development that they can be traced as the causes of all that is most characteristic in his works. There is nothing indeed which sums up the nature of his style as a whole so strongly as German earnestness and sincerity, and the characteristic vein of religious sentiment, which seems to belong to his race.

He did not long enjoy the protection of his parents, but was left an orphan when he was only ten years old. His father can, therefore, have had but little influence upon his musical education; but it is said that the first musical impressions the boy received were from hearing him play upon the violin; and he began to learn that instrument very early under his father's direction. When his father died, his elder brother, John Christoph, took care of him for some years. He lived at Ohrdruff, a place not far off from Eisenach, on the other side of the Thuringian forest. Here John Sebastian began to settle to his musical education; though not to the exclusion of general culture, as he went in for the regular course of study at the "Lyceum" of the town, and learnt his Latin thoroughly enough to be able to make use of his knowledge serviceably later in life.

The violin which his father had begun with, fell to a certain extent into the background, and his attention was given more constantly to keyed instruments. The pianoforte was not invented, but its predecessors, the harpsichord and clavichord, were the most useful and popular instruments of their kind, and upon one or both of these the young musician soon made rapid progress. In fact, his progress was rather too fast for his elder brother Christoph, and jealousy seems to have caused him to put some obstacles in his way. John Sebastian devoured all the music that he could lay hands on, and learnt all the best of it by heart. There was one particular book that he was anxious to have the contents of, which was a valuable collection of the very best and finest organ music by German composers, which Christoph had got together. Christoph did not want his young brother to be level with him in everything, so he carefully kept this book locked up. But John Sebastian's eagerness for it was so great that he finally managed to get it out, possibly by rolling it up and slipping it through the lattice work of the bookcase; and then at night time and by moonlight, whenever the moon was bright enough, he managed slowly to copy it all out. It took him six months to do it, and then at last the elder brother found out what he had been about, and ruthlessly took his own book and the precious copy away.

From such circumstances as these, it is obvious he had soon learnt all he could from his elder brother; and from this time forward the greater part of his education was worked out by himself with extraordinary energy and perseverance. He got some experience of choral music at the school of the Lyceum, for there was a boys' chorus at Ohrdruff, as in many other German towns at that time, and it was an important part of the school course. This chorus used to have to sing motetts and other choral works at all sorts of celebrations, such as marriages and funerals; and the boys also did a great deal of singing before people's houses in the streets, as Luther had done long before in Bach's own native town of Eisenach. John Sebastian had a remarkably beautiful voice as a boy, and he rose to quite an important position among his fellows. But his education here was not destined to continue for long; for when he arrived at the age of fifteen his brother began to find his house and income rather too small to keep more than his own increasing family; and the young musician had to start on his own resources. His beautiful voice seems to have stood him in good stead at this crisis, and he was received into the choir of the church of St. Michael, at Lüneburg; and when his voice broke he was found so serviceable as an accompanist on the harpsichord, and as a player on the violin in the band, that he was still kept on in employment.

He was at this time beginning to show signs of the powers which in later years made him most famous next to his compositions. In Northern Germany there were at that time a good many distinguished organists. At Lüneburg, Bach had chances of hearing some of them, and no doubt learnt a good deal from them. But at no great distance off, at Hamburg, was a greater than any of these, named Reinken, and Bach soon made up his mind he must somehow get there to hear him; so when a holiday came he started off on foot, and trudged away with a cousin called John Ernst, and got safely to Hamburg and heard the famous organist. But one hearing did not suffice for him, and many journeys were made to and fro, to learn what he could from such a master. It had all to be very economically done, and a story was told by Bach himself in later years, which shows how close they had to keep. One time when he had been to Hamburg, and was on his way home, but still far from his destination, he found nearly all his money gone, and sat down on a seat outside an inn taking what tantalising pleasure he could from the savoury smell of edibles that came from within. Suddenly, up above, a window was opened, and a couple of heads of herrings were thrown out near him. Curiosity, or the hopes of lingering fragments of eatable fish, prompted him to pick them up, and, to his surprise, in each there was a very serviceable piece of money. He never succeeded in discovering who was his benefactor; but he made a characteristic use of the unexpected addition to his funds, for he turned about at once and went back to Hamburg to hear Reinken once more, and then had enough left to take him all the way home.

At Lüneburg he had but very poor organs to practise on; but, such as they were, they stood him in good stead; and though there is no account left of the impression his playing made upon any one there, it is obvious from what happened soon after this time that he was arriving at very considerable mastery of his favourite instrument. At the end of three years he moved to Weimar for a short time, and while he was there it so happened that the municipality of Arnstadt—a town not far off—had rebuilt one of their churches, which had been burnt down, and had put a fine organ into it, and were much in want of an organist who could do it justice. Bach happened to go over there to see some of his relations, and played upon the organ. The authorities no sooner heard him than they were convinced he was the man for the place. Before long he was installed, and began from that moment the definite line of that career which made him in the end one of the few greatest among the world's musicians. The music of the place was not in a very inspiriting condition, but he had a good organ to play upon, and a choir to compose for, and opportunities of hearing instrumental music occasionally; and these spurs were enough for the time. He began writing some of the earliest of the long series of church cantatas, and also wrote one of the first and the most curious of his works for the "clavier"—the name commonly given to the old counterpart of the modern pianoforte. This work was the *"Capriccio on the departure of a beloved brother,"* which he wrote when his brother, John Jacob, went off to join the Swedish guard of Charles XII; and this is the solitary example among his works of what is called programme music, each separate movement having a title prefixed which explains its meaning and purpose: such as "A general lamentation by friends," "Friends coming to take leave," an "Aria di Postiglione," and a fugue on a post-horn tune.

Bach lived a quiet life of steady work at Arnstadt for two years, and was always improving and strengthening his powers. But he still felt the need of some guidance. He wanted the opportunity to hear yet more of the performances of the old German organists; for he knew instinctively that no man can arrive at the highest pitch of art without learning all that has been mastered by the best intellects of previous times. At Arnstadt there was little opportunity of improving himself by observing other artists; and he began to be restless, and longed for another expedition like his former ones to Hamburg to hear Reinken. He appears to have become rather negligent of the duties of his office as organist, and it is inferred that he did not keep the choir up to the mark by sufficient drilling and practising. His mind was too strongly occupied by eagerness to develop his own powers to be able to give sufficient attention to choir practices. At last the opportunity came. He had managed to save sufficient money to keep him going for a while; and he asked leave for a holiday for four weeks, and started off again on a long journey on foot to Lübeck in the North. His object was to hear the famous Danish organist and composer, Buxtehude, who had been the most interesting and powerful performer of his time, but by 1705, when Bach was seeking him out, was getting an old man. Nothing is told of their meetings or relations with one another; but it is quite obvious that Bach was not disappointed in the old master, and it can hardly be imagined that Buxtehude, in his turn, can have failed to appreciate and sympathise with a nature which had so much in common with his own. Not very much remains of his compositions, but from what there is it is easy to see how much he influenced the younger artist. There is a richness of counterpoint, and fulness and vigour of harmony, and a glow of noble imagination, about some of his works which make them extraordinarily like Bach's, and in some cases the latter evidently copied the plan and style of the older composer.

The short four weeks passed, and he was due back at Arnstadt, but he could not tear himself away. He felt, perhaps, that the risk of losing his place there was more than worth running for the sake of such an opportunity to learn, as he felt himself to be learning, day by day, at Lübeck. Possibly he was too infatuated to care. Art was all in all to him, and he was yet too young to be hampered with a sense of personal responsibility when such a passion possessed him. He stayed on and on till the end of the year, and it was not till he had been away for four times as long as he had asked for leave of absence that he managed to tear himself away; and having said his last farewell to old Buxtehude, journeyed back to Arnstadt about February, 1706. The consistory were naturally not pleased by his behaviour, and took it seriously into account. They not only objected to his extension of his holiday without asking, but they found many other things in his conduct reprehensible. He had not kept his scholars in order, and he had not had enough rehearsals; his preludes to the hymns were too long; and he used to play such extraordinary harmonies in accompanying the chorales that the congregation got confused. There was a formal examination held, the amusing report of which is still in existence in the form of question and answer between the consistory and Bach. One of the points runs as follows: "We charge him with having hitherto been in the habit of making surprising variations in the chorales, and intermixing divers strange sounds, so that thereby the congregation were confounded. If in future he wishes to introduce some 'tonus peregrinus,' he must keep to it, and not go off directly to something else." Bach's answers were short and not very submissive. He may have felt ashamed of the liberty he had taken in extending his leave, but with regard to his playing he knew quite well what he was about, and that if the consistory did not understand his harmonies that was their stupidity and not his license. But the consistory were really very patient with him, and though they said they must have an answer in eight days, they allowed things to drift on without severer measures, though his answer never came for eight months. They occasionally sent him a reminder of his duty; and latterly they found fresh ground of complaint, for in one of the reports there stand the words, "We furthermore remonstrate with him on his having allowed the stranger maiden to show herself, and to make music in the choir." This sounds as if things were getting seriously strained between the consistory and the organist, and it is evident that they could not go on in such a manner for much longer.

But the mysterious stranger maiden points to the approach of another important event in Bach's life. The daughter of old John Michael Bach had come to Arnstadt after her father's death, and John Sebastian had fallen in love with her, and before long they came to the conclusion they must marry. But Arnstadt was not the place to settle in, and Bach began to look about for a more congenial home.

At length a favourable opening was found at the church of St. Blasius at Mühlhausen. The organist there had just died, and the council that had the duty of electing his successor did not hesitate long when Bach offered himself, and he was safely installed in June, 1707. A little time had to be spent in getting ready for setting up house, and then in three months he went back to Arnstadt to fetch his bride. Mühlhausen was a much better place for music than Arnstadt, but nevertheless it was not destined to keep Bach for long, as a still better opportunity for the development and use of his powers at Weimar offered itself; and in June of the year after he arrived he sent in his resignation to the authorities, who had treated him well and accepted his resignation with evident regret.

At Weimar was the court of a most excellent and earnest man, Duke Wilhelm Ernst, of Saxe Weimar. His interests were chiefly centred in the religion of the German Protestant Church, and he did all he could to strengthen and enliven its influence; and Bach, as a great representative of the best form of music of that Church, was sure of the ready sympathy which is so necessary to draw out an artist's full powers. He had by this time mastered enough of the art of the great organists, such as Reinken and Buxtehude, to go on with own development alone in safety; and in the quiet nine years he lived at Weimar he at length brought his own art to that marvellous pitch of power and perfection which has left him absolutely unrivalled and even unapproached as a composer of organ music in all the history of the world.

The simplest form of musical expression, and the backbone of German religious art, were the famous hymn-tunes known by the name of chorales, which began with Luther, and were produced in considerable numbers by his most ardent and earnest followers. These tunes had all the power of national songs, and were as familiar to all Protestants in Germany as their daily bread; and it so happened that their dignified and noble simplicity made them especially fitted for treatment on the organ. The organists learnt to use them in much the same sort of way as the early Italian composers had used hymns or secular tunes in the vocal masses and motetts. They made them, as it were, the inner thread of the piece they were developing, and wound round their simple melodies many dexterous lines of counterpoint of rich and expressive effect. This was the kernel and centre of their scheme of organ-playing; and generation after generation developed it to greater perfection. Buxtehude had been a great master of the art;

but Bach surpassed every one before or after him by his richness, freshness of invention, and nobility of thought in works of this kind.

Another most important form of organ music was an adaptation of a choral form called the fugue. This, too, had been elaborated by various composers in the course of preceding generations, and was brought to a very high degree of perfection, only leaving, as it were, the top-stone of the edifice to be put on by John Sebastian. The most suitable style of expression for the organ had been developed under these various influences; and soon after his arrival at Weimar the tree which had been so long growing began to come to its fruit; and before the nine years which he spent there were over, many of the works which are familiar to every organist of any taste and ability, and the delight of every one who appreciates great music, were completed. Bach was of all things, first and foremost, an organist. He developed marvellous powers as a writer for stringed instruments and for the clavichord, and his choruses, and arias, and recitatives are as fine as anything of the kind which exists in the world; but behind all these other forms the organ seems to serve as the foundation. Even in writing for voices, or for the violin, or the clavichord, he uses forms of expression which are borrowed from the organ style.

As an organist he certainly had no rival in his lifetime, and he probably has had none since. Many things which he did were totally new to the people of his generation. He could do infinitely more with his fingers than any other man; and the way in which he used to fly about with his feet on the pedals seemed to them almost incredible. But it must be believed that it was not only his agility which astonished them, but also the impressive grandeur of his style.

The time when he was at Weimar is also interesting for the production of some of the most attractive of his church cantatas. These were works which occupied something of the position in German Protestant services that anthems do in the Anglican Church; but they were rather more developed both in style and length, and commonly had a band as well as the organ to accompany them. Bach had, up to the time when he was at Weimar, a difficulty in finding any man who could write a cantata text fit to inspire him. At Weimar he had the good fortune to fall in with a man of really poetical temperament, of the name of Salomo Franck, who wrote many religious poems for him to set in the cantata form; which commonly consisted of a mixed series of choruses, recitatives, and arias, and ended with a chorale. One of the most popular, called *Ich hatte viel Bekümmerniss,* or *My spirit was*

in heaviness, was written by Franck, and was one of the earliest of those
composed at Weimar; and many more noble works of the kind followed
in rapid succession. But in these times Bach was more famous as a
performer than as a composer. He began to have pupils both for organ
and clavier, and to be called to visit various towns to play upon the
church organs for the enjoyment of the local public. In this way he
visited Halle, Handel's native town, and even had overtures made to
him to take the organist-ship there. At another time he went to Leipzig,
where he played the organ in one of the principal churches, and
conducted the performance of the cantata, *Nun komm, der Heiden
Heiland.* The most famous of these journeys from Weimar was one
to Dresden in the autumn of 1717. In those days there was a great deal
of music of all sorts going on in Dresden. There was a lively court,
and a theatre, and it was a centre which attracted many musical celebrities. When Bach was there it so happened that one of the most
famous of French harpsichord players was there also, by name Marchand. He had been organist to the King of France, and was a great
favourite with the musical public of Paris; and he really deserved his
fame, for he was gifted with considerable execution and taste; and his
reception at Dresden, where he had played to the king, had been as
favourable as in his native country. When Bach came, people began
to talk about their respective merits, and were inclined to pit them
against one another as the representatives of German and French art.
In the end Bach was driven by his supporters to offer Marchand a sort
of challenge. He was willing that Marchand should prescribe the terms
of the contest, and he would play or read or attempt any other feat of
skill proposed, on the conditions that Marchand would do the same.
The contest was to take place in public, and on the day appointed a
considerable company assembled to witness the curious trial of skill.
Bach arrived and waited long for his antagonist. People became impatient, and a messenger was sent in search of him. But he could nowhere be found, for he had left Dresden that morning by fast coach.
It was supposed that he had come to the conclusion that Bach was too
great an antagonist for his mettle, and had retired with precipitation.
But Marchand was, in fact, a worthy antagonist, and Bach himself was
well acquainted with his compositions for harpsichord before this
time; and, as is natural, the whole story was considered to be greatly
to Bach's honour, and to the honour of German art.

Very soon after this Bach's connection with Weimar came to an
end. He was probably disappointed at a man of far slenderer abilities

being preferred before him as capellmeister there; and when the Prince
of Anhalt Cöthen invited him to come to him as his capellmeister,
Bach readily closed with the offer. This was a comparatively untried
field for him, but it was one which he was quite ready to cultivate. Up
till this time his energies had been chiefly directed to organ and clavier
playing, and composing works for the organ and church cantatas. His
reputation in all these departments had reached a very high point,
but the greater part of his achievements in the line of secular instrumental music was yet to be begun.

Secular instrumental music is the most modern part of the modern
art of music. In the early times, when the art was beginning to grow,
scarcely any attention was paid to it at all; and when people who looked
upon music more or less seriously began to try and make music with
such instruments as they had, they only imitated or made arrangements
of vocal pieces, such as madrigals and motetts. Their instruments were
also very poor in comparison with what are in use in more modern
times. Instead of violins and violoncellos they had cumbrous coarse-
sounding instruments called viols; and instead of the pianoforte they
had the twanging harpsichord, which was almost incapable of expression, or degrees of loudness and softness; or the little clavichord, which
was very capable of expression, but so soft that it could hardly be heard
a few yards off. Before Bach's time things had got better in the matter
of the instruments which were played with the bow like the violin,
but for keyed instruments they still depended on the harpsichord and
clavichord.

There is another point, too, about instrumental music which is
worth considering, which was the slowness with which people develop
what is called execution, or *technique*. Corelli, noble player as he was
on the violin, could not face certain kinds of difficulties, which mere
children in the present day would think nothing of; and in harpsichord
playing it would have been much the same. The reason of such a state
of things in connection with keyed instruments was, chiefly, that they
were so slow in learning the art of fingering. Many men thought it
really did not matter how the fingers were used so long as the notes
were sounded, and up to Bach's time they hardly ever used their thumbs
at all. Even on the organ, great organists like Buxtehude and Reinken
seem only to have used their thumbs in stretches which were too wide
for the fingers alone. In relation to the harpsichord this seems quite
natural, as it was no use striking the keys as players do the keys of the

pianoforte; for however hard they were struck, no difference was made in the loudness of the tone. Consequently, instead of playing with the hand bent or crumpled up, as is done in pianoforte playing, harp-sichord players kept their hands quite flat and their fingers straight out, and wagged them up and down like sticks fastened with a hinge to the knuckles of the hand; and in that position both the little finger and the thumb were too far back to reach the keys without incon-venience. People used to play their scales by turning the middle finger and the third finger over one another as best they could, and they used their little fingers to help them out of occasional difficulties. Just before Bach's time people were waking up to the possibility of using the thumb now and then. Couperin, the famous writer of harpsichord music in the time of Louis XIV. of France, admitted it now and then in his method, but still it must be doubted if he changed the position of the hand enough to make very much difference. Bach, in his turn, seems to have faced the question thoroughly. He appears to have made up his mind to play with the hand bent, and to use the thumb as freely as the fingers, and to turn it under, or to turn the fingers over it un-reservedly. But he still did not get to the system of fingering used in later times, and in playing on the organ he used to prefer getting smooth effects by sliding some of the fingers over one another. When he was settled at Cöthen his mind naturally turned in the direction of using what he had mastered in all these respects; for at Cöthen he was no longer in the position of a mere organist, and if he had been there was hardly any organ worthy of his powers, and the prince, his master, was not wealthy enough to have such an establishment as a big choir or a theatre, but cultivated his musical tastes in the direction of a high class of instrumental music, and it was for this department that Bach now became responsible.

It is a curious instance both of the amount of influence a man's circumstances may have upon his work, and the advantage it may be to train energies deliberately, so as to make the best use of them. When Bach had a good organ at his disposal, and a good opportunity of testing his work and other people's, he wrote organ works; when he had a choir at his disposal he wrote church cantatas; now, at Cöthen, he had good opportunities of trying other people's instrumental works, and observing their effects and how the effects were done, and putting his own work through the same ordeal; and at Cöthen he wrote the larger part of his most important secular instrumental works of all kinds, such as those for the clavier, as it was called; and for the violin, and for various instruments in combination. Among the best known of these in this country [England] is the collection known as the *Forty-eight Preludes and Fugues*. But it was not forty-eight when the collection was first made, but only twenty-four which was enough to run once through all the keys, major and minor. The second book was added considerably later. This collection is called in the German "the well or equal tempered clavier," and serves as a practical assertion of Bach's views on the important point of tuning a keyed instrument. In old days, when men did not use many keys, it was enough to have a few well in tune, and to let the keys with many sharps and flats in them be out of tune. Bach saw clearly that composers could not in the end do without being able to use all keys, and by way of illustrating his opinion he put together this set of preludes and fugues in all the keys, and called it by the name which pointed to its purpose, *The well-tempered clavier;* which means, in other words, the keyed instrument which is tuned equally well for all keys. This work was, with a few of the organ works, the first by which he became known in this country, and has not only been the constant source of happiness, and content, and comfort to most of the musicians of any standing since the beginning of the nineteenth century, but it has all the elements of the most lasting value imaginable. In it men find almost all the shades of feeling they can desire, except such as are tainted with coarseness or levity. The very depths of pathos and sadness are sounded in some numbers, in others there is joy and lightness, in others humour and merriment, in others the sublimest dignity, and in others that serenity of beauty which seems to lift man above himself, and to make him free for the time from the shadows and darker places of his nature. And all pieces alike are cast in a form of most perfect art, and on that scale which can be realised completely at home with no more elaborate resources than one little keyed instrument.

Another collection, which is well known to musicians under the name of the French Suites, is associated with a change in Bach's life which followed one of his most serious domestic calamities.

Bach's master, the Prince of Cöthen, used to go yearly to Carlsbad, and took his musicians with him. For several years Bach attended him. One of these years Bach arrived home after some time of absence with his master, eager for the glad greetings of his wife, and he was met instead with the news that she was already dead and buried. Bach was a man of profound emotions, and he suffered as such men do. But he was strong and brave, and had work to do, and he would not allow his loss to break him down. Before long he was at his accustomed duties, and travelled about much as before. One of his visits took him once more to Hamburg, where old Reinken was still alive and playing his organ, though ninety-seven years old; and Bach had the pleasure of meeting again the old master from whom he had begun to learn so long before, in the days when he trudged over from Lüneburg on foot; and it is a comfort to find that old Reinken appreciated Bach in his turn, and listened to him with interest.

Towards the end of the following year Bach married again. The second wife's name was Anna Magdalena, and she was the daughter of a man called Wülken, the court trumpeter of Weissenfels. About her much more is known than about the first wife. She seems to have been most wonderfully fitted for Bach. She sang, and she played; and, most serviceable of all, she had an excellent clear hand for copying music, and frequently helped her husband in the laborious business of writing out the music he composed. He gave her lessons on the clavier. There are books of the music she used to play, most of it copied out by herself, with a large proportion of her husband's work in them, and with some of his writing too. In these books the famous French Suites soon made their appearance. Bach did not call them French in the first instance, but they were most likely called by that name later, after the suites by famous French clavier composers which consisted of similarly short and concise movements. These suites were musically far the best which had been produced up to that time, and some of them, such as the last two, are among Bach's freshest and happiest works. Besides writing in this way for the clavier, Bach turned his attention to instrumental music of other kinds. The famous suites and sonatas for violin solo, which are still the finest concert pieces of all the greatest violinists of the present day, were composed at this time, and also some suites for orchestra, which are not so often heard. The greater part of the time at Cöthen, about which but little in the way of biographical details has been left, seems to have been devoted to the study and production of such instrumental music; and this was the latest branch of art which he attacked.

Bach's stay at Cöthen lasted till well on into the year 1723. By that time the prince had married, and the new princess having no liking for music, her husband's attention was drawn away into other directions. Bach seemed for the time to be neglected, and he felt that his art was no longer so much honoured as it had been, and the office of Cantor to the school of St. Thomas in Leipzig falling in his way, he accepted it.* It was considered rather a step down for him to become a cantor after having been a capellmeister; but this particular cantorship had always been held by distinguished men, and life in Leipzig had certain decided advantages, so, as he said in a letter to a friend, he "ventured in the name of the most Highest," and having "passed his examination undertook to move to Leipzig."

The cantor's was a curious office. He was elected by the town council, and was considered to be under its supervision. The cantor had to attend to the choir of the school, and to teach them and conduct them when they sang at any festivals; and besides this he was expected to give lessons in Latin to some of the lower classes in the school, to which duties Bach added the directorship of the music in St. Thomas's Church. He was quite ready to perform these various offices, but there were some drawbacks against him. The choir of the school had got into a most unsatisfactory state, and the town council was not the sort of body to understand either him or his difficulties. There was also a consistory which had the right to meddle in the musical arrangements, and between them all it was no wonder that before long there was general dissension and cross purposes. The town council so utterly failed to appreciate him that they addressed a remonstrance to him, and described him as "incorrigible," and resolved to take away his income. Bach was not at all subservient, but he was very much disgusted, and even tried to find some new place more worthy and appreciative of his powers. But fortunately for Leipzig and the cantorship which his name has made famous, the stupidity of the town council did not have its natural results, and Bach remained in this post for the rest of his days. He was fortunate enough to find a real and appreciative friend in a new rector of the school who was elected about this time. This was a very superior man, and an able scholar, named Gesner, who in a short while got the school into very much better condition, and managed to make things go more smoothly with the town council, who, under his influence, had a better chance of understanding their great cantor.

At Leipzig Bach turned his attention again chiefly to church music. In the churches there the musical part of the service was very elaborate, and he had plenty of occasions to write for. One of the earliest works which he produced after his arrival was the music to the history of

* The position did not exactly "fall" in Bach's way. Actually he was one of six candidates who applied for it. After the Leipzig electors had offered the Cantorate to two applicants and were turned down by both, they offered it to Bach, because, as they said, no one better presented himself!—E. S.

the Passion according to St. Matthew, which has become one of the most famous of his works. The idea of appealing to people's emotions in Holy Week by performing a musical setting of this tragic crisis of the story as told in the Gospels had originated long before; and many German composers had undertaken the task before Bach, including Handel. Bach appears of all men to have been most fitted to accomplish the task with all the poetry and devotion it calls for, and even with great dramatic effect at times. In thinking of this great work it is most natural to draw comparisons with Handel's oratorios. It is not strictly an oratorio, though it has some of the external apparatus of an oratorio, such as great choruses, solos, and recitatives, and elaborate accompaniment of orchestral instruments. But the treatment of the subject and the use of these forces is extremely different in the two great masters. In Handel's work there is grandeur, noble feeling, admirable treatment of the voices, and a great deal of the suavity and simple ease of motion which came from his frequent contact with Italians and with the great singers of the opera; but his treatment of his orchestral forces is rather crude and colourless, though vigorous and easily dealt with. Bach's work is, of all things, most thoroughly German. He broods and reflects more than Handel does; he makes superb effects with his voices, but he often treats them more as instruments, or parts of an organ work. The music, on the whole, has much more character, colour, and delicate variety of feeling and subtlety than Handel's; but it is not so direct, and simple. In Handel's work the influence of the opera for good and sometimes for the contrary is often apparent. Bach, on the other hand, had had next to nothing to do with opera at any time; he made use of opera forms in his airs, but the style is far removed from anything connected with the stage.*

Bach wrote other settings of the Passion besides that according to St. Matthew. That according to St. Mark appears to have been lost, but that according to St. John has often been performed in this country, and has been well appreciated. It is not on the same scale as that according to St. Matthew, but has the same noble and poetical qualities. He wrote a great deal of church music on a grand scale besides these works; for instance, the famous B Minor Mass, one of the most gigantic

---

* Yet one of Bach's pupils described the reaction to the first performance of the *St. Matthew* Passion as follows: "Some high officials and well-born ladies in one of the galleries began to sing the first Chorale with great devotion from their books. But as the theatrical music proceeded they were thrown into the greatest wonderment, saying to each other, 'What does it all mean?' while one old lady, a widow, exclaimed, 'God help us! 'tis surely an Opera-comedy!' "—E. S.

choral works in existence, and also the *Christmas Oratorio,* and a grand setting of the Magnificat and an immense number of church cantatas. At Leipzig there was a great demand for compositions of this latter class, and he seems to have been constantly producing fresh ones for performance on Sundays and great festivals at the churches where he directed the music. Before he came to Leipzig he had probably written twenty-nine; while he was there he appears to have produced over two hundred and ninety, some of which have been lost. This enormous mass of work seems all the more amazing when the richness and variety, and the amount of labour he expended over such works, is taken into account. It is not at all a wonderful thing for every-day composers to turn out cheap or popular operas and operettas by the cartload, as French composers have done; but to write nearly three hundred works of one kind, all of which have thought and elaborate artistic workmanship and individual character about them, is an amount of labour which few men in history can rival.

Bach's life continued always in the same quiet and comparatively uneventful way, which was so unlike the busy manager's life, with many journeys to and fro to foreign countries, and the association with people of all ranks and callings in the lively society of London, which was Handel's lot and his natural atmosphere. The limits of Bach's journeyings hardly exceeded a small portion of his native country, and most of the various towns where he occupied different musical posts one after another were close together and in the same district. His music made very small way with the general public in his lifetime, and the connoisseurs of other countries were rather inclined to look down upon him as a crabbed, curious old pedant, who delighted in mechanical ingenuities and tiresome puzzles. This seems quite explicable and natural considering how rare is the gift of appreciating really great music.

But even among the wiser people of his generation and of that immediately succeeding him his style had but little effect. And this is the more remarkable because he was a great teacher of his art, and had very great influence over his pupils, who naturally felt him to be the greatest musician they had ever come across. His most successful pupils were his own sons, several of whom had very great musical abilities. His favourite was his eldest son, Wilhelm Friedemann, and this one, no doubt, had the greatest depth and character of all of them. But he was unfortunately of a wild temperament, and though he produced some noble works, his abilities were wasted by dissipation, and he sank into deeper misery as he grew older, and ended his life in poverty and uselessness. The second son, Philip Emmanuel, gained great fame and did a great quantity of invaluable work, especially as a clavier-player and writer for keyed instruments. But his line was quite different from his father's, and not by any means so lofty in sentiment or broad in style. This was partly owing to a great change which came over the musical world, which will have to be considered later on; and this affected the work of another son, John Christian, even more strongly in the same way. They all of them profited technically by what their father taught them, but his style had reached too high a pitch of feeling for them to grasp, and in the deepest things of expression he was not able to teach them to do anything which can be said to follow naturally from his style. As time went on and he got more advanced in years he grew to like more and more the quiet, orderly life of his home, with its regular round of duties, and leisure for the constant pursuit of that art which men always find to be the more endless in its possibilities of improvement as they get more thoroughly to understand it. His journeys consequently became less frequent; but there was one journey which he took in the latter part of his life which has become famous, both because it shows how highly his powers were appreciated in Northern Germany, and also because it puts a very interesting and famous man in a peculiar light.

That extraordinary man, Frederick the Great, had all his life long taken great delight in music, and in the intervals of fighting, organising, diplomatising, and carrying out more great schemes than any other man alive, he somehow managed to find time, not only to hear the select musicians whom he kept about him, but to play with them pretty regularly of an evening. Philip Emmanuel, Bach's second son, had been appointed one of his musicians as accompanist and so forth, in 1740, and partly through him and partly through other distinguished members of the musical circle at Potsdam, Frederick's curiosity about John Sebastian Bach was roused to a very high pitch, and he wished very much to see and hear him. Bach was too fond of his quiet life at home to be eager about the journey, but he was at last persuaded to undertake it in 1747. He appears to have arrived at Potsdam in the afternoon, and the news was brought to Frederick just as he had got his flute in his hand ready to begin playing at his usual afternoon concert. Frederick was generally as regular and systematic as a good clock, and held discipline and etiquette to be indispensable to the right ordering of human affairs. But his eagerness overcame his usual habits. His flute was laid aside at once with the exclamation, "Old Bach is come!" and Bach was sent for, and was not even allowed time to change his clothes and put on a suit of such respectful colour as was considered proper at a court. When he came in Frederick set him to work at once to extemporise and show his mastery both as a performer and an artist. He gave him a subject for a fugue, which he had to develop at once on the spot to satisfy the curiosity of the king; and he was afterwards taken to try the Silbermann pianofortes, which were then but lately invented, and had been taken possession of by the royal amateur. His powers were tested in all sorts of ways, and the king seems to have shown much appreciation of the difficulties of the science of music by the experiments to which he subjected him. Bach evidently satisfied Frederick's highest anticipations, and was treated with exceptional honour; and after he went home he wrote a sort of memento of the occasion, in which he combined all sorts of wonderful musical contrivances and masterly strokes of art, which he dedicated to Frederick [*Das Musikalisches Opfer*—The Musical Offering].

In his latter days he continued developing instrumental music. He added the twenty-four more preludes and fugues to the collection before described to complete the work which is known in this country as the "Forty-eight." He wrote also some more suites, which are on a grander and broader scale than the French ones, which appeared soon after his second marriage at Cöthen; and he also wrote some works which make nearer approach to the forms of later days, such as the so-called concertos, both for solo instruments, and for combinations like two or three claviers with small orchestra. And all these show, not only that his powers were as strong and his mastery greater as he grew older, but even that he maintained his youthful fire and geniality and freshness till the last.

Every one notices what a strong preference Bach had for fugues; and it perhaps may fairly be said that the form of fugue was as much his natural way of putting his musical thoughts as the sonata later was Beethoven's. But his fugues are utterly unlike any one else's. Most other musicians, when they have been writing fugues, have worked as if ingenuity was the sole aim of their ambition; which makes their productions of this kind belong more to the order of sport than to the order of genuine music. But Bach looked at the form of a fugue not as an end of itself, but as a means of expressing something essentially musical. He had the mastery of the art, elaborate as it is, so completely in his control that he could naturally express in this form things just as sweetly and perfectly beautiful in the highest sense as any spontaneous musical effusion of Schumann or Schubert. No other man in the world has ever written such instrumental fugues, and it may be safely prophesied that no man ever will. Very often his fugues are much less elaborately ingenious than other people's; and very often, too, they do not contain anything like the orthodox amount of technical devices which theorists say are indispensable to a good fugue. He was quite contented to show in a certain number of fugues that he could make more wonderful devices of the fugal kind than any other man, but he did not think it was always necessary to be doing so. He wanted to make music, not puzzles. At the same time he so far divined what was possible even in instruments that he did not possess, that his works of this kind seem naturally to lend themselves to all the highest possibilities of the most perfect modern pianoforte. He himself was not much attracted by the pianofortes he had the opportunity of trying. They were, no doubt, in some ways more or less defective; and it must be remembered, too, that the ways in which the fingers have to be used to get the best effects out of them are so different to the ways he was accustomed to on his favourite little clavichord, that he most likely found he could not produce the peculiar kind of delicate expression he wanted. The pianoforte did not make much way with any of the musicians in those days. His famous son, Philip Emmanuel, still went on calling the clavichord the most beautiful of instruments till long afterwards, and Haydn and Mozart in their younger days still kept to the old harpsichord. There was so much to be done in the way of changing the habits and practice of players in the positions of their hands and fingers, that full appreciation of the way to manage the pianoforte does not seem to have come till a full generation and more after Bach was dead.

Towards the end of his life his eyes began to trouble him. He had always tried them severely from the time when he copied his brother's collection of organ music by moonlight, till his old age; and it is wonderful they served him well so long. It became necessary to risk an operation, and the responsibility was confided to an English oculist who was living in Leipzig. It was tried more than once, but without success, and he became totally blind. His health, which seems to have been wonderfully good throughout till this time, at last gave way, and then the fight was not long. A fever came on, and on the 28th of July, 1750, in the evening, he died, and was buried with sincere and general mourning near the Church of St. John in Leipzig.

Few men of that time were capable of realising the true greatness of the man they had lost. They admired him as a great master craftsman, a great organist, and a powerful controller of all the forces and difficulties of art. It has remained for men of full a hundred years after his time to realise the depth and almost inexhaustible fertility of his genius, and to understand fully the meaning of that saying of Schumann's, that he was a man "to whom music owes almost as great a debt as religion owes to its founder."

Josef Haydn

Abridged from "Men of Music"

By Wallace Brockway and Herbert Weinstock

IN 1795 England was well embarked on that bloody and protracted strife with France that was to end on the field of Waterloo some twenty years later. It was a black year, characterized by bread riots and widespread famine. There were threats against the life of the younger Pitt, whose indomitable spirit alone kept the war going. In October, a hungry mob howled at poor crazy George III on his way to open Parliament. Everyone except the ministry wanted peace, and it seemed that the brave English nation could think of nothing but its misery. Parliament was the scene of acrimonious debate on matters of the gravest import. And yet, at a time when the most trivial motion was made a pretext for embarrassing the government in the voting, the battling Whigs and Tories agreed to honor an Austrian * composer's claim for one hundred guineas. For the creditor was Franz Josef Haydn, who had lately given the people of England such musical fare as they had not enjoyed since the days of Handel.

Of course, some of the more old-fashioned squires may have muttered that the bill was not in the best of taste. It was well known that Herr Haydn had carried away a small fortune from the island, not to speak of a talking bird of inestimable value. A more fastidious man, going off with such spoils, might well have hesitated to bill the royal

---

* The idea that Haydn had some Croatian blood has now been thoroughly discredited.—Authors.

family for the unique honor of appearing at twenty-six command performances.

But the truth is that the excellent businessman who presented the
claim was anything but a fastidious gentleman. He was a peasant, with
a peasant's shrewdness and realism about money matters. That is the
fundamental thing to remember about Josef Haydn, Mus. D. (Oxon),
Kapellmeister to His Serene Highness Prince Esterházy, and the
music that he made. Even in his silkiest peruke and most brocaded
court suit he never forgot his poor and humble origins and, far from
trying to gloss them over, proudly described himself as something made
from nothing. His father was a wheelwright, his mother a cook; both
families were completely undistinguished.

Haydn's father lived at Rohrau, in Lower Austria, and there, in
a poor, almost squalid, house that is still standing, the composer was
born on March 31, 1732. Both of his parents loved music, the father
playing the harp by ear. Their leisure hours were often spent singing
the local folk melodies that Haydn himself was to use as thematic material. The child showed such a lively interest in this homemade music,
and sang so sweetly, that at the age of six he was carried off to near-by
Hainburg by a distant relative who there served as schoolteacher and
choirmaster. His preceptor, though unnecessarily harsh, grounded him
in the fundamentals of violin and clavier, and trained his voice so well
that two years later, when the music director of St. Stephen's at Vienna
was passing through Hainburg, and heard Haydn sing, he asked to
have the boy for his choir. Permission was granted, and Haydn became
a Viennese at the age of eight.

So much legend has clustered around Haydn's life in St. Stephen's
choir school that it is no longer possible to disentangle fact from fiction.
Boiled down to their bare essentials, these often pointless stories testify
not only to his extreme poverty, but also to his intense love of music.
The choirmaster, whose sole interest was to keep his establishment
running on the smallest possible amount of money, did little to encourage Haydn's obvious talent. He was a cruel and exacting slave driver,
and it is amazing that his stern, repressive measures did not crush the
boy's high spirits. There was never any love lost between the two, and
when Maria Theresa complained of Haydn's voice, which was beginning to break, the choirmaster was glad to seize upon the first pretext
for dismissing him. When Haydn was accommodating enough to cut
off another chorister's pigtail, and was summarily thrown out, the

director doubtless congratulated himself on having washed his hands of an insolent practical joker.

Thus, at the age of seventeen, Haydn found himself alone and friendless in the streets of Vienna. This was not quite so bad as it sounds, for though almost a century was to elapse before Johann Strauss made Vienna the symbol of *Schwärmerei,* it was already the scene of gaiety and good fellowship. Musicians of all ranks entertained their patrons and friends with open-air serenades, often scored for full orchestra. Vienna was organized like a luxury liner, with half the population devoted to the full-time business of entertaining a benevolently disposed nobility. The streets were full of friendly people, who were too busy having a good time to stand on ceremony. One of them— a tenor with a wife and child—met Haydn disconsolately roaming about, and generously offered him a bunk in his humble attic. For three years Haydn's efforts to stave off hunger were no more interesting or distinguished than those of any young man in his position: he sang in church choirs, took part in street serenades, and helped out the music at weddings, funerals, and other festal occasions. All this time he studied hard: he learned theory backward and forward, and practiced the clavier. He got hold of six of Karl Philipp Emanuel Bach's clavier sonatas, and studied them so thoroughly that they became the backbone of his own style. In crystallizing the sonata form, Karl Philipp Emanuel had in one respect outdone his illustrious father, who evolved nothing, but perfected forms already at hand. Haydn himself, in both his quartets and symphonies, developed the new form far beyond anything achieved earlier, but its fundamental architecture he owed to the pioneer. Quick to give praise where it was due, he freely admitted this debt, and Bach returned the compliment by proclaiming Haydn his one true disciple.

Spurred on by his studies in theory and his increasing command of instrumental resources, Haydn had begun to compose. Most of his very early works, including a comic opera for which he received the splendid sum of twenty-five ducats, are lost. An indifferent Mass, for which, as one of his firstborn, Haydn had a sneaking partiality, survives. It must be admitted that these first flights add little to his stature as a composer, and at the time added less to his purse. He even had to accept menial jobs to make ends meet. For several years he gave music lessons to a young Spanish bluestocking whose general education was being supervised by "the divine Metastasio." Haydn's meeting with this stuffy but kindly old bachelor set in motion a train of events that determined the entire course of his life. For Metastasio introduced him to another stuffy old bachelor, Niccola Porpora, "the greatest singing master that ever lived." Haydn aspired to study with him, but had nothing to offer in payment except his services as valet and accompanist. Porpora, whose penny pinching was notorious, drove the hardest possible bargain.

Working for Porpora was probably the toughest job Haydn ever filled. Porpora was an irascible old man, embittered by his fruitless rivalry with Handel, unsuccessful quest for high preferment, and the obvious truth that his great days were mostly behind him. Haydn had to bear the brunt of his spleen. But between brushing the *maestro's* filthy clothes and accompanying the Venetian ambassador's mistress at her singing lessons, he somehow managed to get the information he wanted. George Sand has amusingly embroidered the few facts known about this strange relationship in her long but rewarding musical novel, *Consuelo*. Although Haydn, with his usual generosity, admitted his debt to Porpora, it was actually less artistic than social— through him he met many wealthy noblemen and celebrities, among them Gluck, already famous for a long series of conventional operas, but not yet embarked on his stormy career as a reformer. More important to Haydn was a rich Austrian squire, Karl von Fürnberg.

Fürnberg, a man of artistic tastes, who entertained lavishly at his country house outside Vienna, invited the needy young man to assume the direction of the music at Weinzierl. Haydn accepted with alacrity, and in 1755 initiated his long career as a household musician. He was at Weinzierl less than a year, but in that brief time wrote a series of eighteen pieces for strings, which he labeled indifferently *divertimenti,* nocturnes, and cassations. Basing them on the conventional orchestral suite, he gradually refashioned them in the light of the formal hints he had taken from the sonatas of Karl Philipp Emanuel Bach. In this way, Haydn slowly made something new out of the suite, bringing into being, according to the instruments used, his conceptions of the string quartet and the symphony. Naturally, he did not effect this transformation at one sitting or without getting ideas from other composers: the gap between one of the Weinzierl pieces and the *Oxford* Symphony of his last period is enormous. He made many false starts (some of them delightful) before evolving the four-movement symphony and quartet that until yesterday were the formal norms for these media.

Haydn returned to Vienna with money in his pocket and prestige increased. He came perilously near to becoming a fashionable singing and clavier teacher. After three years, during which he seems to have sacrificed his creative ambitions to ready-money teaching and performing jobs, he was rescued by von Fürnberg, who recommended him to Count Maximilian von Morzin, a Bohemian grandee who kept a country establishment far beyond his means. Von Morzin engaged Haydn as his music director and composer at the niggardly salary of two hundred florins yearly—about $100. His new master kept him a scant two years, during which he returned to composition, producing a mass of miscellaneous pieces that have mostly been forgotten.

Now twenty-eight years old, and good Viennese bourgeois he had become, Haydn bethought himself of taking a wife. There were three stumbling blocks in the way of his marriage: his stipend was too meager to support even a frugal bachelor; Count von Morzin never kept a married man in his employ, and the girl of Haydn's choice—a barber's younger daughter—entered a convent. None of these warnings could shake his determination: he wanted to get married, and nothing could stop him. Accordingly, when the calculating barber suggested his elder daughter as a second choice, Haydn rose to the bait. On November 26, 1760, he led the elder Fräulein Keller to the altar. She was three years his senior—and a highly unreasonable woman. From the beginning, this loveless marriage was doomed to failure. Fortunately, Haydn was not a very emotional man, and marrying a harridan could not break his spirit. There were no children to hold them together, and after a few years a separation was quietly arranged, though he continued to support her.

Von Morzin had no opportunity to apply to his musical director his odd rule about married men. His creditors denied him that luxury. Early in 1761, he was obliged to retrench, and his musicians were among the first dismissed. Luckily for Haydn, just before the collapse Prince Pál Anal Esterházy visited von Morzin, and was greatly impressed by Haydn's compositions and by his conduct of the band. He at once offered him a place in his own musical establishment, and so, when he was dismissed, Haydn went almost immediately to the Esterházy estate at Eisenstadt.

Haydn was to remain in the service of the Esterházys until the dawn of the nineteenth century. Because of the medieval temper of the Hungarian squirearchy, as well as the idiosyncrasies of his masters, he was practically a prisoner in the country for almost thirty years. Very occasionally, when he had an acute attack of wanderlust, he resented this enforced isolation. But he was not a man to beat his wings against the bars in senseless fretting—he was inclined to take life as he found it. As a peasant who had come up in the world, homely philosophy was definitely his line, and he almost invariably stuck to it. A Beethoven or a Mozart could not have brooked the soul-sapping monotony of petty court life—either they would have revolted by running away, or would have stifled their anguish in tragic masterpieces. But Haydn was content, even when his fame had spread throughout Europe, to remain the perfect upper servant perfectly performing his daily duties.*

When Haydn first took up his residence at Eisenstadt, he found his duties comparatively light. The musical establishment was small, and besides, he was at first only assistant *Kapellmeister*. In less than a year, however, Prince Pál Antal died, and was succeeded by his more ostentatious brother, who immediately began to expand in all directions. His Serene Highness Prince Miklós Jozsef Esterházy of Galánta, Knight of the Golden Fleece, was known, with the curious understatement of the eighteenth century, as "the Magnificent." Decked out in his renowned diamond-studded uniform, he would be perfectly at home on a De Mille set. When he made his triumphal entry into Eisenstadt after succeeding to his resounding title, the festivities lasted a month, and were on an imperial scale.

But Prince Miklós had something more than a baroque side to his nature. Like all the Esterházys, he loved music, and wanted his artists to be the best in Europe. Accordingly, when his old *Kapellmeister* died in 1766, he promoted Haydn to the post. It turned out that this was a far more important position than his predecessor had held, for Haydn was soon presiding over the musical household of the most spectacular country place east of Versailles. In 1764 the Prince, bored with his two-hundred-room manor at Eisenstadt, had begun a vast Renaissance château directly inspired by a visit to Versailles. Whether Prince Miklós actually aimed at putting Louis XV's nose out of joint will never be known, but it is certain that he dropped eleven million gulden transforming an unhealthy marsh about thirty miles from Eisenstadt into a fairy palace. The cleverest gardeners in Europe worked formal miracles with its unpromising environs, strewing them with the elegant commonplaces of eighteenth-century landscaping:

---

* It is difficult to know how "content" Haydn really was to remain a servant. We do know he took a deep satisfaction in his freedom, once he was able to obtain it. "How sweet a little liberty tastes!" he was later to write. "I used often to sigh for freedom—now I have it. . . . The knowledge that I am no longer a hired servant repays me for all my trouble."—E. S.

grottoes, hermitages, classical temples, kiosks, artificial waterfalls, and —of course—a maze. The park was copiously stocked with game; the streams were sluggish with fish. But more important than these were the spendthrift provisions for musical and theatrical entertainment: the opera house accommodating four hundred spectators and the marionette theater equipped with every imaginable contrivance.

As *Kapellmeister* of one of the most hospitable magnificoes of the age, Haydn held no sinecure. The detail work was tremendous, and despite his fertility, composing must have taken up only a tithe of his time. To get a picture of Haydn's schedule, imagine Toscanini composing almost everything he plays, acting as music librarian, seeing that the instruments are in repair, and sending written reports of his players' conduct to the board of directors of the National Broadcasting Company. Even when the master was away, Haydn had to give two concerts a week to guarantee against the musicians absenting themselves without leave, and to keep them in concert trim. And when Prince Miklós had a houseful of distinguished guests (which was much of the time), Haydn's duties kept him on the run from early morning until the last candle was snuffed.

Haydn spent almost a quarter of a century at Esterház, occupying three rooms in the servants' wing. His relations with the Prince were as warm as the difference in their ranks allowed. True, while still assistant *Kapellmeister,* Haydn had been reprimanded for—of all things—dilatory attention to his duties. And once he made the tactical blunder of mastering the baryton, a kind of viola da gamba on which his master fancied himself a virtuoso. Instead of being pleased, the Prince was annoyed to find a rival in the field. Haydn then showed his native diplomacy by abandoning the baryton except to write some two hundred pieces for it, pieces carefully calculated not to expose the Prince's limitations. He was unfeignedly fond of his patron. After Prince Miklós' death, he wrote:

"My Prince was always satisfied with my works; I not only had the encouragement of constant approval, but as conductor of an orchestra I could make experiments, observe what produced an effect and what weakened it, and was thus in a position to improve, alter, make additions or omissions, and be as bold as I pleased; I was cut off from the world, there was no one to confuse or torment me, and I was forced to become *original.*"

Between Haydn and his musicians the friendliest feelings always prevailed. The junior members of his staff, many of whom studied with him, were the first to refer to him as "Papa Haydn." In truth, he was a father to all his musicians, and was always ready to plead their case. One of the more delicate subjects was obtaining leave for the men, practically cut off from their families by the Prince's morbid affection for Esterház. With rare humorous tact, Haydn once presented a vacation plea by writing the *Farewell* Symphony, in the finale of which the men blew out the candles on their music stands, and stole out, one by one—until, as Michel Brenet says, "Haydn, alone at his desk was preparing, not without anxiety, to go out too, when Nicolas Esterházy called him and announced that he had understood the musicians' request and that they might leave the next day."

But though Haydn and his men craved an occasional vacation, life at Esterház was not too monotonous, and working conditions were— for the period—excellent. Haydn went to work originally for four hundred florins a year, a figure which was almost doubled before Prince Miklós died. Considering that he had no personal expenses, the fact that he saved a mere pittance during a quarter century at Esterház is eloquent of an extravagant wife. But Frau Haydn was not entirely to blame. When the composer was almost fifty, he became involved with the wife of one of his violinists. Little Signora Polzelli, a vocalist briefly employed at Esterház, was only nineteen when Haydn met her. She did not love her husband, and there is little evidence that she cared for the bluff old Austrian. Soon, however, things came to such a pass that the lovers were exchanging pledges that they would wed when death released them from their partners. Polzelli died after a polite interval, but Haydn's wife was disobliging enough to linger until 1800, at which time the now rather faded siren got Haydn to sign a promise to leave her an annuity of three hundred florins. Whereupon she married an Italian, for the money had been her only object all along. Before forcing the promise of an annuity, she had for years been milking Haydn, probably on the strength of an old indiscretion. Only once did he complain, after he had sent her six hundred florins in one year.

The *affaire* Polzelli seems to have been the only wild oat Haydn sowed at Esterház. His mere routine duties ruled out excesses; the special entertainments for the Prince's eminent guests made self-denial mandatory. The gallant Prince Louis de Rohan, later the scapegoat of the "affair of the diamond necklace," stopped at Esterház in 1772, and delighted his host by comparing the château to Versailles. The next year, Maria Theresa was entertained at a three-day festival, for which

Haydn composed the delightful symphony that still bears her name. And so it went, with the palace a scene of constant revelry and music-making. Or Prince Miklós might tear himself away from Esterház for the pleasure of exhibiting his band and its increasingly famous leader. Sometimes he took them to Pressburg, where the Hungarian diet met; one year they went to the imperial palace at Schönbrunn, where Haydn conducted one of his own operas as well as the music at a state dinner. When the Grand Duke Paul of Russia visited Vienna in 1781, Prince Miklós and his orchestra were on hand. Some of Haydn's operas were performed, and the indefatigable *Kapellmeister* composed the six *Russian* Quartets in Paul's honor. The Grand Duchess, who was extremely fond of his music, presented Haydn with a diamond-studded addition to his already imposing collection of royal and noble snuffboxes.

But infinitely more important than Haydn's contacts with the most imposing stuffed shirts of the era was his meeting with Mozart. This was more than a mere momentary crossing of paths. It was a mutual recognition of genius that affected the work of both men, and thus left an imperishable mark on music. Each had something of the highest value for the other, and it is no mere coincidence that their masterpieces were composed after their meeting. They saw each other rarely, but for collectors of great moments be it known that on at least two occasions they sat down to play quartets together, once with Karl Ditters von Dittersdorf and their now forgotten rival, Johann Baptist Wanhal.

And so the years passed gently over Haydn's head. Suddenly, in September, 1790, Prince Miklós died, and the world Haydn had known for almost thirty years came to an end. The new Prince, less interested in the arts than most of the Esterházys, disbanded the musicians—and Haydn, at fifty-eight, was out of a job. This was no great tragedy, for his beloved patron had left him an annual pension of one thousand florins, to which Prince Antal now generously added four hundred more. It might seem that with an assured annual income of almost twice his stipend from Prince Miklós, Haydn was better off financially than ever. But this was not the case. Not only did the bonuses Prince Miklós had given him for special compositions cease, but also he was obliged to live at his own expense. And life in Vienna, to which he naturally gravitated, was expensive. On the other hand, his already great fame brought many pupils flocking to his door, and considerable sums were coming in from his publishers.

For the man who had once been reprimanded for loafing on the job had really produced during his life at Esterház a vast body of compositions. Unlike Hasse, who may possibly have been cheated of immortality when the great Dresden fire destroyed almost all his manuscripts, Haydn, though he lost many scores in a fire at Esterház in 1779, had already published so much that his fame would have been secure if he had never written another note. Roughly speaking, while there he had composed over twenty operas, about ninety symphonies, and more than sixty quartets, besides small orchestral works, pieces for clavier and other solo instruments (including a glass harmonica and a musical clock), chamber music of all varieties, and Masses and other works for solo and concerted voices.

Almost without exception, Haydn's early vocal works are now outside the living repertoire, if, indeed, they were ever in it. Most of them were written to be performed at Esterház, and were born and died there. Haydn himself seems to have had mixed feelings about the operas. On the one hand, he could write with naïve conceit to his Viennese publisher: "If only the French could know my operetta *L'Isola disabitata* and my last opera *La Fedeltà premiata!* I am sure such works have never yet been heard in Paris, perhaps not even in Vienna." The answer is that by 1781, when this letter was written, the French and the Austrians had heard far too many such operas, and Gluck had already won his battle against them. Haydn, who had been taught to write opera according to the old-fashioned recipes of Alessandro Scarlatti and Hasse, was in a saner frame of mind six years later, when he was invited to compose an opera for Prague:

"You ask me for a comic light opera," he wrote. "Certainly, if you are willing to reserve for private use some vocal work of my composition. But if it is intended for performance in the theater at Prague, then I cannot serve you, for all my operas are written for the special conditions of Esterház, and could not produce elsewhere the effect I have calculated upon for this setting. It would be otherwise if I had the inestimable good fortune to be able to compose for your theater upon a completely new libretto. Though, there again, I should run too many risks, for it would be difficult for anyone—no matter whom—to equal the great Mozart. That is why I wish that all music lovers, especially the influential, could know the inimitable works of Mozart with a profundity, a musical knowledge, and a keen appreciation equal to my own. Then the nations would compete for possession of such a treasure. Prague must hold fast so precious a man—and reward him. For without that, the history of a great genius is a sad one, and gives posterity little encouragement to follow the same course. That is why so much fine and hopeful talent unfortunately perishes. I am full of anger when I think that this unique genius is not yet attached to a royal or imperial court. Forgive this outburst: I love the man too much."

Haydn's affection for Mozart was reciprocated. In 1790, when he was invited to visit London, Mozart tried to dissuade him from going. "Oh, Papa!" he exclaimed (though momentarily he seemed like the wise parent), "you have had no education for the wide, wide world, and you speak too few languages."

"My language is understood all over the world," Haydn replied dryly. For he was determined to go. Salomon, the London impresario, had suddenly burst in upon him several days before, saying, "I have come from London to fetch you. We will settle terms tomorrow." That morrow came, and like Satan displaying the nations of the world from the mountaintop, Salomon unrolled his little plan. Haydn heard, was tempted, and fell. Salomon guaranteed him £900 if he would make the trip. The only difficulty, from Haydn's point of view, was that he had to pay his own traveling expenses. However, Prince Esterházy advanced him the money, and after providing for his wife by selling a little house in Eisenstadt that Prince Miklós had given him, Haydn set out for London in mid-December. Mozart, on hand to see him off, burst into tears. "This is good-by," he sobbed. "We shall never meet again." And, indeed, before Haydn returned to Vienna Mozart was dead.

At fifty-eight, the composer set out on his travels with the naïve curiosity of a child. The Channel crossing was rough. "I remained on deck during the whole passage," he wrote, "in order to gaze my fill at that huge monster, the ocean. So long as it was calm, I had no fears, but when at length a violent wind began to blow, rising every minute . . . I was seized with a little alarm and a little indisposition." He landed at Dover, and arrived in London on New Year's Day, 1791. He was received like a sovereign prince: his fame had been trumpeted before him, and the clever Salomon had used the press to raise public interest to fever pitch. His lodgings were besieged by ambassadors and great nobles, and invitations came pouring in by the hundreds. The inescapable Dr. Burney called, and firmly presented him with an ode of welcome. In view of the fact that the terms of his contract called for twenty especially written compositions, including six symphonies, he finally had to move into the country to elude his pertinacious admirers. Unhappily he had arrived in the midst of one of those wars of the impresarios in which Handel had received so many noble scars, and thus his opening concert was delayed. Slurring squibs about him appeared in the newspapers, and doubtless the announcement of an actual date for the first concert narrowly averted a question being asked in Parliament.

All criticism was silenced by the overwhelming success of the first concert. The adagio of the symphony (now known as the *Salomon* No. 2) was encored—in those times a rare proof of enthusiasm. And when the Prince of Wales appeared like a resplendent apparition at the second concert, the newspapers changed their tone. Blending sycophancy with true admiration, they now referred to "the sublime and august thoughts this master weaves into his works." The shrewd Salomon was assisting at an apotheosis. Crowds were turned away from the Hanover Square Rooms for every concert, and Haydn's benefit on May 16 realized £350—almost twice the take Salomon had guaranteed. The first week of July, Haydn journeyed up to Oxford (or, as he wrote it, Oxforth), which, at Burney's recommendation, had offered him a musical doctorate. At the second of the three concerts given there in his honor, the lovely symphony in G major he had written some years before was performed instead of a new work. Ever since known as the *Oxford* Symphony, this delicious musical kitten appealed immediately to the lettered dons and young fashionables.

Haydn was enormously pleased—and a bit flustered. After he received his degree, he acknowledged the applause by raising his doctor's gown high above his head so that all could see it, saying in English, "I thank you." He must have been a rather comic figure, though he wrote home in great glee, "I had to walk around in this gown for three days. I only wish my friends in Vienna might have seen me." Like so many famous men, he was decidedly below middle height. His thickset, flabby body was carried on absurdly short legs. And his face was far from prepossessing, though its features, except for an underslung Hapsburg jaw, were regular. His swarthy skin was deeply pitted by smallpox, and his nose was disfigured by a growth he stubbornly refused to have removed even when John Hunter, the ablest surgeon of the epoch, offered to perform the operation. Haydn realized that he was ugly, and preened himself on the fact that women fell in love with him "for something deeper than beauty."

Susceptibility to women as women made Haydn rather uncritical of them. One was "the most beautiful woman I ever saw"; another, "the loveliest woman I ever saw." These were but glances: his affections were directed toward Mrs. John Samuel Schroeter, a widow of mature years. What began as music lessons ended as something far more intense: she was soon addressing her elderly music master as "my dearest love." As for Haydn, he cherished a packet of her letters until his death, and once said, "Those are from an English widow who fell in love with me. She was a very attractive woman and still handsome, though over sixty; and had I been free I should certainly have married her."

It may be that Mrs. Schroeter's matronly charms played their part in keeping Haydn in London. At any rate, he dallied there until June, 1792—a full year and a half after his arrival—and then set out for the Continent. He traveled by way of Bonn, where the young Beethoven presented himself, and submitted a cantata for criticism. Haydn's generous praise may well have spurred Beethoven to study in Vienna. In December, Beethoven began to take lessons from Haydn. From the beginning, they misunderstood each other: the young musical rebel puzzled Haydn, while the impatient Beethoven rather unfairly regarded his aging teacher as a fogy. Haydn was too old to realize the scope and significance of Beethoven's music—to him certain aspects of it seemed senseless license. But in the course of years, Beethoven came to appreciate his teacher's musical genius. Yet, the relationship between the two men was nothing more than a protracted casual meeting—they were never actually friends, and their influence on each other was negligible. Beethoven said flatly, "I never learned anything from Haydn."

Wanderlust—and a dazzling new contract from Salomon—called Haydn back to England after a year and a half in Vienna. He arrived in London in February, 1794, and it is worth recording that he carefully chose lodgings near Mrs. Schroeter's house. This is the single tantalizing scrap of knowledge preserved about Haydn's love affair during this second visit. Warm though London had been to him when he first reached England, it now offered him an adulation it had lavished on no composer since Handel. After six new symphonies had been performed, the public clamored for a repetition of the first set. His benefit concert netted him £400. The royal family took him up: George III, whose first loyalty to Handel never flagged, was somewhat restrained in his ardors, but the Prince of Wales invited Haydn to Carlton House twenty-six times. It was for these performances that Haydn presented to Parliament his famous bill for the extremely modest sum of £100.

Again Haydn found it difficult to tear himself away: he remained in England for more than eighteen months, playing the social game heavily. During the summer of 1794 he moved leisurely from one spa or country seat to another. His diary is bare of references to music: he was much exercised over the character of Mrs. Billington, the actress, whose frank memoirs were the current scandal. He remarked on the national debt, preserved the Prince of Wales' favorite recipe for punch, and looked in at the trial of Warren Hastings. Not even the price of table delicacies escaped his omnivorous curiosity: "In the month of June 1792 a chicken, 7 s.; an Indian (a kind of bittern found in North America), 9 s.; a dozen larks, 1 coron [crown?]. N. B.—If plucked, a duck, 5 s." Haydn relished a good joke, and the best ones he heard also went into his diary. Certain lines about the comparative morals of English, French, and Dutch women are too graphic for publication. So, busily jotting down fresh items along the way, he returned to Vienna early in September, 1795.

With this second London visit, Haydn wrote finis to his career as a symphonist. That career, extending over more than thirty-five years, had produced no fewer than one hundred and four separate symphonies, many of high quality, but less notable for their variety. The fact that his earliest trial balloons are worthless museum pieces is easily explained: learning to write for the orchestra was to Haydn a slow and painful process completed comparatively late in life, and he had no models. He literally evolved the symphony from the orchestral suite and the clavier sonatas of Karl Philipp Emanuel Bach by laborious trial and error. The wonder is that he found the essential symphonic form as quickly as he did: to perfect it (within his recognized limitations, of course) took years. For almost a quarter of a century he continued to write symphonies for his small court orchestra, many of which are delightful and witty, and almost all of which are within the same narrow range. Their individuality rests on thematic variety alone.

The more Haydn's life and compositions are examined, the clearer it becomes that Mozart provided the stimulus for his emancipation from the stiffness of his earlier manner. The difference between even the finest of Haydn's pre-Mozartian symphonies—the *Farewell* and *"La Chasse,"* for example—and a richly mature work like the *Oxford* is not an obvious one: from first to last, the personality of Josef Haydn dominated, and limited, his symphonic conceptions. But in the later works this personality expressed itself through more ample resources— richer orchestration and untrammeled handling of musical ideas. With Mozart, Haydn finally brought the purely classical symphony as far as it could go without becoming something else. In the twelve *Salomon* Symphonies, the man who evolved a form lifted it to its zenith—a phenomenon unique in musical history.

These twelve symphonies owe their supremacy not only to their freedom of expression, but also to the fact that they were written for the best and largest orchestra Haydn ever knew. It would appear pathetically inadequate beside one of the perfectly trained and equipped orchestras of our own day, but it was capable of effects quite beyond the powers of the little household band at Esterház. In short, before composing for London, Haydn had never had a chance to make the most of his newly discovered resources. It is among the more fascinating ifs of musical history to speculate on what he might have done if he had had this vastly superior organization at his command when he was thirty rather than when he was almost sixty. The answer seems to be, on the basis of everything known about the composer, that we would have many more symphonies as fine as the *Oxford* or the *Salomon* No. 5, in C minor—but nothing different in kind. It took a restless, eternally dissatisfied temperament like Beethoven's to weld the symphony into a tremendous emotional vehicle.

The truth is that Haydn's symphonies perfectly express his personality and its rather limited outlook. Nobody goes to them for the Aeschylean tragedy of Beethoven or the transcendent, unearthly serenity of Mozart—nor can you wallow with Haydn as you can with Tchaikovsky. Haydn is a prose writer, and as such, unequaled. He is the Addison and Steele of music, with the former's flawless touch and the latter's robust humor and lustiness of outlook. Any one of his great symphonies is the man in small:.one and all they breathe his sunny disposition, his wit, his irrepressible high spirits, and his sane and healthy love of life. When his inspiration flagged, his untroubled faith degenerated into smugness, his desire for formal perfection into schoolmasterly finickiness. But his best symphonies are canticles of life enjoyed to the full—works of lively beauty that rank just below the best of Mozart and Beethoven. "Haydn would have been among the greatest," Bernard Shaw once wrote, "had he been driven to that terrrible eminence."

When Haydn returned to Vienna he abandoned the symphony, the form with which his name is most popularly connected. He was sixty-three years old, and some of his well-meaning admirers had begun to treat him as though he were dead. They invited him to Rohrau, and showed him a monument to his fame. His reaction is not recorded, but he was properly overcome with emotion when he visited the house where he had been born. He knelt down, solemnly kissed the threshold, and pointing dramatically at the stove, declared that on that very spot his musical career had begun. Despite this premature commemorative service, he returned to Vienna, and continued to be thoroughly alive.

The main reason for Haydn's return from England had been a pressing invitation from a new Prince Esterházy, who wished him to resume his old position. Haydn consented, for the duties were comparatively light, entailing a few months each year at Eisenstadt, and the composition of some perfunctory occasional pieces, notably an annual Mass on the Princess' name day. But now Haydn was so famous that it was he who conferred an honor on the Esterházys rather than they on him. In fact, excepting Francis II and Metternich, he was the most famous living Austrian. It was natural, therefore, that in 1797, when the Imperial authorities wished to combat revolutionary influences that had seeped into Austria from France, they should ask Haydn to help by composing an air that could be used as a national anthem. Basing it on words by the "meritorious poet Haschka," he not only achieved his ambition of equalling "God Save the King"—he far surpassed it. *Gott erhalte Franz den Kaiser,* musically the finest national anthem ever written, served its purpose perfectly until 1938, when it was officially superseded by *"Deutschland über Alles"* and the "Horst Wessel Song." Haydn's deeply felt hymn of loyalty was first sung on the Emperor's birthday—February 12, 1797—at the Nationaltheater in Vienna. Francis II himself attended in state, and on the same day it was sung at the principal theaters throughout the Empire. It has always been the most popular of Haydn's songs.

But "God Save the King" was not the only English music Haydn wished to emulate. While in London, he went to a performance of *Messiah,* during which he was heard to sob, "Handel is the master of us all." Later he heard *Joshua,* and was even more moved, saying to a friend that "he had long been acquainted with music, but never knew half its powers before he heard it, as he was perfectly certain that only one inspired author ever did, or ever would, pen so sublime a composition." Just before Haydn left London, Salomon handed him a sacred text originally contrived for Handel partly from *Paradise Lost* and partly from Genesis. A friend of Haydn's made a free translation of it, and the composer set to work. "Never was I so pious as when composing *The Creation,*" Haydn declared. "I knelt down every day and prayed God to strengthen me for my task." However, things did not go smoothly. At times the infirmities of age dammed up the flow of his creative genius. Like Di Lasso in his old age, Haydn began to suffer from melancholia and nerves, but he had reserves of peasant energy that the pampered Fleming lacked. So he came through with a masterpiece after eighteen difficult months. On April 29, 1798, *The Creation* was first produced privately at the palace of Prince Schwarzenburg, in Vienna. Little less than a year later, it was performed publicly on Haydn's name day—March 19—at the Nationaltheater. It was an immediate success, and soon was being heard by appreciative audiences throughout Europe. Even Paris, which did not like oratorio, capitulated. More, the French performers had a medal struck in homage to the composer. In England, the work, translated back into execrable English, rapidly became a runner-up to *Messiah*.

Time has not been kind to *The Creation:* it has been all but crowded out of the repertoire. There are various reasons for this, the main one being the advent of Mendelssohn and his catchy oratorios. Under this onslaught, only a consistently effective work could hold its place. *The Creation* is by no means consistently effective. Although "The Heavens are telling" is magnificent choral writing, most of the choruses are feeble—an inexcusable fault in an oratorio. As the musical climax comes in the first third, the rest of *The Creation,* despite scattered beauties, is anticlimactic. The exact truth is that after Haydn has created his two main characters, he does not know how to make them dramatic. The best passages are descriptive—a kind of sublime journalism. They are usually solos, and lose nothing in being performed alone. "With verdure clad" is one of Haydn's most exquisite inspirations: blending simple rapture with a rare contemplative quality, it is one of his infrequent achievements in musical poetry. Unfortunately, the fine things in *The Creation* are scattered too sparingly to prevent a performance of the whole oratorio from being a chore to the listener. He rises from his seat with the paradoxical feeling that he has heard a masterpiece—but a very dull one.

Enormously pleased by the success of *The Creation,* the uninspired translator who had provided its text began to badger Haydn to set another of his adaptations—this time of James Thomson's *The Seasons.* The old man was not too pleased with the prospect of more work: he was in failing health, and doubted his strength to complete another large composition. At last he consented, and *The Seasons* was completed in a remarkably short time. Yet it is a work of great length, requiring two evenings for an uncut performance. Generally, it is not inferior to *The Creation*. Certainly it is far livelier, and the fact that it has had to take a back seat is largely due to its comparatively frivolous (and absurdly adapted) text, which is less congenial to stuffy, single-minded oratorio societies. Haydn himself recognized the absurdity of the German words, and was inclined to regard *The Seasons* as a step-child. He once remarked petulantly to Francis II that "in *The Creation* angels speak, and their talk is of God; in *The Seasons* no one higher speaks than Farmer Simon."

Haydn's attitude to *The Seasons* was, to say the least, ambiguous. Nowhere did he more successfully transmute his lifelong love of nature into music.* Page after page is inspired by the Austrian countryside and the manifold aspects of its life. The vivid descriptiveness of this music is its most immediately engaging quality, and it is no wonder that its early listeners delighted in the literal transcriptions of country sounds in which it is rich. But Haydn was furious when these mimetic passages were singled out for special praise: "This French trash was forced upon me," he stormed. His injustice to this delicious work may be traced to a well-founded conviction that the exertion of composing it had finally made him a feeble old man. At any rate, his creative life was over. After composing *The Seasons,* he dragged out eight years, subsisting on the bitter diet of past accomplishments. He lived in a pleasant house in the Mariahilf suburb of Vienna, which his wife had fondly hoped to inhabit "when I am a widow." Why this woman, who was three years Haydn's senior, expected to outlive him is not clear. She died in 1800, and her widower lived the rest of his life in the Mariahilf house.

The last years are a constant record of mental and physical decline. In December, 1803, Haydn conducted for the last time. After that, he was confined to his house by increasing infirmities. His already enormous fame became gigantic: people of rank and eminence besieged his door; learned organizations and musical societies delighted in honoring him. In 1804, he was made an honorary citizen of Vienna. When Napoleon's armies occupied the city, many French officers called upon him to pay their respects. When he was feeling comparatively well, he received his visitors warmly, often showing them his medals and diplomas, and rambling on about his past. But more often than not callers merely confused and upset him, and his only wish was to be

---

* *The Seasons,* in addition to expressing a mere love of nature, had another significance. It was one of the first secular oratorios, and in a way expressed the ideas of human equality and brotherhood that Haydn shared with other members of the eighteenth-century Freemasons.—E. S.

left alone. In 1806 he took steps to discourage visitors by having a card printed, bearing a fragment of one of his vocal quartets, with these words: "Fled forever is my strength; old and weak am I!"

During these last years none were more considerate than the Esterházys. The Prince increased Haydn's pension to twenty-three hundred florins annually, and paid his doctor. The Princess often called on him. In 1808, four days before his seventy-sixth birthday, his admirers wished to make public acknowledgement of their affection. Prince Esterházy's carriage called to take him to the University, where *The Creation* was to be performed. The venerable old man was carried into the hall, whereupon the entire audience rose. He was very agitated. When Salieri, Mozart's famous enemy, gave the sign to begin, the whole house was stilled. Haydn controlled his emotions until the great fortissimo on the words "And there was light." He then pointed upward, and exclaimed loudly, "It came from on high." His excitement increased, and it was thought prudent to take him home after the first part. As he was carried out of the hall, Beethoven pressed forward and solemnly kissed the master's forehead and hands. On the threshold, Haydn raised his hand in benediction: he was saying farewell to Vienna.

Haydn lingered another year, growing constantly weaker and less and less master of his emotions. On May 26, 1809, he had his servants carry him to the piano, where he thrice played the Austrian national anthem with remarkable strength and expressiveness. It was his last effort: he died five days later. The French, who had again occupied Vienna, gave him a magnificent funeral, and Requiems were sung all over Europe.

Our own time is rediscovering Haydn. He was submerged during the later nineteenth century—admittedly a classic, but usually kept on the shelf. In view of the fact that practically only his *Toy* and *Clock* Symphonies were played, he was in danger of being thought of as a children's composer. The renascence of chamber music has done much to rehabilitate him. His more than eighty string quartets, after decades of neglect, are re-emerging as his most characteristic works. They were little publicized during his lifetime because of the very circumstances of performance. They are much heard now, and a society has been formed to record them. They, as much as the symphonies and the fresh and delightful piano sonatas, give point to the saying, "Haydn thought in sonatas." Possibly we hear Haydn best in the quartets, for they are performed today exactly as he wrote them. By their very nature, they cannot seem thin, as the symphonies sometimes do to ears accustomed to the augmented orchestras of Wagner, Strauss, and Stravinsky. Nor have the instruments of the quartet changed since Haydn's day, as the piano has.

Haydn has been called the father of instrumental music, which is true in spirit if not in entire substance. His almost unique ability to create and perfect musical forms was due largely to his freedom from academic dead letter. "What is the good of such rules?" he once asked. "Art is free, and should be fettered by no such mechanical regulations. The educated ear is the sole authority on all these questions, and I think I have as much right to lay down the law as anyone. Such trifling is absurd; I wish instead that someone would try to compose a really new minuet." This liberalism infuriated some of Haydn's pedantic colleagues, two of whom once denounced him to the Emperor as a charlatan. But he was a profound student, and as careful a craftsman as ever lived. When his strength no longer matched his inspiration, he lamented to the pianist Kalkbrenner, "I have only just learned in my old age how to use the wind instruments, and now that I do understand them, I must leave the world."

This free and living attitude toward music is central in Haydn. It allowed him, for example, to use the rich store of folk melody always available to him, and to use it without scruple—Beethoven's debt to him in this respect has not been sufficiently acknowledged. It allowed him to perpetuate the robust jokes of the period not only in his diary, but also in his music. It allowed him to breathe life into the form that Karl Philipp Emanuel Bach had left quivering on the brink of being, and to stamp it with the three-dimensioned qualities of a generous and glowing personality.

Wolfgang Amadeus Mozart

From "A World of Music" (in preparation)

By Elie Siegmeister

EVERY age, every generation one might almost say, forms its own particular image of the great musicians of the past. At the beginning of the nineteenth century, Mozart was beloved and worshiped as one of the great pillars of music. His operas were played everywhere and his music was regarded as full of fire and warmth. Seventy-five years later, in the heyday of turgid romantic emotion, when Wagnerian tempests filled the opera houses, Mozart was looked upon as a *naïf*, a composer of the age of charm and playful innocence. Today, we are beginning to hear his music as richly moving and meaningful, perfect in form, and possessed of a matchless personal emotion.

Yet legends die hard. While Mozart is performed and loved more today than for many decades past, the traditional misconceptions still cluster about his name. There is the conventional fable of the "divine," "childlike" composer, the "seraphic" Mozart, whose music is "beauty unalloyed"; and, finally, the pernicious myth of "Mozart the pure musician," concerned with formal perfection alone.

What lends a certain plausibility to the picture of Mozart as an "innocent" is the fact that it does apply to the early part of his career. The story of the *Wunderkind* reads—and was carefully planned to read—almost like a fairy tale.

Born in the picturesque and still slightly medieval town of Salzburg in 1756, of a typical bourgeois family (his father was musician to the Prince-Archbishop) he quickly rose to intimacy with the wealthy and powerful of the earth. At four Wolfgang began to manifest extraordinary musical gifts, and at six was composing, improvising, and playing the harpsichord, violin, and organ with such virtuosity that his father was already able to exhibit him in public with that shameful lack of decency which was characteristic of the age. An advertisement of one of his concert engagements announced that he would

"play concertos on the harpsichord or the piano, and the most difficult pieces of the greatest masters . . . play a concerto on the violin, accompany on the clavier in symphonies, and, with the keys covered by a cloth, will play as well as if he had the keyboard under his eyes. Further: from a distance he will name exactly any note that may be sounded either separately or in chords on the clavier or on any other instrument, or on bells, glasses, clocks, etc. Finally he will improvise as long as he is desired to not only on the clavier but on the organ, and in any key, even the most difficult that may be stipulated. . . ."

We have pictures of the boy sitting on the Austrian Empress's knee, fêted by the Queen of France, delighting the King and Queen of England, adored and treasured by the nobility of half a dozen countries. Trundled about Europe very much like a wonderful monkey, the little Wolfgang performed musical miracles with an ease and self-assurance that won him fame everywhere.

Growing up, Mozart composed in a dozen different styles, writing little symphonies, sonatas, arias, even whole oratorios and operas, that retain their grace and freshness today. With his amazing facility, he learned to adapt his manner to the taste of each town where he happened to be living, and, in the fashion of the day, accepted and fulfilled commissions to write every kind of music that came along. Yet although Leopold Mozart took the boy to town after town—in the hope of obtaining for him a permanent post as court composer or Kapellmeister in any one of the little Italian or German principalities that maintained musical establishments—the most Wolfgang could earn was bread and butter, and extravagant praise.

"It is true," Wolfgang once wrote from Paris, "that people say the nicest things, but there it ends. They arrange for me to come on such and such a day. When I play, they exclaim, '*Oh, c'est un prodige, c'est inconcevable, c'est étonnant!*' and then, good-bye."

All through adolescence and well into maturity, Mozart's anxious search for a patron and his desire to please one or another noble employer led him to turn out work after work in the charming rococo patterns of the day. Certainly, even in this he surpassed his contemporaries, and his purity and finesse remain still unequaled. Works such as *Haffner Serenade,* the exquisite *Eine Kleine Nachtmusik,* the early symphonies, piano sonatas, and concertos—all these, with their utter clarity, their endless melodic flow and transparency of style, come close to being the purest delight in all music. Doubtless in Mozart's early years, he was content with musical pleasure and formal perfection, which summed up the ideals of the eighteenth-century court circles he aimed to enter.

But does this formal, delightful music represent the goal of the mature Mozart, his unique contribution to art?

There is reason to doubt it. Even if we knew nothing at all of the composer's life, there is the evidence of the music itself: the unmistakable note of tenderness and warmth, the full-blooded characterizations of the operas, the dramatic, introspective quality growing deeper and stronger with each passing year. But, knowing Mozart's life and the Europe he lived in, and comparing it with the continuous development of his music, we are able to form a picture of a Mozart far more real than the one of the story-books.

Already in the 1770's, installed as concertmaster of the Salzburg

Archbishop's orchestra (salary, $75 a year), the adolescent composer became aware of the famous "wave of passions" then sweeping the youth of all the middle classes throughout Europe. Rousseau had celebrated the world of intimate subjective emotions in his *Confessions,* and Goethe had brought the passionate *Sturm und Drang* to fever pitch with his *Werther,* which preached a life of sentimentalism, striving, and anguish.

At the age of seventeen Mozart was making melodies that overflowed with tenderness. Like Cherubino in his own *Marriage of Figaro* he wanted to love and be loved by almost every woman he saw. He began to think constantly of the clash of emotions and personalities and to dream of nothing but drama and opera. At twenty-two he wrote: "I am jealous of all who write operas. When I hear an aria I weep. My fixed idea is to compose operas."

At this point the maturing artist began to be vividly aware of his personal situation and the environment in which he functioned. For years he had been carted around, advertised as a strange wonder of nature, made to perform like a trained seal. He had composed music for everyone and everybody except himself, and had adapted himself to every style: French, German, Italian, Viennese; religious, operatic, austere, gracious, aristocratic, popular. Gradually he began to be aware of his own personality, his rights as a human being.

Here he was, a distinguished, world-famous composer, who had been fêted by all the crowned heads of Europe—yet cramped in provincial Salzburg, bullied and humiliated by an arrogant employer, told when and how to write his music, and where to play it. But this was 1781, eight years before the French Revolution. Could not a man come and go, perform and compose, bring his art to whoever wanted most to hear it?

Mozart had somehow, in some way, been infected with the ideas of equality and the rights of man. While he could still write to order, in any form and style, and turn in not only an acceptable but a thoroughly distinguished performance, he no longer found satisfaction in this subservient role. The young man of semifeudal Salzburg was beginning to believe, as were thousands of his social equals throughout Europe, that even though born a commoner, he had the right to live his own life, come and go as he pleased and write music according to his own lights.

Dangerous thoughts! They were soon to lead the composer into all sorts of trouble.

One can feel the storm brewing in the music of Mozart's twenty-third year. There was already a basic difference in style between the compositions he had to write, and those he really wanted to write. The former, exemplified in the following extract from the *Vesper in C* (composed in 1779 as part of his duties as music maker for the Archbishop), was lovely and tuneful, but thoroughly impersonal and "objective" music—meaning that it was written to order, and very little more. Following the conventional custom of the time, Mozart set the austere scriptural text to a light, operatic melody, complete with vocal embroideries, runs, and coloratura passages.

Charming music, certainly, in the most approved eighteenth-century manner—but practically identical with the work of a dozen other composers, and hardly a thing that Mozart could have felt very deeply.*

In the same year (1779) Mozart wrote another score, the incidental music to a drama dealing with the Egyptian religion—a "modern" subject that was, as we shall see, close to the composer's heart, identified with the symbolism of struggle, Freemasonry, and Enlightenment. Mozart marked the following passage in his *Thamos, King of Egypt* as depicting "Mirza's passionate character":

* In the last ten years of his employment at Salzburg, Mozart wrote 42 important religious works. In his ten years of working as a free lance, he wrote three, of which two remained unfinished.

Here was music in another Mozartean style, music of drama and passion, darkly colored, serious, and full of the emotional outbursts of the *Sturm und Drang*. Compare these two musical passages: note the smoothly flowing, conventional line of the former, the latter's stormy, explosive quality, its sudden changes in pace and intensity. Here was the mark of a new composer, who was to outdistance by far the "gracious" Mozart of court and church. And here, already, was the foreboding of the explosions soon to come in Mozart's own personal life.

In 1781, conditions had reached the breaking point between Mozart and the Archbishop Hieronymus von Colloredo. Jealous of his "servant's" growing popularity and annoyed by his restless desire to write other than church music and to perform at public concerts, Hieronymus began to insist on his feudal prerogatives. Mozart was not to give concerts on the outside; he was not to leave the Archbishop's entourage without permission; he was to be obedient and submissive, eat at the servants' table, and perform various menial tasks assigned him.

Outraged, Mozart decided to break once and for all with his detested employer and strike out boldly for a new, free-lance way of life. The Archbishop's agent sped him on his way with a parting boot in the rear. Fateful gesture! For it was to evoke more reprisals against the dying feudal caste than any nobleman had yet bargained for.

Soon after, Mozart was on his own in Vienna, teaching, giving concerts, and free to follow his bent wherever it might lead. And almost at once it led to the doors of the National Singspiel Theater. This was the institution established by that enlightened monarch, Joseph II, to bring opera to the people of Vienna in their native tongue and style. (All grand opera had hitherto been Italian.) Mozart, who had already written thirteen stage works, but not one (except the *Bastien and Bastienne* of his childhood) in his native language, eagerly accepted his long-awaited opportunity. It was a commission to write *Die Entführung aus dem Serail* (Abduction from the Harem)—a lighthearted, comic, romantic opera in German.

In this work Mozart was able to fulfill himself completely for the first time. Addressed to a popular audience, it was his first really successful stage work, and it remains as attractive today as when first written.

How did Mozart approach the composition of *Die Entführung?* Was it with the attitude of a musician occupied entirely with the creation of "pure forms"? Was he the "objective" composer concerned only with weaving abstract musical patterns regardless of their human meaning?

The passionate, "romantic" quality of the music, and its immediate public success, give the answer. But besides this, Mozart himself stated the dramatic and expressive intentions of his various techniques. In a very interesting letter discussing the composition of one of the arias (*"O wie ängstlich"*), he revealed himself as a composer anxious to portray emotional states with the utmost musical precision. He wrote:

The throbbing heart is foreshadowed by the violins in octaves. You hear the trembling, the uncertainty, the rising of the breast expressed by a *crescendo;* you hear the whispers and sighs portrayed by the muted first violins and a flute in unison.

Here are the passages referred to—first the "throbbing heart" depicted by rhythmical staccato notes in the violins:

Then, the *crescendo* depicting the "rising breast" (note that the melodic line also rises):

These passages, and dozens of others like them in Mozart's operas, show him to be not an "abstract musician" but one who used his art to depict character, mood, and situation—in other words, to depict life.

The lyrical quality of *Die Entführung,* its lovely arias, lusty comic scenes, and the fact that it was the first Viennese grand opera written in the popular style and in German brought it a warm response and gave Mozart hope that he would at last be on a sound financial basis. Three weeks after the première, in August 1782, he married the young and featherbrained Konstanze Weber.

But immediately the couple found the larder almost empty—a

condition that was, except for brief periods, to plague the composer for the rest of his days. Under the charming custom of musical piracy then in vogue, a composer was paid only for the first performance of any work. Thereafter, it might be played any number of times (*Die Entführung*, and subsequently *Figaro, Don Giovanni* and *The Magic Flute* were steady popular successes in a number of cities); but the composer never derived any tangible benefits therefrom.

Small wonder, then, that from 1782 on, Mozart began to accept every kind of musical odd job that came along, to keep body and soul together. In the years between 1782 and 1786, he turned out a vast amount of music in every style—quartets, concertos, arias, serenades, marches, divertimentos, minuets, country dances, music for plays, etc.— but although he sought constantly for a steady position as court composer, he was regularly turned down.

During these years of trial and struggle, Mozart's outlook on life and on his own music was steadily growing. He became increasingly aware of the circumstances in which men lived, and of the power of music as a commentary on life as he saw it. Although his operas are staged today as pretty costume-pieces surrounded by much lovely music, to Mozart they meant more than that; for him there was no dichotomy (as there later came to be for many musicians of the Romantic period) between musical beauty and the depiction of reality.

When, late in 1785, Mozart was approached by the Jewish-born Catholic priest, Lorenzo da Ponte, with the proposal to set to music the latter's libretto drawn from Beaumarchais' comedy *The Marriage of Figaro,* he accepted with great eagerness. Not that there were no possible objections to the scheme. The comedy had been a sensation all over Europe (twelve different German translations appeared in 1785); but it was a "hot" subject—nothing less than a scathing indictment of the vices and brutalities of the aristocracy, a plea for the "common man" of those days. One cannot say Mozart was unaware of the implications of the idea. He had read over one hundred librettos looking for a subject. The play was officially banned in Austria; special permission had to be obtained from the Emperor for its use, even as an Italian opera.

Liberal though he was, Joseph II hesitated long before granting such permission, even though Da Ponte had pruned Beaumarchais' play of many "dangerous thoughts." We are told that Mozart and Da Ponte had many discussions over the text. Yet for all their prunings, the opera emerged as a brilliant satire (in which the music and the text were intimately united) against the lascivious and conniving Count Almavivas, and an eloquent statement of the genius of the Susannas and Figaros—the common folk of the earth. No wonder the democratic citizens of Prague took Mozart to their heart with no less fervor than the citizens of Paris greeted the democratic Benjamin Franklin. The Austrian Emperor, while he admired some of the music, found *Figaro* (of all things) "heavy and lacking in finesse"; and after a few performances it was dropped from the Vienna repertoire.

Was *Figaro* merely another opera that Mozart wrote? Let us not forget that he was a human being as well as a composer; though certain biographers seem to imply that outside of music he had scarcely any mind at all, and sought for nothing so much as to escape reality.* But in fact, had not Mozart himself lived the experiences of *Figaro*? Was he not snubbed, scorned, abused by the very type of aristocrat he depicted in the opera? His opinions of the aristocracy are no secret. They appear often enough in his letters: "The prince is a real blockhead!"—"The honor of being in the Emperor's service does not go very far with me,"—and, most famous of all: "The heart shows the true nobleman, and although I am no count, I am more honorable perhaps than many a count; and whether it be a footman or a count, whoever insults me is a scoundrel."

Compare these sentiments with Figaro's very first aria

Se vuol bal - la - re, Si - gnor Con - ti - no.

Se vuol bal - la - re, Si - gnor Con - ti - no.

"If you wish to dance, my little Count, very well, I will play for you. Come with me, I will teach you how to caper. But with quick thrusts and crafty steps, today with flattery and tomorrow with trickery, I'll upset your every scheme!"

The exquisite melodies of *Figaro*, the wonderful human characterizations, the web of intrigue woven in the music as well as in the text, do not hide the meaning implicit in the whole work, its personal re-

---

* Thus Ernest Newman asserts: "He had virtually no culture in the broad sense of the term. . . . His whole being was musical, and his brain must have been engaged almost without intermission in the production of music. . . . Perhaps he did not care to face unpleasant realities. . . ."

lease for Mozart, and its broader implications as a symbol of the rising democracy of the 1780's.

What makes the pattern of Mozart's later life and music still clearer is the important fact that in 1784 the composer had become a Freemason. In those days the order was a closely knit, liberal, and often underground society, numbering among its members such men as Schiller, Goethe, Voltaire, Benjamin Franklin, George Washington, and many other outstanding figures of the whole period of the Enlightenment. The Masons stood for the basic principles of democracy—commonplaces to us today, but in pre-1789 Europe daring and revolutionary: freedom of speech and religion, freedom of scientific thought, the equality of all human beings, even brotherhood among all races. (Mozart's lodge in Vienna numbered a Negro among its members.)

Now it is sometimes alleged that it was the fashion to join the Masons in those days, that Mozart's membership was merely a matter of form, and that, in any case, the events of his "outer life" had little to do with his "inner experiences"—from which his music presumably evolved. If all this were so, the composer would hardly have bothered to become an ardent proselytizer for the movement (it was he who brought Haydn in, and even his own father, an ardent Catholic). Nor would he have taken the time from his many duties and his pressing need to earn a living to write a considerable amount of music on Masonic themes, including his last and in some ways most personal opera, *The Magic Flute*. We can no more detach Mozart's music from his whole outlook on life than we can detach Bach's music from his religion, or Wagner's music dramas from his conception of the world.

The years after 1785 witnessed the emergence of one masterpiece after another. *Don Giovanni,* commissioned by the citizens of Prague who had been so delighted with *Figaro,* appeared in 1787. Here again is a work that we cannot conceive merely as a collection of pleasing arias and ensemble numbers (which is all that most modern productions are). When we see it as the conflict of a passion-ridden individual with conventional morality, law, and even religion, Mozart's work takes its place as one of the great human dramas of all time, truly worthy to rank with Shakespeare.

There have been many Don Juan plays both before and since Mozart, but most of them have been comic or romantic extravaganzas, either lurid or sentimental in their effect on the audience. Mozart's *Don Giovanni* was neither. In word and music both, the Don is here a tempestuous and unregenerate human being, whose sole justice is his inner impulse, whose sole ethics is his duty to follow the dictates of nature as he sees them. Mozart placed on the stage the very archetype of the complete individualist, struggling to fashion life to his own ideas—a type not unknown in the "outside" world, eleven years after the American Revolution, and four before the French.

True, *Don Giovanni* was portrayed as a villain and a thief, and his end is accompanied by a fine flourish of "righteousness must triumph" —complete with devils, brimstone, and some of the most grandiloquent harmonies in all opera:

But none of the other characters in the opera, for all their outraged virtue, holds the attention of the audience as does the reprehensible Don. Each may have lovely or dramatic arias, comic or tragic passages, but in none does the sense of life, of grandeur and fascination throb as in the music of the wicked hero. His music pulses with a fierce vitality that defies reproof and conquers Hell-fire and damnation. Only an artist imbued with a profound humanism, a sensitiveness to the aspirations and struggles of the individual that were the essence of the Enlightenment, could be capable of such an achievement. Mozart brought opera down off its high pedestal, sheared it of classical gods and heroes, and made it a true reflection of human life itself.* He achieved a fusion of light and serious moods, of "grand opera" and "comic opera," and of popular and symphonic music that few other composers have equaled before or since.

Racked by poverty, sickness, and a constant succession of humiliating experiences, Mozart grew in maturity and depth in the last few years of his life. In those years he composed his great masterpieces of

---

* It is true that even in his last years, Mozart also wrote two real "rococo" operas in the old style. But in both cases, he was obliged to adopt the external mannerisms of traditional opera because of the circumstances of his commissions. *Così fan tutte* (1789) was written for the Viennese court, which relished "intrigue opera"; and *La Clemenza di Tito* (1791) for the coronation of Leopold II as King of Bohemia (Mozart was still hoping for the good court position which never came). Neither work was a complete success, although *Così* contains much charming and delectable music.

orchestral and chamber music, which far outdistanced even his magnificent earlier achievements. In the string quartets dedicated to Joseph Haydn, whom the younger man knew and adored, Mozart developed an expressive and lyric method of writing for the four instruments that was entirely new in his time. It was at one of the performances of these works that Haydn said to Mozart's father, "I declare to you before God, and as an honest man, that your son is the greatest composer I know, either personally or by name." Mozart reciprocated, in equally honest fashion, saying, "From Haydn I first learned how to compose a quartet." Thus was evidenced a genuine and noble friendship rare between two artists as great as these two Austrians.

It is impossible to describe or discuss all the dozens of sonatas, symphonies, concertos, and other instrumental combinations that poured in seemingly endless stream from Mozart's pen in the years of his greatest tribulation. (Among them were compositions for popular dances, as well as pieces for the mechanical organ, for musical clockwork, and even for the instrument Franklin invented, the Armonica; Mozart was not above experimenting with any instrument that came along.) But in this music a new note is heard. Somber, almost tragic colors mingle with the bright ones; complex dissonances, chromatic passages, elaborate contrapuntal forms lend a rich texture and a new depth to the works of this period, and reveal a composer ever more desirous of depicting a world of inner strivings and aspirations that clearly foreshadow Beethoven and even the Romantics.

Mozart was plunged into almost frantic desperation these last few years. His health was rapidly failing, and the constant overwork, poverty, and frustrations that were his began to tell. When he finally landed the much coveted position of "chamber musician and Court composer" to Joseph II (left vacant by Gluck's death in 1787), it was at a salary of 800 gulden instead of the 2000 that had been paid to Gluck. "Too much for what I do, too little for what I could do," said the composer. When in February 1790 Joseph II died, his successor, Leopold II, refused Mozart's request for the position of second Kapellmeister and music teacher to the princesses. Mozart was forced to borrow from friends, pawnbrokers, and usurers, but save as he might, he found it impossible to make ends meet.

Some writers have attributed Mozart's economic failure to some hypothetical "weakness of character" or lack of personal adroitness. Can it be that his whole outlook on life, his pride in his own independence, were repugnant to the aristocrats of the old order on whom musicians were still obliged to depend for a steady livelihood—and that it was *this* that brought about his continual rejections? We know of the court cabals that then existed, and the disfavor into which anyone was cast who was out of line in the least little particular. There was even one instance in which a noble patron tore one of Mozart's quartets (the C Major) to shreds because of its radical dissonances. Doubtless his whole outlook and personality were not the right kind to succeed in that dying old order. A new way of life—for the musician at least—was still waiting to be born.

The deepening of Mozart's musical style is discernible in many of the compositions of his last few years. It is present in the long lyrical theme and the wonderful working-out section of the G minor Quintet (1787), in the C Minor Fantasy for piano, with its remarkable anticipations of Beethoven's *Appassionata* Sonata. We hear it in the magnificent D minor and C minor Piano Concertos (1785-6) and in many other works of that period. Most clearly of all, Mozart's maturity appears in the famous last three symphonies, the E flat, the *Jupiter,* and the G minor—all three composed in the incredibly short period of six weeks! In the musical and technical mastery shown in these symphonies, in the variety of moods expressed in each, in the perfect mating of substance and form, Mozart's individuality shone forth as never before. The Rococo was left behind forever, and .we are placed on the threshold of a magnificent new world.

In May 1791, Mozart began work on the composition that best sums up all the varied aspects of his career: *The Magic Flute.* Conceived by Schikaneder, a leading spirit in the folk theaters of Germany and Austria, it combined a variety of divers theatrical devices with a "magic" plot that also served as a symbolic defense of Freemasonry, outlawed the year before by the reactionary emperor who had succeeded Joseph II.

In *The Magic Flute* there is almost every kind of music, from the most popular to the most serious—the simple folk songs of the Viennese suburbs; the noble austerity of the "ethical" and religious passages; the low comedy of the bird-man, Papageno; the elaborate Italianate arias of the Queen of the Night; the romantic Lieder of Prince Tamino; the deep seriousness of the temple and initiation scenes. Like many other great works of art—Goethe's *Faust,* for instance—*The Magic Flute* is imperfect, mystifying, apparently full of nonsense and contradictions. How could Mozart juxtapose the clowning and bad jokes, the trivial Viennese dance tunes, with the solemnity of Sarastro's hymns of human brotherhood?

In these contradictions and complexities lies the true meaning of a musician like Mozart. For, although he did not think of himself in that way, he was a poet of democracy coming to birth. He himself could not live to see the fulfillment of the movement he was part of—not even the fulfillment of his own music. For only a few months after writing *The Magic Flute* he became grievously ill, and in December, 1791, in the midst of working on his last and most shameful commission,* died in a poverty so bitter that his wife could not even muster up the funds for his funeral expenses. He was buried in a potter's field.

But his art belonged to the music of democracy soon to come into being; direct links bind him to Beethoven and other composers of a freer age. In *The Magic Flute,* as in the democratic world then being built, there were numberless confusions. But there was openness and high purpose and fraternity. The moments of consecration before the temple, the passage through fire and water—were they not symbolic of the devotion and strength of those who strove to create the life we now enjoy? In this music were fugues and chorales and hymns; but along with them were the simplest songs of the Viennese slums and the common suburban theater of the people which at the end was the only one to accept Mozart and give him the wherewithal of life.

In this work, the high-minded Prince Tamino went on his mission in search of high ideals. But at his side, and in Mozart's heart, there was also Papageno, the robust folk character seeking the plain things of life —a glass of wine, a *schönes Mädchen,* lots of none-too-delicate fun, and finally, a bevy of *kleine Kinderlein*. The man of noble mind and the man of the people went together, joined in brotherhood to seek the way to make Light triumph over Darkness. That was Mozart, and the world for which he toiled was the world that Beaumarchais, Franklin, Washington, and Jefferson brought into being.

---

* The writing of the *Requiem* has always been ascribed to the commission of a "mysterious stranger"—a tall, cadaverous man who would not give his name, and who has been presented in ominous manner as a premonition of Mozart's death. Actually the "mysterious stranger" was an emissary of a certain Count Walsegg, who had a passion for ordering musical works of various composers and passing them off as his own. Pressed for funds, Mozart was obliged to compose the *Requiem* whose authorship, for all he knew, would go down in history as being not even his own. After the composer's death, Walsegg relented, and acknowledged the work as Mozart's.

Ludwig van Beethoven

Extracts from "Beethoven"

By Romain Rolland

HE was short and thick-set, broad-shouldered and of athletic build. A big face, ruddy in complexion—except towards the end of his life, when his colour became sickly and yellow, especially in the winter after he had been remaining indoors far from the fields. He had a massive and rugged forehead, extremely black and extraordinarily thick hair through which it seemed the comb had never passed, for it was always very rumpled, veritable bristling "serpents of Medusa." His eyes shone with prodigious force. It was one of the chief things one noticed on first encountering him, but many were mistaken in their colour. When they shone out in dark splendour from a sad and tragic visage, they generally appeared black; but they were really a bluish grey. Small and very deep-set, they flashed fiercely in moments of passion or warmth, and dilated in a peculiar way under the influence of inspiration, reflecting his thoughts with a marvellous exactness. Often they inclined upwards with a melancholy expression. His nose was short and broad with the nostrils of a lion; the mouth refined, with the lower lips somewhat prominent. He had very strong jaws, which would easily break nuts; a large indentation in his chin imparted a curious irregularity to the face. "He had a charming smile," said Moscheles, "and in conversation a manner often lovable and inviting confidence; on the other hand his laugh was most disagreeable, loud, discordant and strident"—the laugh of a man unused to happiness. His usual expression was one of melancholy. Rellstab in 1825 said that he had to summon up all his courage to prevent himself from breaking into tears when he looked into Beethoven's "tender eyes with their speaking sadness." Braun von Braunthal met him in an inn a year later. Beethoven was sitting in a corner with closed eyes, smoking a long pipe—a habit which grew on him more and more as he approached death. A friend spoke to him. He smiled sadly, drew from his pocket a little note-tablet, and, in a thin voice which frequently sounded cracked notes, asked him to write down his request. His face would frequently become suddenly transfigured, maybe in the access of sudden inspiration which seized him at random, even in the street, filling the passers-by with amazement, or it might be when great thoughts came to him suddenly, when seated at the piano. "The muscles of his face would stand out, his veins would swell; his wild eyes would become doubly terrible. His lips trembled, he had the manner of a wizard controlling the demons which he had invoked." "A Shakespearean visage—a King Lear"—so Sir Julius Benedict described it.

Ludwig van Beethoven was born on December 16th, 1770, in a little bare attic of a humble dwelling at Bonn, a small University town on the Rhine near Cologne. He came of Flemish origin. His father was an illiterate and lazy tenor singer—a "good-for-nothing fellow" and a confirmed drunkard. His mother was the daughter of a cook. She had been a maidservant and by her first marriage was the widow of a *valet de chambre*.

Unlike the more fortunate Mozart, Beethoven spent an unhappy childhood devoid of domestic comfort. From his earliest years life was for him a sad, even a brutal, fight for existence. His father wished to exploit the boy's musical talents and to turn him to lucrative purposes as a prodigy. At the age of four he compelled the boy to practise on the harpsichord for hours together and he shut him up alone with the violin, forcing him to work in this way. It is astonishing that the boy was not completely disgusted with music, for the father persisted in this treatment for many years, often resorting to actual violence. Beethoven's youth was saddened by the care and anxiety of earning his daily bread by tasks far too burdensome for his age. When he was eleven years old he was placed in the theatre orchestra; at thirteen he became an organist of the chapel. In 1787 he lost his mother whom he adored. "She was so good to me, so worthy of love, the best friend I had! How happy was I when I could utter that dear name of mother and she could hear it!" She died of consumption and Beethoven believed himself to be affected with the same complaint. Already he suffered continually, and a depression of spirits even more terrible than the physical pain hung over him always. When he was seventeen he was practically the head of the family and responsible for the education of his two younger brothers. He suffered the humiliation of being obliged to beg for a pension for his father, that his father's pension should be paid to himself, as the father only squandered it in drink. These sad experiences made a profound impression on the youth. However, he found great affection and sympathy from a family in Bonn who always remained very dear to him—the Breuning family. The gentle "Lorchen," Eleonore von Breuning, was two years younger than Beethoven. He taught her music and she initiated him into the charms of poetry. She was the companion of his youth and there may have been between them a still more tender sentiment. Later on Eleonore married Dr. Wegeler, one of Beethoven's best friends; and up to Beethoven's last days there existed among the three a deep, steady friendship, amply proven by the regular and loving epistles of Wegeler and Eleonore, and those of their old faithful friend (*alter treuer Freund*) to the dear good Wegeler (*guter lieber Wegeler*). These friendly bonds became all the more touching as old age crept on all three, and still their hearts remained warm. Beethoven also found a safe guide and good friend in Christian Gottlob Neefe, his music master, whose high moral character had no less influence on the young musician than did his broad and his intelligent artistic views.

Sad as was the childhood of Beethoven, he always treasured a tender and melancholy memory of the places where it was spent. Though compelled to leave Bonn, and destined to spend nearly the whole of his life in the frivolous city of Vienna with its dull environs, he never forgot the beautiful Rhine valley and the majestic river. *"Unser Vater Rhein"* (our father Rhine), as he called it, was to him almost human in its sympathy, being like some gigantic soul whose deep thoughts are beyond all human reckoning. No part is more beautiful, more powerful, more calm, than that part where the river caresses the shady and flowered slopes of the old University city of Bonn. There Beethoven spent the first twenty years of his life.

In November, 1792, Beethoven removed to Vienna, the musical metropolis of Germany. The Revolution had broken out. It threatened to spread over the whole of Europe. Beethoven left Bonn just at the moment when the war reached it. On his way to Vienna he passed the Hessian armies marching to France. In 1796 and 1797 he set the war poems of Friedberg to music: a Song of Farewell, and a patriotic chorus, *Ein grosses deutsches Volk sind wir* (A great German people are we). But it was in vain that he sang of the enemies of the Revolution; the Revolution overcame the world—and Beethoven with it. From 1798, in spite of the strained relations between Austria and France, Beethoven became closely connected with the French, with the Embassy and General Bernadotte, who had just arrived in Vienna. In this intercourse strong republican sympathies showed themselves in Beethoven, and these feelings became stronger and stronger with time.

A sketch which Steinhauser made of him at this time gives a good idea of his general appearance at this period. Beethoven looks very young for his age, thin and straight, very stiff in his high cravat, a defiant, strained look in his eyes; he knows his own worth and is confident of his power. In 1796 he wrote in his notebook: "Courage! in spite of all my bodily weaknesses my genius shall yet triumph. . . . Twenty-five years! that is my age now. . . . This very year the man I am must reveal himself entirely." Both Madame von Bernhard and Gelinck say that he was extremely proud, with rough and clumsy ways, and spoke with a strong provincial accent. Only his intimate friends knew what exquisite talent lay hidden under this rough exterior. Writing to Wegeler about his successes, the first thought that springs to his mind is the following: "For example, I meet a friend in need; if my purse does not allow me to help him at once, I have only to go to my work table, and in a short time I have removed his trouble. . . . See how charming it is to do this." And a little further on, he says: "My art shall be devoted to no other object than the relief of the poor" (*Dann soll meine Kunst sich nur zum Besten der Armen zeigen*).

Trouble was already knocking at the door; it entered—never more to leave him. Between 1796 and 1800, deafness began its sad work. He suffered from continual singing and humming in his ears. His hearing became gradually weaker. For several years he kept the secret to himself, even from his dearest friends. He avoided company, so that his affliction should not be noticed. But in 1801 he can no longer remain silent; and in his despair he confides in two of his friends, Dr. Wegeler and Pastor Amenda. "My dear, good, loving Amenda, how often have I longed to have you near me! Your Beethoven is very unhappy. You must know that the best part of me, my hearing, has become very weak. Even at the time when we were together I was aware of distressing symptoms which I kept to myself; but my condition is now much worse. . . . Can I ever be cured? Naturally I hope so; but my hopes are very faint, for such maladies are the least hopeful of all. How sad my life is! For I am obliged to avoid all those I love and all that are dear to me; and all this in a world so miserable and so selfish! . . . How sad is this resignation in which I take refuge! Of course I have steeled myself to rise above all these misfortunes. But how is this going to be possible?" And to Wegeler: "I lead a miserable life indeed. For the last two years I have completely avoided all society, for I cannot talk with my fellow-men. I am deaf. Had my profession been any other, things might still be bearable; but as it is, my situation is terrible. What will my enemies say? And they are not few! . . . At the theatre I always have to be quite near the orchestra in order to understand the actor. I cannot hear the high notes of the instruments or the voices, if I am but a little distance off. . . . When anyone speaks quietly I only hear with difficulty. . . . On the other hand, I find it unbearable when people shout to me. . . . Often I have cursed my very existence. Plutarch has guided me to a spirit of resignation. If it be possible at all, I will courageously bear with my fate; but there are moments in my life when I feel the most miserable of all God's creatures. . . . Resignation! What a sorry refuge! And yet it is the only one left to me!"

This tragic sadness is expressed in some of the works of this period, in the *Sonate pathétique* Op. 13 (1799), and especially in the Largo of the Piano Sonata in D, Opus 10, No. 3 (1798). It is a marvel that we do not find it in all the works; the radiant Septet (1800), the limpid First Symphony (C major, 1800), both breathe a spirit of youthful gaiety. There is no doubt that he is determined to accustom his soul to grief. The spirit of man has such a strong desire for happiness that when it has it not, it is forced to create it. When the present has become too painful, the soul lives on the past. Happy days are not effaced at one stroke. Their radiance persists long after they have gone. Alone and unhappy in Vienna, Beethoven took refuge in the remembrances of his native land; his thoughts were always of Bonn. The theme of the Andante for the Variation in the Septet is a Rhenish song.

Troubles of another kind were soon to be added to his physical sufferings. Wegeler says that he never knew Beethoven to be free of a love passion carried to extremes. These love affairs seemed to have always been of the purest kind. With him there was no connection between passion and pleasure. The confusion established between the two things nowadays only shows how little most men know of passion and its extreme rarity. Beethoven had something of the Puritan in his nature; licentious conversation and thoughts were abhorrent to him; he had always unchangeable ideas on the sanctity of love. He was always falling violently in love and ceaselessly dreaming of its happiness, only however to be deceived and to be plunged in the deepest suffering. In these alternating states of love and passionate grief, of youthful confidence and outraged pride, we find the most fruitful source of Beethoven's inspiration, until at length his fiery, passionate nature gradually calms down into melancholy resignation.

In 1801 the object of his passion appears to have been Giulietta Guicciardi, whom he immortalised in the dedication of the famous (so-called) *Moonlight* Sonata, Opus 27 (1802). "I now see things in a better light," he writes to Wegeler, "and associate more with my kind. . . . This change has been brought about by the charm of a dear girl; she loves me and I love her. These are the first happy moments I have had for two years." He paid dearly for them. From the first, this love made him feel more keenly the misery of the infirmity which had overtaken him and the precarious conditions of his life which made it impossible for him to marry the one he loved. Moreover, Giulietta was a flirt, childish and selfish by nature; she made Beethoven suffer most cruelly, and in November 1803, she married Count Gallenberg. Such passions devastate the soul; indeed, when the spirit is already enfeebled by illness, as was Beethoven's, complete disaster is risked. This was the only time in Beethoven's life when he seems to have been on the point of succumbing. He passed the terrible crisis, however, and the details are given in a letter known as the *Heiligenstadt Testament* to his brothers Carl and Johann, with the following direction: "To be read and carried out after my death." It is an outcry of revolt, full of the most poignant grief. One cannot hear it without being cut to the heart. In that dark hour he was on the verge of suicide. Only his strong moral force saved him. His final hopes of recovering his health disappeared. "Even the lofty courage which has hitherto sustained me has now disappeared. O Providence, grant that but a single day of real happiness may be mine once again. I have been a stranger to the thrill of joy for so long. When, O God, when shall I feel joy once more? . . . Ever again? No, that would be too cruel!"

This love of his, this suffering, this resignation, these alternations of dejection and pride, these "soul-tragedies" are all reflected in the great compositions written in 1802—the Sonata with the Funeral March, Opus 26; the *Sonata quasi una Fantasia,* Opus 27, No. 1; the Sonata called the *Moonlight,* Opus 27; the Sonata in D minor, Opus 31, No. 2, with its dramatic recitatives which seem like some grand yet heart-broken monologue; the Sonata in C minor for Violin, Opus 30, dedicated to the Emperor Alexander; the *Kreutzer* Sonata, Opus 47; and the Six Religious Songs, heroic yet grief-laden, to the words of Gellert, Opus 48. The Second Symphony, in D (1803), reflects rather his youthful love; and here one feels that his will is decidedly gaining the upper hand. An irresistible force sweeps away his sad thoughts, a veritable bubbling over of life shows itself in the finale. Beethoven was determined to be happy. He was not willing to believe his misfortune hopeless, he wanted health, he wanted love, and he threw aside despair.

In many of his works one is struck by the powerful and energetic march rhythms, full of the fighting spirit. This is especially noticeable in the Allegro and the Finale of the Symphony in D, and still more in the first movement, full of superb heroism, of the Violin Sonata dedicated to the Emperor Alexander. The war-like character of this music recalls the period in which it was written. The Revolution had reached Vienna. Beethoven was completely carried away by it. "He spoke freely amongst his intimate friends," said the Chevalier de Seyfried, "on political affairs, which he estimated with unusual intelligence, with a clear and well-balanced outlook. All his sympathies leaned towards revolutionary ideas." He liked the Republican principles. Schindler, the friend who knew him best during the last period of his life, said: "He was an upholder of unlimited liberty and of national independence. . . . He desired that everyone should take part in the government of the State. . . . For France he desired universal suffrage and hoped that Bonaparte would establish it, thus laying down the proper basis of human happiness." A Roman of the revolutionary type, brought up on Plutarch, he dreamt of a triumphant Republic, founded by the god of victory, the first Consul. And blow by blow he forged the *Eroica* Symphony (1804), the *Iliad* of Empire, and the Finale of the Symphony in C minor, 1805 to 1808, the grand epic of glory. This is really the first music breathing revolutionary feeling.

Beethoven's spirit reveals itself coloured by the reflections of these great wars. Evidences of this (perhaps unconscious to him) crop up everywhere in the works of this period, in the *Coriolanus* Overture (1807), where tempests roar over the scene; in the Fourth Quartet of Opus 18, the first movement of which shows a close relation to this Overture; in the *Sonata Appassionata*, Op. 57 (1804), of which Bismarck said, "If I heard that often I should always be very valiant"; in the score of *Egmont;* and even in his Pianoforte Concertos, in the one in E-flat, Opus 73 (1809), where even the virtuosity is heroic; whole armies of warriors pass by. Nor need we be astonished at this. Though when writing the Funeral March on the death of an hero (Sonata, Opus 26), Beethoven was ignorant that the hero most worthy of his music— namely Hoche, the one who approximated more closely than Bonaparte to the model of the *Eroica* Symphony—had just died near the Rhine, where indeed his tomb stands at the top of a small hill between Coblentz and Bonn. . . . He had twice seen the Revolution victorious in Vienna itself. French officers were present at the first production of *Fidelio* in Vienna in November, 1805. It was General Hulin, the con-

queror of the Bastille, who stayed with Lobkovitz, Beethoven's friend
and protector, to whom he dedicated the *Eroica* and the C minor Symphony. And on 10 May, 1809, Napoleon slept at Schönbrunn.

Beethoven suddenly broke off the C minor Symphony to write
the Fourth at a single sitting without his usual sketches. Happiness had
come to him. In May, 1806, he was betrothed to Theresa von Brunswick. She had loved him for a long time—ever since as a young girl she
had taken piano lessons from him during his first stay in Vienna. Beethoven was a friend of her brother Count Franz. In 1806 he stayed with
them at Martonvasar in Hungary, and it was there that they fell in love.
The remembrance of these happy days is kept fresh by some stories in
some of Theresa's writings. "One Sunday evening," she says, "after
dinner, with the moon shining into the room, Beethoven was seated at
the piano. At first he laid his hands flat on the keyboard. Franz and I
always understood this, for it was his usual preparation. Then he struck
some chords in the bass and slowly with an air of solemnity and mys-
stery drifted into a song of John Sebastian Bach: '*If thou wilt give me
thy heart, first let it be in secret, that our hearts may commingle and no
one divine it.*' My mother and the priest had fallen asleep, and my
brother was dream gazing, whilst I, who understood his song and his
expression, felt life come to me in all its fullness. The following morning we met in the park and he said to me, 'I am now writing an opera;
the principal character is in me and around me wherever I go. Never
before have I reached such heights of happiness; I feel light, purity and
splendour all around me and within. Until now I have been like the
child in the fairy story, picking up pebbles along the road without
seeing the beautiful flower blossoming close by.' . . . It was in May,
1806, that I became betrothed to him with the ready consent of my
dear brother Franz."

The Fourth Symphony, composed in this year, is a pure fragrant
flower which treasures up the perfume of these days, the calmest in all
his life. It has been justly remarked that at this time "Beethoven's desire
was to reconcile his genius as far as possible with what was generally
known and admired in the forms handed down by his predecessors."

This profound peace was not destined to last although love exercised its soothing influence until 1810. Beethoven doubtless owed to it
the self-mastery which at this period enabled him to produce some of
the most perfect fruits of his genius: that great classical tragedy, the
Symphony in C minor, and that delicious idyll of a summer's day, the
Pastoral Symphony, 1808. The *Sonata Appassionata,* inspired by Shake-

speare's *Tempest,* the Sonata which he himself regarded as his most powerful one, appeared in 1807 and was dedicated to Theresa's brother. To Theresa herself he dedicated the dreamy and fantastic Sonata in F-sharp, Opus 78 (1809).

It is difficult to divine what was the barrier which separated these two from the consummation of their love. Was it the lack of fortune or the difference in social position? Perhaps Beethoven rebelled against the long period of probation which was imposed on him or resented the humiliation of keeping his love secret for an indefinite period. Perhaps, impulsive and afflicted as he was, a misanthrope too, he caused his loved one to suffer without wishing it and gave himself up to despair in consequence. The fact remains that the engagement was broken off, although neither seems ever to have proved faithless.

Even to her last day (she lived till 1861) Theresa von Brunswick loved Beethoven, and Beethoven was no less faithful. In 1816 he remarked, "When I think of her my heart beats as violently as on the day when I first saw her." To this year belong the six songs, Opus 98, which have so touching and profound a feeling. They are dedicated "To the loved one far away" (*An die ferne Geliebte*). He wrote in his notes, "My heart overflows at the thought of her beautiful nature; and yet she is not here, not near me!" Theresa had given her portrait to Beethoven, inscribed, "To the rare genius, the great artist, the generous man. T.B." Once during the last year of his life a friend surprised Beethoven alone, and found him holding this portrait and speaking to himself through his tears: "Thou wert so lovely and great, so like to an angel!" The friend withdrew, and returning a little later found him at the piano, and said "Today, my old friend, there are no black looks on your face." Beethoven replied, "It is because my good angel has visited me." The wound was deep. "Poor Beethoven," he said to himself, "there is no happiness for you in this world; only in the realms of the ideal will you find strength to conquer yourself."

In his notebook he wrote: "Submission, complete submission to your destiny. You can no longer live for yourself, only for others. For you there is happiness only in your art. O God, give me strength to conquer myself."

Love then abandoned him. In 1810 he was once more alone; but joy had come to him and the consciousness of his power. He was in the prime of life. He gave himself up to his violent and wild moods regardless of results, and certainly without care for the opinions of the world and the usual conventions of life. What, indeed, had he to fear or to be careful of? Gone are love and ambition. Strength and the joy of it, the necessity for using it, almost abusing it, were left to him. "Power constitutes the morality of men who distinguish themselves above the ordinary." He returned to his neglect in matters of dress, and his manners now became even freer than before. He knew that he had the right to speak freely even to the greatest. "I recognise no sign of superiority in mankind other than goodness," he writes on 17 July, 1812. Bettina Brentano, who saw him at that time, says that "no king or emperor was ever so conscious of his power." She was fascinated by his very strength. "When I saw him for the first time," she wrote to Goethe, "the whole exterior world vanished from me. Beethoven made me forget the world, and even you, O Goethe. . . . I do not think I am wrong in saying this man is very far ahead of modern civilisation." Goethe attempted to make Beethoven's acquaintance.* They met at a Bohemian spa, Töplitz, in 1812, but did not agree well. Beethoven passionately admired Goethe's genius; but his own character was too free and too wild not to wound the susceptibilities of Goethe. Beethoven himself has told us of this walk which they took together, in the course of which the haughty republican gave the courtly councillor of the Grand-duke of Weimar a lesson in dignity which he never forgot.

"Kings and princes can easily make professors and privy councillors; they can bestow titles and decorations, but they cannot make great men, or minds which rise above the base turmoil of this world . . . and when two men are together such as Goethe and myself these fine gentlemen must be made conscious of the difference between ourselves and them. Yesterday, as we were returning home on foot, we met the whole of the Imperial family. We saw them approaching from a distance. Goethe let go my arm to take his stand by the roadside with the crowd. It was in vain that I talked to him. Say what I would I could not get him to move a single step. I drew my hat down upon my head, buttoned up my overcoat, and forced my way through

---

* "Goethe's poems give me real happiness," he wrote to Bettina Brentano on 19th February, 1811. And also: "Goethe and Schiller are my favourite poets, together with Ossian and Homer, whom, unfortunately, I can only read in translations." It is remarkable that Beethoven's taste in literature was so sound, in view of his neglected education. In addition to Goethe, who he said was "grand, majestic, always in D major" (and more than Goethe), he loved three men, Homer, Plutarch and Shakespeare. Of Homer's works he preferred the *Odyssey* to the *Iliad*; he was continually reading Shakespeare (from a German translation) and we know with what tragic grandeur he has set *Coriolanus* and *The Tempest* in music. He read Plutarch continually, as did all who were in favour of the revolution. Brutus was his hero, as was also the case with Michael Angelo; he had a small statue of him in his bedroom. He loved Plato, and dreamed of establishing his republic in the whole world. "Socrates and Jesus have been my models," he wrote once in his notebooks.

the throng. Princes and courtiers stood aside. Duke Rudolph raised his hat to me, the Empress bowed to me first. The great of the earth know me and recognise me. I amused myself in watching the procession pass by Goethe. He remained on the roadside bowing low, hat in hand. I took him to task for it pretty severely and did not spare him at all."

In 1812 the Seventh and Eighth Symphonies were written during a stay of several months at Töplitz. These works are veritable orgies of rhythm and humour; in them he is perhaps revealing himself in his most natural and as he styled it himself, most "unbuttoned" (*aufge-knopft*) moods, transports of gaiety contrasting unexpectedly with storms of fury and disconcerting flashes of wit followed by those Titanic explosions which terrified both Goethe and Zelter and caused the remark in North Germany that the Symphony in A was the work of a drunkard. The work of an inebriated man indeed it was, but one intoxicated with power and genius; one who said of himself: "I am the Bacchus who crushes delicious nectar for mankind. It is I who give the divine frenzy to men."

The year 1814 marks the summit of Beethoven's fortunes. At the Vienna Congress he enjoyed European fame. He took an active part in the fêtes, princes rendered him homage, and (as he afterwards boasted to Schindler) he allowed himself to be courted by them. He was carried away by his sympathy with the War of Liberation.

After this hour of glory comes the saddest and most miserable period. Vienna had never been sympathetic to Beethoven. Haughty and bold genius as he was, he could not be at ease in this frivolous city with its mundane and its mediocre spirit, which Wagner laughed to scorn later on. He lost no opportunities of going away; and towards 1808 he thought seriously of leaving Austria to go to the court of Jerome Bonaparte, King of Westphalia. But Vienna had abundant musical resources; and one must do it justice by saying that there were always noble *dilettanti* who felt the grandeur of Beethoven, and who spared their country the shame of losing him. In 1809, three of the richest noblemen of Vienna, the Archduke Rudolph (a pupil of Beethoven), Prince Lobkovitz, and Prince Kinsky undertook to pay him annually a pension of 4,000 florins on the sole condition that he remain in Austria. "As it is evident," they said, "that a man can devote himself entirely to art only when he is free from all material care, and that it is only then that he can produce such sublime works which are the glory of art, the undersigned have formed a resolution to release Ludwig van

Beethoven from the shadow of need, and thus disperse the miserable obstacles which are so detrimental to his flights of genius." Unhappily the results did not come up to the promises. The pension was always very irregularly paid; soon it ceased altogether. Also Vienna had very much changed in character after the Congress of 1814. Society was distracted from art by politics. Musical taste was spoilt by Italianism, and the fashionable people favoured Rossini, treating Beethoven as pedantic. Beethoven's friends and protectors went away or died: Prince Kinsky in 1812, Lichnovsky in 1814, Lobkovitz in 1816. Rasumovsky, for whom he had written the three admirable Quartets, Opus 59, gave his last concert in February, 1815. In 1815 Beethoven quarrelled with Stephen von Breuning, the friend of his childhood, the brother of Eleonore. From this time he was alone. "I have no friends. I am alone in the world," he wrote in his notebook of 1816.

His deafness became complete. After the autumn of 1815 he could only communicate with his friends by writing. The oldest conversation-book is dated 1816. There is a sad story recorded by Schindler with regard to the representation of *Fidelio* in 1822. "Beethoven wanted to conduct the general rehearsal. . . . From the duet of the First Act, it was evident that he could hear nothing of what was going on. He kept back the pace considerably; and whilst the orchestra followed his beat, the singer hurried the time. There followed general confusion. The usual leader of the orchestra, Umlauf, suggested a short rest, without giving any reason; and after exchanging a few words with the singers, they began again. The same disorder broke out afresh. Another interval was necessary. The impossibility of continuing under Beethoven's direction was evident; but how could they make him understand? No one had the heart to say to him, 'Go away, poor unfortunate one, you cannot conduct.' Beethoven, uneasy and agitated, turned from side to side, trying to read the expression of the different faces, and to understand what the difficulty was: a silence came over all. Suddenly he called me in his imperious manner. When I was quite near to him, he handed me his notebook, and made signs to me to write. I put down these words: 'I beg you not to continue; I will explain why at your house.' With one leap he jumped from the platform, saying to me, 'Let us go quickly.' He ran straight to his house, went in and threw himself down on a sofa, covering his face with his hands; he remained like that until dinner-time. At the table it was impossible to draw a word from him; he wore an expression of complete despondency and profound grief. After dinner when I wanted to leave him, he kept me, expressing a desire not to be left alone. When we separated, he asked me to go with him to his doctor, who had a great reputation for complaints of the ear. During the whole of my connection with Beethoven I do not know of any day which can compare with this awful day of November. He had been smitten to the heart, and until the day of his death, he retained the impression of this terrible scene."

Two years later, on 7 May, 1824, when conducting the Choral Symphony (or rather, as the programme said, "taking part in the direction of the concert") he heard nothing at all of the clamour of the audience applauding him. He did not even suspect it, until one of the singers, taking him by the hand turned him round; and he suddenly saw the audience waving their hats and clapping their hands. An English traveller, Russell, who saw him at the piano about the year 1825, says that when he wanted to play quietly the notes did not sound and that it was very moving to follow in silence the emotion animating him expressed in his face, and in the movements of his fingers. Buried in himself, and separated from all mankind, his only consolation was in Nature. "She was his sole confidant," says Theresa von Brunswick, "she was his refuge." Charles Neate, who knew him in 1815, says that he never saw anyone who loved flowers, clouds and nature so devotedly; he seemed to live in them. "No one on earth can love the country so much as I," wrote Beethoven. "I love a tree more than a man." When in Vienna he walked round the ramparts every day. In the country from daybreak till night he walked alone, without hat, in sunshine or rain. "Almighty God! In the woods I am happy, happy in the woods, where each tree speaks through Thee. O God, what splendour! In the forests, on the hills, it is the calm, the quiet, that helps me."

His mental restlessness found some respite in Nature. He was harassed by financial cares. He wrote in 1818: "I am almost reduced to beggary, and I am obliged to pretend that I do not lack necessities;" and at another time: "The Sonata Op. 106 has been written under pressing circumstances. It is a hard thing to have to work for bread." Spohr says that often he could not go out on account of his worn-out shoes. He owed large debts to his publishers and his compositions did not bring him in anything. The Mass in D, published by subscription, obtained only seven subscribers (of whom not one was a musician). He received barely thirty or forty ducats for his fine Sonatas, each one of which cost him three months' work. The Quartets, Opp. 127, 130, and 132, amongst his profoundest works, which seem to be written with his very heart-blood, were written for Prince Galitzin, who neglected to pay for them. Beethoven was worn out with domestic difficulties, and with endless lawsuits to obtain the pensions owing to him or to retain the guardianship of a nephew, the son of his brother Carl, who died of consumption in 1815.

He had bestowed on this child all the care and devotion with which his heart overflowed. But he was repaid with cruel suffering. It seemed that a kind of special fate had taken care to renew ceaselessly and to accumulate his miseries in order that his genius should not lack for food. At first he had a dispute over Carl with his mother, who wanted to take him away.

Then his nephew, so passionately loved, proved unworthy of the confidence of his uncle. The correspondence between Beethoven and him is sad and revolting, like that of Michael Angelo with his brothers, but more simple and touching.

After having cherished all kinds of dreams for the future of his nephew, who was not lacking in intelligence and whom he wished to take up a University career, Beethoven had to consent to make a merchant of him. But Carl frequented gambling dens and contracted debts: By a sad phenomenon, more frequent than one believes, the moral grandeur of his uncle, instead of doing him good, made him worse. It exasperated him, impelling him to revolt, as he said in those terrible words where his miserable soul appears so plainly, "I have become worse because my uncle wished me to do better." He reached such a state that in the summer of 1826 he shot himself in the head with a pistol. He did not die from it, but it was Beethoven who just missed dying. He never recovered from this terrible fright. Carl recovered; he lived to the end to cause suffering to his uncle, whose death he hastened in no slight measure. Nor was he with him at the hour of his death. "God has never abandoned me," wrote Beethoven to his nephew, some years before. "He will find someone to close my eyes." This was not to be the one whom he called "his son."

It was from the depth of this abyss that Beethoven undertook to chant his immortal *Ode to Joy*. It was the plan of his whole life. As early as 1793, he had thought of it at Bonn. All his life he wished to celebrate Joy, and to make it the climax of one of his great works. He was always striving to find the exact form of the Hymn, and the work where he could place it. He was far from being decided, even in his Ninth Symphony. Until the very last moment, he was on the point of putting off the *Ode to Joy* to a Tenth or Eleventh Symphony. One ought to notice that the Ninth Symphony is not entitled *Choral* Symphony, as it is now invariably called, but *Symphony with a Final Chorus on the Ode to Joy*. It narrowly missed having another conclusion. In July, 1823, Beethoven still thought of giving it an instrumental Finale, which he used later on for the quartet Op. 132. Both Czerny and Sonnleithner say that even after the performance in May, 1824, Beethoven had not abandoned this idea.

He found great technical difficulties in introducing the Chorus into the Symphony, as is shown by Beethoven's notebooks and his numerous attempts to make the voices enter at another part of the work and in a different manner. In the sketches for the second subject of the Adagio he wrote, "Perhaps the Chorus could enter conveniently here." But he could not decide to part from his faithful orchestra. "When an idea comes to me," he said, "I hear it on an instrument, never on a voice." So he put the entry of the voices as late as possible. At first he wanted to give the instruments not only the recitatives of the Finale but even the Theme of Joy itself.

At the moment when the Theme of Joy appears for the first time, the orchestra stops abruptly, thus giving a sudden unexpected character to the entrance of the Song. And this is a true touch; this theme is rightly divine. Joy descends from heaven enveloped in a supernatural calm; it soothes the suffering with its cool breath; and the first impression that it makes is so tender as it steals into the sorrowing heart, that a friend of Beethoven has said "One feels inclined to weep, as one looks into those soft, calm eyes of his." When the Theme passes first to the voices, it is the basses who present it first with a solemn and rather weighty character. But, little by little, Joy takes possession of us. It is a real battle, a fight with sorrow.

This Titanic work overcame the indifference of the public. The frivolous crowds of Vienna were moved for an instant, but they still favoured Rossini and his Italian operas. Humiliated and saddened, Beethoven was on the point of going to live in London and thought of giving his Ninth Symphony there. A second time, as in 1809, some noble friends sent him a petition beseeching him not to leave the country. They said: "We know that you have written a new composition of sacred music in which you have expressed sentiments inspired by your profound faith. The supernatural light which penetrates your great soul illumines the work. We know besides that the garland of your inspired symphonies has been increased by an immortal flower. . . . Your absence during these last years has troubled all those whose eyes are turned to you. Everyone sadly thought that the man of genius placed so high amongst living beings remained silent whilst another kind of foreign art sought to plant itself in our country, causing the productions of German art to be forgotten. . . . From you only, the nation awaits new life, new laurels, and a new reign of truth and beauty, despite the fashion of the day. . . . Give us the hope of soon seeing our desires satisfied. And then the springtime which is coming will blossom again doubly, thanks to your gifts to us and to the world!" This noble address shows what power, not only artistic but also moral, Beethoven exercised over the *élite* of Germany.

Beethoven was deeply moved by these words. He stayed. On May 7th, 1824, the first performance in Vienna of the Mass in D and the Ninth Symphony took place. The success was amazing; and his greeting almost of a seditious character, for when Beethoven appeared he was accorded five rounds of applause; whereas according to the strict etiquette of the city, it was the custom to give three only for the entrance of the Royal Family. The police had to put an end to the manifestations. The Symphony raised frantic enthusiasm. Many wept. Beethoven fainted with emotion after the concert; he was taken to Schindler's house where he remained asleep all the night and the following morning, fully dressed, neither eating nor drinking. The triumph was only fleeting, however, and the concert brought in nothing for Beethoven. His material circumstances of life were not changed by it. He found himself poor, ill, alone but a conqueror: conqueror of the mediocrity of mankind, conqueror of his destiny, conqueror of his suffering.

He had then completed the object of his whole life. He had tasted perfect Joy. Would he be able to rest on this triumph of the soul which ruled the tempest? Certainly he ought to feel the relief from the days of his past anguish. Indeed his last quartets are full of strange forebodings. But it seems that the victory of the Ninth Symphony had left its glorious traces in its nature. The plans which he had for the future: the Tenth Symphony, the overture on the name of BACH, the music for Grillparzer's *Melusina,* for Körner's *Odyssey* and Goethe's *Faust,* the Biblical oratorio of *Saul and David,* all show that he was attracted by the mighty serenity of the old German masters—Bach and Handel—and more still to the light of the South—the South of France or Italy, where he hoped to travel.

Dr. Spiker, who saw him in 1826, said that his face had become smiling and jovial. The same year when Grillparzer spoke to him for the last time, it was Beethoven who had more energy than the worn-out poet. "Ah!" said the latter, "if I had a thousandth part of your strength and determination!" Times were hard; the monarchial reaction oppressed their spirits. "The censors have killed me," groaned Grillparzer. "One must go to North America if one wishes to speak freely." But no power could put a stop to Beethoven's thoughts. "Words are bound in chains, but, happily, sounds are still free," he wrote to the poet Kuffner. Beethoven's is the great voice of freedom, perhaps the only one then of the whole of German thought. He felt it. Often he spoke of the duty which was imposed on him to act by means of his art "for poor humanity, for humanity to come, to restore its courage and to shake off its lassitude and cowardice." "At the present time," he wrote to his nephew, "there is need for mighty spirits to lash into action these wretched rebellious human souls." Dr. Müller said in 1827 that "Beethoven always expressed himself freely on the subjects of government, the police, the aristocracy, even in public. The police knew him, but they looked on his criticisms and satires as harmless fancies, and they did not care to interfere with the man whose genius had such an extraordinary reputation." * Thus nothing was able to break this indomitable will. It seemed now to make sport of grief. The music written in these last years, in spite of the painful circumstances under which it was composed, has often quite a new, ironical character of heroic and joyous disdain. The very last piece that he finished, the new Finale to the Quartet, Op. 130, is very gay. This was in November, 1826, four months before his death. In truth this gaiety is not of the usual kind; for at times it is the harsh and spasmodic laughter of which Moscheles speaks; often it is the affecting smile, the result of suffering conquered. It matters not; he is the conqueror. He does not believe in death.

It came, however. At the end of November, 1826, he caught a chill which turned to pleurisy: he was taken ill in Vienna when returning from a journey undertaken in winter to arrange for the future of his nephew. He was far from his friends. He told his nephew to go for a doctor. The wretch forgot his commission and only remembered two

---

* In 1819 he was followed by the police for having said aloud that "after all, Christ was only a crucified Jew." He was then writing the Mass in D. That work alone is enough to show the freedom of his religious inspirations. No less free in politics, Beethoven boldly attacked the vices of the government. He attacked, amongst other things, the administration of justice, hindered by the slowness of its process, the stupid police regulations, the rude and lazy clerks in office, who killed all individual initiative and paralysed all action: the unfair privileges of a degenerative aristocracy, the high taxation, etc. His political sympathies seemed to be with England at that time.

days after. The doctor came too late and treated Beethoven unskilfully. For three months his iron constitution fought against the illness. On January 3rd, 1827, he made his well-loved nephew his chief executor. He thought of his dear friends on the Rhine; he wrote again to Wegeler: "How I would like to talk with you! But I am too weak. I can do no more than embrace you in my heart, you and your Lorchen." Poverty would have made his last moments more gloomy, had it not been for the generosity of some English friends. He had become very gentle and very patient. On his death-bed on February 17th, 1827, after three operations and awaiting a fourth, he wrote with perfect calmness, "I am patient, and I think that all misfortune brings some blessing with it." This boon was deliverance—"the end of the comedy," as he said when dying. We might say rather the end of the *tragedy*. . . . He died in the climax of a violent storm, a tempest of snow, heavily punctuated with terrible thunder claps. A strange hand closed his eyes, March 26th, 1827.

The Romantic Movement

Abridged from "Music, History, and Ideas"

By Hugo Leichtentritt

THE romantic movement in literature and art is the significant characteristic feature of the nineteenth century. In music it was so powerful, so productive of new and impressive results, that more recent music cannot be properly comprehended at all without an acquaintance with the various factors that make up the romantic work of art. Germany and France, more than other countries, were the home of these romantic ideas. To trace them back to their origin will help in making clear their nature and their meaning as reflected and reëchoed in music.

It is extremely difficult, perhaps impossible, to define clearly and briefly the nature of the romantic work of art in all its subtlety and complication. But by a number of antitheses and contrasting terms the direction, at least, may be indicated in which one is to look for romantic traits. For instance, the classical form in music, painting, architecture has a tendency toward concentration; it is a closed form; whereas in the romantic style there is an open form, a loose construction, something "eccentric," as opposed to the concentric classical tendency. One may oppose the classical feature of clear-cut contour to the romantic predilection for picturesque, colorful treatment and shadowy contours. Or one may speak of the rationalistic, logical traits of classical style, of its love for harmonious proportions, in contrast to the experimental, fantastic, and irrational features of romantic art. Or one may contrast the objective, orderly, positive, clearly assertive classical manner with the subjective, irregular, hypothetical, and vague romantic statement. The universal tendency of classical art is replaced, at least in the earlier romantic phase, by national traits and by an outspoken glorification of the artist's own race. The changeful character of romanticism, however, is revealed by the fact that later it returns to the cosmopolitan ideal, amalgamating these contrary national and cosmopolitan aims by a number of ingeniously devised methods, as may be perceived in the music of Chopin, Liszt, Berlioz, and Wagner.

How close these contrasting styles come occasionally may be exemplified by certain works of Bach, where fantasy and fugue in the same work of art represent two different manners of artistic expression without losing connection and unity. Such works are Bach's Chromatic Fantasy and Fugue, the G minor Fantasy and Fugue for organ, and the Prelude in E flat minor and its fugue in the first part of *The Well-Tempered Clavichord*. In all these cases we have a fantasy or prelude of romantic nature coupled with a fugue of the severest classical structure. Imagine a work of art that omits these structurally severe fugues and is made up of pieces like the Bach fantasies and preludes just mentioned, and one will have a fairly adequate idea of what is called romantic music. Whatever appeals primarily and very strongly to the imagination and the emotions, and stresses these fantastic and emotional qualities with all the means that are available, may justly be called romantic.

The modern romantic movement flows in two different streams in Germany and in France. German romanticism springs from a purely ideal source, French romanticism from a revolutionary and militant spirit. The causes for the rise of the romantic movement in these two countries were similar, but the reaction to the new romantic ideas was as different as the German and French character and temperament. The cool, rationalistic attitude of mind of the eighteenth century and the revival of classicism had more or less exhausted their vital power toward the end of the century. Scorning logic, mathematical exactness, and scientific clearness, the long-repressed power of imagination now demanded its rights again. The years from about 1780 to 1830 in

Germany and Austria mark the struggle of the rising romantic spirit with the still powerful classical spirit, a struggle finally decided after the death of Beethoven and Goethe in favor of romanticism. But even after the victory of romanticism the struggle goes on, with reversed signs, so to speak, minus instead of plus; the classical spirit reënters, and a reaction in favor of classicism exists side by side with romantic exuberance. This unceasing mixture of classic and romantic traits, recurring always in different proportions, can be clearly observed in the music of Felix Mendelssohn, in the later music of Schumann, and in Brahms.

The early German romanticism of about 1775 makes its first appearance in literature, whence it is later transferred to music. The so-called *Sturm and Drang* period, the storm and stress period of young Goethe, Herder, Schiller, and such lesser writers as Lenz, Klinger, Bürger, Heinse, and the brothers Stolberg, is the dawn, the early spring of German romanticism. It began with an influx of English ideas— with an admiration for Shakespeare, who in Germany was considered the ideal romantic artist, for the poems of Ossian, and for the old ballads collected by Bishop Percy. The traits that characterize this literary movement a generation later are reflected in music. Among them are an opposition to academic rules and tradition; an outburst of nationalism; a craving for liberty; the consciousness of the value and power of individuality, of original genius; an enthusiasm for the distant past, especially the Middle Ages, for folk lore, for the mystical; and a pantheistic religious feeling that is opposed to dogmatic, confessional faith.

If we analyze romantic traits still further, we finally arrive at a number of concrete facts, criteria of the romantic style. There is, for instance, the expression of national patriotic sentiment instead of the former cosmopolitan tendency of the classical style. As early as the eighteenth century German, French, and Italian music were clearly distinct from each other—think of Bach, Rameau, Scarlatti—yet these distinctions were only the natural consequence of the composer's descent, and we scarcely ever find the desire to glorify one's own national music by belittling the achievements of other countries. On the contrary, in Germany, for example, though they naturally accentuated German traits, the greatest musicians of the eighteenth century were cosmopolitan in the widest sense of the term. Bach was a close observer and student of Italian and French music; what we call the Bach style is a compound of German, Italian, and French traits, and it is by no means certain that the German traits exceed the French and Italian traits taken together. In the case of Handel, it is almost impossible to estimate justly whether German, Italian, or English traits predominate in his music. Mozart, too, had the astonishing faculty of assimilating whatever seemed valuable to him, no matter whether it came from Germany and Austria or from Italy and France. When we approach German romanticists like Weber and Schumann, however, the international aspect almost disappears, and characteristically German features are deliberately brought out; a new charm, a strong flavor is sought in them. The same trait can be observed in Russian music, in the Polish accent in Chopin, the Bohemian in Smetana, the Scandinavian in Grieg.

This national aspect includes the use of folk lore and folk song, an outstanding romantic trait. The predilection for folk lore in German poetry began with Herder, Goethe's older friend, and came to its climax in the epoch-making collection of German folk songs edited by Arnim and Brentano under the title *Des Knaben Wunderhorn* in 1805. Even the title is romantic to the core: "The Boy's Magic Horn." The horn is the romantic instrument in German music, with its sound full of longing, of *Sehnsucht,* and "magic," of course, is a thoroughly romantic epithet. "Des Knaben" also has a romantic ring; it means not the school boy but the grown youth, filled with youth's vague emotional turmoil, sensibility, and excitability.

When we come to the romantic composers, Weber, Mendelssohn, Schumann, and Brahms, folk song assumes an importance that it had not had since the sixteenth century, the great classical epoch of German folk song. In Norway, Bohemia, Hungary, Poland, and Russia it becomes essential as the basis of the new national art that is an outcome of the great romantic movement all over Europe. It is only necessary to recall names like Chopin, Glinka, Rimsky-Korsakov, Mussorgsky, Grieg, and Smetana, to perceive how powerful the influence of folk song became in the nineteenth century.

Chopin's melodic material is Polish. Though Chopin spent nearly twenty years in Paris, the most cosmopolitan city of the world, though he was welcomed in the most exclusive Parisian society, his soul and his art remain Polish, and what little admixture there is of French and Italian traits seems like a slightly foreign flavor, marring a little the otherwise delightful purity of his Polish music. He was profoundly influenced by German music; yet he has a way of making this German current almost disappear for most listeners. His method of melodic invention combines the manners of Haydn and Mozart, but with reference to Polish national music instead of Austrian. Haydn's rustic quaintness and Mozart's elegance both reappear, but translated into Polish and transferred to the romantic idiom that is characteristic of the nineteenth century.

Another characteristic feature of all romantic art is the new meaning which nature, especially landscape, gains for art. This can be perceived in poetry as well as in painting and music. The romantic artist is interested not in the details of a landscape, in an exact, photographic, objective copy of actual experience, but in projecting his own emotional world into his vision of a landscape. The difference between unromantic and romantic landscape painting in music can be illustrated by a comparison of Haydn and Weber. In his oratorios, *The Creation* and especially *The Seasons,* Haydn is a delightful realist. These scores are full of charming, idyllic bits: the lion roars, the cock crows, the birds call and sing, the dogs race, panting in the excitement of the hunt; the beauty of flowers, of the hills, plains, and fields, of sunrise and sunset, of rain and tempest is suggested. Haydn's model was Handel, who is unsurpassed as a landscape painter of the old school, but Haydn's own love of nature and delight in its beauty made him even more inventive of charming descriptive touches. This representation of nature, however, remains merely descriptive and does not go beyond the idyllic stage. Mozart has almost no interest in nature; Beethoven's interest in it is limited to its sublime aspect, with rare exceptions, as in the *Pastoral* Symphony, which indeed has a decidedly romantic atmosphere.

It was left to Weber's genius to discover the soul of nature for music. In this respect his opera *Der Freischütz* is epoch-making. The permanent quality of this opera is not in its plot, which is dramatically weak, but in its power of revealing in sound the soul of a landscape, of evoking the *Stimmung* of the dark forests. It is not only that the elemental aspect of the German forest is translated into sound—the forest with its countless dark trees, with its clouds and winds, its friendliness and its mystery; the way in which it influences the people inhabiting it is also suggested most characteristically. The dark nocturnal powers of hell, projected into the bright sunlight of day, give *Der Freischütz* its weird and fantastic atmosphere, its romantic color; and the power to evoke such landscape impressions by the peculiar color of orchestral sound is one of Weber's greatest achievements. The *Wolfsschlucht* scene in *Der Freischütz* has become an arsenal from which all later romanticists in opera—Marschner, Nicolai, Berlioz, Liszt, Wagner—have drawn their implements for producing fantastic sound effects. Neither Berlioz' *Symphonie fantastique,* in itself a great masterpiece of romantic landscape color, nor Wagner's *Flying Dutchman,* nor *Siegfried,* to mention only the greatest achievements, could have come into existence without the vital and fascinating model set by Weber's *Freischütz.*

Fairyland and the phantoms of the air had been introduced into German literature by Norse myth and English ballads, by Ossian, and by certain Shakespeare plays, and music soon found new attractions in these fantastic visions. Schubert tried his hand here occasionally (as, for instance, in the magnificent setting of Goethe's *"Erlkönig"*), though he did not compete with the achievements of Weber and Felix Mendelssohn.

Light, aerial, fairy music is a specialty of Mendelssohn's in which he has never been surpassed. Many of his scherzos have a delightfully fantastic play of the most delicate tones, suggestive of a dance of spirits that float in the air like clouds, soaring lightly in most graceful undulations, hardly touching the ground with their nimble feet, wrapped in veils, like clouds or smoke mounting toward the sky. For example, there is the wonderful scherzo of the octet. Though written by a boy of sixteen years, its light and delicate touch reveals the firm, sure hand, the alertness of imagination of a master. And his ever-fresh young music to Shakespeare's *Midsummer Night's Dream,* with its marvelous overture, is the product of a precocious genius of seventeen years. A more sinister aspect of the fantastic world of spirits appears in his splendid music to Goethe's *Walpurgisnacht.*

But it was not only the fairy scherzo that was created and cultivated by Mendelssohn. He also sought to give musical impressions of landscapes. In his *Italian* and *Scotch* Symphonies he succeeds in evoking in the mind of the listener the impression of characteristic local color that is suggestive of Italian and Scotch scenery, and his *Fingal's Cave* overture has earned for him the praise of so severe an opponent as Richard Wagner, who called Mendelssohn a great landscape painter in music with reference to this particular overture. Certainly it gives a wonderfully vivid impression of the surging sea, of waves resounding in rocky caves, of the harsh cry of the sea gulls, the odor of the salt air, the sharp flavor of sea weed, and the melancholy soul of this northern scene. What a masterpiece of romantic imagination and romantic tone-painting!

This tendency to escape from the sober drudgery of ordinary life into the fantastic world of the imagination was strengthened in Germany by political events. The democratic, liberal flare-up of the European powers against Napoleon's tyranny was of short duration. After the battles of Leipzig and La Belle Alliance [Waterloo] in 1814, after the capture of Napoleon himself, reactionary tendencies in Germany and Austria speedily extinguished the youthful spirit of liberty, and the national enthusiasm accumulated in the so-called War of Liberation in Germany soon found no other outlet for its high-strung ecstasy than romantic poetry and literature. Here, at least, imagination was free to indulge in adventurous flights—the more remote, the better. Too close touch with the actual state of affairs invited trouble with the reactionary governments. These were the days when the struggle of the Greeks for liberty from Turkish bondage made a sensational stir in western Europe, and Lord Byron's active participation is an episode of genuine romantic idealism. The Polish revolutionaries of 1830, in their luckless revolt against Russian oppression, were surrounded with an aureole of romantic glamour, especially in Paris, where Frédéric Chopin and the Polish poet Mickiewicz headed a distinguished colony of homeless Polish fugitives.

The same reactionary spirit was also dominant in France. But the French people, less patient than the Germans and already practiced in revolution, were quicker to revolt, and the short revolution of 1830 marks the first powerful wave of the romantic movement in France. Starting much later than German romanticism, the movement in Paris was more violent and much faster in its rise. It is interesting to note that the outbreak of the revolution in Brussels in 1830 which resulted in Belgium's becoming an independent state followed a performance of Auber's opera, *La Muette de Portici* [*Masaniello*]. Even Wagner points out the revolutionary character of this opera. In fact, the French romantic movement is much more highly inflamed by the revolutionary spirit, is much more violent, radical, and extreme than the unrealistic German romanticism. Making a hasty review of what happened in the romantic ecstasies of the early thirties in Paris, we note in literature the exciting dramas of Victor Hugo, the extravagantly fantastic lyricism of Hugo and Alfred de Musset, the beautiful elegiac poetry of Lamartine. In music, also, exciting events abounded. Paganini was the great sensation. His marvelous feats of virtuosity, the strange and fascinating novelty of his art, the demoniac aspect of his violin-playing and of his personality combined to make him a very potent factor in romantic music. Franz Liszt and Hector Berlioz both received decisive impulses from his extraordinary art. Berlioz' *Symphonie fantastique* is the strongest expression of the bizarre traits in which French romanticism revels. Whereas German romanticism has something of a *paradiso* character, the work of Berlioz centers habitually around the *inferno* aspect. Meyerbeer's operas, *Robert le Diable, Les Huguenots,* and *Le Prophète,* also have this diabolic aspect in parts.

It has been pointed out that masters like Gluck, Cherubini, and Spontini, though foreigners, gained their fame in Paris and became leaders of French opera. The French metropolis asserted its strange power of assimilation again in the case of Meyerbeer, the German Jew. Meyerbeer and the French Jew Halévy, the composer of the admirable opera, *La Juive,* by universal consent of their contemporaries took a position at the head of French opera. In conjunction with Felix Mendelssohn they form a trio of world-famous Jewish musicians. This is not chance, but a conspicuous sign of the times. The liberal, tolerant, cosmopolitan attitude of the romantic spirit is manifest in the quick rise to eminence of a number of Jewish composers, for the first time in history, after the emancipation of the Jews in European countries, which in itself was an outcome of the romantic attitude. Meyerbeer, Mendelssohn, Halévy, Hiller, Offenbach, and later Goldmark, Rubinstein, Joachim, Mahler, and scores of famous violinists, pianists, singers, and conductors, show how cordially the romantic nineteenth century welcomed the musical excellence of the highly gifted Jewish people. But the paradoxical romantic mind could house side by side apparently incompatible and opposite tendencies. Thus we find along with this large, tolerant, cosmopolitan spirit a nationalism that was narrow, intolerant, and extreme. Richard Wagner, who was surrounded by Jews and highly indebted to Jewish artists and Jewish intellectuals, started * the anti-Semitic wave which attained its full force only two generations later, in our own day.

Another characteristic romantic trait is the mutual approach and the mixture of the various arts. The musical world up to this time had been a world quite separate from poetry and painting, though sometimes the various arts had met on common ground, each, however, maintaining its own nature. But the romantic ideal consisted in mixing the various arts, in making music poetical and picturesque, and poetry musical. The glorious German song created by Schubert, Schumann, and Brahms could arise only in a romantic period, for the new romantic idea of the marriage of poetry and music was its esthetic

* This is highly debatable. Certainly Wagner shared in the contemporary anti-Semitic feeling, but it can hardly be said that he "started" it.—E. S.

basis. The old pre-Schubertian song keeps poetry and music cleanly apart. To the soberly recited verses a tune is added, and a thin, unpretentious accompaniment joins music and words together, loosely and superficially. Romantic song is very different: poetry, vocal melody, and instrumental accompaniment are no longer put together loosely but are so thoroughly composed, in the literal sense of the word—that is, mixed together—that tune and words cannot be sharply separated. The three factors together create something new, so that the words interpret the meaning of the music just as the music unveils the inner sense of the words, and the rhythms and harmonies of the instrumental accompaniment give characteristic color, light, and shade, accents and climax, and thus paint the scene of the poem.

Just as music and poetry formed an intimate union in the romantic era, so music and painting became affiliated. Color in the proper sense is a new aspect of romantic music. Conceptions of light and shade, of fine gradations between lighter and darker color, had thus far been found in music only accidentally and exceptionally. In the romantic work of art the idea of color becomes an indispensable factor, and its realization was achieved by an admirable refinement of harmony and of orchestration. Romantic harmony is identical with chromatic harmony. The frequent use of chromatic progressions lessens the distinction between major and minor tonalities and increases immensely the possibilities of varying cadences and modulations from one key to another. One may even say that this sensitive new harmony is the principal achievement of the romantic movement in music, inasmuch as it added something that had not existed formerly in such intensity and richness. Schubert's music is full of the new major-minor tonality, partaking at the same time of both major and minor, soaring from somewhere in the air between the two, and thereby achieving that peculiarly indefinite romantic color which is neither bright daylight nor dark night but various shades of twilight. But the real creator of the magnificent romantic harmony in all its varying aspects is Frédéric Chopin.

It is too little known that Wagner's and Liszt's sensational chromatic harmony is a daughter of Chopin's harmony, that Chopin was the discoverer of this new land of luminous shadows, of transitions from brighter to darker levels of sound, of genuine scales of musical color. For Chopin tonality is no longer, as in classical music, a constructive feature but in the main a coloristic value, a *valeur,* as the French impressionistic painters say. Chopin, the real father of impressionistic music, is much more concerned with these picturesque *valeurs* than with any other aspects of tonality. For him modulation gains a new sense. In classical music modulation was a formal constructive feature, devised in terms of space or time; establishing a key, departing from it, and finally returning to it was an indispensable proceeding in the classical scheme. Chopin does not ignore or deny this constructive function of tonality, but his passionate interest and delight belongs to the picturesque veiling or masking of tonality, to giving music those innumerable delicate nuances of color which romantic painting in France also seeks, especially that of Delacroix, Chopin's close friend. Delacroix once criticized his older colleague, the great classical painter Ingres, saying that Ingres knew only about *coloration,* not about *couleur.* These two terms might also be applied to Chopin's harmony as compared with the harmony of the classical masters. In Gluck, Haydn, Mozart, and Beethoven, melodic design and contour line were of prime importance; harmony gave color to the design in the sense of *coloration.* With Chopin, however, the conception of *couleur,* of color as an independent primary factor in music, gained ground, so far as music permits color to predominate without losing all coherence and melodic sense. More precisely, one might say that the essential and characteristic trait of Chopin's romantic music is melody conceived in terms of color, of constantly changing color, of color in motion, in flow.

In such an art the distinction between light and shade, warm and cool color, necessarily becomes of prime significance, and consequently all available means, including rhythm and dynamics, are employed toward that end. Chopin's tempo rubato, his abundance of dynamic and agogic signs, *sforzati,* sudden irregular dramatic accents, syncopations, his exciting crescendos and his languishing diminuendos and pianissimos, his voluptuous, exhausted *fermati,* his accelerandos, *ritenutos,* sudden changes of tempo are means to express the romantic visions of light and dark color with all their inexhaustible transitions. Romantic painting in France, particularly that of Delacroix, also knows these dynamic accents. Chopin's genius, however, was not concerned with taking over these modern sensational traits into music merely for the sake of giving his art the appearance of being up-to-date. These means were needed to express the exaltations, the longings, despairs, the passionate outbursts and fantastic visions of his romantic soul, his unique personality; and this complete agreement of a powerful individuality with the artistic expression of its emotional world gives Chopin's music its lasting value, beyond the unavoidable change of artistic tendencies and creed. As musician Chopin is closely akin to the romantic poets of the first order, like Byron and Shelley, the greatest English exponents of the romantic movement, which in England was concerned much more with poetry than with music.

Nor is it by chance that the rise of romantic music is more closely allied to the piano than to any other instrument. Neither the organ nor strings nor wind instruments are so admirably fitted for this new passionate music as the pianoforte. The older forms of the piano, the clavecin, cembalo, spinet, and clavichord, were ideal instruments for the piano music of the eighteenth century, for Couperin, Rameau, Bach, Handel, Scarlatti, and Mozart. But these delicate thin-toned instruments had no possibilities for the new romantic music, and by the invention of new technical devices which changed its character completely the spinet was adapted to the demands made upon it. Hammer action gave the piano a more brilliant, metallic, and powerful tone, but even more important is the pedal, which permits the prolongation of sound, a device unknown in the old short-toned cembalo. It is true that the organ, even more than the piano, also has the power of prolonging tone at will. But there is a great difference between the sustained tone of the organ and that of the piano, and this very difference gives the piano its power of producing the romantic spell, of revealing color, atmosphere. The prolonged organ sound is rigid; it seems to increase in volume, to gain in loudness and penetration, whereas the pedal tone of the piano is not rigid but shades off most delicately, growing softer and softer and finally fading away. This colorful resounding tone, this blending of chords into each other, this *Rauschen,* as the Germans say, using a term not known in any other language, this fascinating and fantastic play of sounds in the air, derived from the Aeolian harp, is the romantic ideal of sound, and this is the chief reason why romantic music is in the main piano music. The pedal has been called the soul of the piano, and indeed with its help the great romantic masters, Chopin, Schumann, and Liszt—to a certain extent Beethoven and Schubert—discovered a new world of fantastic, immaterial sound. These pedal sounds cannot be realized by any other means. Neither the organ nor the orchestra can replace the modern piano. Pedal resonance is to sound what the air, the sunlight penetrating layers of clouds, is to color in painting. It makes possible an amazing variety of color effects, and Chopin, Schumann, and Liszt with admirable inventive genius achieved a practical realization of these captivating possibilities, these fleeting shadow effects.

In Robert Schumann we see the incarnation of the romantic spirit. For the most part his romantic qualities are derived from and nourished by literary sources. Jean Paul Friedrich Richter, E. T. A. Hoffmann, Rückert, Eichendorff, Heine are the poets congenial to him. No composer before Schumann had ever devoted his art to making his music "poetic" to a comparable degree. For Schumann "poetic" is a synonym for "musical," and for him the essence of music, its artistic flower, must needs be poetic. The poetic quality he seeks to achieve is that ideal aspect, that elevation above the commonplace, that escape into a world of fantasy which is the desire and final aim of the romantic soul. It is true that much of the music of Bach, Mozart, and Beethoven has a quality of idealism, but romantic idealism is·very different from classical idealism. Schumann's romanticism is of an extremely individual type, quite different from that of Weber, Mendelssohn, Chopin, Liszt, and Marschner. What interests Schumann most is not nature and landscape painting, fantastic visions of fairyland, as in Weber and Mendelssohn; it is not the picturesque sound-fantasy of a Chopin, but rather the poetic exaltation, youthful exuberance, and soulful lyricism of romantic art. In short, he is concerned not so much with the frame, the outer aspects, of the romantic feeling as with its inner aspects. This tendency places him in close contact with the romantic novelists, Jean Paul and E. T. A. Hoffmann, whose writings deal not only with humorous, grotesque, and strange—even abnormal —types of people but also with beautiful and enchanting ones. Schumann's dance fantasies, *Papillons, Faschingsschwank aus Wien, Davidsbündler,* and especially the immortal *Carnaval,* show us this aspect of his art most delightfully. What a difference between this fantastic German dance music and Chopin's hardly less fantastic valses, polonaises, mazurkas, which are so genuinely Slavic in character!

Though Schumann is rarely beyond criticism technically, though his weaknesses in construction, in form, in polyphony, and in orchestral treatment are evident, yet the emotional power of his music is so great that in the works of his best and earliest period he reaches his aim in spite of his handicaps. In many of the Schumann melodies there are a poignant expression, a cry of the heart, a touching accent, a purity and sincerity of feeling so irresistible in their effect that even after a century his strange expressive power has not perceptibly lost its strength. What ties musical souls to Schumann is not his intellectual achievement, which is very slight in comparison with that of other great masters, but the emotional aspect of his music. In this field his achievements are indeed almost incomparable, and the strange, magical charm that emanates from his music has been one of the strongest factors in shaping later music in Germany, France, and Russia. The Schumannesque melodic type is noticeable fifty years later. Gounod and Saint-Saëns, Bizet, César Franck, and Massenet are full of it; Liszt, Rubinstein, Brahms, Tchaikovsky, Borodin, and Rimsky-Korsakov revel in it. Schumann the composer of songs takes us into a fascinating magic land. Here is lyric vocal music fully suited to the romantic exaltations, the fantastic poetry of such writers as Heine, Eichendorff, Rückert, and Platen. There is hardly anything in the immense compass of music that equals certain Schumann melodies in the power of evoking strong emotion, of making tears rush to the eyes, of arousing outbursts of delight—and all this is accomplished with a touching purity and sincerity, a chasteness of feeling very different from Chopin's sensuous refinement, from Wagner's burning passion and voluptuous impetuosity.

The predilection of the romantic masters for short pieces in one movement is a very striking and characteristic feature. They are not interested in complicated design but in inspiration, poetic ecstasy, a mysterious, fantastic background. The fact that the quick flame of fervent inspiration is likely to consume itself as quickly and thus lose its power of incantation seems to be the psychological reason for the somewhat fragmentary aspect of romantic music. The intellectual power necessary for the magnificent architectural structures of a Bach, Handel, or Beethoven is absent from romantic music. The interest is centered on creating not a cyclical work of powerful construction but a short piece, or a loose bundle of short pieces, flaring up in inspiration for as long or as short a time as the flame may burn. Music of pointedly characteristic mood, *Stimmungsmusik,* is the signature of romantic art, of pieces like Chopin's nocturnes, preludes, *études,* valses, mazurkas, polonaises, ballades, and scherzos, Mendelssohn's *Songs without Words,* Schumann's suite-like dance fantasies—his *Carnaval, Kreisleriana, Faschingsschwank aus Wien,* and *Davidsbündler.*

Another characteristic feature of music in the nineteenth century is the rise of national schools. In 1800 there were three great countries that had been rivals in music for centuries—Italy, France, Germany. In 1900, however, a number of newcomers claim attention. There is the Polish music of Chopin, the Russian music of Glinka, Mussorgsky, Borodin, Tchaikovsky, and Rimsky-Korsakov; there is the Norwegian music of Grieg and Sinding, the Danish music of Niels Gade, the

Finnish music of Sibelius; Hungary has its Franz Liszt, Bohemia its Smetana and Dvořák. It is true that music had been practised in all these countries long before 1800, but it gained international validity only in the course of the nineteenth century. Formerly, it had been a provincial dialect, a folk-lore idiom of characteristic traits but narrow scope; in the romantic epoch this nationally limited folk lore expanded into a well-developed language and assumed a style, form, and content that made it interesting to the musical world at large.

During the nineteenth century the position of music was fundamentally changed as a result of the great changes in political and economic conditions and the revolutions of the technical age. Music now became a democratic affair, supported chiefly by the middle classes and maintained by their thriving commercial prosperity. It was no longer exclusive, aristocratic, as in the eighteenth century; neither was it proletarian, as it tends to be in the twentieth century; it kept a middle course. Publicity became an essential condition for its successful existence. Public concerts, symphony orchestras, quartet societies, piano and song recitals, oratorio choruses, music festivals, public opera houses were attainments of the nineteenth century toward which only faint starts had been made up to 1800. Increased ease of travel, the rise of daily newspapers, with musical criticism as an essential feature, increased speed of international communication through the telegraph, the press, and improved mail facilities all helped music in many ways. A prodigious increase in the printing of books and music created new and extensive fields of activity; education of the masses of the people led millions of people toward art and literature; in fact, an enormous new public grew up, eager to experience what art and artists had to offer. Yet this immense widening of artistic activities had its dangers and drawbacks. Art was too often commercialized and was exploited financially to an unprecedented degree. As a consequence it descended to a very low level: late nineteenth-century popular music, for example, is tainted with a vulgarity that is quite new in the history of music. The striving for sensational effect and catering to a vulgar taste prostituted the noble art of music and adulterated its former purity.

One of the more positive attainments of the nineteenth century, however, is the art of reproductive music, which scored triumphs such as had never before been achieved. Wonderfully gifted and accomplished artists interpreted the works of the great masters with an impressiveness and a suggestive power unknown to former ages: pianists like Chopin, Mendelssohn, Liszt, Rubinstein, Bülow, Tausig, d'Albert, Paderewski, Busoni; violinists like Spohr, Paganini, David, Joachim, Wilhelmj, Vieuxtemps, Wieniawski, Sarasate, Ysaÿe; conductors like Weber, Wagner, Berlioz, Bülow, Richter, Nikisch, Mottl, Mahler; world-famous string quartets, like the Joachim, Rosé, and Bohemian quartets; scores of admirable *Lieder* singers and opera singers.

An acquaintance with the inexhaustible treasures of music, accumulated for centuries, was thus spread far beyond a little circle of fastidious connoisseurs. Toward this discovery and interpretation of lost and forgotten works of art, great and important contributions were also made by the science of musical research, musicology, as it is now called. A quite important achievement of the romantic spirit (chiefly German) not only in music but in all fields of art and science is historical investigation based on love and respect for the great deeds of the past. Thus Mendelssohn's discovery and first performance in Berlin, 1829, of Bach's *St. Matthew* Passion is an outcome of this romantic attitude toward historical research. This memorable performance marks the beginning of the great Bach movement in Germany, which a century later had not yet come to a rest. German musicological research, so fertile for the better knowledge of our great art, with all its brilliant achievements, is a child of the romantic movement.

Musicians of high rank once more became ambitious to excel as writers. This ambition was foreign to Handel, Bach, Haydn, Mozart, Beethoven, and Schubert, though it had been common in the two preceding centuries. But the logical, scientific method of the earlier musician-writers is very different from that of the romantic writers, for whom essay writing was not a professional pursuit but a means of getting relief from their artistic nervous hypertension. In this class we find E. T. A. Hoffmann, Weber, Robert Schumann, A. B. Marx, Berlioz, Liszt, Wagner, Bülow, and others. Professional musical journalism and criticism also had an increasing importance in the nineteenth century. The modern critic through his regular, often daily, columns in the newspaper has become a power the like of which had never existed before in the world of music.

Music now began to attach great importance to contents, meaning, expression. The unpretentious play of sounds of the later eighteenth century seemed shallow to romantic musicians. The Dionysian romantic art demanded not a severe ethos but rather an exciting pathos. An ecstasy of creative impulse, the sexual impulse in a sublimated form, dominates the music of Schumann, Chopin, Liszt, and especially Wagner. Magic charms, a revival of the ancient Orphic mysteries, and an orgiastic passion flame up in the arch-romantic *Tristan und Isolde* music. In less pretentious, less powerful romantic music nervous sensibility is the most characteristic trait. The language of the heart means more to the romantic artist than the cold clarity of logic. For romantic music inspiration in its literal meaning—something breathed into the soul, something of heavenly origin, given by the grace of God—is the divine spark which ignites the fire of artistic creation. The role of fantasy becomes of prime importance. Strictly formal problems are of secondary importance, though of course even romantic music could not afford to neglect them. They were refashioned for their new task, which was less architectural, less constructive and mathematical than previously, and associated more closely with poetry, drama, and painting. Sound and color were primary factors, and rhythm, associated with bodily activity, with gesture and elementary vitality, received a new glorification.

Franz Peter Schubert

Abridged from "Studies of Great Composers"

By C. Hubert H. Parry

FRANZ SCHUBERT was born on January 31st, 1797. The stock he came from was a thoroughly plebeian one, for his grandfather had been a Moravian peasant. His father had come from the country to Vienna, where he became a parish schoolmaster. He married a woman by the name of Elizabeth Vitz, who was a cook, and had fourteen children, several of whom died young. Franz was the youngest son of the first family, separated from his eldest brother Ignaz by a space of twelve years, and from the brother Ferdinand, to whom he was most deeply attached, by three years. Schoolmastering was a characteristic occupation of the family. Franz's uncle was a schoolmaster, and these two brothers became so also, as soon as they were old enough, and Franz himself, in his turn, had for some time to adopt the same calling.

The family also had musical tastes. Both Ignaz and Ferdinand played the violin and the father played the 'cello, and they were fond of making music together. The brothers became Franz's first masters, and as soon as he got beyond their capacities, which did not take long, he was passed on to the parish choir-master Michael Holzer, who taught him the violin and pianoforte, and organ, and some harmony. Holzer was immensely impressed with the boy's powers, and said afterwards: "If ever I wished to teach him anything new, I found he knew it already. I cannot be said really to have given him lessons at all; I merely amused myself, and looked on." The truth of the matter appears to have been that Franz's friends and neighbours were scarcely thorough musicians enough to know what to do with him, and many people consider that it was a great misfortune that he was not more thoroughly drilled in his youth in the mechanical part of art. But at least it can be said that mechanical drilling and discipline could not have improved the sensitive impressionableness which was the source of his masterpieces in song writing; and it might have taken away some of his spontaneity and originality for the sake of what a theorist would consider correct and well-balanced treatment.

He developed a beautiful voice as a boy, and was taken first into the choir of the Lichtenthal, the parish where the family lived; and from there he was advanced at the age of eleven years to the school that was called the Convict, where boys were educated for the choir of the Imperial Court chapel in Vienna. In this school his musical opportunities were a good deal improved. Besides singing, the boys had a regular little band in the school, which was good enough to play the simpler kinds of symphonies that were popular in those days. Franz took his place in the band at once, as his violin practice at home and his natural ability gave him some advantages; and it is also recorded that they won him at once a good friend. At the time he arrived in the school a boy called Spaun was the best violin player and led the band; and one day hearing some one playing unusually well behind him he turned round to see who it was, and found it was "a small boy in spectacles called Franz Schubert." Spaun was nine years older than Schubert, but the latter's ability bridged over the gulf which often separates boys of such different ages, and Spaun became one of his truest and most helpful friends. Franz was very poor, and Spaun appears to have been rather better off, and did not neglect any opportunities to help his small friend. The impulse to try his hand at composition seems to have taken possession of Franz by this time, but it was hindered by the difficulties of getting anything to write on. Among other kindnesses Spaun helped him in this respect, and when he found what Franz's talents were took good care they should not be wasted for want of paper.

As time went on Franz rose to be quite an important individual in the school. He became first violin in the boys' band, and his school-fellows looked upon his compositions as marvellous. But he had no one to direct him or advise him, and his early works were for the most part wild and irregular attempts to express himself with no better guidance than his own instincts, and the knowledge he had of such models as the works they performed at the school. He wrote hugely long pianoforte pieces, and songs, overtures, quartetts, variations, and church music; and in 1813 he produced his first orchestral symphony, which was his last composition as a boy at the Convict, for his time there came to an end in that same year, and he went to live at home again.

The life at this school seems to have been a hard one, especially for a boy as poor as Franz was. A letter of his to one of his brothers, written late in the year before he left, gives a strong impression of the absence of any sort of enervating luxury: "I have been thinking a good long time about my position, and find that it's well enough on the whole, but might be improved in some respects; you know that one can enjoy eating a roll and an apple or two, and all the more when one must wait eight hours and a half after a poor dinner for a meagre supper. The wish has haunted me so often and so perseveringly that I must make a change. The few groschen my father gave me are all gone to the devil; what am I to do for the rest of the time?

'They that hope in thee shall not be ashamed.'

So thought I. Suppose you advance me a few kreuzers monthly. You would never miss it, whilst I should shut myself up in my cell and be quite happy. As I said, I rely on the words of the Apostle Matthew, who says, 'Let him that hath two coats give one to the poor.' Meanwhile I trust you will listen to the voice, which appeals to you to remember your loving, hoping, poverty-stricken—and once again I repeat poverty-stricken—brother, Franz." Besides poverty, the boys suffered bitterly in the winter from living and working in unwarmed rooms, so altogether the picture is a very harsh one to contemplate; but, nevertheless, the school afforded some advantages to Schubert, for there he had a good deal of experience of solid music, and plenty of sympathy from the other boys; and there also he made some excellent friends who were faithful to him all through life.

When he got home he found one great change; for his mother had died the year before, in 1812. But there is very little recorded of the effect it had upon him or upon the ways of living at home, and before long his father was married again; and the new wife did not come up to the conventional and traditional reputation of a stepmother, but treated Franz well, and appears to have been regarded by him with affection.

It was now necessary that he should do something definite for his living, and being somewhat in dread of being taken off as a soldier, he shortly became a schoolmaster at his father's school, where he taught the lowest class. This, of course, entailed a considerable amount of drudgery, but he somehow managed to find time to pour out a constant flood of new works, and even to have lessons in composition from old Salieri, who was then *Kapellmeister* of the Viennese Court, and had a great reputation among his contemporaries.

The extraordinary impulse to compose, which seems to have possessed Schubert more powerfully than any other composer known to history, drove him to try his hand in various directions. The year after he left the Convict school he produced a mass for the Lichtenthal church, where his old master Holzer still reigned over the choir. The work was well performed under the boy's own direction, with some very good musicians among the performers, and was received with enthusiasm by his friends and relations, including Salieri, who appears to have been very complimentary, and to have publicly recognised Franz as his own pupil. Another large work soon followed, which was no less than an opera called *Des Teufels Lustschloss,* and this was followed by another mass, and various other works of large calibre.

But among these, and in some ways more important than any of them, are the first great songs, which made their appearance about this time. A most extraordinary thing about them is that in this line he seemed to require no preparation or education; for some of his very finest songs were produced within the year of leaving the Convict, and while he was still endeavouring to imbue infantile minds at his father's school with the elements of knowledge. In some branches of art, such as symphonies, he began at rather a low and uninteresting level, and went on growing and gaining in mastery all through his life. But the tamer style of his instrumental works was probably owing to the same causes which made his song-writing so very remarkable. In instrumental music he was rather at sea at first; and from lack of education and advice he did not know what to aim at, or how to carry on the music in an interesting way. But in relation to songs the want of discipline had its advantages, for it left him all the more open to the impression which the poet produced upon him, and the music seemed to come out as a natural reaction from it. The poems themselves seemed to supply him with the principle of form upon which to construct his music, and with the best musical ideas to intensify the situations; and even with a characteristic style. So he needed no guidance but the receptiveness of his nature to lead him at once to his goal.

It was as early as 1815 that he produced one of his most famous and most powerful songs. The subject is a weird ballad by Goethe called *The Erl-King,* in which a father is represented carrying his child on horseback through a wild night in winter. The terrified child fancies it sees the Erl-King, and that he is calling it to come to him. The father tries to pacify the child, and assures it that there is nothing but waifs of cloud and howling of wind. The fancied voice of the Erl-King mockingly calling the child to come to him is heard, and the excitement waxes wilder as the child's terrors increase, and the despairing father urges on his horse and folds the child closer to his breast. In vain. For when he arrives at his own door the child is dead.

It was a splendid opportunity, and splendidly did Schubert master it, and gave it an impressiveness and a power which no reading of the poem by itself could approach. He gives the impression of the wild elements, and of the headlong career through the night; the terror of the child, the anxiety of the father, and the mocking summons of the Erl-King; and combines it all in sounds which rush with excitement ever increasing from moment to moment, till with their arrival at the door of their home, the music, like their headlong career, stops suddenly, and in a stillness of despair the father's horror at finding his child dead in his arms is simply told in seven quiet words, which supply exactly the dramatic effect that is wanted. This was one of Schubert's earliest songs, and it contains all the marks of the artistic song in complete maturity. Such an effect of course cannot be obtained by the voice alone on the old methods, but the most elaborate resources of instrumental music have to be employed to express the terrors of the situation, while the voice at times does little more than declaim the words. But Schubert never meant to degrade the voice to a secondary position, or let the song be a pianoforte piece with a voice to explain what it was about. His instincts brought him to make use of all the opportunities at his disposal to convey the poet's meaning in musical terms. Sometimes in other songs the voice is far more musically prominent, and the pianoforte has little more than a subordinate accompaniment, in the usual sense of the term; but that is in cases where it seemed right and possible to him to treat the poem in such a way. In most cases where he is dealing with an impressive poem the balance between the voice and the instrument is such as to give to each the full share in conveying the poet's meaning that it is capable of.

The story of the first appearance of *"The Erl-King"* has been told by Schubert's friend Spaun, who called upon him at his home one afternoon in 1815, and found him in a state of excitement over Goethe's ballad, which he had only just come across. The song was finished and written out before the evening, and they took it to the Convict, where some of the old friends were gathered, and they tried it together. As was very natural, they were rather bewildered than pleased with it. Everything thoroughly genuine and original puzzles people at first, and in this instance the work was not only very much out of the beaten track, but extremely wild and dramatic into the bargain; so it is not to be wondered at that his audience did not take it all in at once. But they admired and loved Schubert too well to discourage him, and before long all his friends had learnt to understand and delight in it.

The rapidity with which he wrote this famous song is characteristic of him. He devoured everything that came in his way in the line of lyrics, and scarcely ever paused to consider whether the poetry was good; but if it conveyed any impression to his mind, he set it at once. At one time he lived with a poet, by the name of Mayrhofer, whose acquaintance he made in 1815, and they used to sit in their room together, the one writing poetry and the other music; and as Mayrhofer finished a poem he would toss it across to Schubert, who read it through, and began to make the music for it directly. As a rule this speed was almost a necessary condition of Schubert's work in all branches of art. He had no taste for the patient balancing, considering, and rewriting one word again and again, which was characteristic of Beethoven. The thought possessed him, and must go down on paper, and luckily, in the matter of recording what was in his head he was tolerably certain of the effect he wanted. What he wrote expressed what he meant, and that was enough for him. At the same time, though he did not often alter works when once written with a view to improving them, he improved immensely in successive works; especially in such more arduous kinds of composition as symphony and quartett, because there was in his nature an appreciation of possibilities beyond his first efforts in such lines. In song writing it was difficult to find how to do better than he did even before he was twenty years old.

He was still slaving at the school, and pouring out ceaseless floods of music in the intervals of work, when a new friend sought him out, and at least for a time helped to put him in a position more suitable for his genius. This was a certain Franz von Schober, a young man of some means, who had met with his songs, and had been very much struck by them. He called upon Schubert, and was very much impressed by the apparent unfitness of things in a composer of such extraordinary powers devoting his strength and many hours daily to the education of small infants; and proposed that Schubert should go and live with him, and pursue his art more freely and with less interruption. This generous proposal was accepted, and as Schubert's temperament was for the most part easy and accommodating, the arrangement answered very well as long as it lasted. Schubert devoted himself to composition and congenial company, and his moderate wants were provided for chiefly at von Schober's expense. He never troubled himself to think much about providing for the future.

Meanwhile his compositions were not making any great way. His friends appreciated him fully, but the public knew next to nothing about him, and publishers would not so much as look at his works, or even accept them as a gift. The friends he had made hitherto had scarcely been in a position to help him before the public, but soon after making von Schober's acquaintance, he had the good fortune to make friends with a famous singer and actor called Vogl, whose position in the world as a highly cultivated, enthusiastic, and intelligent man, gave him the very best opportunities of serving any one in whose abilities he believed. Spaun has given an account of their first meeting in Schober's rooms. Vogl had been persuaded by Schubert's friends to see him, and arrived one evening. Schubert with shuffling gait and incoherent stammering speech received his visitor. Vogl, the man of the world, was quite at his ease, and taking up a sheet of music paper, which lay close by, began humming the song Schubert had written on it. Then he tried one or two more, and ended by saying, "There is stuff in you, but you squander your fine thoughts instead of developing them." He was not carried away by enthusiasm all at once, and made no promise that he would come back again. But he made the acquaintance of more of the songs, and became more and more impressed with the style of the music; and then he began to go and see Schubert oftener, and Schubert in turn began to pay Vogl frequent visits. Vogl gave him excellent advice, and helped him in the choice of poems, discussed and criticised, and—practically more useful than all—he began singing

Schubert's songs in the many houses in Vienna where he was welcome, and sometimes took Schubert with him to accompany him. In this way began the friendship which had the most important effect upon Schubert's career.

To this same period, or near it, belong some of the few remains which exist of written expressions of Schubert's own, which throw some light on his character. Fragments of a diary of 1816 contain the most curious passages, such as aphorisms, exclamations, criticisms, and but few biographical details. One passage which gives a clue to his musical mood at the time is interesting. It is of June 13th. "This day will haunt me for the rest of my life as a bright, clear, and lovely one. Gently, and as from a distance, the magic tones of Mozart's music sound in my ears. With what alternate force and tenderness, with what masterly power did Schlesinger's playing of that music impress it deep, deep in my heart. Thus do sweet impressions, passing into our souls, work beneficently on our inmost being, and no time, no change of circumstances, can obliterate them. In the darkness of life they show a light, a clear, beautiful distance, from which we gather confidence and hope. Oh, Mozart! immortal Mozart! how many, and what countless images of a brighter, better world hast thou stamped on our souls!"

Three days afterwards come the words, "Today I composed for the first time for money—namely, a cantata for the name-day festival of Herr Professor Watteroth von Dräxler. The honorarium 100 florins, Viennese currency." Then follow a whole string of general remarks which have nothing to do with one another, and tell nothing of his life except in so far as they illustrate the state of his mind. Such as: "Natural disposition and education determine the bent of man's heart and understanding. The heart is ruler; the mind should be. Take men as they are, not as they ought to be. Town politeness is a powerful hindrance to men's integrity in dealing with one another," and so on, whole pages in a single day. The marvel of it is that he could find time to write so much, when he was incessantly producing one composition after another, and at such a pace that it is wonderful how he could even put it all down.

He made an attempt every now and then to get some fixed musical appointment which might bring him in a little money regularly. In 1818 he was invited to go with the family of a Count Johann Esterházy, to their country-house at Zelesz in Hungary, to make himself generally helpful in musical ways, and to give the daughters music lessons. All the members of the family were musical. The Count and Countess and their two daughters all sang, and the two latter also played on the pianoforte; and they had with them a friend, the Baron von Schönstein, who had a fine voice and sang well, and soon entered into Schubert's songs. The opportunity had in it some decided advantages for Schubert; the country was beautiful and healthy; and the company was good; and, moreover, he had opportunities of hearing Hungarian music in its own home. He was naturally attracted by the style of it, as many other great musicians have been; and he wrote down many of the tunes which he heard sung or played by gipsies or servants. Among other results was a very fine *Divertissement à la hongroise,* which is said to have been founded on some tunes he heard a kitchen-maid singing as he and the Baron von Schönstein were coming in from a walk.

But Schubert was not altogether in love with his circumstances. He was too much of a Viennese, and could not get on without his friends, and the characteristic ways they used to live together. He gives his view of things in a letter to his friend Schober: "No one here cares for true art, unless it be now and then the Countess." And after a few reflections on his art and work he sums up his company as follows: "The cook is a pleasant fellow: the ladies' maid is thirty; the housemaid very pretty, and often pays me a visit; the nurse is somewhat ancient; the butler is my rival; the two grooms get on better with the horses than with us. The Count is a little rough; the Countess proud, but not without heart; the young ladies good children. I need not tell you, who know me so well, that with my natural frankness I am good friends with every one."

He probably went back to Vienna, and his loved companions there, about the end of 1818; and it must have been near that time that he went to live with the poet Mayrhofer. The friends were extremely intimate, and called one another by queer nicknames, and were very fond of rough joking and banter, which showed that their animal spirits were very much alive in those days. Schubert was constantly busy producing music, and had his mind so entirely centred upon that occupation, that he is said to have slept in his spectacles, to be ready to begin writing directly he woke. He used commonly to work till dinner time, after which he liked to go for a walk in the country; and the evening was often divided between some friend's house, a theatre, and finally a *Gasthaus,* where the friends sat smoking and drinking beer or wine, and making merry after the manner of

Viennese till the small hours of the morning. From this it would appear that Schubert's only regular working time was the morning, into which he could squeeze some five or six hours. But that did not preclude his working at other times when the mood came upon him. He wrote his songs anywhere and at any time when the thoughts came to him, or a poem moved him; and even works on a considerable scale were sometimes written at the spur of the moment in out-of-the-way places. It sounds rather an easy, happy-go-lucky kind of life; but when he did work he must have worked thoroughly and rapidly, and got the best out of himself.

Owing to Vogl's advocacy, Schubert's name was brought more and more before the world; and in 1820, a comic operetta called *Die Zwillingsbrüder* was performed in one of the Vienna theatres, and a work called the *Zauberharfe* was also performed later in the same year; so things must have seemed to be growing a little brighter for him. In the next year a more important event occurred, which was the first publication of some of the songs. This consummation was at last brought about owing to some concerts which were given in the house of people called Sonnleithner, one of whom had been at school with Schubert, and had cherished his friendship, as all men seem to have done when they had once won it. At these concerts many of Schubert's works were performed, and among them some of his finest songs. The audience was so much pleased that every one began to think a decided effort ought to be made to enable people to possess such treasures.

Schubert's friend Leopold Sonnleithner, and Gymnich, an amateur who sang the songs admirably, made up their minds to try and find a publisher. They searched in vain. The publishers thought the works too difficult, too uncommon, and that the composer's name was not known enough. Finally, in despair of succeeding any other way, Schubert's friends determined to publish sets of songs on their own account, and get the copies subscribed for among the people who came to the Sonnleithners' concerts, and other friends. A selection was made, and the publications began in April, 1821, and continued for the rest of the year at intervals. The friends did all they could to bring the songs before the public and keep the interest alive, and the result was that sufficient copies were sold to encourage the cautious publishers to go on bringing out more of them at their own expense. This to a certain extent improved Schubert's position as a composer, and the sale of copies even put him for the moment in funds; and this was perhaps the most successful financial result his compositions ever brought him, for in the whole course of his life the publishers could never be induced to give him more than the most absurdly trifling sums, even for his most attractive songs. About the highest price he ever received is said to have been 3*l*. [less than $15] and for some of his best, quite late in his life, he got 10 *d*. [20 cents] apiece.

[After two unsuccessful operatic ventures in 1822-23, Schubert began] a full-sized romantic opera, in three acts, called *Fierabras*. The words were put together by a man called Josef Kupelwieser, and were all about contests of Franks and Moors, and kings and knights and noble ladies. Of this Schubert really had some hopes of getting a performance, as the libretto, foolish as it seems, was already accepted by the manager of one of the theatres before he began to write the music. As soon as the words came to him he set to work and wrote at a most astounding speed. According to the dates given he wrote the whole of the first act, which is 300 pages of manuscript, in seven days, and the whole opera, which filled up more than three times as many pages, was composed and finished in every detail between May and September; though he appears to have been so ill at some time between those two dates that he had to go to a hospital. As soon as it was finished, and before the fate of its performance was decided, he was engaged upon yet another work for the stage, called *Rosamunde,* the words of which were supplied by that absurd old poetical aspirant, Wilhelmina von Chezy, who wrote the words of Weber's *Euryanthe.* The story was called *Rosamunde, the Princess of Cyprus,* and was of the same preposterous romantic texture as Weber's opera, and had the same pernicious effect upon the fortunes of the music associated with it. It was not so much of an opera as a play with incidental music to it, and it did not take Schubert long to write his share; but his share was a beautiful contribution, and far too good to be dragged down into oblivion by the foolishness of the words. It was performed in 1823, and the music was well appreciated; but so much depended upon the play that the combination was an inevitable failure, and the music as well as the literary part was laid aside and forgotten. Long after, in 1867, the work was found in the cupboard where it had been left, by Sir George Grove,* when he was hunting for relics and forgotten beauties of Schubert in Vienna; and much of the music has subsequently been revived in concert-rooms, and is always received with

* And young Arthur Sullivan, who had joined with Grove in the quest of lost Schubert works.—E. S.

delight by all lovers of Schubert. In the same year he wrote many more beautiful songs, among which the most celebrated are a set of twenty, called *Die Schöne Müllerin,* upon which he was engaged at different times in intervals of work upon the opera *Fierabras*—some of the songs being said to have been written while he was ill in the hospital.

Early in the next year the fate of *Fierabras* also was decided. It was returned to him unperformed, and without any prospect being held out of his ever hearing a note of it. These repeated disappointments seem at last to have seriously depressed him. Several written expressions of his about this time show how he felt them. In a letter to the brother of the friend who had put the poem of *Fierabras* together he pours out his grief: "I feel myself the most unhappy, the most miserable man on earth. Picture to yourself a man whose health can never be reestablished; who, from sheer despair, makes matters worse rather than better; a man whose most brilliant hopes have come to nothing, whose enthusiasm for the beautiful (an inspired feeling at least) threatens to vanish altogether; and then ask yourself if such a condition does not represent a miserable and unhappy man. Your brother's opera was declared impracticable, and no demand of any sort was made for my music. Thus I have composed two operas to no purpose whatever."

Belonging to the early months of the same year there remain several entries in his diary, which tell nothing of his outward life, but express pointedly the deep sorrow and depression of his inner man. Grief and bitterness is in every line, and all the consolation which he gets is that grief is better for a man's soul than happiness, and that his best productions spring from his sorrow, and "those works which are the product of pain seem to please the great world most."

In the same year in which *Fierabras* was rejected he took another expedition to Zelesz in Hungary, to stay with the Esterházys, and make music with them as before; and no doubt it did him a great deal of good. A letter to his favourite brother Ferdinand contains allusions to tears which he had shed, and former sadness, but his general frame of mind seems better. But indeed there was enough to make him depressed. The very fact that his friends believed in him so thoroughly, and had looked upon him for so many years as a favourite genius, served to throw the perpetual want of success, and the reiterated rebuffs he received, into darker relief. Few men could have borne such trials so patiently, or with such constant returns of good spirits after occasional fits of gloom; and it was probably the constant outpouring of composition which prevented his dwelling upon his position.

Nothing occurred to mark the course of his life for some time after this beyond the appearance of fresh compositions. The chief events which happened in the following years were two more attempts to gain a definite musical post, such as might supply him with a small but regular income and a definite position among his fellow-artists, but they both came to nothing. Another interesting event was the visit to Beethoven's bedside just before that great master died. Schindler, Beethoven's admirer and biographer, was a great believer in Schubert, and tried to bring them together, but had failed till the end was manifestly approaching. When Beethoven was laid up with his last illness Schindler got some of Schubert's best songs to show him. Beethoven became very much interested in them, and was much surprised when he heard what an enormous quantity of such works Schubert had produced. He is reported by Schindler to have said, "Truly Schubert has the divine fire in him." It is probable that it was owing to these favourable expressions that Schubert was persuaded to visit the great man's bedside. Very few words were said, but they must have been such as to show Schubert that Beethoven had found out his gifts and appreciated them. He went again later, but at that time Beethoven was not able to speak, and could only make signs with his hand, and within three weeks after he was dead. At the funeral Schubert was one of the torch-bearers. When he and two of his friends were returning they stopped at a *Gasthaus,* and Schubert and his friends each drank one glass of wine to the memory of the great man departed, and a second to the one of the three who should first follow him. Schubert little thought then how short his own time was destined to be.

About this time he began to receive communications from publishers with a view to bringing out more of his music, and also some encouraging proposals to write work specially for sundry societies; and in the same year he was elected a member of the representative body of the Musical Society of Vienna, which he regarded as a pleasant honour. He went on with composition with even greater ardour than ever, and by the spring of 1828 had finished his greatest symphony, the only one which was destined to be thoroughly characteristic of him and also complete; and other instrumental works, such as sonatas, and a very fine quintett for strings, a cantata called *Miriam's War Song,* and numbers of songs, succeeded one another rapidly. He seemed to think it was time to give less attention to songs and more to works on a larger scale, as he said to a friend that "he hoped to hear no more about songs, but to devote himself to opera and symphony."

In March, for the first time in his life, he gave a public concert in the hall of the Musikverein of Vienna; the programme included part of a string quartett of his, a trio for pianoforte and strings, music for men's chorus, and several fine songs. Many excellent performers came forward to help him, among them his old friend Vogl; and it shows how his genius was beginning to become known and appreciated, that the hall is said to have been fuller than ever was remembered before, and the people were delighted. The good attendance also brought about 32*l.* into his pocket, which must have made him feel quite rich. As was usual with him, his friends got the benefit of his prosperity, and he spent his wealth royally as long as it lasted, and by summertime he was as badly off as ever. The idea of going for another excursion into the lovely country of Styria was again entertained, but had to be given up because of the low state of his funds, and he had to remain in Vienna all the year round.

Early in September he went to live with his brother Ferdinand in a house in the suburb called the Neue Wieden. He had been bothered with an old trouble of inclination of blood to the head, and giddiness, and it was thought it would do him good to be nearer to the country, and to have readier opportunities of getting away for exercise and fresh air. The house they occupied was a new one, and it is supposed this aggravated his unhealthy and over-strained condition. He became decidedly ill, and doctors had to be called in. Then he picked up a little, and went for a five days' excursion with some friends into the neighbourhood of Vienna, visiting among other places the grave of Haydn at Eisenstadt. He seems to have regained some of his usual gaiety for the time, but when he got back to Vienna the illness returned.

One evening, when having supper with some friends at an hotel, he suddenly threw down his knife and fork, saying the food tasted like poison. He still walked about a good deal after this, but he took scarcely anything to eat and got steadily worse. But he did not seem to have any anxiety about himself, and spoke to the composer Lachner, who came to see him, of his intended work on a new opera he had in hand called *Graf von Gleichen.* He went to hear music, and was very much excited over a performance of one of Beethoven's latest quartetts. Among other ideas he had one of developing his mastery of counterpoint more thoroughly: a purpose which arose from his becoming acquainted with Handel's works so late in life; and he applied to a man called Sechter, who was considered an authority in that branch of art, to give him lessons; and the matter even went so far that he went to see Sechter and discussed what would be the best books to work upon, and arranged dates for the lessons. The last music he heard publicly performed was a mass by his brother Ferdinand, which was done in the church at a village called Hernals on the 3rd November.

When he got home again he was very tired and ill, and grew worse day by day. He wrote to his old friend Schober: "I am ill. I have eaten and drunk nothing for eleven days, and am so tired and shaky that I can only get from the bed to the chair and back." And he asked for some books to amuse him, suggesting some of Cooper's novels. Some of his friends came to see him, but there seems to have been a dread of infection, and he had not so much company to cheer him as was desirable. He occupied some of his time correcting proofs of the latest set of his songs, called *Winterreise,* and still had hopes of doing more work. But after a few days he became delirious, and the doctors announced that he had typhus fever. The faithful brother Ferdinand attended him constantly. Franz was possessed with strange fears, and asked: "Brother, what are they going to do with me? I implore you to put me in my own room, and not to leave me in this corner under the earth. Don't I deserve a place above ground?" Ferdinand did all he could to quiet him, and assured him he was in his own room; but Franz only shook his head, saying, "It is not true, Beethoven is not here." He never became himself again, but died on Wednesday, November 19, 1828, only thirty-one years old. Two days afterwards the funeral took place, and his body was borne, accompanied by many friends and admirers, to the cemetery at the village of Währing, where Beethoven had also been buried; and it was deposited as near as possible to the last resting-place of that great master, towards whom in his latter years he had been so strongly drawn by sympathy and admiration. Many performances were given and articles written in honour of his memory; and the proceeds of concerts and subscriptions were enough to pay for a monument over his grave, upon which were appropriately inscribed the words:

"Music has here entombed a rich treasure, But still fairer hopes."

Several great musicians have been cut off before what might be fairly considered the prime of their life and vigour, but of all the greatest ones Schubert's time was shortest; yet in those few thirty-one years of life he produced such an enormous quantity of music that the amount would have been noticeable even if his life had been rather longer than most men's. He wrote over 500 songs, at least seven entire symphonies, and two incomplete ones, of which latter, one is among his most beautiful and popular works; over twenty sonatas; numbers of string quartetts, six masses, and other large and fine examples of church music; several operas, part songs, cantatas, overtures, and so forth. His rapidity of thought and of writing must have been marvellous. As fast as he finished one thing he generally began another, and often wrote several songs in a single day; and those not songs of the cheap, ephemeral description, familiar in modern times, but works of art, with real thought and point and good workmanship in them.

Robert Schumann
By Daniel Gregory Mason
Article in The International Cyclopedia of Music and Musicians

ROBERT ALEXANDER SCHUMANN, born at Zwickau, Germany, June 8, 1810, was the youngest son of a hard-working bookseller and editor, August Schumann, who surrounded his boyhood with literary influences but died too early to help him through the struggles of youth. He had some desultory education in the universities of Leipzig and Heidelberg, dreamed a good deal at the piano and over the favorite fantastic authors of the romantic style, especially Jean Paul Richter, whom he idolized and imitated in his own youthful writings, and reluctantly, at his mother's behest, made rather an empty pretense of studying law. But all the while he was inwardly following what another student, of a later day, has happily called his "busy thoughts, that hardly knew whether to be poems or music." He resolved to become a great pianist, and in his impatience invented a device which held the intractable fourth finger immobile while the others practised—with the result of laming his hand for life.

This weighted the scales for composition, about his gift for which he was at first singularly uncertain. "Now and then I discover," he wrote his mother when he was twenty, "that I have imagination, and perhaps a turn for creating things myself."

Thanks to his piano teacher, Friedrich Wieck, father of the Clara Wieck who was later to become, as Clara Schumann, the guardian angel of his genius, his mother's opposition to his music was overcome. He threw himself ardently into the study of composition, partly under the guidance of Heinrich Dorn, but even more alone—for his independent nature obliged him to find out everything for himself. This is amusingly illustrated in his letters of 1832. In January he writes: "I shall never be able to amalgamate with Dorn; he wishes me to believe that music is fugue—heavens! how different men are." Yet in July his word is: "Bach's *Well-tempered Clavichord* is my grammar. The fugues I have analyzed down to their smallest details; this is of strengthening effect on one's whole being, for with Bach nothing is half-done, morbid, everything is written as if for eternity." Schumann's cordiality of nature, however, would not let him underrate Dorn; he later described him as "the man who first gave a hand to me as I climbed upwards, and, when I began to doubt myself, drew me aloft so that I should see less of the common herd of mankind, and more of the pure air of art."

The first great jet of Schumann's music, streaming from his freshly awakened mind in inexhaustible profusion all through the third decade of his life and up to the verge of his marriage, and comprising his works from Opus 1 to 23, is all for the piano. And when, before or since, has the art of music seen a jet of greater genius shot forth by one man in one decade? Here are the *Papillons,* the *Davidsbündlertänze* —so autobiographic with their strange title—the *Carnaval,* that motley series of vivid tableaux, the *Fantasiestücke,* the exquisite, inimitable *Kinderscenen,* penetrating to the heart of childhood as Stevenson later did with poetry, the *Kreisleriana* and the *Novellettes.* Here, in larger forms requiring greater sweep and an even more powerful originality, are the *Toccata,* three sonatas, the great *Fantasie,* and above all the *Symphonic Etudes,* a work in which the structural strength of the classic is united with the freshness and color of romantic art.

The whimsicality of the young composer is seen in all these works in the boldness of their rhythms, especially their use of strong dislocations of accent and long-continued syncopations, and in the unconventional harshness of their frequently dissonant harmonies (the great stumbling-block, probably, for Schumann's contemporaries, who greatly preferred to him the suave and clear Mendelssohn). Parry has said that Schumann "loved to dream with the pedal down." The phrase throws a flood of light on the clashing sonorities of these youthful works.

The *Davidsbündlertänze* (a long word for "Dances of the David Club") are, as we said, autobiographical, together with the *Carnaval*. To understand them we have to consider as forming really one personal approach to art what often are distinguished as two sides of their composer, what we like to call the "critical" and the "creative." (These two sides are in reality, as Schumann's life so clearly shows, but different aspects of a single loyalty to music.) As Schumann passed into his early twenties his first exuberance sobered into a sense of responsibility to music, which he gradually saw to be in his day as much misregarded as mere entertainment, a mere pretext for the silly idolizing of virtuosi, as it is in ours. To see this evil was to take action against it. Against these Philistines who prostituted art he and his friends, modern Davids, must fight, uniting themselves into a group half real and half ideal in his ever-fanciful mind, called the David Club. And no idealist was ever a more effective realist; for Schumann actually founded in 1833 a paper called the *Neue Zeitschrift für Musik,* which he edited for ten years, and which did incalculable service in encouraging real music and discouraging mediocrity and sham. When later he wrote a preface for a volume of his writings drawn from it,* he explained its purpose characteristically thus:

The musical situation was not then [i.e. in April, 1834, when the first number appeared] very encouraging. On the stage Rossini reigned, at the piano nothing was heard but Herz and Hünten; and yet but a few years had passed since Beethoven, Weber, and Schubert had lived among us. One day the thought awakened in a wild heart, "Let us not look on idly; let us also lend our aid to progress, let us bring again the poetry of art to honor among men."

So was formed the David Club, of which their leader composed the dances in his Opus 6. But this leader was not one but two, since some of the pieces were signed "F" and some "E." Who but Schumann would have thought of such a device? So real to him were his fancies that he gave himself a dual personality, figuring the impetuous, passionate side of his nature as Florestan and the contemplative, dreamy side as Eusebius. The more thoughtful dances, the tender No. 2, for instance, and the almost timid No. 5, are by "E," while "F" is bold in No. 3, headlong in 9, and delightfully witty in 12. The first (begin-

---

* Translated as *Music and Musicians,* a volume all music lovers should read and reread.

ning with a motto by Clara Wieck, with whom by 1837 both "F" and "E" were already in love), and the next to the last are by both of them; but a lovely coda, looking back over the whole, is added by Eusebius, who, we are told in a note, "felt it almost too keenly—and much happiness shone in his eyes."

The phantasmagoria is even richer in *Carnaval*. Writing it a year or two earlier, when he had still a boyish infatuation for Ernestine von Fricken, whom he met in the town of Asch, Schumann pays her a delicate compliment by founding it on the notes A-S-C-H (in English: A, E-flat, C, B-natural) and subtitling it "Little Scenes on Four Notes." In these magical pages the figures of carnival—Harlequin and Pierrot, Columbine and Pantaloon—touch elbows with Florestan and Eusebius, drawn to the life, and with their friends Estrella (Ernestine von Fricken), Coquette (possibly the same), Paganini, Chiarina—the high-spirited Clara Wieck, here almost domineering— and Chopin, to whom Schumann pays even more intimate though no less admiring tribute than when in the *New Journal* he saluted him with the famous phrase, "Hats off, gentlemen,—a genius." * The whole ends with a rousing march of the Davidites against the Philistines, in which the old fogies, typified by the traditional "Grandfathers' Dance," with its lumbering rhythm, naturally get the worst of it.

Schumann had a contempt for the kind of facile criticism, praising everything, that he called "honey-daubing," and once said: "The critic who dares not attack what is bad is but a half-hearted supporter of what is good." In his criticisms he is never afraid to attack the "grandfathers"—the merely conservative and reactionary, or the purveyors of pretty piano virtuoso pieces and Italian operas ("butterfly-dust" was another of his descriptions) that held the public of his day enthralled. His attacks on certain virtuosi and on opera purveyors like Meyerbeer, in the *New Journal,* are courageously outspoken. Yet everything he thought sincere, no matter what its limitations, he greeted hopefully. Indeed, he is sometimes blamed because some of his swans turned out to be geese. Those who blame him might profitably take a leaf from his own book. Gabrilowitsch is nearer right when he exclaims admiringly: "The first and holiest duty of a critic—as pointed out by Robert Schumann (the greatest musical critic that ever lived)— is to encourage the great artist and to facilitate an understanding between him and the public."

* Not Brahms, as frequently wrongly stated. The phrase was prompted by Chopin's *Là ci darem* variations.

Eighteen hundred and forty was called by Schumann his "Song year." In it the long opposition of Clara's father to her love for the young composer was finally overcome, and they were married in September. The long doubt and anxiety and the final joy inspired Schumann to write a profusion of songs almost as bewildering in its variety as the long series of piano works that preceded it. To name only a few sets, there are the *Myrtles,* Opus 25, containing the exuberant "Dedication" and the subtle haunting "Nut-tree"; the *Song-ring,* to texts of Eichendorff, with the impassioned and soaring "Spring Night"; the *Poet's Love* (*Dichterliebe*) cycle, to poems of Heine; and, perhaps most characteristic of all, the *Woman's Love and Life* (texts by Chamisso) in which he shows as tender an imagination and sympathy for women and their point of view as in the *Scenes from Childhood* (*Kinderscenen*) he showed for children. No wonder the production of all this beauty set him almost beside himself with joy.

"I can hardly tell you," he writes Clara, Feb. 19, 1840, "how delightful it is to write for the voice, and how agitated and excited I am when I sit down to work." Again, only three days later: "Since yesterday morning I have written about twenty-seven pages of music [the *Myrtles,* Opus 25] and I can tell you nothing more about it, except that I laughed and cried with delight." And about the middle of March: "Here is a slight reward for your last two letters—my first published songs. While I was composing them I was quite lost in thoughts of you. If I were not engaged to such a girl I could not write such music."

When they were actually married, and especially when later the children began to come, all sorts of new duties and insights crowded in on the hitherto irresponsible young dreamer, and his music so deepened with his character that songs were no longer enough, he had to turn from them to symphonies; as W. J. Henderson happily expresses it: "The tumult of young love lifted him from the piano to the voice. The consummation of his manhood, in the union with a woman of noble heart and commanding intellect, led him to the orchestra." Thus if 1840 was the "Song year," 1841 might be called the "Symphony year." And similarly, to look forward a little, 1842 could be named the "Chamber music year," 1843, the "Choral year." The curious habit Schumann had of thus taking up one department of music at a time may be traced in part to the intensity with which he threw himself into whatever interested him, in part to his consciousness of his technical shortcomings, and to his wish to surmount them as far as possible by concentrated study.

In writing for the orchestra, it has to be admitted, Schumann, in spite of the freshness and beauty of his ideas, and the finding sometimes of the perfect setting for them (as in the lovely Romanza, for example, of the D minor Symphony) was at a disadvantage. He did not understand any of the orchestral instruments as he intimately understood the piano; he was uncertain in writing for them, and tried to "play safe" by doubling several of them sometimes on the same melody, with the result of cancelling, dulling, and spoiling the effect of them all; and even his ideas, short and not lending themselves to wide sweeps, were less happy for the orchestra, which needs space and broad masses, than for the more intimate and sensitive piano. Schumann, whose ingenuity with the piano was so inexhaustible, lost all sorts of opportunities when confronted with the less familiar orchestra. The First Symphony originally began with a horn call meant to be stirring, but actually, because of certain limitations of the horn, almost laughable until the abashed composer changed it. In the Second Symphony, after writing a fascinating scherzo for whirling violins he continued to use the violins in its trio until, so the story goes, Mendelssohn suggested the natural, almost obvious contrast of the wood-wind instruments.

Yet, whatever their limitations, with what freshness, what exuberance of genius Schumann filled his faulty symphonies! The first, the so-called *Spring* Symphony in B flat, was sketched (as Clara noted in her diary) in four days of the January following their marriage, conducted by Mendelssohn on the last day of March, and received by the Leipzig public on the whole with favor, though with some bewilderment. In April and May a new work was sketched, the so-called Overture, Scherzo, and Finale, Opus 52, virtually a symphony without slow movement. Then on the last day of May Clara noted in her diary: "As yet I have heard nothing about it, but from Robert's way of going on and the D minor chord sounding wildly in the distance, I know already that another work is being created in the depths of his soul." This was in fact the beginning of the long and chequered career of what eventually became his Symphony No. 4, in D minor, Opus 120. The following autumn, on Clara's birthday, September 13, her husband presented her with the first version of the symphony, writing in their joint diary: "One thing makes me happy—the consciousness of being still far from my goal and obliged to keep doing better, and then the feeling that I have strength to reach it." He had need of strength. He was dissatisfied with his first version, performed at the end of 1841, and retired it for no less than ten years. In 1851 he rewrote it, undoubtedly improving it greatly on the whole, thanks to his then greater experience and maturity, and having great success with it. Yet Brahms, who owned the score of the first version, had a good word to say for that too. "Schumann was so upset," writes Brahms, "by a first rehearsal, which went off badly, that he subsequently reinstrumentated the symphony afresh at Düsseldorf, where he was used to a bad and incomplete orchestra. The original scoring has always delighted me. It is a real pleasure to see anything so bright and spontaneous expressed with corresponding ease and grace. . . . Everything is so absolutely natural that you cannot imagine it different."

To the same year of 1841 belongs the beginning of another of Schumann's very greatest works, the Piano Concerto in A Minor. In that year he produced its first movement, called at first Fantasie, and completed it in 1845 by adding the lovely contemplative Intermezzo with the soaring 'cello melody, and the heaven-scaling finale. Whatever reservations we are obliged to make about Schumann's use of the orchestra (and even this glorious concerto suffers from imperfect orchestration) he is always happy when there is a piano; and the concerto is not only one of his great masterpieces but one of the supreme piano concertos in all literature.

Of the five chamber-music works to which Schumann set himself in 1842, the three String Quartets, Opus 41, the famous Piano Quintet, Opus 44, and the Piano Quartet, Opus 47, it may again be said that technically the most successful are those in which he can fall back upon his favorite instrument. The great brilliance of the popular Quintet (which did perhaps more to spread his reputation than any other piece) is in large part due to the piano writing; and per contra certain movements in the quartets for strings alone, such for instance as the Adagio of the first one, where the style is obviously influenced by the piano, are for that very reason not entirely happy for strings.

If we look deeper, however, going beyond the technical to the emotional and the intellectual, we realize that the string quartets are the profounder works, containing some of their composer's greatest music. . . . This is as we should expect, for Beethoven had shown that the quartet is the fit medium for deep spiritual expression, and Schumann's exuberant nature had been deeply spiritualized by the sufferings and difficulties of his middle years: Florestan had become a little chastened, but Eusebius was finer and sweeter than ever. Life had indeed not been easy for him. His introspective pondering tendency made it difficult for him to adapt himself to others. He was entirely wrapped in his thoughts, silent in company, so absent-minded that when conducting he sometimes forgot to beat. Music absorbed him completely; the constant pursing of his lips in an incipient whistling of the melodies in his mind night and day affected even his appearance, as can be seen in his photographs.

This concentration on his inward mental life, in fact, was morbid in its intensity: he wrote his three quartets in about a month, in the early summer of 1842; the first movement of the last quartet is dated July 18, the second July 20, the third July 21, and the fourth July 22. Equally morbid was his taciturnity: once when he was visited by a musician, Herr Witting, commissioned to ascertain the tempi of one of his works, he received him amiably enough, asked him if he smoked, and then without offering him a cigar relapsed into silence. Presently Herr Witting asked him again about the tempi. Schumann roused himself to ask again "Do you smoke?", and again resumed the silent communion with his own cigar. A third time the same thing happened and Herr Witting reluctantly took his departure. No doubt Schumann's mental illness, of which he had a slight attack as early as his 23rd year and which finally crushed him at 44, was in some way connected with this intense concentration, unrelieved by diversions or physical exercise.

The need of earning a livelihood, too, coming with wife and children, pressed cruelly so subjective a nature. His nervous constitution seems not to have been strong enough to bear the rough-and-tumble of worldly struggle, superimposed on the excitement of composition. His happiest and most productive years, those spent at Leipzig up to 1844, were not free from frequent attacks of exhaustion and terrible depression, and his move to Dresden, where he lived from 1844 to 1850, was in part undertaken in quest of rest and quiet. As a teacher he was a failure, sitting through an hour sometimes with hardly a comment. As a conductor he was ineffective, as he himself sadly realized. Clara, ambitious, more "practical" in worldly ways, and energetic to the point of obstinacy, could not recognize his defect, and pushed him to do what he could not do. The Schumanns moved to Düsseldorf in 1850 in the hope of increasing his income by conducting, but Robert was obliged gradually to give place to his assistant. From a money-earning point of view even his composition was too difficult, too new, too far ahead of his day, for him to win by it anything like the quick recognition of his friend Mendelssohn. Once at a musicale where Clara played, a gentleman to whom he was introduced as her husband inquired, "And are you, too, musical, Mr. Schumann?"

Pathetic is the gradual failure of powers once so inexhaustible. In some of his later ambitious works, the choral *Paradise and the Peri* for example, and the opera *Genoveva,* we see flashes of the old—or rather the young—Schumann, but they flash from masses of smoldering notes that not even his genius can kindle. This is true also, on the whole, of the two violin sonatas of 1851, and even of the trios, the first and second dating from 1847, the third from 1851 again. There are returns of all the old fire in single works all through these years—in the Andante and Variations for two pianos of 1843, the year of *Paradise and the Peri*; in the *Manfred* music of 1848; in the third, so-called *Rhenish* Symphony of 1850 with the solemn Cathedral movement. But for the most part Schumann is but going by habit through the motions of a process once full of zest. By 1854, his 44th year, his health failed altogether, and in his misery he threw himself into the Rhine. He was rescued, and lived two more years in a private asylum at Endenich, near Bonn in the Rhineland, where he died, in Clara's arms, July 29, 1856.

Schumann's artistic importance as one of the most original of the composers of the "romantic" group that followed Beethoven combines its claim on our interest with the appeal of his rarely sympathetic personality. He is one of the most lovable men in the whole history of music. Everything about him wins our admiring affection: the fresh youthful note in his music, with its heaven-soaring melodies, clashing harmonies, and rushing rhythms; the impetuous, uncalculating generosity of his nature, as shown in his letters as well as his music; his very weaknesses—such as the frequent ineffectiveness of his writing for orchestra, the unhealthy subjectivity of his temperament, even his tragic loss of mental power in middle life and early death; and above all, his ardent loyalty to his great fellow-musicians. If all the world loves a lover, then no one can help loving Schumann.

Unhappy as was Schumann's fate in this world, his life was in a deeper sense a happy one, because of his ardent devotion all through it to a cause greater than himself—the cause of beautiful music. His worship of Bach, his championship of contemporaries like Chopin, his delight in the discovery in Vienna of the manuscript of Schubert's C major Symphony and in the performance of it by his friend Mendelssohn, his joy at the very end in the discovery of the young Brahms—the "young eagle," he called him—all these were the preoccupations of a happy man. The happiest of all the feelings is admiration, and Schumann had a rich store of it. "Few critics," says Ernest Newman, "have written so lovingly of lovable things, there is a pure ecstasy in his best talk about Schubert or Bach or Beethoven that thrills us even now, after the lapse of 70 or 80 years." It is now 100 years, but time has no power over beauty. . . . In the autumn before his final seizure Schumann wrote in a letter: "I have begun to collect and draw up my thoughts about the young eagle; I should dearly like to be at his side on his flight over the world." The wish was denied him. Yet in a deeper sense Schumann's native air is the clear empyrean of music; and whoever cleaves it feels his spirit to be not far away.

Felix Mendelssohn

From "Alla Breve"

By Carl Engel

THE lives of so many great composers are one long record of struggle, poverty, and disappointment, that Felix Mendelssohn's career would be remarkable if for no other reason than the advantages, the affluence and the success which he enjoyed during his lifetime. His family was Jewish, and of humblest origin. His grandfather, the eminent philosopher Moses Mendelssohn, when young, had still to suffer under the humiliating restrictions which, until the end of the eighteenth century, actually segregated all Jews in the towns of Europe from the normal life of the community. This sage and emancipator gradually conquered the prejudices of the Christians and the bigotry of his own people; he made a position for himself in German literature, was the close friend of the poet and dramatist Lessing, and practically opened to his race the door that gave it access into modern society. Abraham (the second son of Moses and father of Felix), who later in his life said laughingly: "When a boy, I was known as the son of my father; now I am known as the father of my son!" possessed qualities which, peculiarly Jewish, entitle him to not a little of the glory that distinguished the Mendelssohn family; and these qualities were precisely those of an excellent son and an ideal father.

Abraham was clerk in the banking house of Fould in Paris, when he married Lea Salomon, the daughter of a rich merchant in Hamburg. He became associated with his elder brother, who conducted a banking and brokerage business in Hamburg. It was the time of the Napoleonic invasion. War means the destruction of much property; it is also the germ of new fortunes. Abraham settled with his family in Berlin, in 1811; he was a shrewd business man, and the banking house which he founded was still in existence, still conducted by his descendants, until the Nazis saw fit to "liquidate" the Jewish race in Germany. Abraham made excellent use of his riches in cultivating arts and letters, which had played such great part in the life of his father. His tastes were shared by his wife, a gifted musician, who spoke several languages, and read the old Greek and Latin authors in the original.

It was into this atmosphere of ease and culture that Felix was born at Hamburg, February 3, 1809. Both he and his sister Fanny, four years his elder, showed early signs of great musical talent. Their mother gave them their first music-lessons; soon they were ready to receive instruction from the best teachers that the father's money could procure. C. F. Zelter, the friend of Goethe, was chosen to teach Felix composition. The boy made wonderful progress. In the art-loving home of the Mendelssohns, all musicians and artists of renown that lived in or passed through Berlin, convened for the famous Sunday evening concerts, the program containing always one or more compositions by the young prodigy. In 1821, Zelter took Felix on a visit to Goethe, at Weimar, where the boy played and extemporized to the great delight of the Grand Old Man. Felix had inherited his grandfather's gift of expression, and the letters of his youth give vivid accounts of his experiences. Throughout his life he kept up a lively correspondence with his relatives and friends, which makes excellent reading.

Abraham took his son to Paris in 1825 and asked Cherubini's advice whether or not the boy should continue to pursue a musical profession. Cherubini left no doubt in the father's mind, if any there was; but Abraham would not consent to leaving his son with Cherubini in Paris, and took him back to Berlin, where he kept him under his parental guidance and authority.

In 1826, Felix wrote the overture to Shakespeare's *Midsummer Night's Dream*, a work which discloses the full ripeness of his musical genius. His first larger opera was performed in Berlin, in 1827, but owing to a poor libretto it had only mediocre success. Intrigues at the opera house added to the young man's annoyance, and the incident was the beginning of a distinct dislike that Mendelssohn felt ever after for Berlin. During his musical studies he had become engrossed in the works of Handel and Bach, then hardly known by the general public. It is not one of Mendelssohn's smallest merits to have rediscovered these works; and his performance of Bach's music for the *Passion according to St. Matthew* on March 11, 1829, at Berlin, will ever remain a memorable date in the history of music.

Sent by his father, who always acted as his son's adviser, he traveled to Switzerland and Italy, to France, and in 1829 to England, where he achieved triumphs as pianist, composer, and conductor. He visited England nine times, and traveled through Scotland and Ireland, finding inspiration wherever he went—witness his *Italian* Symphony, *Scotch* Symphony, "Venetian Gondolier Songs," *Hebrides* Overture, *Calm Sea and Prosperous Voyage,* and many other compositions. His famous *Songs without Words* were really sketches of a traveler, written for the delectation of those who had stayed at home. They may have the slightness of such sketches, but they also have the vividness of indelible impressions made on a sensitive and cultured mind, and are drawn with infinite charm and grace.

Mendelssohn acted as conductor at various music festivals, and spent a short time as music director in Düsseldorf, where his oratorio *St. Paul* was brought out in 1836. Like his brother and his two sisters, he was brought up in the Christian religion, and in 1837 married the daughter of a Protestant clergyman. His appointment as conductor of the Leipzig Gewandhaus orchestra, in 1835, had given him at last a position worthy of his extraordinary talents. His influence made Leipzig the center of musical life in Germany; his founding of the Leipzig Conservatory of Music, in 1843, created an institution which long remained a model of its kind. On his last visit to England, in 1846, he produced at Birmingham his oratorio *Elijah.*

On his return to Leipzig, he began to feel the effect of overwork; he resigned the conductorship of the orchestra. The death of his beloved sister Fanny broke his heart; he passed away November 4, 1847.

Only at the end of his days did Felix Mendelssohn learn to know the sorrow of bereavement and the tragedy of human helplessness. But then it was too late for him to voice his grief in tones. As his life was full of sunshine, so is his music; the overpowering, elemental note is missing even in his largest works. He was a classicist by education, and a romanticist through contagion. Weber's music decidedly influenced him. Fairy tale and folk lore attracted him as much as it had the older master. Hence his music for _A Midsummer Night's Dream_, for Goethe's _First Walpurgis Night,_ the fragments of an opera _The Loreley,_ and his overture _The Lovely Melusine._ He wrote several choral works besides his two oratorios, much chamber music, and a violin concerto that is especially noteworthy. All of his music bears the stamp of refinement, the glitter and opulence of the surroundings that made his short life an unusually active and happy one.

Frédéric Chopin

Abridged from "Men of Music"

By Wallace Brockway and Herbert Weinstock

THERE are still many people who persist in thinking of Chopin as a more or less inspired dilettante and evoker of small musical moods. Yet, he was the most truly original of all composers.* He arrived almost immediately at a personal idiom that is absolutely unmistakable—an original style so pervasive that a fragmentary bar or two will serve to identify a composition as his. With a rare sense of what kingdom he could make his own, he chose to write music for the piano. He never composed an opera or an oratorio, never a symphony, never even a string quartet. These large forms he left to others, and cultivated his own garden. He worked in a dozen or more forms, several of them of his own creation. He is the composer par excellence of inexhaustible variety in infinite detail. Nor, except when he tried to force his idiosyncratic poetry into some larger classical form, did his Flaubertian feeling for the musical _mot juste_ interfere with his respect for the architecture of a composition as an entity.

Chopin has never lacked champions, but there is no doubt that his intelligent self-limitation has acted adversely on his fame. The

* This chapter is written on the assumption that Chopin was a great composer—this as a warning to any violent dissenters from this opinion. The writers know that no argument, however good, would make these dissenters change their minds.—Authors.

very pervasiveness of his idiom has acted no less adversely. In a certain limited sense, all of his music sounds alike: in their peculiar melodic line and rhythms, their acid-sweet harmonic sequences, their persistent trend to the minor, and their lavish use of ornamentation, the *oeuvres complètes* of Frédéric-François Chopin are a singular phenomenon whose component parts have a deceptive—and, to some, a monotonous —similarity. The elements that shaped his musical language are easy to isolate. Partly Polish, he was the first to introduce a Slavic note into Western music—the experiments of earlier composers, who cast Slavic folk melodies into the absorbent, neutralizing classical mold, do not affect the argument. He was a neurotic, and his music often expresses a hypersensitive, decadent, and rather feminine personality. Further, he lived in a time and place overfriendly to the flowering of such a personality, and therefore it is no accident that this pampered Pole who spent most of his creative life in Paris wrote the most characteristic musical illustrations of French romanticism.

Chopin is always spoken of as a Polish composer. With more justice, he could be called a French composer. His mother was Polish, he spent the first twenty years of his life in Poland, and he was always violently patriotic—from a safe distance. On the other hand, his father was French, and it was in France, under French influences, that he wrote most of the music by which he is today remembered. Nicolas Chopin, his father, was an *émigré* who had been stranded in Warsaw by the failure of the French snuff manufacturers for whom he had worked. Becoming a tutor in the home of Count Skarbek, he had married the Countess's lady in waiting, Justina Krzyzanowska, herself of noble birth. Frédéric-François, their second child and only son, was born on February 22, 1810, at Zelazowa-Wola, a small village near Warsaw, where the Skarbeks had a country place. The Chopins shortly removed to Warsaw, Nicolas began teaching in several schools (he soon opened a successful tutoring academy of his own), and their home became a favorite resort of artists and intellectuals. They were neither poor nor rich—always comfortable, with money enough for an occasional small luxury. Nicolas was a flautist, Justina a singer of pleasing voice, and the eldest child, Ludwika, played the piano. We must conceive of music, then, as always going on in this pleasant household, and of the fond parents violently distressed when they saw that their infant son reacted with floods of tears to the sound of music. They thought he hated it, and it was only when he began to pick out tunes on the piano that they realized he had been crying for joy. They had a hysteric on their hands, not a music hater.

And so, at the age of six Frédéric began to take lessons from a solid and withal sympathetic Czech piano teacher, Adalbert Zywny, for whom he always entertained a lively feeling of gratitude. Zywny was a devotee of Bach, and trained the boy on *The Well-Tempered Clavichord,* thus giving a firm foundation to his pianism. Not the most brilliant of virtuoso prodigies, Frédéric nevertheless publicly played a concerto on his eighth birthday. The noblemen, and even more the noblewomen, who made up the audience were enchanted by the tiny, winsome child, and from that day until his death Chopin was the darling of the Polish *haute noblesse*—an excellent buffer against the cruel world. He took to his noble admirers as much as they to him.

Frédéric began to dabble with little compositions of his own almost as soon as he could play the piano. His father, without any demur, sent him to Joseph Elsner, the best composition teacher in Warsaw, and a widely known and all too prolific composer. He instantly recognized that Chopin's were no usual gifts, and allowed him what certain austere critics have considered too much leeway in developing them. Chopin realized his debt to Elsner, and the bond between them lasted throughout his life. These lessons with Zywny and Elsner constituted his entire formal education, with the exception of three years at the Warsaw Lycée, where he took no interest in his courses. He passed them by the skin of his teeth, and was graduated at the age of seventeen —a slender, dandified, effeminate boy, whose pallor and feeble physique told of a hothouse life divided between the music room and the salons of high society.

Chopin craved adventure, adventure to him meaning life as it was lived in the cosmopolitan centers of Europe. In 1828, he got a glimpse of Berlin as the guest of a family friend who went there to attend a scientific congress presided over by the eternal Alexander von Humboldt. He stared wistfully at Spontini and Mendelssohn, but was too timid to introduce himself. He reveled in the sumptuous stagings of several operas, and wrote home that Handel's *Ode for St. Cecilia's Day* "most nearly approaches my ideal of sublime music." After this tactful and far from intoxicating fortnight's introduction to the great world beyond the Polish frontier, Chopin was back in Warsaw absorbed in musical study and composition. The advent of Johann Nepomuk Hummel, that phenomenal ambassador of the eighteenth century to the nineteenth, aroused the lad's restlessness; that of Paganini made it intolerable. Furthermore, he was racked by all the torments of calf love: the object of his passion was a pretty soprano, but Chopin had not the courage to declare himself, and merely suffered and talked about his "ideal."

Nicolas Chopin decided that such agony and nostalgia should be indulged, and accordingly, in the summer of 1829, the money for a Viennese trip was somehow found. In Vienna, Frédéric succumbed gracefully to a slender success. He found, to start with, that a publisher was on the verge of issuing his variations for piano and orchestra on *"Là ci darem"* from *Don Giovanni.* Then he was persuaded, almost against his will, to give a concert "in a city which can boast of having heard a Haydn, a Mozart, and a Beethoven." He was needlessly nervous, for the concert was so successful that, a week later, he had to give another. The critics were extremely friendly, and there was a flurry in the female dovecotes. There were a few dissenters: Moscheles said his tone was "too small," and one woman was heard to say, "It's a pity he's so insignificant-looking."

Chopin returned home sighing more woefully than ever for his soprano and bored to death with the attractions of Warsaw. His letters to Titus Wojciechowski, the confidant of his maidenly hopes and fears, quiver with self-pity and verbal breast-beating. This no doubt thoroughly masculine young man seems to have been for some years a surrogate for various girls Chopin lacked the guts to speak out to. There is something decidedly ambiguous about these letters, with their kisses, embraces, and wheedling sentimentality, gently chiding "my dearest life"—Titus!—for his unresponsiveness. There is no suggestion of the overtly abnormal anywhere in Chopin's life, and indeed he outgrew his effusive outpourings to men friends, but without developing into an aggressive male. It is impossible fully to understand his music unless we recognize the generous feminine component in his nature.

Warsaw held Chopin for little more than a year, during which time he fretfully and vaguely made and unmade plans for the future. He thrice played successfully in public, the third time with his pretty soprano as assisting artist—which may well have been the climax of his intimacy with her. At last he made up his wavering mind: on November 1, 1830, he left Warsaw. He was still vague about his plans, his itinerary was "parts unknown," but for the time being he was going to Vienna with Titus Wojciechowski. As he passed through his birthplace, Elsner had a cantata performed in his honor, and then presented him with an urnful of Polish earth—an appropriate if incommodious gift, for Chopin never returned home. Early in October, he arrived in Paris, intending merely to see the sights and meet the important musicians. Instead, he stayed for the rest of his life.

The slight, blond-haired young Pole with the prominent aquiline nose, who arrived on the Parisian scene in the second year of Louis-Philippe's reign, already had a small fame. He was known in his homeland and in a few cities outside as a pianist whose delicate style and exquisite nuances made overhearing him in a large hall something of a problem. He was by now the composer of several ambitious piano works with orchestral accompaniment, not to speak of a number of smaller pieces for piano alone.

Chopin was next to penniless, but there seemed no doubt that among the many publics Paris could offer, there must be one for him. A debut concert, arranged for December, 1831, was postponed until late February. Then the critic Fétis, who had a strong aversion to praising anyone, shouted his approval, and Mendelssohn, though he was wont to speak condescendingly of the composer as "Chopinetto," warmly applauded the pianist. The concert enhanced Chopin's reputatation among musicians, but only a few Polish émigrés had bought tickets, and his pockets remained empty. Three months later, he played with equally depressing financial results at a fashionable charity concert, and was so dejected that he decided to move to America. Unfortunately for the muse of comic history, Chopin never had a chance to add another by no means needed note of color to Andrew Jackson's United States. Fortunately for him, he accidentally met Prince Valentin Radziwill, who was aghast at the idea of Chopin departing for such savage shores. He persuaded him to try his luck at Baron Jacques de Rothschild's. There, amid some of the best names in the *Almanach de Gotha,* he conquered Parisian society, and came away with a prince, a princess, a duchess, and a count as his sponsors. As a result, with engagements to play, and with plenty of lessons at twenty francs a head, his financial problems were solved for over a decade.

Chopin never deplored the inroads of society on his time: he had a well-developed frivolous side, adored the company of beautiful women of rank, and unfolded all his petals in a really select gathering. Once he had entree, he gave much attention to the business of cutting a fine figure in Parisian high society. He kept his own carriage, was something of a clotheshorse, and in many respects was quite like one of the young swells of the Jockey Club. His social vices were characteristic of the highborn Pole domiciled in Paris: he was snobbish to the point of stupidity, and often treated those he considered his inferiors with brusque discourtesy. Of a part with this was his fanatical contempt for Jews—unless they happened to be a Rothschild, a Mendelssohn, or a Heine. He used the epithets "Jew" and "pig" interchangeably for anyone who incurred, even unwittingly, his disfavor. Ever a sensitive plant, imbibing his impressions, and most of his nonmusical ideas, from his immediate ambience, Chopin did not think out these absurd attitudes, but accepted them as unthinkingly as he did the fashion of wearing yellow gloves.

The Chopin of the overheated ballrooms with countless countesses moving in the candlelight was the composer of the valses—less than a score spaced over almost twenty years. There are valses in all moods—gay, insouciant, disdainful, *dolce far niente,* somber, languorous, pensive—all evoking the ballroom and the spirit of the dance. Only rarely, however, are they truly dance music, and never are they valses in the good, forthright Johann Strauss tradition. They have rhythm, and when this rhythm is not too vagrant, parts of them could be used in a ballroom. As it is, several of them have been orchestrated for ballet—witness those in that appalling choreographic museum called *Les Sylphides.* It takes a ballet dancer, disciplined to cope with all manner of musical surprise, to follow the subtle retards and accelerations of Chopin's perplexing conception of unchanging three-four time. The valses are really just what Chopin intended them to be—piano pieces, salon pieces to be played intimately. They are all charming, many of them enjoy world-wide popularity, some of them have moments of exquisite tenderness and meditation. Yet, with the possible exception of the C-sharp minor, they are without the special tang and color of Chopin, the revolutionary of the pianoforte. The valses are Chopin's trivia.

The truth is that the valses, having their source in no deep emotions, but bubbling off the surface of Chopin's life, could never rise above charm. Yet, he could make other dance forms the vehicles of eloquent emotion. Such were the polonaise and the mazurka, where the fact that they were Polish dances touched off a complex of personal feelings—patriotism, homesickness, pride of race, a realization of exile —that make them spiritually sincere, artistically creative as the valses almost never are.

The polonaise, which in Liszt's deft but insensitive hands became an omnibus of piano effects, in Chopin's was a magnificent catch at lofty and poetic moods. In this superb dozen of epic dances—great vigorous dances for noble men—it is hard to find the Chopin whom John Field (himself a minor poet at the keyboard) described as "a sickroom talent." With the exception of the clangorous *Militaire,* the polonaises have seldom won the great popular favor they deserve: they are too difficult for any except the strongest and most agile virtuoso; they are entirely beyond the reach of the amateur, who can manage a valse or a prelude. Yet, even a long-neglected polonaise can be dusted off, and used by a great pianist to bring down the house. In capable hands they are absolutely sure-fire. The main reason for this is that, apart from their specific musical beauties, they are amazingly exciting.

For expressing more intimate and evanescent moods than seem native to the polonaise, Chopin turned to another Polish dance— the mazurka. He wrote fifty-six mazurkas of amazing variety, but almost all intensely Slavic in feeling. Many have recourse to the most exotic harmonies and melodic intervals. The way they break the rules, sometimes to produce an authentic Slavic effect, sometimes out of sheer disdain, infuriated the theorists of the day. Even the much freer rules of modern harmony might not admit some of these strange progressions, but the ear—music's best arbiter—allows them because they seem to arise inevitably out of the whole design and context of the music. Lovely, haunting, eerily seductive though they are, the mazurkas have never been concert hits, not because audiences would not like them, but because they offer few big chances to heroic virtuosos. This is perhaps just as well: the mazurkas would lose some of their bloom at the hands of keyboard giants in the wide spaces of the concert hall. They need, far more than the valses, and quite as much as the preludes, the small room, the right time, the personal touch.

The year 1835 was one of the stormiest in Chopin's life. In the first place, he became deeply depressed by the public's tepid reaction to his playing—he foolishly matched his salon touch against Liszt's thunderous pianism in large halls, and naturally cut a poor figure. In early April, the two of them played at a charity concert, and the applause for Chopin was almost as delicate as his playing. He concluded gloomily that he had better stick to composing, and said unhappily to Liszt: "I am not fitted to give concerts. The crowd intimidates me; I feel asphyxiated by its breath, paralyzed by its curious look, dumb before the strange faces; but you, you are destined for the crowd, because when you do not captivate your public, you have the wherewithal to overpower it." A spiteful remark. Was he implying that what Liszt could not do legitimately, he accomplished with sex appeal and piano-pounding? After this, Chopin rarely played in public. His reputation as a keyboard sorcerer depends almost exclusively on the reports of friends and fellow musicians who heard him play his own compositions at private musicales.

The figure Chopin cut at these aristocratic gatherings healed whatever wounds'his vanity suffered at the hands of the larger public. He was a male coquette—there are abundant traces of coquetry in his lighter pieces—and many of his usually inconclusive romances began as he poured out his ardent Slavic soul at.the keyboard and swept his ·susceptible audience with his lustrous eyes. There was something about this slight, poetic-looking exquisite that would have made conquests easy for him if he had had more sheer male drive. But so shrinking was he that the woman had to be the aggressor, and there is good reason for believing that he did not have his first sexual experience until 1834 or 1835, when he was seduced by a misunderstood wife, the talented and glamorous Countess Delphine Potocka. There was real affection between them, but the liaison was cut short when her jealous husband, by stopping her allowance, forced her to return to Warsaw.

Apparently while suffering from this deprivation, Chopin went to Carlsbad to visit his parents. After two happy months, not realizing that they would never meet again, he left them and went on to Dresden to see the Wodziński family, friends of his childhood. There, or the following year at Marienbad, he seems to have offered marriage to the youthful Countess Marja Wodzińska, though evidently without being passionately in love with her. The details of the affair, about which so many doleful conjectural pages have been printed, remain extremely obscure. Certain it is that Count Wodziński objected to a musician son-in-law, but just as certainly Chopin for two years looked forward to marrying Marja. He was longing for a wife and home—the specific Marja was a secondary consideration. In 1837, while he still considered himself plighted to her, she made it clear, by the cold tone of her letters, that marriage was out of the question.

If these abortive relationships, these yearnings for romance, these searchings for lasting love, have a musical gloss, it is pre-eminently in the nocturnes. Unlike the mazurka or polonaise, the nocturne is a fluid mood piece, not a distinct musical form. What gives Chopin's nocturnes their family resemblance is precisely their yearning, searching, often darkling mood. In the hands of Haydn and Mozart, a *notturno* had been an orchestral serenade. John Field, the Irish virtuoso who was St. Petersburg's most fashionable piano teacher in the early nineteenth century, published the first piano pieces to be called nocturnes, by which he meant evocations of night moods, and Chopin, who knew Field, appropriated the idea. Field, to judge by his sane, pellucid nocturnes, felt the same by night as by day. Not so Chopin, whose moods deepened as the shades of night fell. His nocturnes are the music of exacerbated nerves. Their sickly phosphorescence illumines the jungle places, the tropical miasmas of his psyche. They express not only Chopin the thwarted lover, but Chopin the neurotic, the ambivalent, the decadent. In some respects, the nocturnes, which so often exaggerate his idiosyncrasies to the point of caricature, are the most Chopinesque of all his works. They have ended by doing a disservice to his reputation, for it is upon oversentimentalized interpretations of them by oversentimental pianists that the conception of Chopin as "the Polish tuberose" chiefly rests.

An excellent corrective for this one-sided conception of Chopin is furnished by the four scherzos, the most human and variable of which—that in B-flat minor—was published the very year his hope of settling down with the Wodzińska was dashed. The scherzos are stalwarts, and the first three are works of impassioned vigor. Like the three giant polonaises, they demand great strength, a bravura technique, and an understanding of musical Byronics. They have little if any likeness to earlier scherzos, which developed out of the minuet, and which, in the hands of Beethoven, became pieces of titanic playfulness. They are almost equally distant from Mendelssohn's gossamer adaptation of the classical scherzo.

In composition Chopin could find release for ordinary emotional pressures, but in the case of Marja Wodzińska he could not thus exorcise the specter of his shattered hopes. His health suffered, and he sank into ominous lethargy. When he did not rally, two of his friends coaxed him into going with them to London. They were gone less than a fortnight—but long enough, it has been said, for the combination of English weather and his lowered vitality to impair Chopin's congenitally weak lungs. He returned home suffering in body and mind, and might well have surrendered himself completely to despair and disease if the entire course of his life had not been changed by one of the most remarkable women of the nineteenth century—George Sand. They had met in the winter of 1836 at the home of Liszt's mistress, the Countess d'Agoult, and were on friendly terms even before his ill-advised English journey. Almost immediately after his return, they were seen everywhere together. By the summer of 1838, they were so intimate that they spent their vacation together at Nohant, her château in the Loire country. Thus began the most publicized love affair in musical history.

At first Chopin had found Mme Sand repellent, but before he knew precisely what was happening to him, her enveloping sympathy had lapped him in the mother love he yearned for. He became enslaved. Nothing else explains a man so prim about moral appearances (he broke off friendly relations with Liszt because he had used Chopin's rooms for an assignation) going off to spend the summer with this dumpy sibyl, for it was as much as a young man's reputation was worth to be seen in her company in those days. He then threw discretion farther to the winds, and spent a wet, miserable winter with her on the island of Majorca. Chopin was desperately ill during this nightmarish honeymoon: he and Mme Sand and her children were objects of vengeful suspicion by the superstitious natives (primarily because they did not go to church), and were starved into seeking refuge at an abandoned monastery, where they put up for several wretched months. His ill-heated, damp cell and the vile food again wrecked his health, and when finally they made their escape from the island, Chopin, suffering constantly from hemorrhages, was carried aboard the stinking freighter in an advanced stage of phthisis. Eventually the weary travelers put in at Marseilles, and there Chopin recuperated slowly before returning to Nohant for the summer.

A novelist, faced with the problem of solving the fate of so wrecked a hero as Chopin was when he landed at Marseilles, might be excused for incontinently killing him off. Not being a fictionist's puppet, Chopin chose to live ten years more. Not only that, he brought back with him from Majorca, besides two polonaises and a ballade, the twenty-four preludes of Opus 28.

The refining of these preludes had been somehow accomplished in the sordid misery of the Majorca winter. Now, after the healing months in Marseilles and Nohant, Chopin returned to Paris and entered upon one of the most productive periods of his life. He was unquestionably much in love with Mme Sand, and through her achieved a kind of emotional stability he had craved and needed. His work benefited: "His melodies are purer, his rhythms more virile, his harmonies richer," William Murdoch has noted. "Something has happened that has broadened every idea, made nobler every inspiration and given greater shape to every conception." Settled down in

Paris in the same house with Mme Sand, Chopin worked at his art with a passion, a concentrated fervor that, in the brief space of two years, produced a spate of splendid new pieces, many of them on an unwontedly large scale. The first to see the light of day after the preludes was that amazing suite of pieces Chopin chose to call the B-flat minor Sonata. Hearing it for the first time, Schumann declared, "To have called this a sonata must be reckoned a freak, if not a piece of pride; for he has simply yoked together four of his maddest children. . . ."

The very keystone of Chopin's greater art belongs to this remarkable period of unstinted creativeness. The F minor Fantaisie has been called "a Titan in commotion," and all sorts of programs have been suggested for it, one more absurd than the other, as if Chopin could not have reared this vast fabric without binding it together with trivial anecdotage. Even he himself had a program for it—according to Liszt, whose biography of Chopin must be taken as a floral tribute rather than a source of information. The Fantaisie is a big composition in every sense: the themes are not only very beautiful but also extremely malleable and susceptible to development; the large design is carried out with complete success, sustained by passionate and unfaltering intellectual attention.

The creative effort that had produced within two years such a ponderable and splendid part of Chopin's lifework was superhuman in a man who was slowly dying. It could not be kept up. The story of his life after 1841 is one of decline, and for six years its pattern was unvarying. Every summer he went to Mme Sand's château at Nohant, where her sensible nursing helped him gather strength for the autumn and winter season in Paris. Every winter he had a few pieces ready for his publishers, and he always had strength enough to quarrel with them over terms. Otherwise these years passed almost without incident.

Troubled and increasingly weakened by his disease, he turned over fewer and fewer compositions to his publishers each year. Yet, as late as 1845, he signed the fine B minor Sonata. In 1847, after signs that it might drag on wearily until one of them died, his romance with George Sand came to an abrupt end. For some years she had been addressing him playfully as "my dear corpse": now he truly looked like one—an ailing wisp of a man who weighed less than a hundred pounds. His purse, too, was almost empty, and though every added exertion meant agony, he had to do something to fill it. His friends and publishers persuaded him to give a concert. On February 16, 1848, he made his first public appearance in six years, playing a long and taxing program, including the piano part in his 'Cello Sonata, the last extended work he composed. The concert was a great social and financial success. Chopin played exquisitely, but almost fainted after the last number. It was his farewell to the Paris public, which in this case consisted of royal dukes, members of the peerage, and Chopin's pupils.

At this juncture, his devoted friend and pupil, Jane Wilhelmina Stirling, a Scotswoman of ample means, induced him to go to England. She took care of all details of the trip, and hired rooms for him in London, where he arrived late in April, 1848. He played privately at several fine houses, refused an invitation from the Philharmonic—"I would rather not—they want classical things there," he wrote—and met shoals of celebrities, including Carlyle and Dickens. At first, the critics and musicians were inclined to welcome Chopin, but as he evinced such a decided preference for playing privately, their enthusiasm cooled, and he was set down as a society snob. He grew more and more unhappy. Critical unfriendliness, bad weather, and ever-waning health added to his depression. He longed for the lost peace of Nohant.

In January, Chopin returned painfully to France. As his train neared Paris, he mused bitterly on that ill-advised hegira from which he was returning. "Do you see the cattle in that meadow?" he asked his valet. "They've more intelligence than the English." When he arrived, he took it as a last evil omen that the only doctor in whom he had confidence had died in his absence. No longer able to teach, much of the time unable even to sit up, Chopin had no way of earning a living. Income he had none, for he had always sold his compositions outright—on a royalty basis he would have been assured of a handsome living.

Out of the past, almost as if the last act of the drama of Chopin's life demanded her presence, came Delphine Potocka. When they had met, many years before, she had enchanted him with the thrilling quality of her voice, and now one of his few pleasures was to hear her sing. A few days before he died, she came to his bedside, and sang an aria by his beloved friend Bellini. Chopin was fully aware that his days were numbered. With perfect composure, he asked his sister to burn his unpublished manuscripts. "I owe it to the public and myself to publish only my best works," he explained. "I have kept to this resolution all my life—I wish to keep to it now." As the end approached, he was tormented by the fear of being buried alive, and one of his last acts was to scrawl a note asking that his body be cut open before burial. On the night of October 16, 1849, a Polish priest gave him extreme unction. His doctor then asked him whether he was suffering, and he whispered, *"Plus"*—no longer. He died early the following morning.

At Chopin's request the Mozart Requiem was sung at his funeral in the Madeleine. Lablache, who had sung the bass part at Beethoven's funeral, now sang it at Chopin's. The great world of society and art attended reverently, and among those who followed the hearse to Père Lachaise were Meyerbeer and Delacroix. Buried with him was the urnful of Polish soil Elsner had given him almost twenty years before.

Hector Berlioz

From "Alla Breve"

By Carl Engel

BERLIOZ left a detailed account of his life, begun in 1848 at London and carried down to New Year's Day of 1865. We also have much of his personal correspondence. Letters and autobiographies are perhaps the most interesting part of literature. But autobiographies are not always trustworthy documents. Only a few are the calm, enlightened review of facts, the dispassionate probing into causes and effects, the entertaining and instructive painting of characters and customs which are no more. Frequently such accounts are intended as apologies or glorifications of the writer, and as posthumous attacks upon dead adversaries. The Memoirs of Berlioz suffer from this fault to a not inconsiderable, but highly excusable, degree. Godlike as were his aspirations, his soul was human; he was misunderstood and maligned in his youth, grew old in disappointment and vexation. He had the morbid need of self-revealment. That he should have used the pen so extensively, and often caustically, in his own defence is but natural; nor is it to be regretted by posterity, for his pen was brilliant.

Hector Berlioz was born December 11, 1803, at Côte-Saint-André, a small place near Lyons, in the south of France. His father was a physician, intelligent and broadminded, absorbed in his profession. His mother was a fanatic and intolerant Catholic. Berlioz was ever a victim of his shortcomings, which were the result of parental short-sightedness. Although he did not fail to give early signs of musical talent and temperamental impulsiveness, his technical training and moral discipline were vague and ineffective. He learned to play the flute and guitar, after a fashion, and was brought up with the idea that he should end as an honorable country doctor.

He was sent to Paris to study medicine. The French capital, in the first half of the nineteenth century, was still reverberating with the clangor of the revolution and the wars of Bonaparte. New governments followed each other in quick succession. Revolutionary and bellicose was the romantic spirit that possessed the literary and artistic generation of the day. Young Berlioz, ardent and exalted, was suddenly brought face to face with a realization of his secret dreams. He was swept off his feet. Having drunk from the pure essence of Gluck, Beethoven and Weber, he could no longer stand the heavy atmosphere of the dissecting room. He discarded his books on anatomy and pathology for treatises on harmony and counterpoint.

Berlioz was twenty-two years old when he entered the Paris Conservatory and became a pupil of Reicha, after having taken a few lessons from Lesueur. Conspicuous in dress and manners, his fine head crowned with a leonine crop of hair that quivered like aspen leaves at his impassionate gestures, he could not help attracting the attention of everyone. Notwithstanding the remonstrances of his father and the actual curses of his bigoted mother, to whom music was an agent of the devil, he pursued his studies. He suffered want, earning a pittance by singing in the chorus of a third-rate theater, and contracted debts in order to perform the works he was now beginning to compose. These works inflamed the younger and progressive element with wild enthusiasm; they scandalized the fogies. Fétis, the studious musicographer and Berlioz' lifelong enemy, wrote in 1835, after some of the composer's greatest and most magnificent orchestral pieces had already been heard in public: "According to my belief, the things that M. Berlioz writes do not belong to what I am accustomed to consider as music, and I am absolutely certain that the conditions of this art are unknown to him." Fétis saw only the flaws, and was blind to the light of genius. But flaws there were, and even Schumann, who had been the loud and staunch defender of the younger Berlioz, could write in later years to the historian Ambros: "Time makes us severer.

In some of Berlioz' recent works there are things which one can't forgive a man of forty."

With due allowance made for such blemishes, there remains the work of a giant, an innovator, without whom music would have lost much that was fructifying; there remain the vast conceptions of an inspired brain, hewed in large masses of tone; there remain, above all, the creation of the modern orchestra and the establishing of the "program" symphony, two things which his contemporaries and successors eagerly appropriated. Heine called him "the lark with eagle wings."

Only after several attempts did he succeed, in December, 1830, in winning the Rome Prize with a cantata sufficiently academic in style to pass the judges. This was three years after his first great emotional crisis, brought on by an Irish actress, Harriet Smithson, who gave English performances of Shakespeare in Paris. Berlioz greatly admired Shakespeare, as he did Goethe and Byron. He lost his head completely over his Ophelia, walking the streets day and night like one demented. A *grande passion* was essential to his nature, and to accelerate creation nothing served him so well as love fulfilled or unrequited. The unapproachable Miss had passed from the scene, however, when Berlioz set out for his sojourn in the Eternal City, as a pensioner of the French Government. It was then Marie (Camille) Mocke, a youthful and coquettish pianist, who had captivated his heart. He tore himself away and arrived at the Villa Medici about the middle of March, 1831.

When by the first of April he was still without word from Marie, he fled from Rome and got as far as Florence, where he fell ill. Upon learning that Marie had meanwhile married M. Pleyel, he swore vengeance, meditated the murder of the faithless one, and instantly proceeded on his homicidal errand. But he had a timely change of mind, was conscience-stricken, simulated an attempt at suicide, wrote to the painter, Horace Vernet—the director of the Villa Medici—and received a paternal and forgiving answer. He returned to Rome, but never liked the city very much. In 1832 he left the Villa, not without having made love to Vernet's daughter, for whose hand he asked Madame Vernet in a letter dispatched as soon as he arrived in Paris.

But here an unexpected discovery gave events a different turn. He found that Harriet Smithson was again in town, and the old fire flamed up more violently than ever. Not with ordinary wooing did he want to win her, but by the impact with his *Fantastic* Symphony (first performed in December, 1830, and then revised), a tremendous work for those days, and reflecting with dramatic vividness the emotions—real and imagined—that his love for Harriet had awakened. Miss Smithson heard the symphony at a concert on December 9, 1832. The composer's magnetic personality, the impression produced by his remarkable work on an audience which, though it contained enough hostile reactionaries, gave overwhelming signs of its admiration, combined to achieve the desired effect. After parental objections were overridden, the marriage finally took place on October 3, 1833. It was not a happy union. The wife grew more and more jealous, the husband disillusioned. Conditions became intolerable and a separation followed. In 1843, after so many artistic, pecuniary, and domestic misadventures, Berlioz left Paris for a concert tour through Germany, Austria, and Russia. He was accorded everywhere the warm and intelligent reception that his compatriots had refused him.

Liszt, in particular, espoused his cause and performed his works when called to direct the musical affairs of Weimar. The operas of Berlioz were heard in Germany before France knew them. But it is not as an opera composer that he excelled. Neither the Shakespearean *Beatrice and Benedict* nor the romantic *Benvenuto Cellini* has found a permanent place in the operatic repertory. *The Trojans,* suggested by Virgil's tale of Æneas, fared no better. The dramatic symphony *Romeo and Juliet* (1839) constituted a departure; as novel as the form, as characteristic are the contents of this splendid work. All things considered, it ranks perhaps highest among the composer's creations. His early reading had furnished the inspirational germ for most of his later compositions. Shakespearean was the subject for the overture *King Lear,* for the orchestral fantasy *The Tempest.* We find Byron's glowing flame in the symphonic poem *Harold in Italy* (1834) and the *Corsair* Overture. Goethe is responsible for *The Damnation of Faust* (1846), the work that did most to earn the composer posthumous laurels.

Berlioz, a child of his age, was chivalrous. When Harriet was dying in 1854, his affection for her was still alive. As he had sung his love in his *Fantastic* Symphony, where the obsessing idea of the beloved had taken musical shape in an equally obsessing theme—the first true specimen of the *Leitmotiv*—so did he mourn for her in his funeral music of Ophelia. Death, in the soul-searching days of romanticism, was a solemn and spectacular thing. No one represented it more dramatically than did Berlioz in his Requiem Mass (1837). It is, with the *Fantastic* Symphony, Berlioz' most astonishing achievement in orchestral technique. His instinct for unusual and graphic instrumentation was infallible. His treatise on the instruments of the orchestra is the work of a shrewd analyst, deft craftsman, and sensitive poet.

Berlioz had found, early in life, that his literary and critical gifts were more dependable breadwinners than was his musical genius. As a critic on several newspapers, notably *Le Journal des Débats,* which he joined in 1838, he became a power and a sort of oracle. He did not hesitate to avow his antipathy to Wagner. Seldom did he set down anything but his candid opinion. He never used his influence for selfish ends. His sharp wit, his enlightening observations, make good reading in a day when most of the works and persons that formed the objects of his criticisms live only by the praise or censure he bestowed on them. Having survived a second wife, having buried a son of his first marriage, and also his sister, he was left solitary, a prey to his dejected moods. He died on March 8, 1869. A grand and pathetic figure was this hyperemotional dreamer and combative originator.

Franz Liszt

Abridged from "Alla Breve"

By Carl Engel

THE life of Liszt was brilliant, spectacular. Drab words can give only a glimpse of it. A youth, portrayed by the music-mad Ingres as a dreamy Apollo in London-tailored clothes, his golden curls were the admiration of all romantic women in the romantic Paris of 1830, while his demoniacal hands were the dread and envy of his pianistic rivals. At seventy, robed in priestly black, the white curls that framed his warty, wrinkled face were still coveted by doting femininity, his fingers still conjured up enchantment from out a case of wire strings: his spirit had not aged. His personality and manners, not less than his art and wit, made him beloved by all. No man of his time was more truly the *grand seigneur* of music, or the fairy-godfather of struggling talent. In the Parisian salons of the July monarchy he was a peer of Chopin, Victor Hugo, George Sand, and Heine. Between rapid-fire runs and octave trills he could shrewdly discuss Saint-Simon's *nouveau christianisme* or political and social problems. He was at ease strolling with Napoleon III on the terrace of the Tuileries, or with Pius IX in the gardens of the Vatican. Whether living with the astonishing Countess d'Agoult on the shores of Lake Geneva, or at Weimar's "Altenburg" with the solicitous Princess Sayn-Wittgenstein in attendance; whether in the blaze of a crowded concert hall or in cloistral retirement at Santa Francesca Romana, with the ruins of the Forum at his door, the various scenes in this unparalleled career were always of a sort to keep the tongues of Europe wagging, to satisfy the public's craving for picturesque effects and sentimental complications.

Born at Raiding, near Oedenburg in Hungary, on October 22nd, 1811, Franz Liszt was fortunate in having a musical father who gave the boy his first piano lessons and left nothing undone to develop the exceptional abilities of his son. Aged nine, Franz played before an audience of Hungarian nobles, who were so impressed that they contributed to a fund which permitted the father to give up his position as farm superintendent of Count Esterházy, and take his little prodigy to Czerny in Vienna. In 1823 Beethoven heard him play, and embraced him—the latter is authenticated, the former at least doubtful, considering the great man's tragic deafness. At the age of twelve Liszt was taken to Paris, where he created a *furore*. Cherubini would not accept him at the Conservatoire, under the pretext that he was a foreigner. Reicha became his teacher in composition; on the piano there was little left for him to learn. Switzerland and London were next to hear him. For the long journeys in his traveling coach, he carried with him a little silent clavier to keep in daily technical training. After his father died, in 1827, Liszt taught and concertized in order to support his mother. He soon amassed a fortune. In the winter of 1833-34 he met Countess d'Agoult. Liszt vainly tried to escape the charms of this politico-poetic Circe. Their attachment created a scandal. It proved anew that our moral code was drawn up without consulting genius. One of their three children, Cosima, was married to Hans von Bülow, and later to Richard Wagner. Four years they lived within the tolerant confines of the Helvetian republic, or traveling in Italy. Then Liszt resumed his concertizing. With a large gift of money from the proceeds of his recitals, he made possible the completion of the Beethoven monument at Bonn. In 1844, growing misunderstandings led to the final separation from the Countess. His wanderings lasted till 1847, carrying him through Germany, Russia, Sweden, and Spain, fêted wherever he went. The University of Königsberg, where Kant had lectured, gave him a doctor's degree. Kings and Emperors had to be content to offer him orders, jewels and other costly trifles. Having entered into very cordial relations with the reigning house of Saxe-Weimar, in 1848, he accepted the Grand-duke's offer to become director of the court opera and concerts. From 1848 to 1861 he resided more or less permanently in the "city of the Muses," forever distinguished by Goethe and Schiller; but even in later years he liked to return to this charming quiet spot among the wooded mountains of Thuringia. During this period he wrote his most important orchestral works. In his symphonic poems he followed the example of Berlioz, but with a greater felicity in the choice of his subjects, with a broader command of sensuous melody, and with a richer palette of instrumental colors. *Dante, Tasso* and the *Faust* Symphony contain remarkable inventions in tonal beauty. By applying his methods of orchestration to the piano, he augmented its range and endowed it with a new wealth of dynamic shadings and contrasting sonorities.

During this first Weimar period he became the champion of Wagner. Memorable letters were exchanged between Liszt and Wagner, who, as a political exile from Germany, was not able to hear the first performance of his *Lohengrin* on August 28, 1850. Liszt's influence quickened the advance of music incalculably. Berlioz found in him an enthusiastic interpreter. These progressive tendencies met, as usual, with attacks from the reactionary elements and, tired of petty cabals, Liszt left Weimar in 1861 and went to Rome, where he resided until 1870. His religious contemplations led him to study the old liturgical chants and sacred music; he was prompted now himself to write for the church. As his pupils and admirers had followed him wherever he went, so did they soon gather round him in the Eternal City, and he again held his court. He taught, composed, encouraged—always kind and hospitable—enjoying a glass of cognac and a rubber of whist, notwithstanding his clerical aspirations. He took the lower orders in 1865, and thereafter Abbé Liszt wore the Roman frock.

In 1875 he was made director of the musical Academy in Budapest, dividing his time between the Hungarian capital, Rome, and Weimar, to which old associations drew him ever again. His declining years were dimmed by the rising star of his son-in-law, Richard Wagner, who helped himself to much of what Liszt had created. Carrying his train of disciples the length and breadth of Europe, spending royally of his wisdom and encouragement, he ended his earthly travels at Bayreuth, on July 31, 1886, during a visit to the Wagnerian Mecca. Thus died he who was counted on as an added attraction to the "shrine"

—lonely and unconsidered—in the midst of the festivities presided over by his preoccupied daughter Cosima.

The number of Liszt's compositions is very large. Not all of them withstand the wear of time. They can be classed roughly as, first, his piano music; second, his orchestral tone poems; and third, his religious music. Each of these classes may be subdivided into the many *pièces d'occasion,* compositions written, as it were, to order, and those which are the spontaneous work of his own choosing and devising. His songs, while they are interesting and often beautiful, are rather "contrived" than inspired. It was only natural that the virtuoso should write to dazzle the public. He did it with his *Hungarian Rhapsodies,* his Études and Concertos. He could also be simple, and wove intimate confessions into the shorter sketches that illustrate, autobiographically, some memorable hours in his journeys and emotional life. His church music, after all, is not that of an ingenuous mind, but betrays a sort of dilettante asceticism. He emphasized the obvious effects of the most effective ritual in Christendom. When he played some of his church music for Wagner, at Venice, in 1883, the latter remarked: "Your God makes a lot of noise." In a work like his *Legend of St. Elisabeth* the composer's dramatic and religious instincts mingle in more fruitful union. His "program symphony" was the model for a long line of successors, who must trace to him what they learned about the art of evoking mental conceptions and distinctive moods through aural sensations. *Till Eulenspiegel* of Richard Strauss, Rachmaninoff's *Isle of the Dead,* and Debussy's *La Mer* are descendants of Liszt's *Mazeppa, Battle of the Huns, Les Préludes,* and all his other orchestral pieces broidered upon the woof of some poetic or pictorial subject. But his contribution to music, as such and apart from programmatic associations, is the really vital service he rendered his art. Gifted with an ear that caught some of the unheard harmonies still stored beyond the threshold of consciousness, and opening the door for an instant, he let a fresh gust of sounding beauty into the world.* He was the only composer of the nineteenth century who would have understood and liked the music of the early twentieth, because, among all the musicians of his time, he had the farthest vision and the least conceit.

* Also—many musicians would say—much claptrap and vulgarity.—E. S.

Richard Wagner

Abridged from "A History of Music"

By Paul Landormy

RICHARD WAGNER was born in Leipzig, May 22, 1813. His father, a police clerk, died six months after his birth.* A little later his mother remarried, in Dresden, her second husband being the actor, dramatic poet, and painter Ludwig Geyer, who in turn died in 1820. Wagner followed the classic curriculum of study with brilliant success, and his teachers destined him for a career as a philologist. Yet he thought in first instance of poetry and the drama, and then of music. In 1833, he wrote *Die Feen,* which he could not manage to get performed. In 1834, he was appointed director of the Magdeburg Theater, and composed *Das Liebesverbot* (The Prohibition to Love), a very free adaptation of Shakespeare's *Measure for Measure,* which was performed in 1839 without much success. He then married an actress, Minna Planer. After remaining a short time at the Königsberg Theater, he spent two years (1837-1839) as orchestra conductor of the Riga Theater. It was there that he began to compose *Rienzi.*

From the beginning of his life Wagner was subjected to all sorts of diverse influences. His stepfather wished to have him study painting. Yet he grew weary of "drawing eyes indefinitely." He was surrounded only by theatrical people. His sister Rosalie made her début at fifteen; his sisters Clara and Louise were also actresses; his brother too, abandoned the study of medicine in order to become a comedian, and of his two daughters † one, Johanna, was later destined to sing Elizabeth in *Tannhäuser* admirably. Wagner knew his way about the stage at an early hour. At the same time he himself had no leanings toward an actor's career. Yet at first he dreamed of writing dramas. When thirteen, after having translated the first twelve chants of the *Odyssey,* and become an enthusiastic admirer of Shakespeare, he outlined a tragedy in which forty-two persons died in succession, and then

---

* The debate as to whether Wagner did or did not have "non-Aryan blood" in his veins still continues. However, the whole matter is quite unimportant, since it has not yet been demonstrated that blood type has any relation to musical type.—E. S.

† That is, the brother's daughters. Johanna Wagner was Richard's niece.—E. S.

reappeared as ghosts in order not to leave the stage deserted before the end of the play. His musical vocation did not show itself until very late, and he never attained virtuosity on any instrument. "Throughout all my life," said he, "I never learned to play the piano."

Weber and Beethoven revealed music to Wagner. Since 1817 Weber had been the conductor of the Dresden Opera, and Ludwig Geyer was one of his most enthusiastic partisans. Young Wagner became one as well. After having heard the first performances of the *Freischütz,* he murdered the overture at the piano. And twenty years later, when he heard the *Freischütz* at the Paris Opéra, he cried: "Ah! my wonderful German fatherland, how I love you, how I cherish you, though only because the *Freischütz* was born on your soil! How I love the German people who love the *Freischütz* and who, even today, believe in the marvels of the most naïve legends; who, even today, though having reached the age of virility, still react to those sweet and mysterious terrors that thrilled their hearts in the days of their youth!"

In 1827, at Leipzig, Wagner heard the symphonies of Beethoven —who had just died—at the Gewandhaus concerts. He experienced a profound emotion. And, suddenly, he set to work to compose a sonata, a quartet, a grand aria, without the faintest knowledge of harmony. He soon realized his ignorance, and took a few lessons from a teacher who merely succeeded in quickly disgusting him with the arid study of the chords. He again abandoned theory, and composed a rather disheveled overture which was performed in 1830, but of which not a trace remains. Returning to harmony, he covered it in its entirety as well as counterpoint, in the course of six months, under the guidance of Theodore Weinlig. He then composed a sonata, a polonaise, a fantasy for piano, some overtures, two symphonies, and finally, in 1833, his opera *Die Feen,* which was not staged, but some fragments of which were presented in concert form. The subject of this youthful work already presaged that of *Lohengrin,* for the fairy Ada is metamorphosed into a statue because the mortal Arindal is weak enough to doubt his beloved for a moment.

The years Wagner passed at Magdeburg, Königsberg, and Riga were onerous years. His duties as an orchestra leader were taxing and unrewarding. Wagner was often in want at this time, especially after his marriage. He was feeling his way. The revolutionary ideas of 1830 first aroused his enthusiasm, and, applying them to his art, he declared war on tradition and scholastic subtlety, and no longer acknowledged anything but the free melody of the Italians, whose type he found in

Bellini's *Norma.* "Song, song and still more song," he cried, "Germans that you are!" Yet he may have noticed that he went too far in his admiration of the Italians, for he adds: "One must belong to one's own day, find new forms suited to the new times. The master who does this will write neither in the Italian nor in the French style—nor yet in the German." It was under the influence of these ideas that he wrote his *Liebesverbot.* He even sought a subject for a comic opera; yet he called a halt. He realized that he would stray were he to follow the road of "easy music." Then, in 1838, he undertook a work of greater length, *Rienzi,* without giving thought to its time of completion or place of performance.

Rienzi is a type of the pure and heroic tribune who wishes to deliver the Roman people from the yoke of the nobility, and who in the end is himself abandoned in a cowardly manner by the people he wished to deliver. At the moment Wagner was under the influence of the "historical opera," which was triumphing in Paris: *William Tell,* by Rossini, dates from 1829, *La Muette de Portici,* by Auber, from 1828, *Robert le Diable,* by Meyerbeer, from 1831, *Les Huguenots,* from 1836, and *La Juive,* by Halévy, from 1835. As Wagner said later: "I saw the subject of my *Rienzi* through the Grand Opéra opera-glasses"—that is to say, as a spectacle production in five acts, with large ensembles, hymns, processionals, military scenes, ballets, great arias and duos written in a style consistently pompous and oratorical.

In 1839 a new period began in Wagner's life. Driven from Riga by a rival's intrigues, he took the road to France, bringing with him his sketch of *Rienzi,* which he hoped to have performed at the Paris Opéra.

He reached Paris together with his wife Minna and a magnificent Newfoundland dog, but without any money. Meyerbeer gave him some recommendations, introduced him, and patronized him. Wagner composed romances for the *salons,* romances which were not understood. He wished to have his *Liebesverbot* performed at the Renaissance, and at that moment this theater went bankrupt (1840). He offered to write the music for a *vaudeville* by Dumanoir, the *Déscente de la courtille;* but even this purely scenic task was not intrusted to him. He presented the scenario of his own opera, *Der fliegende Holländer* (The Flying Dutchman), to the director of the Opéra. The subject aroused the director's enthusiasm, and for 500 francs he bought the right to have it set to music—by another composer! In 1841, at a concert arranged by the music publisher Schlesinger, Wagner's overture, *Christopher Colomb,* was played, but the orchestra was poor and the public remained indifferent. Then the blackest misery overtook Wagner. He did anything and everything to make a living; arranged operas in the fashion of the day for flute, for clarinet, for cornet; corrected music proofs; and undertook the most ungrateful assignments for French and foreign magazines. He soon grew disgusted with Paris and its dilettantism. His one consolation was hearing the Beethoven symphonies, notably the *Choral* Symphony, conducted by Habeneck, at the Conservatoire concerts, and his mind germinated all sorts of prolific ideas. "If I were to compose an opera according to my own feelings," he wrote, "it would drive away the public, since it would contain no airs, no duos, no trios, nor any of those pieces which are stitched together nowadays, somehow or other, to make an opera; what I should like to compose I could find neither singers to sing nor a public to hear." He turned again to composition. During the winter of 1839-1840 he wrote the *Faust* overture, and then completed *Rienzi* and sent his score to Dresden, where he hoped to have it performed. In 1841, at Meudon, he completed the musical outline of *The Flying Dutchman* in seven weeks, and at the same time received the glad tidings that his *Rienzi* was to be performed in Dresden. He left France April 7, 1842, and went to Germany overland.

On October 20, 1842, *Rienzi* was performed in Dresden with great success; on January 2, 1843, *The Flying Dutchman* was received with the same favor, in appearance at any rate; for in reality the public had not entered into the spirit of the new musical drama. Wagner was appointed conductor at the Dresden Opera with a salary of 1,500 *Talers* per annum.

Already, in this first essay of Wagnerian art, we observe symbolism detach itself. Like Ulysses or the Wandering Jew, The Flying Dutchman is punished for having strayed too far from his native land: his adventurous spirit is his misfortune. He must return to his hearth, or rather, he must find a hearth, though it be in the regions of the ideal. All of Wagner's heroes thus seek the road of true happiness, the meaning of life, the way of salvation. And always, in his dramas, there is a savior, a redemption through love, pity, or sacrifice. But in *The Flying Dutchman* the problem of redemption is presented, as yet, only in an obscure manner.

From a purely musical point of view *The Flying Dutchman* marks Wagner's break with the ancient operatic forms; there are no more numbers detached one from the other, and joined together as well as circumstances permit, to make a veritable Arlequin's suit, devoid of continuity and succession. The musical drama becomes a symphony built up on one or more themes, which have a poetic or dramatic signification, the *Leitmotiv* ("leading motives"). In place of juxtaposing themes which are always new and different, the composer develops a small number of ideas closely linked together by the bonds of polyphony. "I well remember," says Wagner (in his *A Communication to My Friends*), "that before passing on to a realization, properly speaking, of *The Flying Dutchman,* I composed the text and the melody of Senta's ballad in the second act. Unconsciously I deposited in this number the thematic germs of the entire score. It was a concentrated image of the whole drama as it outlined itself in my thoughts. . . . When, finally, I passed on to composition, the thematic image which I had conceived opened out of its own accord, like a kind of network over the whole score. And without my actually willing it, so to speak, it was sufficient for me to develop, in a sense conformable to their nature, the various themes contained in the ballad, in order to have before me, in the form of well-characterized thematic constructions, the musical image of the principal lyric situations in the work."

The Flying Dutchman scored no more than a partial success. After the triumph of the first evening, the press showed itself unfavorable, and the public at the following performances maintained an attitude of reserve. *Rienzi* was redemanded, and *The Flying Dutchman* disappeared from the announcements.

Wagner then began to write his *Tannhäuser.* Tannhäuser was an actual historical personage, a thirteenth-century Minnesinger. An old folk song tells how he went to the mountain of Venus (Venusberg), where he was loved by the goddess for a space of a year. Seized with remorse, however, he invoked the aid of the Virgin Mary, left the mountain, and made a pilgrimage to Rome to obtain the pardon of the Holy Father.

"In his hand the Pope held a rod made of a dry branch. 'When this rod puts forth leaves,' said he, 'God will once more grant you grace.' The knight returned from the city, sad and with a grieving heart. . . . And he took his way to the mountain to remain there throughout all eternity. 'I return to Venus, my tender lady, to whom God himself sends me!' But on the third day the dry branch put forth green leaves. Then the Pope sent messengers throughout every land to discover the whereabouts of Tannhäuser. But Tannhäuser had re-entered the mountain to rejoin the lady of his heart. And for this reason, Pope Urban is condemned to eternal damnation."

Wagner combined this legend with the famous legend of the poetic tourney at the Wartburg. In a mediocre poem of the thirteenth century we find an account of this curious struggle, in which the vanquished forfeited his life by the hangman's hand. Wagner made his Tannhäuser the Minnesinger who is unfortunate in the Wartburg tourney, and invented the character of Elizabeth, who saves the knight.

He commenced work with febrile impatience, feeling that he was destined to produce a masterpiece; he was afraid of dying before he completed the opera. At last, in 1845, the score was finished. (He revised it in 1847 and 1861.)

There are some evident analogies between *The Flying Dutchman* and *Tannhäuser*. We have the same romantic stage-setting; and the idea of a redemption through love dominates the entire work. Venus represents not only love alone, but terrestrial happiness under all its forms, worldly success, and the activities which lead to that success. Yet true happiness is not of this kind: salvation lies in renunciation, of which Elizabeth gives Tannhäuser an example; for she loves Tannhäuser, is loved by him, and gives him up in order to save him.

In *Tannhäuser* the action is more picturesque and more dramatic than in *The Flying Dutchman*, the dramatic personages are more vitally alive and better characterized, the inner drama is developed in a far broader and more ample manner.

Lohengrin soon followed *Tannhäuser*. The book was written in 1845, and all the music composed in a year's time. The first performance did not take place until 1850, in Weimar, under the direction of Liszt.

According to Wagner, *Lohengrin* represents "the most tragic situation of our epoch," the irremediable misunderstanding which separates the souls of the chosen from the obscure throng toward which they are propelled by the impulse of an irresistible affection. Lohengrin is Wagner himself, who feels that he is isolated and powerless in the midst of contemporary society, unintelligent and inimical. Wagner suffered from this isolation; he demanded that he be not discussed, he wished to be loved without having to declare whence he came, what he wished to do, his name and his titles. To trust and to believe, without seeking to know, such is the secret of happiness for others and for oneself. But Wagner is not beloved and he returns to his solitude. Elsa is "the spirit of the people." She is naïve, spontaneous, all love. Yet, just as Lohengrin, the "initiate," turns to love, Elsa, who "loves," turns to science, and her fatal and inevitable error is her ruin. It may be that the unhappiness of these two beings is due to the fact that Lohengrin is a sage, a proud rather than a simple spirit, a creature of instinct, like Siegfried and Parsifal. Only the inconscient are happy, and the kingdom of the skies is the inheritance of the humble.

It was at the time that he wrote *Lohengrin* that Wagner, perhaps, most bitterly felt his moral isolation. He had to suffer at the same time from the injustice of the critics, who treated him as a charlatan; the hostility of the connoisseurs, furious enemies of all that was new; the ill will of the Baron von Lüttichau, intendant of the royal theater, whose sole object was to thwart all his attempts at reform at the Dresden opera; and finally, the implacable jealousy of Meyerbeer, who barred the road to Berlin against him, and prevented his works from being performed there. Wagner's pessimism rose to great heights of excitement: he accused society as a whole, he adopted the revolutionary opinions which, as a consequence of the movement of 1848, had spread through France and throughout Germany. He joined the Socialist party. He took part in a revolt and, in order to escape a judicial sentence, was obliged to flee to Switzerland, where he took refuge in Zürich.

There he abandoned politics and once more took up his art. His friends and admirers aided him to subsist. He communed with himself and began the publication of his most important theoretic writings. At this time (1848-1854), under the double influence of Feuerbach's philosophy and events at Dresden, Wagner turned atheist and became an anti-Christian. He adjudged the world evil, yet firmly hoped that the revolution would soon inaugurate a new era of universal felicity for mankind.

At the same time Wagner formulated his ideas regarding art in a manner well-nigh definitive. In *Das Kunstwerk der Zukunft* (1849), and his *Oper und Drama* (1851), he developed his conception of the "popular" or "communistic" drama, which cannot be realized without the collaboration of the people. Thus, in ancient Greece, in the days of Æschylus and Sophocles, the poet was no more than the carrier of the word of the people, the genius of the race; the tragedies were performed before the people as a whole, and the people supplied the actors. All the arts, poetry, music, the dance, architecture, co-operated in a sort of religious ceremony in which beauty was made manifest to all under sensible, material, and living forms. Afterwards, to their disadvantage, the arts were disassociated. The question, for the modern artist, is not that of adapting poetry to music or music to poetry; each art must follow her own laws; yet unity is obtained when poetry and music co-operate to the same end: to express *the human action*.

Underlying the singer's melody, the orchestra should not, as in the operas, voice a mere accompaniment, one as foreign to the melody as the melody is to the drama. The orchestra should no longer be "a gigantic guitar." It must express what song does not say, it must elucidate: (1) Gesture. (2) The psychic state of the personage whose song merely reveals to us one of its isolated elements. (3) The past and the future in their relation to the present (presentiments and recollections), and here it is that the *leitmotiv* plays a large part. The orchestra should resemble the chorus in the ancient Greek tragedy, ever present and commenting on each event; it should assure the continuity, the interconnection of the parts of the work.

No sooner had Wagner formulated his ideas with regard to the musical drama, than he undertook to give them a grandiose application in a colossal work, *The Nibelungen Ring*, a vast trilogy, preceded by a Prologue, whose four parts, *Das Rheingold* ("Rhinegold"), *Die Walküre* (The Valkyrie), *Siegfried*, and *Götterdämmerung* (The Twilight of the Gods), were meant always to be represented on four successive evenings. The Trilogy comprises a double drama: the death of the gods and the deliverance of humanity. The elements of the work were borrowed from old Germanic and Scandinavian legends.

This tremendous poem comprises a very complex philosophy. In it Wagner in turn presents himself as a *socialist,* as when he curses gold and its fateful power, and predicts the regeneration of humanity through love; as an *anarchist,* when he condemns law and the conventions, justice founded on injustice, and makes Siegfried, the hero of freedom, a foil for Wotan, the god of contracts; as a *pagan,* when he depicts this same Siegfried as "the most perfect of men," although he only follows his instincts, is ignorant of morals, and lives without either god or law; as a *Christian,* when he admits that Brünnhilde and Siegfried may atone for the sins of Wotan through their own merit, and thus assure the redemption of mankind; as a *pessimist,* because, according to Wotan, wisdom consists in not wishing to be; and finally, as an *optimist,* since the reign of love may render life worth living.

This diversity of ideas and sentiments, often antagonistic, which has inspired the Trilogy, may be summed up in an antinomy, a contradiction of law, present in Wagner's own nature. On the one hand, his ardent temperament, his passionate desire to live and be happy, tended to make him an optimist and a pagan. On the other, reflection turned him to pessimism, and he consoled himself with the negation of "the wish to live," and the affirmation of an ideal, a "salvation" more or less Christian in character. We should neither be astonished nor irritated by the contradictions of a philosophy essentially in a formative state, and which does not pretend to constitute a fixed system. It is the very richness and diversity of a work such as the Trilogy which makes its grandeur: it reveals to us the whole of man. When we estimate the distance traversed by Wagner in passing from *Tannhäuser* to the *Ring,* from the musical point of view, it is evident that after the progress already so clearly indicated by *Lohengrin,* Wagner had by now come into full possession of the means of expression he needed in order to realize his artistic thought. Henceforward we find no trace in his works of the methods of operatic procedure; his style is essentially personal. There are no more airs or duos, or anything resembling them; the scenes are linked without lack of continuity; music's only task is to comment the drama. The vocal phrase departs further and further from the conventional formulas of Italianism; the harmony grows richer and more complex; the polyphonic development of the leading motive lends the entirety of one work, or even of an entire cycle like the Trilogy, the appearance of a gigantic symphony. Wagner no longer need modify his art in any way; it is sufficient for him to apply it to different ends in order to produce a variety of incomparable masterpieces.

In 1854 Wagner had completed *The Rhinegold* and the greater part of *The Valkyrie,* and had written half of *Siegfried* as well. Yet the artistic production of these works did not suffice him. He craved contact with the public, the practical realization of his art dreams, and suffered from his inaction in exile. His dramas were produced without him, far away from him, in Germany. He was parted from his dearest friends. And he entertained no hope of being able to re-enter his own land, for reaction was triumphant in France and in Germany.

On January 15, 1854, he wrote Liszt: "Not one of these past years has gone by without, once at least, my having come face to face with the idea of the extreme solution, without my having thought of putting an end to my life. My entire existence has been destroyed and ruined. Oh, my friend! at bottom art for me is no more than an expedient which enables me to forget my distress, nothing more."

It was during that very summer of 1854 that one of Wagner's friends gave him *The World as Will and Idea,* by Schopenhauer.

Wagner immediately adopted the doctrines of the great pessimist, so entirely in tune with his own feelings, and declared that Schopenhauer's thought had been subconsciously present in his own mind before he, Wagner, had actually realized it; and that only now did he understand the profound meaning of his preceding works.

He believed that in the *Nibelungen Ring* he had written a revolutionary and optimistic cycle; in reality, the Trilogy, despite himself, conveyed the absolutely pessimistic conclusion that the world is irremediably evil, and that nothingness is worth more than life.

At the same time a crisis of feeling completed the upset of Wagner's soul. For a long period serious dissension had reigned between his wife Minna and himself. Minna regarded Wagner as a visionary egoist, who ruined his own life and stupidly sacrificed the happiness of a devoted helpmeet to his unrealizable political and artistic dreams. After numerous disputes, Wagner broke with her in 1851. In 1852, in Zürich, he made the acquaintance of a certain Wesendonk and his wife, who soon became his most loyal and devoted friends. In 1857 he accepted their hospitality in the small cottage they offered him near their own villa, "Green Hill." An increasingly tender intimacy developed between Wagner and Mathilde Wesendonk; and they soon realized that a redoubtably passionate love drew them to one another. Yet they hesitated to do aught which might be base and cowardly. They decided to separate. Wagner left for Venice, after having definitely broken with Minna, who sadly rejoined her family in Saxony. Of this swift emotional tragedy one legacy is left us—*Tristan und Isolde.*

In 1854 Wagner already had written Liszt: "Out of compassion for the most beautiful dream of my life, for love of young Siegfried, I must complete my *Nibelungen*. Seeing, however, that throughout my existence I have never tasted the joy of love in its perfection, I wish, with the fairest of all dreams, to raise a monument, compose a drama in the course of which this wish for love will be gratified to entire satiety. I have in mind the plan for a *Tristan and Isolde,* a work absolutely simple, yet brimming over with the most intense vitality; and I should like to wrap myself around with the folds of the sable banner which floats above its final scene and die." In 1857 Wagner abandoned the Trilogy and commenced the score of *Tristan* (1857-1859), partly for practical reasons, since he wished to compose a drama of smaller dimensions, which could easily be staged in Germany, but above all in order to give his heart an opportunity of pouring out all the amorous distress and despair which filled it.

The fundamental idea of *Tristan* is that passion has imprescriptible rights, superior to all law and to the judgment of man, provided it be absolute, doomed, and willing to accept death as its sole refuge. *Tristan* among all Wagner's works is the most passionate and disconsolate. Here we have the greatest love to which the world has given birth, and also the most frightful state of being which may be assigned to mortals. This life is accursed. One is compelled to wish for nothingness, for "night," the blindness of will. Those who are truly happy are Tristan and Isolde, reunited in death. Unfortunate is King Mark, who remains among the living!

The music of *Tristan* may be classed with that which is not judged, not criticized; it takes entire possession of the listener, penetrates to the very depth of his soul, possesses him and leaves him exhausted. "The world is poor indeed," says Nietzsche, "for him who has never been ill enough to savor this hellish voluptuousness."

Tristan completed, Wagner finally wished to re-establish his contact with the public; he wished to do battle with the artists, the critics, the crowd, to be in the vanguard of the strife. He left for Paris, where he managed to have his *Tannhäuser* accepted for performance at the Opéra; yet the personal intervention of the Emperor Napoleon III was necessary to dominate the ill will which opposed him. The score, thrice performed (March 13, 18, and 23, 1861), failed beneath the hisses of an odious cabal. The members of the Jockey Club, deprived of their ballet; Wagner's German rivals, headed by Meyerbeer; and, finally, the majority of the newspaper men, sold out to these two powerful parties—managed to make further performances an impossibility.

Now Wagner, taking advantage of an amnesty, could finally return to Germany. He then attempted, though in vain, to have the leading German opera houses accept his *Tristan;* all the managers refused it. He undertook tours in order to spread a knowledge of his works in Germany, Austria, and Russia. But soon he hardly knew where and how to act in their behalf, so thoroughly was he persuaded that all his effort was lost, that he could count on neither moral nor material success.

It was at this moment that King Ludwig of Bavaria summoned him, and offered him all the resources necessary to the final realization of his artistic dream. "So great is my joy," wrote Wagner, "that it has crushed me!" Model performances of *Tannhäuser* and *The Flying Dutchman* were given in Munich; then came *Tristan's* turn (1865), and it was mounted under exceptional circumstances. Unfortunately, court intrigues rendered Wagner's relations to Ludwig increasingly difficult. He was finally obliged to leave Bavaria, and retired to Switzerland.

There Wagner passed some of his happiest years (1866-1872), those which he spent at Triebschen, near Lucerne, in a little mansion on the bank of the lake, where Cosima, the daughter of Liszt and the wife of the conductor Hans von Bülow, soon joined him, carried away by an irresistible passion. After having obtained her divorce, she was to marry Wagner in 1870, and to present him with a son, Siegfried, in honor of whose birth he composed the *Siegfried Idyll*. "I would sell all the rest of my affiliations with humanity for a song," Nietzsche said somewhat later, when he had become Wagner's enemy, "yet for nothing in the world would I efface from my life those beautiful days at Triebschen, days made up of confidence, serenity, sublime hazards, profound moments." It was there, in the calm and the plenitude of his happiness, that Wagner finished his *Meistersinger,* and well-nigh completed the Trilogy (taken up again in 1865 and terminated in 1874).

The initial idea of *Die Meistersinger* harked back to 1845, a period when Wagner had fallen out with the Dresden critics. He thought of staging the eternal struggle of genius against pedantry and routine. The figure of Hans Sachs, the shoemaker celebrated by Goethe, had been popularized by a drama of Deinhardstein (1827) and by a comic opera of Lortzing (1840). Wagner also was acquainted with Wagenseil's old *Nuremberg Chronicle,* and *The Cooper of Nuremberg,* by Hoffmann. Yet he had soon abandoned his project, and did not resume it until 1861, after his return from exile, while the work was not definitely taken up until 1867.

Die Meistersinger offers a striking contrast to *Tristan.* In the former we have an overflowing of life and joy. A host of personages mingle their various passions in a crowded action. Comic episodes alternate with the most serious or poetic scenes: we find once more, transformed and rendered unrecognizable, the choruses and ensembles of the older opera. Lichtenberger with reason regards the *Meistersinger* as a species of "interlude" in Wagner's accomplishment. Yet, underneath the outward semblance of a merry and mocking satire on the artistic morals of Germany, is ever hidden the same philosophy, the same leading thoughts, the same dominating sentiments.

Walter von Stolzing personifies the rights of genius as opposed to the routine of the pedants. He is of noble blood; he has dwelt far from cities in his lonely manor-house. In the winter he reads the poetry of Walter von der Vogelweide. In summer he wanders through the forest, and it is thus that he has become a poet himself, without ever having learned the rules of his art.

The *"Meistersinger"* [Mastersingers] are the upholders of tradition; their zeal is estimable, yet their talents are mediocre. They are good craftsmen with a limited intellectual horizon, and of a suspicious trend of character. Sixtus Beckmesser represents all the defects of the corporation carried to excess: he is stupid, jealous, invidious, and even dishonest, and saves himself from contempt only by means of ridicule. Yet Beckmesser is an exception. In general the Mastersingers are good fellows, a trifle vain, but generous, like Pogner.

The true sage of the drama is Hans Sachs, "the last representative," says Wagner, "of the creative and artistic spirit of the people." He wishes to reconcile the rights of genius with the rules of art, the liberty of inspiration with the discipline of tradition. He desires that art be no longer withheld from the people, that the people be its judge, and herein he is opposed to the masters who despise the vulgar.

Aside from the comedy of manners, the *Meistersinger* includes a drama of passion which plays in the inmost heart of Hans Sachs, and, though hardly touched upon in the poem, is especially stressed in the music. Hans Sachs loves Eva and sacrifices himself so that she may marry Walter. "My child," Hans Sachs tells Eva, "I know the sad tale of *Tristan and Isolde*. Hans Sachs is wise and does not crave the sorry happiness of King Mark." He is well aware that true happiness does not exist, that here below all is illusion. "Madness, madness! All is but madness! The chronicles of the cities, the histories of the peoples, is replete with every sort of madness. The peaceful citizens of Nuremberg themselves a short time ago were seized with an attack of madness. Why? Because an evil gnome had passed above the old city, because a glowworm sought its mate in vain, because the elder-trees were in blossom, because it was Saint John's Eve. . . ." Yet Hans Sachs is not a genuine pessimist. He believes in the virtue of sacrifice; life has a meaning for him. We may already anticipate Wagner's return to the idealistic optimism which manifests itself in *Parsifal*.

This last evolution of Wagner's thought is betrayed first of all in his writings: *Die Kunst und die Revolution* (1864); *Deutsche Kunst und Deutsche Politik* (1865); *Beethoven* (1870); and *Kunst und Religion* (1880). His doctrine of nature and of life has completed itself; his pessimism now is no more than its initial moment. The wish to live no longer seems evil to him, if it does not remain egoistic; the universe should and can be regenerated. Man's fall is due to the capitalistic and militaristic state, to a church overjealous of its temporal power, to moral utilitarianism, to materialistic science, to industrialized art. His fall is due also to race intermixture. The Germans have remained the least contaminated; from them will proceed regeneration and redemption.* And art shall lead the peoples into the paths of salvation. Hitherto art has lowered herself to copy vulgar reality, and amuse a surfeited and corrupted public. Her function is a nobler one. The modern artist is called upon to take up the heritage of the priest: "an art-work is the living representation of religion."

Yet in this case the character of a theatrical representation, however, would have to be modified profoundly. As early as 1850 Wagner had entertained the idea of a playhouse especially constructed in the country, whose performances would serve no industrial end. In the Preface to his poem of the *Ring* (1862) he appealed to the public for aid to realize his project. In 1871, after the German victory over France, Wagner thought the nation ripe for the effort he expected her to make. He inaugurated a public subscription, and at the end of five years the model stage was built in Bayreuth. Wagner did not wish the enterprise to pay anyone a profit. The performances were to be given by the public for its own satisfaction at its own expense. In 1873 and 1874, when the continuance of the work was placed in jeopardy, Wagner was offered notable sums to transplant his stage to Baden, London, and Chicago. He refused. It was Ludwig II of Bavaria who made it possible for Wagner to complete his Festival Playhouse, by advancing the necessary sums in 1874 and 1876, the money being advanced on the royalties accruing to him from the Munich performances of his dramas.† In 1882 Wagner was obliged to give up his first idea: he turned Bayreuth into a paying opera house, yet only on condition that the monetary returns would be reserved to increase the reserve fund of the undertaking, and would never be diverted to other uses.

It was in this Bayreuth house, within this special and impressive frame, on a stage which concealed an invisible orchestra, before an auditorium plunged in darkness, in the presence of a public impenetrated with a kind of religious fervor, that in 1882 the first perform-

---

* The reasons why the Nazis have made Wagner their idol are obvious.—E. S.
† The Bayreuth Theater was formally opened with the first performance of the entire *Ring*, in August, 1876.—E. S.

ance of *Parsifal* took place. Wagner was to die soon after, in Venice, on February 13, 1883.

Wagner was acquainted with the Parsifal legend at the time he wrote his *Lohengrin*: Lohengrin was the son of Parsifal. And Wagner had dreamed, before writing *Parsifal,* of a *Jesus of Nazareth;* and then of a Buddhist drama, *The Victors* (1856). It was in the spring of 1867, on Good Friday, that he heard "that sigh of profoundest pity which of old had resounded from the Cross at Golgotha, and which, on this occasion escaped from his own breast." He then wrote the lines in which Gurnemanz explains to Parsifal the Good Friday magic spell. It was the first sketch of the new drama. This sketch was rounded out in 1865, the poem was completed in 1877, and the music in 1882.

Three figures dominate the entire action: that of Kundry, the sacrilegious woman who had insulted the sufferings of the Crucified with impious laughter; that of Amfortas, the king of the Grail, captivated by Kundry's charms, who expiates his sin in anguish; and finally, that of Parsifal, the "innocent with the pure heart," destined to "save" Amfortas, when he has come to understand the mystery of human suffering, the illusion of desire, and the vanity of sin.

Thus, in his old age, Wagner was able to reconcile the contradictory tendencies of his own nature in the mystic affirmation of a salvation through renunciation, and an optimistic belief in a supernatural felicity, closely akin to the Christian ideal.

Wagner's personality was, perhaps, the most powerful and richest expression of the German genius of the nineteenth century. It comprises at the same time the Teutonic romantic aspiration, its mystic morality, its democratic, socialistic, and nationalistic dream, its pantheism and spirit of synthesis. This art, heavy, overweighted, less pure than classic art, yet profoundly moving, infinitely subtle, brims over with humanity beneath its complicated legendary and symbolic apparatus. It renewed and amplified the technical resources of the language of music, and offered musicians of the future a wealth of discoveries. "It is," says Nietzsche, "something German in the best and in the worst sense of the word, something complex, shapeless, inexhaustible, in the German fashion. It has a certain strength essentially German, an invading plenitude of the soul which does not shrink from hiding beneath the refinements of decadence; which, perhaps, otherwise, does not feel wholly at ease; a faithful and authentic image of the German soul, at once young and very old, at the same time more than matured, yet with too rich a future. This type of music is the most exact expression of what the Germans think: they belong to the day before yesterday and the day after to-morrow, they have not yet attained to the present day." If we make allowance for the exaggeration of this criticism, the judgment of this great enemy of Wagner nevertheless presents some of the most penetrant views which have ever been offered with regard to his works.

Johannes Brahms

Abridged from "Men of Music"

By Wallace Brockway and Herbert Weinstock *

LESS than half a century after the death of Johannes Brahms, the phrase "the three B's"—Bach, Beethoven, and Brahms—has such wide currency that it no longer evokes surprise or protest. When Hans von Bülow first sprang the phrase, he drew a double wrath upon himself: there were those who thought that he was taking a belated revenge on Wagner for a personal injury, and there were those who thought that he was violating the loftiest canons of his profession (as well as ordinary common sense) by raising a parvenu to the supreme fellowship of the greatest masters. A third party dryly concluded that he was merely giving a friend a hand up. Few—and least of all, Brahms himself—took the bracketing seriously. Today the only comment it causes is, among dissenters, a pursing of the lips or a shrug of the shoulders, but though they may consider it fantastic, they cannot laugh it off. For Brahms's reputation has grown vast, and his cohorts have waxed numerous and vociferous. In point of fact, Bülow's words contain, if interpreted sanely, an indisputable truth: that is, if they are taken to mean that Brahms's conscious artistic genealogy was predominantly classical, no one can refute them. In his persistent and masterly use of counterpoint, Brahms was among Bach's fairest children; in his

---

* In a sense, this is one of the most controversial articles in this volume. The authors are distinctly of their own mind about Brahms, and—though I certainly do not agree—I say more power to them! The reader may compare their view with that of Olin Downes (pp. 180-187). The difference shows how little we may expect universal agreement among various writers on music.—E. S.

conception of the larger musical forms he stemmed from, and added little to, Beethoven. These are facts, and not in the realm of controversy. But only the most perfervid Brahmsian can accept without question the other implication of "the three B's": that Brahms is one of the three greatest composers who ever lived.

One of the best antidotes to an overestimate of Brahms that can end only by doing him a grave disservice is to read what he had to say about himself. "I know very well," he remarked in his old age, "the place I shall one day have in musical history: the place that Cherubini once had, and has today." Brahms's modesty was excessive. He declared that he and his contemporaries made a living out of composing only because the public had forgotten so much of the music of the past. Once, after playing Bach's Violin Sonata in C major with Joachim, he threw to the floor his own sonata in the same key, exclaiming, "After that, how could anyone play such stuff as this?" Possibly few great composers have not had these moments of feeling small beside Bach, but Brahms also had a perhaps exaggerated reverence for masters whose genius did not, at best, exceed his own. Witness his almost servile remark about Mendelssohn: "I'd give all my compositions if I could have written such a piece as the *Hebrides* Overture!" He thought of himself as a good composer whose duty it was to work as hard as possible on what ideas came to him, and to publish only what dissatisfied him least. He was pre-eminently an artisan, with an almost medieval feeling for his craft, and quite content to let the products of his workshop speak for themselves. Such a man with such stern ideals could only be embarrassed by Bülow's ballyhoo. Everything that was deepest in his character revolted against claiming too fair a kingdom for himself or aiming at too easy a success.

Although born [1833] in the slums of a vast commercial city, Brahms was a peasant of the peasants, and so he remained all his life. This does much to explain the temperance of his ambitions, the obstinacy of his ideals, and the rather static quality of his genius. Even when his fame made him the intimate of royalty, he never by a single action showed that he had "gone up in the world." He remained true to his own past and his family's. His father had come to Hamburg from the barren and sparsely populated marshlands of the Elbe estuary; his mother was a proletarian of the same great city. Johann Jakob Brahms, a stupid musical Jack-of-all-trades who eventually attained the eminence of first double-bass at the municipal theater, at the age of twenty-four married Johanna Nissen, a woman of some superiority, but seventeen years his senior, ugly, crippled, of irascible and dominating temper. This inevitably mismated'pair had three children, of whom the composer was the second. Separation was the foreordained end of such a marriage, but Brahms, who was deeply devoted to his mother, managed to stave it off until 1864, when the jealousy of the seventy-five-year-old woman drove her husband from the house.

We do not know whether it was Johann Jakob's undoubted passion for music, or merely a desire to add to the family income, that made him decide upon music as a career for Johannes. It does not seem that he had any grandiose plans for the boy: he envisioned him, almost certainly, as walking approximately in his own footsteps. He undertook his son's musical education himself, soon exhausting his own limited knowledge. As the Brahmses could not afford a piano, at the age of eight Johannes was sent to a modest little pedagogue to learn that useful instrument. He was so apt that within a year or so he was much in demand in what his cautious biographers gloss over as "humble places of entertainment" or "sailors' taverns." These were brothels, and according to Brahms himself, he was the darling of the prostitutes, who thought it fun to try to arouse his immature emotions. It is impossible to overestimate the influence of these odd experiences on Brahms's sexual make-up: he depended all his life on prostitutes for physical release, and withdrew from a relationship with a decent woman as soon as an overt amorous element showed itself. The "women in Brahms's life" are anonymous.

Little Johannes was not exclusively a redlight-district virtuoso. He attended the local schools, such as they were, and continued his musical studies. In 1843, his teacher pled with Eduard Marxsen, Hamburg's leading music master, to take the boy. Marxsen consented reluctantly to give him an occasional lesson, and Brahms made his public debut at a concert arranged to defray the costs of this more expensive instruction. He played, besides a few solos, the piano part in chamber works by Mozart and Beethoven. Marxsen, finding him a willing slave to music, gradually undertook not only to perfect his piano technique, but to teach him composition. Shortly, Brahms was grinding out an interminable series of potboilers—mostly arrangements of popular tunes of the day. His ambition was to become a fine composer, but before he succeeded in writing anything he cared to publish under his own name he had published 151 ephemera under the pseudonym of G. W. Marks, as well as a few he considered somewhat better, attributing these latter to the cacophonously named Karl Würth. Music lessons and compositions, combined with schoolwork and night jobs, wore him out. He was rescued by a family friend who treated him to two summers in the country, but even then he worked, making the hundred-and-twenty-mile round trip every week.to take his lesson, and conducting a rural chorus. Rest and fresh air did wonders, and when he returned to Hamburg in the fall of 1848, he was glowing with that rugged good health that scarcely varied for half a century.

On September 21, Johannes Brahms gave his first public recital, showing the classical rectitude of his taste by venturing a Bach fugue— an unheard-of feat of daring in those days. At another recital the following April, he gave Hamburg its first taste of Brahms the composer, with a fantasy that has not survived. On the whole, these first attempts at a serious career were disappointing, and he had to resume his hack labors. But these could not hold him long, for he had been fired by two experiences: he had heard the already famous Joachim, only two years his senior, play Beethoven's Violin Concerto, and had met the brilliant Hungarian-Jewish violinist, Eduard Reményi. Joachim stirred him more deeply than he realized at the time. Reményi, with his extravagant collection of travelers' tales, captivated him with a vision of that great world Brahms in later years came, if not to detest, at least to disregard. He fretted more than ever under a hateful routine, but found precisely the solace his artist's soul needed in composing the two piano sonatas, scherzo, and songs that now constitute his first four opus numbers.

Just about the time of Brahms's twentieth birthday, Reményi again appeared on the scene with a tempting offer to take him as accompanist on a vagabond concert tour. At Hanover, they fell in with Joachim, who enraptured Brahms by expressing an understanding admiration for his compositions. After arranging a court concert for Reményi and Brahms, Joachim, who at that time was still warmly espousing the cause of the *Zukunftsmusiker,* sent them off to Weimar with a generous letter. Although Liszt was lavish with his praise, Brahms was so disgusted by the trumpery court politics of the Altenburg that he disdained to give its master his meed of flattery. This was fatal to any real *rapprochement* between them, particularly as Brahms found little to admire in the "music of the future." He decided to move on, leaving Reményi swooning under the spell of Kundry Liszt. He did not miss the young Hungarian: musically, Reményi gave Brahms little that he could use except a smattering knowledge of gypsy folk tunes.

On September 30, 1853, Robert Schumann wrote in his diary, "Brahms to see me (a genius)." For after the disheartening visit to Liszt, Joachim had persuaded his friend to go to Düsseldorf. The Schumanns received the handsome young fellow with open arms. As a bosom friend of Joachim's, he was welcome, and when he played his music for them, they treated him at once as an equal. Brahms, still vexed by the artificial ways of the Altenburg, gave his heart immediately to his new friends, who (he could not but remind himself) were, for all their simplicity and forthrightness, two of Europe's leading musicians. Clara was to become his friend for life. Robert, with but three years before him, and those clouded, at once translated enthusiasm into action. He successfully urged a publisher to issue some of Brahms's early compositions, but almost more effective in establishing his protégé's name was the farewell article he wrote for the *Neue Zeitschrift für Musik*. Called "New Paths," this high-flown panegyric hailed Brahms as "vouchsafed to give the highest and most ideal expression to the tendencies of the times, one who would not show us his mastery in a gradual development, but like Minerva spring fullarmed from the head of Zeus." The article aroused wide interest in the newcomer, but there were plenty, particularly among the adherents of the Neo-Germans, who felt that the Elijah of romanticism was casting his mantle over the wrong man. Worse, they whispered that this violently enthusiastic manifesto was proof of the rumors that Schumann was losing his mind. The fact was that he had written "New Paths" in one of those dazzlingly lucid intervals that preceded his collapse: less than six months after his meeting with Brahms, he was incarcerated in a madhouse. During the period of Schumann's insanity, Brahms visited him as often as he could, and was to the unhappy wife and mother a tower of strength.

What was the music that had stirred the weary Schumann to his swan song? Appropriately enough, it was as romantic music as Brahms ever composed. It consisted of three piano sonatas, a scherzo, and some songs, besides certain compositions that Brahms, tempering Schumann's enthusiasm, refused to publish because they did not come up to his own standards. The Scherzo—the first piece he played for both Liszt and Schumann—is a bright youthful display, rather empty, rather dazzling, and altogether as near to pure virtuoso music as any he ever contrived. The C major Sonata is not entirely successful: Brahms here uses the sonata form awkwardly, academically rather than spontaneously, and much of the result is so unpianistic as to seem an extended sketch for an orchestral work. Yet it is vigorous, confident, always provocative in thematic material, manfully reverent in its obvious Beethoven worship. In short, possibly the most satisfactory Opus 1 ever composed. The F-sharp minor Sonata is a cold and rather dour work that pianists rightly consider thankless. The F minor Sonata— the last Brahms ever wrote for the piano—is important. Though far too long, and in a medley of styles, it yet contains many consecutive pages of beautiful music. There are still Beethoven echoes, especially in the development of the first movement, but here already are Brahms's widely spaced harmonies, broken chords, and perilous modulations, as well as the trick of carrying a melody on the inner notes of chords. The scherzo reads like a Brahms rewriting of parts of the *Carnaval,* but the andante is the kind of music fully matured Brahms was to turn into sheer magic.

The total effect of these early piano works suggests a composer of genius who has not yet found his métier. The extravagance of the romantic material in them tends to obscure what on analysis appears equally obvious—that Brahms was faithfully, if not always happily, devoted to the sonata form as Beethoven left it. Those who can bear to study a work like the C major or F minor Sonata as a laboratory specimen can uncover the whole catalogue of Brahms's artistic virtues and vices. Their proportion may vary, but the dichotomy remains. It is less noticeable in the four ballades composed little later than the pieces that inspired Schumann's eulogy: Brahms never carried out his intentions more successfully than in the archaic and severely pared *Edward Ballade,* based on an old Scots poem. All the ballades hint that Brahms's genius as a composer for the piano would find its happiest outlet when freed from the conventions of the sonata.

It is probable that the four ballades were the last of Brahms's music that Schumann ever heard. Certain it is that Brahms played them to the dying master during one of his sane interludes in the madhouse. About the same time, Brahms delighted Schumann with a set of "Short Variations on a Theme by Him. Dedicated to Her." This not very inspired composition is interesting for two reasons: it is a trial flight in a form that Brahms was to infuse with new meaning, and it is dedicated to Clara. During the last two years of Schumann's life, Brahms had become warmly devoted to her, so warmly, indeed, that there was gossip about them. There were some who went so far as to whisper that he was the father of Clara's last child, and now, almost half a century after their deaths, people are still guessing and theorizing about the status of their relationship. In the absence of any documents except their increasingly ardent letters, it is possible to belong to one of two camps. One holds that it was a high-minded, purely platonic friendship based on a common grief and common sympathies and interests. The other, referring to them as Johannes and Clara (the analogue of Richard and Cosima), takes a Freudian point of view.

Robert Haven Schauffler, without committing himself to what actually took place between them, summed up the case for the prosecution. It is, briefly, that Brahms (clearly the victim of a mother fixation) chose Clara, fourteen years his senior, as a mother surrogate. It is significant, perhaps, that he occasionally addressed her as *"meine liebe Frau Mama."* Grief and mutual admiration brought them together under highly emotional circumstances, and it may be that Brahms persuaded the distraught woman to become his mistress. This school of thought makes much of the fact that Brahms and Clara, less than a year after Schumann was incarcerated, went on a five-day pleasure trip with only her maid to chaperon them. This sounds incriminating, but certain physiological and psychological peculiarities in Brahms's development as a functioning male suggest that, whatever their impulses may have been, they could not have been lovers at this time. In the first place, Brahms's voice did not change until 1857, at which time also his beard began to grow. Secondly (and Mr. Schauffler is authority for this astute conjecture), it seems likely that Brahms's mother fixation and infantile erotic experiences in brothels made him incapable of consummating a physical relationship with a decent woman. His whole life bears out this contention.

At first, Clara's friendship for Brahms asserted itself in a helpful and practical way. Then, as always, she had more pupils than she could handle, and she turned several of them over to Brahms. Some of them happened to be well-born ladies from Detmold, and they, with the help of a good word from Clara (who had fine connections everywhere), wangled a semiofficial appointment for him at this sleepy little town, where the Prince of Lippe held his court. There, from 1857 to 1859, Brahms spent a portion of each year, giving lessons to the Prince's sister, conducting a chorus of doting *Fräulein,* and presiding over the court orchestra. Here was an ideal place for thinking things out. The decisions Brahms came to musically he expressed only in music, and they are not easy to express in words. Briefly, he went to Detmold saturated with the type of romanticism summed up in Schumann, and, after much vigorous self-criticism and experimentation, emerged as a Brahmsian, which is the only accurate description of a man who is variously called a neoclassicist, an eclectic, or a classical romanticist, depending on what measuring stick is used. Certainly, those who think exclusively of the contour and emotional atmosphere of the overwhelming majority of his themes are justified in calling him a romanticist; those who focus their attention on the way he handles his musical material are equally justified in calling him a classicist. Between them they have a complete judgment of one who, starting with classical sympathies, ran the gauntlet of romanticism, and came out with an eclectic style that eventually became as idiosyncratic as Chopin's.

To the Detmold period belong Brahms's first three compositions for orchestra. Two of these—extended serenades or *divertimenti*—are of little more than historical interest. Both are excessively long and excessively dull, though the second of them, in A major, is suave enough in its instrumentation, chiefly because Brahms reorchestrated it many years later. Their discursiveness and blurred outlines suggest that he was wise in never again venturing to use the classical-suite form. Yet, composing them was of incalculable value in putting him at ease among the instruments of the orchestra. The scoring of the D minor Piano Concerto, effected at about the same time, is still not of the happiest, but clearly shows not only the solid results of working on the serenades, but also the fruits of directing his own band.

On January 22, 1859, Brahms played the D minor Concerto in Hanover. It was a failure. Five days later he played it at a Gewandhaus concert in Leipzig. It was roundly hissed, and he himself, as a pianist, with it—a fact that was instrumental in causing him to abandon a possible virtuoso career. Hamburg was kind to the concerto, but only the first time, for when it was repeated there a year later, it was received with icy silence. While Brahms was inclined to view all this merely as a temporary setback, enough rancor simmered in his mind to lead him to the only foolhardy act recorded of him. The *Neue Zeitschrift für Musik,* then an organ of the Neo-Germans, published an article stating that almost every good composer in Germany belonged to the Liszt camp. The idea was certainly a silly one, if for no other reason than that it made a Hungarian cosmopolitan the arbiter of German music. Brahms and Joachim fell into a rage and, with two less-known musicians, signed a manifesto attacking the article. Then they began collecting other signatures, but it was accidentally published without these. The reverberations were far-reaching, particularly as Wagner, too, had been tacitly aspersed in the manifesto. Brahms was unwittingly jock-eyed into being a paladin of the anti-Wagnerians, and worse, the in-censed Wagner was moved to discharge the vials of his wrath on the imprudent Brahms. Without wishing to, he had created overnight a powerful bloc of vituperative enemies who for years delayed the full appreciation of his music.

In 1860, Brahms gave up his connection with Detmold, and for three years made his headquarters in or near Hamburg. Here he organ-ized a women's choir, for whom he drew up a quaintly medieval char-ter and wrote much of his smaller choral work. Often he took his ladies into the country, and practiced out of doors; as he was a stubby little man, he often chose the branch of a tree as his podium. Anyone who glances at a chronological list of Brahms's compositions will notice that this period is one of his least productive, but its barrenness is more apparent than real. He was either actually at work on several major compositions or thinking them out. One of them—*Ein deutsches Requiem,* his most pretentious choral work—was not completed until 1866; the First Symphony took more than twice that long. The spate of song continued unabated, and he also wrote a considerable amount of chamber music.

On this thirtieth birthday, when the decrepit Vienna Singakade-mie invited him to become its director, he accepted with joy this oppor-tunity to settle permanently in the city that had seemed so pleasant to him on his single visit. Although within a year he gave up the Sing-akademie post as a bad job, Vienna remained his headquarters for the rest of his life.

The first major work completed by Brahms after settling in Vienna had a curious history. In 1862, he had written it as a string quintet, but had been much dissatisfied when the Joachim Quartet and an extra 'cellist played it over for him. He then revised it as a sonata for two pianos, and was even more dissatisfied. Late in 1864, he again rescored it, this time for piano, two violins, viola, and 'cello, and so, after these almost unexampled labor pains, the famous F minor Piano Quintet came into the world. It is possibly the best of a large group of baffling pieces that some have not hesitated to call the crown of Brahms's achievement. In speaking of his chamber music, Edwin Evans, the English musicologist, says that in it "Homer never nods," but omits the pertinent fact that Brahms is never Homer. It is perfectly true that the chamber works, from the B major Piano Trio (1853) to the clarinet sonatas (1894), maintain a uniformly high level. But that high level is nevertheless far from epic grandeur. If you are a really devout Brahmsian—if the things Brahms says inevitably hit an answering chord in your psyche—then there is hardly one of his chamber pieces that will not be a favorite of yours. But if your criteria of enjoyment emphasize the way things are said, then much of Brahms's chamber music may well rub you the wrong way. It is not that Brahms did not know the native speech of his instruments. But he was not infallible. The chamber works are one and all spotted with thick, muddy passages * that suggest not so much lack of taste as actual insensitivity to effect.

In all, Brahms composed two dozen chamber works, seven of them duet sonatas and the rest for three or more instruments. A sextet in G major written about the same time as the Piano Quintet is of peculiar biographical interest. Of it Brahms said earnestly to a friend: "In this I have freed myself of my last love." One of the themes is built on the sequence A-G-A-D-E, and so refers to a certain Agathe von Siebold, who had a small slice of Brahms's heart for rather more than a year. He had come across her in Göttingen in 1858. It is not clear why he was attracted to her: Agathe was a plain-featured young woman of slight charm. Perhaps he merely fell in love with the way she sang his songs. At any rate, he was soon writing more of them just for her, and what Clara Schumann saw of their relationship was enough to make her jealous. Despite this, they exchanged rings, and the girl seems to have considered herself betrothed to Brahms. When a common friend chided him for keeping Agathe dangling, Brahms wrote her a passionate love letter with the news that he longed to hold her in his arms, but could not consider marriage. This paradox was too much for Agathe, who, moreover, was thoroughly respectable. Five years later, as a final salving of his conscience, Brahms composed a tribute to her in the G major Sextet. This tepid romance was probably the closest he ever came to marrying, but it was by no means the last of his heart flutterings. One of his most famous songs—the *"Wiegenlied"*—was dedicated to a former inamorata on the birth of her second child.

With all his friends, Brahms suffered from loneliness, which he combated by frequent travel. Besides professional touring as far afield as Budapest, he roamed the resort towns of Germany, Austria, and Switzerland, and in later life often visited Italy, which he came to love. An innate dislike of all things French and English made the Rhine the

---

* There is some foundation for this statement, but it seems to me far too sweeping, and—though no Brahmsian myself—I must emphatically dissent.—E. S.

barrier of his westward wanderings, and he took no pains to conceal his ungracious attitude toward those nations. From about 1857 on, Brahms was free of financial worry, for his music was selling well, and he could easily afford to indulge his taste for summer rambling, particularly as his scale of living was simple. After resigning the direction of the Singakademie in 1864, he went to Baden-Baden to spend the season with Clara Schumann and her family. There he met Turgeniev, with whom he discussed plans for an opera, which fortunately (for Brahms was anything but a dramatic composer) remained at the discussion stage. His mother died the following year, and he had the tough assignment of getting his father to the funeral. Although profoundly affected by this loss, he accepted his father's remarriage, a few months later, with cheerful equanimity, and even grew very fond of his stepmother and her crippled son.

It has often been carelessly said that the death of his mother led Brahms to compose *Ein deutsches Requiem*. The facts are actually these: he had begun it years earlier, while still affected by Schumann's death, and had worked at it sporadically. By 1867, the six sections of the work as originally projected were finished, and the first three were given at Vienna on December 1. The performance was rowdy rather than reverent, the audience hissed, and for a time Brahms was in eclipse. On Good Friday of 1868, all six sections were produced so well at Bremen that the *Requiem* was immediately established as an important work. It was not until this year that Brahms wrote a new section for soprano solo to commemorate his mother; this is now the fifth part of the *Requiem*. The whole work was finally sung under the happiest auspices at the Gewandhaus on February 18, 1869, under the baton of the careful Karl Reinecke, a friend of Schumann and Mendelssohn. It was soon popular throughout Germany, and was the first large composition by Brahms to achieve world-wide fame.

Ein deutsches Requiem is scored for chorus, soloists, and orchestra, with organ ad libitum. It is not a Requiem in the traditional sense: that is, it does not follow the specific liturgical text of a Requiem Mass. It is a Protestant work built on words chosen by Brahms himself from the German Bible, which he knew intimately from cover to cover. The outstanding musical feature of this vast work is that it is a veritable compendium of technical effects. Every contrapuntal resource is laid under contribution, often to excess, chiefly in certain fugal passages, which though marvels on paper are confusing in performance. Here, again, Brahms draws out some of his best effects to the point of boredom. The result is a general amorphousness that is not sufficiently compensated for by many passages of real beauty. The whole *Requiem* is instinct with earnestness, with a genuine reverence for the sacred texts that makes one wish the results were better. Yet the total effect is one of noble dreariness. There are factors quite independent of Brahms's musical limitations,that had their part in flawing the *Requiem*. No soul-lifting faith in the transcendental aspects of religion shines from it. Brahms had no such faith. At best, he had a homely respect for the Good Book. He repeatedly stated, for instance, that he had no belief in life after death. Without absolutely echoing the brash Shaw of the early nineties, who said that listening to the *Requiem* was a sacrifice that should be asked of a man only once in his life, it may be said that the reputation of this interminable work is, among critics, justifiably waning —with no especial loss to Brahms's position. Perhaps quite the contrary.

During the very years Brahms was toiling over the completion of this solemn monument, he tossed off several groups of small pieces that have done more service to his reputation among music lovers than a dozen *Requiems* would have. The sixteen waltzes for piano duet, now more familiar as solos, are among the most sure-fire encore music ever composed. They are delicious little masterpieces, deceptively simple and engagingly unpretentious, yet made with exquisite care and subtlety. The A-flat major Waltz shares with the *"Wiegenlied"* top popularity among Brahms's original compositions. His arrangements of twenty-one Hungarian Dances, the first two books of which were issued as piano duets in 1869, were, however, the earliest of his compositions to gain a large popular audience. He was the first composer who ever became comfortably well off from the sale of his music alone, and the widespread demand for certain of the Hungarian Dances was the foundation of his not inconsiderable fortune. Three years later, he published piano-solo arrangements of the first two books, and these, with Joachim's versions for violin and piano, added still further to their popularity. In 1880, Brahms issued the third and fourth books for piano duet. Although these pieces are also heard as solos, they are not his own arrangements. Nor are the many orchestral transcriptions usually Brahms's own: he orchestrated only three of them—the first, third, and tenth. No matter how he issued them, he was careful to say that the Hungarian Dances were merely "arranged by Johannes Brahms," though a few of the melodies were his own. This scrupulousness did not avert charges of plagiarism by Reményi and others. Brahms's publisher issued a pamphlet containing the facts in the case, but the composer himself held aloof from the unsavory mess. He was content to have enriched the repertoire with these clever, vibrant, and rhythmically vigorous dances, whose popularity to this day is undiminished.

In February, 1872, Johann Jakob Brahms died, leaving his wife and stepson in Johannes's care. This duty he interpreted generously. His father's death drew him more closely to the widow, and he remained on the most intimate terms with her for the rest of his life—far more intimate, indeed, than with his own brother and sister, neither of whom he liked. Fortunately, money was no problem to him, and in the fall, his circumstances improved still further, when he was appointed to succeed Anton Rubinstein as director of the Gesellschaft der Musikfreunde, far and away the best of Vienna's choral organizations. The Gesellschaft found their new chief a strict and rather terrifying taskmaster, and it is evident that his severity of taste was not altogether palatable to the members of the chorus. As Roman Catholics, they were a little bewildered by the Protestant music of Bach and Handel, but Brahms's three years' tenure of office was in the main beneficial to their morale and standard of taste.

More than fifteen years had passed since Brahms had completed a purely orchestral composition. In 1873, while summering at the beautiful lakeside resort of Tutzing in the Bavarian Alps, he began and finished what some have pronounced his most consistently successful orchestral work—the *Variations on a Theme by Josef Haydn*. Brahms had found the theme in some recently unearthed manuscript material —incidentally, it is by no means certain that it was Haydn's to begin with. The fact that the theme was labeled *Chorale St. Antoni* [*sic*] led Brahms's first biographer to interpret the *Haydn* Variations as something so Lisztian as scenes from St. Anthony's temptations. Whether or not Brahms had a struggle between good and evil in mind when he wrote them (which, to say the least, seems unlike him), they stand in no need of a program. The theme is an attractive one, square and vigorous, and quite as well suited for comment as that of the *Handel* Variations. In the eight variations and finale, Brahms sets the orchestra ablaze in a manner quite unusual for him, with masterly efficiency using every color resource of his enlarged band, with its extra horns, trumpets, and kettledrums.

The *Haydn* Variations are almost as compendious in their musical erudition as the *Paganini* set for piano, but are utterly free from any pedantic or artificial feeling. Again Brahms interprets the variation in the freest way, and again it sets his imagination free. Yet, the total effect is one of almost incredible unity, of absolutely satisfying form. The music is joyful and (what is even rarer in Brahms) frankly sensuous. The whole composition is irradiated by a kind of luminous sanity. This does not mean that the coloring and mood are always bright: they are actually sometimes dark and somber. But when the wind choir reiterates the theme triumphantly at the close of the finale, it is with no mere unimaginative smugness. If the *Haydn* Variations can be made to symbolize anything, it is Brahms the man accepting all human experience as his province. It is a rare view, and may not be entirely welcome to those who prefer their Brahms dispensing an unleavened brand of thick Teutonic philosophy. Yet there is no doubt that the *Haydn* Variations brought him his first triumph as an orchestral composer, and that even the critics who had snubbed his D minor Piano Concerto echoed the enthusiasm with which Vienna greeted the Variations when they were first played on November 2, 1873. Today they stand in the shadow of the more pretentious symphonies, but they are played often enough to give us a chance to realize how great Brahms could be when his creative powers were unhindered by a hankering after a traditional formalism he was destined never to master.

The salutary effects on Brahms of not having to conform to the restrictions of the sonata form are illustrated most clearly in his more than two hundred songs, written over practically the entire span of his creative life. The best of these are exceedingly fine, and it may seem strange that only one—the flawless *"Wiegenlied"* (1868)—has attained that thoroughly universal popularity which so many of Schubert's songs, and not a few of Schumann's, enjoy. But a moment's reflection will reveal the reason. They are without the feckless spontaneity, the effortless melody of Schubert, and also lack that profoundly sympathetic understanding of the poetic line that informs the best of Schumann's songs. Brahms is often positively insensitive to the precise rhythmic demands of his text, to such an extent that singers are sometimes forced to mispronounce words in order to do justice to the musical beat. In this he affords an instructive contrast to Hugo Wolf, who at times went to the opposite extreme of sacrificing purity of musical contour to an ironclad reverence for the poetic meter. Although most of Brahms's songs are love songs, they sing of, or comment upon, what seems a rather passionless love—they are reflective, nostalgic, pessimistic, even aloof. Almost without exception, they lack drama. One of the most dramatic—*"Vergebliches Ständchen"*—is cast in an innocuously light mood. We are left to gather that for the most part Brahms was afraid to touch the heavier emotions. The intensely passionate *"Von ewiger Liebe"* is not Brahms at his most characteristic, but it is his greatest song.

Most of Brahms's songs are of high musical interest quite apart from their relation to their texts. Looked at merely as a fusion of melody, harmony, and rhythm, such a song as the *"Sapphische Ode"* is a beautiful and moving piece of music. It would be just as effective written to another set of words. Not a few of Brahms's happiest melodic inspirations are to be found in his songs, and invariably they are handled with tact and finesse. Even when the results are not very good as songs, they are still good Brahms—fine music-making.

Except for songs and choral pieces, Brahms published little during his years as director of the Gesellschaft der Musikfreunde. This is the best evidence that he took his job seriously and performed his duties conscientiously. It is impossible to guess what a prolonged tenure of this exacting position would have done to his career as a composer, but the nature of most of his compositions completed during these years does suggest that he might have been permanently sidetracked. The ostensible reason for his resignation in 1875 was that he was annoyed by the machinations of one of his predecessors, who was plotting to get the directorship back. Actually, Brahms must have left official life with relief, for great projects were pressing for completion, and he needed leisure to carry them out. For years he had been at work on a symphony. He was now forty-two years old, and it was still incomplete. Within little more than a year after leaving the Gesellschaft, he had finished the First Symphony and sketched the Second. He was feverishly at work when, in 1876, he was invited by Cambridge University to visit England to receive an honorary doctorate of music. Brahms refused to go. He said that he disliked "concerts and other disturbances"; his friends said that he hated the English and feared the sea. The most likely explanation of his rather churlish refusal (which he repeated in 1892) was that he was too pressed to take time off. At any rate, that same summer saw the completion of the First Symphony. Within a decade he had put the finishing touches to his Fourth and last.

Brahms's four symphonies are the most eloquent and decisive commentary on the prophecy contained in Schumann's *Zeitschrift* article, assuming that in hailing Brahms as the "Messiah of music . . . he who was to come," Schumann meant the successor of the great classical masters, specifically Beethoven. Color is lent to this interpretation by

Schumann's own growing classical bent in the last years of his life. There is no doubt that Brahms took Schumann's incautious words with grave seriousness, and throughout his career endeavored to fill the role in which Schumann (rather than his own innate tendencies) had cast him. Although he never postured as a great master, Brahms felt his mission confirmed when Bülow pronounced his First Symphony "Beethoven's Tenth." Bülow set a style: devoted Brahmsians almost inevitably refer to the four symphonies as "the greatest since Beethoven." Anti-Brahmsians and middle-of-the-road admirers unite in pointing out that it is precisely in the symphonies that Brahms failed most signally to measure up to the demands of the larger classical forms.

That Brahms viewed the writing of a symphony with more than ordinary apprehension is indicated by the chronology of his orchestral work. He had published two serenades of quasi-symphonic scope, a large piano concerto, and the *Haydn* Variations before completing a symphony on which he had been at work for almost twenty years. Begun in Brahms's early twenties, the C minor Symphony is nevertheless by no means a youthful work. It represents a considered whipping into shape by a fully matured man. It is unfortunate that we have no revealing notebooks to show us the early ideas out of which, twenty years later, Brahms evolved this symphony. Certainly, as it stands, the C minor has had any young quality taken out of it. It is predominantly a dour work and, except for the introduction to the first movement and the finale, could be interpreted as the last composition of an embittered old man. The introduction is an effective swirl of nebula—music of enchanting loveliness in itself. Its presence needs no excuse, but its function is problematical. If out of it rose the vigorous germinative themes essential to the construction of a recognizable symphony,* it might seem as much a stroke of architectural genius as the sublime adagio introduction to Mozart's E-flat Symphony. But nothing of this sort takes place. Instead, the invertebrate nature of the introduction pervades the first three movements. Suddenly, in the finale, Brahms hits upon a truly energizing first theme, about which it might be carping to say that it is in part lifted from the choral finale to Beethoven's Ninth Symphony were it not for

---

* The authors get themselves into quite an argument here. If the opening notes of the Introduction—

are not a "germinative theme" (they appear some 30 or 40 times in various forms during the first movement), I wonder what is?—E. S.

the fact that zealots of the Brahms cult make such a point of repeating the master's famous growl when someone mentioned this resemblance: "Any fool can see that!" The point is that this Beethovenian theme, whether hit upon by accident or purposely, is just the right sort of material on which to erect a soundly constructed symphonic movement. This Brahms proceeds to do with complete success. But it must be said that a triumphant conclusion—almost a swift victory march—after three vast movements of transitional music produces an odd effect.

The Second Symphony, the most cheerful of Brahms's larger compositions, is attractively bucolic in nature. It has often been called his "Pastoral" Symphony, but the implied comparison must not be strained. The D major contains, in fact, better music than Beethoven's Sixth, but is not so well constructed.* Also, programmatic effects were foreign to Brahms's Dorian conception of symphonic dignity. The scoring is light and clear. The instrumentation is, for Brahms, unusually transparent— free of the sluggish turgidity that so often clogs the machinery in his other symphonies, and sometimes makes them difficult to follow. The circumstances of the composition of the D major Symphony—it was composed during the summer of 1877, on the shores of the Wörthersee, a beautiful Austrian lake—doubtless have much to do with its spontaneous quality. Two of Brahms's most seductive melodies appear in the first and third movements respectively, and the whole is liberally sprinkled with delights. The entire allegretto enjoys a popularity of its own: it is, after all, much like a theme and variations, and naturally Brahms is at his happiest in it. As a suite of attractive symphonic effects, the D major is not surpassed by Brahms's other symphonies, but even more than the others, it lacks the perfectly achieved cohesiveness that is the hallmark of a true symphony.*

In 1883, Brahms composed a third symphony, and began to sketch a fourth. The first of these, in F major, is the shortest of all his symphonies, but often seems the longest because of its heroic cast and grandiosity. A few attentive listenings to it should dispel forever the notion that Brahms is essentially a classical composer. It begins with a burst of romantic virtuosity, and is steeped throughout in an almost Schumannesque romanticism. In the first two movements, Brahms seems to be speaking *in propria persona,* a persuasive romantic poet uninhibited by any sense of duty to the great classical dead. The breathless flow of melodic beauty is nothing short of intoxicating, and momentarily, at least, we scarcely care that we are listening to a free fantasia rather than

* I'd be willing to offer a prize for any *proof* of these statements.—E. S.

to a symphony. After these heroic draughts, the third and fourth movements are tepid and unadventurous. The skeleton in Brahms's closet is indeed neoclassicism—a very self-conscious neoclassicism—and its bones rattle throughout the andante and the allegro. In no other large work is the descent from mountain to plain made so rapidly. The idiom suddenly becomes harsh and monotonous, the melodic line studied. The whole symphony sags, and in trying to find distinction for this industrious classicizing Brahms descends to real ugliness in his orchestration. Had Richard Strauss concocted some of this, we should say that he was orchestrating a sandbank, and compliment him for doing it perfectly. The last half of the F major Symphony has given those critics who make a specialty of judging a composer by his lapses something to hold on to: from it, more than from anything else, has come Brahms's reputation as a harsh melodist and a muddy orchestrator.*

Brahms lived to be almost sixty-four years old, but he finished his last symphony when he was only fifty-two. In many respects, the E minor is the most remarkable of the four, just as it is the least conventional. In movement sequence it violates some of the most time-honored canons of the symphonic form: it begins with an allegro, moves on to an andante, then to another allegro, and ends with a third allegro, *energico e passionato,* that is actually a passacaglia—a theme and variations in triple time. It begins and ends tragically, violating another supposed rule that even a tragic symphony must close on a yea. Be it said that Brahms's innovations are, in themselves, completely successful, and that none of his other symphonies so consistently holds the attention as the Fourth. It is unquestionably one of the sovereign works for orchestra, never for a moment devoid of great melodic inspiration, and orchestrated sensitively, sometimes brilliantly. Coming after the spacious but mysterious and darkly questioning first movement, the melancholy, tender andante, and the robust good-humored allegro giocoso, the majestic passacaglia, with the mind-dazzling variety of its thirty variations and finale, is as inspired a conception as the grand fugue of the *Handel* Variations.

For some years Brahms had intended to compose a violin concerto for Joachim, and during the summer of 1878, having returned to the Wörthersee, did so. Joachim naturally introduced it, at the Gewandhaus, on New Year's Day, 1879. The public reaction was cold, and it

* Again I dissent, and bid the reader once more to consult Mr. Downes on p. 185, as well as Mr. D. G. Mason on p. 531. For a vote on the side of Messrs. Brockway and Weinstock, read the statement on Brahms's symphonies quoted from Tchaikovsky, p. 531.—E. S.

took years of proselytizing on Joachim's part to get it accepted widely. That it is today solidly established is a tribute to the great violinist's conviction that he was advertising a masterpiece. Again Hanslick was a dissenter and a powerful deterrent to immediate acceptance. Many still agree with him. The D major Violin Concerto is as uneven as the Third Symphony. It has an absorbingly beautiful, if rather errant, first movement, a hopelessly inadequate second, and a sometimes exciting, but far from perfectly achieved, finale. Except for the cadenza, which Brahms leaves to the soloist's taste (Joachim's or Fritz Kreisler's is ordinarily used today), it is not a display piece for the soloist, whose role, indeed, is sometimes worse than secondary. Bülow, in one of his acidulous and bitter-truthful moods, once said that Max Bruch had written a concerto *for* the violin, Brahms a concerto *against* the violin. The roles of solo instrument and orchestra are best balanced in the first movement—an emotional, nobly speaking allegro. The andante is ruined by flagrantly inept orchestration: the thin note of the oboe carrying the main theme is swamped by too massive accompaniment, and the solo violin's comments are insignificant and weak. In the finale, there is much fine gypsy music of bravura cast, but here Brahms, halfway to success, swamps the solo instrument itself.*

Late in 1879, the University of Breslau informed Brahms that it intended to honor him with a Ph.D. Possibly to the surprise of the University authorities, he accepted graciously, and bethought himself of some music fitting to the occasion. Let us, under the guidance of Sir Henry Hadow, follow his ruminations at the lovely summer resort of Ischl: "A ceremonial of so solemn and academic a character naturally demanded an unusual display of learning. Symphonies were too trivial, oratorios were too slight, even an eight-part *a cappella* chorus in octuple counterpoint was hardly adequate to the dignity of the occasion. Something must be done to mark the doctorate with all the awe and reverence due to the Philosophic Chair. So Brahms selected a handful of the more convivial student-songs and worked them into a concert overture which remains one of the most amusing pieces of pure comedy in the whole range of music." This rollicking piece was the still immensely popular *Academic Festival Overture*. Oddly enough, when performed under Brahms's direction at Breslau, on January 4, 1881, it was received with less enthusiasm than its perfect gauging to the occasion deserved. It may be that the presence on the program of the *Tragic Overture*, also

* Let the reader—and *hearer*—judge for himself.—E. S.

completed at Ischl the preceding year, explains the audience's low spirits. This is a gloomy, not to say dull, work. Although Brahms insisted that he had no specific tragedy in mind, it has been guessed that the overture was meant as a prelude to *Medea, Hamlet, Macbeth,* or *Faust.*

It was not until the summer of 1881 that Brahms physically became the familiar bearded figure of most of his portraits. He began the composition of the B-flat Concerto smooth-shaven, and emerged with a heavy beard. The growing of this famous ornament, which became more and more luxuriant with the years, has been interpreted by Freudian critics as a compensatory gesture for " the smooth cheeks of his early twenties." In view of the fact that the hoarseness of Brahms's voice from middle age on was due to his having artifically lowered its pitch, this explanation has some slight plausibility, though it is almost negated by the fact that he grew his beard in the very heyday of excessive hirsuteness. The most likely reason is that Brahms grew tired of shaving and of wearing a tie. His careless dress became proverbial, his old brown overcoat and battered hat one of the sights of Vienna. About this stubby, rather paunchy little man there was small glamour. The ashes of interminable cigars fell unheeded on his waistcoat, and were smudged in. He was a heroic beer drinker, withal a connoisseur, and his taste in food was heavily German. As he aged, his hosts of friends regarded Brahms with affection, his appearance and habits with delighted amusement, though his wide acquaintance with ladies of easy virtue, who often greeted him brightly on the street, embarrassed them. Until the very end of his life, people remarked on his piercing, extremely blue eyes, fair skin, and magnificently domed forehead, and it was these characteristics that, much to Brahms's amused gratification, led a geographer to include his portrait in a textbook as a typical representative of the Caucasian race.

As Brahms neared fifty, his life settled more and more into a routine of summer composing and winter touring. He kept his quarters in Vienna, but as soon as the weather warmed, he was to be found at one of his favorite mountain resorts—Thun, Mürzzuschlag, or Ischl—and there he did most of his creative work. In the winter, his tours often served to introduce his latest compositions to a growing public. Whenever possible, he spent a part of each year in Italy. The Third Symphony, for example, was begun at Ischl during the summer of 1882, and finished at Wiesbaden the following year. On December 2, Richter led the Vienna Philharmonic in a successful *première,* following which Brahms introduced the symphony at various places, notably at Berlin early in 1884.

Almost ten years more of life remained to Brahms—years of meager outward eventfulness, but sweetened, on one hand, by lavish official and public recognition, and on the other, saddened by the loss of beloved friends of long standing. In 1889, Franz Josef, Emperor of Brahms's adopted country, bestowed the coveted Order of Leopold on him, and the same year, his birthplace pleased him even more by giving him the freedom of the city. Brahms ordinarily refused to wear his numerous decorations, but relaxed during solemn state dinners at the Meiningen ducal *Schloss,* and amused himself by wearing the whole lot. Generally speaking, pleasures outweighed sorrows. In 1892, however, the still young Elisabeth von Herzogenberg died, and for months Brahms was inconsolable. He was growing old, and could not lose himself so completely in composition as had been his wont earlier in life. Fortunately, at Christmastime, he was reconciled to Clara, whose growing touchiness had caused a break between them in 1891. He managed to see her at least once a year for the next three years, perhaps feeling that each time might be the last. And in May, 1896, when Clara was almost seventy-seven, the dreaded news came in a telegram from her daughter Marie: "Our mother fell gently asleep today." Brahms was at Ischl, and the telegraph people had had difficulty in finding him. He set off at once for Frankfort, read in a newspaper that the funeral was to be at Bonn, and reached there just in time. A few months less than forty years before, he and Clara had walked beside the bier of Robert Schumann.

At Clara's funeral, weakened by fatigue and grief, Brahms caught a chill from which, in a sense, he never recovered. By September, it was obvious to his doctor at Carlsbad that he was dying of a liver complaint. When he returned to Vienna the next month, his altered appearance shocked all his friends. It seemed that he had grown old and feeble overnight. He grew steadily worse, and when 1897 came around, knew that he would not get better. On March 7, he attended a Philharmonic concert, and heard the great Richter do a superb job of his Fourth Symphony. It turned out to be an intensely emotional occasion for all concerned: after each movement, the music was wildly cheered, and at the end of the finale, when Richter indicated Brahms's presence, the audience rose as a man, and saluted him. Almost sobbing out his emotion, the old man bowed, and then stepped back into the shadow of the box. Less than a month later, on April 3, 1897, he died of cancer of the liver. He died with tears in his eyes—he had loved life, and hated to give it up.

Peter Ilyich Tchaikovsky
By Daniel Gregory Mason

Article in The International Cyclopedia of Music and Musicians

PETER ILYICH TCHAIKOVSKY was born at Votkinsk, in the government of Vyatka, Russia, May 7, 1840, second in a family of five sons (the two last ones twins, whom he loved as if he had been their father) and one daughter, to whom he was tenderly devoted. Once in his early teens when he was in school at St. Petersburg and his mother started to drive to another city, he had to be held back while she got into the carriage, and the moment he was free ran and tried to hold the wheels.

There is an anecdote of Tchaikovsky's earliest years that gives us a clue to the paradox of his personality. Passionately kissing the map of Russia and then, one regrets to state, spitting at the other countries, he was reminded by his nurse that she herself was French. "Yes," he said, accepting her criticism with perfect sweetness and affectionate docility, "I covered France with my hand." The child is father of the man; here we have already Tchaikovsky's strange two-sidedness: on the one hand his intense emotionality in all personal matters, his headstrong impetuosity, leaping first and looking afterwards; on the other his candor and modesty, his intelligent acceptance of criticism, even his carefulness and good workmanship—he had "covered France with his hand"! If he had only been able to reconcile that lifelong feud between his over-personal heart and his magnanimous mind, he would have been saved endless suffering. But he could not: in his music his self-criticism, as one of his best biographers, Edwin Evans, has remarked, "came after and not during composition"—he destroyed score after score. And in daily life he never learned to apply the advice of a wit to the victim of a temperament like his: "Less remorse and more reform."

As a youth he reluctantly studied law, as much bored by it as Schumann had been, and even became a petty clerk in the Ministry of Justice. But in his early twenties he rebelled, and against his family's wishes had the courage to throw himself into the study of music at the St. Petersburg Conservatory. He was a ready improviser, played well for dancing, and had a naturally rich sense of harmony, but was so little schooled as to be astonished when a cousin told him it was possible to modulate from any key to any other. He went frequently to the Italian operas which at that time almost monopolized the Russian stage, and laid the foundation of his lifelong love of Mozart; but he had no acquaintance with Schumann, and at 21 did not even know how many symphonies Beethoven had composed. He was an ardent worker nevertheless, and once when Anton Rubinstein, his teacher of composition, asked for variations, he sat up all night and brought in two hundred. Is not that already the very picture of a facility almost fatal?—a facility which in even so fine a work as the Trio transforms an unoffending Russian folk tune into a waltz, a mazurka, and even a fugue, like a conjurer drawing rabbits out of a hat!

Early in 1866 he removed permanently to Moscow, with which all his later musical fortunes are associated, accepting a teaching post in the new conservatory just established by Rubinstein's brother Nicolas. His early attempts at composition, largely because of that same fatal facility, had displeased himself as well as his friends; on one of them, with that same impersonal candor always flashing out from him, he had scribbled the words: "dreadful muck." Yet now he had the courage to attempt his first symphony, "Winter Dreams." Musically it is not of great importance, any more than are indeed the second and third, one strongly "folk" and the other rather featureless, in spite of a beautiful slow movement. But the First Symphony is interesting biographically for two reasons. Over it, to begin with, its composer worked his too-delicate nerves into a state of almost pathological strain that was to recur at intervals all his life. He suffered from insomnia, a sensation of hammering in the head, and even hallucinations; and so painful was the whole experience that he never again composed at night.

Of more importance is the vivid example his symphony gives us of the contrast between his passionately narrow attitude in personal relations and his magnanimity and candor whenever he could get away from the stifling atmosphere into the free air of impersonal art. His eager wish for a performance of the symphony in St. Petersburg, where his works had so far been badly received, was peremptorily refused by his old teacher, Anton Rubinstein. Here was the kind of slight that any composer finds hard, but above all a morbidly shy man like Peter Ilyich, with his easily hurt pride. "This was the last straw," writes

Evans—"he never forgave Anton Rubinstein—he included in his dislike the Directors of the Music Society, the Press, and even the St. Petersburg public. It was the last time he asked to have a work performed
there." And no doubt this "complex," as a psychologist would be justified in calling it, was intensified by the great success of the symphony,
a year later, in Moscow, when the young composer was called unexpectedly to the stage—terribly nervous, carelessly dressed, holding his
hat in his hand, and making clumsy bows.

So much for the personal side. Now for the impersonal. Decades
later, hardly more than a year before his death, he was asked for his
memories of Rubinstein. "In him," he wrote in answer, "I adore not
only a great pianist and composer but a man of rare nobility, frank, loyal,
generous, incapable of petty and vulgar sentiments . . . a man who
towered far above the common herd. . . . I took him an overture, *The
Storm,* guilty of all kinds of whims of form and orchestration. He was
hurt, and said that it was not for the development of imbeciles that he
took the trouble to teach composition. I left the Conservatory full of
gratitude for my professor."

Those who patronizingly regard Tchaikovsky as a neurotic will do
well to ask themselves how many artists there have ever been who
would be capable of such a disinterested detachment. But he goes further.

"I have always regarded him," he continues, " as the greatest of
artists and the noblest of men, but I shall never become his friend.
. . . It would be difficult to explain the reason. I think my *amour propre*
as a composer has a great deal to do with it. In my youth I was impatient
to make my way. . . . Painful as it is, I must confess that he did nothing, absolutely nothing, to forward my plans. The most probable explanation of this mortifying luke-warmness is that Rubinstein *does not
care for my music, that my musical temperament is antipathetic to him.*
[Tchaikovky's own italics.]

"I still see him from time to time," ends the letter, "and always
with pleasure. At the time of his jubilee I had the happiness of going
through much trouble and fatigue for him. . . . If I have told too little
it is not my fault, nor that of Anton, but of fatality."

Another letter equally lovable in its magnanimity is the long one
—too long to quote here—of Jan. 5, 1878, to his benefactress, Nadejda
von Meck, about the Russian Nationalists or *Kutschka* (literally
"Bunch") of St. Petersburg, placed by circumstances and to some extent
by tastes in opposition to himself and his Moscow fellows, but always

treated with consideration by him. The essence of the opposition was that the Kutschka—Balakirev, Rimsky-Korsakov, Mussorgsky, Borodin, and César Cui—were fanatical Nationalists, believed that music began and ended with folk song, were all, except Rimsky, rather amateurish in technique, and tended to regard Tchaikovsky—the glibness of whose poorer moments indeed gave them some excuse—as a "featureless eclectic." Some of them, notably Cui, were scarcely civil in the things they said of him. He, on the other hand, describes in his letters their merits as well as their defects with surprising freedom from bias. For example: "The young Petersburg composers are very gifted, but impregnated with the most horrible presumptuousness and a purely amateur conviction of their superiority. Rimsky-Korsakov is the only one among them who discovered . . . that their doctrines had no sound basis, that their denial of authority and of the masterpieces was nothing but ignorance. . . . Cui is a gifted amateur. Borodin possesses a great talent, which has come to nothing because fate has led him into the science laboratories instead of a vital musical existence. Mussorgsky's gifts are perhaps the most remarkable of all, but his nature is narrow and he has no aspirations towards self-perfection. Besides, his nature is not of the finest quality, and he likes what is coarse, unpolished, and ugly. . . ." "What a sad phenomenon," he sums up. "So many talents from which, with the exception of Rimsky, we can scarcely dare to hope for anything serious. But all the same, these forces exist. Thus Mussorgsky, with all his ugliness, speaks a new idiom. . . . We may reasonably hope that Russia will one day produce a whole school of strong men who will open up new paths in art."

The first decade of Tchaikovsky's life in Moscow was one of much struggle, intensified by several attacks of the nervous depression and morbid self-disgust always dogging him, of first meeting with some of his great contemporaries, such as Turgenev, Tolstoi, Berlioz, Liszt, Saint-Saëns, and Wagner, of an abortive love-affair with the opera-singer Désirée Artôt, and above all of a varied production of many kinds of music, of all types from operas to string quartets, which laid the foundation of his skill and fame. Most of the operas, written hastily, uncritically, and sometimes on wretched librettos, were failures, the scores of which in a number of cases he himself destroyed. At the other end of the gamut of musical style are the three String Quartets (1871, '74, and '76). All have interest but none quite achieve the reticence and reserved beauty of true quartet style. The *Andante cantabile* movement of the first, Opus 11, founded on a folk song the composer heard whistled by a house painter, has become deservedly famous. The third, in E-flat minor, contains music of a funereal solemnity and tragic feeling anticipating the *Pathetic* Symphony. By far the most successful of all these early works are the orchestral ones where Tchaikovsky's passionate emotion and flair for gorgeous coloring have full sway: not perhaps the symphonies (No. 2, 1872, and No. 3, 1875) but more dramatic conceptions like *The Tempest* (overture, 1873), the tone poem *Francesca da Rimini* (1876) and two masterpieces, *Romeo and Juliet* composed in 1869, and produced and revised a year later, and the magnificent Piano Concerto in B-flat minor, composed in 1874, at first intended for Nicolas Rubinstein, but owing to his indifference dedicated instead to Hans von Bülow. These works, both by quantity and quality, amply justify the solid and gradually spreading reputation of the middle seventies.

Then came a double crisis, involving two women, one of whom, touching Tchaikovsky on his personal and most vulnerable side, nearly wrecked him, and the other, lending timely aid to the impersonal artist in him, the side of him that was truly great, turned his life to new fruitfulness. Antonina Ivanovna Milyukov hurled herself at his head, declaring in a letter her love for him. He, through misplaced chivalry, was quixotic enough to marry her, July 6, 1877. Within a month he discovered their utter incompatibility and on the 26th wrote that a few more days of such life would have driven him mad. He left her for most of the summer, but made another attempt in early September to live with her in Moscow. Before the month was out he fled to St. Petersburg, arrived in complete nervous collapse, and was taken to the hotel nearest the station, where he became unconscious for 48 hours and then passed into a high fever. Ordered by the doctors to leave Russia, he gradually regained strength at Clarens, a quiet village on Lake Geneva, where he later did some of his best work. Neither partner to this unfortunate marriage had any blame to give the other.

Nadejda Filaretovna von Meck, the widow of a wealthy railway engineer, had fallen under the spell of Tchaikovsky's music the year before, had given him several commissions, and had begun the long correspondence with him that reveals for us so much of his inner life. Nine years older than he and living in a socially different world, rich and apparently somewhat spoiled and autocratic but at any rate sincere in her love for his music, she had the good sense or the good luck (it is hard to tell which) to stipulate from the first that they should have no personal intercourse. They could not, to be sure, avoid one or two casual meetings at musical events, but it is said they never spoke to each other—they who wrote so inexhaustibly. Nothing could have been better suited to the queer psychology of Tchaikovsky. Secure from upsetting attacks on his personal privacy, he was provided, from 1877 on, not only with an income of 6,000 rubles, which enabled him to give up teaching, but with a tireless listener to all his opinions, beliefs, impressions, hopes, despairs, and aspirations.

Almost at once he resumed work on the splendid Fourth Symphony which he had begun before the unfortunate marriage; and early in 1878 finished it, and also his most successful opera, *Eugene Onegin*. That same year he wrote at Clarens the immensely popular Violin Concerto. *Manfred* followed in 1885; the Fifth Symphony in 1888; another successful opera, *Pique Dame* (The Queen of Spades), in 1890; the *Casse-Noisette* (Nutcracker) Ballet, from which the delightful Suite is drawn, in 1891. In these prosperous years his fame all over the world was rapidly increasing; he visited most of the European capitals for performances of his works; and there even began to be Tchaikovsky Festivals. Under the genial influence of all this sunshine he partially forgot, or put aside, his shyness, and took up the baton again, at first with many qualms, but gradually with so much assurance that in 1888 he made an international conducting tour, appearing in Leipzig, Hamburg, Prague, Paris, and London. Three years later he even ventured to come across the Atlantic and conduct his own works in New York at the ceremonies opening Carnegie Hall, as may be read in his letters in amusing detail of his triumphs and homesickness. And for the summers there were a series of modest but comfortable country houses in Russia where he could compose in peace, from Maidanova, with which he began, to Klin, near Moscow. Only at the end of 1890, three years before his death, came the inevitable rupture with Madame von Meck, and by that time he was financially independent, so that the break affected his spirits more than his music. In 1893 he wrote at Klin his most famous work, the *Pathetic* Symphony, and conducted it at St. Petersburg on Oct. 28. It was coolly received, and he did not live to witness its success. Only a few days later he drank a glass of unfiltered water, and died of cholera, Nov. 6, 1893.

Tchaikovsky's life seems to have been, even more than most lives, a curious mixture of successes and failures, the failures mostly due to his morbid subjection to moods and his tendency to leap before he looked, the successes due to his sincerity, intelligence, modesty, and candor. It is the fashion nowadays to paint his faults almost more than life-size. We are told, for instance, that his style is eclectic, at its worst miscellaneous. He wrote, it is pointed out, in such a jet of impulse that whole works give the impression of being accidentally what they are —the Second Symphony so "folk," for example, and the Third so facile and cosmopolitan. Already we have mentioned the almost department-store-like jumble of styles in the variations of the Trio. The piano music is much of it only higher salon music; parts of the Sextet are pretty-pretty Italianism; even so fine a work as the Fifth Symphony breaks into a waltz rather too easily—and so on.

One answer to this criticism is that Tchaikovsky has the merits of his defects, and that this uncritical jet of emotion often produced the loveliest melodies. There are more haunting tunes in his pages than we can count: the folk tune in the *Andante Cantabile,* the song *"Nur wer die Sehnsucht kennt,"* the noble horn-theme in the slow movement of the Fifth Symphony, the swaying love-song from *Romeo and Juliet* and the delicious moment for muted strings that follows it. Of course tunes are not favored by the sophisticates who take so severe a view of Tchaikovsky, but the plain man likes them, and most candid musicians not led astray by theories will agree with the plain man.

A variant of the criticism of facile eclecticism that perhaps deserves more attention is the charge of careless development of ideas, acceptance of rubber-stamps, and in particular the obvious use of sequences. Here again we must distinguish the element of justice in the criticism from finical fault-finding. Some of the sequences, it must be confessed, in their over-obviousness are distressingly banal: such, for instance, as the perfectly self-satisfied evolution of platitude that makes up a good deal of the opening theme of the Piano Sonata in G major. But compare those tragic sequences, inevitable in the good sense, big with fate, that carry the opening of the Finale in the *Pathetic* down to the lowest depths. Evidently there are sequences *and* sequences. He who abuses them, as Tchaikovsky does in his lazy moods, vulgarizes his music; but he who avoids them altogether becomes merely unintelligible. So with the much-decried Tchaikovskyan climaxes. There is something a little trying in the foregone way he piles in the brass, "swearing a theme," as someone said, "through a stone wall." But where are there greater moments, in dramatic orchestral music, than some of his terrifying pedal points?

And after all he was, as psychologists say, "a sensitive," though a sensitive of high intellectual endowment, and his virtues as well as his faults are those we must expect. "It would be vain to try to put into words," he writes Mme. von Meck, in the famous letter about the Fourth Symphony, "that immeasurable sense of bliss which comes over me directly a new idea awakens in me and begins to assume a definite form. I forget everything and behave like a madman. Everything within me starts pulsing and quivering; hardly have I begun the sketch ere one thought follows another. In the midst of this magic process . . . some interruption wakes me from my somnambulistic state. Dreadful are such interruptions." And he goes on to say regretfully how even in the greatest masters we find moments of such interruption, when "the organic sequence fails, and a skilful join has to be made." Elsewhere with his usual delightful candor he confesses: "Such hindrances are inevitable: hence the joins, patches, inequalities, and discrepancies. I cannot complain of lack of inventive power, but I have always suffered from want of skill in the management of form."

Such a thing of shreds and patches (even if splendid ones) as the opening movement of the Fifth Symphony shows that here he has keenly diagnosed his own weakness. But how many perfect movements are there in modern symphonies? Has even Brahms written anything else so all-of-a-piece as the finale of his Third Symphony? And who in the nineteenth century has ever imagined a more magnificent opening than the fanfare of brass with which the Tchaikovsky Fourth begins, even if it is not quite kept up through the rest of the movement? Who has made a nobler tragic end to a piece of music than those solemn drum-haunted final pages of the *Romeo and Juliet?* The wonder about this composer is, in fact, not that his work is full of imperfections and that he can seldom sustain a whole movement at the height of its greatest passages, but that being, as he was, a "sensitive," and as he himself said, "no Beethoven" (when someone compared his Fourth to Beethoven's Fifth), he yet frequently touches the heights. But he cannot dwell there; and there is something winning about the very weakness, so human, that brings with it so many blemishes, especially as he is so honest, so modest, about them all. "I confess," he writes in a letter towards the end of his life, "that the post-Beethoven music offers many examples of prolixity. . . . Is not Brahms a caricature of Beethoven? Is not this pretension to profundity and power detestable, because the content which is poured into the Beethoven mould is not really of any value? Even in the case of Wagner (who certainly has genius) wherever he oversteps the limits it is the spirit of Beethoven which prompts him." (It does not matter whether we agree with Tchaikovsky's judgments: in any case his sincerity is lovable.) "As regards your humble servant," he concludes, "I have suffered all my life from my incapacity to grasp form in general. I have fought against this innate weakness, not—I am proud to say—without good results; yet I shall go to my grave without having produced anything really perfect in form."

But how "human, all too human," are these weaknesses, after all—and what beauty and power we find in spite of them in all his greatest works! Our winnowing is, no doubt, severe. Of the operas we have to discard nearly all but *Eugene Onegin* and perhaps *Pique Dame*. The choral music is comparatively unimportant. Of the chamber music the quartets contain single attractive movements, but on the whole are justly neglected; and the Trio, despite the nobility of its opening, the charm of the variation theme, and the haunting beauty of one variation (in C-sharp minor with the piano arpeggios) is overpretentious, melodramatic, almost orchestral in style (Frederick Stock has orchestrated it) and as we have seen eclectic to the point of miscellaneousness. The piano music is mostly light and merely pretty or sentimental, or else, like the G major sonata, pompous and inflated in the manner of Liszt. The songs we remember for a few especially fine examples: *"Nur wer die Sehnsucht kennt,"* "Don Juan's Serenade," "Invocation to Sleep," and the magnificent, unjustly neglected "Pilgrim's Song."

That leaves the orchestral music and the concertos; and even here, while there are many splendid things, there are few perfect ones. Here, to be sure, the conventionality of conductors has narrowed the field unjustly. The war-horses, such as the last two symphonies, the *1812* Overture and the *Casse-Noisette* Suite, are played to death, while many fine works are neglected. (One might mention particularly the orchestral suites, all of which contain fine movements. The variations in the Third Suite have been justly compared to the Elgar *Enigma* Variations.) But even in the works kept in the repertory, what unevenness we find! They all rise to nobility, some to sublimity, and—even the early *Romeo and Juliet,* one of his most inspired works—they all sink to banality, glibness, and rubber-stamp. But they will not be forgotten for a while yet—there is too much beauty in them, too rare a sincerity.

And it is comforting to remember that Tchaikovsky himself knew that and drew solace from it, for all the sufferings of his too personal temperament. Always he escaped from the sadness of the merely personal into the joy of impersonal art. It is well to remember that in spite of all the sentimental nonsense that has been written about his pessimism, in spite of his own morbid fears—his constant cry that he was growing old and losing his powers, that he must stop composing, that he was *homme fini,* his powers went on ripening to the end. The over-personal little boy who had kissed the map of Russia died murmuring the name of the benefactress he thought had deserted him —Nadejda Filaretovna. But he who had "covered France with his hand"—the free mind open to criticism, the modest and impartial intelligence, the good workman, knew that his last work had been his best. As he left the hall after conducting that initial, not much acclaimed performance of the *Pathetic* Symphony, Oct. 28, 1893, nine days before his death, he told his friend Glazunov that for the first time in his career he had come away from hearing one of his compositions "with a feeling of complete content." So, after all, he was a happy man.

Russian Composers

Extracts from "A History of Music"

By Paul Landormy

IT IS WITH *Michail Glinka* (1804-1857) that Russian opera begins to take on a truly national character. He was born of a noble family. In his childhood he dreamed only of music. He was educated at the pedagogic Institute for the Sons of the Nobility. There he learned Latin, French, German, English, and Persian. He played the piano and violin. His studies completed, he amused himself, upon his return beneath the paternal roof, by conducting a small orchestra which played the works of Cherubini, Méhul, Haydn, Mozart, and Beethoven. He then entered the ministry of roads and communications, and began to frequent the artistic world, where he met Prince Galitzin and the Tolstoi brothers. On occasion he figured as a singer and actor.

In 1830 he set out for Italy. "Homesickness for my native land," he said at a later period, "little by little led me to think of writing Russian music." Then he went to Berlin, where he studied composition with Dehn. It was his fixed wish to create a genuine Russian national opera. "Not only with regard to subject, but musically as well, do I want my dear compatriots to be entirely at home in it."

He returned to St. Petersburg and entered into relations with Pushkin, Gogol, and Kubolnik. Soon Jukovski suggested a subject to him: "Ivan Sussanin," whose story may be epitomized as follows: In 1613 the Poles invade Russia, seeking to seize the person of the young emperor, Mikhael Fedorovitch Romanov. Ivan Sussanin sacrifices himself in order to save his sovereign. He leads the Poles astray in an impenetrable forest, while he advises the emperor to gain a safe hiding-place. Intermezzos are supplied by a festival in the Polish camp, and the entry of the Tsar into his capital. *La Vie pour le Tsar* (*A Life for the Tsar*) was performed for the first time on November 27, 1836.

The music of this opera was still quite composite in character. The Italian influence dominated in the majority of the arias sung by the principals. Yet folk songs frankly Russian in type also were presented in the score, with their rhythms in 5/4 and 7/4 time, and their strange harmonizations. *A Life for the Tsar* scored a decided success, and one which had a prodigious repercussion throughout Russia, despite opposition on the part of a section of high society. It was "coachman's music," said aristocratic amateurs.

In 1842 Glinka's *Russlan and Ludmilla,* whose libretto is mediocre but which is often superior in musical value to *A Life for the Tsar,* was performed. In certain pages there are brilliant Oriental color effects to be admired.

Alexander Dargomijsky (1813-1868) continued the work of Glinka. [He began to compose in childhood.] He became a distinguished musical amateur. Then, after having met Glinka, he began to work in earnest. He was the composer of *The Russalka* and *The Stone Guest.* Dargomijsky played an important part as president of the *Société de musique russe,* and exercised a very happy influence on the young artists who, succeeding him, banded together to take charge of the nationalist musical movement in Russia, those artists known as "The Five": César Cui, Balakirev, Borodin, Mussorgsky, and Rimsky-Korsakov, the "powerful group," as they called themselves; the "coterie," as they were termed by their enemies.

It was in 1856 that Balakirev and César Cui met and became friends. They were joined soon after by their companions. "Dramatic music," so they said, "should always possess an intrinsic value, like absolute music, one derived from its text." They wished to prevent the sacrifice of musical beauty for the benefit of spectacular splendor and the external entertainment represented by the ballet, for the virtuosity of the operatic soprano, the "stunts" of the tenor with his high C-sharp.

César Cui (1835-1918), professor of the art of fortification at the Engineering Academy of St. Petersburg, played a part quite subordinate among The Five. His operas, *Le Prisonnier du Caucase, Le Fils du mandarin, William Ratcliffe, Angelo, Le Flibustier,* all said and done, are merely estimable works.

Mily Balakirev (1836-1910), after studying mathematics and natural history, taking Glinka's personal advice, devoted himself exclusively to music. Balakirev's influence on his companions who formed the group of The Five was at first a dominating one; he was their educator. Gifted with a musical instinct, prodigiously sure, he was almost entirely ignorant of the art of composition. He had practically no theoretical knowledge, and he taught that experience could be adequately acquired by practice. In his youth his preference inclined to Glinka, Schumann, the Beethoven of the last period, and Berlioz. He despised Haydn, Mozart, and Chopin, and hardly knew Liszt and Wagner. In 1862 he founded a free school of music in St. Petersburg, and from 1867 to 1870 he conducted the concerts of the *Société de musique russe.* He then became director of the singers of the Imperial chapel. His most notable works were a symphonic poem, *Tamar,* music for *King Lear,* and an Oriental fantasy for piano, *Islamey.*

Alexander Borodin (1834-1887) descended on his father's side from the Princes Imeretinsky—the last kings of Imeretia, "the loveliest of those ancient kingdoms of the Caucasus, where the flora of the Orient flourished in the shade of eternal snows." The ancient kings of Imeretia boasted their descent from David, and bore the harp and the sling in their coat of arms. Borodin was at first an army physician, then professor of chemistry at the Academy of Medicine and Surgery in St. Petersburg. He was a curious character, absorbed with the preoccupations of a somewhat confused charity, never finding time to visit his chemical laboratory, or, what is still more to be regretted, opportunities for making the most of his admirable musical gifts. "He adopted young children," Rimsky-Korsakov tells us, "whom he brought up in his house. He took many poor relatives who fell ill or lost their minds into his home. Borodin nursed them, placed them in hospitals, and visited them there. . . . His wife suffered from asthma and did not sleep, and Borodin tended her at night."

His domestic life was completely disorganized. He ate at all those hours when people do not eat. And when, by chance, Borodin happened to think of turning to the piano, he gave up the idea for fear of waking some parent or friend, "asleep on the couch, or simply stretched out on the floor." It is clear that, under such conditions, Borodin wrote only a small number of works. He left two symphonies, a symphonic poem (*In the Steppes of Central Asia*), some chamber music, and an unfinished opera, *Prince Igor,* which Rimsky-Korsakov and Glazunov completed, and which was performed in St. Petersburg in 1890. The subject of *Prince Igor* is the expedition of the Russian princes against the Polovtsi, a savage tribe identical in origin with the ancient Turks, who invaded Russia in the twelfth century. The score of *Prince Igor* comprises pages of surprising beauty, notably the famous *Polovtsian Dances,* whose charm is so penetrant and whose vitality so intense.

Nicholas Andreivitch Rimsky-Korsakov (1844-1909), at first a naval officer, devoted himself entirely to music at an early age. In 1871, when he had as yet benefited only by the advice of Balakirev, he was appointed professor of composition at the St. Petersburg Conservatory. He himself admitted at the time that he was almost wholly ignorant of what he was to teach. In particular, he had no more than a very vague idea of counterpoint and fugue. He set to work courageously, however, and little by little became a remarkable technician. Rimsky-Korsakov, finally, was the only one of The Five who took the trouble to study the theory of his art in detail.*

His considerable output comprises the symphonic poems, *Sadko, Antar, Scheherazade,* a *Capriccio espagnol,* several string quartets, and a large number of operas: *Pskovityanka* (*The Maid of Pskov,* 1873), *A May Night* (1880), *Snegurotchka* (*The Snow-Maiden,* 1882), *Mlada* (1893), *Sadko* (1897), *Mozart and Salieri* (1898), *Tsar Saltan* (1900), *Koshtchei the Immortal* (1902), *Pan Voyevoda* (1905), *Tale of the Invisible City of Kitezh* (1906), and *Le Coq d'or* (1910, posth.).

A close relationship is manifest in the inspiration of Balakirev,

---

* Rimsky-Korsakov, of course, merits a more extended treatment than it has been possible to give him here. He was not only the composer of many pleasurable works—he was also one of the most brilliant orchestrators of all time, whose influence on modern orchestration has been incalculable. For fuller details of his extremely interesting career, see his *Autobiography, My Musical Life.*—E. S.

of Borodin, and of Rimsky-Korsakov. Fancy is less spontaneous, perhaps, in the case of the last-named, who devotes more care to solidly
balanced construction. Yet we are struck by the points these three
artists have in common: the powerful originality of Slavic or Asiatic
folk songs, whose themes in bizarre modes, with their broken rhythms,
their capricious outlines, their subtle and passionate sensuality, they
imitate and borrow, and whose use lends their music an incomparable
flavor. They possess a marvelous instinct for colorful harmonization and
orchestration, and know how to draw all sorts of brilliant, scintillant,
ingratiating effects, effects strangely seductive, from the instrumental
combination.

Modeste Mussorgsky

From "A World of Music" (in preparation)

By Elie Siegmeister

AMONG composers of the nineteenth century there is none whose
artistic achievements and whose influence on the recent course of music
have been so little understood as Modeste Mussorgsky. What we hear
of his—*Boris Godunov* in a bowdlerized version, sung in Italian; *Pictures at an Exhibition* in Ravel's brilliant orchestral dress; and the "Song
of the Flea" done by would-be comic bassos—gives but the vaguest
picture of the man and his significance to the art of music. Appearing
towards the end of the Romantic age, whose last exponents were
beginning to plunge music into the morass of hysterical emotionalism
and introspection, he was like a fresh wind blowing. His was a new
course for music, and he stood alone in his time; without him none of
the biggest men of our time—not Debussy, Ravel, Stravinsky, Bartók,
or Prokofiev—would have found their paths so easily, or turned music
in the directions it has since taken.

The facts of Mussorgsky's life are simple. His was not one of
those extravagant careers that were then so popular. Born in the little
Russian village of Karevo on March 21, 1839, of a well-to-do family
(though his grandmother had been a serf), he entered a military
career, and in his late teens was a dashing young officer, fond of drink
and hard living and adored by the ladies. At nineteen, however, he
resigned his commission, and left this career behind him to devote

himself to composing. From this point on, the story of his life is that of his compositions. In 1868 he set one act of Gogol's comedy, *The Marriage;* in 1869 he wrote *Boris,* which after several revisions forced on him by the St. Petersburg opera management was produced in 1872. In 1873 he began work on the opera *Khovantchina,* and the following year on the comic opera *The Fair at Sorochintzy*—neither of which he had the time or strength to complete. For all during these years, Mussorgsky worked five or six hours of each day as an ill-paid clerk in various government offices, dragging out an impoverished existence. His early friendships with the other members of the famous Five (Rimsky-Korsakov, Borodin, Balakirev, Cui) petered out in the last ten years, owing to his musical intransigeance and the manner of his personal life. At the end he was completely abandoned and alone, and, after his death in 1881, his music was almost completely forgotten by performers and the public for over thirty years. Even today there is no company in America able to do justice to his truly great stage works, and no singer who even attempts to perform more than five or six of his epoch-making songs.

What was Mussorgsky's distinctive achievement? He opened the doors of European art music to a host of fresh and revolutionary technical procedures: new scales, rhythms, harmonies, and tone colors that had flourished vigorously in the peasant music of Slavic countries and Asia, but had never before been admitted into Western art. Yet, daring though it was, Mussorgsky's new musical outlook and technique did not result from any abstract esthetic speculations. They arose out of a strong and purposive view of life and out of the musician's realization that the Romantic musical language was wholly inadequate to express that view.

To Mussorgsky, as to few composers before or since, the life of the common people was a wellspring of artistic power. He was in closest sympathy with the so-called *Narodniki*—those sons and daughters of the Russian aristocracy and middle class who, stirred by the misery of the peasants in the 1860's, left their homes and professions and went to live in the villages, to help, uplift, and teach the common people—and to learn from them. His brother Filaret once wrote in a letter: "In boyhood and youth, as well as in his later years, my brother Modeste had a special predilection for everything concerned with the people and the peasantry. Even the Russian *muzhik* was a human being in his eyes."

Mussorgsky saw peasant music not as picturesque local color, as did other so-called "Nationalists," but as the language and expression of the great mass of humanity—joyful, suffering, or healthy. He was the first highly skilled professional musician to take motives from the life and music of the humble and translate them into art-forms without trying to "uplift" or "purify" them according to conventional concert-hall standards. Because of the ruggedness, simplicity, and daring realism of his style he earned the almost unanimous condemnation of the professional musicians of his time—particularly of those who held the reins of musical power—the critics, conductors, directors of conservatories and opera houses.

Like other Russian artists of his time—Gogol and Dostoevsky in literature, Nekrassov in poetry, and Riepin in painting—Mussorgsky broke the Romantic illusions of "pure beauty," "grand" and "ideal" art, bringing his experience of life as he saw it directly into his music. Like the others, too, he had numerous brushes with the government censors. Several of his songs were banned altogether, and scenes from *Boris* were cut before the work could be mounted. Oskar Riesemann tells us that when *Boris* was finally removed from the repertoire of the Imperial Theater, it was as a result of word from "on high" (the Tsar himself).

Certainly Mussorgsky had plenty of reasons for railing at fate. But because his aim was "to give yourself wholly to mankind . . . say to mankind a new word of friendship and love, right out, till it echoes over the whole breadth of the Russian plains," he was able to create an art transcending personal sufferings, drawing strength from its identification with common humanity.

Mussorgsky, like so many other Russians of his time, was a realist —but not of the back-alley variety. Mechanical imitation of natural sounds, in the manner later made famous by Richard Strauss,* did not interest him. The Russian composer conceived music as a reflection of and commentary on the essential lives of the common men and women he saw about him in the Russia of the 1860's and 1870's. Realism was not, of course, invented by Mussorgsky, for it was already well established in the literature, painting, and drama of his time. But it required daring and vision to apply it to music, still considered largely an art of dreams and introspection.

Keenly aware of his position in music, Mussorgsky stated his aims

---

* For example, the "bleating of the sheep" passage in *Don Quixote,* or the ringing of an alarm clock and the sound of water flowing into a bathtub in the *Symphonia Domestica.*

in no uncertain terms. "Life, wherever it is shown; *truth*, however bitter; speaking out boldly, frankly, point-blank to men—that is my aim," he cried out; and further: "The artistic presentment of beauty alone is sheer childishness, fit for the babes and sucklings of art. To trace the finer characteristics of human nature and of the mass of mankind . . . that is the mission of the artist. . . . I am a realist in the *higher sense*—i.e., my business is to portray *the soul of man in all its profundity.*"

Mussorgsky's seventy-odd songs, two completed operas, and two unfinished ones are a series of human documents in which the whole mass of the Russian people of that time are portrayed with dramatic vividness. The range of themes, emotions, and characters extended far beyond the refined concert-hall canons of what was "fit for art"; no scene was too "crude," no emotion too vigorous, no human being too humble, to find a place in the composer's music.

Because of this, he did not idealize nor prettify the common people; he presented them as he saw them, with all their humor, high spirits, and healthiness, and also their misery, ignorance, and sorrow. He shows us the serf, the drunken coachman, the homeless tramp, the old woman beggar taunted by a street urchin. In *The Nursery*, he gives us with remarkable fidelity the speech and fantasy of children. *The Fair at Sorochintzy* depicts the crowd of merchants, peddlers, and gypsies shouting their wares; *Khovantchina*, the superstitious horde of Old Believers intoning their ancient chants; "Fair Savishna," the cry of the village idiot tormented by the local belle to whom he makes love; and *Boris Godunov*, a crowd of ragged *muzhiks* roused to anger.

When he portrayed those he loved, Mussorgsky worked in broad fresco strokes. But he could also apply his precise, objective technique to the keenest psychological analysis. The characterizations in *Boris*— of the Overseer, of Prince Shouisky, of the Boyars, and of the conniving Dmitri—are sharp and unerring. The Tsar himself is a magnificent personality study, in which external pomp and majesty are combined and dramatically contrasted with the inner terrors and psychological conflicts of the man. The Hallucination and Death Scenes of the opera attain a graphic and dramatic power almost unparalleled. The songs "Death the Commander," "A Ballade," and the four "Dances of Death" are vivid presentations of psychological conflict and human anguish never approached before in the domain of the song—and seldom since. In them Mussorgsky made use of techniques later developed by Debussy, Schönberg, and Alban Berg; but none of these later musicians was ever to equal the musical simplicity and telling power of the Russian.

In others of his songs, Mussorgsky's realism takes the form of a keen, merciless satire. "The Goat" portrays a grotesque old roué. In "The Classic" we have a picture of the self-satisfied music critic for whom "modern" dissonances (this was in 1870) meant the "death of art." "The Seminarist" is a comic masterpiece, in which the religious student, droning Latin declensions, forgets himself and mingles into them his dreams of the village Pope's buxom daughter, getting his ears boxed for his pains.

The fact that Mussorgsky's music did not appeal to conventional musical circles and was regarded as dangerous by the régime itself did not lead him to change his style in any way. In a sense it strengthened his convictions. In 1870, the composer wrote in a letter to a friend: "The banning of my song 'The Seminarist' may be taken as a sign that musicians are now gradually beginning to be raised from the ranks of nightingales, wandering minstrels, and moon-struck gallants and admitted as members of the human race. At the same time, even if they were to ban every single thing I write, I should still go on working as long as strength lasts, for I am not easily thrown off my balance, and a prohibition such as this serves only to fan more fiercely the fire of my enthusiasm."

To Mussorgsky, musical technique was entirely determined by its appropriateness for a given subject matter. Since for him "art was a way of communicating with one's fellow creatures" it is not surprising to find the composer dispensing with all purely formal musical devices that did not serve to transmit the psychological and dramatic matter.

At the same time, seeking a musical language that would faithfully convey the elemental, rough, ironic, violent, and naïve materials of his own vision, Mussorgsky found himself inventing new technical means, or adapting devices of popular music never before used so freely by serious composers.

Of course, elements of folk music had, as we have seen, been used by professional musicians from time immemorial. But in the vast majority of cases, the fierce, vigorous qualities of the people's art were polished and "made presentable" before being admitted to the salon or concert hall. In the music of the Renaissance, in Haydn, Mozart, and even the nineteenth-century "nationalists" who were Mussorgsky's contemporaries and friends, the simple strength of folk music was usually somewhat diluted. The rude melodies were more or less softened and prettified, the strange scales generally revamped into the conventional major and minor, the rough natural harmonies and free, irregular rhythmic designs distilled into more "logical" patterns. Dvořák's symphonies, for example, were cast in the academic Sonata form, and the folk themes introduced were made to behave according to all the rules of the game. Even in Rimsky-Korsakov and Borodin, peasant melodies and rhythms were almost always used as "local color" in a more or less traditional musical framework.

But Mussorgsky, perhaps because he was closer to common life than any other professional musician of his time, did not hesitate to carry out the implications of his material fully—to ignore the major and minor scales, the rules of regular rhythm and the traditional laws of harmony, even to dispense with the basic canons of "musical logic," "orderliness," and "good taste," when the need arose.

The very opening scene of *Boris Godunov*, for example, presents a crowd of peasants beseeching the Tsar for bread:

"What kind of music is this?" the professional critic might have exclaimed—and did. For here is neither regular tonality, rhythm, nor musical form.*

In the second scene of the opera, a drunken friar tells a wild story of ancient battle between Russians and Tatars:

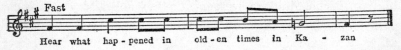

Here again the unusual [Phrygian] scale gives a distinctive flavor to the melody.

* In the orthodox key of F minor, there should be at some point, as every piano student knows, an E-natural; it is totally lacking here. The shifting time signatures (3/4 and 5/4) made no sense in classic practice. The measure phrasing is unorthodox as well (four measures answered by five).

The first measures of *Pictures at an Exhibition* introduced an alternating meter (5/4 and 6/4)* which gives the special character to so many of Mussorgsky's compositions:

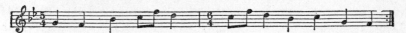

Mussorgsky did not invent these unorthodox musical practices, nor did he use them merely in order to be "different." They were part and parcel of the folk music of the Russian people, which he had known from early childhood, and which he never ceased to study and collect in the villages. His feeling for realism told him that the plain characters that peopled his songs and operas should speak in a language normal and natural to them. It was for this reason, not for "color," that Mussorgsky's own melodic creation was a natural development of the style of Russian (also, on occasion, of Ukrainian, Tatar, Polish, and Jewish) folk music.

The broadened conceptions of scale and rhythm which the composer of *Boris* derived from the people's music opened many musical possibilities unknown to Romantic musicians, and exploited fully only by twentieth-century composers. But even more daring was the Russian's treatment of harmony: his use, for example, of unusual chord combinations to portray the weird and fantastic (as in *A Night on Bald Mountain,* and in the famous Hallucination Scene in *Boris*). Mussorgsky also loved clanging bell harmonies, in which several tonalities seem to be fused into one great resonance. Most famous of these is the opening of the Coronation Scene from *Boris*.

It was these highly original devices—of such great significance for the development of "modern" composers twenty to forty years after Mussorgsky's death—that led one critic to describe the composer's work as "a perpetual strumming on the piano with the loud pedal down most of the time." He could be as delicate and ethereal as anyone when the subject called for it (witness the exquisite Prelude to *Khovantchina*); but when it was a matter of depicting a conflict of wills—as in the end of the Coronation Scene, when the people struggle with the Tsar's guards—he found the exactly appropriate dissonances with which to do it.

It is scarcely necessary to adduce any further examples of Mussorgsky's fresh approach to the materials of music—an approach that is still "modern" today. Suffice it to say that the composer's musical

* Other unusual rhythms used by the composer were 7/4 and 17/4 time.

vision was so far in advance of the official artistic views of his time that his music went practically unrecognized. The one opera of his own that Mussorgsky heard—*Boris*—was produced over the strenuous opposition of the musical authorities, and only because the leading prima donna of the opera house threatened to resign were it not mounted. Even then, Mussorgsky was obliged to make extensive cuts, and—far worse—to insert an artificial love scene in his music drama of the Russian people. (Who ever heard of an opera without a love scene?) *Boris* aroused tremendous enthusiasm among contemporary audiences, especially among the students, stirred by its scenes of peasant uprisings and its political symbolism. But, unfortunately, the Tsarist officialdom at length appreciated this symbolism too, and in spite of its popular success, *Boris* was finally removed from the boards without explanation.

The time had not yet come when a composer whose aim was to create music of, for, and by the people could devote himself to this aim without paying a bitter penalty. Mussorgsky's payment was a lifetime of incessant drudgery and the virtual ostracism imposed on his music by the great ones of the musical world. When Mussorgsky's operas were eventually revived, twenty to thirty years after his death, it was only in the considerably polished version of the faithful Rimsky-Korsakov, who in all sincerity "corrected" some of Mussorgsky's "mistakes." Rimsky feared—and not without justice—that unless he sweetened the pill opera managers would never swallow it. Even today *Boris* is performed in this country only in the shorn and disfigured "edited" version.

While Mussorgsky's music in its original form is still largely unknown to the wide audience of music lovers, its composer's labors were not in vain. For the scores are all here (in the recently published Soviet edition of the original texts), and will some day unquestionably win the recognition that is their due. But equally important is the vast and fruitful influence they have had on the music of our time. For, in the deepest sense, many of the best composers of the last generation and this have been Mussorgsky's children.

Giuseppe Verdi

Abridged from "Alla Breve"

By Carl Engel

THREE centuries of Italian opera lie between the first real attempt at this form of musico-dramatic expression, the *Dafne* of Rinuccini, and *Falstaff*, the octogenarian Verdi's last and finest work for the stage. Rinuccini's poem with the music by Peri and Corsi was performed privately in Corsi's house at Florence, some time after 1594 and before 1597. Between 1600 and 1800, the mythological subject of Daphne's change into a laurel tree, as related in Ovid's *Metamorphoses,* had been used by no fewer than fifteen composers, including Handel. At about the same time that the circle of Florentine dilettanti was experimenting with "chanted plays," substituting the solo voice with instrumental accompaniment for the then prevailing type of choral part-writing (chiefly unaccompanied), Shakespeare was immortalizing the character of Falstaff in his *Henry IV* and *The Merry Wives of Windsor*. Falstaff had appeared in fourteen different operas before Arrigo Boito, poet and composer, wrote his libretto for Verdi, whose opera was first presented at La Scala in Milan, on February 9, 1893.

Giuseppe Verdi was born October 10, 1813, at Roncole, a village near the little town of Busseto, in the former grand-duchy of Parma. He was therefore only seven months younger than Richard Wagner. At the time of his birth, Italy formed part of the French empire, under Napoleon I. At Napoleon's abdication in 1814, the duchy of Parma was allotted to Marie Louise, Napoleon's dethroned wife and daughter of the Austrian emperor. The subsequent rule of persecution and oppression, however, was inspired by Vienna. Verdi's youth and musical development coincided with the period of Italian struggle for emancipation from the Austrian yoke. His parents made a meager living by keeping an inn and a small shop in Roncole. Although brought up in the humblest surroundings, it was fortunate that Giuseppe found incentive and understanding for his talents in a community which was intensely musical. The village organist gave him his first lessons; the father bought him a rickety little spinet. In time he was sent to Busseto, three miles distant from Roncole, to get what rudimentary knowledge the schoolteacher had to impart. While still a mere lad he was chosen to succeed the old organist at Roncole, who had died. Every Sunday and holiday saw him on the highroad, walking the three miles from Busseto to the little village church, where, to the great pride not only of his parents but of all the worshipers, "Giuseppino" fingered the clattering keys and occasionally stretched his little foot for a deep pedal note that mightily reverberated from the vaulted roof.

Busseto enjoyed the distinction of possessing an orchestra formed by capable amateurs, under the direction of a musician named Provesi. One of the leading spirits in this little band was a distiller, Barezzi, a friend of old Verdi's. When Giuseppe had finished his school education, he entered the employ of Barezzi, who housed and treated him like a son. Barezzi possessed a thing very rare for those days, a grand piano of Viennese make; he also possessed a pretty and musical daughter, Margherita. Young Verdi was much attracted by both the precious instrument and the charming girl. His studies in counterpoint and composition were now directed by Provesi. The town of Busseto granted him a stipend which enabled him to seek further and better instruction in Milan. But upon his asking for admission to the Milan conservatory of music, it was refused by the director on account of "lack of technical equipment." Perhaps this is not so surprising as it may seem. The academic training essential in an institution of that kind, Verdi had not acquired. Had he been brought up in a manner conforming to these academic standards, his natural impulse might have been dwarfed or diverted. He might have become an obscure composer of creditable masses and motets. As it was, he had been permitted to "grow up musically" in an unsophisticated world where a "tune" counted for everything, where popular taste was all for *le belle romanze*. However, while the doors of the august conservatory remained closed to him, he found an excellent teacher in Vincenzo Lavigna, conductor of the orchestra at La Scala, the grand opera house of Milan. This association with theatrical circles had a directing influence upon Verdi's development. He began to compose more ambitious works, but none of them had significant merits. Upon the death of Provesi, in 1833, the boy of twenty was invited to return to Busseto and become the successor of his old master as conductor of the little orchestra and organist at the cathedral. He did not obtain the latter position, because of strong objections from part of the town authorities to whom the young man's musical tendencies seemed altogether "too worldly." But Barezzi received his protégé with open arms, and two years later accorded him the hand of Margherita. The little town did not offer room enough for Verdi's ambition; therefore he went, with his wife and two little sons, to Milan in 1837, intending to enter the operatic field. He found a librettist in the nineteen-year-old poet Temistocle Solera, and in 1839 the first fruit of their collaboration, *Oberto, conte di San Bonifacio,* was successfully produced at La Scala. All seemed to point to a splendid future for the youthful composer. He was commissioned to write a comic opera, and was in the midst of his work, when his wife and both his children died within the space of two years. Under such mental stress it was impossible for him to give of his best. Although he completed the opera, it was a failure. Discouraged by so much misfortune, he retired to Busseto. But he found that only renewed activity could really bring the oblivion he sought, so he finally returned to Milan. The director of La Scala offered him a libretto that had been rejected by Otto Nicolai, composer of *The Merry Wives of Windsor.* The libretto was that of *Nabucco,* a biblical story. Verdi felt attracted by the subject, and went to work. The success of the première on March 9, 1842, decided Verdi's future. The leading soprano in the cast of *Nabucco* was Giuseppina Strepponi, who later became Verdi's second wife.

From that point on, Verdi's career resembled that of all other Italian opera composers who had preceded him. Failures alternated with successes. A constant demand for new works left no time to ponder over either. The old "opera d'obbligo" was still necessary to the Carnival season, and every year witnessed these rival productions in all the larger cities of Italy. On February 11, 1843, *I Lombardi,* at La Scala, confirmed Verdi's operatic ascendancy. Rossini had given up writing operas; Donizetti had but five more years to live, with his mental powers beginning to give way; Bellini had died, thirty-three years old, in 1835. That Wagner's *The Flying Dutchman* was the contemporary of Verdi's *Nabucco* is of interest, considering that it was thirty years before the Italian's work became in the slightest degree akin to the German's novel procedures. Eleven operas had followed *I Lombardi* (with only *Ernani,* first performed March 9, 1844, as a striking success) before *Rigoletto,* on March 11, 1851, set Venice literally wild with enthusiasm. The text, fashioned upon Victor Hugo's *Le Roi s'amuse,* had to be subjected to various revisions before the Austrian censor would pass it. Verdi was known for his patriotic sentiments. Northern Italy was infested with spies, paid by the Viennese police. Any allusion, however veiled, to governmental abuses or longings for independence was ruthlessly prosecuted. *Rigoletto* was followed in quick succession by *Il Trovatore* and *La Traviata.* When *Il Trovatore* was sung for the first time, in Rome on January 19, 1853, the Tiber had overflowed the streets of the city. Yet, ankle-deep in water, people stood at the gates from nine o'clock in the morning, on the day of the first performance, in order to gain admission. *La Traviata* seemed doomed to failure, owing to the poor interpreters at the première. Verdi remained silent for four years. In 1855 followed *The Sicilian Vespers,* written for the Opéra in Paris. *Un Ballo in Maschera* again attracted the censor's attention in 1858, and the murdered King Gustavus III of Sweden had to be turned into a "Governor of Boston," the opera coming too soon after the attempted assassination of Napoleon III by the Italian Orsini. But Napoleon, stirred to action at last, espoused the cause of Italy against Austria, and after the battles of Magenta and Solferino, in June, 1859, the dream of a United Kingdom of Italy was nearing its realization. The name of VERDI, standing for Vittore Emanuele Re d'Italia, became the battle-cry of the patriots.

The last in this almost uninterrupted chain of operas was also the revelation of a new and greater Verdi. It was *Aida,* written upon command of the Viceroy of Egypt, finished in 1869, and performed at Cairo in 1871. The composer could not be persuaded to cross the Mediterranean. When the opera was given in Europe, Verdi had the satisfaction of winning serious and enthusiastic consideration from even the sternest music critics, who had up to that time spoken lightly of his "melodic facility and harmonic shallowness." But what seemed to these critics the composer's splendid swan-song was in reality only the first of three works which ultimately showed Verdi's genius at its full stature. After another pause of eighteen years he gave the world his magnificent *Otello.* In his eightieth year, 1893—as though at last in the happy calm of old age he had rediscovered the humorous vein that fifty-three years ago the annihilation of his young family had cut —he wrote that masterly *Falstaff,* perhaps the finest of all Italian comedy-operas, sparkling with youthfulness and subtle musical wit, the ultimate proof of Verdi's consummate artistry.

No sum of honors or distinctions could induce Verdi to abandon the quietude of his country estate Sant' Agata near his native Busseto. As a landed gentleman he preferred to live the summers amid surroundings beloved since childhood; his winters were passed mostly at Genoa. He died in Milan on Jan. 27, 1901.

Much of Verdi's inspiration responded to a purely popular note. No composer's melodies have been sung and whistled by a greater number of people than his. A Requiem Mass, composed in 1874 in memory of the poet Manzoni, is more theatrical than churchly, and it can hardly be counted a departure from Verdi's style. The public of Italy that attended the first opera performance at Venice in 1637 had grown into the public of the world. And that public looked to Verdi for its greatest joys, with almost fanatic devotion. His last two operas, revealing all his ripened mastery, are not those most often performed. It is still the wealth of sensuous melody contained in *Rigoletto, Il Trovatore* and *Aida* that sends thrills through the crowded opera houses of both hemispheres and perpetuates the glory of Italian opera in the work of Italy's greatest *maestro.*

Claude-Achille Debussy

Adapted from "A History of Music"

By Paul Landormy

CLAUDE-ACHILLE DEBUSSY was born August 22, 1862, at Saint-Germain-en-Laye. His home surroundings were quite unmusical, and his father had destined him for a navy career. Notwithstanding, his musical vocation showed itself at a decidedly early age, and he entered the Conservatoire in 1873. In 1877 he obtained a second piano prize; but all recognition in harmony was refused him. On the other hand, the first prize in accompaniment was awarded him in 1880, and the Prix de Rome in 1881, the latter for his cantata *L'Enfant prodigue.* Meanwhile he had spent a short time in Russia, which gave him an opportunity of hearing works by Rimsky-Korsakov, Balakirev and Borodin, and, in particular, the free improvisations of the genuine Russian gypsies.

From Italy Debussy sent on a brace of works to the Institute, *Le Printemps* and *La Damoiselle élue,* which latter was in part refused; *Le Printemps* was looked upon as scandalous. Debussy at once objected to the performance of his *Damoiselle élue* at the concert solemnly organized through the offices of the Institute, according to the tradition which thus rewards the Prix de Rome winners for their labors; and the first hearing of the work was given by the *Société nationale*.

An old music lover then called Debussy's attention to *Boris Godunov*. Soon after, Debussy set to music the *"Ariettes oubliées"* of Verlaine (1888), and Baudelaire's *"Cinq Poèmes"* (1890). He made the acquaintance of Stéphane Mallarmé, whose home was the meeting-place of so many young artists, poets and painters in particular, and the sanctuary of the symbolist movement. There he met Gustave Kahn, Henri de Régnier, Pierre Louÿs, Francis Viélé-Griffin, Stuart Merrill, Verlaine, Whistler, etc.

Following his instinct, Debussy had approached the artists who not only could understand him, but also could aid him to perfect his intellectual development. In 1892 he wrote his first symphonic poem, *Prélude à l'après-midi d'un faune,* inspired by one of Stéphane Mallarmé's poems; and then he set to work to compose his *Pélleas et Mélisande,* which was destined to keep him busy for ten years. However, in 1893 he produced a string quartet, broad and poignant in inspiration; and in 1894 his *Proses lyriques,* for which he himself had supplied the literary texts.

In 1898 appeared the marvelous *Chansons de Bilitis,* and the three *Nocturnes* for orchestra, and Debussy's fame began to spread beyond the circle of his more intimate friends. He also essayed musical criticism, in which he displayed a subtle wit, original, concise, clear-cut, and free-spoken.* The performances of *Pélleas et Mélisande* at the Opéra-Comique (1902) finally revealed the new genius to all musicians.

Thenceforward Debussy was famous. The impassioned discussions which raged about his name merely added to his glory.

He himself led the existence of a recluse, and hardly showed himself. He devoted himself entirely to his work, and one by one, as though regretfully, yearning for a perfection which was never satisfied, he gave his publishers long-considered compositions in which his ambition to give thought its clearest expression in the briefest compass was increasingly evident. The *Préludes* for piano, in this respect, are especially significant.

* In his critical writings he affirms his predilections, which are significant: he prizes above all else works in good taste. His heroes are Racine, Watteau, Couperin, Rameau, Mozart. He cannot forgive Wagner his grandiloquence, and also reproaches César Franck, declaring that his sentimental effusions betray a lack of good form.

For a whole year, beginning with August, 1914, Debussy ceased to write. He was destined to die a few years later (1918), waging against his bodily sufferings, against daily and hourly martyrdom, the heroic struggle of genius which, to its last hour, insists upon its strength and its freedom.

Two extra-musical influences contributed to direct Debussy's footsteps in his search for the paths which would lead him to a full outpouring of his originality: symbolist poetry and impressionistic painting.

Debussy, who, as we have said, was an assiduous frequenter of the gatherings in Mallarmé's home, there found his dislike for the artifices of romanticism confirmed. More and more, he rejected the precepts of that musical rhetoric which is merely the art of development carried to excess, the art of drawing from a theme more than it does or should contain. Like Verlaine, he detested eloquence. He did not wish to take advantage of us. He limits our enjoyment in order to make it the more complete. He is always fearful of wearing out our patience. He is discreet.

He took pleasure in a kind of naturalistic revery which attempts to draw from things a poetry eluding the vulgar; yet an immediate, unpremeditated poetry, a poetry not systematically composed by intellectual effort, in the style of romantic poetry, but a naïve poetry, self-born of the spontaneous correlation of sensations, emotions, and images.

Impressionistic painting, too, affected Debussy's art. Monet, Renoir, Sisley, Pissaro sought to reconcile their aim of painting the most prosaic details of modern life with a deep idealism. They were concerned only with impressions, and thought less of line than of color.

And this very thing might be said of Debussy, that he preferred *color* to *line,* that is to say, *harmony* to *melody.* His music at times seems to be composed of tonal splashes in juxtaposition. At any rate, he abandoned the great sentimental themes of romantic music. He, too, noted down his fleeting impressions. Debussy wished to convey to us a sensation of the light, the vague, the unreal, and not to insist on the all too solidly established aspects of reality.

As to the musical influences to which Debussy reacted, they were many in number. First of all were those of his teacher, Massenet, still quite noticeable in his earlier works, *La Damoiselle élue* and the *Arabesques* for piano, for example.

Then there was Chabrier's influence, easily noticeable in the works of the same period, and in places, that of Wagner, from which he did not at once free himself. In this connection it is interesting to reread the *Cinq Poèmes* by Baudelaire.

Massenet and Chabrier, the one as regards voluptuous tenderness, the other ironic fantasy, continued to inspire Debussy in spirit. Yet their methods soon ceased to suffice for the exigencies of a sensitive nature richer and more varied than their own. Debussy at an early stage realized the necessity of developing a technique very different from that of his French predecessors.

In his researches he was above all guided by the example of the Russians. Mussorgsky was mainly responsible for pointing out to him the road to a less restricted harmony, a musical idiom freed from the rules of its ancient logic, and, on occasion, a way of leading vocal melody almost parallel with the outline of ordinary speech, in short intervals, and in relatively rapid utterance.

Rimsky-Korsakov and Borodin gave Debussy a glimpse of all the resources, in part unexplored, of the ancient modes, of the extra-classic scales, and of a novel use of orchestral means.

It might be added that a freakish French musician, more inventor than creator, Erik Satie, the composer of the *Sarabandes* (1887), the *Pieces in the Form of a Pear,* the *Bureaucratic Sonata,* and other fantastic products of a whimsical yet quite elegantly witty imagination, furnished certain elements of that new language which the composer of *Pélleas* used for loftier ends.

No matter how much credit be given his predecessors and the influences which led him to the path of his discoveries, Debussy none the less remains an extraordinary inventor of new procedures, as well as a creator of unexpected emotions.

Never, perhaps, in the whole history of music, has so brusque and radical a change in technique been witnessed. The whole edifice of traditional harmony was overturned.

In place of our individual scales, major and minor, the "connecting ties" common to all melody, we find a host of different scales, scales on different degrees, scales with a lowered or a raised fifth, five-note scales, whole-tone scales, etc.

Instead of the fundamental differentiation between chords as consonant and dissonant, all chords are regarded as consonant. There are no more resolutions, no more correct and incorrect combinations. The new chords are developed out of the encounter of sounds formerly regarded as barbarous, and excluded from music.

At first Debussy appeared to be no more than a revolutionary, an anarchist. He was reproached with writing music which was no music, since it violated all accepted rules. Is it necessary to recall that rules are only developed after the event, by the analysis of the masterworks of the past, and that they are modified whenever an innovating genius creates a form of beauty hitherto unknown?

And besides, all those formulas by means of which Debussy's critics at first endeavored to define his style fell short of the mark. In reality, Debussy destroyed nothing, he gave up nothing. He did not break with tradition. Debussy, according to the dictates of the moment, made use of all the resources already acquired by musical art. In his own manner he was well able, for example, to develop the themes in his quartet, which is "cyclic" in form; to employ old consonant harmonies; to use "leading motives," as in *Pelléas;* lovingly to draw the outlines of a slow, extended melody with sinuous curves complaisantly spread out. He was not systematic to the point of robbing himself of the accumulated resources of the past. Yet he threw wide the gates to the future!

For all the importance of Debussy's technical innovations, they do not comprise his whole art. The point is to understand how they are connected with his own mode of feeling, his own character, his own genius.

He was at once classed as an *impressionist,* and the word applies— if it be correctly understood. One might say, in fact, that Debussy's art is an impressionistic art, because he does not stress it, does not dwell on it, does not force it. We are affected, yet his touch is light, at times a simple allusion. He never repeats a blow which has found its mark. This makes his art appear but skin-deep, and yet it is profoundly penetrant. One must be able to grasp his meaning from a hint. It is the antipode of Wagnerian music, and of all romanticism.

He is a dreamer who does not seem to believe in the reality of life, and lives in a dream. Even in objects themselves he seizes only an illusory semblance with which he enchants himself, and a vain and hidden charm which he discloses to us.

He indolently allows himself to drift with the capricious current of his sensations, his images, and his emotions. He does not care to build up either his life or his joys. He abandons himself to the "innocent and effortless movement of instinct." This superrefined nature is above all captivated by naïveté.

In external actualities he is attracted by all that is fugitive and mysterious, all that lends itself to the ambiguity of symbolism, to the caprice of fantastic interpretation.

Nothing delights him more than that which, in inanimate matter, has a movement which assumes the aspect of life, and an illusive psychic sensibility. The water, the air, the winds, all that is fluid, all that has emotion, that reflects, that flashes or caresses—especially water—appeals to him and holds his attention, and he is its incomparable poet-musician (*Le Jet d'eau, Nuages, La Mer*).

No musician has spoken better of "the little ones," has addressed himself to them more simply, without any "writing down," without any sentimental silliness, but with vivid, direct, intuitive sympathy (*Children's Corner*).

Yet his is no devout soul, no religious soul predisposed to faith, bending down to other beings, in order to question their mystery. He believes only in the universal illusion.

His scepticism often inclines him to tenderness, to pity for every living being suffering from that fundamental deception life represents. His scepticism is expressed in irony also. It is an irony which is not cruel, the irony of a man who at heart is kind and simple. His malice is that of a child. At times Claude Debussy is only a big boy who likes to amuse himself. It was in such a mood that he wrote his *Minstrels* and *General Lavine*.

A free spirit if ever there was one, Debussy eludes the narrow limitations of those definitions of his talent and his art which a hasty, too often partial, examination first suggests. Capable of diverting us, or setting us dreaming, as his mood may dictate, he also has the power to unseal for us the broad, deep springs of pity and tragic awe, and to strike our soul with terror.

Maurice Ravel

By Gilbert Chase

From "Great Modern Composers," ed. by Oscar Thompson

MAURICE JOSEPH RAVEL, the greatest French composer since Debussy, was born (1875) in the French-Basque town of Ciboure, adjacent to Saint-Jean-de-Luz (Basses-Pyrénées). His father's family was French-Swiss; his mother was of Basque descent. A few weeks after his birth, his parents moved to Paris, where Maurice was educated. His father, an engineer, was a musical amateur, and, though Maurice showed no overwhelming inclination towards music, he was encouraged to take lessons in piano and harmony from about the age of twelve. His first piano teacher was Henri Ghis, and he took lessons in harmony from Charles-René, who recognized the musical individuality of his young pupil. In 1889 he was admitted to Anthiome's preparatory piano class at the Conservatoire, and two years later passed into Charles de Bériot's class. He also studied harmony under Emile Pessard, and (from 1897) counterpoint under André Gédalge and composition under Gabriel Fauré.

Gédalge has testified that Ravel was a brilliant student of counterpoint. But from the first he showed a penchant for unorthodox harmonic combinations, and he delighted in playing the unconventional pieces of Chabrier and Satie. Though these composers exerted a certain influence upon him, at the age of twenty he already possessed a highly personal and novel style, as shown by the *Menuet antique* for piano of 1895, followed in 1895-96 by the *Sites auriculaires* for two pianos, containing the Habanera which was later incorporated into the *Rapsodie espagnole*.

Under the enlightened guidance of Fauré, whose character was free from academic rigidity, Ravel's artistic personality was able to develop spontaneously and to achieve that synthesis of classical balance and daring innovation which was to remain a basic feature of his music. Nevertheless, he had to contend against academic opposition, critical injustice, and public indifference before attaining his undisputed place in the foremost rank of French composers. He made his public debut as a composer in 1898, when the *Sites auriculaires* were performed at a concert of the Société Nationale de Musique, and the following year the same organization gave his *Ouverture de Shéhérazade* for orchestra and the *Pavane pour une infante défunte* for piano. One critic described the Overture as "some Rimsky-Korsakov rehashed by a Debussy-ist who is eager to equal Erik Satie."

During the next few years he composed three striking masterpieces, the *Jeux d'eau* for piano (1901), the String Quartet in F (1902-03), and the song-cycle *Shéhérazade* (1903). Yet during this period he was to feel the sting of academic hostility. In 1901 he competed for the Prix de Rome, but received only the second prize. He competed for the famous prize again in 1902, and in 1903, both times without success. Finally, in 1905, when for the fourth time he presented himself as a candidate for the award, he was not even passed at the preliminary test, intended only to eliminate incompetent contestants. And this in spite of the fact that he was nearing the age-limit and had a right to expect the customary leniency under such circumstances. This high-handed procedure aroused a storm of protest in French musical circles, leading to a change in the directorship of the Conservatoire.

Though the gates of official success were closed to him, Ravel now produced an unbroken succession of works marked by such originality and perfection that his unmistakable genius had perforce to be acknowledged. The *Miroirs* for piano (1905) showed that he was exploring, technically and poetically, a new world of keyboard music. And the pianistic horizon was further enlarged by the three pieces comprising *Gaspard de la nuit* (1908). In the field of vocal music, he developed a distinctly personal style of lyrical declamation in the *Histoires naturelles* (1906)—a style tinged with malicious irony and dry humor. This type of vocal declamation, supported by a very subtle and piquant orchestration, was given a more extensive development in the one-act comic opera *L'Heure espagnole* (1907), produced at the Opéra-Comique on May 19, 1911. In spite of its witty and vivacious quality, this work did not enjoy an immediate success; but after its revival at La Monnaie, Brussels, in 1921, and at the Paris Opéra in 1922, it was more warmly received. It was given at Covent Garden, London, in 1919; in Chicago and at the Lexington Theater, New York, in 1920, and at the Metropolitan Opera House, 1925.

Another work of Hispanic inspiration composed in 1907 was the pungently evocative *Rapsodie espagnole* for orchestra. To this period belongs also the work which is regarded as Ravel's masterpiece, the ballet *Daphnis et Chloé,* composed in 1909-11 on a commission from Serge Diaghilev, who produced it with his Russian Ballet at the Châtelet, Paris, on June 8, 1912. In the form of two orchestral suites, this is one of the most frequently performed works in the modern symphonic repertoire. This score represents the culmination of Ravel's inspiration: the harmonic texture is complex and elaborate without abandoning the basic principle of tonality; the instrumentation evokes a shimmering array of tone-tints, yet remains always an integral part of the musical fabric; the melodic lines are pure and graceful, the form is organic and perfect.

As if realizing that harmonic and instrumental elaboration could go no further without sacrificing some of this essential clarity of form and line, we now find Ravel turning towards a simplification of style. This is to be noted in the *Trois Poèmes de Mallarmé* (1913) for voice, piano, string quartet, two flutes, and two clarinets, in which each instrument is treated as a soloist, and also in the Piano Trio (1915), in which the evident influence of Saint-Saëns confirms the composer's preoccupation with clarity of form. The tendency towards simplification is continued in *Le Tombeau de Couperin* for piano (1914-17), of which four numbers were orchestrated in 1919. In this work Ravel affirms his strong spiritual ties with the eighteenth century, when the intellect and the emotions had a mutual respect for each other, and inspiration and formality walked naturally together.

During the World War of 1914-18, Ravel, though of frail physique, served as an ambulance driver at the front until his health gave out and he was obliged to undertake a rest cure. In 1920 he composed one of his very few works written directly for the orchestra, *La Valse,* a somewhat cruel evocation of a vanished era, musically very effective. In 1920-22 came the compact Sonata for violin and 'cello, and then Ravel turned again to the stage with the opera-ballet *L'Enfant et les sortilèges* (1924-25), produced at Monte Carlo in 1925 and at the Opéra-Comique in 1926.

In 1928 he was commissioned to write a ballet for Ida Rubinstein. As he had produced his most artistic composition on a commission from Diaghilev some twenty years before, so he now produced his most popular composition on a similar commission from Mlle. Rubinstein. This was the famous *Boléro,* given at the Paris Opéra in November, 1928. This extraordinary orchestral tour de force is based simply on the repetition of a single theme, in unvarying rhythm, remaining in the key of C major almost to the very end, and continuing throughout in a gradual crescendo. It took the world by storm, and was heard in every variety of instrumental arrangement, including versions for jazz band, making Ravel's name known even to the masses who cared little about "serious" music.

Though greatly esteemed in the musical world, Ravel up to this time had not been a really popular figure. Since the war he had lived and worked in seclusion at his villa in Montfort l'Amaury, about 40 miles from Paris, avoiding public activity of any kind. After the success of *Boléro,* however, he became the most popular musical figure in France. He was repeatedly invited to appear as guest-conductor of his own works, and on every such occasion was enthusiastically acclaimed, though he was not a skilful or effective conductor. He was slight in build, and his movements were angular and precise. His features were sharp and intelligent, the lips thin, with a hint of irony in the set of the mouth.

From 1930, the composition of two piano concertos occupied Ravel simultaneously. One of these was the Concerto in G major, a scintillating work full of novel effects, first performed at Paris on Jan. 14, 1932; and the other was the Concerto for the Left Hand, written for the one-armed pianist Paul Wittgenstein, by whom it was played for the first time in Vienna on Nov. 27, 1931, Ravel conducting. These two works, so widely dissimilar, illustrate Ravel's capacity for creative renewal. But his creative career came to an end with the three songs for baritone and orchestra entitled *Don Quichotte à Dulcinée,* composed in 1932. After this he was stricken with a brain ailment which eventually caused his death. He died in a Paris clinic, following an operation, on Dec. 28, 1937, at the age of 62.

It may be truly said of Ravel that his art was his life. He never married. He shunned the outward signs of fame: twice he refused membership in the Legion of Honor. He visited the United States in 1928, made several trips to England, and toured Europe as guest-conductor of his own works in 1932; but he did not travel extensively. His chief hobby was the collecting of curios and bibelots, of which his house was full. He had a keen sense of humor and enjoyed playing practical jokes upon his friends. He did not care for teaching, but gave lessons to a few pupils, of whom the most distinguished was the English composer, Ralph Vaughan Williams.

At the outset of his career Ravel was accused of plagiarizing Debussy. Though this groundless accusation has been amply refuted, it may be well to compare the art of Ravel with that of Debussy in order to bring out the essential difference between them. Both composers received their musical training at a time when the autocratic sway of Wagner's music was at its height, and both revolted against this hegemony, refusing to be caught up in the post-Wagnerian movement of the César Franck school. Thus they had a common starting-point, further emphasized by certain common influences: the Russian "Five," Chabrier, Erik Satie. But even in this matter of influences, there were important divergencies. Among the Russians, Debussy was more influenced by Mussorgsky, Ravel by Rimsky-Korsakov; among the Romantics, Debussy inclined towards Chopin, Ravel towards Liszt; and among immediate precursors, Debussy felt the spell of the sensuous and sentimental Massenet, while Ravel was attracted by the suave and precise Saint-Saëns. While Debussy gravitated inevitably towards Impressionism, Ravel from the outset remained a classicist at heart, not exempt from a touch of that scholasticism which Debussy held in horror.

Harmonically, the musical language of Ravel is clearly differentiated from that of Debussy. Though Ravel made use of the chord of the major 9th which Debussy so fully exploited, it is the chord of the 11th harmonic, based on the principle of natural resonance, which is characteristic of Ravel's harmonic idiom. The whole-tone scale so frequently employed by Debussy is rarely to be met with in Ravel.* Both composers made use of the ancient Greek modes, a result probably of the Russian-Byzantine influence. Ravel is more daring than Debussy in his use of appoggiatura chords, and of appoggiature either unresolved or resolved upon other appoggiature. But it should be observed that Ravel takes care not to destroy the principle of tonality, which forms the foundation of his harmonic structure. He embellishes the structure with a profusion of bold, elaborate, and subtle ornamentation; but he is too much of a classicist to undermine the foundation. Unlike Schönberg, therefore, he does not evolve a new harmonic system, but renovates the old.

It is very probable that in his piano music Debussy owed something to Ravel. Striking similarities have been pointed out between Debussy's *Estampes,* which appeared in 1903, and Ravel's *Jeux d'eau,*

* The most conspicuous exception is to be found in the *Habanera.*

published in 1902. Ravel's piano music is unquestionably of the utmost originality and importance; its historical significance lies in the restoration of a tradition which had been allowed to languish for more than half a century. *Jeux d'eau* stems directly from Liszt, reviving the tradition of pianistic virtuosity which aims at exploiting all the technical resources of the piano while placing them at the service of poetic and descriptive ideas. In *Miroirs* and in *Gaspard de la nuit,* Ravel carries the art of pianistic evocation to new limits of imaginative and technical subtlety. The piano music of Ravel calls for a new technique and a new emotional approach; the pianist Gil-Marchex remarked that one of his pieces (*Le Gibet*) required no fewer than twenty-seven different methods of touch.

Ravel is rightly regarded as a master of orchestration. Yet it is necessary to emphasize the fact that he never indulges in instrumental effects for their own sake, but conceives his orchestration as an integral part of his musical thought. Paradoxically, this is true even when he orchestrates works originally written for piano, as in the *Pavane pour une infante défunte, Alborada del gracioso, Ma Mère l'Oye,* and *Le Tombeau de Couperin.* When transferring his piano music to the orchestra, he conceives it anew in terms of this medium and the result therefore is a fully organic and autonomous work of art. Roland-Manuel has observed that Ravel's orchestral music makes greater demands upon the virtuosity of the instrumentalists than upon the initiative of the conductor. This is because his instrumentation is so calculated and precise. Thus Vuillermoz aptly remarked that "There are several ways of performing Debussy's music; but there is only one way of playing Ravel's."

Ravel's music has been compared to those formal French gardens in which the trees and shrubs are trimmed to precise shapes, and the flowers laid out in well-ordered patterns. The unique quality of his genius consists in his ability to achieve such originality and variety of expression within the bounds of these formal restrictions. He has been accused of lacking emotional depth and power; it is true that he refused to wear his heart on his sleeve, though he was by no means devoid of sensibility; his emotion is intense and concentrated rather than diffuse and expansive. It has been pointed out that he lacked the capacity for creating in the larger forms, such as grand opera, the symphony, and the symphonic poem. But, since the only valid measurement of music is qualitative rather than quantitative, this is less an indication of his limitations than of the special bent of his temperament. Within the forms that he chose to cultivate, his inspiration seldom waned, his artistry never lost its consummate skill. Even those who hold that there is too much artifice in his art must admit that he conceals this artifice with infinite grace.

PART SIX

In Our Time

VI. In Our Time

IF I were to start this chapter in the style of a radio quiz, I might put the following question to the reader: Which one of our newest composers provoked the following reaction from a famous critic, and what was the work that did it?

"It is a strange state to which the great improvements in the technical and mechanical arts have brought our newest composers. Their productions are no longer music; they go beyond the level of human feelings, and no response can be given them from mind and heart."

But the question would be definitely an unfair one, because this criticism was made *not* of a work by Hindemith, Cowell, Bartók, or one of our young atonalists, but of one by Ludwig van Beethoven—of his Fifth Symphony, in fact; and the critic was none other than Goethe!

Nothing would be easier than to find similar criticisms of many other works which we now regard as great masterpieces, but which when first written were considered experimental, even "unmusical," essays by the "newest composers." Of course, such criticisms were less frequent in those periods when musicians followed traditional pathways, writing in a manner that was acceptable to all because it had already been used a thousand times.

But at periodic intervals in history, music, after flowing along in a perfectly calm and well-behaved fashion for generations, suddenly seems to go into violent eruption. Young men emerge who write works apparently violating all the respectable rules of beauty, harmony, and good taste. They provoke diatribes and debates, plunge the professors and critics into angry confusion, awaken enthusiasm among the new generation, and ultimately go down in history either as fools or as creators of a new musical epoch. Such sudden upsets were brought about in 1600 by the creators of the opera; in (about) 1750 by the

565

"modernists" who introduced the symphony form; in 1800 by Beethoven; at ever shorter intervals since by Berlioz, Wagner, Mussorgsky, Debussy; and finally, by the composers of our own time.

Perhaps the musical changes of the past two generations have been more drastic than most previous ones. I say "perhaps," because these artistic shocks always seem more violent when we are very close to them; two or three decades later, many of the most "revolutionary" and bitterly condemned works have a strange way of becoming "classics." Fifteen or twenty years ago, Stravinsky's *Sacre du printemps* caused many old Philharmonic subscribers to quit their seats in ostentatious disgust. Routine critics denounced it as the work of a lunatic or a charlatan; one of my college professors even asserted that you could play the work backwards and no one would know the difference!

Today the "daring innovations" of the 1910's and 1920's hardly make a splash in the concert hall. The dissonances, complex rhythms, and novel orchestral effects no longer sound so shocking as they once did—or even shocking at all; indeed, audiences have learned to find many of them quite pleasant. Not only the *Sacre du printemps* but many another "modern" work has settled down to a respectable popularity in the concert hall, among them Falla's *Three-Cornered Hat*, Ravel's *Daphnis and Chloe;* Debussy's *La Mer* and *Iberia;* Stravinsky's *Fire-Bird* and *Petroushka;* Prokofiev's *Peter and the Wolf* and his two violin concerti; and at least three symphonies by Shostakovich.

But even more than this, so-called "modern music" has passed from the concert hall to the workshops of the Broadway dance arrangers and the fabricators of Hollywood and radio background music. The discords and rhythmic distortions of the swing and boogie-woogie brethren, played in juke-boxes from the Bronx to Kalamazoo, have begun to outdistance some of the most audacious novelties of the 1920 *avant-garde*. Cacophonous harmonies, frenetic rhythms, and atonal melodies, once performed only in the select circles of the Guilds and Leagues, are now heard as accompaniment to movie comedies and "epics," animated cartoons, radio "mysteries" and soap operas, documentary films, recitals of modern dance, and other non-concert activities. The innovations of the 1920's have been recognized in most quarters as definite additions to the language of music, and many of the erstwhile "lunatics" and "charlatans" have been invited to professorships at our most respectable universities.

Even the critics, after damning them for twenty years, have begun to recognize that—like the new literary techniques of Joyce, Proust, and Virginia Woolf, and the innovations brought to painting by Cézanne, Van Gogh, Matisse, and Picasso—the new outlook and procedures of contemporary composers have enriched and refreshed the art of music.

It is, in a sense, in order to understand and evaluate these, that our whole survey of music is of value. For today it cannot be enough, as it was formerly, for the listener to "appreciate" only the music of the past, and to let the present go hang. It is as much his job as it is that of the composer to mold the art of the present, and, by his understanding, his active participation in musical life, his positive support or rejection, to determine which music shall and which shall not live. The time is past when it was the prerogative of self-appointed committees, directors, conductors, and critics to have the final word on the direction of music. In a democracy, that should be the concern and decision of the whole democratic body of music makers and listeners.

In spite of the recognition already won by certain contemporary works, there are still many intelligent and sensitive musicians and listeners who sincerely wonder why modern music must be so different from that of the great masters. Why must much of it be so violent, discordant, difficult to grasp? Is it not the work of tricksters, pretenders, untalented men who could not write a simple melody if they tried, and who hide this inability beneath a mass of intellectual and technical complications? And why cannot composers of today continue to write expressive melodies, lovely harmonies, and pleasing orchestral sonorities like those of the nineteenth century?

These questions, which recur repeatedly in connection with contemporary music, especially on the occasion of a first performance, are perfectly understandable, and in many instances more than justified. New art is frequently difficult to absorb, but newness can never be a compensation for a lack of genuine musical substance. Unfortunately, in the 1920's many bogus musicians attained considerable notoriety for themselves and for "modern music" by writing such works as a Ballet for Airplane Motors, a Sonata for Double Bass and Piccolo; a Concerto for Tin Whistle and Orchestra. Freakish stunts of this kind were often far more publicized than many genuine and sincere contemporary works, causing not a few listeners to conclude that *all* composers who use an unfamiliar musical language are members of the lunatic fringe.

Furthermore, as in every other generation, there are not a few composers writing music in the "modern" style today whose creative gift is quite limited. They may, on the other hand, possess an enormous talent for technical brilliance or one—no less important in the modern world—for making "connections." Since both the latter gifts often make a more rapid impression than the genuine musical one, it often happens that the works of inferior "modern" musicians are played for a time much more often than those of really gifted ones. The listener of 1942 subjected to a program of mediocre contemporary music may impatiently declare, "This modern stuff is terrible; give me the classics any day."

But let us suppose the same listener were transported back two centuries to 1742, a period of contrapuntal music. Today, with hindsight, we think of that as the "glorious age of Bach." But the listener of 1742 would scarcely have considered the music of his time in that light, for Bach was practically unknown then. He would have to judge the contrapuntal style by the productions of Bohm, Telemann, Froberger, Marchand, and other such worthies, and might have reasonably concluded, with a yawn, "This contrapuntal stuff is terrible—give me the classics any day." The listener of 1842—which we now think of as the Romantic age—would have been far less familiar with the music of Schubert and Schumann than with that of Kalkbrenner, Spohr, and Moscheles—on the basis of which he might very justifiably have concluded, "This Romantic stuff is terrible . . . etc."

One cannot judge the merits of a particular musical style by the works of its less inspired exponents. "Modern music" is not condemned as an artistic language because fifty or a hundred mediocre musicians use it to write works that are commonplace or dull. If one first-rate composer can say something exciting and memorable in this language, then it has contributed something fresh and worth while to music.

In the last fifty or sixty years many new composers have arisen. Most have been just a flash in the pan. Some, whose early work promised big things, have died strange spiritual deaths, while their bodies lived on and their pens continued to turn out score after meaningless score. Typical of these is Richard Strauss, once the author of brilliant and rebellious works, but a has-been for almost thirty years and now a contemptible instrument of the Nazis.

Others have risen in the Europe of the 1920's and 1930's—a world sick with inner decay—with a sense of striving, of protest, and in some cases of magnificent achievement that will almost certainly remain for the future. Of all these I have selected eight—Stravinsky, Bartók, Falla, Honegger, Hindemith, Berg, Prokofiev, and Shostakovich—as the most representative of our present epoch. Although they are by no means the only significant European composers,* their work seems to symbolize the aspiration, conflict, despair, and finally the coming rebirth not only of European music but of European culture as a whole.—E. S.

Listening to Modern Music

The chapter "The Tolerant Ear" in "Of Men and Music"

By Deems Taylor

IF RALPH WALDO EMERSON is not the patron saint of all those who write on controversial subjects, including music, he ought to be. For it was Emerson who invented that God-given line about consistency being "the hobgoblin of little minds." My other favorite author is Walt Whitman, with his "I contradict myself? Very well, I contradict myself"—or words to that effect. All of which is a more—or less—graceful way of leading up to the fact that, having just pleaded for a revival of intolerance in listening to new music, I am about to plead, with equal eloquence, on the other side. In short, while I do feel that a good many of us could afford to be a bit more honest in expressing our musical dislikes, we might, on the other hand, be a little slower in forming them; we ought to be quite sure that we know what it is that we do not like about music that repels us.

Let me get to my text. It is a letter from a radio listener to the Philharmonic-Symphony concerts, and reads, in part, as follows:

"I have been listening for many years to the works of the great masters as rendered by the best orchestras on two continents, and think I know a little about good music. But I am unable to appreciate the modern composers. Such music seems to me to be without melody, harmony, or form, and literally gives me a pain. And yet there must be something in it, or the great orchestras would not play this kind

---

* Although Stravinsky, Bartók, and Hindemith are now living in the United States, they are still—together with Prokofiev and Shostakovich—outstanding representatives of European music.

of music. What must I listen for? How should I listen? There must be something I have missed, and I am sincere in my desire to know what it is. I am sure there are thousands like myself, asking the same questions. Could you say a few words on this subject some time? I feel that many of your listeners would be grateful for some advice on this point."

Naturally, I cannot undertake to write an exhaustive and authoritative treatise on How to Listen to Modern Music, for the three excellent reasons that I haven't space enough, you haven't patience enough, and I don't know enough. But I might be able to make a few suggestions that would possibly be useful to anyone hearing ultra-modern music for the first time.

First and foremost, when you sit down to a piece of ultra-modern music, try to rid yourself of . . . fear. I make that suggestion in all seriousness. Don't be afraid. It may seem silly to imply that people are frightened by modern music. Just the same, I think they are. A good deal of the fury with which people denounce the new and unfamiliar in art is the result of a very real terror. Let me illustrate.

When I was a good deal younger than I am now—in fact, when I was four years old—my most precious possession was an iron fire engine drawn by two galloping iron horses. That engine and its horses never left me. It stayed with me through the day and went to bed with me at night. One day, when I was supposedly playing with it, contentedly, my mother came into the room and found me dissolved in tears. After a good deal of questioning she found out what the trouble was. I forget how I worded my explanation, but the gist of it was that I had just realized that when I grew up I wouldn't be able to play with my fire engine any more. She tried to comfort me by assuring me that I could have my engine as long as I liked; that I could play with it even when I was grown up. "But," I said, miserably, "I'm afraid I won't *want* to."

I think that particular fear lies at the root of a great deal of people's unwillingness to give even a first hearing to modern music. It's a sort of "I'm-glad-I-don't-like-lemonade-because-if-I-did-I'd-drink-it-and-I-hate-it" attitude. How many times I've heard people say, "Well, if *this* is music, what's going to become of Bach and Beethoven and Mozart and Wagner?" We're really afraid of getting to like this new stuff, for fear that it might destroy our taste for the older music that we've known and loved all our lives.

Or, if our reactions are a little less naïve, we have a subconscious —or perhaps conscious—fear that if too many people grow to like this new music the old will lose its popularity, orchestras will stop playing it, singers and instrumentalists will stop putting it on their programs, and we shan't be able to hear the classics any more.

Now granted that you may be haunted by that fear, look about you—or rather, use your ears. Is Bach extinct because Strauss wrote *Ein Heldenleben?* Is Beethoven on the ash-heap because Stravinsky wrote *The Rites of Spring?* Is Wagner no longer heard because Debussy wrote *Pelléas et Mélisande?* Has Brahms been scrapped to make room for Shostakovich? If the history of the race tells us anything, it tells us that art is not a branch of the automobile industry or the millinery trade. This year's model does not render last year's model obsolete. The music you have always liked will continue to be played. There is no limit to the library of the world's music. There's plenty of room on its shelves for new scores, without throwing out any old ones.

Another thing of which not to be frightened. Don't be too much impressed by what people have to say about how this ultra-modern music marks a complete smashup of all our previous conceptions of what music ought to be, the destruction of all pre-existing laws of melody, harmony, and whatnot. Some of the most repellent characteristics of much modern music have been in existence for centuries. In the Confucian temples of China, for instance, the priests sing certain prescribed hymns in unison; but every priest is at liberty to choose whatever key is best suited to his voice. That's polytonality. The so-called harmony of the Middle Ages would sound unbearably awkward and ugly to us. There is much talk of twelve-note scales and quarter-tones today. In Hindu music today, as there always has been, there are sixty-three well-defined different scales. So don't get to thinking of this break-up of existing musical theories in terms of the fall of the Roman Empire or the destruction of civilization. It's only the breakup of a lot of rules made up by people who weren't composers. The so-called laws of musical theory are rules of procedure, codified from what composers of the past did more or less instinctively, in order to allow composers of the present to write music that will at least be inoffensive.

Great music can be written that conforms to the strictest rules ever laid down. But the fact that music conforms to the rules is no guarantee that it will be great. Bach and Mozart and Beethoven broke as many rules in their day as Schönberg is breaking in his. Most great composers are esthetic anarchists; so don't let people scare you by tales of the Red menace. Particularly, don't let us critics frighten you. The people who stand most stubbornly in the way of progress in any art are generally the very people who know most about it. They *know* what rules are being broken, and are correspondingly horrified. The general public likes the new work or doesn't like it, and so keeps it alive or kills it.

Furthermore, if you honestly want to understand this new music, don't pay much attention to what its composers have to say about it. Every artist desires ardently to be understood, and his natural impulse is to burst into words in order to help you see what he is driving at. But music happens to be a language—a very definite language—for the expression of just those ideas and moods and emotions that cannot be expressed in words. So don't trust words. If a piece of music can be completely expressed in words, and the intellectual ideas of which words are the supreme medium, there never was any need to compose it.

And don't wonder what Beethoven or Wagner would have said of it. If what their fellow composers had to say of their music is any criterion, Beethoven and Wagner would loathe it. Don't take the word of the past, no matter how great a past. Ancestor worship does not make for a healthy nation or a healthy art. God help us if the younger generation ever stops being the despair of its grandparents, or turns out no music of which its spiritual ancestors would have thoroughly approved.

Another thing. If music means anything to you, if it is a source of pleasure, inspiration, or spiritual nourishment to you, you owe something to music. It is your duty to help to keep it a living, growing art. You must not be selfishly content merely to sit in the shade of the tree. Water it occasionally. The least you can do, as a lover of music, is to be willing to listen to what a new composer has to say, whether you like it or not. People write me despairing letters, pointing out our dearth of great composers, our lack of a Beethoven, a Wagner, or a Brahms. I don't say that that is true or not true. I don't know. But if it is true, at least let us make it possible for the great man to get a hearing when he does arrive. And make no mistake. When he does arrive, many of you will not like him. To some of us at least, Debussy's *Afternoon of a Faun* is one of the loveliest pieces of music ever written. Even those who may not care for it hardly find it ugly or incoherent. Yet at the first performance of the *Faun* there was a riot in the hall. The audience laughed and yelled and hissed and whistled so loudly that the piece went virtually unheard. That was in 1894, less than half a century ago. The human ear is a very adaptable instrument.

"All right," you say, "I'll listen. Now what do I listen for?" That question is not so easy to answer. Or perhaps it is. I think I would say, listen for the same things that you expect to find in any piece of music; but don't make your definitions too rigid. There are four elements that are present in any piece of good music: melody, which is design; harmony, which is color; rhythm, which is proportion; and form, which is the ground plan. Listen for them. Ask yourself, does this music contain themes that possess a definite contour and outline, regardless of whether they happen to please me or not? Do they exist? Granted that its harmonies may offend my ear, is there any element of contrast among them? Is there any discernible difference between one ugly chord and another, or is the general impression of all this cacophony one of monotony? Does the music possess some underlying rhythmic pattern that keeps it going, or does it give the effect of moving in a circle? Does it possess any plan that I can discern, no matter how unfamiliar or unlike the traditional forms? Does it seem to possess a beginning, and middle, and an end, or does it just start and stop?

Now a word of warning about the harmony. Bear in mind that in recent years composers have taken to using strongly dissonant chords very often not as harmony is conventionally used, but to give an effect of color. It is a device that is hard to explain in words. One simple example is the silver-rose theme in Strauss's *Der Rosenkavalier*, where the celeste plays a series of chords that has nothing in common with the harmony of the strings that underlie it. If you're familiar with that theme, you can't deny that the dissonant harmonies give it a silvery, metallic quality that has nothing to do with the tone quality of the instruments that are playing it. Look for a similar intention in a piece of new music before you decide that the composer was just trying to annoy you with a series of discords.

One thing about form. Music has always been inspired by the mediums through which it is transmitted—in other words, has always been written for whichever medium would give it the most performances. If Haydn and Mozart and Beethoven wrote a great many symphonies and string quartets, one reason is that almost every wealthy man of their times maintained a private orchestra or a private quartet. He would order a new symphony or a new piece of chamber music much as you would order a new overcoat. Today there are no more private orchestras and very few patrons. But one medium that is becoming increasingly hospitable to composers is the theater.

Now stage music must base its form, not on a musical structure, but on a dramatic one, which is frequently quite foreign to musical logic. To develop a musical idea clearly and coherently takes a certain amount of time; but when music accompanies a dramatic story, or the gestures of a pantomimist, it must frequently turn in its own length, so to speak, long before it would naturally do so. The consequence is that, when such music is played on a concert stage, without the panto-mime or the ballet as a clue to what it is trying to express, it is often likely to sound formless and incoherent. Parts of Stravinsky's *Petroushka* and *The Rites of Spring,* for instance, are almost meaning-less without the accompanying stage action. This is no fault of the music; it is the fault of playing the music out of its proper place—ex-hibiting the costume, so to speak, without bothering to bring on the actor. Bear that handicap in mind when you listen to a new ballet or pantomime in concert form.

And now, having dutifully listened, suppose you still don't like this new music? Hear it again. Give it several hearings, if you possibly can, no matter how much they may hurt. And then, if you are absolutely sure that you really don't like it, or that you really do, don't be afraid to say so. Don't be afraid to be wrong. Don't pretend, either way, out of deference to your friends, or a fear of being thought old-fashioned. Furthermore, if you dislike one ultra-modern work, don't take it for granted that no ultra-modern music is for you. On the other hand, don't assume that every new piece, however outrageous, is the voice of the future. The proportion of rubbish to great music that is being written today is what it always has been: about ninety per cent.

When we hear two men speaking in a foreign language, if we don't happen to know that language, everything they say sounds like gibberish. Only after we have begun to grasp their language can we decide whether they are talking wisdom or nonsense. Composers today are experimenting with a new musical language. There is as yet no dictionary for it, and no way of studying it except to listen to it with-out panic and without mental reservations. And the more we listen, the better able shall we be to weigh and estimate the value of what present-day composers are saying. Some of them are just talking pig-Latin; but others may be saying something that we may all, some day, be grateful to hear.

How I Wrote Petroushka and Le Sacre

By Igor Stravinsky

Extracts from his "Autobiography"

ONE day, when I was finishing the last pages of *L'Oiseau de feu* in St. Petersburg, I had a fleeting vision which came to me as a complete surprise, my mind at the moment being full of other things. I saw in imagination a solemn pagan rite: sage elders, seated in a circle, watched a young girl dance herself to death. They were sacrificing her to propitiate the god of spring. Such was the theme of the *Sacre du printemps*. I must confess that this vision made a deep impression on me, and I at once described it to my friend Nicholas Roerich, he being a painter who had specialized in pagan subjects. He welcomed my inspiration with enthusiasm, and became my collaborator in this creation. In Paris I told Diaghilev about it, and he was at once carried away by the idea.

At the end of August I went to Switzerland with my family. Before tackling the *Sacre du printemps*, which would be a long and difficult task, I wanted to refresh myself by composing an orchestral piece in which the piano would play the most important part—a sort of *Konzertstuck*. In composing the music, I had in mind a distinct picture of a puppet, suddenly endowed with life, exasperating the patience of the orchestra with diabolical cascades of *arpeggi*. The orchestra in turn retaliates with menacing trumpet-blasts. The outcome is a terrific noise which reaches its climax and ends in the sorrowful and querulous collapse of the poor puppet. Having finished this bizarre piece, I struggled for hours to find a title which would express in a word the character of my music and consequently the personality of this creature.

One day I leapt for joy. I had indeed found my title—*Petroushka*, the immortal and unhappy hero of every fair in all countries. Soon afterwards Diaghilev came to visit me at Clarens, where I was staying. He was much astonished when, instead of sketches of the *Sacre*, I played him the piece which I had just composed and which later became the second scene of *Petroushka*. He was so much pleased with it that he would not leave it alone and began persuading me to develop the theme of the puppet's sufferings and make it into a whole ballet. While he remained in Switzerland we worked out together the general lines of the subject and the plot in accordance with ideas which I suggested.

We settled the scene of action: the fair, with its crowd, its booths, the little traditional theater, the character of the magician, with all his tricks; and the coming to life of the dolls—Petroushka, his rival, and the dancer—and their love tragedy, which ends with Petroushka's death. I began at once to compose the first scene of the ballet, which I finished at Beaulieu. While there, I frequently saw Diaghilev, who was at Monte Carlo. By mutual agreement, Diaghilev entrusted the whole *décor* of the ballet, both the scenery and the costumes, to Benois. Diaghilev soon went off to St. Petersburg, whence he wrote at Christmas, asking me to join him there for a few days, bringing my music so that Benois and his other collaborators might see it. I went in some trepidation.

As soon as I arrived I let my friends hear what I had so far composed for *Petroushka*—namely, the two first scenes and the beginning of the third. Benois immediately began work, and in the spring he joined us at Monte Carlo, whither Diaghilev and I had returned.

When I returned to Beaulieu, I resumed work on my score, but its progress was interrupted. I became seriously ill with nicotine poisoning, and was at the point of death, this illness causing a month of enforced idleness. I was terribly anxious about the fate of *Petroushka,* which had at all costs to be ready for Paris in the spring. Fortunately I recovered my strength sufficiently to enable me to finish my work in the ten weeks which remained before the beginning of the season. Towards the end of April I set out for Rome, where Diaghilev was giving performances at the Costanzi Theater during the International Exhibition. There *Petroushka* was rehearsed, and there I finished its last pages.

And now for the *Sacre du printemps.*

As I have already said, when I conceived the idea, immediately after *L'Oiseau de feu,* I became so much absorbed in the composition of *Petroushka* that I had no chance even to sketch preliminary outlines. After the Paris season, I returned to Oustiloug, our estate in Russia, to devote myself entirely to the *Sacre du printemps.*

Although I had conceived the subject of the *Sacre* without any plot, some plan had to be designed for the sacrificial action. For this

it was necessary that I should see Roerich. He was staying at Talach-
kino, the estate of Princess Tenichev, a great patroness of Russian art.
I joined him, and it was there that we settled the visual embodiment
of the *Sacre* and the definite sequence of its different episodes. I began
the score on returning to Oustiloug, and worked at it through the winter
at Clarens.

I worked continuously at the score of the *Sacre* at Clarens throughout the winter of 1912-13, my work being interrupted only by inter-
views with Diaghilev, who invited me to the first performances of
L'Oiseau de feu and *Petroushka* in the different towns of Central Europe where the Russian Ballet was on tour.

My first journey was to Berlin. I very well remember the performance before the Kaiser, the Empress, and their suite. The program
consisted of *Cléopatre* and *Petroushka.* The Kaiser naturally gave preference to *Cléopatre,* and, in complimenting Diaghilev, told him that
he would send his Egyptologists to see the Ballet and take a lesson from
it. He apparently thought that Bakst's fantastic coloring was a scrupu-
lously historical reproduction, and that the potpourri of the score was
a revelation of ancient Egyptian music. At another performance, when
L'Oiseau de feu was given, I made the acquaintance of Richard Strauss,
who came on to the stage and expressed great interest in the music.
Among other things, he said something which much amused me: "You
make a mistake in beginning your piece *pianissimo;* the public will
not listen. You should astonish them by a sudden crash at the very start.
After that they will follow you, and you can do whatever you like."

I have now come to the spring season of 1913 in Paris, when the
Russian Ballet inaugurated the opening of the Théâtre des Champs-
Élysées. It began with a revival of *L'Oiseau de feu,* and the *Sacre du
printemps* was given on May 28 at the evening performance. I have
refrained from describing the scandal which it evoked; that has already been too much discussed. The complexity of my score had demanded a great number of rehearsals, which Monteux had conducted
with his usual skill and attention. As for the actual performance, I am
not in a position to judge, as I left the auditorium at the first bars of
the prelude, which had at once evoked derisive laughter. I was disgusted. These demonstrations, at first isolated, soon became general,
provoking counter-demonstrations and very quickly developing into a
terrific uproar. During the whole performance I was at Nijinsky's side
in the wings. He was standing on a chair, screaming "Sixteen, seventeen, eighteen"—they had their own method of counting to keep time.

Naturally the poor dancers could hear nothing by reason of the row in the auditorium and the sound of their own dance-steps. I had to hold Nijinsky by his clothes, for he was furious, and ready to dash on to the stage at any moment and create a scandal. Diaghilev kept ordering the electricians to turn the lights on or off, hoping in that way to put a stop to the noise. That is all I can remember about that first performance. Oddly enough, at the dress rehearsal, to which we had invited a number of actors, painters, musicians, writers, and the most cultured representatives of society, everything had gone off peacefully and I was very far from expecting such an outburst.

Now, after the lapse of more than twenty years, it is naturally difficult for me to recall in any detail the choreography of the *Sacre* without being influenced by the admiration with which it met in the set known as the *avant-garde*—ready, as always, to welcome as a new discovery anything that differs, be it ever so little, from the *déjà-vu*. But what struck me then, and still strikes me most, about the choreography, was and is Nijinsky's lack of consciousness of what he was doing in creating it. He showed therein his complete inability to accept and assimilate those revolutionary ideas which Diaghilev had made his creed and obstinately and industriously strove to inculcate. What the choreography expressed was a very labored and barren effort rather than a plastic realization flowing simply and naturally from what the music demanded. How far it all was from what I had desired!

In composing the *Sacre* I had imagined the spectacular part of the performance as a series of rhythmic mass movements of the greatest simplicity which would have an instantaneous effect on the audience, with no superfluous details or complications such as would suggest effort. The only solo was to be the sacrificial dance at the end of the piece. The music of that dance, clear and well-defined, demanded a corresponding choreography—simple and easy to understand. But there again, although he had grasped the dramatic significance of the dance, Nijinsky was incapable of giving intelligible form to its essence, and complicated it either by clumsiness or lack of understanding. For it is undeniably clumsy to slow down the tempo of the music in order to compose complicated steps which cannot be danced in the tempo prescribed. Many choreographers have that fault, but I have never known any who erred in that respect to the same degree as Nijinsky.

In reading what I have written about the *Sacre*, the reader will perhaps be astonished to notice how little I have said about the music.

The omission is deliberate. It is impossible, after the lapse of twenty years, to recall what were the feelings which animated me in composing it.

Igor Stravinsky

From *"Men of Music"*

By *Wallace Brockway and Herbert Weinstock*

AFTER ten years of shadowboxing, Igor Stravinsky * still retains the crown of modern music. He retains it because there is no one to dispute his supremacy. Sibelius, though using as many modern means as he needs, is at heart a traditionalist who has found the essence of classicism. There have been challengers, more or less serious, whom Stravinsky has not even had to vanquish, for they have eliminated themselves simply by not getting into the heavy-weight class. First it was Ravel, then Falla; even the mathematician Schönberg was spoken of as a dangerous rival. The weary king retains his crown, but unless he shows his royal will shortly, it will be time to declare the throne vacated, and a democracy established.

There is between Stravinsky's career and that of Richard Strauss a parallel so tragically close that one wonders whether a twentieth-century composer can live fully in the world, and yet come to the fullest fruition.† They both started out tepidly with Brahmsian echoes: Strauss, as the better-taught man, produced his academic symphony at an earlier age than Stravinsky, who merely dabbled in music until his early twenties. Both quickly spouted revolutionary works, threw off fireworks for a couple of decades, and then fizzled out, though in different ways. Strauss's creative energy dried up. Stravinsky, always an experimentalist, continued to experiment. But for a number of reasons, his later experiments have failed. By a strange coincidence, their careers as composers that matter stopped just short of their fiftieth year. Neither of them has shown the staying power of a Haydn, a Wagner, a Sibelius—a Verdi. Still, there is the ghost of a chance that Stravinsky,

---

* Born at Oranienbaum, June 17, 1882.
† Both Prokofiev and Shostakovich seem to have done this—E. S.

who is only fifty-seven years old,* may come through with another masterpiece. It is too early to write his epitaph.

In many respects, Stravinsky's early life was conventional for a major Russian composer. The second- and third-rate Russian musicians were prodigies, and went early to academies of music; the geniuses came late to music, and ended up by teaching themselves. The Five were young-gentleman dilettantes who entered music by the back door. Tchaikovsky, though he eventually acquired a solid academic grounding, did not start formal training until after his twentieth year. Stravinsky, not having Tchaikovsky's overmastering urge to devote himself to music, in 1905 docilely finished a law course at the University of St. Petersburg because his mother wished him to. The next year, his mind still not made up about becoming a professional musician, he married his second cousin.

There is something incredibly lackadaisical, something whimsical, about Stravinsky's inability to grow up. At this time, he was a typical gifted futilitarian from a Chekhov play. Yet his background was musical. His father was an opera singer of some renown, and his mother knew music at least well enough to enjoy reading opera scores. Not the least surprising thing about Stravinsky is that he was no prodigy. His parents viewed his childish musical efforts with indulgent amusement: they did let him study the piano, but he had to pick up the rudiments of harmony and counterpoint by himself. Soon he tried compositions of his own—little more than written-down improvisations. But it is uncertain how long his musical maturity would have been delayed if he had not met Rimsky-Korsakov's son at the university. In 1902, while traveling in Germany, Stravinsky, by his chum's wangling, got to show the pedantic master some of his *juvenilia*. Rimsky was not enthusiastic: he advised the boy to go on with law and, if he wished, to take private lessons in harmony and counterpoint. He unbent enough to offer to look at any future pieces by his son's friend. Five years were to elapse before Stravinsky, having done everything the great pundit asked of him, and having frequently consulted him about his confessedly desultory work, showed Rimsky a large composition that his adviser thought fit to be performed.

Stravinsky's Opus 1 and Opus 2—respectively a symphony and a song cycle with orchestral accompaniment—are rarely given. By 1908, however, he was at work on three compositions that have, in some form or other, kept a precarious hold on public attention. The first

* This article was written in 1939.—E. S.

was an opera, *Le Rossignol,* with which he struggled, off and on, for six years. The second was the orchestral *Scherzo fantastique.* The last was a little tone poem called *Feu d'artifice,* which he sent to Rimsky on his daughter's wedding, as the master had expressed an interest in its composition. "A few days later," Stravinsky says in his autobiography, "a telegram informed me of his death, and shortly afterwards my registered packet was returned to me: 'Not delivered on account of death of addressee.' " In honor of his teacher, he then composed a *Chant funèbre,* the score of which vanished during the Russian Revolution.

The *Scherzo fantastique* and *Feu d'artifice* were the means of bringing fame and fortune to their composer, for in the audience at the Siloti concert where they were first performed on February 6, 1909, sat the greatest talent scout of the century—Serge Diaghilev. Something in these fast, crackling pieces, with their knowing echoes of Paul Dukas's popular *L'Apprenti sorcier,* enthralled him. With his usual impetuosity, Diaghilev instantly commissioned Stravinsky to orchestrate a Chopin nocturne and valse, to be used in the forthcoming performance of the Ballet Russe's version of *Les Sylphides.* Stravinsky was made. His adaptations turned out to be most satisfactory, and later that year the impresario telegraphed him to compose a completely new work for the Ballet Russe's 1910 season at the Opéra.

The result of Diaghilev's confidence in his find was *L'Oiseau de feu,* the first real modern ballet. Not only did it inaugurate Diaghilev's custom of commissioning entire ballets, but it set the precedent of the composer consulting both the choreographer and the *décor* artist during the course of composition. The brilliant Opéra audience that made the opening of *L'Oiseau de feu,* on June 25, 1910, the notable event of the Paris season saw, in effect, the perfectly functioning collaboration of Stravinsky, the choreographer Fokine, and the scene painter Golovin. Thamar Karsavina was the Firebird, Adolf Bolm the Prince. We who have too often seen a tired version of *L'Oiseau de feu,* with faded sets and bedraggled costumes and bored dancers, can scarcely imagine the incredible glamour of the original production. Stravinsky, who was making his first visit to Paris, found himself famous overnight—the most fêted hero of smart Paris society. For years *L'Oiseau de feu* remained a favorite of balletomanes, and spread Stravinsky's name across the world. Shortly after the *première,* he made a selection of excerpts from the ballet, and this rather hasty business served for some years as an orchestral suite. In 1919, however, he reorchestrated and re-edited the suite, and this carefully constructed potpourri is, even twenty years later, his most popular concert piece. Abounding in vivid color, romantic melodies, and easy, fruity emotion, *L'Oiseau de feu* is as ingratiating as *Scheherazade*. Only the *Dance of Kastchei,* the fourth of the five sections of the suite, might hit the conservative in the midriff: its irregular pounding rhythm and jagged harmonies, the sheer physical excitement of this diabolic music —all foreshadow the cometlike anarch of *Le Sacre du printemps.* The rest of the suite might be not quite first-rate Rimsky. It is fading rapidly. But fortunately, it was the *Dance of Kastchei* that the composer was to use as a springboard.

While composing *L'Oiseau de feu,* Stravinsky toyed with the idea of doing a ballet based on the ancient pagan rites of his native land. He discussed the matter with the painter Roerich, but the difficulties of the task deterred him momentarily. Keeping it cubbyholed in his mind, he turned to another idea he found equally fascinating—the composition of a large orchestral work with an important piano part. Speaking of how this unnamed piece happened to develop into *Petroushka,* Stravinsky has written, "In composing the music, I had in my mind a distinct picture of a puppet, suddenly endowed with life, exasperating the patience of the orchestra with diabolical cascades of arpeggios." As soon as he played over the manuscript to Diaghilev, the impresario, though he had been expecting to hear the pagan ballet music of which rumors had reached him, was excited, and persuaded his friend to enlarge it to ballet size. Wandering across Europe, from Switzerland to France, and from France to Russia and Italy (for Stravinsky, like all Russians, is a tireless traveler), the composer, adding touches to *Petroushka* along the way, finally settled down in Rome, and completed the score on May 26, 1911, three weeks before his twenty-ninth birthday.

Only eighteen days later, Diaghilev sumptuously mounted *Petroushka* at the Châtelet in Paris. Again a galaxy of talents gave added éclat to a new ballet by a man who was already hailed as one of the first of living composers. This time Nijinsky danced the Clown, Bolm was the Moor, and Karsavina the apex of the tragicomic triangle. It was admitted at once that a perfect ballet had been written, the principal reason being that nowhere before or since has such wholly danceable action been allied to such vividly illustrative music. While previous composers had generously borrowed Russian material, Stravinsky, with the help of the learned and sensitive Alexandre Benois (despite his name, also a Russian), had, in this tale of a St. Petersburg carnival, caught the very essence of theater Slavdom.

In the *Dance of Kastchei,* a new voice had been heard, but it was still uncertain what that voice would say. *Petroushka* ended all doubt. It was undeniably an anarch's voice, but hostility was not yet aroused. This anarch was an amusing one. Yet, the leap from *L'Oiseau de feu* to *Petroushka* is immensely wider than that from *Petroushka* to the next ballet Stravinsky wrote—that ballet which literally caused a riot, and organized powerful forces against his music. In *Petroushka* gone are the romantic melodies and charming Rimskyan harmonies. In a work just as brimful of color, Stravinsky has primitivized his palette. The raw, sharp color of *Petroushka* has its analogue in the choppy, mechanized rhythms, which tend to dominate among the various musical elements. Stravinsky broke even more violently with the past in the harmonies. For the first time, a composer wrote simultaneously in two clashing keys. The effect, far from being ear-shattering, is strange, acrid, deliciously different. Bitonal counterpoint is being born under our very noses, but we scarcely notice it, much less damn it, for, as Gerald Abraham has shrewdly noted, "Both contrapuntal strands are absurdly easy to follow."

In 1921, Stravinsky "began a task which enthralled me—a transcription for the piano which I called *Trois Mouvements de Pétroushka.* I wanted this to provide piano virtuosos with a piece having sufficient scope to enable them to add to their modern repertoire and display their technique." Those who have heard Artur Rubinstein, to whom the *Trois Mouvements* is dedicated, play it, will realize how perfectly the composer has succeeded. The transcription is one of the few notable large pieces of post-Debussyan piano music. In addition to being a work of distinction and beauty, it illustrates the changed point of view from which postwar composers considered the piano. No longer the vehicle of fluctuant, cloudy impressionism, of curtains of sound, it began to be treated as a percussion instrument—something that could be properly thumped, banged, struck, and otherwise attacked. Now a projector of significant noise, it might be considered a congeries of small drums tuned to various pitches. This conception has led to the anarchic extravagances of Henry Cowell, and has its golden mean in the piano compositions of Serge Prokofiev, and in Stravinsky's own Concerto, Capriccio, and Concerto for two unaccompanied pianos.

After *Petroushka* was produced, Stravinsky returned to Russia and his idea of a pagan ballet. He stayed there until winter in order to complete the scenario with Roerich, after which he moved to Switzerland, to Clarens, almost sacred to him because it had often sheltered his hero Tchaikovsky. There, after other visits to Paris, Bayreuth (which moved him to irreverent laughter), and Russia, he finished *Le Sacre du printemps* in March, 1913. He looked forward to the staging of this very complicated ballet with trepidation, for the choreography had, at Diaghilev's insistence, been entrusted to the maladroit care of Nijinsky. His worst fears were realized. Nijinsky was both incompetent and unreasonable, and though the *corps de ballet* was working against a deadline, his inability to follow the bar-by-bar significance of the score took the form of demanding an absurd number of rehearsals. Despite all the resulting contretemps, the invitation dress rehearsal went off well.

Not so the *première*. The first performance of *Le Sacre du printemps,* at the Théâtre des Champs-Elysées, on May 29, 1913, was a scandal unmatched in the annals of music. Jean Cocteau, the star reporter of smart Paris, so describes it: "Let us now return to the theater in the Avenue Montaigne, while we wait for the conductor to rap his desk and the curtain to go up on one of the noblest events in the annals of art. The audience behaved as it ought to; it revolted straight away. People laughed, booed, hissed, imitated animal noises, and possibly would have tired themselves out before long, had not the crowd of esthetes and a handfull of musicians, carried away by their excessive zeal, insulted and even roughly handled the public in the loges. The uproar degenerated into a free fight.

"Standing up in her loge, her tiara awry, the old Comtesse de Pourtalès flourished her fan and shouted, scarlet in the face, 'It's the first time in sixty years that anyone's dared to make a fool of me.' The good lady was sincere: she thought there was some mystification."

The cause of all this disturbance was the most beautiful, the most profoundly conceived, and most exhilarating piece of music thus far composed in the twentieth century. By some odd freak of genius, Stravinsky, a straitlaced devotee of Greek Catholicism, had become an earth-worshiper, and written a hymn of pantheistic exaltation. For *Le Sacre* is in truth exactly what Stravinsky called it: an act of faith

The *Great Sacred Dance,* in which the scapegoat maiden dances herself to death, is the high-water mark beyond which the brutal mod-

ern technique has not gone, possibly cannot go. Its constantly changing rhythms thudded out in screaming, searing discords engender a
physical agitation in the listener that is closely akin to sexual excita-
tion, acting chiefly on atavistic, deeply veneered strata of being. Music,
beginning with the rewritten Venusberg scene from *Tannhäuser,*
and proceeding through *Tristan und Isolde* to much of Strauss and the
now unheard tone poems of Alexander Scriabin, was tending inevitably
to this glorification of the physical, and for decades was busily stripping
away veil after veil of respectability. Once Stravinsky had completed
the process, imitators were quick to take a hint. For instance, Prokofiev's
clever but derivative *Scythian Suite* came a year later than *Le Sacre.*
But gradually, music (largely under Stravinsky's own tutelage) has
been turning away from these scandals to desiccated forms of experimentation which, momentarily at least, seem to remain localized in the
laboratory of the past. It is not a little odd that Stravinsky, whose pantheistic vision reduces Wordsworth's or Thoreau's to spongecake,
should have become the leading medium in those ectoplasmic spin-
nings out which have thus far characterized the career of musical neoclassicism. Because *Le Sacre* is Stravinsky's overtowering masterpiece,
everything he has done since is necessarily something of an anticlimax.
But the anticlimax is most depressing when he is in full flight from
the genii he uncorked in *Le Sacre,* and retreating headlong into the
arms of Tchaikovsky, Pergolesi, Handel, and Bach. As his artistic
remorse becomes unbearable, it may be that he will go farther, and
retreat into Palestrina, Des Prés, and Jubal.

Before Stravinsky went off into those experiments in pure rhythm
which were clearly prognosticated by *Le Sacre* he completed the opera
he had begun in 1908. He had written but one act of *Le Rossignol*
then, and it was only in 1914 that he found time to compose the last
two acts. Meanwhile, a lot of water had gone under the bridge, and
there was a huge disparity between the styles of Act I and Acts II and
III—far more disparity than was required by the change in scene and
mood in the Hans Christian Andersen fairy story. Although Diaghilev
gave *Le Rossignol* a sumptuous mounting, the opera was not a success. Then Diaghilev suggested staging it as a ballet. But Stravinsky
said no: he would, instead, take material from the last two acts, and
adapt it as a symphonic poem that could be used for a ballet. This was
Le Chant du rossignol, a glittering simulacrum of real Chinese music,
the composer's last fling with the musical paintpot. Hereafter his color

was to be applied gingerly and, in many places, to be reduced to black and white. *Le Chant du rossignol* is attractive picture-book music, and is unduly neglected.

Beginning with *Trois Pièces pour quatuor à cordes,* composed in 1914, for nine years Stravinsky sent forth from his studio a series of small compositions that have the air of being experiments with one or more aspects of musical technique. As these bloodless fragments appeared, they were greeted by Cocteau, Boris de Schloezer (who has constituted himself Stravinskyographer extraordinary), and other less talented but equally thuriferous critics with clouds of incense that simultaneously gave the occasions a religious tinge, and served to obscure the paltriness of the music. According to these official communiqués from the Étoile sector, it seemed that Stravinsky had always just completed a masterpiece that would alter the whole face of music. In 1918 it was *L'Histoire du soldat* that was crowned by the Académie Cocteau; in 1920 it was *Pulcinella,* in 1922 *Le Renard. Le Soldat* and *Renard* were experiments in timbres and rhythm; *Pulcinella* was an experiment in melodies (since Stravinsky had so few of his own he used Pergolesi's). Poor, half-starved things that they were, they have scarcely had the energy to last twenty years. The best parts of them, the parts when they are suddenly galvanized into life, are evidence that at moments Stravinsky realized he was a Russian, and forgot he was a member of an esoteric Parisian coterie.

In a somewhat different category is *Les Noces villageoises,* a secular ballet-oratorio, first performed in Paris in June, 1923. This tale of a Russian village wedding, though it began as more experimentation in timbre and rhythm—Stravinsky discarded several instrumentations (including one with mechanical pianos, which were found impracticable) before hitting on the final one—ended up as something far more formidable. It is scored for four pianos, seventeen percussion instruments, solo voices, and chorus. Some have called *Les Noces* Stravinsky's masterpiece. It is, for perhaps half its length, as exciting as a tribal chant. After that, its lack of color palls, its insistent rhythms numb rather than excite, and the voices distort the delicate balance of timbres. They become overprominent, inescapable, exacerbating. It may be said that it was exactly this maddening iteration at which Stravinsky was aiming: if so, he has succeeded. But whereas *Le Sacre* maddens and exhilarates, *Les Noces* maddens and leaves you exhausted. This is sensationalism pure and simple, and it is all very cleverly done. In *Les Noces* Stravinsky has interpreted the idea of catharsis not as a purging of the blacker humors, but as a draining of vitality. It is precisely a deathly work.*

Stravinsky's feverish search for the new, constant change of technique, and bald refusal to repeat himself make the comparison with Picasso inevitable. Both are expatriates from countries with strong folk traditions: both have become Parisians and, by extension, internationalists. Here the comparison ends. Picasso is a tireless experimenter in new techniques and new styles, and has as wholly discarded his Spanishness as Stravinsky his Russianness. But the painter, though he may not produce an immortal work of art each time he changes his manner, shrewdly knows that the new canvases can be accepted or rejected at a glance by the sophisticated eye, which, after all, is the only eye he paints for. The musician contrarily has failed to realize that the sophisticated ear has a limit of toleration. It can take in an almost unlimited amount of discord, polyrhythm, atonality, and novel timbre, but it cannot, will not, endure for long the musical analogues of a Picasso puzzle. Stravinsky's refusal to admit this handicap of a temporal art is odd if not stupid. His later compositions have a limited meaning to the unaided ear, however sophisticated: to be fully understood, they would need perfectly trained groups of listeners, each equipped with a full score. Obviously, this is not one of the desiderata of a sensual art.

With *Les Noces,* Stravinsky's interest in the nerve-twisting possibilities of rhythmic pulse culminated. Worse was to follow. Having devitalized his audiences in *Les Noces,* he now proceeded to devitalize himself. His principal aim in most of the compositions he has written since 1923 is to make them sound as little as possible like his own. It has been a difficult task, but in some of them he has done it flawlessly. The composer's retreat into the past—away from both his achievements and his experiments—began with the *Octuor* (1923), and by the time of the Piano Sonata, the following year, he no longer looked over his shoulder. A landmark, or a tombstone, along this tragic road of misguided genius is *Oedipus Rex,* a pompous, turgid, and altogether prolix opera-oratorio, after Sophocles—and Handel. Cocteau made a fine translation of the Greek play into French, and then his version was translated into Latin by the Rumanian poet, Jean Daniélou.

Let us hear Stravinsky's own explanation of this piece of what the old Comtesse de Pourtalès would have been justified in calling

---

* *Les Noces* has its faults, to be sure; but I cannot agree with this wholesale condemnation. If there is one thing the work has, it is vitality.—E. S.

"mystification": "What a joy it is to compose music to a language of convention, almost of ritual, the very nature of which imposes a lofty dignity! One no longer feels dominated by the phrase, the literal meaning of the words. . . . The text then becomes purely phonetic material for the composer. He can dissect it at will and concentrate all his attention on its primary constituent elements—that is to say, on the syllable. Was not this method of treating the text that of the old masters of austere style?" The answer to Stravinsky's rhetorical question is no. Stravinsky was using Latin because it was denatured of meaning; Palestrina (who may fairly be taken as one of the "old masters") was using Latin because it was fraught with the most profound meanings and emotions he knew.*

It seemed, in the two ballets that followed *Oedipus Rex*, that Stravinsky was faced with complete loss of creative potency. *Apollon Musagète* is an inane group of musical statuary, *Le Baiser de la fée* a nosegay of weakest scent "inspired by the Muse of Tchaikovsky," and quoting some of Piotr Ilyich's most sentimental trivia. But in 1929 came the Capriccio for piano and orchestra that could, at the moment, have been interpreted either as a sign of real life or as the last galvanic spasm of a dead man. There is a quality in it that might be called a memory of emotion: otherwise, the Capriccio is facile, clever, and pallid. The hope that the Capriccio was indeed a symptom of life was quickened the next year—1930—when the Brussels Philharmonic Orchestra gave the world *première* of the *Symphonie de psaumes*. Stravinsky, with a complete lack of humor, had put on the title page "composed for the glory of God and dedicated to the Boston Symphony on the occasion of the fiftieth anniversary of its existence." It is a setting for chorus and orchestra of Latin versions of the thirty-eighth, thirty-ninth, and fortieth Psalms, the first two fragmentarily, the last *in toto*. As Stravinsky is an intensely religious man, it seemed reasonable to suppose that he would have written deeply felt religious music, which —despite his many pronouncements against emotional content in music—might move the listener as well as the composing artist. Actually, except in those portions when his sheer musical talent momentarily released him from the grip of his own esthetic, the *Symphonie de psaumes* must be chalked up as just another experiment. For two movements, the good things are spaced closely enough to make it im-

---

* The criticism is excellent. It is interesting to note that the "old masters" Stravinsky used as models were those of the stilted, artificial Baroque court opera, not the great Renaissance composers. See the discussion of Baroque opera, pp. 259, 263.—E. S.

pressive, and occasionally moving, as nothing of Stravinsky's had been since *Les Noces*. The third movement has been dismissed by some critics as sentimental trifling: this would in itself be egregious in a setting of the fortieth Psalm. But the sad truth is that even the sentimentality is not genuine. It rings about as true as the halo Del Sarto put about the head of his peasant mistress when he was manufacturing a religious picture.

Despite its lapses, its blotches of bad taste, the *Symphonie de psaumes* kept hope alive for the patient. After all, he was only forty-eight years old. But almost a decade has passed, and though Stravinsky may be leading a rich interior life, he has passed none of it on to the public. A scant half-dozen large works have come from his workshop, all solving special musical problems (for he is always very plausible about the *raison d'être* of each of his compositions). Those that it has been possible to hear have been deader, drier, and more forbidding than those immediately antedating the Capriccio. The most recent of them to be given publicly was *The Card Party,* a ballet "in three deals," representing the actual course of three poker hands. It is as trivial, and not nearly so charming, as Delibes' most obscure and forgotten ballet. Stravinsky has reached the nadir. At the present writing, there seems no reason to believe that he will ever write another important composition.

It is fascinating to ponder the strange arc of Stravinsky's career. Many explanations have been advanced, all with grains of truth in them. Stravinsky is a complex personality, and it is not easy to chart the future course of his career or explain the vagaries of his past. Some have said that Diaghilev acted as his Svengali, and that Stravinsky's vitality waned with Diaghilev's. There are those who say that quite the opposite was the case, and that, by focusing Stravinsky's attention on rhythm (the prime requisite of ballet music), Diaghilev precipitated the drying up of his creative powers. They insist that Stravinsky had little melodic gift to start with, and that rhythmic preoccupation sapped that little. There can be no doubt, too, that expatriation hurt Stravinsky. Russians must go back. Even the Paris-loving Turgeniev went back, and recently we have seen the onetime internationalist Prokofiev returning to the Soviet Union with happy results. But the Russian Revolution completed Stravinsky's subjugation to his adopted land. He became a French citizen in 1934.

The natural tendency in discussing the composer of such dehumanized music is to forget the personal element completely. Yet

Stravinsky is by no means a Martian. There are plenty of Americans who remember his first visit to our shores in 1925, when he seemed like a herald angel, like the harbinger of a new dispensation in art. Despite his unpoetical resemblance on the podium to a trained seal, one was tempted to say of the composer of *Petroushka* and *Le Sacre,* "I too have once seen Shelley plain." He still comes to America from time to time—a little, hurried man, awkward in his gestures, and looking myopically from behind horn-rimmed spectacles. Alas, alas! we should have seen it on his first visit: Stravinsky looks like a business-man, and nothing else. It is difficult to think of him as the composer of two or three indubitable masterpieces, even more difficult to think of him as holding the future of music in his (much photographed) hands. And when he takes up the baton, and begins to conduct another of his recent compositions, we can be sure that the future of music belongs to other, younger men.

Béla Bartók

Abridged from "Twentieth Century Composers"

By David Ewen

WHEN Béla Bartók was twenty-four years old (his formal music study had by this time come to a close) he spent a few days at the country home of a friend in the interior of Hungary. While there he acci-dentally overheard one of the servants singing to himself a tune so exotic in character and content that he asked its source. The servant explained that he had acquired the melody from his mother who, in turn, had heard it as a child-in-arms from her parents. Upon further questioning, the servant disclosed the fact that there existed a large number of similar melodies—all Magyar in origin—which were sung in the smaller towns of Hungary, bequeathed from one generation to the next.

This was Bartók's first realization that there existed a storehouse of Hungarian folk music far different from the weeping sentimentality and meretricious decorations of the melodies publicized by Brahms and Liszt as authentic Hungarian folk music—and a folk music which was a much truer expression of the Hungarian people. The sentimental songs that had been recorded by Brahms in his dances and Liszt in his Rhapsodies—and which were identified by the rest of the world as indigenously Hungarian—were not Hungarian in origin, as Bartók knew well. They had been imported into Hungary by itinerant gypsy caravans who, in turn, had created this music from an indiscriminate *mélange* of influences acquired from the many countries they visited. As Bartók studied the songs hummed to him by the servant, he realized that here—and not in mawkish gypsy airs—was the musical tradition of his country.

His curiosity aroused in this little-known music of his own country, Bartók decided to travel extensively throughout the land to collect folk-song data. He visited the more remote corners of Hungary, small hill towns and secluded villages nestling in the valleys. There he lived with the peasants, sometimes worked with them in the fields, frequently drank liquor with them—and at all times made copious notes of the songs he heard.

During this trip, he stumbled across a fellow-musician, Zoltán Kodály. Kodály, who was later to occupy a position next to Bartók as an outstanding Hungarian composer, was a member of the faculty of the Royal Hungarian Academy where Bartók was soon to teach the piano. They were not a little surprised to meet each other in so far-flung a district of Hungary. Their surprise, however, expanded to amazement when they learned that they were on a similar mission; for Kodály, too, had learned of the existence of native Hungarian folk music and was in search of it. They decided to join forces, copying on paper the songs they heard peasants sing.

For the next ten years, Bartók—frequently aided by his friend Kodály—consecrated himself to the herculean task of unearthing Hungarian folk music and bringing it to the notice of the music-world. During the next decade, he wandered from the Carpathian Mountains to the Adriatic, from western Slovakia to the Black Sea—always equipped with notebook and a recording apparatus—making copious notes. In that time he collected more than 5,000 folk melodies which had been the property of the Hungarian peasant for generations but which, strange to say, were almost completely unknown in the large cities of Hungary, not to mention the rest of the world. Several thousand of these folk melodies were published, under the editorship of Bartók and Kodály.

These excavations had an effect analogous to Pedrell's explorations in Spanish folk music; they revealed to the world that Hungarian folk music possessed an individuality which the gypsy song, known to the rest of the world, could not even faintly suggest. Hungarians are not, by temperament, a mawkishly sentimental race. They are made of sterner stuff—made hard and callous by suffering and labor. To a great extent they are a reticent folk.

True Hungarian folk music is not so tinklingly melodious, so emotionally uninhibited, so pleasingly seductive to the ear as gypsy airs. It is much severer in structure, with hard surfaces of sound. Authentic Hungarian folk songs are constructed from modal scales (and, like all modal music, have a subtle and elusive charm which is not always perceptible on first hearing) and highly intricate rhythmic patterns. They are frequently drenched with somber grays, far different from the vivid purples of gypsy music.

As with Manuel de Falla of Spain and Ralph Vaughan Williams of England, Béla Bartók's devoted researches in folk music influenced his musical writing. But this influence has been much more elusive and less strongly accentuated in Bartók's works than in those of the other two composers. At first hearing, Bartók's principal works do not flaunt their national influence. His music is strongly modern, sometimes atonal in harmony, avoiding the more obvious patterns of melody and employing a highly individual harmonic language. With the exception of his children's pieces, he never uses folk songs directly. Even the more recognizable technical qualities of the Hungarian folk song are not discernible in his music at first glance.

It is only after an intimate familiarity with Bartók's music that its affinity with Hungarian folk music becomes apparent. Like the folk song, his melodies are often derived from the modal scales. Like the folk song, Bartók's rhythms are complex, with edges as pointed as the blade of a saw. As in the folk song, there is often a shadow of somber despair hovering over his music. Bartók is too much the individualist ever to be an imitator. But he has permitted the spirit of the Hungarian folk song to touch his own music ever so lightly and to spread over it a spell, as though it were a faint perfume.

Béla Bartók was born in Nagyszentmiklos, Hungary (now Jugoslavia), on March 25, 1881. His father, the director of an agricultural school, died when the boy was eight years old. The burden of supporting the family fell upon the shoulders of the mother who, assuming the profession of schoolteaching, was forced to travel frequently from one section of Hungary to another, teaching in its various schools. Thus, as a mere child, Bartók acquired a knowledge of the many-patterned customs of his country-people.

Despite his nomadic life, his education was not neglected. Revealing unusual musical aptitude, he was launched in the study of the piano at the age of six. At nine he was already creative, producing a group of small pieces for the piano. A year later, he made his first public appearance as pianist.

When Béla reached his twelfth year, his mother acquired a post in Pressburg, at the time the most advanced musical city in Hungary. There, she placed the boy under competent musical teachers. Laszlo Erkel was engaged to teach him the piano, and Ernst von Dohnányi— four years Bartók's senior—became his friend and adviser. Under their guidance Bartók's musical progress was fleet.

In 1899, upon the advice of Dohnányi, Bartók entered the Royal Hungarian Academy of Music, where he was enrolled as a piano student of Stephan Thomas and as a pupil of composition of Koessler. He remained in the academy for four years, earning recognition as one of its most brilliant pupils.

Following his graduation from the Academy, Bartók knew desperate poverty. He did some concert work as pianist, made some musical arrangements, and engaged in some teaching. But his earnings from all three were hardly sufficient to supply him with necessities. Poverty and suffering did not smother his contagious enthusiasm and his enormous zest. A scholarship, won in 1905, helped him for a time. But not until 1907, when he was engaged as teacher of the piano at the Royal Academy, was he guaranteed comfort.

During these student days, Bartók was subjected to several important musical influences. The first of these was Brahms, whose romanticism Bartók frequently attempted to ape in his first works. Then he heard a performance of Richard Strauss's *Thus Spake Zarathustra,* which profoundly affected him. He felt now that in Strauss's pungent and dramatic writing, musical expression had achieved its apotheosis, and for several years, Strauss was his idol. Finally, Bartók found Liszt—Liszt who at first had repelled him because of his pseudo-Hungarian effects but whose great significance he now realized.

Bartók's earliest works—such as the *Rhapsody* for piano and orchestra and the first Suite for orchestra, both composed during his student days—were, therefore, obviously derivative. In fumbling for his own vocabulary, Bartók freely borrowed that of those composers who had impressed him most. But—for all its imitative strains—there was already perceptible the shadow of Bartók's later personality, particularly in his riotous rhythms and in his almost barbaric savagery of speech.

It was in 1905 that Bartók was first attracted to Hungarian folk music. Between 1905 and 1914 he divided his time among his intensive travels throughout Hungary in search of native musical material, his teaching assignments at the Royal Academy (after 1907), and, most important of all, his creative work.

Bartók's struggle for recognition as a composer has been a bitter one; and not even today can we say that he has achieved full victory. His purely personal style has brought him lifelong antagonism and misunderstanding. His music, compounded of asperity and desiccated emotions, was bitterly condemned. Such an early work as *Kossuth,* a symphonic poem composed in 1903, found an enthusiastic audience because, strongly imitative of Richard Strauss and drenched with nationalistic ardor, it was easily comprehensible to the musical intelligence of early-twentieth-century Hungary. But as Bartók's personality evolved and became integrated, and as he achieved his own individual speech, the music public turned sharply away from him. In the *Two Portraits* for orchestra and the *Bagatelles* for piano, he emerged with his peculiar counterpoint, with a melody that was severely outlined, and with emancipated rhythms. With the First String Quartet he definitely blazed his own trail.

During the first World War, Bartók lived in complete seclusion, occupying himself with his creative activity. His industry remained unaffected by the trying conditions brought on by the War and the physical suffering to which his country was subjected. It was at this time that he received one of the few successful ovations that had been accorded to him during his career. In 1917, a ballet, *The Woodcut Prince,* was performed in Budapest to what was probably the first welcome sound of applause and cheering that Bartók had heard as a composer in more than a decade.

Subsequently his fame grew slowly but inevitably. An opera, *Bluebeard's Castle,* was found in 1918 to be a remarkable fusion of drama in music; its composer therefore received a handsome measure of praise from the critics. So has the pantomime, *The Wonderful Mandarin,* because of the dramatically conceived musical score, in spite of the hostility of certain audiences. Finally, three additional string quartets—in which Bartók has achieved his most compressed and incisive writing—a Dance Suite for orchestra (1923), a *Rhapsody* for violin and orchestra, dedicated to Joseph Szigeti (arranged by the composer, also, for violoncello and orchestra, in honor of Pablo Casals), and a Concerto for piano and orchestra (one of the most pulsating and dynamic pieces of music of our time)—these have earned for Bartók the designation of Hungary's greatest living composer.

Yet it would be extravagant to say that Bartók has achieved that worldwide fame that he deserves. For one of the most uniquely endowed and imaginative composers of today, and one of the most alive and vital forces in twentieth-century music, Bartók has never been accorded a fame commensurate with his genius and his significance.

Manuel de Falla

By Harold C. Schonberg

From "The American Music Lover," Vol. 7

MANUEL DE FALLA belongs to that small group of living composers who have written music that is assured of immortality. He has not composed much—at least, not much in comparison with Hindemith, Strauss, or Sibelius; but most of the music he has composed bears the mark of original and fastidious genius. His gifts were nurtured, in part, on his studies in France, where he came under the influence of Debussy, Ravel, and Dukas. This alone, however, does not account for the searching, introspective quality of his compositions. All during his life Falla has had a horror of prostituting his talents in any way, or of publishing works that he felt could be improved. Always he has displayed an almost disconcertingly high set of values. As a student he refused offers to write Spanish operas after the hackneyed pattern; in Paris he indignantly refused to adopt French nationality, though it would have assured the production of his works. The kind of mentality shown by these actions is evident in the music, which displays strong individuality and a stubborn refusal to comply with anything but the composer's artistic dictates.

Certain broad influences are apparent. The workmanship often suggests Ravel, there is an impressionism that faintly recalls Debussy, and a mysticism and rich, chromatic harmony that might be traced to Franck. But of actual stylistic influences there are few in Falla. He studied in France, but he is one of the few Spanish composers who have rejected French methods and techniques. He is a Spanish nationalist, but more; he is a poetic composer.

Falla was born in Cadiz, Nov. 23, 1876. He was taught the piano by his mother; later he studied under Pedrell and Trago. In 1905 he won a prize with his first great work, *La Vida Breve* (which was not produced until 1913). In 1907 he was in Paris, where he earned the respect and friendship of Ravel, Debussy, and Dukas. When the War broke out he returned to Spain, finally making his home in Granada in 1921. Today the composer lives in Argentina. Among his most important works are: *El Retablo de Maese Pedro* (1919), *El Amor Brujo* (1915), *El Sombrero de tres picos* (1919), *Noches en los jardines de España* (1909-15), the Concerto for harpsichord and small ensemble (1923-26), 4 *Pièces espagnoles* (1919), *Fantasia Boetica* (1919), *Siete canciones populares españolas* (1914), other songs, and guitar works.

Not only the greatest Spanish composer, Falla is one of the supreme musicians of our day. Far from being an esthetic recluse, he has adopted the best elements of impressionism and atonality and has united them into an intensely personal idiom. Although he is a master of orchestration—not even Ravel could surpass the gorgeous texture that Falla can create—he never abuses that facility, as Ravel sometimes did. Like all the great nationalists Falla transcends his medium. That is, one is first conscious not of exotic colors and folk melodies, but of musical content, form, and workmanship. Naturally the Spanish element predominates. The composer first and last is a nationalist, but he has raised his nationalism to that degree wherein a purely local flavor assumes a universal aspect.

Like Ravel and Sibelius, Falla has achieved a synthesis of modernist theories with the established vocabulary of the past. He is definitely of the twentieth century, but has not discarded the established system of tonality. Indeed he most decidedly rejects the atonal system. He has written: "It is a widespread error, the belief that modernity in music depends on a prodigality of harmonic dissonances. This is to such an extent untrue that I make bold to declare that the modern spirit in music can subsist in a work in which only consonant chords are used, and what is more, in music consisting only of an undulating melodic line. The modern spirit resides mostly in the three fundamental elements of music: rhythm, modality, and melody, used as a means of evocation. The music of Schönberg is atonal, and to this grave error is due the unpleasant effect produced by some of his music. But fortunately the majority of modern musicians observe the laws of tonality, considering them rightly as immutable." Yet Falla does not hesitate to introduce bold dissonances into his music when he feels that they will enhance its emotional content. His remarks may perhaps be construed as directed against that school which uses dissonance for sensational effects. For Falla is not a conservative, as his remarks might suggest. It is a fair assumption that by dissonance he means the type that is the studied outgrowth of a theory of composition, rather than the dissonance of Ravel or Sibelius, which is a natural adjunct to expressive means.

Arthur Honegger and "King David"

Abridged from the chapter "Composer Versus Time" in "Of Men and Music"

By Deems Taylor

WHEN I was in high school I remember being much impressed to learn that Thomas Gray worked on his *Elegy Written in a Country Churchyard*—how many years was it?—Seven?—Thirteen? I seem to have forgotten. At any rate, it was a long time, sufficient to leave me with a firm subconscious conviction that creating a notable work of art is a slow business. Most of us assume, I think, that the amount of time an artist has spent on a given piece of work has direct relation to its value. Unfortunately for the infinite-capacity-for-taking-pains theory, this is by no means invariably true. Whistler could turn out one of his nocturnes in a day, achieving a result that a lesser painter could not have equalled in a year. Arthur Honegger, the Franco-Swiss composer,* owes his reputation as an important contemporary composer to a work that took less than four months to write—his oratorio, *King David*. Six months before it was first performed, Honegger had not the faintest notion that he was going to write it. The story of how he came to do so is not unamusing.

* Born at Le Havre in 1892.—E. S.

In Mézières, a town not far from Lausanne, in Switzerland, there was a sort of experimental stock company known as the Jorat Art Theatre. It was started in an abandoned car barn by two brothers named Morax, and later, when it became prosperous, moved into an old wooden concert hall. It was very much like one of our own community playhouses, in that its actors, and its musical and mechanical departments, were largely amateurs.

One of the founders of the theatre, René Morax, was a dramatic poet; and some time in 1920 he wrote a biblical drama on the life of King David, which he was planning to produce at his own playhouse and for which he intended to employ considerable incidental music. As he wanted the play to go on in the early summer of 1921, whatever music it needed would have to be written in a hurry. He tried an eminent French composer first; then one a little less distinguished, then another a bit less distinguished than that. None of them would undertake the work on account of the extremely short time allowance.

At last, having exhausted most of his list of candidates, Morax struck bottom. He approached Arthur Honegger. The young Swiss at the time had achieved a certain amount of—well, not so much fame as notoriety—through his activities as one of the *Groupe des Six*. This was a sort of club of young musicians who had banded together with the idea of giving concerts and getting publicity for their own work and that of their fellow members. The other members of the group were Georges Auric, Louis Durey, Darius Milhaud, Francis Poulenc, and one woman, the composer-pianist, Germaine Tailleferre. Among them they created quite a commotion in Paris musical circles; but although they did attract a measure of rather horrified attention from the conservative musicians, their names did not loom very large on the general musical horizon.

Honegger was, therefore, rather a forlorn hope for Morax. The young composer accepted the commission at once, and started to work late in February, 1921. On April 28 following, nine weeks later, he finished the score. The play and the music went into rehearsal at once, and on June 11, 1921, three months and seventeen days from the time the score was begun, *King David* had its first performance in the rickety Théâtre du Jorat in Mézières, Switzerland. It was a great success from the beginning, and the music attracted so much attention that Honegger conceived the idea of grouping the musical numbers into the form of an oratorio—or, as he prefers to call it, "A Symphonic

Psalm," and turning the dialogue of the original play into a spoken narrative to be delivered between the numbers.

He did this, incidentally revising the original orchestration. For the Mézières production he had been allowed only fifteen players, including a piano and a harmonium. The revised version calls for a symphony orchestra. In its oratorio form, *King David* was performed first in Paris, at the church of St. Germain-en-Laye, during the summer of 1923. Its popularity, however, soon took it out of the confines of church performances; it has been done in concert halls and theaters throughout Europe and America. Its first performance here was one given by the Friends of Music in the Town Hall in New York, on October 26, 1925.

Despite Honegger's new term for his work, "Symphonic Psalm," *King David* is essentially a dramatic oratorio, somewhat on the style of Mendelssohn's *Elijah*. It is not, however, a sacred oratorio, strictly speaking, for although the story is a Biblical one, the text does not all come from the Bible. The presence of the Narrator is not quite so much of an innovation as it appears to be. Narrators were used in oratorios and cantatas as far back as the seventeenth century. I do think, however, that the Narrator adds greatly to the dramatic interest of this work, for what Honegger has done is to throw away the old-fashioned recitative passages, whose chief function was to carry the story along, and which, even in the greatest oratorios, have no tremendous musical value, and put them into the mouth of a single speaker, who is thus able to communicate the narrative much more clearly and rapidly than a singer could.

In Paris, in 1926, not long after the first American performance of *King David,* a friend of mine, an American newspaper man, told me of an interview he had just had with Honegger. After talking about this and that, the American said: "Now in planning this work, did you have any novel style or form in mind? Just how did you conceive the general plan of the score?"

"No," said Honegger, "I didn't. I had only a little over two months in which to write the thing, and I had no time for theories. I did start out with the idea of writing the music in the general style of Bach. Well, after working about ten days at that, I realized that if I wrote the whole work in Bach's elaborate contrapuntal style I'd never get through in nine weeks. Counterpoint takes too long to work out. So then I decided to continue in the style of Stravinsky. Well, after about ten days at that, I realized that I'd never be through in time if I went in for Stravinsky's complicated harmonic progressions. Too many notes to write."

"How did you write the rest?" said the American.

"Oh," said Honegger, "I just fell back on Massenet."

Paul Hindemith

From *"Twentieth Century Composers"*

By David Ewen

PAUL HINDEMITH was born on November 16, 1895, in Hanau, Germany. His love for music became apparent at such a tender age that he began the study of the violin and the viola even before he could read or write. His parents objected violently to his musical preoccupations. Rather than renounce music, he ran away from home. For an extended period, beginning with his eleventh year, he earned his livelihood by playing in cafés, dance bands, and movie houses. However, he did not neglect his own musical development. In the Hoch Conservatory of Frankfurt, where Hindemith was a pupil of Arnold Mendelssohn and Bernhard Sekles, he received a comprehensive training not only on the viola and the violin but also in harmony, counterpoint, and composition. He was a brilliant pupil and captured many school prizes. It was while he was still a pupil at the Hoch Conservatory that he began composition seriously.

In 1915, Hindemith joined the orchestra of the Frankfurt Opera House as concertmaster. He remained there until 1923, rising to the post of conductor. Meanwhile, his importance as a musician had branched out generously into several significant directions. He founded and became the violist of the Amar String Quartet—a powerful force for the dissemination of propaganda for modern chamber music throughout Germany. He had likewise attracted notice as a composer. In 1921, 1922, and 1923 his early chamber music was featured prominently at the Donaueschingen Festival in Baden-Baden—so prominently that his music was soon the feature attraction of the festival. In 1922, his Second String Quartet (Opus 16) was successfully performed in Salzburg, followed one year later by a triumphant performance of the Clarinet Quintet (Opus 30).

Hindemith's musical style was not completely personalized until 1925, with a *Kammermusik*—a concerto for piano and twelve solo instruments—introduced at the Festival of Modern Music in Venice. In his work, Hindemith revealed forcefully a tendency which had been asserting itself spasmodically in his previous works—a tendency which extended as far back as Bach. In his previous works—particularly in the sonatas for violoncello and piano and for viola and piano, and in his magnificent song-cycle *Das Marienleben* based on poems of Rainer Maria Rilke—Hindemith disclosed a strong predilection for polyphonic writing; in the *Marienleben,* frequently, the melodic line of the solo voice moves completely independent of the piano accompaniment. However, counterpoint became fully integrated into Hindemith's style with the *Kammermusik* of 1925. From this time on, his music was to be a combination of Bach's polyphonic principles with the harmonic, rhythmic, and melodic innovations of twentieth-century music. He was, with rare felicitousness, to infuse the modern spirit into old forms. His music, for all its leanings on seventeenth-century counterpoint, is crisp in idiom, often stingingly acid, strong-fibered in architecture, muscle and sinew rather than heart and nerves. Yet it derives from Bach its sense of perpetual movement, the lucid clarity of its construction, and the inextricable unity which binds it into a coherent whole. It was this strange marriage of modern musical devices with Bach polyphony that tempted more than one critic to refer to these works of Hindemith as "Brandenburg Concertos upside down."

In 1926, Hindemith's name assumed especial significance in the world of modern music when his *Meisterwerk,* the opera *Cardillac,* was introduced at the Dresden Opera under the baton of Fritz Busch. This was not Hindemith's first venture into operatic form. In 1921-2, he had produced a series of three one-act operas whose rawness and immaturity have relegated them to an obscurity they probably deserve. The year after that, a play with incidental music, *Tuttifantchen,* was given a first performance in Darmstadt—an opera which proved to be so inept a union of drama and music that, shortly after the first performance, a quip was circulated throughout Germany which quoted the composer as saying, "Never again, as long as I live, will I compose an opera of which I haven't read the text!"

Cardillac was, however, Hindemith's first mature and full-grown composition in operatic form. The opera was based upon E. T. A. Hoffmann's novel, *Das Fräulein von Scuderi.* The scene of *Cardillac* is seventeenth-century Paris where Cardillac, a goldsmith of singular ingenuity in fashioning things of a delicate beauty, plies his trade. It is soon discovered that a curse pursues all those who buy Cardillac's works of art. An officer, who is in love with Cardillac's daughter, determines to solve the mystery of the curse and learns that Cardillac is a diabolical murderer who injects into his molds a lethal poison.

In *Cardillac,* Hindemith did not blaze new trails for the music-drama as Alban Berg did, for example, in *Wozzeck. Cardillac* is an opera in traditional form, a combination of arias, duets, recitatives, etc. Its great strength lies in its architectonic construction, the design of which is as taut as a violin string. One critic astutely remarked that in *Cardillac* Hindemith applied the form of some of his concertos: the first act resembles an exposition, the second act a development, and the third act something of a recapitulation. In style, the opera has the compactness of writing, the terseness of expression, the lucidity of structure, and the moving beauty of polyphony which mark the best pages of Hindemith's chamber works. There are few moments in modern opera so deeply stirring as the final scene of the opera.

Cardillac definitely placed Hindemith at the head of the younger German composers—"the most full-blooded talent," as Hugo Riemann called him. His creative significance brought him in 1927 a professorship in composition at the Berlin Normal School as well as a membership to the German Academy—an amazing distinction for a composer who had only recently seen his thirty-second birthday.

Cardillac was followed by a still more sensational opera which, for a time, enjoyed an overwhelming vogue among German music-lovers. It was *Neues vom Tage,* produced in Berlin in June, 1929, when it received an electric response from the audiences. Built about a libretto which was a swiftly moving and acid comment on modern life, written with the raciness and gusto of a tabloid news column, *Neues vom Tage* delighted a jazz-mad era. The opera, for all the sparkle and vitality of its score, is, however, the most transitory of Hindemith's works; its greatest appeal lay in its timeliness. Tabloid realism is certainly unsuitable for the composition of inspired music, and his earnest attempt to treat the plot flippantly in his music was, for the most part, futile. His hand was too heavy for such absurdities; his music too severe.

It was the inartistic theme of *Neues vom Tage,* as well as such works as the *Kammermusik No. 5,* a concerto for viola and orchestra (whose last movement appeared to be a satire on a German military march), and such *Gebrauchsmusik* as his manufactured pieces for pianola, radio, talking screen, and even ether-wave instrument, that aroused the dispieasure of the Kulturkammer of the Nazi government.

At about this time Hindemith visited Paris and London. On January 22, 1936, he was scheduled to introduce his latest work, *Der Schwanendreher* (concerto for viola and small orchestra) at a concert at Queen's Hall under the auspices of the B.B.C. The death of King George V cancelled the prospective concert. It was decided to substitute on that date a special studio concert in memory of the King, with Hindemith playing some appropriate music on his viola. For three days, Hindemith searched musical literature for some appropriate work for viola and orchestra, but could find nothing. He decided, therefore (since the concert was only two days off), to compose an original work for the occasion. That morning he set to work upon *Funeral Music,* a composition for viola and string orchestra. Late that afternoon the work was completed. The following day it was rehearsed. And the evening after that it was given its first performance on a nationwide broadcast.

"Such a feat," remarked the English critic Walter Leigh, "can rarely have been accomplished since Handel's day in the sphere of serious music. Only a composer with a complete mastery of technique and an exceptionally fertile invention could perform it successfully. It is the more remarkable because the work bears no trace of speed, other than its simplicity; and this very simplicity is one of its great merits."

In the spring of 1937, at an invitation of the Elizabeth Sprague Coolidge Foundation, Paul Hindemith came to the United States for the first time. He was forty-one years old now, but—in the almost boyish expression of his round face and the ingenuous quality of his eyes—he appeared much younger, so much younger that it seemed difficult to believe that for more than a decade already he has been a dominant figure in the world of modern music. The regal reception that Hindemith was accorded not only by the outstanding musical organizations of this country but by the music public as well was an eloquent tribute to a great musical figure—and an eloquent answer to the country, across the ocean, that had ejected him because he was "an unwholesome influence."

Alban Berg and "Wozzeck"

The chapter "A Masterpiece" in "Of Men and Music"

By Deems Taylor

I HAVE already mentioned the possibility that before long composers would arrive to whom the strange harmonic and rhythmic idiom of so-called ultra-modern music would be their natural musical speech, and whose talents would be patent even to those who happened to dislike their music. The statement was over-cautious. Such a composer has arrived, in my opinion, and has produced at least one musical work of enduring value. He will not produce another, more's the pity. He was Alban Berg, the Austrian composer * who died not long ago, at fifty, long before his task was finished. The work that he produced is his opera, *Wozzeck,* which, to one of its hearers at least, towers high above most contemporary music. I am not sure that I like *Wozzeck;* I cannot quite imagine dropping in at a performance of it at the Metropolitan to hear that delicious bit in the third act. Still—I might. And I do consider it an authentic work of genius.

Wozzeck made its initial appearance at the Berlin Staatsoper on the night of December 14, 1925. Savagely attacked from the start, and as savagely defended, it made its way through the opera houses of Germany and Austria, and for a time was a favorite topic of debate in European musical circles. It reached this country six years later, when it had two performances by the Philadelphia Opera Company, under Leopold Stokowski. I saw them both, and I shall not soon forget them.

Berg arranged his libretto from a play by George Büchner, a curious and tragic early nineteenth-century combination of scientist, mathematician, and poet, who died in 1837, in his twenty-fifth year. The manuscript was lost at the time of its author's death, and was not found and published until 1879. Originally in some twenty-odd loosely connected scenes, it was compressed by Berg into fifteen, distributed equally through three acts.

The story of *Wozzeck* is, briefly, the story of a poor devil. Nominally, Wozzeck is a conscript, a captain's orderly, garrisoned in a small German town, but in a broader sense he is the common man of any

* Born in Vienna, 1885; died there, 1935.—E. S.

604

time and place, the eternal underdog, the little fellow at the bottom of the pile. He is a stupid, trustful fool, bullied by his captain, who loves to jeer at his thick-wittedness, and exploited by the town doctor, who uses him for some idiotic experiments in psychiatry. Dumb brute as he is, he has got himself a mistress, Marie, whom he worships and who has borne him a child. Marie, who was a rather shopworn blossom even when Wozzeck gathered her, wearies of him and falls a willing victim to the wiles of a handsome dog of a drum-major. The captain and the doctor have great sport hinting to Wozzeck that he has been betrayed. He rushes to Marie, bewildered and suspicious. She laughs at his forebodings; furious, he raises his hand against her. "Don't touch me!" she screams. "Rather a knife in my heart than a hand laid upon me!"

Baffled and jealous, he wanders into a summer garden, where he sees Marie and the drum-major dancing. He goes back to the barracks, but he cannot sleep. The drum-major comes in, drunk, taunts Wozzeck with his conquest, and when he refuses a drink, beats him up. The poor, half-mad, abandoned lover takes Marie for a last walk in the country, by a pond. There he stabs her. He goes back to a tavern, but the revellers look at him in horror; there is blood on his hands. The knife! He must find the knife. He goes to the pond once more, but the knife is gone. Wholly mad now, he wades in the pond, and is drowned. The doctor and the captain happen by, and hear his dying gasps; but they hurry away. In the town, the children hear the news of the murder, and rush to tell Marie's little son that his mother is dead. But he is too young to understand. They run off, leaving the little boy riding his hobbyhorse.

Grewsome as this story may sound, outlined thus baldly, it is told with such pity, in language and scenes of such simple pathos, that its horrors are softened, quite dimmed, in fact, by the spectator's profound sense of sympathy and pity for its people in general and Wozzeck in particular. For its expounding, Berg wove a musical integument of enormous complication and great dramatic power. He was, as you have been told many times, a pupil of Arnold Schönberg, and his score is written in the atonal manner of his master—that is, in complete disregard of what are still the orthodox notions of concord and discord. The orchestral voices go their way in what seems like complete independence, in totally unrelated keys, and in rhythms as complex as the harmony.

But, like it or not, the music of *Wozzeck* is not to be dismissed with a word—or with many words. It is music written by a man who has enormous talent for the theater, who can isolate, as it were, the emotion of a scene, and convey it, who has an unerring sense of timing and an almost unfaltering command of climax. *Wozzeck* is a true music drama, written by a dramatic artist of the first order.

What impresses one first of all about the score of *Wozzeck* is the technical mastery of its composer, his complete control of his medium. Berg himself has written that the composer of opera must be a super stage director, a statement whose truth ought to be—and is not—self-evident to any assiduous opera-goer. For it is the composer who, in the last analysis, not only establishes the mood of the scenes, but dictates the pace at which they are taken, the pauses between speeches, the time allowed for stage business, the emphasis and inflections with which the speeches are delivered, the very speed with which the curtain goes up and down. To be a master-musician avails an operatic composer very little if he be not also a man of the theater.

And this Berg is. Throughout the three acts and fifteen scenes of his astonishing opera he seldom relaxes, and never loses, his hold upon the hearer. He displays an admirable sense of just how long the tension of a given mood can be sustained without snapping, how long or short an interlude should be, just what sort of music is needed to effect the transition between two disparate scenes, exactly where the music should be lyric, where graphic and dramatic, where reflective.

The score of *Wozzeck* is an extraordinary contrapuntal achievement. It is not, perhaps, the sort of counterpoint that would appeal to a German musical scholar of the old school. Hearing it, Jadassohn would probably go mad, and Fuchs would assuredly hang himself. Bach, however, while he might have made a wry face over it, would have rendered its creator a grudging respect. For the voices in Berg's orchestra are manipulated with great skill. Their progressions have little to do with accepted notions of concord and key-relationship; but they are real progressions. His canons are canons, and his fugues are real fugues.

The least successful element in the work seems to me to be the vocal writing. Berg's idea, presumably, is to get away from the idiom of traditional operatic singing, to make the musical speech of the singers approximate the rise and fall and intonation of the spoken speech of actors. Much of the time he directs them to use a tone that preserves the relations of the written notes to one another, without trying for exact intonation (a procedure that is almost imposed by the impossibility of singing true notes against an atonal orchestra). This is an excellent idea, but in carrying it out he elects to write the vocal parts in a register that is practically impossible for the singers. The Captain, sung by a tenor, spends most of his time in a register that would be comfortable only for a contralto. Wozzeck must be prepared to negotiate a low E natural in the bass clef, yet sings most of his lines in a fairly high tenor register. Berg, who would not dream of asking a French horn to spend half the evening screaming away on its top C, does not hesitate to demand that Marie do just that.

As a result, the actors neither speak nor sing. They just holler. On the rare occasions when they do manage to sing-speak as Berg demands, their vocal loops and nosedives are so abrupt and far-reaching that they sound like bad actors ranting. When it comes to reading lines, Berg could have learned something from almost any good American stage director.

But far more important than Berg the technician is Berg the artist and thinker. He has caught and intensified with amazing power the mood of terror and nameless horror that hangs over the story of Wozzeck. The plot is only a framework for the inner, personal drama that he sets to music. Most of the time his music is not objective at all. It concerns itself, not with the external horrors of lust and murder, but with the secret terrors of the mind, the thoughts that gnaw the brain like maggots, the chucklings and whisperings of the little devils of madness.

Even when his music is descriptive it contrives to be introspective, to be both a picture and a comment. The distorted harmonies of the band in the beer garden, the drunken dissonances of the revelers, contrive to saturate the scene with the nightmare quality of a Goya etching. The rising tide of swirling chromatics that engulfs the orchestra after Wozzeck's death is the voice of the water as it must have sounded in the ears of the dying man. The incredible interlude that follows the murder scene—a stupendous unison *crescendo* on the note B—creates in the brain the same intolerable tension that slow realization must have wrought in the brain of the poor, bewildered murderer.

The music is, of course, almost wholly dissonant. There is hardly a chord that does not bristle with unreconciled sharps and flats, scarcely a progression that does not bite like acid. Yet there is a curiously reassuring quality in Berg's music. You feel that he is writing, not to a formula, but from necessity. The music is so completely appropriate to the dramatic theme that it is easy to believe that it is not the only music its composer can write. His themes have bite and salience; they stand on their own feet and move of their own vitality. Upon occasion he can write simply, almost diatonically. The interlude between the second and third scenes of the first act; Marie's *berceuse* and her recital of the story of Mary Magdalene; the last intermezzo of the third act, and the pitying and rueful finale—all these possess a quality of lifting and eloquent beauty that speaks to the heart direct, needing neither analysis nor explanation.

I have never heard any excerpts from the score of *Wozzeck* played in concert. It is quite possible that, divorced from the stage action of which it is so eloquent an interpreter, the music might sound arbitrary and formless. That, however, is only a negative way of saying that it fits its own frame to perfection, that its creator, in setting out to write a musical setting for a drama that would express not only its action but its emotional overtones, has succeeded, as Debussy did in setting a not dissimilar drama, in producing an unforgettable masterpiece.

Sergei Prokofiev

By Nicolas Slonimsky

From "Great Modern Composers," ed. by Oscar Thompson

THE young years of Sergei Prokofiev are vividly described by him in an excerpt from his autobiography, published in the Moscow monthly, *Sovietskaya Musica,* of April, 1941. "I was born in the village of Sontzovka, in the Ekaiterinoslav government, which is now in the Dniepropetrov district, at 5 o'clock in the afternoon, on April 11, 1891, according to the old style, which corresponds to April 23, new style. My father was director of the estate of the Sontzovs. This estate comprised large expanses of the steppe, and the owners never lived there. My mother played the piano rather well, chiefly Beethoven and Chopin, and this gave me a taste for serious music from my youngest years. When I was three years old I bumped my forehead against an iron trunk, and the bump stayed for something like twenty-five years.

A painter who did my portrait used to touch the bump and say, 'Well, perhaps your whole talent is in this bump.'

"When I was five and a half years old, I improvised a little piece and played it several times. My piece was in F major, minus the B-flat, which however, should not be interpreted as a predilection for the Lydian mode, but should rather be ascribed to the fear of touching a black key. It is hard to imagine a more preposterous title than the one I assigned to this creation, *The Hindu Gallop*. At that time there was a famine in India, and the grown-ups read about it in the papers and discussed it, while I listened."

At the age of six, Prokofiev was already able to write down his new compositions, a waltz, a march, and a rondo, and in June, 1900, at the ripe age of nine, completed an opera, *The Giant*. It was in three acts and six scenes, and it was duly performed in the following summer in the estate of Prokofiev's uncle, where Prokofiev's family was visiting. Of course, the opera was written in piano score, without orchestration. Prokofiev tried to compose a more ambitious opera entitled *On the Desert Island* but could not get beyond the overture. He played this overture for Taneiev in Moscow, and Taneiev suggested a regular study of harmony and composition. Prokofiev was lucky in his first teacher, Reinhold Glière, with whom he began serious study in the summer of 1902. Prokofiev picked up the necessary science very quickly, and, guided by Glière, concocted a full-fledged symphony in G major, in orchestral score. Glière showed it to Taneiev, who smilingly remarked that the harmonies were rather elementary, mostly the three principal triads. Prokofiev was hurt by this remark, but, then, when some eight years later he, as a promising modernist and rebel played his Études, Op. 2, for Taneiev, the latter had different criticism to offer: "Too many false notes."

Prokofiev was with Glière again in the summer of 1903, and wrote, under his guidance, an opera based on Pushkin's *Feast During the Plague*. This time it was a real opera, with an overture in sonata form.

In February 1904, the twelve-year-old Prokofiev had an audition with Glazunov, who was impressed with the boy's talent and suggested that he should be enrolled in the St. Petersburg Conservatory, where Glazunov was teaching. The Prokofiev family heeded Glazunov's advice, and Prokofiev entered the St. Petersburg Conservatory in the spring of 1904, producing at the examination a large portfolio of compositions which included four operas, two sonatas, a symphony, and a number of piano pieces. He was immediately accepted, and began the study of harmony and counterpoint with Liadov, and orchestration with Rimsky-Korsakov.

While continuing his academic studies, Prokofiev composed in a manner not approved by his Conservatory teachers. On Dec. 31, 1908, he appeared for the first time in public at a concert of the Contemporary Music Society in St. Petersburg, playing seven piano pieces. He was seventeen years old at the time, and his appearance produced a flurry of excitement. There were reviews in the papers. One in the St. Petersburg *Bulletin* said: "If all these rather confused pieces are to be regarded as a composer's first attempts, there might be found in them occasional flashes of some talent."

In the summer of 1908, Prokofiev composed another symphony, of which only the Andante was preserved. The thematic material of this Andante was later incorporated into his Fourth Piano Sonata. In the same year he began to study piano with Essipova and conducting with Tcherepnin. Although still a student at the Conservatory, he digressed in his compositions from the required academic manner. His *Sinfonietta,* composed in 1909, was a work so mature in its new style and technique that Prokofiev thought it worth while to use the music twenty years later for a revised version. Accordingly, it bears a double opus number, 5/48.

The year 1910 brought two symphonic poems, *Rêves* and *Esquisse automnale. Rêves* is dedicated to Scriabin and represents one of the rare instances in which Prokofiev showed interest in Scriabin's music. *Esquisse automnale* was inspired by Rachmaninoff, particularly by his *Isle of the Dead.* It was subsequently revised, and achieved its final form twenty years later.

The earliest composition of undoubted significance was the First Piano Concerto, written in 1911. This is a work in which Prokofiev's definitive style is clearly outlined. There is the familiar boisterousness, the "football" quality that aroused so much admiration (and indignation) among Russian musicians and critics. The Concerto is episodic in its development, but its episodes are firmly interconnected, following, with some modifications, the form of a sonata. In the summer of 1911, Prokofiev wrote a one-act opera, *Magdalene,* to a story of fifteenth-century Venice. He revised this opera in 1913, but never orchestrated it. During his Conservatory years he worked on another opera, *Undine,* of which he composed three acts.

It was in his piano music of the early period that Prokofiev found his true style. He wrote the First Piano Sonata in 1909, the Second in 1912, and the Third in 1917. Ten piano pieces, written between 1908 and 1913, were assembled in a suite, and published under Opus No. 12. In 1918, Jurgenson accepted from Prokofiev several piano compositions, and paid him 100 rubles for the First Piano Sonata, and twelve miscellaneous pieces. The same publisher paid 200 rubles for the Second Sonata, and 500 rubles for the Ten Pieces, Op. 12. The titles of some of these pieces reflect Prokofiev's early addiction to the grotesque. Other titles, such as *Suggestion diabolique, Élan,* etc., may reflect the Scriabin influence.

On March 6, 1910, Prokofiev performed his Sonata, Op. 1, and Four Etudes, Op. 2, at the thirteenth "musical exhibition" in Moscow. In the summer of 1911 his two symphonic sketches, *Rêves* and *Esquisse automnale,* were performed by a summer orchestra, and in the following summer, Prokofiev appeared as pianist with the same orchestra in his First Piano Concerto. On Sept. 5, 1913, Prokofiev played his Second Piano Concerto at a summer orchestra concert in Pavlovsk, a suburb of St. Petersburg. This performance created an uproar. The St. Petersburg *Gazette* wrote caustically: "Prokofiev sat at the piano, and began to dust the keys, or perhaps, try which key sounds higher and which lower. All this in a sharp, percussive manner. The audience was puzzled. Some were indignant. . . . The young composer's Concerto concluded on a mercilessly dissonant combination of brass instruments."

Prokofiev selected the First Piano Concerto as his graduation piece, and played it at the commencement of the St. Petersburg Conservatory on May 24, 1914, with the student orchestra conducted by Tcherepnin. He received the first prize, a grand piano, but the decision of the jury was far from unanimous, and Glazunov himself voted against Prokofiev.

In his autobiography, Prokofiev makes an important analysis of the creative evolution of his style:

The principal lines which I followed in my creative work are these: The first is classical, whose origin lies in my early infancy when I heard my mother play Beethoven sonatas. It assumes a neo-classical aspect in the sonatas and the concertos, or imitates the classical style of the eighteenth century, as in the Gavottes, the *Classical Symphony,* and, in some respects, in the *Sinfonietta.* The second is innovation, whose inception I trace to my meeting with Taneiev, when he taunted me for my rather "elementary harmony." At first, this innovation consisted in the search for an individual harmonic language, but later was transformed into a desire to find a medium for the expression of strong emotions, as in *Sarcasms, Scythian Suite*, the opera *The Gambler, They Are Seven*, the Second Symphony, etc. This innovating strain has affected not only the harmonic idiom, but also melodic inflection, orchestration, and stage technique. The third is the element of the toccata, or motor element, probably influenced by Schumann's Toccata, which impressed me greatly at one time. In this category are the Études Op. 2, Toccata Op. 11, Scherzo Op. 12, the Scherzo of the Second Piano Concerto, the Toccata in the Fifth Piano Concerto, the persistent figurations in the *Scythian Suite, Le Pas d'acier*, and some passages in the Third Piano Concerto. This element is probably the least important. The fourth element is lyrical. It appears at first as lyric meditation, sometimes unconnected with melos, as in the *Fairy Tale* Op. 3, *Rêves, Esquisse automnale, Legend*, Op. 12, etc., but sometimes is found in long melodic phrases, as in the opening of the First Violin Concerto, the songs, etc. This lyric strain has for long remained in obscurity, or, if it was noticed at all, then only in retrospection. And since my lyricism has for a long time been denied appreciation, it has grown but slowly. But at later stages I paid more and more attention to lyrical expression.

I should like to limit myself to these four elements, and to regard the fifth element, that of the grotesque, with which some critics are trying to label me, as merely a variation of the other characteristics. In application to my music, I should like to replace the word grotesque by "Scherzoness," or by the three words giving its gradations: "jest," "laughter," "mockery."

By 1914, Prokofiev's style may be considered as established. It contains the elements of humor as well as the lyrical qualities. The short piano pieces which created early popularity for Prokofiev, particularly *Fugitive Visions*, have endured. The secret of the charm of these pieces, most of them very brief, consists in Prokofiev's unfailing ability to invoke a mood, comical, mock-sentimental, or movingly lyrical, as the case may be. In 1914, Prokofiev composed his first important orchestral work, the *Scythian Suite*. In some respects it is a counterpart of Stravinsky's *Le Sacre du printemps*. There is the same invocation of the remote past of pagan Russia, the same primitive directness. The harmonic writing of Prokofiev, however, is much more transparent than Stravinsky's of that period. Prokofiev conducted the first performance of the *Scythian Suite* in Petrograd on Jan. 29, 1916.

In his Incantation for tenor, chorus, and orchestra, *They Are Seven*, based on the old Sumerian legend of seven demons, and written in 1917, Prokofiev went much farther. Here, the melodic line becomes nearly a function of verbal inflection, and the harmony a background of solid dissonance. As if to counterbalance this outburst of elemental force, Prokofiev, in the same year, composed his *Classical* Symphony. This work remains Prokofiev's most popular orchestral piece. Its technique of sudden shifts of tonality, deceptive cadences, and leaping melodic intervals, has remained the most characteristic feature of Prokofiev's style.

Prokofiev's first important opera was *The Gambler,* after Dostoevski, composed in 1915-16. Its style derives from the realism of Mussorgsky; there is even literal imitation, as in the musical picturization of the whirling roulette. Prokofiev revised the score of the opera for its production in Brussels, which took place on April 29, 1929. In 1917 Prokofiev made the first sketches of his ballet *The Buffoon,* usually known as *Chout,* which is the French transliteration of the Russian word for buffoon. In the same year, 1917, Prokofiev wrote the First Violin Concerto. This work reflects very strongly the influence of the Russian national school, particularly Rimsky-Korsakov and Glazunov.

Prokofiev conducted the first performance of the *Classical* Symphony in Petrograd on April 21, 1918, when the famine and disruption of civilian life had reached a high peak. Armed with a recommendation from the Commissar of Education, Lunatcharsky, Prokofiev left Russia by way of Siberia and the Pacific, and on Sept. 18, 1918, arrived in New York. In America, he made several appearances as pianist, playing his own works. His first opera production took place in Chicago, when the Chicago Opera Company presented, on Dec. 30, 1921, his fantastic opera, *Love for Three Oranges,* to the story by Carlo Gozzi. The March and the Scherzo from this score subsequently became popular as orchestral numbers. In Russia, *Love for Three Oranges* was produced on Feb. 18, 1926, in Leningrad.

In 1922, Prokofiev made his home in Paris, and there he entered into close association with Serge Diaghilev, the famous impresario of the Russian Ballet, who was just resuming his post-war season in Paris. Prokofiev had given to Diaghilev his ballet *The Buffoon,* which was produced in Paris on May 17, 1921. It remained in the repertoire of the Russian Ballet until the dissolution of Diaghilev's enterprise. In the form of an orchestral suite, *The Buffoon* has also enjoyed many concert performances. In 1925, Prokofiev wrote a ballet entitled *Le Pas d'acier* (The Steel Leap) which represented the spirit of industrial and social growth in the new Russia. It was, of course, a stylization, a Westerner's view, of the outward aspects of Soviet Russia, but psychologically it was a preparation for Prokofiev's return to his native country. *Le Pas d'acier* was produced in Paris by Diaghilev on June 7, 1927.

In 1927, Prokofiev made a concert tour in Russia, playing and conducting his works. He was received with a cordiality that showed that he was regarded in Russia not as an emigrant, but as a Soviet citizen at large. Returning to Paris, he wrote another ballet for Diaghilev, *L'Enfant prodigue,* which was produced in Paris on May 20, 1929, the last year of Diaghilev's life. Prokofiev's last ballet of the Paris period was *Sur le Borysthène,* commissioned by Serge Lifar, and produced by him at the Paris Opéra on Dec. 12, 1932.

Another important association was that with Serge Koussevitzky, who opened his Paris series of orchestral concerts in 1921, and who gave several first performances of Prokofiev's works—the Second Symphony (June 6, 1925), the First Violin Concerto (Oct. 18, 1923), as well as repeat performances of the *Scythian Suite,* the *Classical* Symphony, March and Scherzo from the opera *Love for Three Oranges,* and the Suite from *The Buffoon.* As the head of the Russian Publishing House in Paris, Koussevitzky has published a number of Prokofiev's works. For the 50th anniversary of the Boston Symphony Orchestra, Koussevitzky commissioned Prokofiev to write a symphony. This was Prokofiev's Fourth, and it was performed by the Boston Symphony Orchestra on Nov. 14, 1930. This Fourth Symphony included thematic material from the ballet *L'Enfant prodigue.*

In the meantime, Prokofiev continued his concert activities as a pianist in Europe and America. He gave the first performance of his Third Concerto in C Major with the Chicago Symphony Orchestra on Dec. 16, 1921. This Concerto reveals Prokofiev's characteristic qualities, the aggressive "football" technique, and gentle lyricism, with just a suspicion of irony. His Fourth Concerto was a commission by the one-armed pianist, Paul Wittgenstein, and was accordingly written for the left hand alone. The Fifth Concerto in G Major was performed by Prokofiev with the Berlin Philharmonic on Oct. 31, 1932.

In 1934, Prokofiev went back to Russia and reëstablished his status as a Soviet composer. But he had to undergo a period of adjustment, for Soviet musical life differed in many respects from that of the western world. He also had to withstand initial criticism of some of his compositions, as, for instance, his *Symphonic Song,* first performed in Moscow on April 14, 1934. In Russia Prokofiev completed his Second Violin Concerto, in G Major, written in a broad melodic manner, and with full regard for the capacities of the instrument. It was first performed not in Russia, but in Madrid, on Dec. 1, 1935. He also wrote a Concerto for violoncello and orchestra, performed for the first time in Moscow on Nov. 26, 1938.

In 1936, Prokofiev wrote his *Russian Overture,* based on national themes. This work comes close to the dominant Soviet movement, characterized by "national framework" and "contemporary content." In 1937, Prokofiev asserted even more definitely his adherence to Soviet ideas in his Cantata, written on the occasion of the 20th anniversary of the Soviet Revolution and composed to the texts from the speeches and writing of Marx, Lenin, and Stalin.

The role that Diaghilev's ballet played in Prokofiev's Paris days was filled in his Soviet period by the theater and the motion picture. For the films, he wrote the score to *Lieutenant Kijé,* based on the story of Tsar Paul's mistake in reading an officer's name, as a result of which a fictitious officer was created to receive the Tsar's honors. This theme suited Prokofiev's satirical talent, and the music was successful. From it Prokofiev made an orchestral suite. His greatest success in the field of theatrical music, however, was achieved in his fairy tale for children, *Peter and the Wolf,* which was first produced at the Children's Theater in Moscow on May 2, 1936. In this score each character is illustrated by an instrument, to enable the children to learn orchestral timbres. Peter was characterized by strings, his grandfather by the bassoon, the bird by the flute, the duck by the oboe, the cat by the clarinet in the low register, and the wolf by three horns. Also, each character was assigned a motive—an unexpected application of the Wagnerian principle, otherwise so alien to Prokofiev's music.

In the field of ballet, Prokofiev wrote a score on a Shakespearian theme, *Romeo and Juliet.* The production took place in Moscow on Nov. 24, 1936.

In connection with the revival of interest for the Russian past, a motion picture, *Alexander Nevsky,* was produced in 1938, and Prokofiev composed the musical score for it. The story celebrated the rout of the Teutonic Knights on the frozen surface of Lake Peipus on April 5, 1242. Prokofiev expanded this music into a cantata, and conducted it in Moscow on May 17, 1939. When the cantata was repeated during the November Festival in the same year, it was extremely well received, and the Soviet newspapers extolled Prokofiev's music with unreserved praise. The musical style of *Alexander Nevsky* is a compromise between Prokofiev's early modernism of the period of the *Scythian Suite,* and the new conception of a nationally Russian style, derived mainly from Borodin, and, to a lesser degree, from Mussorgsky. Hence, the luxurious orchestration, with bells, xylophones, and—an innovation—the Cuban instrument, maracas.

After the composition of *Alexander Nevsky,* Prokofiev turned his attention to Soviet opera. He selected a subject from the civil war in the Ukraine. The original title of the opera was *I am the Son of a Working People,* but Prokofiev later changed it to the name of the hero, a Red Army warrior, *Simeon Kotko.* The opera was produced in Moscow on June 23, 1940, and enjoyed considerable success. In December, 1940, Prokofiev completed a new opera, this time to a play by Sheridan, *The Duenna.* He sketched the opera *A Monastery Wedding* and a ballet *Cinderella* in 1941.

His active interest in the stage had not diminished his energies in the field of instrumental music. On Feb. 11, 1940, he completed the composition of his Sixth Piano Sonata. If in the field of stage music Prokofiev seems to simplify his musical language to make the production less hampered by avoidable complexities, in his instrumental music he applies the sharpest point of polyphonic dissonance.

Though Prokofiev does not occupy any teaching position, he exercises the greatest influence on young Soviet composers, and shares with Miaskovsky and Shostakovich the highest stellar position on the Soviet musical horizon.

Dmitri Shostakovich

By Nicolas Slonimsky

From "Great Modern Composers," ed. by Oscar Thompson

DMITRI SHOSTAKOVICH was born in Leningrad (then St. Petersburg) on Sept. 25, 1906, and thus was barely eleven years old at the time of the Soviet Revolution. He belongs, then, to the generation of Russian composers whose adolescence and adult life have passed under the Soviet regime. Undoubtedly, his is the most brilliant name among Soviet composers.

Shostakovich studied at the St. Petersburg Conservatory with Nikolaev (piano), Sokolov (harmony and counterpoint), and Steinberg (composition). He began composing at an early age, and at thirteen wrote a Scherzo for orchestra. He graduated in piano in 1923, and in composition in 1925. The first public performance of his music took place in Leningrad on May 12, 1926, when his Symphony No. 1 in F minor was performed under the direction of Nicolai Malko. This symphony, composed when Shostakovich was nineteen years old, has proved the most durable and the most successful of his works, and has since held a permanent place in the orchestral repertoire not only in Russia, but also in the United States. Academic in its form, and couched in the orthodox four movements, it is, however, very original in its melodic and rhythmic elements. Its themes are alternately gay, to the point of boisterousness, and lyrically meditative, tending at times toward undisguised sentimentality.

These two contrasting elements remain the chief characteristics of Shostakovich's music. Often the gaiety of the first element reaches pure grotesque, while the meditative quality approaches the sentimentality of a Russian gypsy song. Superseding both, there is a dramatic power in Shostakovich's music, in a twentieth-century Beethoven manner. In common with other Soviet composers, Shostakovich regards Beethoven as a model of true "people's music," and applies Beethoven's fundamental qualities of drama, humor, and sentiment to the new uses.

Shostakovich's Second Symphony represents his first attempt to inject social meaning into music. It is subtitled *Dedication to October*, with reference to the October Revolution (November, according to the new style of Russian Calendar), and it was first performed at the tenth anniversary of the Revolution, Nov. 6, 1927, in Leningrad. This symphony has a choral ending with the text of a Soviet poet, glorifying Lenin and the Revolution. The harmonic and contrapuntal idiom of the Second Symphony is constructivist, or formalist, to use the term critically applied by Soviet musicians to this type of writing. Shostakovich here uses, for instance, such formal patterns as a nine-part canon on a chromatic theme, in which different instruments enter at the interval of a sixteenth note, so that, in the end, chords of nine chromatics move in parallel blocks. Another instance of formal complexity is polyrhythmic counterpoint of two, three, four, and five notes to a beat. He introduces a factory whistle in the orchestration.

The Nose, an opera written at the same period as the Second Symphony, also belongs to the constructivist type of composition. Shostakovich had absorbed the lessons of contemporary German opera, and the technique of writing of Schönberg, Křenek, Hindemith, and Alban Berg. Operas and orchestral works by these western masters were widely performed in Leningrad in the late twenties, and Shostakovich had the opportunity to study their effect. For his text, Shostakovich selected Gogol's fantastic tale of the nose which became detached from a customer's face in a barber's chair, and began to live an independent life as a petty government official. Although the orchestra of the opera is a small one, the percussion instruments are greatly increased in number. The part of the Nose itself is to be sung with the nostrils closed, to produce a nasal effect. When the opera was presented for the first time in Leningrad on Jan. 13, 1930, the direction of the theater thought it prudent to announce it as an "experimental spectacle."

Equally satirical is Shostakovich's first ballet, *The Golden Age* [or *The Age of Gold*], produced in Leningrad on Oct. 26, 1930. The ballet represents the dissolute atmosphere of a large capitalistic city, and among the characters there is a Fascist. Shostakovich often works on several compositions at the same time—a symphony, an opera, a piece of chamber music. At the time he was writing *The Golden Age,* he was also composing one of his most important works, his Third Symphony.

As in the Second Symphony, so in the Third (subtitled *May First*) Shostakovich uses a choral ending, as a Soviet equivalent of the *Ode to Joy* in Beethoven's Ninth Symphony, a tribute to the new social regime. Regarding his attitude, Shostakovich made a statement to the *New York Times* of Dec. 5, 1931: "I am a Soviet composer, and I see our epoch as something heroic, spirited, and joyous. . . . Music cannot help having a political basis—an idea that the bourgeoisie are slow to comprehend. There can be no music without ideology. The old composers, whether they knew it or not, were upholding a political theory. Most of them, of course, were bolstering the rule of the upper classes. Only Beethoven was a forerunner of the revolutionary movement."

Both the satirical and dramatic elements find their expression in Shostakovich's opera *Lady Macbeth of the District of Mzensk,* which he himself described as a "tragic satire." It was written between 1930 and 1932, and first produced in Leningrad, on Jan. 22, 1934. The book, taken from a short story by the nineteenth-century Russian writer Leskov, portrays a strong-willed woman who, stifled in her ambition, and seeking an outlet for her energies, poisons her husband at the instigation of her lover. In the introduction to the program book of the opera, Shostakovich states his intention to treat the Russian Lady Macbeth as "a positive character, deserving the sympathy of the audience." Concerning the musical idiom of the opera, he writes: "The musical development is projected on a symphonic plan, and in this respect my opera is not an imitation of old operas, built in separate numbers. The musical interludes between the scenes are continuations and developments of the preceding musical idea, and have an important bearing on the characterization of the events on the stage."

The opera, which was performed in Leningrad under the title *Katherina Izmailovna,* after the name of the heroine, was extremely successful, and the press hailed it as the greatest achievement of Soviet operatic art. It was produced in America at the Metropolitan Opera House on Feb. 5, 1935, by the Cleveland Orchestra, Artur Rodzinski conducting, and singers of Art of Musical Russia. The production was more realistic than in Russia, and the symphonic interlude, with suggestive trombone glissandos, while the lovers retire behind the curtains of a bedroom on the stage, scandalized many.

But what seemed the peak of Shostakovich's popular achievement nearly proved his artistic undoing. On Jan. 28, 1936, *Pravda,* the organ of the Communist Party of the Union of Socialist Soviet Republics, published an article, condemning the opera and its tendencies, and raised the question, fatal to a Soviet composer, whether the success of *Lady Macbeth* among the bourgeois audiences abroad was not due to its confused and politically neutral ideology, and to the fact that it "tickled the perverted tastes of the bourgeois audience by its jittery, noisy, and neurotic music." The opera was accused of vulgar naturalism and esthetic snobism. The writer of the article was outraged by the attempt to "solve all problems on the merchant twin bed," and by the author's expressed sympathy with the murderous heroine. The article had a profound effect on Soviet musicians, and opened a series of discussions in which not only Shostakovich himself but also his erstwhile exegetes were attacked. It must be said, however, that performances of the opera continued in Leningrad, though not in Moscow, and Shostakovich's teaching positions were not imperiled by the wave of criticism.

Shostakovich's ballet, *The Limpid Stream,* picturing life on a Soviet collective farm, and originally produced in Leningrad on June 4, 1935, was similarly condemned in another *Pravda* article, after its Moscow production. This time Shostakovich was accused of over-simplification and a flippant treatment of Soviet characters. His position was thus placed in double jeopardy, both for his innovation and for his simplification. The Leningrad publication, *The Worker and the Theater,* described Shostakovich as "the foremost representative of tendencies harmful to Soviet art: pathological naturalism, eroticism, and formalistic fastidiousness, as in *Lady Macbeth of the District of Mzensk,* and, at the same time, primitivistic schematicism, as in *The Limpid Stream.*"

Although Shostakovich publicly expressed agreement with the points of the *Pravda* articles, he found it extremely difficult to re-form his musical lines and to formulate a new stylistic credo. The Fourth Symphony, which he wrote in that difficult year 1936, was put in rehearsal by the Leningrad Philharmonic in December, 1936, but was withdrawn by the composer after he heard it and observed the reactions of the players.

Despite this additional setback, Shostakovich set to work on a new symphony, his Fifth. It was performed by the Leningrad Philharmonic on Nov. 21, 1937, and provoked bursts of enthusiasm in the press. The English-language newspaper, *Moscow Daily News,* carried a long despatch from Leningrad which described the new symphony as "a work of great depth, with emotional wealth and content," and welcomed the liberation of the composer from the "fetters of musical formalism." The Soviet writer Alexei Tolstoy wrote emotionally in *Izvestia* of "the sense of joy, of happiness that bubbles in the orchestra, and is carried into the hall like a spring breeze," and spoke of the symphony as satisfying the chief requirement of the art of socialist realism, the self-formation of the individual in society. The aviator Gromov, celebrated for his flight to America over the North Pole, joined the professional reviewers in their praise for Shostakovich, and his newly found symphonic style. The Fifth Symphony quickly became as popular as the First. It had its American premiere at a broadcast concert of the National Broadcasting Company, in New York, on April 9, 1938, Artur Rodzinski conducting.

The Fifth Symphony does not represent a radical departure from Shostakovich's highly individual style, but rather summarizes all its most striking qualities, and infuses the music with great dramatic and dynamic power. Its four movements follow the classical model, and its opening bars are ostentatiously Beethoven-like, but the essence is Shostakovich's. The two chief characteristics of his talent, the rhythmic vitality and a songlike nostalgia, once more assert themselves as powerful incentives to musical pleasure.

In an interview published in the Moscow paper, *Soviet Art,* of Nov. 20, 1938, Shostakovich announced his plans for a choral symphony, which he visualized as a monumental work dedicated to the memory of Lenin, with the text by national poets of the Caucasus.

These plans did not materialize, and when his Sixth Symphony came to performance, in Moscow, on Dec. 3, 1939, it was a different work, without chorus and without Lenin's name. The work was only moderately successful, but the reception at subsequent performances raised it in popularity almost to the level of the Fifth. Written in a romantic vein, it is as infallibly "effective" as most of Shostakovich's music.*

Shostakovich is as successful in his chamber music as in his symphonies. Invariably, he adheres to the classical model, usually in four movements, with an allegro in sonata form, a slow second movement, a scherzo, and a brilliant finale. The writing for the instruments is always clear, and not over-difficult technically. There are some characteristic devices, such as a glissando in the string instruments, and the use of extreme registers in unison. Of chamber music, the important works are the 'Cello Sonata (1934), the String Quartet (1938) and the Piano Quintet (1940). The performance of the Quintet at the November, 1940 Festival in Moscow, with the composer at the piano, was the occasion of critical jubilation almost as great as after the performance of the Fifth Symphony. On March 15, 1941, the Soviet Government granted Shostakovich a "Stalin prize" of 100,000 rubles for the composition of the Quintet. Another recipient was Miaskovsky, who received a prize for the same amount for his 21st Symphony.

An Interview with Nina Shostakovich

From Information Bulletin, Embassy of the USSR, July 18, 1942

WE FIRST met fifteen years ago [said Nina Shostakovich, wife of the composer, in an interview given to the Soviet press]. Dmitri had just returned from an international competition of musicians in Poland, where he won a certificate of honor. We were both studying in the Physio-mathematics Department of Leningrad University.

He was a very bashful, modest young man, but he was already fully matured as a man and musician. He was particularly proficient in mathematics and the exact sciences; on the other hand, he did not like foreign languages.

In 1922, when Dmitri was 16, his father died and the family

---

* For an account of Shostakovich's Seventh Symphony, see page 242.—E. S.

found themselves in straitened circumstances. The composer began his working life in the capacity of piano player in a small Leningrad movie house. But this career was destined to failure. Dmitri's direct, spontaneous nature caused his downfall. An American comedy was being shown with huge success three times daily. Every time certain scenes flashed on the screen, the piano was silent and the audience heard the piano player burst into laughter, enjoying the antics of the comedian. For this unseemly behavior, the administration decided to part company with the youthful pianist.

Since we first met, the years have changed Dmitri very little. Perhaps he has acquired somewhat more dignity and is less tempestuous and nervous. Five years after we met, we were married. Dmitri is very devoted to his family, especially to our children. But his life is by no means confined to his family and personal well-being. He simply can't exist without the radio and newspapers. I think he subscribes for every newspaper published throughout the Soviet Union.

Our two children, Galya and Maxim, are fair-haired and blue-eyed, like their daddy. As yet we aren't attempting to make musicians of them, but nonetheless they both perkily and fairly accurately sing some of his melodies, even his symphonic works. Their most popular tune just now is the theme from the first movement of the Seventh Symphony. They often beg their father to play for them, and they clamber onto the lid of the grand piano and sit as quiet as mice, all ears. We even took them with us to the general rehearsal of the Seventh Symphony. There they sat in the director's box, and when Professor Samosud, the conductor, asked them, "What have you come to listen to?" they replied, "Our symphony!" But in the middle of the first movement Maxim suddenly started "conducting" with such desperate energy that he had to be taken home.

How does Dmitri work? Well, he demands no special working conditions. He just sits down at his writing desk and writes—morning, noon, evenings. At night he sleeps. If it isn't singing or shouting, noises don't affect him at all. The door of the room where he works is usually open, and often the children romp around in his room. Sometimes Galya climbs onto his knees while he is composing, but in such cases she sits quietly. While Dmitri was finishing the final bars of the Seventh Symphony, for instance, friends who had come in were chatting and joking in the room where he sat. He composes swiftly, writing the score straight through, usually without changes or deletions. Dmitri has a great capacity for work and once having started a composition he is wholly engrossed.

Even during air raids he seldom stopped working. If things began looking too hot, he calmly finished the bar he was writing, waited until the page dried, neatly arranged what he had written, and took it down with him into the bomb shelter. Whenever he was absent from home during an air raid alarm he always 'phoned me asking me not to forget to take his manuscripts down into the shelter.

He is highly critical toward his work, particularly from the viewpoint of time. Once the work is finished, he cools down, so to say, to again warm up and become entirely engrossed with the next work. He almost never reverts to what he has already written and, therefore, already experienced. It is far simpler for him to write anew than to remold a finished work. The Fourth Symphony, for example, never saw daylight because the instrumentation of a few bars of the finale failed to satisfy Dmitri and he could not contemplate rewriting them.

For a long time my husband could not reconcile himself in thought to the necessity of leaving Leningrad. The tense battle for existence waged by his native city, the particularly close companionship under strenuous wartime conditions—all this made him suffer keenly in the unaccustomed safety of Kuibyshev, far from the front lines.

One of Dmitri's distinguishing characteristics is his extraordinary, almost bureaucratic conscientiousness and scrupulousness in whatever he may be engaged in. When the Conservatory fire-fighting brigade of which he was a member was barracked, he punctiliously obeyed all regulations and flatly refused repeated suggestions that special allowance be made for him. If anti-typhoid vaccinations are announced, Dmitri is sure to be the first to arrive, and sometimes the only one to show up. At concerts he arrives before the cloakroom attendant, and always turns up ahead of time for duty at the Composers' Union. He is always afraid of being late.

He is terribly enthusiastic about whatever he is doing. He is a great sports fan. Before the war—heat or cold, rain or snow—there was not one soccer, ice hockey, or boxing match he would miss. As a Conservatory student he would even shirk a lesson to run off to the stadium. At home, in Leningrad, he instituted a special "debit-credit ledger" in which he would diligently enter all games won or lost by all the soccer teams during the current sports season. From various towns, to this very day, soccer players keep Dmitri fully posted on the "situation." He is very fond of volleyball, is an enthusiastic player, and doesn't brook any disrespect toward this game. His favorite entertainment is the circus. At one time he went in for motoring. With his usual punctiliousness he got his driver's license, but was too cautious a driver; when he drives, for example, he never takes the children. Chekhov, Gogol, Saltykov-Shchedrin, and Maupassant are his favorite authors.

What else can I tell you about Dmitri? He's unusually modest, and, putting it mildly, he doesn't like performing at concerts. He's always highly agitated when he gives a public performance. But his greatest bane is having to be filmed. He can't stand being photographed either. The result is a scowling face. There's only one single snapshot in existence of Dmitri laughing. I took that myself!

What I Believe

By Dmitri Shostakovich

From "New Masses," August 4, 1942

THE great patriotic war we are now conducting against German fascism, the most dangerous enemy mankind ever had, has served to unify and bring closer than ever before all the nations inhabiting the USSR.

The Russian people to which I belong were always distinguished by their undying interest in science, culture, and arts. We are proud of our science: it has contributed a great deal to human thought. We are proud of our literature: it has created heroes reflecting the entire development of human society. We are proud of our music and our arts: they gave the world works of inimitable strength and became some of the most precious contributions to the treasury of world culture. Pushkin, Leo Tolstoy, Tchaikovsky and Glinka, Mussorgsky and Repin, Pavlov and Setchenov—a whole Pleiad of magnificent creators in science and cultures—are all sons of my people. Suvorov and Kutuzov, two great military leaders who repeatedly vanquished the enemies of our country, glorified Russian arms and made famous the heroism of the common Russian soldier—all sons of my people. There is virtually no single sphere of culture, science, military arts in which my people have not contributed glorious pages and given mankind magnificent monuments.

The war forced upon us by the contemptible Nazis has aroused in our people not only wrath and hatred against the invaders. It has called forth a great upsurge of creative activity and kindled the flame of daring thought. Our people know no fear in this struggle. Thousands of heroes go into battle for our country and, without sparing their lives, fight with a courage and fearlessness that electrify the whole world. At the front, in advanced positions, and behind the fighting lines, the people of our country display not only the greatest moral stability, courage, and devotion, but also a tremendous force of creative spirit and constructive might. And this strength of theirs brings us the certainty that no matter what trials we may have to suffer, no matter what burdens of war may fall upon our shoulders, we will stand it all, fight, and overcome it all, and we will emerge victorious. The proud Russian people who never before surrendered will go through all the storms and trials of battle and will be victorious.

By every means available to the artist, we must rouse in our people the spirit of faith in the triumph of their task, rouse their forces, and summon them to heroic achievements in battle and in labor. No artist can create anything of significance if he is isolated from the people, if he tries to escape the events of the day in some ivory tower. The artist thus isolated from the people, from their thoughts and dreams, hopes and aspirations, who escapes the stern facts of war, is inevitably condemned to creative stagnation, to a miserable existence. The artist dies as soon as he becomes an introvert.

The great masters of culture whose names we honor, and whose thoughts have been for us a book of learning and great revelations, have always distinguished themselves by the fact that they knew their people, shared their joys and grief, felt their living impulses, and were always in the front ranks of all the people's struggles. And they, these masters of word and brush, music and stage, loved their people, suffered with their agonies, wept with their tears, were stirred with their passions, and burned with their dreams and thoughts. Pushkin has no more remarkable pages than those in which he wrote of his love for country and people. Gogol, Tolstoy, Chekhov, Turgenev, have no more colorful pages than those in which they spoke of their compatriots, the Russian folk, the Russian people, the Russian soil. The works of the great Russian composer Glinka, that most modest of all great composers, were so closely linked with the creative efforts of the people that he used to say: "We do not create, the people create; we only record and arrange." The great lyricist and master of musical art thereby underscored his close ties with the Russian people and their magnificent wealth of creative effort.

And yet these ties do not signify that the artist simply borrowed from the creative genius of the people. For the composer, for example, it does not mean simple use of folklore. Tchaikovsky's great works— his Sixth Symphony, the ballet suites, *The Sleeping Beauty, The Swan Lake,* and the *Nutcracker*—are deeply national works, and we all accept them as such. To learn ceaselessly from the people, to grasp everything the people create, to be worthy of the time period in which we artists live—therein lies our task.

This war is a great test for our artists, musicians, authors, scientists. Only those of strong spirit and courageous heart can pass this test with honor and good name. The war has imposed a great mission upon every one of us. There are not and there cannot be in our country any citizens aloof from this great struggle. "Everything for the front, everything for victory," is the slogan for men and women. The self-sacrifice of the workers, the hardest labor of the collective farmer, the persistence of the scientist, the courage of the constructor, the lyricism of the poet, the creative flight of the composer—all must be consecrated and freely given, to the last drop, to our sacred aim for which we live and breathe, for our victory.

The future historian of our days will note one special circumstance: in a country engaged in fierce struggle against a deadly enemy— fighting on land, in the air, and on water, for its freedom and independence, putting forth the greatest efforts of all of its citizens—the life of science, art, and culture did not slow up, did not quiet down. On the contrary, the patriotic upsurge enveloping the peoples of the Soviet Union became a remarkable soil in which, during these days of war, rise ever newer achievements in art. Our theaters produce new plays, work out new characters, and awaken in our people noble and heroic sentiments. Along with the presentation of new works, we continue carefully and painstakingly the presentation of the greatest creations of world art of the past. Our Philharmonic Orchestras are conducting their current concert season with great success. Our soloist musicians, with their deep understanding of the musical works, continue to make us composers happy. Our demanding Soviet audiences avidly continue to crowd our concerts and plays.

This fact, so remarkable and pleasing to us, is terrifying for the

Hitlers and Goebbels. We can proclaim to the world that during these days of bloody battles and ceaseless thunder of guns, music never became silent in besieged Leningrad. Art, which in any other country would have had to step aside at such times and find shelter in the quiet zones far from the fighting lines, became in our country a new type of armament striking the enemy. Such facts must bring us Soviet composers not only a sense of great satisfaction, but a sense of great responsibility.

During the period of this patriotic war, our composers have created a whole series of interesting works. The composers know that every new work, if written by the hand of a man who loves his country and who has found the proper colors for the expression of his thoughts, is like a great salvo of fire at the enemy. While we love each other deeply, we demand at the same time a great deal from each other. And thus we find a great wealth and variety of types in our music, in all that we now write. From the simplest song to the great canvases of operatic and symphonic art, Soviet music performs a great and useful service to the country.

The task of our musical art consists in creating works consecrated to the present day and its great events. These works must be right up to the moment, sharp and exciting. But the timeliness of the theme does not mean that we may lower the standard demanded for the artistic content of the work. We must also create alongside the smaller works, great monumental pieces, great by their scale and magnificent by their content. We must learn from the great artists of the past how to serve our people in their hour of trials.

We have done a great deal of useful work, but we must do immeasurably more and better. We think too much of our own future to stop at present achievements. A great writer was once asked, "Which one of your works do you consider the best?" To which he replied: "It hasn't been written yet." We must be eternally dissatisfied with our achievements, great as they may be. This is much better than complacence or boastfulness. For us, these achievements must become only the impetus to still greater achievements, more persistent labor, new creative flights.

We Soviet musicians are constantly searching for new style. We must continue to go further and further ahead, ceaselessly perfecting ourselves, never for a moment stopping, never for a moment forgetting that our art serves our people, is necessary for our people because it helps achieve victory.

We enjoy the greatest support of our state, we are surrounded by the care and love of the government and the people. We must justify the confidence reposed in us and the hopes placed on us. "Forward to new shores," said the great Russian composer Mussorgsky. "Forward to victory" is the slogan of Soviet musicians, the heirs and successors to the great traditions of world musical culture.

Music in the Films

From "Our New Music"

By Aaron Copland

WITH the radio and the phonograph, the music track of the sound film must be set down as a revolutionizing force in today's music. The medium is so new, and the possibilities so vast, that this brief article can hardly do more than introduce the subject. Even so, it treats of little more than the Hollywood aspect of film music. Though artistically of a low order, historically the music of the West Coast is certain to loom large in any stocktaking of filmdom's musical achievements.

Everyone is so prepared to hear the worst about Hollywood that it is a pleasure to be able to start these observations on a cheerful note. The best one can say about Hollywood is that it is a place where composers are actually needed. The accent is entirely on the living composer. Day after day and year after year there are copyists, instrumentalists, and conductors who do nothing but copy, perform, and conduct the music of contemporary composers. Theoretically, at any rate, the town is a composer's Eldorado.

For the movies do need music and need it badly. By itself the screen is a pretty cold proposition. In Hollywood I looked at long stretches of film before the music had been added, and I got the impression that music is like a small flame put under the screen to help warm it.

It is this very function, however, which so often gives the composer a minor role. There is no sense in denying the subordinate position the composer fills. After all, film music makes sense only if it helps the film; no matter how good, distinguished, or successful, the music must be secondary in importance to the story being told on the screen. Essentially there is nothing about the movie medium to rule out any composer with a dramatic imagination. But the man who insists on complete self-expression had better stay home and write symphonies. He will never be happy in Hollywood.

Whether you are happy or not largely depends on two factors: the producer you work for and the amount of time allotted for completing the score. (I am assuming that the film itself is an intelligent one.) The producer is a kind of dictator, responsible only to the studio executives for every phase of the picture's production. This naturally includes the musical score. The trouble is not so much that these producers consider themselves musical connoisseurs as that they claim to be accurate barometers of public taste. "If I can't understand it, the public won't." As a result of this the typical Hollywood composer is concerned not with the reaction of the public, as you might think, but with that of the producer. It isn't surprising therefore, that all film music originating in Hollywood tends to be very much the same. The score of one picture adds up to about the score of any other. You seldom hear anything fresh or distinctive partly because everyone is so intent on playing safe. A pleased producer means more jobs. That alone is sufficient to explain the Hollywood stereotype of music.

The demand for speed from the composer is familiar to anyone who has ever worked "in pictures." The composer may sit around no end of time, waiting for the picture to be done; as soon as it's finished the director, the producer, the script writer—everybody—is in a frightful hurry; valuable time is passing, and the studio has visions of the money it is losing each day that the film is not in a theater. It is difficult to make studio executives realize that no one has yet discovered how to write notes any faster than it was done *circa* A. D. 400. The average movie score is approximately forty minutes long. The usual time allotted for composing it is about two weeks. For *Of Mice and Men* I had about six weeks, and I believe that other composers insist on that much time for writing an elaborate score.

The purpose of the film score is to make the film more effective; that's clear enough. But I don't think anyone has as yet formulated the perfect solution for this problem. In fact, I came away with a sense of the mysterious nature of all film music. In retrospect, I can see three important ways in which music helps a picture. The first is by intensifying the emotional impact of any given scene, the second by creating an illusion of continuity, and the third by providing a kind of neutral background music. Of these three, the last presents the most mysterious problem—how to supply the right sort of music behind dialogue.

Intensification of emotion at crucial moments is, of course, an old tradition of theater music. True, it is no more than the Hearts-and-Flowers tradition, but still, perfectly legitimate. The one difficulty here is to get the music started without suddenly making the audience aware of its entrance. To use a favorite Hollywood term, you must "steal the music in."

Obvious, too, is the continuity function of music. Pictures, jumping from episode to episode, from exterior to interior, have a tendency to fall apart. Music, an art that exists in time, can subtly hold disparate scenes together. In exciting montage sequences where the film moves violently from shot to shot, music, by developing one particular theme or one type of rhythmical material or some other unifying musical element, supplies the necessary continuous understructure.

But "background" music is something very special. It is also the most ungrateful kind of music for a composer to write. Since it's music behind, or underneath, the word, the audience is really not going to hear it, possibly won't even be aware of its existence; yet it undoubtedly works on the subconscious mind. The need here is for a kind of music that will give off a "neutral" color or atmosphere. (This is what creates the indefinable warmth that the screen itself lacks.) To write music that must be inexpressive is not easy for composers who normally tend to be as expressive as possible. To add to the difficulty, there's the impossibility of knowing in advance just what will work in any given scene. If one could only test the music by adding it to the scene before it is shot or have the music performed while the actors speak their lines! But this is utopian. Once the scene is done and the music is added, the result is fairly problematical. Even dubbing it down almost below the listening level will not always prove satisfactory.

If Hollywood has its problems it has also its well-known solutions. Most scores, as everybody knows, are written in the late-nineteenth-century symphonic style, a style now so generally accepted as to be considered inevitable. But why need movie music be symphonic? And why, oh, why, the nineteenth century? Should the rich harmonies of Tchaikovsky, Franck, and Strauss be spread over every type of story, regardless of time, place, or treatment? For *Wuthering Heights,* perhaps yes. But why for *Golden Boy,* a hard-boiled, modern piece? What screen music badly needs is more differentiation, more feeling for the exact quality of each picture. That does not necessarily mean a more literal musical description of time and place. Certainly very few Hollywood films give a realistic impression of period. Still, it should be possible, without learned displays of historical research and without the hack conventions of symphonic music, for a composer to reflect the emotion and reality of the individual picture he is scoring.

Another pet Hollywood formula, this one borrowed from nineteenth-century opera, is the use of the *leitmotiv*. I haven't made up my mind whether the public is conscious of this device or completely oblivious to it, but I can't see how it is appropriate to the movies. It may help the spectator sitting in the last row of the opera house to identify the singer who appears from the wings for the orchestra to announce her motif. But that's hardly necessary on the screen. No doubt the *leitmotiv* system is a help to the composer in a hurry, perhaps doing two or three scores simultaneously. It is always an easy solution mechanically to pin a motif on every character. In a high-class horse opera I saw this method was reduced to its final absurdity. One theme announced the Indians, another the hero. In the inevitable chase, every time the scene switched from Indians to hero the themes did, too, sometimes so fast that the music seemed to hop back and forth before any part of it had time to breathe. If there must be thematic description, I think it would serve better if it were connected with the underlying ideas of a picture. If, for example, a film has to do with loneliness, a theme might be developed to induce sympathy with the idea of being lonely, something broader in feeling than the mere tagging of characters.

A third device, and one very peculiar to Hollywood, is known as "Mickey-Mousing" a film. In this system the music, wherever possible, is made to mimic everything that happens on the screen. An actor can't lift an eyebrow without the music helping him do it. What is amusing when applied to a Disney fantasy becomes disastrous in its effect upon a straight or serious drama. Max Steiner has a special weakness for this device. In *Of Human Bondage* he had the unfortunate idea of making his music limp whenever the clubfooted hero walked across the scene, with a very obvious and, it seemed to me, vulgarizing effect. Recently Mr. Steiner has shown a fondness for a new device. This is the mixing of realistic music with background music. Joe may be walking around the room quietly humming a tune to himself (realistic use of music). Watch for the moment when Joe steps out into the storm, for it is then that Mr. Steiner pounces upon Joe's little tune and gives us the works with an orchestra of seventy. The trouble with this procedure is that it stresses not so much the dramatic moment as the ingenuity of the composer. All narrative illusion is lost the instant we are conscious of the music as such.

It may not be without interest to retrace some of the steps by which music is added to a film. After the picture is completed, it is shown in the studio projection room before the producer, the director, the studio's musical director (if any), the composer and his various henchmen, the conductor, the orchestrator, the cue-sheet assistants, the copyists—anybody, in fact, who has anything to do with the preparation of the score. At this showing the decision is reached as to where to add music, where it should start in each separate sequence, and where it should end. The film is then turned over to a cue-sheet assistant whose job it is to prepare a listing of every separate moment in each musical sequence. These listings, with the accompanying timing in film footage and in seconds, is all that the composer needs for complete security in synchronizing his music with the film. The practised Hollywood composer is said never to look at a picture more than once. With a good memory, a stop watch, and a cue sheet, he is ready to go to work. Others prefer to work in the music projection room where there are a piano, a screen, and an operator who can turn the film on and off. I myself used a movieola, which permits every composer to be his own operator. This is a small machine that shows the film positive through a magnifying glass. Using the movieola, I could see the picture whenever and as often as I pleased.

While the music is being written, the film itself is prepared for recording. Each important musical cue must be marked on the film by some prearranged signal system that varies in every studio. These "signals" show the conductor where he is. If he wants to hit a certain musical cue that, according to the cue sheet, occurs at the forty-ninth second, the film must be marked in such a way as to indicate that spot (always with sufficient warning signals), and if the conductor is competent he can nearly always "hit it on the nose." In Hollywood this knack for hitting cues properly is considered even more important in a conductor than his ability to read an orchestral score. Another method, much more mechanical but used a good deal for Westerns and quickies, is to synchronize by means of a so-called "click track." In this case, the film is measured off not according to seconds but according to regular musical beats. There is no surer method for hitting cues "on the nose." But only the experienced composer can ignore the regularity of the beat and write his music freely within and around it.

For the composer the day of recording is perhaps the high point. He has worked hard and long and is anxious to test his work. He hears his music sounded for the first time while the film is being shown. Everything comes off just as it would in a concert hall. But if he wishes to remain happy he had better stay away from the sound-recording booth. For here all the music is being recorded at about the same medium dynamic level so that later on the loudness and softness may be regulated when the moment comes for rerecording.

Rerecording takes place in the dubbing room. This is a kind of composer's purgatory. It is here that the music track is mixed with other sound tracks—the dialogue, the "effects" track, and so forth. It is at this point that the composer sees his music begin to disappear. A passage once so clear and satisfying seems now to move farther and farther off. The instant a character opens his mouth, the music must recede to the near-vanishing point. This is the place that calls out all a composer's self-control; it's a moment for philosophy.

From the composer's standpoint, the important person in the dubbing room is the man who sits at the controls. It is he who decides how loud or soft the music will be at any given moment, and therefore it is he who can make or ruin everything by the merest touch of the dials. But surprisingly, in every studio these controls are in the hands of a sound engineer. What I don't understand is why a musician has not been called in for this purpose. It would never occur to me to call in an engineer to tune my piano. Surely only a musician can be sensitive to the subtle effects of musical sound, particularly when mixed with other sounds. A Toscanini would be none too good for such a job—certainly a sound expert is not qualified.

While on the subject of sound levels, I might as well mention the unsatisfactory way in which sound is controlled in the picture theater. The tonal volume of a picture is not set for all time; no mechanical contraption permanently fixes the loudness or softness of the music. The person who decides on the sound levels is not even the film operator but the individual theater manager, who is, of course, susceptible to advice from Tom, Dick, and Harry sitting anywhere in the house. People who love music tend to prefer it played loudly. Those who don't care for it especially want to hear it only at a low level. So no matter how much care is taken in the dubbing room to fix proper tonal levels, the situation will remain unsatisfactory until a method is found to control the casual and arbitrary way in which dials are set in the theater operator's booth.

Hollywood, like Vienna, can boast its own star roster of composers. Alfred Newman, Max Steiner, Victor Young, Anthony Collins, are composers created by the film industry. It is easy enough to poke fun at the movie music they turn out as so much yardage, but it would at the same time be foolish not to profit by their great experience in writing for the films. Newman, for example, has discovered the value of the string orchestra as a background for emotional scenes. Better than the full orchestra, the strings can be depersonalized. This is important in a medium where the sound of a single instrument may sometimes be disturbing. Another secret of movie music that Steiner has exploited is the writing of atmosphere music almost without melodic content of any kind. A melody is by its nature distracting, since it calls attention to itself. For certain types of neutral music, a kind of melodyless music is needed. Steiner does not supply mere chords but superimposes a certain amount of melodic motion, just enough to make the music sound normal and yet not enough to compel attention.

Composers who come to Hollywood from the big world outside generally take some time to become expert in using the idiom. Erich Korngold still tends to get overcomplex in the development of a musical idea. This is not always true, however. When successful, he gives a sense of firm technique, a continuity of not only feeling but structure. Werner Janssen, whose score for *The General Died at Dawn* made movie history, is still looked upon as something of an outsider. He shows his pre-Hollywood training in the sophistication of his musical idiom and in his tendency to be overfussy in the treatment of even the simplest sequence. Ernest Toch, who belongs in the category with Korngold and Janssen, wrote an important score for *Peter Ibbetson* several years ago. On the strength of this job, Toch should be today one of the best-known film composers. But unfortunately there aren't enough people in Hollywood who can tell a good score when they hear one. Today Toch is generally assigned to do "screwy music." (In Hollywood music is either "screwy" or "down to earth"—and most of it is down to earth.) Toch deserves better. The latest addition to Hollywood's roster of "outsiders" is Louis Gruenberg, who composed a distinguished score for *So Ends Our Night*.

The men who write Hollywood's music seem strangely oblivious of their reputations outside the West Coast. I have often wondered, for instance, why no concerted effort has ever been made to draw the attention of music critics to their more ambitious scores. Why shouldn't the music critic cover important film *premières?* True, the audience that goes to the films doesn't think about the music and possibly shouldn't think about the music. Nevertheless, a large part of music heard by the American public is heard in the film theater. Unconsciously, the cultural level of music is certain to be raised if better music is written for films. This will come about more quickly, I think, if producers and directors know that scores are being heard and criticized. One of the ways they will find out what's good and what's bad is to read it in the papers. Let the press now take this important business in hand.

The Growth of Radio Music

Abridged from "Music Comes to America"

By David Ewen

THERE are fifty-one million radios in actual use throughout the country. Almost every other person in the United States can, with the turn of a switch, come into direct contact with the greatest available operatic, symphonic, and chamber music. What this means in terms of educating the masses can only be guessed at on the basis of what already has been accomplished in some twenty years.

Twenty years of experimenting in the transmitting of programs over the air was the background for the first successful broadcast. In the early 1900's, Lee De Forest—generally credited with being the inventor of the radio—broadcast from the stage of the Manhattan Opera House, via Marconi air waves, an aria from *Carmen* sung by Mariette Nazarin. For the first time, through squeals and roars, a human singing voice was sent over the air waves. But not even the most farsighted could have guessed that in this primitive experiment lay the embryo of an epoch-making instrument.

But experiments went on apace. On Christmas Eve, 1906, Reginald Fessenden transmitted a musical program "successfully." On March 5 of the following year De Forest brought his equipment to the

Tellharmonic Hall in New York to broadcast the *William Tell Over-ture*. Somewhat later—on January 20, 1910—De Forest was responsible for the first broadcast to take place on the stage of the Metropolitan Opera House when portions from *Cavalleria Rusticana* and *Pagliacci*, both with Caruso, were sent through the air and picked up by fifty radio amateurs, several ships in the Brooklyn Navy Yard, and a group of invited guests in a Times Square hotel.

Not until 1920 was the first radio station to come into existence. Shortly after the close of the World War, Dr. Frank Conrad, an engineer in Westinghouse, built a transmitting set in his garage. His hobby was to send out programs of recorded music, interspersed with news and some personal comments. His programs, received by numerous amateurs over an extended area, met with such an enthusiastic response that Westinghouse realized for the first time what a force the radio could become if given the proper direction. With the aid of Dr. Conrad, Westinghouse organized a pioneer radio station for the purpose of publicizing its electrical products. In November, 1920, it sent out its first national broadcast by reporting the presidential election. Meanwhile, on August 20, 1920, the first commercial station had begun regular broadcasting—WWJ in Detroit.

Other radio stations mushroomed up throughout the country. In 1922 WEAF in New York put on the first known commercial program, advertising a New York real estate company. In the same year, on August 3, the first radio sound effect was produced by WGY, Schenectady, when the slamming of a door was simulated by the banging of two pieces of wood in front of the microphone. In 1926 the first major radio network came into existence, formed by the National Broadcasting Company. Already the role to be played by great music in radio was suggested when the inaugural program of the network, on November 15, featured Mary Garden, Titta Ruffo, Harold Bauer, the New York Symphony Society, and the Oratorio Society of New York. In 1927 a second radio network was created by the Columbia Broadcasting System.

Those were the days when the crystal set was making way for the battery set. Jazz and light salon music dominated the programs. Radio executives said that great music would never find an important place in radio because radio depended for its existence on mass consumption, and who ever heard of mass consumption of great music? Many great artists considered it below their dignity to appear before a microphone. Those were the days when good music meant Victor

Herbert and more Victor Herbert, or a fifteen-minute violin program by Godfrey Ludlow, or a half hour of "slumber music" at the hour of midnight. Those were the days when music had to be listened to through major air disturbances and static, when the musician acidly spoke of the radio as "De Forest's prime evil."

But the experiments in the laboratory continued indefatigably. Electricity replaced the battery. The superheterodyne set and the Magnavox loud-speaker became obsolete. The quality of transmission was improved with the elimination of much of the static. A quality of reception was finally achieved in which the programs could be heard undistorted by extraneous noises.

As reproduction over the air became more faithful, good music began to acquire a slowly increasing importance. Two early broadcasts of good music—a performance of *Aïda* from the Kingsbridge Armory in New York and a concert of the New York Philharmonic from the Great Hall at the College of the City of New York—proved that there was an audience for more serious musical efforts. Hesitantly—in spite of their so-called better judgment—radio executives meted out the dribs and dabs of good music. In 1926 John McCormack and Lucrezia Bori were sponsored on a joint program, and they received an avalanche of congratulatory letters. In the same year Walter Damrosch became musical director of the National Broadcasting System and directed twenty weekly symphonic broadcasts during the season—the first extensive series of symphonic concerts over the radio. It was estimated that the combined audience for this series of concerts was 200 million.

In 1927 the first regular series of opera broadcasts was undertaken from the stage of the Chicago Civic Opera. Concerts by the Boston Symphony and the New York Philharmonic were also transmitted during the same year. In 1928 Damrosch inaugurated his Music Appreciation Hour for the nation's schoolchildren, and he was sponsored by General Electric to present symphonic concerts for adults. In 1929 Leopold Stokowski and the Philadelphia Orchestra associated themselves with the radio, beginning a relationship which was to have a far-reaching result on the quality of orchestral transmission. Other great orchestras, numerous opera stars, and virtuosos, even a few chamber-music ensembles, joined the ever-growing parade of musicians to the microphone. And, to the amazement of radio executives who had always felt that great music was for only a limited audience, the more frequently good music was put on the air, the larger the audiences grew and the more enthusiastic became the reception.

Even so adamant a foe of the radio as Gatti-Casazza, general manager of the Metropolitan Opera House, was eventually won over. For several years officials of the National Broadcasting Company had appealed to Gatti-Casazza for permission to broadcast opera performances directly from the stage of the Metropolitan. Gatti-Casazza was stubborn in his refusal because, he felt, radio was not sufficiently developed to permit an artistic transmission of good music, particularly good opera. He finally decided to permit a trial broadcast, the result of which was to influence his future decision. He and his musical staff visited a private studio of the N. B. C. to listen to the relay of a performance of *Madama Butterfly*. Gatti-Casazza was so impressed by the quality of the reproduction that, then and there, he decided that his fears had no basis whatsoever. On Christmas Day, 1931, the first broadcast of a full opera from the Metropolitan took place—Humperdinck's *Hänsel and Gretel*—inaugurating the history of broadcasts from the Metropolitan Opera House.

Two years before this the New York Philharmonic had begun its historic series of Sunday afternoon broadcasts. Two of America's leading musical institutions were now permanent fixtures on the radio. They were to have their audiences of several million devoted listeners. The mail to the Metropolitan following each broadcast (not only in grateful appreciation for the performance, but also to acquire information about the operas and their composers) was so great that it inspired the creation of the Metropolitan Opera Guild in 1935, drawing the bulk of its membership from radio listeners. Its publication, *Opera News*, reaches all radio subscribers with full information about each opera broadcast. A similar organization was created by the New York Philharmonic primarily for its radio audiences.

The horizon was ever expanding. More and more great music assumed roles of importance in radio broadcasting. International broadcasts, inaugurated in 1931 with a performance at Covent Garden, brought the major European festivals to the American home. Chamber music, long considered the property of the élite, came to the air. In 1929 the Perolé String Quartet introduced the first extensive series over the radio, devoted to chamber music literature—on WOR. In 1934 the N. B. C. Music Guild was founded to present chamber music four times a week. The first opera written expressly for radio—*The Willow Tree*—was created by Charles Wakefield Cadman in 1931 and was broadcast over N. B. C. Five years after this, the Columbia

Broadcasting System launched an ambitious program for commissioning special symphonic works exclusively for radio performance, recruiting some of the foremost American composers for this purpose.

The N. B. C. Symphony Orchestra—now one of the great symphonic organizations—was founded in 1937 to bring Toscanini to the
radio. Leading commercial sponsors found that great music was an
effective salesman for their products: Ford, General Motors, Philco,
Chesterfield, Firestone, General Electric, and others reached for a
large audience through broadcasts of great symphonic music.

At least one commercial station discovered that good music pays
—WQXR in New York, the programs of which are, for the most
part, transmissions of the greatest available recorded music. Broadcasting recorded music, of course, was not the innovation of WQXR.
The New York Municipal station, WNYC, had inaugurated a Masterwork Hour many years before WQXR came into existence, and later
extended its programs to include many other hours of good recorded
music. Other small commercial stations throughout America also devoted an hour or so a day to programs of great music through records.

There remains to speak about those significant figures who have
been major influences in the growth of good music over the air. One
of the earliest of these was, of course, Walter Damrosch, who resigned
his position with the New York Symphony Society to devote himself
exclusively to radio work. "I had always dreamt of the time when I
could reach through music a wide and limitless audience," he said.
"Radio magically offered me the means. I realized that with one performance I could reach more people through the radio than I could
previously in five years of concert work." He was one of the first to
bring concerts of great symphonic music to the radio—at a time when
it was felt that there were simply no audiences for such programs.
His broadcasts in 1926, 1927, and 1928 set the stage for all future
symphonic broadcasts. Equally important, Damrosch was the first to
realize the value of the radio as an educational medium. In 1928 he
inaugurated his famous Music Appreciation Hour for schoolchildren.
His audience has grown from 1½ million to an estimated 5 million
listeners, relayed to some 70,000 schools throughout the country. He
became the music teacher to a nation—a voice known almost to every
schoolboy and schoolgirl. A few years ago, on a visit to the West,
Damrosch was invited by a public school principal to address his
children at the assembly. Damrosch offered to come on the condition

that he be allowed to appear without an official introduction. The principal promised. He merely announced that he had the honor to present a man known to all of them. Damrosch arose and quietly began: "Good morning, my dear children"—his radio greeting. Immediately a furor arose among the children. "It's Papa Damrosch!" they cried. Damrosch had required no introduction.

Other musical figures have also been of consequence in radio's musical development. On September 18, 1927, a young American conductor, Howard Barlow—who had up to that time had only a limited experience as a conductor—made his radio début by performing excerpts from Deems Taylor's *The King's Henchman* over the Columbia network. He said:

I was certainly nervous before the performance began. I pictured the "mike" as a central spot from which countless wires, endless in length, stretched all over the country. I felt like a tiny fly caught in the center of a spider's web. But when the music started, and I felt the baton in my hand, I forgot everything but music.

Barlow was soon afterward appointed conductor of the Columbia Broadcasting Symphony Orchestra, ultimately increasing its membership from its original sixteen musicians to thirty, then to sixty-seven. His regular symphony concerts over the air helped to create a new standard for orchestral programs in which modern music—particularly works by American composers, many of them especially commissioned by the network—received flattering attention.

Frank Black succeeded Walter Damrosch as musical director of the National Broadcasting Company in 1928. For a long time Black had urged radio officials to pay greater attention to good music. He had approached the National Broadcasting Company with the idea of directing a thirty-piece string symphony orchestra in a regular series of concerts. The idea was rejected as too highbrow. For a while Black contented himself with random assignments given him to conduct special radio concerts. His following grew until the company finally permitted him to organize his own string orchestra for regular radio performances. As a conductor of his Sinfonietta, and as musical director of the National Broadcasting Company, he has been one of the truly progressive forces for good music. To realize the lofty musical aims of its director, one need only consider one of his more recent radio series —devoted exclusively to the music of young and less-known American composers. A unique feature of this series was that each new composition was performed twice on the same program, before and after an explanatory commentary.

Radio found another vital influence in Alfred Wallenstein, who deserted the first 'cello desk of the New York Philharmonic Orchestra in 1935 to become music director of WOR. In this post he conducted many important concerts of the Sinfonietta and Symphonic Strings (both of which he founded), succeeding in resurrecting many masterpieces of music long forgotten. Besides these orchestral concerts, he directed many series of concerts of unquestioned artistic importance, including a Sunday evening series devoted to all the church cantatas of Bach, a Saturday evening series of Mozart operas, and a midweek series of all the piano concertos of Mozart, with Nadia Reisenberg as soloist.

Davidson Taylor, music director of the Columbia Broadcasting System, was responsible for bringing great chamber music to radio prominence. He was also originator of the plan to commission American composers to write music especially for radio use. Ernest La Prade, director of music research of the National Broadcasting Company, brought many important small ensembles to the microphone, particularly during the series of concerts prepared by the N. B. C. Music Guild. Deems Taylor, music consultant of the Columbia Broadcasting System and commentator for the New York Philharmonic concerts on Sunday afternoons, has humanized music through his informal talks.

In 1939 a national survey among radio listeners revealed the fact that 62.5 per cent of the radio public listened to programs of serious music. In 1940 it was estimated that serious music over the major networks consumed nearly 2000 hours.

"All musicians must feel gratitude to the radio," said Lily Pons in an interview. "It has done so much for musical taste. Even in the ten years that I have been here I see a great difference in what people like to hear. You will be surprised at how much better selections the people ask for. They get to know concert works. I can see this in my tours."

José Iturbi has told two anecdotes in the *Pictorial Review* which eloquently demonstrate how good music over the air is continually finding a larger and more responsive audience:

I was riding on a bus between two Missouri cities. It was Sunday afternoon, and the program from Carnegie Hall was being broadcast. The bus carried a radio; the set was turned down in volume. A distinguished violinist began to play just as we reached the outskirts of a small town in a slight traffic jam. Someone turned the radio up, and finally, as we weren't getting anywhere, he remarked: "Does anyone object if we pull up to the side of the road and hear the rest of this number?" No one objected. The driver turned off the motor and twenty-three passengers listened with a great deal of pleasure.

Driving to New York after a concert in Williamstown, Mass., I stopped for coffee at a lunchwagon in the Connecticut countryside just as a Sunday evening symphonic program went over the air. What happened amused me greatly. There was a good deal of clatter and rattle among the diners. First the counterman stopped washing dishes and listened. A man rattling his cup next to me set it down carefully—and listened. The waitress, stacking dishes on a small table, stopped her activities, sat down—and also listened. The place was comparatively quiet, but the counterman wasn't satisfied. He scowled at four hamburgers sizzling on the griddle and carefully removed them one by one. We all sat there for the remainder of the program, when the waitress confirmed our verdict by remarking: "Gee, that was swell!"

These two anecdotes could be multiplied by a hundred to prove that, through the radio, good music is reaching the average man in the street.

Why Not Try the Air?

By Davidson Taylor

From "Modern Music" for January 1938

WHEN we were children, they used to tell us that if a tree falls and no one hears it fall, it makes no sound. Well if music plays and no one hears it played, it makes no noise. Of course, a tree falls only once. But new music is played twice only if someone who heard it the first time liked it.

First performances of American music are comparatively rare, and repetitions are much rarer. How then can we have great composers? Greatness in music may be unimportant, and sincerity or individuality enough. But all musicians are fundamentally interested only in great music, or the greatness they can find in good music, or what goodness they can find in bad music. The demerits of a piece really interest only the writers. But however you may feel about criticism as a vocation or a pastime, you are interested in the prospect of great American music, and would like to hear some.

This age shows an unparalleled apathy toward new music of permanent aspirations. Cecil Gray (a thoroughgoing and respectably prejudiced historian) said recently that at no period of music history has the public cared so little about contemporary works and he could not give a reason for this unresponsiveness. I know a composer of unusual talent, vitality and perspective who says in his black moments that if everyone should stop composing tomorrow, and not start again for a hundred years, nobody would notice.

In September 1937, six well-informed Parisian musicians were talking about the French composers of the hour; at the end of their tepid enumeration, they burst into a gloria about the early songs of Gounod which were just being unearthed. There, it appeared, was something really worth performing. Look what a fuss has recently been made over the revelation of the "lost" Schumann Violin Concerto. Maybe the modern musician should aim to become what Melville calls "a mere painstaking burrower and grub-worm of a poor devil of a Sub-Sub Librarian."

Perhaps it would be best for an American of today to spend his time making Charles Ives's later scores more practical for performance. Ives received all too few performances of his music while he was writing it. He seldom got to try out what he had put on paper, and now he is too ill to write. It was not fantastic for him to contemplate a work for seven orchestras and a chorus of thousands, while nobody was taking the trouble to play his string quartets, which are quite easy.

Composers it seems, go right along composing, even though what they write may be unwanted. For whom are they doggedly preparing all these scores? For Carnegie Hall, which was politely bored when Barbirolli gave Bartók's *Music for Strings, Percussion, and Celesta* the best performance we may ever hear of this piece in New York? For the critics who said it was "much ado about nothing," and remarked that it was easy to "whip such a thing into shape?"

This masterly piece was not even hissed. During the past four seasons, I have heard only one hiss in Carnegie Hall, that of a lone soul when Koussevitzky did Prokofiev's *Scythian Suite*. Everybody smiled. It was positively heartwarming.

The figure of the composer as a popular hero is temporarily extinct. The honest men who are writing for themselves alone admit they find it cheerless. Some still write only for their clique, but the clique is very tired of claquing.

In the face of such facts, the radio broadcasting networks play new music, commission new music and give prizes for new music. Why? Because the audience for new music is now the radio audience. I believe this because, in the line of duty, I have read at least seven thousand music fan letters during the past eleven months. Among the writers were violent objectors to modern music, and for these articulate partisans we should all be grateful. But the objectors were overwhelmingly in the minority, and often they were people who were primarily concert-goers, or disappointed performers. The great majority of persons who wrote these letters wanted to hear new music, and particularly new American music. Since the radio stations are interested in giving the public what it wants, they are giving their public this new music.

During 1937, the Columbia Broadcasting System played the works written for the first Columbia Composers' Commission by Howard Hanson, Walter Piston, William Grant Still, Aaron Copland, Roy Harris and Louis Gruenberg. The National Broadcasting Company commissioned Gian-Carlo Menotti to write a radio opera. C.B.S. announced the second Columbia Composers' Commission, with works ordered from Jerome Moross, Robert Russell Bennett, Leo Sowerby, Nathaniel Dett, Quincy Porter and Vittorio Giannini. N.B.C. announced the winners of its Music Guild Award for chamber music (Mitya Stillman, Alois Reiser and Rudolf Forst). On the Columbia Workshop, a radio music-drama by Marc Blitzstein, *I've Got the Tune,* was commissioned and performed. Previous to 1937, N.B.C. had engineered through Deems Taylor its Orchestral Awards (won by Philip James, Max Wald, Carl Eppert, Florence Galajikian and Nicolai Berezowsky). At various times, Bernard Herrmann has composed thirty dramatic scores to order for C.B.S.; he has also written seven melodramas for full orchestra and speaking voice at the network's request, and supplied his *Nocturne* and *Scherzo* on order from Howard Barlow for the Columbia Symphony Orchestra. This list does not attempt to include world premières of new works via radio, American premières on the air, or first broadcasts of new pieces.

The radio audience listened to this music and asked for encores. It is impossible to quote the letters on various broadcasts at much length. However, on October 17th, 1937, C.B.S. put on a two-hour broadcast of nothing but commissioned works in its series called Everybody's Music, and here are a few typical comments on the occasion:

Baltimore: "Vigorous and prolonged applause for the two-hour broadcast this afternoon. Add stamping of feet and even standing on the chair."

Chattanooga, Tennessee: "It was a rare treat. The music was full of variety, interest and color, and gave the vast audience a splendid idea of what our American composers are able to do."

Alton, Illinois: "Permit me to express my gratitude for the privilege of attending the premières of six new American compositions written especially for radio. You are bringing to residents of the most remote villages the exciting experience of hearing a first performance of a symphonic work, an opportunity formerly possible only to the big-city-dweller. There must be many other listeners like me who hope to hear them again on the radio, every one of them. A great day for the radio audience!"

Spokane, Washington: "Thank you for another of the most enjoyable programs on the air. I welcomed the opportunity to hear the music of Aaron Copland and Roy Harris. The entire program is making the *best* music everybody's music."

Columbus, Ohio: "Let anybody have a fine orchestra playing old accepted masterpieces. By demonstrating that music is a living, vital force, and that we have composers of note in this country, you are rendering a far greater service to the cause of music."

Milwaukee: "We who are ordinary citizens are grateful that American composers are at last having an opportunity to present their works to the nation at large through the medium of radio."

Charleston, West Virginia: "It was a pleasure to hear history made in the field of music."

In the United States we have seen a whole nation which was musically informed in only a few centers develop an appetite for music in the space of less than two decades. Out in the former Miserere Belt, where hearing records of the *Peer Gynt* suite used to constitute the event of many a sensitive listener's season, auditors have become accustomed to Brahms and Stravinsky, via radio, and they know what to think of these gentlemen. For most of this audience, the question of whether a piece is new or old is no more important than whether it was written in the morning or at night. Musical appetites are jaded only in the centers which are surfeited with sensation. Despite all commentators, radio audiences form their own method of approach to composers. There is a demand for new music on the air, and the demand has just begun.

Since composers need a public, why should they prefer to address a sated minority instead of an avid majority? Radio has shown its willingness to produce new works which are adapted to the medium. Yet the scores which come to radio stations every week are generally written with no knowledge of studio conditions, no regard for the instrumentation of studio orchestras, and no consideration of the microphone whatever. Even when they are possible for network production, they are impossible for the hundreds of stations which have more limited orchestral apparatus. Why should a concert performance mean more to a composer than a radio performance?

When a piece of music is broadcast, millions of people learn to reckon with the composer as an artist, whether they like him or not. These same people would probably remain unaware of his very existence if his works were played only in the concert hall. I should like therefore to point out to composers a few ways in which the radio audience differs from the audience to which they are accustomed to address themselves.

It is an ungregarious audience. It consists of single isolated individuals, or of isolated small groups. It does not respond as elements of a mass. It generally listens under quiet, friendly, homelike circumstances.

It is a blind audience. It cannot care whether the conductor beats one-in-a-bar by a rotary or a piston motion. It doesn't notice whether the players are wearing tails or shorts. It will not see you when you bow.

It is an intimate audience. Nothing except the transmission mechanism comes between you and it. And the same mechanism comes between it and Berlioz, so you and he start even.

It is an impatient audience. If you do not captivate it, off you go with the simplest twist of the wrist. No amount of ballyhoo will make it love you if you treat it hatefully.

It is unprejudiced. Many of its number are not certain whether you are living or dead, and few of them consider it bad taste for you to be the former.

It is unanalytical. It wants to be moved, amused, lulled, diverted, touched, shaken, delighted, transported, sobered, reassured. But it does not want to pick you to pieces.

It is simultaneously immense. Whereas millions used to be able to hear a piece during the course of a century, now millions can hear it within the space of an hour. A whole nation can form an opinion on a presidential move overnight, and that same nation can form an opinion on a piece of music overnight.

How much attention should the composer pay to such an audience? Well, he must decide how much attention he will pay to any audience, and this is a point few artists ever decide to their own satisfaction. It is considered moral among musicians to say that one should write solely what he hears with his inner ear, and pay no attention to the multitude. However, it is impossible for a composer who writes for radio to be unconscious of his audience. He can take one of two courses with regard to it: he can try to please, or he can despise it. It is perfectly respectable to take either. Yet I wonder whether any composer who really despised his public ever succeeded in pleasing it.

At one stage in radio, Hindemith had the greatest power of any composer to infuriate listeners. No matter what his theories might have been, broadcasts of his music brought in unanimously vituperative letters. Then suddenly one spring morning in 1937, the Columbia Broadcasting System carried an hour and three-quarters of Hindemith's music from Washington, with the composer participating as violist. The letters which came were not numerous, but they were all friendly. That night, I had dinner with a charming old lady from Iowa who had heard and liked the broadcast. She had become conscious of music only through radio. I asked her what piece she liked best, and she said, "The piece he played on the violin." It was the sonata for viola alone which was the bitterest and most uncompromising work of that stringent one hundred and five minutes.

One thing is certain: the composers who neither know nor care what the public thinks are living in a dream-world all their own. They can never really know what the public thinks if they decline to write for the medium which reaches it most efficiently today. The great American composers will write for radio, and they will write much. Air carries sound, but no sound travels in a vacuum.

Music and the Phonograph

From "Music Comes to America"

By David Ewen

THE greatest force in making America a country of music lovers has unquestionably been mechanization. A developed concert life, expanding educational resources, growing musical institutions, increasing audiences—these were, of course, significant in the evolution of a musical culture. But in the face of mechanization which, literally, brought the art of music into every household, all other influences assume secondary importance. Inevitably, the process by which an uneducated and uninformed public is trained to visit the concert hall or opera house regularly is, at best, a slow one. Over a period of fifty years there has been noticeable development in this direction. But the transformation of America into a musical country would not have been consummated in fifty or a hundred and fifty years if mechanization had not entered upon the scene. Through machines, the mountain came to Mohammed: music came to the average American—and into his living-room.

"Mechanical music," "canned music," "robot music," "tin-box music"—the epithets hurled at it were many and varied. Yet, in spite of derogatory sneers, its importance in the cultural growth of America assumed Gargantuan proportions. Your ordinary citizen, to whom the music of Bach and Sibelius was as remote as, say, the poetry of a Donne or the paintings of a Correggio, began to familiarize himself with the works of these and other masters. Music more and more filled a role in his everyday life.

In the beginning there was the Swiss music-box, pleasantly tinkling a single folk song or popular air in the American home. Then, in the 1900's, came the mechanical player piano, the first important mechanized musical instrument. Arthur Whiting wrote in the July, 1919, *Yale Review:*

> The early model of the player had the exuberant spirits of a machine gun. The notes of Mendelssohn's *Spring Song* were shot out like bullets so that the musically timid hastened to take cover. . . . In the overwhelming solos there was no recognition of the principles which underlie playing; no

648

important or unimportant sounds; no increase and decrease of volume. Such crudeness, however, soon gave place to machine-like imitations of light and shade, to sound emphasis of the melodic line and variations of speed.

Ultimately, this primitive piano player developed into the Ampico, the Duo Art, the Welte Mignon—a rather faithful reproduction of the greatest performances of concert pianists. The player piano became a fashion and a fad in the American home. Chopin, Beethoven, and Liszt, at the hands of Paderewski, Rosenthal, or Godowsky became the evening entertainment in the nation's parlors.

The player piano had been preceded (but was eventually displaced) by a still more important reproducing instrument: the phonograph. The latter was hardly more than a toy for adults in the closing years of the nineteenth century, producing sounds the identity of which were not always recognizable. Yet it became (almost overnight) the greatest single missionary for great music in this country.

Its history must form a salient part of the musical story of America. Born in 1877, the year in which Edison first took out a patent for a reproducing machine, its growth was rapid. In 1888 Edison perfected the wax cylinder. On May 16 of the same year, Emil Berliner, inventor of the disc which was to replace the cylinder, gave a demonstration before members of the Franklin Institute of Philadelphia. By 1896 the flat disc was sufficiently developed to permit extensive reproduction of great voices. By 1900 recordings were prepared commercially. Maria Michailova was the first important singer to record commercially. Enrico Caruso was the first of the great Italian tenors to be featured on records; it was the phenomenal sale of Caruso's records which converted the recording of music into a tremendous industry. Independent companies then arose to put on the market the singing of many other outstanding singers.

Despite the fact that these great voices were often submerged under the surface noise of the needle scratch, despite the fact that it was not often easy to discern the artistry of the performer in the squeals and snorts that emerged from the horn, the public was delighted with this musical novelty, which it called a "screech box." In 1903 Columbia issued the first of its "Celebrity Discs," featuring a list of artists including Jean de Reszke, Sembrich, Scotti, Schumann-Heink. Victor (which had been on the market for several years, reissuing European recordings) followed suit with an artists' list of its own. Recorded music was proving to be more and more practicable. Artists who only a few months earlier had been jeering at this new contraption were hurrying to put their signatures on recording contracts. Within a few years there was hardly a singer of note who was not making records: Louise Homer, Campanari, Emma Eames, Gadski, Nordica, Lilli Lehmann, Journet, Caruso, and innumerable others. The great instrumentalists also were engaged for records. First came Joachim and Sarasate; after them, Mischa Elman, Maud Powell, Kreisler, Kubelik, Paderewski, and Pachmann.

The ornate mahogany cabinet of the Victrola now occupied something of an imperial position in the living-room of the middle-class American family. Relaxation came with the cranking of the talking machine for a program of good "canned music." The sale of serious music records reached ever-soaring heights, achieving, in 1921, the sales peak of ten million discs. The American was being educated in music *en masse*. Opera excerpts took precedence: the sextet from *Lucia* (sung by Caruso, Tetrazzini, Jacoby, Amato, Journet, and Bada, and priced at $8.00 for one side); Galli-Curci and her electrifying coloratura voice in the "Bell Song" from *Lakmé;* Titta Ruffo injecting a note of burlesque with his breath-taking incantations of *Figaro! Figaro! Figaro!;* the incomparable Enrico laughing through his tears in *Vesti la giubba.* Light concert numbers also enjoyed prodigious sales: Alma Gluck singing the *"Elégie"* of Massenet to a sentimental background of her husband's violin; John McCormack nostalgically remembering Ireland; Kreisler playing of love's joys and sorrows with his characteristic Viennese charm; the Elman tone, opulent in the Schubert *Ave Maria* or the Tchaikovsky *Mélodie;* the pyrotechnics of the prodigy, Jascha Heifetz, in incredible digital exploits through music of Wieniawski and Sarasate; the great pianists sentimentalizing with a Chopin Nocturne, the Mendelssohn *Spring Song,* or the opening movement of Beethoven's *Moonlight* Sonata.

For many years the recording apparatus was too insensitive to reproduce authentically anything beyond a solo voice and piano accompaniment, or a single instrument; an attempt to record an orchestral accompaniment for an opera aria, tried in 1905, failed dismally. But experiments continued. In a few years, several groupings of instruments, and finally a full orchestra, were capable of being transferred to the disc. In 1917 three great orchestras joined the Columbia list of celebrities: the Chicago Symphony conducted by Stock, the Cincinnati Orchestra under Kunwald, and the New York Philharmonic with Josef Stransky. Victor followed the lead: in 1918, the Boston Symphony appeared on the red label, in 1919 the Philadelphia Orchestra under Stokowski, and, in 1921, the orchestra of La Scala under Toscanini. At first, orchestral music came in four-minute (or, at most, eight-minute) excerpts: *Hungarian Dances* by Brahms, the second movement of Beethoven's Fifth Symphony, the last two movements of the Mozart E-flat major Symphony (the symphonic movements always badly truncated), and the more familiar passages from the Wagner music dramas.

Thus, America was learning its music piecemeal—four minutes at a time. It was being given a hurried familiarizing sip at a strange potion before being asked to drain the entire cup. Eventually it was no longer content with a mere taste: finally, in place of encore numbers, truncated orchestral pieces, and opera arias, it demanded complete symphonies, concertos, operas, and masses.

In her autobiography, *An American Musician's Story,** Olga Samaroff-Stokowski gives an admirable description of the early years of recording from the point of view of the recording artist:

Artists usually lunched with officials of the company when they recorded in Camden. . . . Possibly the overindulgence in iced tea accounted for the nervousness which caused me to play a wrong note or two in every record I made of Mendelssohn's *Spring Song.* When I played it through for the sixth time, there was not a single mistake until the very last measure, which thereupon brought forth my despairing "damn."

"Never mind, Madam," said one of the recording experts who officiated on such occasions. "The same thing happened to Caruso the last time he was here. He was ready to cry. It just gets you sometimes."

Even without heat and too much iced tea, there was something peculiarly unnerving about the buzzer that dominated life during the process of making phonograph records. After everything had been adjusted, and all possibility of outside noises eliminated (you had to be sure your piano stool did not squeak and reasonably certain you would not have to blow your nose), there would be two peremptory buzzes which meant "get ready"; they were followed by a minute suspense during which you reached an agonized conviction that you did not know a single note of the piece you were going to play; finally, a single, fateful buzz started you off as though someone gave a violent shove to a sled at the top of a steep toboggan slide. . . .

Recording was young. . . . Electric recording had not been perfected and experimentation was going on in every direction. From the start, however, the musicians and recording companies were engaged in a long drawn-

* New York: W. W. Norton & Company, Inc., 1939.

out conflict. The *casus belli* was the choice of music to be recorded. The musicians wanted to record great music; the recording companies demanded popular music. . . . The opera singers had a relatively easy time, although even they were lured by the almighty dollar into sentimental renderings of songs like *The Little Gray Home in the West* which earned fortunes for all concerned. But at last many really good operatic arias came within the category of "popular music." Relatively few great instrumental compositions did.

Orchestras, string quartets, and solo instrumentalists battled with manifold difficulties. Aside from the questions of popularity, the compositions they particularly wished to record were usually too long to fit the time limit of the record. The largest record only played four minutes and fifty seconds for each side of the disc. Unless the musician was willing to make inartistic cuts, long compositions necessitated a series of records that were unpopular at the time because they were too expensive, and—according to the prevailing psychology—too "highbrow" for the general public. . . .

Very often a battle with the company on the choice of music would result in a sort of compromise. For instance, they would let me play a Rhapsody of Brahms, if I would consent to record the *Spring Song* of Mendelssohn. . . .

The acoustical problems of phonograph recording still require a special technique of performance. In the old days, however, before electric recording was developed to the point of being usable, difficulties were still greater. Singers had to be moved about while singing so as to increase or lessen the distance between them and the recording apparatus according to the volume of tone they produced. An overloud tone caused "blasting," the recording studio term for the raucous sound it produced. The acoustical funnels hanging over a piano which transmitted the sound-vibrations to the wax matrix had to be carefully placed. The difference of a hair's breadth in their position might cause certain tones to obtrude themselves with an unpleasant quality. A pianist in those days was obliged to operate within a very limited tonal gamut. A very soft tone did not record clearly, if at all. A *fortissimo* tone caused "blasting." Naturally, the restraint necessitated by these limitations interfered with freedom of musical feeling. It was as though a painter were forced to work with a palette from which some of the most important colors were removed.

When the radio became a fad, it was generally believed that the phonograph was through. Since, with the twist of a dial, the radio loud-speaker would disgorge a good variety of popular and semiclassical music, the effort of cranking a phonograph and changing records every four minutes grew to be too taxing. Finally, both phonograph and the library of records were relegated either to the cellar or the attic—and, seemingly, to obsolescence. The imperial corner in the living room now belonged to the superheterodyne.

Yet, just when a dirge was being intoned for the passing of the phonograph, something approaching a miracle took place in the recording industry. Like the Phoenix of fable, it was to rise suddenly from its own ashes, to become even more significant than it had been before. Unexpectedly, the phonograph not only came back to its one-time popularity after suffering a period of complete discard, but also achieved new heights of artistic importance.

In 1930, when virtually every other industry in America was threatened by collapse, the phonograph reached an altogether new five-year high. In 1937 the Victor Company triumphantly announced that in that year its sale of serious music exceeded that of 1930 by 535 per cent. Since 1937 the graph on the sales chart has been consistently mounting. In 1939 there was a sale of fifty million records, five million being serious music—a rise of one and a half million in the serious-music field over the preceding year. In 1940 almost ten million serious-music records were sold. More than 300,000 phonograph machines were bought in 1940, bringing the total number of phonographs in use above the four-million mark.

Actually, what brought about the recrudescence of the phonograph was that very thing which, at first, was believed to be its ruin. The radio did not destroy the phonograph. On the contrary, it succeeded in bringing to it a new lease on life.

For one thing, the perfected radio brought to the science of recorded music a revolutionary method. Formerly, reproduction on records had been achieved acoustically. The performer, or performers, played into a large horn which was used to converge the sound and increase its intensity at the recorder with sufficient power to cut into a wax disc, which in turn became the matrix for the records. This method succeeded in only approximating on discs the tone qualities of the voice and solo instruments. It failed to reproduce an orchestra or chorus with any degree of clarity or sharpness of detail.

The radio, however, introduced the use of the electric microphone into recording. The sound is now uttered into a microphone (just as in the broadcasting studio) and thence transmitted to an amplifier that enormously increases its power. The output of the amplifier goes to a device called a "cutter," which is essentially a phonograph pick-up driven electrically instead of mechanically. This "cutter" drives grooves into the wax disc.

From the radio, too, the phonograph acquired an altogether new type of loud-speaker in which the amplification is achieved through radio tubes. Electrical recording voiced through this new type of speaker finally brings a fidelity to musical recording almost lifelike in its quality. For the first time, recordings succeeded in converting symphonic and choral music cleanly, clearly, and sonorously. For the first time, the disc succeeded in catching exact shades of tone qualities from the different instruments. And, for the first time, a tonal range could be reproduced spanning the low notes of the bass and the high notes of the piccolo. The professional musician or astute music lover could no longer sneer at recorded music or refer to it as "canned." Recorded music had achieved, through its radio innovations, so human a quality that it could now afford esthetic pleasure to even a discriminating ear.

There is a radical difference between the demand for records before 1920 and the present demand. This, in itself, is an illuminating commentary on the growth of musical intelligence in this country in recent years.

Before 1920 people who bought records generally emphasized the importance of the interpreter over the music itself. Today, it is the music and not the artist that sells the records. People demand, first of all, a specific work; then, and only then, are they interested in the performer. A recent survey among several gramophone shops in New York revealed to this writer that Kreisler or Heifetz playing a musical trifle will not sell one-tenth so well as these artists interpreting a work of major musical significance. Twenty years ago or so the best Kreisler sellers were his Viennese bonbons—*Liebesfreud, Liebesleid, Schön Rosmarin.* Today these Viennese morsels are fabulously outsold by his interpretations of the concertos of Beethoven, Brahms, and Mendelssohn.

Another important difference distinguishes the record buyers of before and after the phonograph's renascence. Formerly buyers preferred one-record excerpts of the major musical works. In 1926, however, the first album set came into being, presenting a large work in its entirety. It met with such an enthusiastic response that, thenceforth, phonograph companies revised their entire recording programs to put emphasis on album sets. Today, albums of an entire symphony or concerto or string quartet or opera find a ready market—even though a work, in its entirety, may cost as much as $10 or $15.

A third, and probably the most significant, difference between the record buyers of these two periods is the conversion of interest from thrice-familiar classics to less familiar masterpieces. The great symphonies of Beethoven, Tchaikovsky, Brahms are, of course, consistently good sellers—so much so that the companies have found it profitable to issue them in several different recordings by different orchestras and conductors. But the best-seller lists of records during the past two years or so in record shops throughout the country have disclosed some startling information. Sibelius sells better than Tchaikovsky; Bach better than Dvořák; Mozart better than Chopin. Many times Bach has achieved the status of a best seller—though this is largely because of the appeal of Stokowski's orchestral transcriptions.

Again and again record collectors have proved their eagerness to explore completely unfamiliar realms of the musical art. It is for this reason that the record lists of recent years have been frequently more progressive than the programs of concert halls. Old music, long suffering neglect and obscurity, finds an eager public. Within the past few years the following works, rarely heard in public performances, have been steady sellers: Pergolesi's *Stabat Mater,* Scarlatti's sonatas for harpsichord, Bach's *Peasant* and *Wedding* cantatas, harpsichord fantasias of Telemann, early American music, cantatas of Buxtehude, early symphonies by Stamitz, Purcell's music for chamber orchestra, works by Grétry, Lully, Rameau. These works constitute only a small fraction of the library of unexplored musical masterpieces which appear regularly on the record lists.

Modern music also finds a great demand. The piano concerto of Jean Françaix appeared on records a year before it was given its American première in New York. The Violin Concerto of Ernest Bloch and the Second Violin Concerto of Prokofiev were familiar to record owners months before they became known to New York concertgoers. Many other compositions appeared on records almost immediately after their premières—works like Shostakovich's Fifth Symphony, Bartók's *Mikrokosmos,* Bartók's *Contrasts,* Rachmaninoff's Third Symphony. The recording catalogues now boast a well-represented cross section of the music of our time. Besides, a conscientious attempt has been made by the phonograph companies to record every major work of the leading composers. Richard Strauss, Sibelius, Roy Harris, Delius, Ravel, Stravinsky are represented on discs by virtually every one of their important works.

PART SEVEN

Music of America

VII. Music of America

UNTIL not so very long ago it was fashionable among certain musical sophisticates to speak of American music with an air of knowing condescension. "Yes, yes," we can hear one of them saying: "we are such a *delightfully* immature nation, with our Stephen Fosters, MacDowells, Victor Herberts, and Gershwins, but" (and here the speaker's voice rises in a dramatic crescendo) "have we yet produced a Bach or Beethoven?" And, if this seemed not enough to clinch the matter, he threw in a few phrases about our supposed lack of traditions, the absence of "genius" among us, our insensitivity to "higher values." Such remarks were supposed to settle the question of American music once and for all.

People such as these, who could often tell you about the history of the madrigal and whistle all the tone poems of Sibelius, had usually never heard a note of William Billings, Charles Ives, or Morton Gould, had never heard Leadbelly, Aunt Molly Jackson or Woody Guthrie * sing, and knew nothing at all of what has been happening musically in Oklahoma and Massachusetts, in Alabama and South Brooklyn, these many years.

Fortunately this type of critic has become rarer nowadays, while public interest in our native music has grown by leaps and bounds. People who never before gave the matter a thought are now beginning to wonder what American music is. Is it jazz, blues, folk songs, spirituals, musical comedy, boogie-woogie, or some of these modern symphonies or cantatas we hear on the radio? Now that Toscanini has given his benediction to the *Rhapsody in Blue,* and other leading conductors and soloists have begun to feature the works of young American composers, as well as the more traditional music of our country, wide masses of people are beginning to take pride in our national

* Three of America's best folk singers.

culture, in the music that is distinctly our own. Yet they want to know which is most representative of us—Cole Porter, Oscar Levant, Benny Goodman, Duke Ellington, Charles Ives, Morton Gould, or Aaron Copland; "Go Down, Moses," "Old Dan Tucker," "John Henry," "Smoke Gets in Your Eyes," "Star-dust," "Old Man River"; *Porgy and Bess, The Cradle Will Rock, Ballad for Americans,* a jam session, or those tricky sonatas one hears at League of Composers' concerts.

The answer, of course, is—all of them. They are all unmistakably part of our music and of us—the naïve and sophisticated, the vigorous and sensitive, the square-dance songs, Hollywood tunes, theater works, symphonic compositions, patriotic cantatas, the century-old ballads and "experimental" works written only last year. All are part of our exciting American past and our present coming-of-age as a nation in the musical world.

But while in a sense our music-making all stems from one single impulse, it is also a web of many different strands. Broadly speaking, it is possible to distinguish four important segments: * (1) the music of early America, (2) our folk music, (3) popular music: jazz and swing; and, newest of all, (4) our symphonic and concert music. More important to the future of American music than our brilliant concert life, splendid orchestras, virtuosi, and the millions spent each year for recordings, radio, and opera, is this ripening of our native musical consciousness. For there can never be any true music in a country until the great international traditions of culture are wedded to the local popular style—until one indivisible national language, indigenous to the soil and the people, emerges.

We are passing through this stage right now. For a long time we borrowed our standards of art-music wholesale from Europe, making no effort to acclimate them to our temper and spirit. So long as we did that, attempts to create American art were dry and sterile, and our composed music remained merely a matter of luxury and prestige, never expressive of the plain American man.

But today we are discovering our roots in the present and past; young composers by the dozen are springing up, depicting our native backgrounds, our traditions of democracy, our rich folk heritage. As we turn eagerly towards the present and future of American music (which now shares with England and Russia the privilege of carrying on world music), we should know our beginnings, and realize that even in its very early days America was no arid desert.—E. S.

* Part VII will discuss each of these in turn.

Music in Early America

By Elie Siegmeister

IN COLONIAL New England and Virginia, native music was alive so early that in 1625 a scandalized minister was crying out against "lascivious dancing to wanton ditties"; and a century later another divine was still thundering against the "foolish songs and ditties" that "hawkers and peddlers carry to all parts of the country." For ballad-singing was a favorite form of social entertainment in an age when there were no movies nor radios and very few books or newspapers to turn to during the long winter evenings.

In Revolutionary times, the first distinctively native songs— "Springfield Mountain," "Paul Jones' Victory," "Chester," "Yankee Doodle," and the "Ode on Science"—arose as part of the growth of an independent American culture. The very first known native composer, the urbane and charming Francis Hopkinson, was also a signer of the Declaration of Independence, thereby forging a link between American music and the struggle for freedom that has never since been broken.

Many of the Founding Fathers were passionate lovers or practitioners of music. Jefferson used to rise at five in the morning to practise the violin; his expense books record many a purchase of "the latest minuets" and of fiddle strings for string-quartet sessions; and he was well acquainted with the technique and construction of various instruments. Samuel Adams organized the people of Boston into secret singing clubs to stir up enthusiasm for independence. And Thomas Paine wrote at least two fine songs, "The Liberty Tree" and "Bunker Hill." In addition to having made a famous ride, Paul Revere might go down in history as having been the engraver of the first volume of original hymns and anthems ever published in this country. And Benjamin Franklin—most versatile of all—not only was a writer of ballad verses and a music publisher, but even invented a new musical instrument—the glass Armonica, for which Gluck, Mozart, and Beethoven composed a number of pieces.

Perhaps the most interesting figure among early American musicians was the tanner, patriot, and composer, William Billings

(1746-1800). It is said that he wrote his early compositions in chalk on the hides with which he worked. Lame, one-eyed, and possessed of a thunderous voice and even more thunderous manner, Billings rushed boldly in where others feared to tread, publishing six volumes of original songs between 1770 and 1794. His so-called "Fuguing Tunes" were erratic, cantankerous, and often highly successful ventures into the realms of higher composition—daring, when one considers the primitive state of church music in Boston of those days. Billings's music is often crude, to be sure, but it is not lacking in a genius of sorts, and a typically American enthusiasm and flair for the vigorous and unconventional. At least half a dozen of his pieces are gems that have awakened real enthusiasm when performed for audiences today.

Like other composers of early America, Billings introduced each of his collections with a "literary" preface. These prefaces give an insight into the curious nature of the man and the conditions under which he worked.

Prefaces to "The New England Psalm Singer" (1770) and "The Singing Master's Assistant" (1778)

By William Billings

THE NEW ENGLAND PSALM SINGER

PREFACE

To all Musical Practitioners:

Perhaps it may be expected by some, that I should say something concerning rules for Composition; to these I answer that Nature is the best Dictator, for all the hard dry studied Rules that ever was prescribed, will not enable any person to form an Air any more than the bare Knowledge of the four and twenty letters, and strict Grammatical Rules will qualify a Scholar for composing a Piece of Poetry, or properly adjusting a Tragedy, without a Genius. It must be Nature, Nature must lay the Foundation, Nature must inspire the Thought. But perhaps some may think I mean and intend to throw Art entirely out of the Question, I answer by no Means, for the more Art is display'd the more Nature is decorated. And in some sorts of Composition, there is dry study required, and Art very requisite. For instance, in a Fugue, where the Parts come in after each other, with the same Notes; but even there Art is subservient to Genius, for Fancy goes first, and strikes out the work roughly, and Art comes after and polishes it over. . . .

For my own Part, as I don't think myself confin'd to any Rules for Composition laid down by any that went before me, neither should I think (were I to pretend to lay down Rules) that any who came after me were any way obliged to adhere to them, any further than they should think proper. So in fact I think it is best for every Composer to be his own Carver. Therefore upon this Consideration, for me to dictate, or pretend to prescribe Rules of this Nature for others, would not only be very unnecessary, but also a great Piece of Vanity.

It would be needless in me to attempt to set forth the Usefulness and Importance of Psalm-singing, which is so universally known and acknowledged, and on which depends no inconsiderable Part of the Divine Worship of our Churches. But thus much I would say, That he who finds himself gifted with a tunable Voice, and yet neglects to cultivate it, not only hides in the Earth a Talent of the highest value, but robs himself of that peculiar Pleasure, of which they only are conscious who exercise that Faculty. . . .
Boston, October 7, 1770.

ADVERTISEMENT

To the generous Subscribers for this Book:

The Author having to his great loss deferred the Publication of these Sheets for Eighteen Months, to have them put upon American Paper,* hopes the delay will be pardoned; and the good Ladies, Heads of the Families into whose hands they may fall, will zealously endeavour to furnish the Paper Mills with all the Fragments of Linnen they can possibly afford: Paper being the Vehicle of Literature, and Literature the Spring and Security of human Happiness."

[Billings did not believe in praising the Lord in solemn hymn tunes sung in dreary fashion, but urged his readers to sing his "Fuguing Tunes" with energy and resolution:—E. S.]

If you fall in after a rest in your part you must fall in with spirit, because that gives the Audience to understand another part is added,

* This was during the boycott on all British imports—a boycott of which Billings, as a good patriot, heartily approved.—E. S.

which perhaps they would not be sensible of if you struck in soft. In 'fuguing' music you must be very distinct and emphatic, not only in the tune but in the pronunciation; for if there happens to be a Number of voices in the Concert more than your own, they will swallow you up. Therefore in such a case I would recommend to you the resolution (though not the impudence) of a discarded actor who after he had been twice hissed off the stage, mounted again and with great assurance thundered out these words, 'I will be heard.'

[In his first volume, Billings had informed the reader that he had a second all prepared and ready to be issued. But the Revolution intervened, and it was not until eight years later that *The Singing Master's Assistant*—later known as *Billings' Best*—made its appearance, with the following address to the reader:—E. S.]

THE SINGING MASTER'S ASSISTANT

PREFACE

No doubt you (do, or ought to) remember that about eight years ago, I published a Book entitled, The New England Psalm Singer, etc. And truly a most masterly and inimitable Performance I then thought it to be. Oh! how did my foolish heart throb and beat with tumultuous joy! With what impatience did I wait on the Book-Binder, while stitching the sheets and putting on the covers, with what extasy, did I snatch the yet unfinished Book out of his hands, and pressing it to my bosom, with rapturous delight, how lavish was I, in encomiums on this infant production of my own Numb Skull? Welcome; thrice welcome; thou legitimate offspring of my brain, go forth, my little Book, go forth and immortalize the name of your Author; may your sale be rapid and may you speedily run through ten thousand Editions, may you be a welcome guest in all companies and what will add tenfold to thy dignity, may you find your way into the Libraries of the Learned. Thou art my Reuben, my first born, the beginning of my strength, the excellency of my dignity, and the excellency of my power. But to my great mortification, I soon discovered it was Reuben in the sequel, and Reuben all over; for unstable as water, it did not excell. But since I have begun to play the Critic I will go through with my Criticisms, and endeavor to point out its beauties as well as deformities, and it must be acknowledged, that many of the pieces are not too ostentatious, as to sound forth their own praises; for it has been judiciously observed, that the oftener they are founded, the more they are abased. After impartial examination, I have discovered that many of the pieces in that Book were never worth my printing, or your inspection; therefore in order to make you ample amends for my former intrusion, I have selected and corrected some of the Tunes which were most approved of in that book and have added several new pieces [*Sic*], which I think to be very good ones; for if I thought otherwise, I should not have presented the book to you. However, I am not so tenacious of my own opinion, as to desire you to take my word for it; but rather advise you—purchase a Book and satisfy yourselves in that particular, and then, I make no doubt, but you will readily concur with me in this certification, viz., that the Singing Master's Assistant, is a much better Book, than the New England Psalm Singer. And now Reader I have no more to say."

[Billings's most popular song was "Chester." An ardent lover of independence, the composer had already published the tune with the following verse in 1770—six years before the Declaration of Independence:

Let ty-rants shake their i - ron— rod, And slav-'ry clank her— gall - ing chains, We fear them not,— We trust in— God, New— En-gland's God— for - ev - er— reigns.

By 1778 "Chester" had become the *Marseillaise* of the Revolution, sung by every soldier from Maine to Georgia. But the original verse was not enough for the fiery Billings, and when *The Singing Master's Assistant* appeared it contained the following graphic, embattled verses:

"Howe and Burgoyne and Clinton, too,
    With Prescott and Cornwallis join'd,
        Together plot our overthrow,
            In one Infernal league combined.

"When God inspired us for the fight,
    Their ranks were broke, their lines were forc'd,
Their ships were Shelter'd in our sight,
    Or swiftly driven from our Coast.

"The foe comes on with haughty Stride,
    Our troops advance with martial noise,
Their Vet'rans flee before our Youth,
    And Gen'rals yield to beardless boys.

"What grateful Off'ring shall we bring,
    What shall we render to the Lord?
Loud Hallelujahs let us Sing.
    And praise his name on ev'ry Chord."

Although Billings's music was widely sung throughout early New England, and he was a protégé of Governor Samuel Adams, he lived in the traditional manner of all composers—in poverty. Like Mozart, when he died in 1800 there was no money to purchase a tombstone. He lies in an unmarked grave, somewhere on Boston Common.—E. S.]

Planning an Orchestra

By Thomas Jefferson (in a letter)

In a letter of June 8, 1778, in the very midst of the American Revolution, Thomas Jefferson was dreaming of the day when he might establish a private orchestra at Monticello, on the pattern of the manorial bands then common among European landowners. His dream of an American Esterházy was fated never to be realized, but it is interesting to note that among his plans for the promotion of the good life in the land of freedom, the founding of orchestras was not neglected. —E. S.

MUSIC . . . is the favorite passion of my soul. . . . The bounds of an American fortune will not admit the indulgence of a domestic band of musicians, yet I have thought that a passion for music might be reconciled with that economy which we are obliged to observe.

I retain among my domestic servants a gardener, a weaver, a cabinet-maker, and a stone-cutter, to which I would add a *vigneron* [vine-grower]. In a country [like Italy] where music is cultivated and practised by every class of men, I suppose there might be found persons of those trades who could perform on the French horn, clarinet, or hautboy, and bassoon, so that one might have a band of two French horns, two clarinets, two hautboys, and a bassoon without enlarging their domestic expenses. A certainty of employment for half a dozen years, and at the end of that time to find them, if they choose, a conveyance to their own country, might induce them to come here on reasonable wages. . . .

On Setting Words to Music

By Benjamin Franklin

From the "Pennsylvania Magazine," 1776

Benjamin Franklin's keen interest in problems of musical style and his considerable knowledge of the techniques of composition are revealed in a letter he wrote from London. The statesman's brother had sent him a poem from America, with the request that Franklin find a composer in England to set it to music. The fact that Franklin, replying, preferred a melody "made by some country girl in the heart of Massachusetts" to the mannered style of the sophisticated English composers reveals two things of interest.

First, it is evidence that folk singing and the ability to make melodies for words were very much alive among common Americans of pre-Revolutionary days. Second, it attests the preference of the most civilized of the Founding Fathers for our native folk style, as against the over-refined techniques of Europe.

Franklin's indictment of Handel was perspicacious, and in a sense still holds today, for the German composer was in fact indifferent in his musical treatment of the English language. Finally, the Philadelphia printer's analysis of the violence done our mother tongue by opera composers and singers might well be studied in many music conservatories and singing studios even today.—E. S.

(*Letter from Benjamin Franklin to Mr. Peter Franklin*)

DEAR BROTHER:

I like your ballad, and think it well adapted to the purpose of discountenancing expensive foppery, and encouraging industry and frugality. If you can get it generally sung in your country, it may probably have a good deal of the effect you hope and expect from it. But, as you aimed at making it general, I wonder you chose so uncommon a measure in poetry, that none of the tunes in common use will suit it. Had you fitted it to an old one, well known, it must have spread much faster than I doubt it will do from the best tune we can get composed to it. I think, too, that if you had given it to some country girl in the heart of Massachusetts who has never heard any other than psalm tunes, or Chevy Chase, the Children in the Wood, the Spanish Lady, and such old simple ditties, but has naturally a good ear, she might more probably have made a pleasing, popular tune for you, than any of our masters here, and more proper for your purpose; which would best be answered if every word, as it is sung, be understood by all that hear it, and if the emphasis you intend for particular words could be given by the singer as well as by the reader; much of the force and impression of the song depending on these circumstances. I will however, get it as well done for you as I can.

Do not imagine that I mean to depreciate the skill of our composers here; they are admirable at pleasing practiced ears, and know how to delight one another; but in composing songs, the reigning taste seems to be quite out of nature, or rather the reverse of nature, and yet, like a torrent, hurries them all away with it—one or two, perhaps, only excepted.

You, in the spirit of some ancient legislators, would influence the manners of your country by the united powers of poetry and music. By what I can learn of their songs, the music was simple, conforming itself to the usual pronunciation of words, as to measure, cadence, or emphasis, etc.; never disguising and confounding the language by making a long syllable short, or a short one long when sung. Their singing was only a more pleasing because a melodious manner of speaking; it was capable of all the graces of prose oratory, while it added the pleasure of harmony. Most modern songs, on the contrary, neglect all the properties and beauties of common speech, and in their place introduce its defects and absurdities as so many graces.

I am afraid you will hardly take my word for this; and therefore I must endeavor to support it by proof. Here is the first song I lay my hand upon; it happens to be a composition of one of our greatest masters, the ever famous Handel. It is not one of his juvenile performances before his taste could be improved and formed; it appeared when his reputation was at the highest, is greatly admired by all his admirers, and is really excellent in its kind. It is called the "Additional favorite song in Judas Maccabeus." Now, I reckon among the defects and improprieties of common speech the following:

(1) Wrong placing the accent or emphasis by laying it on words of no importance, or on wrong syllables.

(2) Drawling; or extending the sound of words or syllables beyond their natural length.

(3) Stuttering; or making many syllables of one.

(4) Unintelligibleness; the result of the three foregoing united.

(5) Tautology; and

(6) Screaming without cause.

For the wrong placing of the accent or emphasis, see it on the word their, instead of the word vain, in the following instances.

With their   vain___   mys   te - ri - ous   art___

And on the word from, and the wrong syllable, like:

God - like   wis - dom   from___   a - bove

For the drawling, see the last syllable of the word wounded:

Who— can heal— the wound - ed heart.

For the stuttering, see the ne'er relieve, in

Ma - gic—— charms can ne'er—— re - lieve— you

Here are four syllables made of one, and eight of three; but this is moderate. I have seen in another song (that I cannot find) seventeen syllables made of three, and sixteen of one; the latter, I remember, was charms, viz: cha-a-a-a-a-a-a-a-arms.—Stammering with a witness! For the unintelligibleness, give this whole song to any taught singer, and let her sing it to any company that have never heard it; you will find that they will not understand three words in ten. It is therefore that, at the oratorios and operas, one sees with books in their hands all those who desire to understand what they hear sung by even our best performers.

For the tautology, you have it in the endless repetitions.

As to the Screaming, no one who has frequented our operas but will painfully recall instances without number.

I send you enclosed the song, with its music at length. Read the words without the repetitions. Observe how few they are and what a shower of notes attend them. You will then, perhaps, be inclined to think with me, that though the words might be the principal part of an ancient song, they are of small importance in a modern one; they are in short, only a pretense for singing. I am, as ever,

Your affectionate brother,

B. FRANKLIN

P.S. I might have mentioned inarticulation among the defects in common speech that are assumed as beauties in modern singing. But as that seems more the fault of the singer than of the composer, I omitted it in what related merely to the composition. The fine singer, in the present mode, stifles all the hard consonants, and polishes away all the rougher parts of words that serve to distinguish them from each other, so that you hear nothing but an admirable pipe, and understand no more of the song than you would from its tune, played on any other instrument. If ever it was the ambition of musicians to make instruments that should imitate the human voice, that ambition seems now reversed, the voice aiming to be like an instrument. Thus, wigs were first made to imitate a good natural head of hair; but when they became fashionable, though in unnatural forms, we have seen natural hair dressed to look like wigs.

While the compositions of Billings and the musical enthusiasms of the Founding Fathers seemed to augur well for the early development of a genuine American music, it was not in the realm of the opera and concert that this was to take place. For almost a hundred years, Americans created little of importance in the so-called higher forms. It was from this fact that there arose the myth of American unmusicality that plagued us for so long.

Although we can find little of importance in American artistic music during the whole nineteenth century, once we turn from the concert hall and opera house to the places where plain Americans have lived—the prairies and mountains, farms and river-boats, lumber camps, cotton fields, village churches and dance halls—we find a rich, vital body of common music created by our forefathers ever since the country was young.—E. S.

Our American Folk Music

From "A World of Music" (in preparation)

By Elie Siegmeister

WHAT is American folk music? Well, it is hard to give an exact definition or even to find a decent name for it. But call it folk music, ballads, work songs, spirituals, popular song, traditional music or blues, it is the stuff our people have been humming, crooning, whistling, shaking a foot to, blowing a harmonica or scratching a fiddle at for the past three hundred years or so. Daily life in colonial times provided its first themes and patterns, the events of the Revolution gave it spark and fire, and already with "Yankee Doodle" and "Springfield Mountain" our tunes had a distinctive twist and flavor.

The century-long westward migrations of the Pioneers gave birth to a whole body of native melodies: "Shoot the Buffalo," "The Promised Land," the swaggering "El-a-noy," the melancholy "Poor Wayfaring Stranger." * There were camp-meeting songs, fiddle jigs and clog dances, wagon and river-boat tunes, "play party" melodies and minstrel refrains. The Forty-niners have their tunes, the Abolitionists theirs, the woodsmen their rousing shanty songs. Slavery brought forth the Negro spirituals and Civil War days the "Battle Hymn," "Slavery Chain Done Broke at Las' " and many another song of freedom.

The opening of the Far West gave rise to a new literature of cowboy and railroad songs, and the industrialization of the South added the chants of steel-laying gangs and mill-workers to the older plantation melodies, cottonfield reels, Creole dances and street cries.

If we include the chanties of the old-time sailormen, the calls of the "canawllers," the work songs of miners and sharecroppers; the innumerable "ballets" of Kentucky moonshiners, Vermont old maids and those who go a-sparking "up on Old Smoky"; children's game songs, prison moans, banjo and guitar "breakdowns," folk hymns, nonsense songs, Blues, chain gang and "wanderin' " tunes, we have a vast body of music with distinctively American traits. Besides its sheer musical fascination, it tells us much of the life and spirit of the plain people of this country.

Today collections of American folk music are being made in almost every state. There is scarcely a region that has not contributed: the Appalachians, the South, New England, the Midwest, and the Far West. Vermont, once considered by some a dour, unmusical land, has two hundred songs, many of local origin. Florida, not especially noted for native production, recently turned in a thousand. Ohio, Nebraska, Michigan, and Oklahoma have yielded a rich harvest of ballads old and new. Even New Jersey and Brooklyn have handed in their shares! The Library of Congress, according to latest report, has more than thirty thousand recordings of native songs, and there are thousands more in other collections.

Of this great total, many songs are, of course, variants of certain

* For the melody, see p. 19.

basic originals. But this should not lead us to believe, as some apparently still do, that all the folk songs heard in this country are merely survivals of old English ballads brought over by the early settlers. Even that brilliant collector, Cecil Sharp, was so convinced of the British lineage of all music found here that he included "Kentucky Moonshiner," "Come All You Arkansas Girls" and the Negro work chant, "Swannanoa Tunnel" (which tells of working on the B.&O. Railroad) in his collection entitled *English Folk Songs from the Southern Appalachians*.

Certainly the early English settlers brought over their native music. So did the Irish, Dutch, Spanish, Africans, Scots, and French who came to this country. Out of the intermingling of all these and out of the new conditions of life on this continent came a distinctively American musical speech.

Especially interesting are the ways in which English ballads, changed by the local environment, contributed to the growth of American style. True, many of the oldest of these melodies, like the basic elements of the English language, have survived intact in various parts of this country (often in versions far more beautiful than those which have remained current in the mother country itself). But in many cases these ancient ballads have been completely transformed. Thus, Barbara Allen—in the seventeenth-century London version a noble beauty who died of love's grief and was buried in the "high churchyard"—has emerged in our South after three centuries as a Negro desperado, "Bobby Allen," whose corpse is shipped out of a railroad station in Dallas, Texas, leaving his relatives "squallin' and holl'in' with grief." It is also encountered in a western version in which the body is borne on a buckskin pony for burial in the Arizona desert. The melodies as well as the words of these songs bear about as much relation to the originals as the speech of Southern Negroes or Western Cowboys does to Restoration English.

Many different strains have added in a similar way to our musical brew. Irish jigs furnished the pulse for "Jefferson and Liberty," "When Johnny Comes Marching Home," and "Pat Works on the Railway." The Scottish snap entered into "Tom Bolynn," "Weevily Wheat," and many a fiddle reel. The Pennsylvania Dutch gave us hymns, lullabies, and the traditions of the Bethlehem choirs. The sprightliness of French dances comes out in the rhythms of Louisiana Creole music. African rhythms entered into Minstrel songs and remained in much American Negro music. Even distant Poland added the swing of her peasant dances: a popular mid-century Minstrel tune, "Walk Jaw-bone," follows the *Krakoviak* almost note for note:

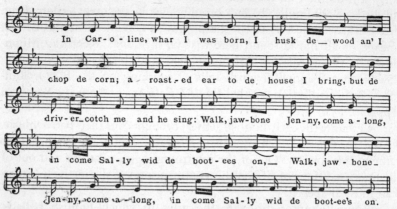

In Car-o-line, whar I was born, I husk de__ wood an' I chop de corn; a roast-ed ear to de house I bring, but de driv-er__cotch me and he sing: Walk, jaw-bone Jen-ny, come a-long, in come Sal-ly wid de boot-ees on,__ Walk, jaw-bone__ Jen-ny, come a-long, in come Sal-ly wid de boot-ee's on.

Hungarian, Jewish, Slovak, and Spanish melodies and rhythms were subtly distilled into the songs of miners, cowboys, and factory workers, and into our popular music for a century and more.

But it is not only out of traditional sources that our folk songs have come. Local events—"The Jam on Gerry's Rocks," the death of Casey Jones or Jesse James, a murder in West Virginia, or a wreck on the Santa Fé Railroad—have given rise to typical native expressions. Music-hall, Minstrel, and vaudeville tunes have sometimes contributed melodies for these.

Country folk often pick up a popular city tune and pass it off as a folk song. Frequently I have been told, "And now I will sing you one I made up myself"—and then heard a garbled version of an 1890 tear-jerker that no doubt traveled out to the provinces via some wandering peddler. I recently heard a country fiddler play a slightly rusticated version of an erstwhile Tin Pan Alley favorite, claiming it was an old jig.

Even in the early days the boundary between folk and "popular" songs was extremely vague. "Lord Randall" and "Hangman, Slack Your Rope," considered among the most typical of the older folk songs, were performed in music halls by professional singers over two hundred years ago. That most folklike of childhood favorites, "Frog Went A-Courtin'," was actually copyrighted and published more than three centuries ago. "Old Dan Tucker," a characteristic square-dance melody today, was written in 1830 by Dan Emmett, and was for years a "hit tune" with all Minstrel bands. "Sweet Betsy from Pike," "Red River Valley," and "Buffalo Gals"—among the most typical of our folk tunes—were originally written by professional "popular" composers.

The process of appropriation of "popular" music by the folk worked the other way, too. Professional writers, from William Billings through the Minstrel composers and Stephen Foster, never hesitated to "borrow" a good folk theme. Julia Ward Howe set the words of the "Battle Hymn" to the melody of a spiritual popular among Negroes. More recently, "Casey Jones," "The Wreck of the Old 97," "Short-'nin' Bread," and many another have been brought up from the South to furnish grist for the Broadway mill. Jazz writers, as we shall see, continue the time-honored tradition.

Just as folk and popular styles were interchanged, so were Negro and white. During slavery and afterwards, colored singers used melodic phrases of many white spirituals and ballads in fashioning their own songs. The harmonies of Negro spirituals to a certain extent reflect traditional Protestant four-part hymn-singing; but the complex rhythms of the Negro's religious songs were unquestionably his own. Early white spirituals and hymns were completely lacking in the typical syncopations and other rhythmic devices that abound in the Negro sacred songs.

On the other hand, Negro rhythms and melodies passed at an early date into the white man's Minstrel music, and thereby into square-dance and vaudeville melodies that became popular throughout the country. And, even more recently, white country folk of the South continued to adopt Negro styles (just as Broadway writers do), turning them into their own expression. The melody of a beautiful "Okie" migrant song, notated only a few years ago, is in the typical Negro twelve-bar Blues pattern:

I'm goin' where them chil-ly winds don' blow, dar-lin'
ba-by, Goin' where them chil-ly winds don' blow, dar-lin'
babe, an I'm goin' to my dark lone-some home.

Yet, in spite of the indubitably American character of our folk songs, were someone to ask just what is distinctively American about them in a *musical* sense, a precise answer would not be easy. For the greater part of the American flavor comes from the actual *quality of sound* of this music—the characteristic intonations of voice, fiddle, and banjo, unmistakable to the ear, yet difficult to set down in notation.

The differences in style among the various types of native song and among the different regional groups (New England, Deep South, Creole, Far West, etc.) make generalizations precarious. But broadly speaking, it is hard to mistake the American singing style: the semi-nasal, drawling, or guttural tone and the impersonal manner of performance. The true folk performer sings "straight"—without shading, change of nuance, or emphasis. He never dramatizes his delivery, since for him the music itself conveys all the drama or emotion needed.

Characteristic also are the catches, scoops, and slides in the voice, and the sudden falsetto quirks. These inflections, found in New York State as in Kentucky, can only be suggested in musical notation—as in the following transcription of the colonial ballad, "Springfield Mountain": *

But apart from their performance style, our traditional refrains have certain purely technical features that distinguish them from music written by professional composers.

Most obvious is the fact that most of them consist of a single melody, performed by an individual singer or fiddler, without accompaniment of any kind.† Since the entire musical effect must be achieved in the one singing line, many American folk melodies possess a musical completeness not found in "popular" tunes, which are designed to sound against a harmonic background.

* To give this ballad its full flavor, the grace notes should be sung in a sharp falsetto, swooping down to a normal chest tone on the regular notes.

† The main exceptions are dance tunes, frequently accompanied by banjo or guitar, and Negro work songs and spirituals, often (though not always) sung in choral harmony.

A melody such as the Kentucky folk-hymn, "The Saint's De-light," is a complete, self-contained musical form, without any harmony whatsoever:

In the absence of any harmonic rules to pin them down, our folk tunes often take unusual, and delightful, melodic byways. This hobo melody (which I collected in New York State in 1941) has a casual way of roaming from major to minor and back again, without a moment's warning:

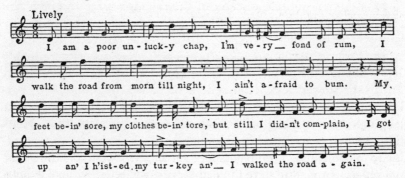

The purely melodic character of much of our folk music has other important consequences. First, the variety of scale employed. Folk singers use our familiar major and minor, but also the so-called "modal" scales not conventionally found in popular music. The performer of "I Walked the Road Again" also sang an old love ballad "Fare You Well, My Own True Love" (quoted below) whose distinctive melodic flavor depends largely on this "modal" scale pattern. The use of the different modes adds much to the musical interest and variety of folk melodies.

It is a striking characteristic of our folk songs that they commonly use only the primary tones of the scale. The ornamental half-tones found so often in sentimental popular melodies rarely occur in a true folk song. This economy of technical means gives folk music much of its strong, elemental quality.

One disconcerting thing about our folk music is that the form of any given song is seldom completely fixed. In some cases there are almost as many versions as there are singers. In the absence of any printed notation and of any instrument to fix the pitches, the same singer may perform a melody in a slightly different way each time he renders it. Thus performance is not merely repetition, but in a sense a continual varying and re-creating of a given theme. When recording, I have often asked a folk singer to repeat a melody three or four times. Tones which at first sounded like sharps sometimes turned out to be naturals on repetition; and on a third hearing would on occasion fall halfway between sharp and natural.

The same rhapsodic manner of performance creates a special type of rhythm as well. The Kentucky housewife and the Oklahoma blacksmith do not have any abstract conception of time values. To them, rhythm is entirely a matter of the rounded curve and inflection of an entire melody, rather than any rigid division into mathematically laid out "beats" and "measures." In instrumental pieces and dance songs, it is true, the untrained performer will often maintain a strongly accented pulse that does not vary from one end of a tune to the other. But in the slower, less rhythmic type of ballad, the duration of particular tones and the number of beats in a phrase often depend on the length of the verse and on the inflection of individual words. Sometimes the singer will give a certain phrase *three* quarter-notes (according to our reckoning); on repeating the melody, *four;* and a third time the phrase is found to have three and one-half beats (7/8 in our notation)—all this without the performer's being aware that he has made any change whatsoever in the three renditions!

This free, spontaneous feeling for rhythm accounts for the apparent metrical complexity of folk songs such as "Fare You Well, My Own True Love": *

---

* A similar type of rhythm is also found in folk music of other countries, and in compositions in folk style. See the themes of Mussorgsky, on pp. 542, 543.

Such complexities, however, are more apparent than real. While they impress the trained musician, neither the singer nor the average listener is conscious of anything out of the ordinary, for to the ear "Fare You Well" has a completely natural, easy flow. The difficulty lies not in the rhapsodic nature of folk rhythm, but in our system of time notation, utterly inadequate to record any but the symmetrical type of rhythm for which it was originally designed many centuries ago.

Another rhythmic device that occurs frequently (though not exclusively) in American traditional music is syncopation—accents on the off-beat. Found today in work chants, reels, nonsense songs, and fiddle tunes, the earliest notated examples in our music occurred in the first Minstrel songs (and, as we shall see, were probably derived from Negro sources.) "Old Dan Tucker" contained rhythmical groupings such as those marked by horizontal brackets in the following:

Though most folk performers know even less of the formal technique of music than a schoolboy, it does not follow that "there is nothing to" the making of their music. Many folk singers today—Leadbelly, Aunt Molly Jackson, George Edwards, and Joshua White—have distinctive, individual qualities of style that mark them as outstanding artists in their field. The gift for improvisation and invention is much more widespread among the average population in unsophisticated folk culture than in educated society. Today folk improvisation remains richest in the Appalachians and in the Deep South, where there are comparatively fewer radios than elsewhere.

Country instrumentalists, too, have a special feeling for their instruments and a style of playing that has a tang of its own. Square-dance tunes like "Sally Goodin" are often played all the way through on two strings, requiring unusual tunings of the fiddle not practised by educated violinists:

Individual banjo-pickers, guitarists, fiddlers, and harmonica-players sometimes have an amazingly intricate technique. If you have never heard one of those one-man singing, foot-tapping, guitar-and-harmonica teams perform "The Fox Hunt," it is an experience to look forward to. The racy melodies and crisscrossing rhythms, the mingled shrieks and yodels, rise to a contrapuntal pandemonium at the catching of the fox. The rhythmic inventiveness and virtuosity displayed could well be the envy of many professionals.

Dependent as it is on the memory and mood of its performers, folk music is in perpetual flux. In a growing democratic culture such as ours, where men are continually changing their homes and occupations, music changes with them. The complex migrations and counter-migrations of footloose Americans ever since the earliest days were no more fantastic than the strange journeys, transformations, cross-matings, and rebirths of our folk songs.

Thus, in the early 1800's a lusty sea chanty about Captain Kidd was brought by some retired sailor to the South, and there it was transformed into a lovely camp-meeting song. Religious folk hymns, fitted out with new words and played in livelier fashion, turned up as dance melodies on the frontier. A sentimental ballad from the East, "Bury Me Not in the Deep, Deep Sea," carried out to Idaho or Wyoming by some rover, emerged with a Western twang as the Cowboy classic, "Bury Me Not on the Lone Prair-ee." A song collector in Ohio gathered one of the most lovely versions of the old Scotch ballad "The Gypsy Laddie" from a Russian Jew who had learned it from the Mormons in Utah!

American folk music is not something one tires of. Unlike the more spectacular "popular" music, folk melodies do not grow old, nor do they die in a month or a year. They are built to last, and some of them have lasted a dozen generations and are still going strong. Yet this music is not something quaint or antique; it is a living art in which the common people of our own day continue to express their feelings in simple yet perfect form. It is music which has vitality and beauty for the twentieth century, not only as material to be used in a symphony or opera, but in and for itself.

When the boll weevil hit the South, a farmer sang:

O, de boll wee-vil am a lit-tle black bug, come from Mex-i-co, dey say; come all de way from Tex-as jes' a-look-in' for a place to stay, jes' a-look-in' for a home _____ • jes' a-look-in' for a home

The tune was simplicity itself, and its dry, self-mocking, typically American humor expressed the mood of planters and share-croppers everywhere. It was not long before the "Boll Weevil" traveled along the musical grapevine through a dozen states, emerging in a different form in each of them.

When drought and dust storms came, folks sang "I'm Goin' Down the Road Feelin' Bad"; when Pretty Boy Floyd met a dramatic end his fate was recorded by the people, too. They sang "WPA Blues," the "Ballad of the TVA," "Ku Kluck Klan," and many another, telling of the loved and the hated things in their lives. And today, in the midst of a war for freedom, new ones are springing up from the hearts of the people: "The Ballad of Dorie Miller," "Truck-Patch Trooper," "I'm a Pea-Pickin' Poppa," and "Round and Round Hitler's Grave." Folk song, the natural expression of our people who "don't know anything about music," is the deepest, most democratic layer of our American musical culture.

Early Negro Music

By Elie Siegmeister

THE music of the American Negro is at once the most readily recognized and the least understood of our national traditions. While the public is familiar with many of the well-known Spirituals, it is too often prone to regard these as all there is to Negro music; or else it regards Negro music in terms of a few clichés: "blackface" songs, "mammy" songs, "plantation" songs, and so forth—most of which are not Negro music at all, but white composers' stereotypes of the black man's music.

Negro art is rich and varied, perhaps one of the richest of our national traditions, and it has played a basic role in our musical culture. As early as Revolutionary times, no less a person than Thomas Jefferson noted the musical gifts of the slaves. In his *Notes on Virginia* (1781), he wrote:

"In music the blacks are more generally gifted than the whites, with accurate ears for tune and time, and they have been found capable of imagining a small catch. Whether they will be equal to the composition of a more extensive run of melody, or of complicated harmony, is yet to be proved."

In the early nineteenth century, many Southern plantations had bands of Negro musicians, who accompanied their singing on the fiddle, banjo and "bones." For understandable reasons, the early records of Negro music are few and far between. But in 1867 a remarkable book appeared, *Slave Songs of the United States,* collected and published by three enthusiasts. Not only was it the first substantial collection of Negro spirituals, reels, dance tunes, etc., ever published, but it contained graphic descriptions of the various types of the black man's music, and an appreciation of the difficulties of setting it down in our musical notation.

The following extracts from this volume discuss Negro music as it was in Civil War times: work songs, ballads, and "shouts," as well as the fascinating question of how these evolved.

Songs of Slavery

From "Slave Songs of the United States"

By William F. Allen, Charles P. Ware, and Lucy McK. Garrison

WE MUST look among their non-religious songs for the purest specimens of Negro minstrelsy. It is remarkable that they have themselves transferred the best of these to the uses of their churches—I suppose on Mr. Wesley's principle that "it is not right the Devil should have all the good tunes." Their leaders and preachers have not found this change difficult to effect; or at least they have taken so little pains about it that one often detects the profane cropping out, and revealing the origin of their most solemn "hymns," in spite of the best intentions of the poet and artist. Some of the best pure Negro songs I have ever heard were those that used to be sung by the black stevedores or perhaps the crews themselves, of the West India vessels, loading and unloading at the wharves in Philadelphia and Baltimore. I have stood for more than an hour, often, listening to them, as they hoisted and lowered the hogsheads and boxes of the cargoes; one man taking the burden of the song (and the slack of the rope) and the others striking in with the chorus. They would sing in this way more than a dozen different songs in an hour; most of which might indeed be warranted to contain "nothing religious"—a few of them, on the contrary, quite the reverse—but generally rather innocent and proper in their language, and strangely attractive in their music; and with a volume of voice that reached a square or two away. That plan of labor has now passed away, in Philadelphia at least, and the songs, I suppose, with it; so that these performances are to be heard only among black sailors on their vessels, or " 'longshore men" in out-of-the-way places, where opportunities for respectable persons to hear them are rather few.

What makes it all the harder to unravel a thread of melody out of this strange network is that, like birds, they seem not infrequently to strike sounds that cannot be precisely represented by the gamut, and abound in "slides from one note to another, and turns and cadences not in articulated notes." It is difficult to express the entire character of these Negro ballads by mere musical notes and signs. The odd turns made in the throat, and the curious rhythmic effect produced by single voices chiming in at different irregular intervals, seem almost as impossible to place on the score as the singing of birds or the tones of an Aeolian Harp.

The best that we can do with paper and type, or even with voices, will convey but a faint shadow of the original. The voices of the colored people have a peculiar quality that nothing can imitate; and the intonations and delicate variations of even one singer cannot be reproduced on paper. And I despair of conveying any notion of the effect of a number singing together, especially in a complicated shout, like "I can't stay behind, my Lord," or "Turn, sinner, turn O!". There is no singing in parts, as we understand it, and yet no two appear to be singing the same thing. The leading singer starts the words of each verse, often improvising, and the others, who "base" him, as it is called, strike in with the refrain, or even join in the solo, when the words are familiar. When the "base" begins, the leader often stops, leaving the rest of his words to be guessed at, or it may be they are taken up by one of the other singers. And the "basers" themselves seem to follow their own whims, beginning when they please and leaving off when they please, striking an octave above or below (in case they have pitched the tune too low or too high), or hitting some other note that chords, so as to produce the effect of a marvellous complication and variety, and yet with the most perfect time, and rarely with any discords.

The true "shout" takes place on Sundays or on "praise-nights" through the week, and either in the praise-house or in some cabin in which a regular religious meeting has been held. Very likely more than half the population of the plantation is gathered together. Let it be the evening, and a light-wood fire burns red before the door of the house and on the hearth. For some time one can hear, though at a good distance, the vociferous exhortation or prayer of the presiding elder or of the brother who has a gift that way, and who is not "on the back seat,"—a phrase the interpretation of which is "under the censure of the church authorities for bad behavior"; and at regular intervals one hears the elder "deaconing" a hymn-book hymn, which is sung in two lines at a time, and whose wailing cadences, borne on the night air, are indescribably melancholy. But the benches are pushed back to the wall when the formal meeting is over, and old and young, men and women, sprucely dressed young men, grotesquely half-clad field-hands—the women generally with gay handkerchiefs twisted about their heads and with short skirts—boys with tattered shirts and men's trousers, young girls barefooted, all stand up in the middle of the floor and, when the "sperichil" is struck up, begin first walking and by-and-by shuffling round, one after the other, in a ring. The foot is hardly taken from the floor, and the progression is mainly due to a jerking, hitching motion, which agitates the entire shouter and soon brings out streams of perspiration. Sometimes they dance silently, sometimes as they shuffle they sing the chorus of the spiritual, and sometimes the song itself is also sung by the dancers. But more frequently a band composed of some of the best singers and of tired shouters stand at the side of the room to "base" the others, singing the body of the song and clapping their hands together or on the knees. Song and dance are alike extremely energetic, and often, when the shout lasts into the middle of the night, the monotonous thud-thud of the feet prevents sleep within half a mile of the praise-house.

As to the composition of these songs: "I always wondered," says Col. Higginson, "whether they had always a conscious and definite origin in some leading mind, or whether they grew by gradual accretion, in an almost unconscious way. On this point I could get no information, though I asked many questions, until at last, one day when I was being rowed across from Beaufort to Ladies' Island, I found myself, with delight, on the actual trail of a song. One of the oarsmen, a brisk young fellow, not a soldier, on being asked for his theory of the matter, dropped out a coy confession. 'Some good speritulals,' he said, 'are start' jess out o' curiosity. I been a-raise a sing myself, once.'

"My dream was fulfilled, and I had traced out, not the poem alone, but the poet. I implored him to proceed.

" 'Once we boys,' he said, 'went for tote some rice, and de nigger-driver, he keep a-callin' on us; and I say, "O, de ole nigger-driver!" Den anudder said, "Fust ting my mammy told me was, notin' so bad as nigger-drivers." Den I made a sing, just puttin' a word, and den anudder word.'

"Then he began singing, and the men, after listening a moment, joined in the chorus as if it were an old acquaintance, though they evidently had never heard it before. I saw how easily a new 'sing' took root among them."

A not inconsistent explanation is that given [in] an Address delivered by J. Miller McKim, in Sansom Hall, Philadelphia, July 9, 1862:

"I asked one of these blacks—one of the most intelligent of them—where they got those songs. 'Dey make 'em, sah.' 'How do they make them?' After a pause, evidently casting about for an explanation, he said: 'I'll tell you, it's dis way. My master call me up, and order me a short peck of corn and a hundred lash. My friends see it, and is sorry for me. When dey come to de praise-meeting dat night dey sing about it. Some's very good singers and know how; and dey work it in—work it in, you know, till they get it right; and dat's de way.' A very satisfactory explanation; at least so it seemed to me."

Negro Work Songs and Blues
From "On the Trail of Negro Folk Songs"

By Dorothy Scarborough

THE Negro, by nature rhythmical, works better if he sings at his labor. He seems to lighten his toil, perhaps even to forget the fact that he is working, if he has a song to help him on. As a soldier can march with less fatigue if inspired by the music of a band, so a Negro's hoe or axe swings more easily to the beat of a ballad or the sighing swing of a spiritual, or any sort of song he chants at his task. He can work not only more pleasurably to himself, but more profitably to his employer, for he moves faster and accomplishes more if he sings. This is well recognized by those who employ bands of Negroes at various types of work, as on construction gangs and the like, and the fact is taken advantage of. Singing is encouraged—not as an art, but as an economic factor in efficiency. Song leaders are chosen, formally or informally, their responsibility being to speed up the effort of the workers. Sometimes these men are paid more than any of their comrades, and are required to do nothing but direct the songs.

Frances Gilchrist Woods has told me of such methods being used twenty-five years ago in the phosphate mines in Florida. The song leader would be called a "Phosphate Jesse," and all he had to do was to inspire the singing. Under the thrill of music, the workers would compete madly with each other to see who could "lay the rest out," until all but one had dropped in exhaustion, almost denuded of clothes. Song leaders also directed the singing of Negroes in the turpentine camps in Florida, Mrs. Woods says. The men who worked at "box-chopping," or chopping the trees to let the turpentine run out into the boxes placed to receive it, had their own special songs.

There is a good deal of singing in tobacco factories in the South today, but less than formerly, since machinery has been substituted to do what once was done by hand. In the old days, the workers sang in chorus at their task; and now that the roar of wheels would drown out their voices, in some factories the machinery is stopped for brief periods during the day and the toilers rest themselves by singing.

The cottonfield has heard much of this communal singing, as any Southerner knows. J. E. Morrow reports a scene from Texas:

"A number of 'hands' were in a cotton patch, and they constantly sang as they went down the rows. Groups of kindred spirits would sing one song together, or each sing a stanza alone, as fancy suggested. One of the favorites was this. One of the groups in the cotton patch— and the fastest—had for its leader an old man. He was apparently tireless, or so engrossed with his singing that he never slacked exertion. His favorite was the first stanza in this song. As he sang, the others added their contribution, with the following composite result:

" 'Wouldn't drive so hard, but I needs de arns.*
Wouldn't drive so hard but I needs de arns.
Snatchin' an' a-crammin' it in my sack,
Gotter have some cotton if it breaks my back,
Wouldn't drive so hard, but I needs de arns,
Wouldn't drive so hard, but I needs de arns.' "

Work is dignified when it is shown to be important enough to have a song addressed to it, when it is lyrically apostrophized. The Negro has little of the detached, impersonal attitude towards life or any aspect of it, but thinks and speaks subjectively. Even the street cries in the South are musical, as Harriet Kershaw Leiding has shown in her interesting booklet about Charleston, *Street Cries of an Old City*. So, in New Orleans, the chimney-sweep announces himself by a weird

* "Arns" = earnings.—E. S.

cry, half wail and half chant, which can scarcely be imitated, but which is very impressive: *Ramonée la cheminé latannier!* And Miss Emilie Walter has given me the cry of the watermelon vendor in South Carolina: "Barka-lingo, watermelon! Barka-lingo, watermelon!" with its musical intonations and echoing fall.

In Texas, especially at Waco I am told, the bootblacks sing at their work, songs passed from one to another, or improvisations, which they call "shine reels," and which serve not only to entertain the customer whose shoes are being polished, but to make less weary the waiting time for those who have not yet ascended the throne. The boys who black the shoes of the Baylor University students are, or used to be several years ago, adept at remembering or improvising these reels. Early Busby gave me one recently that he recalled having heard sung at these bootblack establishments.

> "Where wuz you, Sweet Mama,
>   When de boat went down?"
> "On de deck, Baby,
>   Hollerin', 'Alabama boun'!' "

Work songs of the Arkansas Negroes have been collected by Mrs. Richard Clough Thompson of Pine Bluff. She gives a woodchopper's song, which must be impressive, intoned in the solitude of the woods, as the chopper wields his shining axe to bring down one of the big trees. The song of the Negro is more philosophic in its acceptance of inevitability than is that of the poet of *Woodman, Spare that Tree,* and its solemn tones have harmonious accompaniment in the ringing sound of the axe as it strikes the tree trunk.

> Ole Mister Oak Tree, yo' day done come!
>   Zim-zam-zip-zoom!
> Gwine to chop you down an' cahy you home!
>   Bim, bam-biff-boom!
>
> Buhds in de branches fin' anodder nes'!
>   Zim-zam-zip-zoom!
> Ole Mister Oak Tree, he gwine to hees res'!
>   Bim-bam-biff-boom!
>
> White folks callin' for day wahm wintah fiah!
>   Zim-zam-zip-zoom!
> Lif' de axe, Black Boy, hyah, hyah, hyah!
>   Bim-bam-biff-boom!

Mrs. Thompson says: "It is difficult to represent the musical sounds of the refrain, which are like hissing, humming, whistling and long-drawn-out crooning tones emphasized by the blows of the axe."

[*Blues have, of course, become a basic part of our popular music. But until recently, little was known of their true origin. Here Miss Scarborough describes her visit to W. C. Handy, composer of the St. Louis and many other famous blues.—E. S.*]

To my question, "Have blues any relation to Negro folk song?" Handy replied instantly: "Yes—they are folk music."

"Do you mean in the sense that a song is taken up by many singers, who change and adapt it and add to it in accordance with their own mood?" I asked. "That constitutes communal singing, in part, at least."

"I mean that and more," he responded. "That is true of course of the blues, as I'll illustrate a little later. But blues are folk songs in more ways than that. They are essentially racial, the ones that are genuine,—though since they became the fashion many blues have been written that are not Negro in character, and they have a basis in older folk song."

"A general or a specific basis?" I wished to know.

"Specific," he answered. "Each one of my blues is based on some old Negro song of the South, some folk song that I heard from my mammy when I was a child. Something that sticks in my mind, that I hum to myself when I'm not thinking about it. Some old song that is a part of the memories of my childhood and of my race. I can tell you the exact song I used as a basis for any one of my blues. Yes, the blues that are genuine are really folk songs.

"Here's a thing called *Joe Turner Blues,* written around an old Negro song I used to hear and play thirty or more years ago. In some sections it was called *Going Down the River for Long,* but in Tennessee it was always *Joe Turner.* Joe Turner, the inspiration of the song, was a brother of Pete Turner, once governor of Tennessee. He was an officer and he used to come to Memphis and get prisoners to carry them to Nashville after a Kangaroo Court. When the Negroes said of anyone, 'Joe Turner's been to town,' they meant that the person in question had been carried off handcuffed, to be gone no telling how long."

I asked him if the blues were a new musical invention. He said: "No. They are essentially of our race, and our people have been singing like that for many years. But they have been publicly developed and exploited in the last few years. I was the first to publish any of them or to feature this special type by name." He brought out his *Memphis Blues* in 1910, he said.

The fact that the blues were a form of folk singing before Handy published his is corroborated by various persons who have discussed the matter with me, and in Texas the Negroes have been fond of them for a long time. Early Busby, now a musician in New York, says that the shifts of Negroes working at his father's brickyard in East Texas years ago used to sing constantly at their tasks, and were particularly fond of the blues.

Handy commented on several points in connection with the blues —for instance, the fact that they are written all in one tone, but with different movements according to the time in which they are written. The theme of this modern folk music is, according to Handy, the Negro's emotional feeling quite apart from the religious. As is well recognized, the Negro normally is a person of strong religious impulse, and the spirituals are famous as expressing his religious moods; but they do not reveal his nature. The Negro has longings, regrets, despondencies, and hopes that affect him strongly, but are not connected with religion. The blues, therefore, may be said to voice his secular interests and emotions as sincerely as the spirituals do the religious ones.

Handy said that the blues were different from conventional, composed music, but like primitive folk music in that they have only five tones, like the folk songs of the slavery times, using the pentatonic scale, omitting the fourth and seventh tones. He says that while most blues are racial expressions of Negro life, the form has been imitated nowadays in songs that are not racial. While practically all the music publishers refused to bring out his compositions at first, now most of them publish blues.

Even though specific blues may start indeed as sheet music, composed by identifiable authors, they are quickly caught up by popular fancy and so changed by oral transmission that one would scarcely recognize the relation between the originals and the final results—if any results ever could be considered final. Each singer adds something of his own mood or emotion or philosophy, till the composite is truly a communal composition. It will be noted in this connection that one of the songs announces of itself that, while it is first published in seven verses, people will soon be singing it in one hundred verses. The colored man appropriates his music as the white person rarely does.

What Is Jazz?

From "A World of Music" (in preparation)

By Elie Siegmeister

WHAT is Jazz? A music with many faces. The term has been used to describe more different types than almost any other musical term in the dictionary. There is "hot" jazz, and "sweet" jazz. There is the raucous, improvised variety played on broken-down honky-tonk pianos, and the elegant "symphonic" variety, scored by conservatory-trained arrangers, performed by ninety-nine-piece radio orchestras. Almost every type of music has been turned into jazz: Negro spirituals, nursery rhymes ("Itiskit Itaskit"), mountain ballads ("Careless Love"), Yiddish folk songs (*"Bei mir bist du schön"*)—and also Chopin's *Fantaisie Impromptu,* Ravel's *Pavane,* even a melody from Tchaikovsky's Fifth Symphony. Some assert that jazz is not the music played, but the manner of playing it, while others maintain that the only true jazz was that played by such-and-such a performer in New Orleans, St. Louis, or Chicago fifteen years ago.

But whatever it is, one thing is certain: jazz did not spring out of nowhere. It has its roots in our people, and its antecedents in the popular music of an earlier period. There is a line—perhaps an indistinct one, but a line nevertheless—starting possibly in the earliest minstrel songs, passing through the "plantation melody" days, the vaudeville tunes of the '70s and '80s, to the era of the cake-walk in the '90s. The 1900's brought forth ragtime and the one-step. The "pats," "jubas," "reels," "stomps," "drags," "hoe-downs," and the Creole dance tunes of New Orleans entered in between 1900 and the first World War, and finally the Blues came up from the canebrakes to the marts of Broadway. Between 1910 and 1925 various groups, notably the almost legendary Dixieland Band, made their appearance in metropolitan centers, and the new and lusty offshoot from the old branch was already in full bloom: Jazz. Its history is shrouded in anecdotes, memories, fantasies, and conjectures; but the fact remains that by about 1915, there it was.

During the first World War and the troubled decade that followed, the vigorous newcomer spread infectiously through this country and abroad. In an amazingly short time, people were singing and dancing to jazz in Paris, London, Cairo, and Hongkong. The victrola took it to the Polar regions, and the radio to the remotest mountain communities. In a dozen countries internationally known composers, among them Ravel, Stravinsky, Milhaud, and Hindemith, recognized it as a fascinating style and wrote pieces in which they tried to catch the spirit of *le Jazz Américain*. There has probably never been any other type of music that spread with such rapidity, or was so widely sung in the four corners of the earth.

Jazz has been hailed as the most truly representative American art, and condemned as a nervous expression of modern life. To the jitterbug it is an ecstatic ritual; to the intellectual "expert," a rediscovery of the primitive roots of music. The sentimental adolescent finds in it a world of dreamy romance; the radio sponsor, a means of promoting his products. Millions who have no theories about it eat, work, ride, dance, go to sleep with the radio tuned to jazz. It has become so common a part of daily life that we are likely to forget how it started and why.

The following articles by Winthrop Sargeant, Louis Armstrong, Benny Goodman, and George Gershwin discuss its origin and character.

Jazz, Hot and Hybrid
Extracts from the book of that title

By Winthrop Sargeant

WHAT is jazz? When three or four Negro musicians get together in a New Orleans dive and loose their enthusiasms in a collective improvisation, does that constitute jazz? And if so, when a commercial Tin Pan

Alley tunesmith writes a melody and (if he is a sufficiently good musician) an accompaniment down on paper, is that jazz? Is jazz, as Paul Whiteman wrote, "not the thing said but the manner of saying it"? Or is it, as Gershwin and others have attempted to make it, a legitimate basis for composition in the larger European forms? Is it the system of rhythmic and harmonic formulas exhibited in the average piece of popular sheet-music, or the carefully rehearsed and arranged body of sound that issues from a swanky dance orchestra, or, as the swing-music enthusiasts will have it, the purely improvised product of a "hot" ensemble? Are all these merely different varieties of jazz, or is jazz some sort of essential element that manifests itself in one way or another in all these various forms or results of musical activity?

The American Negro's music has usually been classified according to the social function in connection with which it has appeared. The music of the dance-hall has been known as "jazz" or "ragtime"; that of the religious service as "spirituals"; that accompanying the labor of the cottonfields and the chain-gangs as "work songs." "Blues" has been the term applied to a certain variety of secular song of lamentation. This classification is perhaps not without its usefulness in certain connections, but from the purely musical point of view it is somewhat unsatisfactory. Not only does the musical expression included under these categories overlap from one to the other, obscuring any precise lines of demarcation, but the categories themselves encompass types of music that are essentially different from each other. Thus a "spiritual" may be (1) the spontaneous expression of a shoutin' congregation in the act of worship; (2) a more or less traditional melody that is made the subject of repeated and differing versions by such a congregation; (3) a melody of similar type that has been taken over by a more or less musically sophisticated Negro chorus, carefully rehearsed and performed in the concert hall; (4) a religious song, originally of improvised character, that has been written down, given "form" and a piano accompaniment by a musically educated person and presented on the program of some well-known Negro baritone or tenor; (5) a religious composition written by a White or other sophisticated musician in imitation of the Negro idiom; (6) a White hymn tune that has got woven into the fabric of a Negro religious service, been remembered by someone and transcribed back into the notation of the White man's vocabulary; and, no doubt, several other things. "Jazz" may include: (1) the sort of spontaneous improvisation known as "hot" jazz or "swing music"; (2) the rehearsed music played by a large professional dance orchestra in pseudo-Negroid manner including occasional solos and "breaks" that are technically "hot"; (3) rehearsed music by a sophisticated orchestra based on Tin Pan Alley tunes of purely European character which are subjected to the process known as "jazzing"; (4) the same type of music based on a tune pirated from the work of some classical composer; (5) something written down on paper by a Tin Pan Alley composer in imitation of the Negro method of playing, and so on.

The only outstanding musical difference between these two categories is that the spirituals are preponderantly vocal and that jazz is preponderantly instrumental, and this far from absolute distinction is of slight importance in its bearing on musical form and style. Actually the "spiritual" of the shoutin' congregation has more in common with hot jazz than it has with the "spiritual" sung by the highbrow Negro concert singer. And the carefully and deliberately arranged and notated "spiritual," which is made the subject of "interpretations," is in some ways more akin to certain varieties of "sweet" jazz than it is to the spontaneous outpouring of religious emotion peculiar to the naïve rural Negro by whom all true spirituals are originally conceived. The need of another classification for musical purposes is obvious, one based on differences in form, technique, and method of creation, rather than differences in social function or in the character of accompanying texts.

Certain rough distinctions are obvious. The least European, hence the most purely Negroid, variety of Afro-American music is to be found in the embryonic spiritual of the shoutin' congregation. It is less standardized in pattern, more varied in style, freer in form than the hottest of hot jazz. A comparison with African tribal music will show it to be related to its jungle prototypes. Hot jazz, on the other hand, exhibits the influences of sophisticated city life, and something of the standardization usually associated with commercial products. The mere fact that hot jazz is played upon complex standardized instruments of European origin (the influence of the piano keyboard is particularly important in this connection) gives it a sophisticated character totally lacking in the shoutin' spiritual. The human voice, feet, and hands are instruments common to both the American and the African Negro; the piano, trumpet, silver-plated banjo, and saxophone are not.

Nevertheless, hot jazz and the shoutin' spiritual are in certain respects remarkably similar. Both are largely improvisatory. Both are Negroid in their participative, rather than artist-audience, approach.

Both are far richer in purely Negroid rhythmic and scalar elements than are the more deliberate forms of jazz or of Afro-American religious music.

The term "hot" is, however, a relative one. Much of the music which it commonly designates is only partially improvised. Both in the religious and in the jazz fields, particularly pleasing improvisations are apt to be remembered and repeated more or less intact, to be accorded something of the status of "compositions." Here we have, perhaps, another, though a closely related, variety of Negroid music, slightly more deliberate and clearly crystallized than the purely improvised variety, but still showing most of the traits of Negroid improvisation. Most of what is popularly known (even among swing fans) as "hot jazz" belongs to this category of remembered and repeated, partially rehearsed, music.

JAZZ ORIGINS AND INFLUENCES

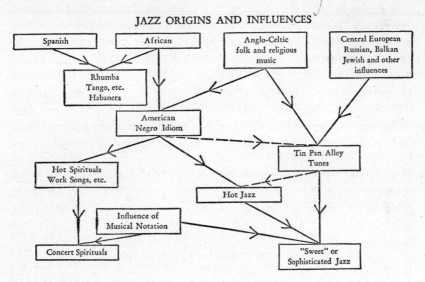

ORIGIN OF THE BLUES SCALE

The widespread popularity of the blues scale in commercial jazz undoubtedly started with the appearance of the blues themselves. And it is probable that the hot, as well as the sweet, jazz player took a cue or two from the blues singers, from the "father of the blues" W. C. Handy, and from other comparatively sophisticated sources in evolving his rapid and complicated use of the same tonal material. It is at any rate true that some of the subtlest music in this genre is to be found in the work of certain of the Negro blues singers who interpreted, or improvised upon, the blue and ragtime tunes of Handy and others.

Supreme among these, according to the connoisseurs of swing, was the Negro singer Bessie Smith. And even the present writer, whose interest in jazz is clinical rather than rhapsodic, must concede that her reputation was a richly deserved one. Hot jazz in general may be a thrilling communion with the primitive soul; or it may be an ear-splitting bore. This writer will not argue the point. But almost any unbiased and musically sensitive person will admit, on hearing them, that Bessie Smith's recordings of *You've Been a Good Ole Wagon, But You Done Broke Down,* and *Cold in Hand Blues* are musical experiences of a high and poetic order. The latter song, in particular, possesses all the simplicity and sincerity that we associate with the finest product of the Negro's musical genius.

Bessie Smith's style represents a conceded standard of excellence in the art of blues declamation. It is both somewhat simpler and somewhat more purely "African" than the style of the average blues singer. She uses a very small range and a very limited scale. *Cold in Hand Blues,* for example, rests almost entirely on a scale of four notes. However complex the harmony underlying her vocal melody, she changes her scalar pattern only rarely and slightly by way of compromise with it. Often her tones do not "harmonize" with the chords of the accompaniment according to the European notion of harmonization. But the sureness and consistency of her deviation from European usage carry with them their own artistic justification. And the effect is undeniably satisfactory. Her treatment of conventional blues tunes is exceedingly free, in the sense that she pays very little attention to the notes, or even the words, of the printed version. As in the case of all true "hot" soloists, the rigid conventional lines of the standard tune on which her improvisation is based often become almost unrecognizable in what she produces. Her freedom of treatment, however, is not the freedom of elaboration. She does not add florid elements to the original tune. She rather subtracts its superfluous elements, pruning it down and simplifying its phraseology; making it, in fact, more truly "primitive."

Bessie Smith's melodic style undoubtedly reflects the influence of a deep-rooted racial musical instinct. While comparatively few of the published spirituals show with any clarity these completely un-European melodic habits we have been describing, a great deal of primitive Southern spiritual singing actually follows them with remarkable consistency. Where the trained and self-conscious Negro chorus is more likely to imitate European or "White" constructions, the little rural congregations of the Deep South, raising their voices in spontaneous religious communion, often drone their more fervent outbursts in the intervals of the blues tetrachords. Even when the medium is speech rather than song, as in sermons and prayers, the blues intonations creep into the texture of their discourse. The Negro preacher will commence his sermon in a matter-of-fact voice, stressing his words carefully so as to convey with the utmost clarity the logic of his thought. As he and his congregation warm to their common devotional task, however, his intonations will begin to crystallize, and soon a frenzy of religious ecstasy will be reached in which his speech becomes a recitative with clearly defined musical values. Very commonly the ecstatic part of such a sermon will be found to rest, melodically, on two or three notes of a blues tetrachord. One sermon, recorded by E. P. Jennings in central Alabama, is sung—or "preached" if you like— entirely on two notes: a tonic, or main declamatory tone, and the "blue" third above it. Both congregation and preacher echo each other frequently in snatches like

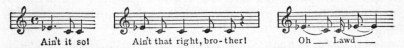

Ain't it so!   Ain't that right, bro-ther!   Oh ___ Lawd ___

The appearance of the blues tetrachord in primitive spiritual singing and even in Afro-American prose declamation should convince the most skeptical of their authenticity as a characteristic Negroid contribution. Regarding the pentatonic and other supposedly Negroid scalar constructions there is legitimate room for controversy. These conductions are common to the folk-idioms of several races, and there is some possibility that they have been borrowed by the Negro. But the blues scale is his own unique product, and its use in American popular music is to be traced directly to his influence.

That the Afro-American has intoned this scale since the earliest days of slavery can hardly be doubted. But its widespread appearance in all sorts of Negro declamation, as well as in the singing of spirituals whose origin is demonstrably at least three generations behind us, suggests a far more venerable pedigree. It is patently impossible for the Negro to have borrowed it. The Whites did not use it; nor has any scalar construction similar to it been used in European music for many centuries.

EVOLUTION OF JAZZ RHYTHM

Just when the Negro's rhythmic contribution began to appear as an ingredient of popular music in this country is something that would be very difficult to determine. The mass of sheet music turned out by the publishing industry did not begin to show its effects in any overwhelming profusion until about 1900. On the other hand it is a certainty that ragtime was played and sung many years before it appeared in print. Its history undoubtedly goes far back in the annals of "minstrelsy," and the minstrel show, according to historians, dates from the early 'forties. It is not at all unlikely that plantation entertainments by Negro slaves, which were imitated by "blackface" Whites in the early minstrel shows, had their accompaniments of syncopated and polyrhythmic music long before even the minstrel as such appeared on the scene.

These, however, are conjectures. The early nineteenth century did not have the blessing of the phonograph, and just exactly how the first minstrels and their Negro models sang will never be known. It is a fact that polyrhythm,* and other characteristic jazz elements, began to appear sporadically in print several decades before the turn of the century.

The early polyrhythmic outcroppings were somewhat reticent. But they are unmistakable. Even as far back as *Turkey in the Straw* or *Old Zip Coon,* which enjoyed popularity at least as early as 1834, we find evidence of the Negro idiom. The first half of the old melody is as prim and severe as any hornpipe. But the last half begins with a little figure—

whose polyrhythmic character is pretty well defined. The "cake walk" figure (♪♩) which appears in the above mentioned phrase from *Turkey in the Straw,* is perhaps the earliest polyrhythmic device to find consistent application in printed ragtime. It was a stock-in-trade formula among ragtime and country dance players in the 'nineties. Several old "buck and wing" dances in Harding's *Collection of Jigs,*

---

* Polyrhythm—a characteristic dovetailing of rhythmic pulses; strictly speaking, the simultaneous presentation of two distinct metrical patterns.—E. S.

Reels, and Dances (copyright 1897) contain it. In the same collection will be found early precursors of the art of "jazzing the classics," still lamentably so popular. In these early examples of musical mayhem the prime mutilator is the "cake walk" figure. Harding's version of *I Dreamt That I Dwelt in Marble Halls* from Balfe's *Bohemian Girl*, for instance, begins in this vein:

RAGTIME

The years that followed—from 1905 to 1910—might, in fact, be spoken of as comprising the "golden age" of ragtime. It was during this period that it reached its heyday as a national institution. America was beginning to dance as never before in its history. Formerly a great deal of our popular music had been written to sing. Now there was an unappeasable need for music to dance to. The sentimental song was giving way, in the public favor, to the "two-step" and its various Negroid derivations. And Tin Pan Alley was scouring the country for material to fill the new requirements.

A purely vocal type of music could never have filled them. The song, as a medium, was too limited in rhythmic possibilities. Ragtime was essentially an instrumental art. Few of the best rags offered melodies that could be sung. None of the really good ones had vocal refrains or were encumbered with words. The song writers attempted for years to capitalize on the trend by writing vocal tunes in which texts extolling the virtues of the dance were accompanied by slightly "ragged" piano accompaniments. The results were usually feeble imitations. One need only examine the so-called ragtime songs of such writers as Irving Berlin and George M. Cohan to be struck with their unimaginativeness in comparison with the real rags of the period. The rags were written by instrumentalists who knew their instruments intimately and exploited their practical potentialities. Few of the big commercial names of Tin Pan Alley knew enough about music in the practical sense to turn out acceptable rags.

The dominating instrument of the period was the piano, and the good rag composers were usually pianists. The standardized dance orchestra had not yet appeared on the scene. The saxophone did not make its entry as a standard component of the jazz ensemble until about 1916. The jazz arranger, whose function in turning vocal "tunes" into acceptable dance music was so important to Tin Pan Alley's later activity, was as yet an unknown quantity. The phonograph had not yet made orchestral dance recordings available to every hamlet and isolated farm-house in the country. The piano, plus or minus a few additional instruments, was what the generality of Americans danced to. Equipped with a "player" mechanism and perforated rolls it took the place later occupied by phonographically recorded music. It was to be heard in every small "nickelodeon" where the products of the budding movie industry were displayed. A player piano was the pride of every reasonably prosperous rural family. And the ability to play some sort of elementary ragtime on the mechanically unassisted instrument was daughter's most admired "accomplishment."

It was under these social and mechanical circumstances that the rag reached its nation-wide popularity. The Negro's piano technique —a curious combination of digital expediency and native rhythmic sense, operating upon a highly complex civilized musical instrument— had already developed into a characteristic idiom. The dance craze and the universal accessibility of the piano combined to make it, for a time, the popular idiom of the whole country.

As it existed between 1905 and 1910 the rag offered the most intricate and interesting rhythmic development that has ever been recorded in our popular printed sheet-music. The rag writers of the early nineteen hundreds used every formula of syncopation, phrase distortion, and cyclical rhythmic structure that ingenuity could contrive. None of the sheet-music industry's subsequent efforts have shown anything of comparative technical complexity. Revivals, in the nature of trick piano compositions, did appear from time to time. Some were clever. Confrey's famous polyrhythmic pieces were essentially rags, and Confrey used the old rag formulas with considerable adroitness. But he added little that will not be found in the rags of the century's first decade. Almost every rhythmic formula subsequently fashionable in "sweet" jazz made its first printed appearance prior to 1910.

By 1910 the rag had become enormously popular, and decadence set in. Public demand brought about wholesale production, and by this time even the least gifted of Tin Pan Alley's hacks knew the tricks of the trade. The rags of subsequent years were numerous and mostly of poor quality. Old formulas were done to death, and individual ingenuity disappeared from the art of rag composition. Contrary to popular belief, and to his own published statement, Irving Berlin was far from being the instigator of the ragtime craze. By the time the uncharacteristic and rather unimaginative phrases of *Alexander's Ragtime Band* appeared in print (1911) the rag, from a creative point of view, was already well on the decline.

The transition from ragtime to jazz has also been made the subject of a great deal of misinformed and unsubstantiated writing. Styles in our popular music have, of course, changed gradually. "Sweet" commercial jazz today is different in many respects from the ragtime of 1910. It is orchestral where ragtime was pianistic. It is suave and sophisticated where ragtime was jerky and boisterous. Its melodies are vocal: based on tunes that are originally created as songs. Its composers and what is more important, its arrangers, are likely to be eclectic in their choice of musical material. Its harmonic and orchestral effects are often borrowed from the romantic and impressionistic composers of Europe. Its general character is more romantic and sentimental, less primitive, than that of ragtime. It is also a more complex product, in which the work of the composer appears as a mere scaffold for the more important activities of the arranger and the instrumentalist.

BLUES

Jazz draws much from the vocal aspects of Negro music, and these aspects were necessarily absent from such a purely instrumental expression as the rag. The blues, publicized and brought to national popularity by W. C. Handy just as the rag craze was beginning to die out, undoubtedly made a powerful contribution to the technique of the commercial jazz artist. Part of this contribution led to greater harmonic and melodic subtlety. Ragtime had been rich in the percussive rhythmic elements of the Negro idiom. But it had contained little trace of the Negro's miraculous instinct for harmonization, and no trace whatever of his beautiful and characteristic style in sustained vocal declamation. These things, or their pale reflections, entered the commercial jazz artist's tool kit with the advent of the blues; and the wind instruments of the jazz band provided him with a pliable medium for their exploitation.

Influenced by the blues, the temper of popular music as a whole became warmer, its melodies smoother and its tempos somewhat more deliberate. The enormous popularity of the tango in the early nineteen-tens testified to the need for a more sustained, romantic type of music to relieve the incessant clatter of the rag. But the tango, with its distinctly Latin emphasis, remained an exotic importation. The blues offered an even slower tempo and a more singable melodic line than the comparatively hectic tangos of the period, and coupled these qualities with an idiom that was already deeply established in the American musical consciousness. They also offered Tin Pan Alley an opportunity to get the public appetite focussed on "tunes" again, which must have been somewhat of a relief to Tin Pan Alley's "composers" after a harassing decade of ten-finger pianism.

The style of commercial dance music, then, changed considerably between 1910 and 1920, when what is known as ragtime passed over into what is known as jazz. But this change—important as it was in the fields of melodic style, harmonization, instrumentation and musical form—was not primarily a change in rhythmic structure. The blues provided Tin Pan Alley with new ways of dressing up the Afro-American rhythmic ingredients. The ingredients themselves did not change.

Thus, from the technical point of view, and where rhythm in particular is concerned, the Negro idiom was established in our popular music long before the much heralded advent of jazz. Even printed sheet music testifies to this fact, and print probably followed practice by a lapse of decades. Or, if you want to define it differently, jazz—as a distinct type of rhythmic expression in music—is a far older phenomenon than popular opinion and the journalistic pundits usually concede.

A great deal of the subtlety of form in hot jazz improvisation is inexpressible in musical notation. In much of its detail it is as free and unpredictable as the emotions of the musicians who create it. But even at its freest, it is remarkable how often it exhibits characteristic, measurable elements.

JAZZ INSTRUMENTS

Not all manifestations of hot rhythm are precisely alike. As in most kinds of music, the limitations and aptitudes of the instruments upon which it is played exercise an influence over the product of the jazz musician. Jazz ensembles are usually divided into three departments known technically as "brass," "reeds," and "rhythm." The first comprises the trumpets, trombones, and other instruments of similar construction and technique. The second is represented by the saxophones and such additions in the way of clarinets, oboes, sarrusophones, flutes, and so on, as happen to be at hand. The third department is that of the drums and of instruments whose function in the ensemble is similar to theirs. The piano, the banjo, and the string bass are commonly included under this head.

Now this conventional division into three departments is not merely an arbitrary classification according to principles of instrument construction. It represents a differentiation of three totally distinct types of improvisatory technique. The hot intonations of a jazz trumpeter are quite different from those of a jazz saxophonist. The former's contribution to the ensemble is, as a rule, more oratorical, less precise and florid, than the latter's. And the jazz banjoist functions differently again from either of the others, hewing far more closely, even in his hot solos, to the strict line of fundamental rhythm.

HOT TRUMPET

The trumpet and the trombone are the declamatory, dramatic, emotional voices of the hot ensemble. More than any of the other instruments they approach the role of the human voice. Their inflections are usually closely related to the inflections of speech and song. They are the spokesmen of complete abandon, of ecstasy, of hysteria. Their utterances are the least formal, the least reserved and the most intimate. They speak like the voices of their manipulators, creating their own words in rhythm and tone-color. On the technical and physical side they are admirably equipped for this purpose. They have a larger practical range of dynamics than any of the other instruments. In the hands of a talented hot player they have an amazing variety of timbre, which is employed much as a vocalist employs the shades of color in his voice. The vibrations of trumpet tone are produced by a part of the player's own body. His lips function as do the vocal cords of the singer. And his medium is correspondingly flexible and responsive.

Hot trumpet (and to a slightly lesser extent trombone) solos thus tend to a greater rhythmic and dynamic freedom than do those of the other instruments. From the abstract musical point of view they are often chaotic, resembling recitative or even prose inflection. And the recitative and prose usually bear a close resemblance to Negro speech in their intonations. Crescendos and climbing phrases are infrequent. Explosive attacks are followed by dwindling tone and descending melodic curves. Artificial mutes, the device the Germans call "*flutterzunge*," and a dozen methods of lip and tongue manipulation result in a complete set of what we might with very little inaccuracy term vowel sounds. If the human voice formed an integral part of the generality of jazz ensembles it might, as far as its musical function is concerned, be lumped with the trumpet and trombone as a member of the "brass."

SAXOPHONE AND CLARINET

Upon the "reeds" devolve the more lyric, what from the conventional point of view would be termed the more "musical," aspects of hot melody. While the "brass" produces the exclamation and the rhetoric, the melodic sense rests mostly with the "reeds." Their utterances are more integrated and civilized. Reed solos, as a rule, are more crystallized in musical form. Separate a brass solo from its context and it means very little. Isolate a reed solo similarly and it will usually make some sort of musical sense. Hot reed improvisations tend to be more florid and complex than do brass. For these melodic peculiarities the instruments of the reed department have their appropriate aptitudes. The saxophone is among the easiest and technically most flexible of all wind instruments, and the clarinet is its close second in these respects. When the violin enters into the hot jazz ensemble, its functions are similar. All of these instruments are facile in the articulation of rapid legato passages. All are suited to a more florid, more precise and less emotional sort of expression. The subtleties of jazz "melody," as that word is commonly understood, rest principally with them.

Under "rhythm" are included those instruments whose principal function it is to maintain the constant throbbing that forms the foundation of the jazz edifice: what we have termed for technical purposes the "normal" or "fundamental" rhythm. Their musical excursions are by no means limited, however, to a mere marking of the pulse in four-quarter time.

JAZZ PIANO

The "rhythm" instrument, par excellence, is the piano. I believe it was Stravinsky who remarked some years ago that the piano is essentially a percussion instrument. As employed by the jazz pianist it certainly falls into that category. It is, in fact, a percussion instrument of enormous resource. It possesses the drum's capacity to mark rhythm with incisive blows; and these blows can be struck with infinite gradations of loudness and softness, so that the subtlest contrasts in accentuation are possible. More than all this, the piano can support two or more rhythmic or melodic voices at once: a counterpoint of rhythms can be played on it with ease. Still more it has a complete scale which permits no end of melodic and harmonic variation. It is little wonder that the piano occupies the chief place among all jazz instruments. Jazz without it is a rarity.

Much of the most detailed and complex rhythmic variation of the hot ensemble will be found in the piano part. Like the other instruments of the "rhythm" department, its role is a comparatively unemotional one. It lacks the personal intimacy of the trumpet, and the sustaining quality for lyric melody that the reeds possess. Its scale is fixed: the pianist cannot produce those alterations in intonation that are so important a part of the more vocal type of jazz melody. Its rhythms are for the most part rigid and precise. Among them the regular pulse of the fundamental rhythm usually has a dominating place.

Within far greater limitations as an instrument, the banjo plays a similar role to the piano's. Its common duty is to mark the pulses of the fundamental rhythm with a series of chords. In fulfilling this duty it is, like the string bass, merely a part of the rhythmic background. Occasionally, however, it steps to the front and takes on the tasks of a full-fledged solo instrument. Though its tone, for this purpose, is comparatively weak, it can accomplish certain things which the piano and the remaining "rhythm" instruments can not. Its scale is not fixed like that of the piano. It can deviate, within the limits of its small sustaining power, from established intonation. And it can produce a certain powerful, twanging pulse for rhythmic purposes that is all its own. Like those of the piano, its rhythms are usually clearly defined.

The guitar often replaces the banjo in the jazz ensemble with musical results that are not very different. The complexities of European guitar technique hold little place in the jazz guitarist's repertoire. As used by him it is, like the banjo, a "rhythm" instrument.

HOT DRUMMING

To the piano and banjo must be added those other indispensable members of the "rhythm" section, the drums. Among these instruments of indefinite intonation a variety of tone-color will be found, ranging from the dull thud of the bass drum to the ticking sound produced by hitting the rim of the snare-drum with a wooden stick. In the "sweet" ensembles a great deal of fancy percussion is usually added in this department including wood-blocks, Chinese tom-toms, gongs, cymbals, triangles, anvils, castanets, Chinese temple bells, vibraphones, xylophones, glockenspiel, celestas, and similar exotic paraphernalia. Needless to say such colorful resources do not lead to better or more interesting drumming. The drummer of the hot ensemble usually limits himself to a bass drum, a snare drum and a modest and easily handled assortment of kitchenware. It is the complexity and imagination of his drumming, rather than the instrument it is played on, that attracts musical attention.

The drummer's rhythms are incisive, absolutely precise, and indispensable to the accent and emphasis of a large ensemble. His role is usually a background affair, but its absence would be quickly noted. What the pianist often does as a counterpoint of rhythms, a good drummer is able to do within a single rhythmic voice by differences in accent and tone-color. His role is even more mechanical and impersonal than that of the other "rhythm" players. From the musical point of view the tap dancer represents a branch of the jazz drummer's art. Though his footwork does not form a standard part of the jazz ensemble, its principles of rhythmic improvisation are precisely similar to those of jazz drumming. The differences, musically speaking, are only differences of instrumental medium. The feet of a Bill Robinson tapping on a wooden floor, and the drumsticks of a Gene Krupa tapping on taut calfskin are equivalent, and all the syncopative and polyrhythmic aspects of jazz rhythm are represented in both their arts.

It is hardly necessary to mention the role of the string bass here, or that of the bass tuba or sousaphone which took its place in earlier jazz ensembles. Both are background instruments, useful to mark elementary rhythms and bass notes of prevailing harmonies. Both are too unwieldy to offer much of interest to the present discussion.

Of the three departments of jazz orchestration the utterances of the "rhythm" and "reed" groups are the most easily notated. Indeed, where the "rhythm" instruments are concerned difficulties in the way of exact transcription seldom present themselves. As is to be expected, a larger proportion of mathematically precise rhythmic patterns is to be found in the solos of both "rhythm" and "reed" sections than in the more hectic, emotional playing of the "brasses." Among their contribution one finds polyrhythm and the other formulas of jazz theory embodied with considerable clarity. Yet even in the declamatory phrases of the "brass" there is often a surprising conformity, in rough outline, to the rhythmic patterns we have been describing.

MUSICAL FORM OF JAZZ

Considered as we consider "musical form" in Western music, jazz has a rather elementary structure. The hot ensemble simply presents a theme, which may be improvised or taken from some popular melody, and proceeds to make a series of rhythmic and melodic variations on it. The harmonic structure of the theme is not altered in the variations. The formula is that usually expressed in theory books as $A+A'+A''+A'''$ etc.; in other words the simple theme-and-variation type of structure.

Within the scheme of this formula there are several common variants. Popular Tin Pan Alley songs usually consist of a "verse," or introductory stanza, and a "chorus," which constitutes the main melody. The phraseological structure of these component parts usually answers to common European principles of song form. In semi-improvisatory jazz performance the "chorus," and variations upon it, usually appear more frequently than the "verse" and its variations. There seems to be no precise rule as to which precedes or follows which. The "verse" may even be omitted altogether, and the "chorus" alone used as the theme for the variations. Phraseological structure is usually in units of four, eight or sixteen measures, except in "blues" which are usually laid out in phrases of twelve measures. There are, of course, exceptional forms to be found in more sophisticated hot playing. Some of these are of "fantasy" or "rhapsody" character. They are not common however. It is notable in this connection that the hot ensemble usually sticks to a single key throughout an entire improvisation. It seldom modulates.

The sweet jazz arranger has, of course, developed his more deliberate and more elaborate recipes for giving a jazz tune extended form. These need hardly concern us at length here. Again the process is one of variation form, the completed orchestral version being known, in the language of the craft, as a "routine." A typical routine is laid out as follows:

Introduction (A short phrase in the key of the composition).
(B) Verse (In the original key).
(A) First Chorus (In the original key with slight change in orchestration).
(A′) Second Chorus (In the original key with altogether different orchestration).
(A″) Third Chorus (In a higher key).
> (This is sometimes known as the "Arranger's Chorus" because of the fact that here the greatest liberties of orchestration and rhythmic variation occur.)
(A) Fourth or Final Chorus (In the original key).

There are, of course, many types of routine, some affected by individual arrangers, others more or less standard.

EVALUATION AND CRITICISM

Such "formal" qualities of jazz as these reflect, obviously, the influence of European musical thought. And this influence is to be felt to a certain extent even in the layout of technically hot recordings, based on Tin Pan Alley tunes. The really characteristic aspects of jazz form, however, lie in a dimension that is foreign to the music of the West. To compare the phraseological structure of jazz with that of European music is thus to point out merely superficial resemblances. The phraseology of jazz is related to a wholly different functional plan. Negroid "swing" is found only in a musical art that is unpredictable and impulsive.

It is obvious that jazz responds in several ways to what is loosely spoken of as the "American psychology"; that while its ancestry may be African and European, it is none the less a peculiarly American form of expression. The spontaneous, improvisatory aspect of jazz is remarkably adapted to the musical needs of a pragmatic, pioneering people. Like the typical American the jazz musician goes his own syncopated way, making instantaneous and novel adjustments to problems as they present themselves. He is little concerned about precedent and is inclined to respect that which "works" rather than that which is laid down in theory books. The discipline of tradition "cramps his style." He cannot abide the idea of foregone conclusions: an art-form that demands a beginning, a middle, and an inevitable end is alien to his psychology. His greatest "kick" is in feverish activity, his goal often somewhat indefinite.

Jazz relies on suspense, on sudden adjustments to the unexpected, for its essential vitality. The best of it is created impulsively, and forgotten almost instantly afterward. From its listeners it invites, not contemplation or applause, but participation. It is a "get together" art for "regular fellows." In fact it emphasizes their very "regularity" by submerging individual consciousness in a sort of mass self-hypnotism.

An objective critical attitude is impossible to one who is actually experiencing the appeal of good jazz. The very act of surrendering to its spell destroys automatically the auditor's sense of values, moral or musical. He becomes one of a crowd, his physical movements, feelings, and even thoughts directed by a powerful collective urge. Thus, in a sense, jazz may be spoken of as profoundly "democratic"; democratic, that is, if one strips the term of its positive moral connotations. In the social dimension of jazz, the individual will submits, and men become not only equal but virtually indistinguishable.

The attendant weakness of jazz is that it is an art without positive moral values, an art that evades those attitudes of restraint and intellectual poise upon which complex civilizations are built. At best it offers civilized man only a temporary escape into drunken self-hypnotism. It does not encourage him to strive after anything. It does not offer him ideals, induce him to sacrifice himself for great causes, instill in him a sense of human dignity. It is a far cry from the jazz state of mind to that psychology of human perfectibility, of aspiration, that lies, for example, behind the symphonies of a Beethoven or the music dramas of a Wagner. Indeed, the mere thought of such a comparison makes one ponder how vast and how conflicting is the range and character of human expression commonly included under the term music.

Jazz has, however, its legitimate claims to serious artistic consideration. Despite its limitations, it possesses the indefinable quality which is the hallmark of genuine musical expression. The quality is an elusive one. Critics and pedagogues have never been able to reduce it to a formula; academicians, whether traditional or modernistic, have never imitated it successfully. Yet it is a quality common alike to Beethoven's Ninth Symphony and the most trivial Neapolitan ballad, and one that is easily recognized by the sensitive music-lover. For want of a better word we can call it vitality. Jazz, like most music that is conceived out of full-blooded emotion to fill a real and thirsty demand, has vitality. And this quality causes it to compare favorably with a vast amount of music by contemporary composers, music which aims high but shows, only too evidently, a lack of impelling purpose, a lack of legitimate function. Jazz does not attempt to sound the profounder depths of human emotion; but it gives a meaningful account of some of the shallows.

It would hardly seem necessary to draw any such comparison between jazz and the music of the masters, were it not for the fact that enthusiasts are continually making exaggerated claims for it as an art-form. A decade and a half ago when Whiteman was first seriously presenting large-scale jazz as a concert art and Gershwin's melodious but technically inept *Rhapsody in Blue* was gaining its enormous popularity, there was much talk of sophisticated jazz as "the music of the future." Some even wondered seriously whether it would replace the art of symphonic music, whether America was not on the brink of a musical renaissance in which the Gershwins, Kerns, Confreys, Berlins, *et al.*, would some day figure as Bachs and Buxtehudes. Even critics and musicians who ought to have known better took the question seriously enough to defend, or to attack violently, the position of jazz as a concert art.

More recently a somewhat similar furor arose over the venerable Negroid art of improvisation which was now dubbed "swing." Learned discussions invaded the musical magazines, it became almost sacrilegious to think of dancing to the hotter types of jazz (though dancing was precisely what it would have moved its unaffected Negro listeners to do). People sat in at "jam sessions" with a reverence that they would hardly have accorded a concert of Beethoven's chamber music, discussed gravely the phrasing of this or that hot-lick virtuoso, wrote books in which the most ridiculous superlatives were applied to the improvisatory blaring and thumping of night-club and honky-tonk musicians. Again, under somewhat different auspices, a somewhat different type of jazz became the rage of the intelligentsia. And again all decent regard for the critical verities went to the winds.

Jazz has, for some reason, always been both the most consistently underrated and the most consistently overrated of all arts. There is no doubt in the mind of any tolerant and reasonably sensitive music-lover that good jazz is an interesting and highly stimulating type of music. But the periodic claims of its hysterical devotees inevitably put sensible people on the defensive. Jazz is not an art in the sense that the fine arts of European culture are, or were. It does not demand the creative activity of unusual minds, or the refinement of the faculties through constant study and practice. The jazz artist is no Beethoven. He has a small talent—a sort of talent that is by no means uncommon. He is a "natural musician," with a feeling for certain Negroid rhythmic and melodic styles. What he does involves little study, no meticulous workmanship, no acquaintance with a great tradition of art. It does not necessarily even involve intelligence. It may, in fact, be laid down as a general rule that the more intelligent he is the worse his jazz, and vice-versa. His product may be charming and stimulating. But to compare it with a symphony or a music drama is very much like comparing a crime report in a tabloid newspaper with a novel by Tolstoi.

Meanwhile it is important to distinguish between jazz in its sophisticated metropolitan form, and jazz as a deep-rooted Afro-American social phenomenon. On one hand we have the chatter and sales-talk of individual jazz artists and their press agents and hysterical admirers;

on the other we have a much bigger and profounder thing—a new musical language growing from the cane-brakes and cottonfields of rural America, affecting every stratum of American society, a language certainly capable of expressing deeper matters than those which occupy the world of sophisticated entertainment. The much-acclaimed hot jazz artists of today, like the much-acclaimed Tin Pan Alley composers of yesterday, are merely flecks of foam on the surface of a deep-flowing current. They do not direct or influence the current itself. The current keeps rolling along far from the music marts of Hollywood and Broadway. Its sources lie imbedded in the American soil, fed by generations of America's most patient peasantry, the Negroes of the rural South.

Swing That Music

Extract from the book of that title

By Louis Armstrong

JAZZ is the granddaddy of today's swing music; and though they both came from the same soil, along the lower Mississippi, they have come to be very different kinds of music, as any good musician knows and any good dancer feels. Jazz came up slowly out of the old Negro folk songs and the spirituals, and the regular beat of the jazz syncopation probably came out of the strumming of the banjos which the slaves had learned to play before the Civil War. Some say it went back to the tom-toms of our people in Africa before we were civilized. Anyway, the Mississippi delta country around New Orleans was the birthplace of jazz, and it was New Orleans which first went crazy about it.

Four years before I learned to play the trumpet in the Waifs' Home (1909) the first great jazz orchestra was formed in New Orleans by a cornet player named Dominick James LaRocca. They called him "Nick" LaRocca. His orchestra had only five pieces, but they were the hottest five pieces that had ever been known. LaRocca named his band "The Old Dixieland Jazz Band." He had an instrumentation that made the old songs sound new. Besides himself at the cornet, LaRocca had Larry Shields, clarinet, Eddie Edwards, trombone, Regas, piano, and Sbarbaro, drums. They all came to be famous players, and the Dixieland Band has gone down now in musical history. Some of the great records they made, which carried the new jazz music all over the world in those days, were: *Tiger Rag, Lazy River, Clarinet Marmalade, Ostrich Walk, Sensation, Livery Stable Blues,* and *Toddlin' Blues.* LaRocca retired a few years ago to his home in New Orleans, but his fame as one of the great pioneers of syncopated music will last a long, long time—as long, I think, as American music lives.

But at the time I am now writing of, 1913, the Dixieland Band was getting to be known about far beyond New Orleans, and it was only three years later that LaRocca opened up at Reisenweber's Restaurant in New York. People in the East were dancing to the kind of sweet and soft ballroom music that Meyer Davis and other famous northern ballroom conductors of that time had perfected.

The Dixieland Band changed everything. Pretty soon LaRocca was taking in as much as a thousand dollars a night, and all of New York was strummin' *Lazy Daddy, Sensation,* and *Toddlin' Blues.* The boys would put a tin can painted "Sugar" out on the dance floor in front of them, and when the people got to dancing hot with the music they'd throw money into the sugar can, plenty. Jazz had "gone East" and made good, and LaRocca really took it there and first put it across. It made an easier road for all the others who were very soon to come. A year or so later the Dixieland went to London and had the same success. London kept them there more than a year. The Dixieland Band never went back to New Orleans. In fact, the great combination broke up before 1922. All the boys had made more money than they ever dreamed there was.

Very few of the men whose names have become great in the early days of jazz and of swing were trained in music at all. They were *born* musicians; they felt their music and played by ear and memory. That was the way it was with the great Dixieland Five. None of them could read. But they were musicians, and they made the world say so.

I must not fail to mention Buddy Bolden. So far as any of us know who were born and brought up in New Orleans, and just about saw jazz born, this boy was really the first of them all. He blazed himself into New Orleans, with his cornet, as early as 1905, and they tell me people thought he was plumb crazy the way he tossed that horn. Buddy got to drinking too much—staying up two or three nights a week without sleep and going right on to work again, just like many hot musicians. He was the rage at all the smart private parties in town. He was gone, as I remember, when the Dixieland came along. But while he was undoubtedly the first great individual jazz player, he never had a band like the Dixieland and never got to be known outside of New Orleans.

Around 1909, when the Dixieland started cutting the hot new music, a lot of players began to take it up in the cabarets, and pretty soon New Orleans was clean mad with it. Many of the old plantation songs and the popular tunes of the day were being played in the new jazz rhythms, and new tunes were being composed that were hotter and hotter. All of a sudden came along those two great songs, *Memphis Blues* and *St. Louis Blues*. My, they were hot and how we all loved them! They were written by a colored composer named W. C. Handy who lived in Memphis. He had caught jazz from some of the players on the Mississippi River boats. Handy's name will go on as long as jazz does because of those two early songs, if for nothing else. He lives today in Harlem, New York, and has his own music-publishing house, and every jazz musician everywhere honors him.

After that, nothing much was played but the new style of music. From the big star cabarets down to the lowest honky-tonks and gin-mills, it was all jazz, and the players who could do best at it were in great demand.

One of the front men was Joe Oliver, later to be known as "King" Oliver; of all the others of that day, "Papa Joe" (as I have always called him) was the one who was to travel farthest along the road that the old Dixieland pioneered.

You'll notice that none of the early orchestras used either the piano or the saxophone. In fact, the sax just came into general use as late as about 1917. Often as not, they didn't even use drums.

One of the hottest clarinetists then was a young genius named Sydney Bachet. He is now a featured man with Noble Sissle's Band, playing soprano sax. Bachet teamed up with Ed Atkins, trombone, and the pair of them struck out from New Orleans to see the world. They actually got to London ahead of the Dixieland, which arrived about the end of 1917, and those two boys took old London by storm. Nobody there had ever heard anything like it. Later on Bachet toured the Continent with Jim Europe's band.

Among others of that original group of great players who lived jazz, ate jazz, and brought jazz into being, I must mention Emmanuel Perez, who played hot trumpet. Emmanuel couldn't speak so much English, but, boy, his horn could talk in *any* man's language! He didn't have an orchestra—he had a ten-piece brass band. It was composed as follows: three trumpets, two trombones, alto horn, baritone horn, E-flat clarinet, bass drum, and snare drum. He called it the "Onward Brass Band." He began playing jazz, in brass, about 1910—I remember as a kid of ten years old I was so crazy about Perez' brass band I would follow them on the streets when they paraded with the Elks and Moose and other societies. Now the marching brass bands in the North never went in for jazz—always straight march time and all that. But in New Orleans it was different. All the brass bands would swing jazz like the orchestras—even the drummer had a swing.

Down there everybody was music crazy. I used to follow brass bands all day. Later on, after I left the Waifs' Home, I joined one of them, the Tuxedo Brass Band. Often we'd play at funerals. We'd play sad music when we took them to the grave; then, when the brother was buried and we were bringing them back to Lodge Hall, we'd play swing music, because they needed cheering up.

"King" Oliver played his trumpet in Perez' Brass Band and also had his own orchestra, "The Magnolia"—another of the finest in New Orleans. His instrumentation was ace trumpet (Oliver himself), clarinet, trombone, guitar, bass violin, violin, and drums—seven pieces.

Jazz began to spread, little by little, onto the big excursion boats that used to play the Mississippi River ports. From New Orleans to St. Paul, from the river on to Chicago, east to New York. That was the path jazz followed. But it took a whole quarter of a century for it to make the trip—and to bring it finally to the music we know today as *swing*.

There are millions of people who don't like or do not yet understand American jazz music; in fact, they seem to hate it. They do not seem to see the difference between trashy, popular jazz and fine swing music. So they will turn off their radios when a fine swing orchestra starts to play; they would rather hear some "sweet" band play—the kind all hot-musicians call *corny*. They do not understand.

A musician who plays in "sweet" orchestras must be like a writer who writes stories for popular magazines. He has to follow the same line all the time, and write what he thinks the readers want just because they're used to it. That keeps him writing the same kind of thing year after year. But a real swing musician never does that. He just plays, feels as he goes, and swings as he feels. That is why real swing musicians are great. They start in and play for fun. Each one plays the instrument he likes best and plays it in his own way, with everything in him. If one of them is lucky and has the breaks and finally gets to be well known and makes some money—well, it's so much velvet! But most of the boys never do. Buddy Bolden was only one of many truly great swing players I have known who never got to be heard of outside a small circle.

For a man to be a good swing conductor, he should have been a swing player himself, for then he knows a player is no good if the leader doesn't let him "go to town" when he feels like going. That phrase "goin' to town" means cuttin' loose and takin' the music with you, whatever the score may call for. Any average player, if he's worth anything at all, can follow through a score, as it's written there in front of him on his instrument rack. But it takes a swing player, and a real good one, to be able to leave that score and to know, or "feel," just when to leave it and when to get back on it. No conductor can tell him, because it all happens in a second and it doesn't happen the same way any two times running. It is just the liberty that every individual player must have in a real swing orchestra that makes it most worth listening to. Every time they play there is something new swinging into the music to make it hot and interesting. *Hot*, as swing musicians use the word, does not necessarily mean loud, or even fast. It is used when a swing player gets warmed up and "feels" the music taking hold of him so strong that he can break through the set rhythms and the melody and toss them around as he wants without losing his way. That creates new effects and is done whether the music is loud or soft, or fast or slow.

You will think that, if every man in a big sixteen-piece band had his own way and could play as he wanted, all you would get would be a lot of jumbled up, crazy noise. This is true with ordinary players, and that is why most bands have to play "regular" and their conductors can't let them leave their music as it is scored. The conductor himself may decide on certain variations—an "arrangement," they call it—but the players have to follow that scoring. In that way the conductor or "arranger" may write some hot phrasing into an old score and, to those who don't know, the orchestra may seem to be "swinging." But when you've got a real bunch of swing players together in an orchestra, you can turn them loose for the most part. "Give 'em their head," as they say of a race horse. They all play together, picking up and following each other's "swinging," all by ear and sheer musical instinct. It takes a very fine ear and some years of playing to do that. That is why there have been so few really fine swing orchestras in the world. First you have to get a combination of natural swing players, and then they've got to learn how to play in and out together as one man. No conductor can make them do it, or even show them much how to. His biggest part is to make suggestions and try to get them into a good humor and then let them alone. And I mean alone! If he doesn't—if he starts telling one man just how to play this part, and another how to play another part— pretty soon he'll ruin his orchestra: he'll have one that just plods along with the score, playing regular, and all the life will be gone out of the men. Swing players have got to have a good time when they are playing and they can't have a good time—playing and rehearsing as they do twelve and fourteen hours a day—if you just make machines out of them.

Swing music is America's second big bid to bring forth a worth-while music of its own. The first big attempt was in the early days of jazz. We can look back now and see the mistakes and see about where jazz got side-tracked. We won't have many excuses if we let today's swing music go the same way. Jazz lost its originality and freshness and stopped growing. It stopped early. As it came to be written down and recorded in all the thousand and one jazz songs of later years, it was not musically rich enough. Take almost any one of those songs, even a big hit, and keep playing it over the way it was composed and written, and pretty soon it gets tiresome and you want to hear a new tune. That is why you got a big vogue for one tune, and then in a few months it sounded stale—and another one would come along. And yet many of those songs had a lot to them underneath. My own swing orchestra can take one of the old favorites, like *Chinatown,* and swing it so that a new kind of beauty and fuller "body" comes into it. Another old-timer we swing is the great pioneer jazz song, *St. Louis Blues.* That was written back in 1914 and it still stands head and shoulders above most. Jazz needed constant improvisation and experimentation before it could grow into a richer music.

The writers of jazz have not developed jazz music much during all these years, although a few men must be given credit. But for the most part the new songs that have been coming out of Tin Pan Alley are not really new at all. They are the same old melodies and rhythms just twisted around in a different way and with different words— coarse beats or sticky sweet phrases and all that, year after year. It makes good musicians tired, and it is no wonder that a big part of the public is tired of it too. And the people who like it least are the swing musicians, for they are the very ones who are doing most to break up these worn-out patterns. The reason swing musicians insist upon calling their music *swing* is that they know how different it is from the stale brand of jazz they've got so sick of hearing. But in the early days jazz wasn't that way at all. It was the first crude form of today's swing—the daddy of swing—and it was "going places" until it got all tangled up in Tin Pan Alley and made fortunes for men who couldn't swing a jew's-harp. That is the real truth.

GLOSSARY OF SWING TERMS

GUTBUCKET—Swing in Blues fashion, disconsolate.

IN THE GROOVE—When carried away or inspired by the music, when playing is exalted spirit and to perfection.

JAM SESSION—An informal meeting of musicians playing for their own amusement, swinging without leadership or score; an experimental session.

PAPERMAN—A musician who plays only written music, as written.

RIDE—Easy-going rhythm.

SCREWBALL—Crazy, extremely unbridled swing.

WHACKY—Same as above, only noisier, more discordant.

OUT OF THE WORLD—Same as "In the Groove."

WAXING—Recording for phonograph records.

ALLIGATOR—A non-playing swing devotee, a listener.

BARREL-HOUSE—Every man for himself, playing without regard for what the others are playing.

CATS—The musicians of a swing orchestra.

LICKING THEIR CHOPS—Getting warmed up to swing.

FRISKING THEIR WHISKERS—Same as above.

COFFEE-AND-CAKE—Very poor pay for a job, often only carfare.

COLLEGIATE—Extremely slow swing music.

COMMERCIAL—Appealing to the uninitiated public, compromise swing.

CORNY—The "razz-mah-jazz" style of the Twenties.

GANG—A medley of songs.

GETTING OFF—Commencing to swing.

LICK—An original interpolated phrasing.

BREAK—Dropping the rhythm for a few beats.

DIXIELAND—The original New Orleans jazz as developed by the famous Dixieland Five.

SOCK CHORUS—Last chorus of arrangement.

MUGGING LIGHT—Soft, staccato swinging.

MUGGING HEAVY—As above, with heavier beat.

WOODSHED—To experiment in private with a new song.

KICKING OUT—Very free, enthusiastic improvisation.

SITTING IN—When an outside musician drops in by invitation to play with a swing band or group.

SWINGMAN—A swing musician.

SENDER—A word or a phrase that sends a band into swing playing, as "Swing it, boys!" or "In the groove!" or "Let's mug one for the folks!"

The Kingdom of Swing

Extract from the book of that title

By Benny Goodman

[*Following a description of his boyhood in Chicago, and his early interest in music, Mr. Goodman tells of his first stage appearance.*]

WHEN I was twelve, something happened that was pretty important to me. Somehow we had gotten hold of one of those old phonographs with a horn, and Charlie used to bring home records. One of them was played by Ted Lewis, who we figured was a pretty hot clarinet player. Charlie used to play this thing by the hour, and after a while I got so that I could play the tune just the way Lewis did. Charlie thought this was too good to keep in the family, and since he was always a promoter at heart, tried to figure out some way of making use of it. He heard that the Central Park Theatre on the West Side put on "Jazz Nights" every Thursday, which was something like an amateur night.

It was quite a thrill when I went there the first time, dressed in a Buster Brown collar, with one of those bow ties. Before this my father, who was very much interested in the Workmen's Circle in Chicago, had taken me to meetings with him several times on Sunday nights, and sometimes I would play if they had a little concert. Charlie got the manager to hear me play, and they put me on. Since I was only twelve, the manager figured he might get in trouble if he put me up on the stage. So I stood down in the orchestra pit, on a box the conductor used. I must have done all right, because a couple of weeks later, when one of his acts folded up, the manager sent for me to fill in. I was out on the street playing shinny, but I grabbed the clarinet and hustled around to the theater, for my first professional engagement. You can imagine how I looked in short pants up on the platform, weighing about seventy-five pounds *with* the clarinet in my hand. It was a daytime show, so that it was all right for me to play from the stage. The applause was nice, but the five bucks they paid me was even better, because it was the first money I ever earned playing clarinet.

[*After playing in a settlement-house band, Benny and his brother Harry got a chance to play with professionals.*]

The combination of the two things—the fact that we began to make some money by playing and were sitting in with professionals—gave us the idea that maybe we could do ourselves some good if we had a regular combination of our own. So Harry and I went looking around the neighborhood for kids who played instruments. We had fiddle, piano, clarinet, cornet, and tuba before long, but the big thrill came when we found a kid who could play both snare *and* bass drums at the same time. We had been playing with separate bass and snare because we always played with band musicians. When we got set up with a real snare and bass combination, we sure felt that we were getting some place. We rehearsed on Friday nights, playing from stocks, but we didn't stick to them much after we got a chorus or two worked out. I always liked to play free, from the very start, and when we got hold of a new chord or a good lick that was thrill like nothing else.

We usually changed around from week to week, playing at the kids' places, but whenever one of the other fellows' folks objected to us playing there, we generally came back to our house. My father was always glad to have us, just as he was always glad to do anything for us kids that he could. He was the one in the family that always encouraged us in our music, and the more we played the better he liked it. I was practicing quite a bit now, and you could hear it all over the house. Together with the "El" that passed by pretty close, it made quite a racket, I guess—and it wouldn't be long before my mother would come to the door and say: "*Genug*, Benny! Still."

We had some pretty promising kids in those little bands. As for style, it was pretty much every man for himself, because none of us knew quite what we were trying to do. My idea of a great clarinet (since I had passed out of the Ted Lewis stage) was Leon Rapollo, who was playing at the Friar's Inn then with the New Orleans Rhythm Kings, and I did my best to sound like him. I never heard him play in person more than once, but there were plenty of good records to study up on.

When I had been playing these jobs for a few months, a lucky thing happened for me, early in 1923. During a dance one afternoon, a fellow named Charlie Podolsky came up to me, and said he liked my playing. The fellows called him "Murph." He was a little older than we were, and had some connections out at Northwestern, where he had a little band and also booked name bands for house parties and proms. Naturally we youngsters thought he was an important guy. He asked me if I would like to play some dates with him. Well, there was no question that I wanted to play, but first I had to join the union. I got my first card soon after that, in the American Musicians' Union, a kind of minor league outfit, when I was still thirteen years old.

I jobbed around with "Murph" quite a bit after that, playing whatever dates there were. I remember some at Northwestern and Chicago U., the first time I ever played college dates. During the day I was still wearing short pants, but when I went out to play a job I looked so young that "Murph" made me get long pants to wear on the band stand. Of course, by this time I had my own clarinet, a swell Martin that my sister Ethel helped me to get. She was also responsible for my first "tux," which I needed for work. At that time she was working for a clothing firm as a bookkeeper, and I went down there to see about a suit. But I was so small that none of the ready-made suits fitted me. So they made one to order for me, for which she paid by working extra. That was the first tuxedo in the Goodman family, a very big thrill.

I also started to pick up sax about this time, and tried to argue the folks at home into seeing that I ought to have it. They thought I should stick to clarinet, but I knew that being able to double would help me get more jobs, so I bought it out of the money I was earning. The folks could hardly believe their eyes when I walked in one night with that big thing under my arm.

Working with "Murph" broke me into the business of playing regularly late at night, and coming home on the Chicago Street Railway or the "El." Sometimes I would fall asleep on the way home, and occasionally I was so exhausted that I left my clarinet on the train, and we'd have to go down to the Lost and Found office the next day to get it back. Being forgetful about my instrument is something that goes on even today.

[*Benny Goodman migrated to New York City, and the next passage describes the situation he found there.*]

To understand the situation in music around 1929, it is necessary to appreciate the fact that the public at large didn't have much contact with the men who actually played the music. They might know about a band by name, but nobody put the names of musicians on the labels of records (as they do now) or featured them outside of a theater—unless they could play "Nola" on a bicycle pump. The leader was the top man, and that's all there was to it.

Consequently, most of the really fine players of the time—fellows like Teagarden, "Bix," Eddie Lang, Jimmy McPartland, Coleman Hawkins, Earl Hines, the Dorseys, Teschmaker, Joe Sullivan, and so on —were known only among musicians. When I say musicians, I mean those fellows who appreciated that style of playing and listened to it by the hour on records (as all of us did). I just mentioned a few colored musicians, but they hadn't come in as yet for much recognition from the public, except if they heard them in some such show as *Blackbirds* or *Shuffle Along,* or up in Harlem at Connie's Inn or the Cotton Club. There were a few enthusiasts around who knew what musicians played every solo on the good records, but they were scattered all over the map.

The result of all this was that musicians who played hot were pretty much of a clique by themselves. They hung around in the same places, made the same spots after work, drank together and worked together whenever they had the chance. A fellow who came to town with something different in the way of style and ideas found that the news traveled pretty quickly. Within a month or so everybody in town would have made the spot where he was working, and passed on his ability. If the verdict was favorable, he would be recognized as having made the grade, and from that time on, various odd jobs might come his way—playing records, or clubbing around when his band was laying off, or getting spots on a radio program. Musicians would tell one another about him, and the contractors would know that so-and-so was the man to have on a certain date, all before the public ever heard of him or even knew he existed.

Along in November, "Red" Nichols got the job to play in the pit for the Gershwin show *Strike Up the Band,* which was just going into rehearsal. For this Babe Rusin came into the band, along with Glenn Miller and Gene Krupa—which made it just about the best line-up of hot men that had yet played a Broadway show.

I lived out in Jackson Heights for a time, and then I took an apartment with Jimmy Dorsey on West 58th Street. I had always liked Jimmy and we got along pretty well together. There was one trouble, however. Both of us were doing a lot of jobbing around, playing record dates and parties or radio jobs as they came along, and the 'phone was ringing practically all the time. That was fine, except that both Jimmy and I played clarinet and sax, and whoever grabbed the 'phone first got the job. Sometimes the race wound up in a tie, and one of us would be accepting the job through the mouthpiece, while the other was finding out where it was through the receiver.

Unfortunately Jimmy and I couldn't get into the same clothes, but there was plenty of swapping in ties and socks. We didn't care much about this, but it was a different proposition when one of us found a good reed. He'd practically have to sleep with it or else it would be gone the next day. Since good reeds are comparatively scarce, it was more likely that we'd be taking turns playing them from one room to the other, with Jimmy giving me his opinion of how the one I had sounded, and vice versa.

Getting a band together is not too difficult if you have plenty of money, or backing, or a name as a leader, or at least a definite job in view. As it happened, when I started out one day in March 1934, I had none of these things. I had an idea of what I wanted to do (not a very clear one at that), the knowledge that there was a job open if I could click; and, of course, I knew a flock of musicians. However, many of the fellows I would have liked to have were tied up with jobs (like Jack Teagarden, whom I naturally thought of right away; he had a contract with Whiteman by that time). They were making pretty good money and were not going to give it up just on a gamble.

What I was looking for primarily were young fellows with good musicianship, who could read and play in tune, also who wanted to play in a free style but never had the chance. Willingness and a spirit of co-operation were also important because, as I said, there was no special thing in view, and the whole scheme might come to nothing.

Moreover, when I explained that I was trying to get a band to-gether that would play dance music in a free and musical style—in other words, in the way that most good musicians wanted to play but weren't allowed to on the ordinary job—I got a response right away.

The point was that no white band had yet gotten together a good rhythm section that would kick out, or jump, or rock or swing—all expressions describing the life and vitality that comes from music that is played at just the right tempo with a lot of enthusiasm and unified rhythm snap; using arrangements that fit in with this idea, which would give the men a chance to play solos and express the music in their own individual way.

It was about this time, or maybe just a little earlier, that large bands became standardized with five brass, four saxes, and four rhythm (piano, guitar, drums, and bass). I would have much preferred this set-up to the one I had with three saxes, but since I played a reed instrument myself that rather made up for it, inasmuch as the budget wouldn't allow an additional man. It's a funny thing how the set-up of a jazz band finally worked around to this combination, because ten men (with at least one fiddle) used to be considered the limit of even a large dance orchestra. But first the banjo went out in favor of the guitar; then the string bass took the place of the tuba; and finally the fiddle disappeared (except in "society" orchestras), leaving only a few specialists—Venuti, Eddie South and Stuff Smith—to show that it had been there.

Gradually arrangers found that three trumpets and two trom-bones give the best effect in the brass section, and that you could do a lot more, in the way of voicing and variety of effects, with four sax than you could with two or three. As for rhythm, it has never been pos-sible to have a band with swing unless you had a really good rhythm section. That was one of our main ideas right from the start.

Getting in front of a band for the first time, working with a bunch of musicians to get some unity out of a dozen different ways of playing, brought a lot of things to my attention I had never been conscious of before. I didn't go at all for the idea of a leader standing in front of a jazz band and making a lot of motions, as if he were conducting some-thing by Bach or Mozart.

With a dance band, what there is in the way of effects has to be done in the rehearsals, or it isn't done at all. My idea was to get good musicians, work on intonation, a blend of tone and uniform phrasing in rehearsals, and then depend on them to take care of themselves pretty much on the stand. The main thing a leader has to do out in front is to kick off the music at the right tempo. If the boys are playing a little too loud or too soft, a simple little gesture, just holding a hand up or something like that, is enough to tone them down or bring them up. When we are playing things in which the various soloists take choruses, a nod of the head or a pointed finger tells the boys who's next, if the piece has no set formula. One finger held up means another chorus for the soloist who is playing, and if I clench my fist the boys know that we take the final chorus of the arrangement on the next time around. As for the kind of "showmanship" that goes with waving a stick, I never cared much for it. Moreover, if I did any conducting, I wouldn't be able to play as much as I wanted—and that was one of the big ideas I had in getting a band together: to be able to play the way I wanted to. I figured that if the music was good, it would sell itself to the public without a lot of gestures.

By the time we finished our job in *The Big Broadcast of 1937,* which was made in the summer of 1936, we had a pretty good idea that the public for real jazz was a big one, and growing all the time. But I don't think that any of us realized how strong a hold it had on the youngsters until a certain day early in March 1937.

We had undertaken to double at the Paramount Theater in New York in addition to playing our job at the Pennsylvania, with no expectation that we would do more than fair business. After all, our only previous theater bookings had been something less than sensational. So when we arrived at the theater for an early morning rehearsal before the first show and found a couple of hundred kids lined up in front of the box-office at about 7 A.M., we couldn't help feeling that every one of our most loyal supporters in the five boroughs was already on hand.

The theater was completely full an hour before we were supposed to go on, and when we finally came up on the rising platform, the noise sounded like Times Square on New Year's Eve. It certainly was a lot different from the days when I played on that same platform with Eddie Paul's orchestra.

The crowd quieted down a little when the band started in, but even on stage you could get an undercurrent of intense excitement. That reception topped anything we had known up to that time, and because we felt it was spontaneous and genuine, we got a tremendous kick out of it. It's only in these latter days, when some of the youngsters just come to cut up, that it gets in our way. After all, if a fellow like Jess Stacy or Ziggy Elman or Vernon Brown gets up to play a solo, he has a right to be heard.

However, we didn't know half the story until we got off the stage and were back in our dressing-rooms. It seems that Willard was sitting in the mezzanine with Bob Weitman, the manager of the Paramount. They got the same thrill out of this enthusiasm that we did, up to the point where a couple of youngsters got up and started to shag in the aisles. Then a few more started to climb over the rail towards the orchestra, and Bob jumped up and rushed out, yelling: "Somebody's going to get hurt there any minute. There'll be a panic."

He ran down the steps to the back of the orchestra, and as soon as the ushers saw him, they snapped to attention and started saluting. "The hell with that," he shouted. "Get down there and stop those kids from killing themselves!"

As he went down the aisle to get the ushers organized, he had to go through the same routine of being saluted by each one before he could get things under control.

By three o'clock in the afternoon, 11,500 people had paid their way into the theater, and the total for the first day's attendance was 21,000.

It was during this engagement that we found out what this particular sort of success means. We played five shows a day at the Paramount, beginning around 10:30 in the morning, and in between the two evening shows we did our usual stint at the Pennsylvania, going back there after the last show (about 10:30) to finish up the dance session, until 2 A.M. Then, of course, there was the radio commercial once a week, with the special rehearsals that go with it. There was also the problem of moving the stuff up to the studio, which in our case is the C.B.S. Radio Theater.

It got so that the only time I saw the sunlight was when we were going to the theater in the morning, because I never got out of my dressing-room during the day, and by the time we went to the hotel in the evening it was dark. I wasn't squawking, of course, because I came up in this business the hard way, and I know that the time to complain is not when there are so many things to do that you haven't the time to do them all, but when you start having time on your hands. But the funny thing is this—when the public wants you, they want you all the time; and when they don't, they don't want you even a little bit.

Right after this we got the first taste of what comes with being a really successful band. I didn't have any more love for one-nighters than I had before, but that summer we filled a schedule of bookings that lasted almost two months, and we never played the same town twice. As a matter of fact, we finished up with a string of thirty consecutive dates on as many nights, in the middle of a broiling mid-West July.

Traveling with a band on tour is the next thing I can think of to moving a circus. There's the music to be taken care of, the instruments to be checked, the trunks and other baggage to keep in line—all of which is in the care of a general handyman, porter, and looker-outer.

On a typical one-nighter around the New York territory, we travel in a Greyhound bus that stays with us throughout the entire tour. Generally it rolls up to the place late in the afternoon, and if we haven't been there before, we have to find out about the P.A. (the public address system) and hook up the one we carry along, if the permanent installation isn't any good. Then the stands have to be set up and the music laid out—and in most places, some kind of rope or a guard rail put around the stand so that we can work without stepping on the fingers of the kids that hang around the band.

By this time Hymie Schertzer's nose for corned beef has led him, without fail, to the best place in town for his favorite food, and a few of the boys go along with him. The rest of us pick out some likely-looking place for the kind of food we want, and get through with the meal just in time to change our clothes and get on the band stand. The crowd starts coming in, the requests start piling up, and another job is under way.

What I admire most in a musician, of course, is really good ideas —the ability to say something with his playing. After that comes competence—which includes a thorough knowledge of his own instrument (and maybe one or two others), the ability to read off a part at sight at least fairly well, and the experience in the business to take care of himself in a pinch. The really good musicians have it in any field, regardless of whether it's jazz or concert music.

For example, two things happened within a few days of each other last winter, when we were at the Paramount in New York. I was playing the Mozart concerto at a Sunday night concert at the Waldorf with an orchestra of Philharmonic men, and as an encore we thought it would be a good stunt to do Alec Templeton's *Bach Goes to Town*. The audience liked it a lot, and we decided to repeat the number. It happened that Buddy Schutz, our drummer, who played the cymbal part that goes all the way through the piece, disappeared when we finished the performance, and figured he was through for the night. So Sol Goodman, the wonderful timpani player of·the Philharmonic, picked up Buddy's part, and played it right along with his own part, at sight, jumping from one to the other as he got the chance. That was real musicianship, and I sure got a kick out of it.

Maybe that's why I am such a bug on accuracy in performance, about playing in tune and with just the proper note values—because I think that a good musician should do that automatically when he sees something in an arrangement. For example, when we first rehearsed Edgar Sampson's *Don't Be That Way,* some of the fellows were playing a triplet uneven—with more time on one note than another—instead of making them all even. Well, we went over that and rehearsed it as carefully as we could, till everybody was playing it just the same way. That was one of the reasons that we got such a terrific rock on that arrangement, and why it turned out to be one of the biggest things we ever had.

That's why I get such a lift out of playing with people like Josef Szigeti, the wonderful Hungarian violinist, or the Budapest String Quartet. Not that I want to make any comparisons between Mozart and Edgar Sampson, or Bartók and Fletcher Henderson; but just as a matter of playing what is written in the score, I discovered that they go about things pretty much the same way.

In rehearsing a Bartók piece I played with Szigeti, I got a marvelous lesson just from working with him, and seeing the way he went about studying something. Most people that come to hear what is called "modern music" in the concert halls just sit down and listen, and when it is over say "I liked that" or "I didn't like that." I don't think they have any idea what a man like Bartók puts into a score, how each note has its own place and meaning. The way Szigeti explained the score, and the way we worked it out in rehearsals—noticing how in one place you'd come across an idea that had first occurred a while back, only here it was in a different rhythm, or turned upside down, or one instrument was playing a part of it while the other instrument answered with a different part—you realized it was all completely logical and carefully worked out.

These links between jazz music and concert-hall music really exist (as more people are finding out all the time) and maybe that explains why I can get a kick out of playing both. In jazz it's the feeling of freedom, of being able to take a chorus in the low register if you feel like it, or go up high if that's the way you happen to want to play it; or—if in the middle of playing *One o'Clock Jump* I hear Jess Stacy get off on a certain train of ideas—of picking it up and playing around with it in my own way; or—if I get an idea for a background phrase to play against the trombone or trumpet solo—to pass it along to the saxes and work it up with them.

In other kinds of music, it's the idea of measuring yourself against what a great composer was thinking, of playing with a fine quality of tone and blending in with the other instruments, phrasing with them, and trying to hit just the right tempo in which the music sounds best. When everything blends, and all the players feel the same idea back of what they're playing—well, that's the thing jazz musicians mean when they say that something swings.

The Relation of Jazz to American Music

By George Gershwin

From "American Composers on American Music," ed. by Henry Cowell

THE great music of the past in other countries has always been built on folk music. This is the strongest source of musical fecundity. America is no exception among the countries. The best music being written today is music which comes from folk sources. It is not always recognized that America has folk music; yet it really has not only one but many different folk musics. It is a vast land, and different sorts of folk music have sprung up in different parts, all having validity, and all being a possible foundation for development into an art-music. For this reason, I believe that it is possible for a number of distinctive styles to develop in America, all legitimately born of folk song from different localities. Jazz, ragtime, Negro spirituals and blues, Southern mountain songs, country fiddling, and cowboy songs can all be employed in the creation of American art-music, and are actually used by many composers now. These composers are certain to produce something worth while if they have the innate feeling and talent to develop the rich material offered to them. There are also other composers who can be classed as legitimately American who do not make use of folk music as a base, but who have personally, working in America, developed highly individualized styles and methods. Their new-found materials should be called American, just as an invention is called American if it is made by an American!

Jazz I regard as an American folk music; not the only one, but a very powerful one which is probably in the blood and feeling of the American people more than any other style of folk-music. I believe that it can be made the basis of serious symphonic works of lasting value, in the hands of a composer with talent for both jazz and symphonic music.

Men of Jazz

Extracts from "Our Contemporary Composers"

By John Tasker Howard

LOUIS ARMSTRONG, one of the very top names in jazz, famous Negro trumpet player; born in New Orleans in 1900, played first there, later in Chicago, and in recent years in New York, various capitals of Europe, and anywhere else he has wanted to. Of him Virgil Thomson has written that he is "a master of musical art comparable only . . . to the great *castrati* of the eighteenth century. His style of improvisation would seem to have combined the highest reaches of instrumental virtuosity with the most tensely disciplined melodic structure and the most spontaneous emotional expression, all of which in one man you must admit to be pretty rare."

William ("Count") Basie, Negro pianist and leader of one of the leading big bands—big, that is, for a "swing" band, consisting of more than a dozen men.

Leon Bismarck ("Bix") Beiderbecke, Chicago cornetist, who, because his untimely death in 1931 ended playing which is described as unique in tone, rhythm, and melodic line, endlessly inventive, yet restrained, is reverenced to an extraordinary degree among swing musicians and enthusiasts.

Jimmy and Tommy Dorsey, brothers, each of whom leads a famous band. Jimmy plays the clarinet and the alto saxophone; Tommy is a virtuoso on the trombone. For Tommy Dorsey's band, Roy Harris wrote his Fourth Symphony.

Edward K. ("Duke") Ellington, who perhaps vies with Louis Armstrong for the title of best-known Negro jazz musician. Ellington, born in Washington, D.C., in 1899, is a brilliant jazz pianist, leader, and composer—not only a collaborator in composition, like all these men, but a composer in his own right. It should be said that the members of his band "compose along with him," but the basic ideas, melodic, orchestral, and formal, are his. His band is one of the larger groups. Through his records and his radio broadcasts, Ellington enjoys one of the biggest reputations in the field. He played for several years in Paris, and is well known throughout Europe as well as at home. *Mood Indigo* and *Solitude* are among his best-known pieces.

Benny Goodman, clarinetist extraordinary, whose talents and whose very well managed publicity together have crowned him "King of Swing." (It is not so many years since Whiteman was the "King of Jazz"; that King is not dead, so long live the Kings!) Nothing is too good for Goodman, neither the Waldorf-Astoria, where he played regularly for a time, nor the Mozart Clarinet Quintet, which he has played and recorded with the Budapest Quartet, nor Béla Bartók, who wrote a work for him and the violinist Szigeti. Conservative critics have found his playing of the classic repertoire perhaps a little academic, but in no way objectionable; commerce has smiled on him, for he has had perhaps the most sensational success of recent years in the field of jazz; and yet the jazz authorities include him in their Pantheon. The gods are not so good to many.

William Christopher Handy, sometimes called the Father of the Blues, composer of the most famous blues tune, the *St. Louis Blues,* born November 16, 1873 in Florence, Alabama, son of a Negro preacher. The *Memphis Blues* is Handy's, too; likewise the *Beale Street* and *Yellow Dog.* The *Memphis Blues* was published in 1912, and the *St. Louis Blues* shortly afterwards; both are still favorite tunes among all types of jazz musicians.

Coleman Hawkins, who, according to Hobson, "has been to the tenor saxophone what Armstrong has to the trumpet." He has been a member of bands led by Joe Oliver, Fletcher Henderson, and "Count" Basie, among others.

The brothers Fletcher and Horace Henderson, the former a noted Negro band leader, and the latter a pianist, arranger, and composer (of the "hot jazz" rather than the "commercial" type). Fletcher Henderson is also a pianist. The Henderson brothers have specialized in scores designed to support and furnish a background for brilliant solo improvising by members of the band.

Gene Krupa, an outstanding jazz drummer. The term "drummer" really means percussionist, of course, for drums are only a part of the equipment of the "rhythm section," which, in addition to piano and plucked string instruments (banjo, string-bass, guitar), includes a battery of what used to be known as "traps." The era of using tin pans, cowbells, and anything else both unconventional and noisy to give the effect of great vitality is largely past. The jazz drummer of today relies on subtler and more genuine means of stimulating his comrades and infusing them with the tempo. It is for them at least as much as for any listeners that he plays.

Meade ("Lux") Lewis, famous "boogie-woogie" pianist, who, at the time (1936) when he made some recordings which have been very popular, was washing automobiles in a Chicago garage. An element of his style is the use of an ostinato figure in the left hand, in some characteristic, rolling rhythm, with free improvisation in the right.

Milfred Mole, trombonist, whose attractive name is immortalized on records made by "Miff Mole and his little Molers."

Loring ("Red") Nichols, who often played with "Miff" and was well known some years ago to record buyers and radio listeners as the leader of "Red Nichols and his Five Pennies."

Joe ("King") Oliver, trumpeter, originally from New Orleans, where he taught and inspired Louis Armstrong to play the trumpet; later of Chicago, where his band at the Lincoln Gardens attracted great attention in the early 1920's.

Bill Robinson, the king of tap-dancers, whose feet are as expressive a pair of musical instruments as any percussion instrument very well could be. Robinson is not as young as he used to be, but as late as the New York World's Fair of 1939 his dancing in *The Hot Mikado* —a partially jazzed version of the Gilbert and Sullivan classic—was telling more than volumes of analysis and criticism ever could about the nature and the origins of jazz.

"Pee Wee" Russell, clarinetist and saxophonist, specialist in improvisation of the "hotter" and "dirtier" variety. (For "dirty," an older generation would have said simply "tough.")

Bessie Smith, "Empress of the Blues," some of whose robust and heartfelt singing was gathered into a special memorial record album shortly after her death in an automobile accident in 1938.

Joe Sullivan, Chicago pianist, whose conservatory training did not spoil him for hot jazz, and who has played with Louis Armstrong, Benny Goodman, and others at the top of the business.

Jack Teagarden, remarkable trombonist, originally from Texas, who has belonged to several leading bands including Louis Armstrong's and Paul Whiteman's. (The latter organization, although it has varied considerably through the years, and has adapted itself to changes in style and taste, has always specialized in the "sweet" or "symphonic" type of jazz, leaving little or no room for improvising. But many of the best improvisers are also first-class technicians on their instruments, and it is as such that such men as Teagarden and Beiderbecke have found places in Whiteman's band.)

Thomas ("Fats") Waller, Harlem-born Negro pianist, who is a brilliant jazz improviser as well as the composer of some published tunes.

Teddy Wilson, young Negro pianist, who has also played the harpsichord both in jazz and in concert performances of eighteenth-century music.

The American Composer

From "A World of Music" (in preparation)

By Elie Siegmeister

FOLK art, stemming directly out of common life, is the deepest, most democratic layer of our musical culture. Jazz, while newer, has formed an equally broad layer of American music. Newest of all, serious music has just begun to strike roots in our native soil and spirit.

Before examining our achievements in this field, it is important to inquire, why were they so late in arriving? Certainly Americans have always loved music; even in the leanest years folk and popular arts, singing and playing instruments have been treasured. Yet in more than a century of national existence we produced no really great serious composer. In an age that brought forth American writers of world rank—Emerson, Thoreau, Poe, Hawthorne, and Whitman—we had no musician of remotely comparable stature. Why did no one emerge in the 1860's to do for our sea chanties what Melville did for the tales of the whalers; and no one to sing in music of lilacs in the dooryard, of Brooklyn Ferry, Lincoln, and democracy—as Whitman did in poetry? Why was there no American to do for our folk traditions what Smetana and Dvořák did for those of Bohemia, Mussorgsky for Russia?

The usual answer is "lack of genius"; but deeper than this were the peculiar conditions of music in the American past.

Serious literature has to a certain extent always been close to, and found an audience among, the plain people of this country. In revolutionary New England, farmers read Homer, the writings of Tom Paine, and the poems of Freneau. Poe, Longfellow, Hawthorne, Mark Twain, O. Henry, Sinclair Lewis, and Carl Sandburg have each appealed to all classes of Americans in their time.

But from an early date, serious music was severed from the common music of the people, becoming the property of a narrow élite. In all countries music in the larger forms has required subsidy or social support of some kind. While the "singing school" for the teaching of psalms and hymns was a ubiquitous feature of pioneer life even in the smallest settlements, the early guardians of the Republic failed to

733

follow France, England, Italy, and Germany in providing public funds for orchestras, opera houses, and a national conservatory. As a result, the patronage of classical music was taken over at an early date by well-to-do private citizens, who found in it not only musical pleasure but a badge of elegance and prestige. The merchants and their wives who for over a hundred years met the deficits and sat on the boards of directors of our orchestras and opera houses relished the exclusiveness of foreign "names." Along about 1830-40 it became tacitly agreed in the "best" circles that good music was foreign music; the only thing an American could produce was cheap minstrel tunes or barroom ballads.

All during the nineteenth century, serious orchestral and opera music (almost entirely European) was confined to a small minority of Americans in a few large cities, while the overwhelming majority of people throughout the country clung to homespun folk songs and ballads, popular tunes, and dances. This separation between native music and the great serious forms was the bane of our musical life for over a hundred years. On the one hand it caused opera and concerts to be surrounded with an "arty" aura that long rendered them suspect in the eyes of common Americans. On the other hand, it led those in control of our highest musical circles to doubt that any American could be a genuine artist. In 1850 Louis Moreau Gottschalk had to win fame in Paris as the "American Chopin" before local managers would book him. A generation later the Fisk Jubilee Singers were accepted in Boston and New York only after the Queen of England and the King of Prussia had acclaimed them. And only a few years ago Marian Anderson was refused by half a dozen agents until Europe gave her its benediction.

Reverence for the imported article was so strong that an American name was a handicap to those embarking on a concert career. Many Johnsons, Thomsons, and Smiths emerged in high-sounding French, German, or Italian disguises. Opera houses would not consider American singers. Even today only one of the regular leaders of our major symphony orchestras is a native American.*

In this atmosphere of un-American snobbery, the native composer

* This should in no sense be construed as a criticism of foreign-born American conductors, most of whom have made magnificent contributions to the development of music in this country; some, in fact, have been more devoted to the cause of the American composer than many native-born conductors. The whole point is that the matter of where a musician was born should simply not enter into consideration in deciding whether he is to be appointed to a conductorship. Unfortunately, it still remains a factor with most directorial boards.

was regarded with amused indifference. Critics, managers, conductors doubted—even denied—that he could ever write "great" music. Visiting lecturers informed us that the Yankee was cold and insensitive by nature. Composers who wished to have their works performed had to ape foreign models.

Obviously, such music, although written by Americans, could hardly express the heart and spirit of this country. All through the nineteenth century, and well into the twentieth, talented composers such as J. K. Paine, MacDowell, Loeffler, Griffes, and others were cut off from the simple materials of native life that had given distinctive content and style to Mark Twain, Walt Whitman, and so many other American writers.

In the past twenty years, and more especially in the last two or three, all this has begun to change. America has become a world power and Americans are looking to their own democratic culture. The snobbish control of music is slowly breaking down; the Diamond Horseshoe is no more. The best in classical music has been opened to the widest audience; and at the same time our own popular and folk traditions have begun to command the respect long overdue.

With the breaking of the barriers between classical and native art, American music is at last coming of age. Not only are there ten times as many composers writing serious music as there were twenty years ago, but this music is growing ever closer to and more expressive of our land and people. Even in operas and symphonies many of our best artists are no longer afraid to be as plain and "homespun" as the people they come from.

This has been a long and slow process, and it is by no means completed at the moment of writing—perhaps it is only now "the end of the beginning." But since the course of our serious music is perhaps the most interesting question of our present musical life, the remaining pages of this book will be devoted to tracing it, in outline at least, from the days of Jenny Lind to the present. Rather than devote half a dozen meaningless lines to every composer who has written or is writing worth-while American music—and there are many—I prefer to select a representative few and give them more adequate treatment. While it is naturally difficult to make a selection from among one's immediate predecessors and colleagues, it is my sincere belief that the composers mentioned from page 749 onward—even though in some cases little known—are among the most gifted of all. In their work, it may be that the future music of America is being revealed.

Concert Music in Barnum's Day

The chapter "When America Was Musically Young"
from "Music Comes to America"

By David Ewen

THE era following the Civil War was one of great fulfillment and still greater promise. It was an age of expansion. New cities arose, industrialization spread, population increased, speculation became rampant, fortunes were made almost overnight. These and other symptoms pointed to the fact that a great country was undergoing growing pains. America was sprawling out in new directions—into the Far West, for example, which was now being built up and populated. A country seeing growth and development in every phase of its activity required more breathing space.

But what of musical activity in America? Was this period of expansion and development, so rich in promise of every kind, bringing with it a new age for the musical life of the country as well?

It was well known that famous European musicians came to this country to give concerts during the nineteenth century and returned to Europe with both well-filled purses and strange tales of American naïveté in music. There could be no denying that America, in music above everything else, was innocent; she was awkward and ingenuous and misinformed as only the very young and uneducated can be. She was sublimely oblivious of any standards of artistic excellence. What concerned her most in music seemed to be the obvious, the meretricious, the sensational. A recognition of values had not yet begun to enter into her musical calculations.

Up to the closing decades of the nineteenth century, Americans regarded concerts as but another form of popular entertainment in the class, say, of the minstrel show, the prize fight, and the circus. As a matter of fact, there were many towns in the South and Midwest which believed that an announced concert would be just a novel variety of the minstrel show. It was the grumble of many who came to attend the orchestral concerts of Theodore Thomas (when that brave pioneer first explored regions formerly untouched by musical civilization) that the evening fell flat because there had been no end men and no jokes. They

736

further lamented that the men of the orchestra had even been too lazy to blacken their faces. When Anton Rubinstein visited Memphis, Tennessee, for a recital, he who was generally considered the greatest pianist of the time was stopped backstage by a helpful stage assistant who advised him to hurry to blacken his face in time for his "show."

It is uniquely appropriate that, when Jenny Lind concertized in America in 1850 (she was the first great singer to tour this country extensively), she should have been under the managerial wing of Phineas Taylor Barnum. It was not for a moment considered bad taste for Barnum to exploit a great artist with the methods used for his circus attractions. He aroused the curiosity of the American public in Jenny Lind's personality by spreading strange and fabulous tales about her virtue and angelic goodness. He inspired awed comments by escorting her from the boat to her hotel with regal splendor: spirited white horses drew her sumptuous carriage. In the evenings he arranged for local singing societies, or firemen bands, to serenade her beneath her window. His flair for igniting the imagination and the enthusiasm of the public for his stellar attraction soon yielded incredible results. Jenny Lind became a vogue, a passion, a disease. Clothing, food, café houses were named after her. Her photographs sold millions of copies. Young women imitated her hair dress and her clothing. Musical numbers were written to praise her charms. And the box office showed commensurate returns. Halls were overcrowded whenever she sang. The crowds came, not to hear a great artist, but to see with their own eyes an apotheosized personality.

Music at the time appealed to American audiences for the very reasons that circuses did. It exploited eccentric personalities. It introduced breath-taking extramusical features. It flaunted unexpected tricks. When it did none of these things, music held no fascination for most of the audiences of the time. Teresa Carreño was publicized throughout the country as "the greatest woman pianist in the world" in much the same manner as the "bearded lady" or the "fattest woman in the world" —not as an artist, but rather as a freak of nature. An infant prodigy of the time, who inspired no end of wonder, was a "Master Marsh" who, at the age of four, was able to play on two drums at one time. Hatton, a pianist highly favored in the middle of the nineteenth century, would appear on the concert stage with a string of sleigh bells fastened to his right leg. When he reached the proper moment in a composition describing a sleigh ride, he would shake his leg; then an assistant on the stage would use an instrument which imitated the cracking of a whip.

"And this thing," reported Dwight's *Journal of Music* (December 18, 1852), "aroused a storm of applause which had no end until it was repeated several times *da capo*."

Volovski, a Polish pianist, toured America with advertisements in which he "guaranteed" to play four hundred notes in one measure; and the singer De Begnis offered the attraction of singing six hundred words and three hundred bars of music in four minutes. Leopold de Meyer announced that he could perform on the piano with fists and elbows, even with a cane. Ole Bull, Norway's greatest violinist, exploited the fact that he could play "miraculous" double-stops on a "flattened fiddle-bridge." Some, like the pianist Henri Herz, even tried to lure audiences into the concert hall by announcing some such irrelevant attraction as the fact that his auditorium would be lighted by a thousand candles! The famous bandleader, Patrick S. Gilmore (Sousa's celebrated fore-runner), thrilled his public by performing musical compositions that called for bells, anvils, and even actual cannon. At the Peace Jubilee concerts of 1869, a performance of the *Anvil Chorus* by Verdi recruited the services of red-shirted firemen who contributed to the sonorities of the orchestra by striking on anvils. George William Curtis wrote that in 1862 the musical tastes of the time "reached an apogee" with *The Battle of Prague,* a cacophonous composition for tin pans written many years earlier.

No wonder, then, that in such a bizarre setting the eccentric French-English conductor, Jullien, should have scored a sensation in 1853. He was America's musician-of-the-hour. His antics delighted America's love for the strange and the unexpected. When he conducted, he had behind him an ornately decorated velvet chair resembling a throne; into this he would sometimes sink with exhaustion at the com-pletion of a musical number. There seemed no limit to the extravagances of his ideas. When he conducted one of his own quadrilles, he would (at a climactic moment) seize the concertmaster's violin and bow or, on other occasions, tear a piccolo from the breast pocket of his velvet jacket. Then, swaying elaborately and accompanying the ecstatic motions of his body with exaggerated grimaces of his face, he would play with the orchestra. Before he conducted music by Beethoven, he would have a pair of kid gloves brought to him ceremoniously on a gold platter. In front of the eyes of the audience, he would put on these gloves and with great dignity proceed to direct the music. For other important works he used a special jeweled baton.

He would frequently perform excellent music: movements from symphonies by Beethoven, Mozart, and even Mendelssohn. But what took America by storm was a rendition of a piece called *The Fireman's Quadrille.* The composition began serenely enough with the strings. Suddenly, from off the stage, the clang of fire bells was heard. An ingenious stage effect simulated fire. Firemen in full regulation attire rushed on the stage with fire hose, pouring actual water on the stage fire. Then, when the fire was extinguished, the firemen ceremoniously left the stage. The music, which had been proceeding undisturbed throughout the entire exhibition, now reached a feverish climax which, sometimes literally, threw the audience into a frenzy. For many years thereafter orchestras and bands throughout the country attempted to emulate Jullien's success by performing *The Fireman's Quadrille,* not quite so elaborately as Jullien, but nevertheless with firemen in full uniform parading up and down the stage.

Sometimes accident helped to provide American concert audiences with unexpected thrills. At one of the concerts of the celebrated Hungarian violinist Reményi (American audiences were particularly partial to Reményi because of his fiddle acrobatics) he amazed his audience by apparently drawing a clear note in crescendo from his violin at the same time that he was going through the intricacies of a solo violin transcription of the funeral music from Handel's *Saul*. How he could draw this pure, clear tone uninterrupted, while his hands were involved in technical intricacies, was a mystery to fascinate a nineteenth-century audience in America. At the end of the performance the audience deliriously acclaimed the violinist. It might be added that this feat bewildered even Reményi himself until, going backstage, he discovered that during the performance someone had gone to the pipe organ and had maliciously sounded the single sustained note throughout his entire performance.

Besides revealing an insatiable appetite for the sensational, American music audiences also disclosed a particular weakness for musical entertainment built on grandiose lines. The bigger the musical project, the better it was appreciated. Recitals by a single artist did not go well. Americans liked variety; they enjoyed a program that featured numerous artists. A concert of sixteen pianists on eight pianos was more likely to appeal than a concert by a single pianist, even if the pianist happened to be a world-famous artist. Concerts featuring a varied group of artists, supplemented frequently by a chorus and an orchestra, were preferred by Americans to an evening of chamber music. Often these concerts, which enlisted the services of a variety of artists, featured strange collaborations. At one concert, for example, Henri Vieuxtemps, Belgium's greatest violinist, appeared on the same program with a concertina artist who delighted his public by crushing his instrument on his nose or forehead.

Americans particularly liked concerts by mammoth orchestras and Gargantuan choruses. A favored entertainment of the time would be, say, a combination of Sousa's band with a major symphony orchestra in the performance of some well-known orchestral piece. The fact that each could have given a better account of itself independently did not disturb the listeners, who were more interested in size, and in massive size, than in the quality of the performance. Thus they went in for festivals with zest—not because these festivals featured unusual choral and symphonic music but, more especially, because they utilized forces of tremendous size. There were such established festivals as those in Worcester, Oberlin, and Cincinnati which, at regular intervals (either annually or bi-annually), presented a cycle of grand-scale performances of symphonies and oratorios. In many western sections of the country all the musical activity would find its annual culmination in festival performances recruiting the orchestras and choruses of several different localities. Sometimes musicians would draw the limelight of attention upon themselves by arranging special festivals, as Gilmore did when he created the "Great Beethoven Centennial Jubilee" and as Theodore Thomas and Leopold Damrosch did after him. Sometimes special occasions brought forth the creation of festive musical celebrations, as the Peace Jubilees in Boston in 1869 and 1872 and the Chicago World's Fair, dedicated musically on October 22, 1892.

These festivals invariably called for unwieldy forces. At the Chicago World's Fair the fact that Theodore Thomas was to conduct "the largest orchestra ever to assemble on one stage" was the magnet used to draw in the audiences. At the Peace Jubilee of 1869 a chorus of 10,000 voices was joined by an orchestra of 1,000. Johann Strauss II, coming to this country for the first time to assist at the Jubilee of 1872, was an attraction not only because his waltzes were known in practically every American household, but more especially because—catering to the tastes of the time—he conducted a fabulous army of singers and orchestra players. His own description of the affair is enlightening:

On the musicians' tribune there were twenty thousand singers; in front of them the members of the orchestra—and these were the people I was to conduct. A hundred assistant conductors had been placed at my disposal to control these gigantic masses, but I was only able to recognize those nearest to me, and though we had rehearsals there was no possibility of giving an artistic performance, a proper production. . . . Now just conceive of my position face to face with a public of four hundred thousand Americans. There I stood at the raised desk, high above all the others. How would the business start, how would it end? Suddenly a cannon-shot rang out, a gentle hint for us twenty thousand to begin playing *The Blue Danube*. I gave the signal, my hundred assistant conductors followed me as quickly and as well as they could and then there broke out an unholy row such as I shall never forget. As we had begun more or less simultaneously, I concentrated my whole attention on seeing that we should finish together too! Thank Heaven, I managed even that. It was all that was humanly possible. The hundred thousand mouths in the audience roared applause and I breathed a sigh of relief when I found myself in fresh air again and felt the firm ground beneath my feet.

Such festivals, developed along prodigious outlines, dramatized music for Americans through means they could best understand and appreciate: display, and the impressiveness of sheer size.

Stephen Foster

By John Tasker Howard

Article in The International Cyclopedia of Music and Musicians

THE American song-composer Stephen C. Foster (born July 4, 1826, died Jan. 13, 1864) was the ninth child of William Barclay Foster, a man active in the business and political life of Pittsburgh when it was still a frontier and river town. Although Stephen showed musical talent from earliest childhood, little was done to encourage it and no effort was made to give the lad musical training. In his youth and early manhood he may have had a few rudimentary lessons from Henry Kleber, a German musician resident in Pittsburgh, but otherwise the little knowledge of musical theory that he gained was entirely self-acquired. His early schooling was received in a local private school, and in 1840 he attended for a short while the Academies at Athens and Towanda, Pa. It was in the Spring of 1841 that his first known musical composition was performed—"Tioga Waltz"—which was played by several flutes at an exhibition of the Athens Academy. In 1841 he entered Jefferson College, but remained there less than a week.

For the next five years he was at home with his family, living principally in Allegheny, Pa., where his father served several terms as Mayor. Family correspondence in these years shows much concern over Stephen's future. Few seemed to understand his "idle, dreaming ways," and his "strange talent for musick." An attempt was made in 1846 to obtain a West Point appointment for him, but it was not successful. He was, however, beginning his career as a song writer, and in 1844 his first published song, "Open Thy Lattice, Love," was issued by G. Willig of Philadelphia. For a social organization called the "Knights of the S.T." he wrote and composed several songs which he introduced to minstrel performers who visited Pittsburgh. Among them were "Old Uncle Ned," "Lou'siana Belle," and probably the famous "Oh! Susanna."

Late in 1846 he went to Cincinnati, where he became a bookkeeper for his brother Dunning, of the firm of Irwin & Foster, commission merchants. In Cincinnati he met W. C. Peters, a music publisher he had known in Pittsburgh. Peters published several of Foster's early songs, from which he was reputed to have made several thousand dollars and for which he gave the composer only a small amount of cash, if anything. These were not the only editions of the songs, however. Because Foster had given manuscript copies to minstrel performers, these copies found their way into the hands of other publishers. Twenty different editions of "Oh! Susanna" were issued in less than three years, nineteen of them pirated. "Oh! Susanna," first issued in 1848, became highly popular with the "forty-niners" who joined the gold-rush to California, and the vogue of the song quickly established Foster's reputation. He accepted royalty contracts with Firth, Pond & Co., of New York and F. D. Benteen of Baltimore, and was able to leave his brother's employ in Cincinnati and to return to his parents' home in Allegheny, where he devoted himself to song-writing as a profession.

In 1850 he married Jane McDowel, and except for short residences in New York and Hoboken, N. J., he lived in Allegheny continuously until 1860, when he removed to New York. It was in the early years of his marriage that his best songs were published—"Old Folks at Home" (1851), "Camptown Races" (1850), "My Old Kentucky Home" (1853), "Massa's in de Cold, Cold Ground" (1852),

"Come Where My Love Lies Dreaming" (1855), and others. Although he received fair business treatment from his publishers, and the sale of his songs brought him an income that in his era should have been sufficient for the needs of his small family of wife and daughter (averaging $1,371 a year from 1849 to 1860, but being much higher in the first years of the decade), his expenses were continually in excess of his income, and on two occasions he was compelled to sell out all future rights in his previous compositions for cash. After his death these rights reverted to his widow and daughter on expiration of copyright, and in the renewal periods (1879-98) yielded a total revenue of $4,199.24.

By 1860 Foster's affairs were at a low ebb, and he decided to take his wife and daughter to New York. It proved to be a highly unwise decision. His powers as a song-writer were distinctly waning, for aside from "Old Black Joe" (1860), and perhaps "Beautiful Dreamer" (posthumous, 1864), none of the many songs of his later years equaled his earlier efforts. The habit of drink fastened itself upon him, and there is some evidence to support the theory that he suffered from tuberculosis. His wife, from whom he had been temporarily separated in 1854, left him again in 1861, and he lived alone in cheap boarding and lodging houses. His death was the result of an accident. In a weakened condition he fell upon a wash-basin or water-pitcher and cut his neck. He was taken to Bellevue Hospital where he died a few days later.

Altogether Foster published 200 songs and instrumental compositions. The latter are negligible, but the best of the songs form the most important group of people's songs that have ever come from the pen of any composer. At least 25 are still constantly sung, and not less than 50 are worthy of preservation. They are probably the most typically American expression that any composer has yet achieved. Born and raised in the interior, Foster was little affected by the foreign immigration of musicians that enslaved the seaboard in mid-century. The influences that molded Foster were inherently American—the minstrel shows and their songs; the singing of Negroes on the wharves of the Ohio River; and the sentimental songs that were carried through the country by the so-called "singing families" in concert.

Although he was a Northerner who never journeyed South until after some of his best Negro, or "Ethiopian," songs were written, he so absorbed the atmosphere of the plantations that Southerners have accepted his songs as an authentic expression. This was probably because he dealt with fundamental emotions which gave his work a universal rather than a local appeal. He found a medium that was simple and sincere, at its best dealing with emotions that are fundamental to all mankind, and at its worst never quite so bad as the other popular songs of his own day, or later.

The twentieth century has witnessed a continuously increasing revival of interest in Foster's music. In spite of the so-called jazz age, his sentimental songs not only retain their popularity, but they are heard more and more throughout the world. Growing interest has also been shown in the life and personality of the composer, and shrines and memorials have been erected to his memory.

Edward MacDowell

Abridged from "How Music Grew"

By Marion Bauer and Ethel Peyser

EDWARD MACDOWELL, born in New York City in 1861, began piano lessons when he was eight. One of his teachers was the brilliant South American Teresa Carreño, who later played her pupil's concerto with many world orchestras. At 15, he entered the Paris Conservatory where he was fellow student with Debussy.

In 1879, MacDowell studied composition at Frankfort with Joachim Raff, one of the composers of the Romantic period. Raff introduced him to Liszt, who invited MacDowell to play his first piano suite at Zurich (1882). The composer's modesty is reflected in these words which Lawrence Gilman quotes: "I would not have changed a note in one of them for untold gold, and *inside* I had the greatest love for them; but the idea that anyone else might take them seriously had never occurred to me." This suite was his first published composition.

In 1888, he established himself in Boston as pianist and teacher. His first concert was with the Kneisel Quartet, and in 1889 he successfully played his Concerto with the Boston Symphony Orchestra. He made tours through the States giving recitals and appearing with the orchestras. Winning immediate recognition, his position as an exceptional composer grew. In 1896 the Boston Symphony Orchestra presented his first piano concerto and his orchestral *Indian Suite* on the same program in New York. Such an honor had never before been shown an American!

In 1896, he became professor of the new Chair of Music at Columbia University in New York City. After resigning his post in 1904,[*] his health broke as the result of an accident, and for several years he was an invalid. All the care of physicians, devoted friends, his parents, and his courageous wife, could not restore his memory, and in 1908, he died in Peterborough, New Hampshire, where he is buried.

MacDowell was a composer for the pianoforte, although he wrote some lovely songs; a few orchestral works, best known of which is the *Indian Suite,* in which he employs Indian themes; and several male choruses written when he conducted the New York Mendelssohn Glee Club. We love and remember him for his *Woodland Sketches, Sea Pieces, Fireside Tales, New England Idyls* (opus 62 and his last work), virtuoso-studies, and the four sonatas—the *Tragica, Eroica, Norse,* and *Keltic.*[†]

Charles Tomlinson Griffes

From "How Music Grew"

By Marion Bauer and Ethel Peyser

CHARLES TOMLINSON GRIFFES (1884-1920) was a poet composer whose early death was a serious loss to America, for everything he wrote was an addition to our music. He was impressionistic in style, and we are grateful for the lovely art songs, *Five Poems of Ancient China and Japan,* three songs with orchestral accompaniment to poems of Fiona MacLeod, ten piano pieces and the Sonata which have never been surpassed in beauty and workmanship by any American, the *Poem* for flute and orchestra, the string quartet on Indian themes, and his orchestral

---

[*] His resignation came as the result of a disagreement with President Nicholas Murray Butler as to the conduct of the Music Department. The full story is related in John Tasker Howard: *Our American Music,* pp. 395-402.

[†] MacDowell was important not only for the quality of the compositions he produced, but in a broader sense because he was the first to show that, given the background and opportunity, an American *could* write serious music of distinction in the larger forms—this, in spite of the fact that he himself detested chauvinism in any form, and did not want to be recognized simply because he was an American.

Much of his music was more popular twenty years ago than it is today. But, whether a large proportion of his compositions survives or not, he gave confidence and a certain standing to his successors. In a more tangible way, his country home—now the MacDowell Colony—provided a summer haven for composers in none too affluent circumstances.—E. S.

tone poem, *The Pleasure Dome of Kubla Khan*. For the stage Griffes composed a Japanese mime-play, *Schojo;* a dance drama, *The Kairn of Korwidwen;* and Walt Whitman's *Salut au monde*, a dramatic ballet.

Griffes was a native of Elmira, New York, and his first studies were made with Miss Mary S. Broughton, who recognized her young pupil's unusual talent and took him to Germany for study. His composition work was done with Humperdinck and Rüfer, and from 1907 until his death he taught music at Hackley, a boys' school in Tarrytown, New York.

Lawrence Gilman, American critic, says of him: "He was a poet with a sense of comedy. . . . Griffes had never learned how to pose— he would never have learned how if he had lived to be as triumphantly old and famous as Monsieur Saint-Saëns or Herr Bruch or Signor Verdi. . . . It was only a short while before his death that the Boston Symphony Orchestra played for the first time (in Boston) his *Pleasure Dome of Kubla Khan** . . . and the general concert-going public turned aside—to bestow an approving hand upon this producer of a sensitive and imaginative tone-poetry who was by some mysterious accident an American. He was a fastidious craftsman, a scrupulous artist. He was neither smug nor pretentious nor accommodating. He went his own way—modestly, quietly, unswervingly . . . having the vision of the few."

Henry F. Gilbert
From "Our Contemporary Composers"

By John Tasker Howard

THE music of Henry F. Gilbert is so racy of the soil that it stamps its composer as one of our first nationalists. He was one of the original

---

* "It was first performed under circumstances that were indeed pathetic, as far as Griffes was concerned, for the labor of its composition was partly responsible for the illness that caused his death. When he knew it would have a performance by the Boston Symphony he set himself to copy out the parts, as all composers must do with a manuscript work unless they can afford to hire a copyist. He was tired and busy with his regular work of teaching music at a boys' school, and when he was finished he fell ill with an attack of pneumonia. Word of his great success was brought to him just before he died."—John Tasker Howard in *Our American Music*.

Wa-Wan group, and his intense nationalism may have been one of the reasons for the tardy recognition he received, particularly in the opening years of the twentieth century. Born in Somerville, Massachusetts, September 26, 1868, he studied first at the New England Conservatory, and then became MacDowell's first American pupil. During his student years, from 1889 to 1892, he earned his living playing the violin for dances and in theaters. This hack work disgusted him, and he determined to keep his music apart from the routine of getting money to feed himself. He became first a real-estate agent, then a foreman in a factory, a raiser of silkworms, and finally a bread and pie cutter in a restaurant at the Chicago World's Fair. There he met a Russian prince who had been a friend of Rimsky-Korsakov, and who, when he recovered from the unconventional advances of the bread and pie cutter, was able to tell the young American much about Rimsky-Korsakov and other members of the "neo-Russian" school.

Gilbert was always interested in composers who used folk songs and native material in their music, and his journeys after 1895, when he inherited a small sum of money, took him wherever he could find kindred spirits. He was so stirred when he heard of the coming première of Charpentier's *Louise* in Paris, knowing that it made use of popular themes, that he worked his way to Europe on a cattle-boat to hear the first performance.

It was not until 1911, when he was forty-two, that he really came to the attention of the musical public. It was in April of that year that the Boston Symphony played the *Comedy Overture on Negro Themes,* which disturbed the audience considerably but impressed itself on its hearers immediately as something new. As Olin Downes remarked, "There were some who thought that the opening was undignified, and stopped thinking at that place."

The *Overture* had originally been intended as a prelude to an operetta based on the *Uncle Remus* tales of Joel Chandler Harris. Gilbert had actually completed his sketches for the operetta and then found that exclusive stage rights had been granted to another composer. So he could use only the overture, which he rescored for a larger orchestra. The first theme was a Negro melody from the Bahamas; the second a tune sung by the roustabouts of the Mississippi steamboats, "I'se Gwine to Alabama, Oh!" The middle section was a witty, rollicking fugue on the "Old Ship of Zion." In spite of the audience's dismay at the first performance, Gilbert had given his material such genuine, spontaneous treatment that he began to be talked about, and two years later he was invited to write an orchestral work for the Litchfield County Festival in Norfolk, Connecticut.

For this occasion he wrote his *Negro Rhapsody,* which pictured first a Negro "shout," alternating a savage dance tune and a spiritual; then a glorification of the spiritual, in which the barbaric elements gradually gave way to the loftier, nobler phase. This final triumph of the spiritual offers a direct contrast to John Powell's *Negro Rhapsody,* in which there is a reversion to paganism.

Gilbert's next work to bring him further recognition was his *Dance in the Place Congo,* based on five songs of the Louisiana Creole Negroes. It was first composed as an orchestral piece, but the composer later wrote a ballet scenario, to which it was finally performed at the Metropolitan in New York, March 23, 1918. This is one of Gilbert's best works. The tropical grace of the Creole tunes is subtly emphasized, while the gloomy, tragic note of the slave dances in the Old Place Congo of New Orleans forms a weird and fantastic background. First comes the *Bamboula,* then some light moments which rise to frenzy, interrupted at last by the booming of the great bell that summons the slaves back to their quarters. Then a pause and a cry of despair.

There were also several works not based on American folk songs. Long before Gilbert gained the recognition that came with the *Comedy Overture,* David Bispham had sung his setting of Stevenson's *Pirate Song* ("Fifteen Men on a Dead Man's Chest"), and the Russian Symphony Orchestra in New York had given a single performance of his *Salammbô's Invocation to Tanith,* for a soprano and orchestra. There was also a Symphonic Prelude to Synge's drama, *Riders to the Sea,* in which Gilbert made use of an old Irish melody. This was first written for small orchestra, to be played at some performances of the drama at the Twentieth Century Club in Boston, in 1904. Later Gilbert expanded the work, and it was performed at the music festival of the MacDowell Memorial Association at Peterborough, September, 1914. He also composed a one-act opera that has not yet been performed—*Fantasy in Delft,* with the scene laid in seventeenth-century Holland. Gilbert lived to be not quite sixty years old, and died May 19, 1928.

Charles Ives

From "A World of Music" (in preparation)

By Elie Siegmeister

IT IS probably no accident that, of all the men who are writing in our time, the first to grasp in his music the true feeling of our land and people was not a professional musician at all, but a New England insurance broker, Charles E. Ives. Born on October 20, 1874, in Danbury, Connecticut, of a musical family (his father was a bandmaster in Grant's army, and an ardent musical experimenter), Ives received a thorough academic training in composition at Yale. But his mistrust of the cosmopolitan musical circles with their classic-worshiping conductors, snobbish patrons, and pontifical critics, made it clear upon his graduation from Yale in 1898 that the kind of music he wanted to write would not be recognized in those circles. Furthermore, Ives could not hold with the then dominant idea of music as something apart from, even opposed to, life as a whole. In an afterword to a collection of his 114 songs, the composer later wrote:

> An interest in any art-activity, from poetry to baseball, is better, broadly speaking, if held as a part of life, or of a life, than if it sets itself up as a whole—a condition verging towards . . . a kind of atrophy of the other important values, and hence reacting unfavorably upon itself.

Although music was his first love, Ives decided against following the career of a professional composer. He worked as a business man by day,* and at night wrote sonatas, symphonies, chamber music, songs, and orchestral pieces which no one ever heard, but which were more revolutionary for the America of those days than the compositions of Stravinsky, Schönberg, Hindemith, and Milhaud were for contemporary Europe.

Ives's participation in the everyday life of Danbury gave him a familiarity with the feelings of average people that few purely "artistic" composers could equal—a knowledge of the ways of ordinary

* His first job was as a clerk in an insurance office. Later he established his own firm, Ives and Myrick, in which he worked until 1930 when he was obliged to retire because of ill health. Ives is at present living in New York.

children, old men, bankers and storekeepers of his own New England. The communal rites, festivities, circus parades, camp-meetings, election rallies, barn dances, Fourth of July celebrations, and the common music that accompanied them were a cherished part of his experience. Ives listened to the tunes of the old minstrel band and theater orchestra; the off-key singing of the congregation at Meetings; the reels and jigs scratched out by Connecticut fiddlers with characteristic Yankee twang; the traditional marches, schottisches and quadrilles played (slightly out of tune) by the village brass band; the singing of the family around the wheezy harmonium; the scrambled medleys of patriotic tunes offered on festive occasions—and all of these entered at one time or another into his music. You can hear "Good Night, Ladies," "Rally 'round the Flag," "The British Grenadiers," "Turkey in the Straw," "The Irish Washerwoman," "Shall We Gather at the River" in his symphonies, his sonatas, and chamber pieces. As he tells us in one of his songs:

I think there must be a place in the soul all made of tunes of long-ago; I hear the organ on the Main Street corner, Aunt Sarah humming Gospels, summer evenings, the cornet band playing in the square. . . .

To Ives, real life experience was a greater stimulus to composition than all the patronage and "prizes" in the world.

Possibly the more our composer accepts from his patrons . . . the less he will accept from himself. . . . If for every thousand-dollar prize a potato field be substituted, so that these candidates of "Clio" can dig a little in real life . . . art's-air might be clearer. . . ."

Ives was not a realist in the obvious sense of the word, but he did weave the scenes, characters, thoughts, and sounds of his environment into his music in a highly suggestive way. The great majority of his orchestral and chamber compositions start with some typical New England or other American scene or subject, introducing in a sort of free rhapsody local sounds, melodies, and incidents together with the composer's own reflections on them.

Ives's music represents an amazing diversity of styles, techniques, themes, and methods of treatment, each fitted to its particular subject. Thus he writes music of bardic violence in his song, "Walt Whitman":

Who goes there? Hankering, gross, mystical and nude; How is it I extract strength from the beef I eat? What is man anyhow? What am I? What are you? . . .

In contrast, his "Thoreau" has the calm, floating atmosphere of the dreamer lost at Walden. The "Housatonic at Stockbridge" is a tone-painting of the quietly flowing river:

Con - ten - ted ri - ver!_____ in thy dream - - y

realm the cloud-y wil - low and the plu - my elm._____

Behind this simple melody there is background of blended harmonies in two keys at once, the mingled chords admirably suggesting the thin Massachusetts summer haze.

The Connecticut composer made use of many "modern" techniques of music—some of them before Stravinsky and Schönberg had been heard of. In fact, Ives's musical experiments were sometimes so complex that many of his orchestral scores strike the most skilled musician as a Chinese puzzle. Even today, when the name of Ives has become almost legendary in American music, none of his large orchestral works has been performed in entirety, for this reason.

Yet this bold venturer into the realm of supercomplex harmonies and rhythms confounds his modernist contemporaries by jumping from the most "advanced" musical effects to the simplest melodies, such as the rousing cowboy ballad, "Charlie Rutlage":

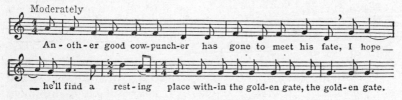

Moderately

An - oth-er good cow-punch-er has gone to meet his fate, I hope__

__ he'll find a rest-ing place with-in the gold-en gate, the gold-en gate.

Ives himself tells us that he published some of his songs without any illusions as to their musical value—or, as he charmingly put it, "to help clear up a long disputed point, namely: which is worse? the music or the words?"

But while taking his modesty into account, we may find value even in the composer's most banal barber-shop melodies, his "corniest" harmonizations. For, seen in the light of his entire production, they do illumine his unannounced purpose—to put America into his music, the good, the bad, and the indifferent.

Ives has been accused of inconsistency of style. But his shiftings from one technique to another always seem remarkably right. The rambunctious blare and pounding fists of "General William Booth Enters Heaven" are right for that poem of the Salvation Army hero; the loping rhythm and hoarse shouts are right for the middle section of "Charlie Rutlage"; dreamy, mellifluous harmonies and a lyrical melodic line are right for the setting of Milton's lines, in the song "Evening." The Connecticut musician might have said, with Whitman, "Do I contradict myself? Very well, then I contradict myself." For the wildness, humor, simplicity, chaos, anger, maudlin sentiment that are to be found side by side in his works are all part of his experience, all part of the world he and we live in. Any deliberate "unity of style" would have been specious and forced.

Charles Ives's music stands as a cornerstone of the "American school" of serious composers. From what he has done a dozen young men have learned. Yet one wonders whether his work will not appear imperfect, incomplete, and uneven to listeners of a future age. For the man's isolation as an artist left two gaps in his work: incomplete craftsmanship, and a lack of feeling for the audience. There was not one important performance of his music until Ives was fifty-three years old. It was unquestionably this that gave an experimental, unfinished quality to his music. How could it be otherwise? A composer needs to hear his work played, and to watch the reactions of those who hear it. Although Ives drew his source material from the plain people, he can scarcely have had the people in mind as an audience for some of the compositions he wrote about them. His imaginative mind, forced into isolation, created some of the finest American music that has yet been written, but also a considerable number of compositions that seem destined for some abstract intelligence instead of the ears of any actual auditors. To my ear, works like the "Concord Sonata" seem overtranscendental, turgid, confusing. Fuller judgment of Ives's position must await hearings of the four symphonies, the many sonatas and orchestral suites, very few of which have as yet been performed.

But if the listener has doubts as to the practicability and ear-appeal of some of Ives's music, so had the composer himself. Of his volume of songs, he says:

Some of the songs in this book . . . cannot be sung. . . . An excuse for their existence . . . is that a song has a few rights the same as other ordinary citizens. . . . If it happens to feel like trying to fly where humans cannot fly—to sing what cannot be sung—to walk in a cave on all fours—or to tighten up its girth in blind hope and faith and try to scale mountains that are not—who shall stop it?

And again Ives reflected:

> Some have written a book for money; I have not. Some for fame; I have not. Some for love; I have not. In fact . . . I have not written a book at all. I have merely cleaned house. . . . It's good for a man's vanity to have neighbors see him—on the clothes line. . . . This package of paper . . . is submitted . . . in the chance that some points for the better education of the composer may be thrown back at him.

Ives would have valued the comments of "neighbors" on what he hung "on the clothes-line." But he was a composer cut off from any "neighbors"—any audience at all. Living in the midst of America, he was talking about America to himself. When some of his works ultimately arrived before the public, it was too late for the composer to profit by the experience. Musical America was not yet ready to receive its own.

George Gershwin

From "Our Contemporary Composers"

By John Tasker Howard

GEORGE GERSHWIN had one of the most appealing melodic gifts among all the song-writers, and was the composer of a remarkable string of musical comedy and revue successes: *La La Lucille* (1919); *George White's Scandals* (1920-24); *Lady, Be Good* (1924); *Oh, Kay* (1925); *Strike Up the Band* (1927); *Funny Face* (1927); *Girl Crazy* (1930); *Of Thee I Sing* (1931); *Let 'Em Eat Cake* (1933). From them came tunes which have not been surpassed in Tin Pan Alley: "Swanee" (interpolated in Jolson's *Sinbad*); "That Certain Feeling"; "Fascinating Rhythm"; "Do, Do, Do"; "Fidgety Feet"; "Maybe"; "Sweet and Lowdown"; "The Man I Love"; " 'S Wonderful"; "My One and Only"; "Embraceable You"; and many others.

He was born in Brooklyn, New York, September 26, 1898. As a youngster he studied piano with Charles Hambitzer and harmony with Edward Kilenyi, and at the age of sixteen went to work for the firm of J. H. Remick & Company as a "song-plugger." He soon began to write his own songs and was launched on a career of remarkable brilliance. But he had "higher" ambitions, for which the Whiteman concert offered him the first good opportunity. The *Rhapsody in Blue* was an instantaneous success, and was listened to with rapture by the great American public, and with interest by numerous serious composers who felt it pointed in a direction that seemed to offer interesting possibilities. Two of the most exaggerated tributes and one of the most acid comments on Gershwin have come from England. In 1930, Albert Coates, noted conductor, ranked the Concerto in F among the "fifty best musical compositions of all time." And Stanley R. Nelson, author of a somewhat fatuous book, *All About Jazz,* wrote of the Tchaikovskian *espressivo* theme in the *Rhapsody,* "To me, this noble tune is one of the most appealing things in all music." On the other hand, the witty young British musician, Constant Lambert, speaks of the *Rhapsody* as "combining the more depressing mannerisms of jazz with all the formlessness of the nineteenth-century fantasia," and one has to admit that the second half of this reproach, at least, is accurate enough.

Gershwin's next venture in the symphonic field was commissioned by Walter Damrosch for the old New York Symphony Orchestra; it was the Concerto in F, written in 1925. For the *Rhapsody in Blue* the orchestration had been prepared by Ferde Grofé, but now that Gershwin had graduated into the ranks of symphony orchestra composers he decided that he must do his own scoring. Still belonging, however, to Tin Pan Alley so far as his income was concerned, Gershwin could afford to do what many of his more distinguished colleagues in the symphonic field must have envied him for—that is, hire an orchestra to play the piece over a few times, and then adjust the orchestration accordingly.

Gershwin played the piano part of the Concerto himself. Damrosch, who conducted, introduced the new work with these remarks:

Various composers have been walking around jazz like a cat around a plate of hot soup, waiting for it to cool off, so that they could enjoy it without burning their tongues, hitherto accustomed only to the more tepid liquid distilled by cooks of the classical school. Lady Jazz, adorned with her intriguing rhythms, has danced her way around the world, even as far as the Eskimos of the North and the Polynesians of the South Sea Isles. But for all her travels and her sweeping popularity, she has encountered no knight who could lift her to a level that would enable her to be received as a respectable member in musical circles.

George Gershwin seems to have accomplished this miracle. He has done it boldly by dressing this extremely independent and up-to-date young lady in the classic garb of a concerto. Yet he has not detracted one whit from her fascinating personality. He is the Prince who has taken Cinderella by the hand and openly proclaimed her a princess to the astonished world, no doubt to the fury of her envious sisters.

Just who the sisters were, Dr. Damrosch didn't specify. But despite his graceful remarks and Gershwin's best playing, the Concerto didn't quite come off as the *Rhapsody* had done, although it enjoyed a considerable popularity for several years.

In *An American in Paris,* also written for Dr. Damrosch, and presented by him on the same program with the first performance of Bloch's *America,* Gershwin found a subject suited to his idiom, and created a very charming and relaxed bit of writing. It had humor and gaiety, two of the things jazz could handle best. And its program— the adventures of an American (recognizably the composer himself) three thousand miles from home—opened the door to a "blue" mood and a blues theme that is one of Gershwin's happiest inspirations.

On February 5, 1932, Gershwin played his Second Rhapsody, for piano and orchestra, in Carnegie Hall, New York, with the Boston Orchestra, under Dr. Serge Koussevitzky. On that occasion, Olin Downes wrote:

The score . . . is the expansion of a five-minute sequence introduced into the picture *Delicious,* a screen comedy drama, based on a story by Guy Bolton, with lyrics by Ira Gershwin and music by George, produced in 1931. The Rhapsody was written in California in the Spring of the same year and later somewhat revised. Some of the comedy scenes showed the streets of New York, and for the five-minute orchestral sequence Gershwin conceived a "rivet theme" to echo the tattoo of the skyscrapers. The Second Rhapsody had originally the title of "Rhapsody in Rivets."

This rhapsody has more orchestration and more development than the *Rhapsody in Blue.* Its main motive is reasonably suggestive of rivets and racket in the streets of the metropolis; also, if you like, of the liveliness and bonhomie of its inhabitants. There is a second theme, built into a contrasting section. Thus jazz dance rhythm and sentimental song are opposed and juxtaposed in this score. The conception is wholly orchestral . . . But with all its immaturities, the *Rhapsody in Blue* is more individual and originative than the piece heard last night. . . . We have had better things from Mr. Gershwin, and we expect better in time to come.

One more serious effort on a large scale was to come from George Gershwin, his "folk opera" *Porgy and Bess,* based on the play, *Porgy,* by Du Bose and Dorothy Heyward, produced by the New York Theater

Guild at the Alvin Theater in the autumn of 1935. It was characteristic that when he did get around to writing a jazz opera he wrote it for the theater, and not for the opera house, so that it might be a good show, and not just a musical triumph. All are agreed that it was the former; on the latter question there were dissenting opinions. Brooks Atkinson, drama critic of the *New York Times,* remarked that "Mr. Gershwin has found a personal voice that was inarticulate in the original play. The fear and the pain go deeper in *Porgy and Bess* than they did in penny-plain *Porgy.*" But he had some sensible objections to make:

These comments are written by a reviewer so inured to the theater that he regards operatic form as cumbersome. Why commonplace remarks that carry no emotion have to be made in a chanting monotone is a problem in art he cannot fathom. Even the hermit thrush drops into conversational tones when he is not singing from the topmost spray in a tree. Turning *Porgy* into an opera has resulted in a deluge of casual remarks that have to be thoughtfully intoned and that amazingly impede the action. Why do composers vex it so? "Sister, you goin' to the picnic?" "No, I guess not." Now, why in heaven's name must two characters in an opera clear their throats before they can exchange that sort of information? . . . To the ears of a theater critic there are intimations in *Porgy and Bess* that Mr. Gershwin is still easiest in mind when he is writing songs with choruses. He, and his present reviewer, are on familiar ground when he is writing a droll tune like "A Woman Is a Sometime Thing," or a lazy darkie solo like "I Got Plenty o' Nuttin'," or made-to-order spirituals like "Oh, de Lawd Shake de Heaven," or Sportin' Life's hot-time number entitled "There's a Boat that's Leavin' Soon for New York." If Mr. Gershwin does not enjoy his task most in moments like this, his audience does. In sheer quality of character they are worth an hour of formal music transitions.

Lawrence Gilman took exactly the opposite view:

Perhaps it is needlessly Draconian to begrudge Mr. Gershwin the song-hits which he has scattered through his score and which will doubtless enhance his fame and popularity. Yet they mar it. They are its cardinal weakness. They are a blemish upon its musical integrity. . . . It is not Gershwin, the apt and accommodating lyricist, who is most conspicuously present in *Porgy and Bess,* but Gershwin the musical dramatist, who has, in certain fortunate moments of this score, been moved to compassionate and valid utterance by the wildness and the pathos and the tragic fervor that can so strangely agitate the souls of men. These pages will abide, and honor the composer, long after the musical-comedy treacle which drips from other pages has ceased to gladden even those whose favor is scarcely worth the price.

In this case, one is tempted to think that it was the drama reviewer who proved the better music critic. Gershwin was so much a natural part of Tin Pan Alley, and jazz was so natural a part of him, that one must doubt whether his effort to make it a mere ingredient of music in the larger forms ever would have succeeded. The larger forms themselves were not anything he came to naturally, and they always fitted him very loosely. Whether he would have grown into them is a question that can never be answered.

For, at a cruelly early age, and with cruel suddenness, death cut him down in the middle of his remarkable career, on July 11, 1937. He was in Hollywood, working on the score of a new picture, *The Goldwyn Follies*. Two weeks before his death he collapsed at the film studios and was taken to a hospital for observation, with his illness tentatively diagnosed as a nervous breakdown. He seemed to recover, but twelve days later again collapsed, and this time X-ray examination showed a fast-growing brain tumor. An emergency operation was performed, but he did not survive it.

No one questions the eminence of George Gershwin in the field of popular song. And if his accomplishments in more pretentious fields are less firmly established, there can be no question that he put ideas into the heads of many composers who, while lacking his free and easy gift of tunefulness, may turn out to be better able than he to embody jazz in a truly symphonic style. Among his engaging small pieces, the delightful *Preludes* for piano, although they have not seemed to fit into any previous part of this discussion, must not be entirely overlooked. Nor must the part that his brother, Ira Gershwin (born December 6, 1896, New York City), played in George's success as adroit and tasteful lyric writer for many of the works mentioned go without acknowledgment.

Aaron Copland

By Marion Bauer

Abridged from "The American Music Lover," Vol. 4

AARON COPLAND was born in Brooklyn, November 14, 1900, and began his musical studies when he was twelve. Among his teachers were Victor Wittgenstein and Clarence Adler for piano, and Rubin Goldmark and Nadia Boulanger for composition. He was the first student of composition to enroll in Mlle. Boulanger's classes, in 1921, at the Fontainebleau School of Music. He remained under her tutelage for three years.

In 1925 he received the Guggenheim Fellowship, which he held for two years. In 1930 he was joint winner in the RCA Victor Company award presented to him for his *Dance Symphony*. He was one of the American composers commissioned by the Columbia Broadcasting System to write a work specifically for radio performance. This *Music for Radio,* subtitled *Saga of the Prairie,* had its première July 25, 1937.

Copland has been a most constructive agent in the development and encouragement of contemporary music and of American composers. This interest in American contemporary music manifested itself in his co-operation with Roger Sessions in the Copland-Sessions Concerts during the seasons of 1928-1931; as first director of the American Festivals of Contemporary Music at Yaddo, Saratoga Springs, for two seasons; as an active member of the League of Composers Executive Board; as a director of the United States Section of the International Society for Contemporary Music; and more recently (1937) as the founder and chairman of the American Composers Alliance, one object of which is to improve the economic status of native composers.

From the first, Aaron Copland manifested an individuality and a musical profile which has developed and matured. As has been the case with innumerable composers, he has evinced definite changes in style. But with Copland, probably because he is a child of his day and age, he has gone from complexity to simplification, from harmonic harshness to a gentler and more amiable mode of procedure. Such was obviously the case with *El Salon Mexico.*

His earlier music might be compared to the abstractionists' paintings in being all angles, lines, and planes. Soft melodic contours, long and involved developments, rich impressionistic harmonies, are absent. His use of the piano is almost invariably percussive, staccato, and dry, as for example in his *Concerto for Piano* (1926), *Piano Variations* (1930), and *Vitebsk—Study on a Jewish Melody* for violin, 'cello, and piano (1929).

Another considerable characteristic of Copland's style is his rhythmic vitality. Youth, exuberance, *élan,* ironic wit, fearlessness even to the point of recklessness, are expressed largely through his rhythms.

This American quality is not due alone to jazz, although with Copland the originality of his rhythmic designs comes no doubt from an inherent response to jazz and a conscious study of its possibilities.

Paul Rosenfeld, in his essay on Copland in *An Hour With American Music,* wrote a decade ago:

> The great interest of his music remains the architectural one, the interest of the independent, projected, self-sufficient object. And in their structurality, their faithfulness to the line of strength, his tonal edifices resemble nothing so much as steel cranes, bridges, and the frames of skyscrapers before the masons smear them with their stonework.

Probably the most frequently heard of Copland's earlier works is *Music for the Theatre.* It is in five movements: *Prologue, Dance, Interlude, Burlesque,* and *Epilogue.* As in so many of his scores, here we find Copland's feeling for jazz and lively rhythms contrasted with serious mood and a classic feeling for form.

Of Copland's ballets, I must take the word of others that he has a flair for this type of music, as I have never seen any of his three works: *Grogh* (1932); *Hear Ye, Hear Ye!* (1934); or *Billy the Kid** (1938). The second of these was presented by the Chicago Grand Opera Company under the direction of Ruth Page. During the instrumental introduction, a series of sensational tabloid headlines, flashed upon the curtain by means of a moving-picture projector, outlined the plot. The entire work was treated satirically and as grotesque. Copland's understanding of jazz, of the American scene, and of irony in music, is given full play.

Copland's new style may have been creeping up gradually on the public, but it took many unawares when his *Music for Radio,* announced as *A Saga of the Prairies,* had its radio première on July 25, 1937. This followed closely on the heels of the play-opera, *The Second Hurricane,* written for and performed by the children of the Henry Street Settlement Music School. Naturally, this music was in a simpler fashion and idiom than his earlier works, though thoroughly original and far from conservative. Likewise, the *Music for Radio* was comparatively simple. Straightforward melodies, colorful harmonization, and effective orchestration made the work one of softer curves and more amiable effects than are regarded as characteristic of Copland.

The Second Hurricane is a two-act "play-opera," on a libretto by

---

* Together with his more recent *Rodeo* (1942), *Billy the Kid* has been consistently programmed since its first performance in 1939.—E. S.

Edwin Denby, which occupies an entire evening in performance. It was first presented by a cast of one hundred and fifty ranging in age from eight to eighteen, at the Neighborhood Playhouse, April 21, 1937 (New York City), under the stage direction of Orson Welles, and the musical direction of Lehman Engel. Copland understands the adolescent mind and character and knows how to control his technique and musical thought so as to write appropriately and effectively for children. There are solo arias for youthful voices, choruses for the children, and choral parts in which the worry of the parents and comrades is expressed for the children who are experiencing the second hurricane alone and separated from the others. The orchestra numbers twenty, and it plays simple music accompanying the songs, all of which are written in a popular style easily assimilated by the young people.

In the *One-Act Play Magazine,* Paul Rosenfeld wrote (Dec. 1938):

The Second Hurricane is one of Copland's attempts to meet the public half way. Yet nowhere has he been guilty of concessions to public bad-taste. The material is concise; and the musical treatment is invariably sensitive and resourceful. The writing for the brass is particularly brilliant and hard of edge. Much of the choral writing is grand. . . . In fact, this revealing little play-opera may be very influential on the future of American music: as a work representative of a new tendency to simplicity without sacrifice of either musical expressiveness or of musical quality.

One of Copland's recent works* is *Outdoor Overture,* written especially for the orchestra of the New York High School of Music and Art, and played December 16 and 17, 1938. Again he has disciplined himself to the point of writing a not too difficult score which the orchestra played with contagious enthusiasm. It is fresh, spontaneous, and wholesome.

Copland states his credo clearly in his book, *What to Listen for in Music,* first in the Preface:

The composer has something vital at stake. In helping others to hear music more intelligently, he is working toward the spread of a musical culture which in the end will effect the understanding of his own creations.

And again the last chapter:

---

* Since 1939, Mr. Copland has written the music for three films: *The City, Of Mice and Men,* and *Our Town* (at the moment of writing he is at work on a fourth, *North Star*), a *Lincoln Portrait* for orchestra, incidental music for the plays *Five Kings* and *Quiet City,* and a Piano Sonata.

What, after all, do we listen for when we listen to a composer? He need not tell us a story like the novelist; he need not "copy" nature like the sculptor; his work need have no immediate practical function like the architect's drawing. What is it that he gives us, then? Only one answer seems possible to me: He gives us himself. Every artist's work is, of course, an expression of himself, but none so direct as that of the creative musician. He gives us, without relation to exterior "events," the quintessential part of himself— that part which embodies the fullest and deepest expression of himself as a man and of his experience as a fellow-being.

Marc Blitzstein

From "Our New Music"

By Aaron Copland

MARC BLITZSTEIN* is a comparative newcomer as far as writing for the stage goes. As a very young man he was something of a problem child. He seemed to have all the necessary requisites for composing— talent, ability, technique—but somehow he had a harder time than most composers in finding out exactly what he wanted to do. From time to time he wrote works destined for the stage, such as the unproduced ballet *Cain,* an unusually promising piece, or the light one-acter *Triple Sec* that found production in a musical revue. But these were only incidental in a fairly long list of concert pieces, few of which actually reached the concert hall. The reason was that not many of them really came off in a way that one could thoroughly approve. Either a composition was too obviously derivative, or it tried too hard to be astonishing, or the style adopted was too rigidly abstract. It wasn't until Blitzstein began writing primarily for the stage that he really found himself.

His stage works belong to a category that is better called musical theater than opera. They are meant to be performed, not by singers with trained voices but by actors who can sing after a fashion. This gives them a reality as stage drama that opera seldom has. At the same time it seriously limits the emotional range made possible in opera by

* Born in Philadelphia, March 2, 1905. In addition to the works described by Mr. Copland, Blitzstein has (since 1937, the year of *The Cradle Will Rock*) written music for the films *Valley Town, The Spanish Earth, Native Land,* and *Night Shift.* As this book goes to press, he is serving in the U. S. Army Air Corps.—E. S.

the complete exploitation of that most expressive of all instruments, the human voice. What Blitzstein has sacrificed in giving up the fullness and amplitude of the operatically trained voice he has gained in the naturalness and charm of the singing actor. There is little likelihood that one will ever replace the other. I myself should not like to see the musical theater accepted as a substitute for opera. But it certainly brings us closer to a realization of that dream of an American grand opera.

Blitzstein's success as theatrical composer rests, thus far, on two works: *The Cradle Will Rock* and *No for an Answer.* He has written, besides, effective scores for a half-hour radio opera called *I've Got the Tune,* scores for some documentary films, and also incidental music for several straight dramas. In his work for the musical theater he has the inestimable advantage of being able to write his own texts. (You have to know how very rare good librettos are to appreciate what that means.) Most commentators are agreed that Blitzstein has an unusual flair for dialogue and lyrics but does less well in the construction of a tightly knit dramatic plot. He will undoubtedly improve in this respect as he adds to his experience in the theater.

In his first full-length work for the stage, *The Cradle Will Rock,* Blitzstein was clearly influenced by the examples of Kurt Weill and Hanns Eisler. The *Dreigroschen Oper* of Weill had set the model: spoken dialogue interspersed with recitative, interspersed with more formal numbers such as solos, trios, and choruses. There was nothing new in the formula itself, for it was mostly a reversion to a pre-Wagnerian kind of opera—with these differences, however: the subject matter was entirely contemporaneous, the solos and concerted numbers were in the manner of popular songs rather than operatic arias and choruses, and the spoken dialogue and the music were more evenly balanced. The whole was something of a cross between social drama, musical revue, and opera. Blitzstein was the first to apply this formula to an American stage work. Some of the tunes that he wrote still showed the Weill or Eisler derivation, but they all had their own character— satirical, tender, bitter, or pessimistic. The prosody, which was subtle and complex, nevertheless had all the naturalness of hard-boiled English as sung in a jazz song—an accomplishment in itself. One innovation peculiar to Blitzstein was introduced: the musical sections, instead of being formally set with definite beginnings and endings, seemed to start and finish casually, so that one was rarely conscious of where the music began and the dialogue left off, or vice versa. Thus the general flow of the stage action was less likely to be cut up mechanically through the separation of speech and song.

Blitzstein brought with him from his experience as concert composer all the formal discipline of the trained musician. He possesses a passionate love of design. One of the most striking characteristics of *The Cradle* was the extent to which every moment in the piece seemed controlled. Nothing was left to chance. Every word in the text appeared to have its set place in the dramatic web, just as in music a theme has its set place in the contrapuntal web. I mention this with some emphasis because it is obviously one of Blitzstein's principal preoccupations and is certain to play a large part in any further work he undertakes.

No for an Answer was an advance on the first work in every way. For one thing it was closer to straight opera than *The Cradle*—there was more continuous singing. Then, too, the choral sections were enormously exciting. Here the lack of trained voices was least apparent. For once the chorus seemed to know what it was singing about, and this, combined with a directness and surety in the thing said, made for a completely infectious enthusiasm. But perhaps Blitzstein's outstanding achievement was the fact that for the first time in a serious stage work he gave the typical American tough guy musical characterization. Just imagine what it means to make a taxi driver sing so that the result sounds natural. In *No for an Answer* the composer has one of the little guys, in this case a panhandler, sing a song in accents so true as to make us feel that no one has ever before even attempted the problem of finding a voice for all those American regular fellows who seem so much at home everywhere except on the operatic stage. If the opera had nothing more than this to recommend it, its historical importance would be considerable.

With *No for an Answer* Blitzstein finally found his own musical style. You can recognize it in the short, clipped musical sentences, the uneven phrase lengths, the nervous energy, the unerring sense of design. There is subtle use of a talky prose rhythm over a musical background that is very personal to the composer. His melodic line, as a rule, is straightforward, but the accompaniments may be exceedingly complex, though almost never obtrusive. Thus, the man in the gallery has a tune to hang onto, and the more erudite listener has added musical interest with which to occupy himself. His style, as musical theater, is always enormously effective, whether the mood is one of heartsick yearning or punch-line sarcasm, social uplift or the dregs of dejection. It is a thoroughly malleable style that can be applied in future to almost any subject matter.

Henry Cowell

From "Our Contemporary Composers"

By John Tasker Howard

HENRY COWELL is the friend of all modern tendencies and the tireless proponent of all modern works. In his books, *American Composers on American Music* and *New Musical Resources;* in the concerts which he has organized at the New School for Social Research in New York, and for the Pan American Association of Composers in Europe and America; in his lectures in many parts of the world; in his quarterly publications and recordings of New Music, issued under that title; and in countless other activities, he has been one of the most ardent and effective champions of modern American music of the nonconformist variety.

Cowell was born in California on March 11, 1897. He studied the violin as a child, but when he was eight he gave his instrument away. He decided that composing was his destiny, and he proceeded to follow it, not deliberately breaking the rules of harmony, but simply not learning them and paying no attention to them. Charles Seeger was one of his teachers, but Cowell is largely self-taught. He is in the truest sense of the word an experimenter, for it is the materials of music and their expansion that chiefly interest him. His early fame came from his use of the term "tone-clusters" and from his employment of them in his music. He was not the first or the only composer to use clumps of tones as sonorous material. Ives had written "chords" that must be played with a board or a ruler. But Cowell specialized in the production of new tone-colors from the piano. He pays no attention to prejudices and habits of thought, such as the notion that the keyboard is the part of the piano that should be used for tone production. No—Cowell rubs, pats, plucks, punches the strings, the sounding-board, the case. And in so doing he has produced some new and wondrous sounds, which have nothing but the unconventionality of their origin against them. Probably he has produced more raw material for composition than actual music;* but that is often true of pioneers.

In 1931, he received a Guggenheim Fellowship for the study of comparative musicology—specifically, the music of exotic and primitive peoples—in Berlin. It was in that same year, too, that Cowell induced Professor Léon Thérémin, inventor of the ether-wave instrument that bears his name, to construct an instrument for the execution of all sorts of complicated rhythms, which they dubbed the Rhythmicon. From one to sixteen sounds in a given time-interval are made by this instrument, at the pitches which correspond to their metric frequency in the overtone series. Cowell has written a four-movement orchestral suite, *Rhythmicana,* in which this instrument is employed.

Cowell's tendencies as a composer are dual. On the one hand, he has a certain Celtic fondness for the weird, the colorful, the whimsical—even, at times, the sentimental. On the other, he is full of the scientific spirit. *Synchrony,* for orchestra and dancers; *Polyphonica,* for twelve instruments; a Piano Concerto—these and many other compositions represent the modern scientific experimenter in Cowell. The Suite for "string and percussion piano" and chamber orchestra (in three movements, "The Banshee," "The Leprechaun," and "The Fairy Bells"), represents the application of his technique acquired by experiment to the ends of expressiveness and color effect.

The list of Cowell's works is far too long for inclusion here. And besides, it is what he stands for, what he has made possible, and what he has done to help his fellow composers that make him most important. Whatever one thinks of the value of his music, or of this innovation or that, or even of much of the music he has helped to make known, he has been a unique and incomparable factor in seasoning our musical fare, and in adding color and life to the American musical scene.

* This is probably truer of many early Cowell compositions than of those he has produced in recent years. Since about 1939, Mr. Cowell's work has entered a new phase, in which there is a distinct feeling for a more melodic and communicative music. In such compositions as *Tales of Our Countryside, Old American Country Set,* and *Gaelic Symphony* for orchestra, and *Shoonthree* (one of 21 works for symphonic band), Cowell has achieved a simplification of his formerly complex materials that makes them impressive and enjoyable as music alone.—E. S.

Morton Gould

From *"Our Contemporary Composers"*

By John Tasker Howard

MORTON GOULD is one of those who have approached jazz "from above" (to use an old-fashioned expression); that is, he did not come to serious music as an alumnus of Tin Pan Alley, but rather the other way around. Born December 10, 1913, in Richmond Hill, Long Island, Gould began to compose when he was four years old, and was something of a pianistic prodigy as well. He studied piano with Abby Whiteside and musical theory with Dr. Vincent Jones, and graduated at the age of fifteen from New York University. In his teens still, he played in public a good deal and attracted some attention as an "elbow pianist"— one, that is, who was not afraid to use his elbows or his whole forearm or anything else that would help him achieve the effect he desired. It would have been easy for him to develop as an eccentric, as so many others have done. But fortunately, financial pressure intervened. He had to earn his living, and Broadway was the best place to do it, he thought. For a time he was on the staff of the Radio City Music Hall, and later of the National Broadcasting Company. Of recent years he has conducted his own programs of "special arrangements" on Station WOR.

Gould has not let his work in the popular field swamp his serious activities, and he has tried to maintain a fruitful connection between the two. He has little use for the "art-for-art's-sake" boys. His *Chorale and Fugue in Jazz* was played by Stokowski and the Philadelphia Orchestra in January, 1936; he has played his Piano Concerto with various leading orchestras; and Fritz Reiner commissioned his *Foster Gallery,* a work based on melodies by the immortal Stephen. He has also written three Piano Sonatas; an *Americana Suite;* a Cantata; a Symphony; and two *Swing Symphonettes.**

* Since this was written, Mr. Gould has written two more *Symphonettes* (one of them *Latin-American*); *Spirituals for Orchestra; A Cowboy Rhapsody; Joshua; Lincoln Legend; Folk Suite,* and a number of other works, many of which have been widely performed. His music is easily among the most popular written by serious composers today. His name is rapidly becoming one of the best known in American music, not only because of his compositions but also through his radio programs, which have at last won the desirable "commercial" status.—E. S.

Paul Creston

From "Our Contemporary Composers"

By John Tasker Howard

BECAUSE of his research in the fields of acoustics, esthetics, musico-therapy, and kindred subjects, Paul Creston might conceivably be placed among the experimenters, but his music does not altogether justify such a classification. Leonard Liebling made this distinction clear when he reviewed Creston's Suite for saxophone (or clarinet) and piano. He wrote:

> Here is something in contemporary style which will please the advance guard and not offend the reactionaries and standpatters. Creston's form and construction move along conservative lines, but his harmonies and rhythms speak the tonal language of the moment. If there is concordance in dissonance, you can find it here, much to the satisfaction of any sort of taste. Freshness in ideas, clever colors, and a certain healthy brightness seem to prove that Creston does not write merely because he has technic, but chiefly because he feels creative urge. His new suite has atonal freedom, with the result that the integrated passage writing is especially alive and flexible.

Creston was born in New York, October 10, 1906, and is self-taught in harmony, theory and composition. He did, however, study other branches of music with Randegger and Déthier, and organ with Pietro Yon. At present he is organist and choirmaster at St. Malachy's Church in New York. He was awarded a Guggenheim Fellowship in 1938, and again in 1939. Among his works are a Prelude and Dance, and a Symphony, for orchestra; a Partita for flute, violin, and strings; and a long list of chamber-music works, several of which have been performed at the Yaddo and the Westminster Festivals, and elsewhere. His *Two Choric Dances* were performed by the National Symphony Orchestra in Washington under Hans Kindler, on March 3, 1940. His Concertino for marimba and orchestra was played at Yaddo in September, 1940. Perkins found it "graceful and melodic and advantageous for the soloist, while not of unusual consequence in regard to its musical ideas." But then, as someone has remarked, it would be hard to be very significant on the marimba.*

Earl Robinson

From "Our Contemporary Composers"

By John Tasker Howard

EARL ROBINSON sprang into sudden prominence in the spring of 1939 with his *Ballad for Americans,* a piece for chorus, solo voice, and orchestra. It is a novel concoction of talk and music, singing the praises of democracy; and it is perhaps for its idea, embodied in a libretto by John La Touche, as much as for its music, that it became immensely popular. It was first introduced in the WPA production, *Sing for your Supper,* where it created a considerable stir. Then it was broadcast on the Columbia Broadcasting System program, "The Pursuit of Happiness," with Paul Robeson taking the solo part. From this hearing its fame and popularity spread—to the symphony orchestras, the movies, and even (although it was of Leftist origin and inspiration) to the Republican National Convention in 1940. Largely on the basis of this great popular success, perhaps, Robinson won a Guggenheim Fellowship for 1940 for work on a musical dramatization of Carl Sandburg's *The People, Yes.* There is no reason to doubt that Robinson may have a fine talent. He has written other songs and choruses with a message, and incidental music for several Federal Theater plays. But there is also no blinking the fact that the *Ballad for Americans* is a bit old-fashioned and theatrical, and that the fact that it came just at a time when people were particularly conscious of the blessings of the American democracy was largely responsible for its success. On the strength of *God Bless America* alone, Irving Berlin would not have been proclaimed a popular hero, either, at any other time. But voicing the sentiments of the people is no

---

* Since 1941 the name of Paul Creston has appeared with increasing frequency on important orchestral programs. Toscanini has played his *Choric Dance No. 2,* with the NBC Symphony and on tour; Stokowski has recorded the Second Movement of his Symphony. In 1943 he won the awards of the Academy of Arts and Letters and of the New York Music Critics Circle.—E. S.

doubt a worthy calling, too, even if no particular originality or distinction is involved.* Robinson was born July 2, 1910, at Seattle. Washington, and educated at the University of Washington.

Alex North

From "A World of Music" (in preparation)

By Elie Siegmeister

ALEX NORTH † is one of the most curious and little-known figures of young America. His music has qualities which are decidedly rare today —graceful charm, easy lyricism, and clean emotional warmth. North developed as a composer through writing "functional" compositions of an especially intricate variety: music for the modern dance.

The musician who works for dancers of the Martha Graham, Doris Humphreys, or Hanya Holm schools is given a task requiring almost mathematical ingenuity. The dancer generally works out her choreography in utmost detail: each beat and step is planned and measured out. The composer, called in when the pattern is all set, is asked to write a score in which every beat dovetails exactly with the movements of the dancer. Most men simply turn in a series of loosely connected musical sequences whose sole merit is that they furnish a background for the choreography.

To write music that will meet these requirements and yet be able to stand on its own as well is a technical and creative feat of the highest order. Alex North's *Slaughter of the Innocents*—written for Anna

* Who knows what is or is not "originality"? Perhaps another generation will look back on some of the "original" composers of our time—whose music means little to anyone but themselves and their friends—and find that their so-called originality was nothing but a stereotype and an escape from life. Perhaps it is more original to be common, to write music which everyone can grasp and sing, and which expresses our American ideals in a much deeper way than *God Bless America.* Earl Robinson's music has played a role in our country's history, and if the composer continues to grow artistically—as his recent Cantata, *Abraham Lincoln Comes Home,* gives evidence of his doing—he may prove to be a far more important artist than many whose technical achievements far outstrip his own.—E. S.

† Alex North was born in Chester, Pa., Dec. 10, 1910. He studied composition with Aaron Copland and Ernest Toch. Besides compositions for the dance, films, and stage, he has written several orchestral works, numerous songs, piano pieces, chamber music works, etc. He is at present in the U. S. Army.

Sokolov's dance on the bombing of Barcelona—is one of the most moving American scores of recent years, even when listened to apart from the dance. The ballet music for *War is Beautiful* used all the resources of contemporary music to deliver a savage attack on Fascist barbarism. (Both scores were written in 1937-8.)

North's uncanny sense of musical timing, derived from his dance experience, enabled him to write a brilliant score for the film *People of the Cumberland.* Here two aspects of the composer's talent found free play: his sense of jazz rhythms and his unusual melodic invention. He is not specifically a jazz composer. But the tempo and the quality of popular rhythm and melody are in his bones; they come out naturally in the midst of any American subject he touches.

This is most clearly illustrated in his Negro Cantata, *Mother.* Here he has evolved a style in which popular and serious elements are so completely fused that there is no longer any question of "how to bring jazz and classical music together." Here they *are* one single American music. In the slow, easy melody with which *Mother* opens, there is syncopation and the Charleston rhythm; but also a serious beauty and dignity never known to Tin Pan Alley. *Mother,* with its direct, effortless melodies and its structural simplicity—a simplicity enriched by all the resources of modern harmony when needed—is definitely music of the American people. It is a strange commentary on our present musical life that this work, written in 1940, has had only one performance to date.

If there is one quality that the music of the "modern" school has lacked it is a healthy, joyous feeling. Certainly our times are as troubled, and the personal hardships of the composer as great today, as they have ever been. Yet there is one difference between the present and the last generation: the musician who has devoted himself to the service of the common people has a future. He is convinced of the triumph of democracy, and in spite of all difficulties his music has the strength that comes from ties with common humanity. He can be, must be, confident and cheerful—yes, even filled with joy in the midst of the world's terrors.

Alex North's children's opera, *The Hither and Thither of Danny Dither,* is symbolic not only of the young American composer, but of all young people in this distraught world. It is the story of a youngster so lost that he does not even know his name. He wanders about the maze of a big city, hoping to find his identity through the newspapers, the radio, the welfare agencies. Finally, he is adopted by the city brats who assure him he need not worry about his name, for they will help him find himself and show that there is still good in the world.

The piece was written when the present War had already broken out. But its warm lyricism, its atmosphere of human sympathy, the love and joy that exudes from this music not only stamp Alex North as one of the inevitable composers of tomorrow, but show that, even in the midst of this great struggle (in which the composer himself is now an active participant) art grows stronger and deeper as it comes closer to the plain people.

Composer in Brooklyn *

From "A World of Music" (in preparation)

By Elie Siegmeister

As I have already mentioned somewhere in this book, the early stages of my career gave absolutely no signs of being a child prodigy's—and I am glad of it. For, music study being what it was twenty-five years ago (practising eight hours a day, exclusive concentration on the "classics," isolation from normal life), I found it repugnant to all my instincts as a boy and even through my college years. I felt at that time, as I still do, that Art with a capital A is a menace; music is one of the elements of a normal American existence, not apart from it. The exoticism of art music in the 1920's seemed alien and meaningless to the people I knew and liked (my part of Brooklyn is a small community pretty much like any other small town in America).

So that, while I wrote fugues and sonatas for Seth Bingham's composition class at Columbia, my heart wasn't in them. The first work that showed a spark of my own was a weird song, "Rosenbloom is Dead," inspired by an incident that occurred in 1925 on our Brooklyn street. When friends went around the house chanting its refrain, I knew I was a composer. My first ambitious work was a cantata to words of Carl Sandburg.

After several years of serious study (with Wallingford Riegger

---

* With apologies to Aaron Copland, who described himself (in *Our New Music*) as "Composer *from* Brooklyn." I am in fact an interloper on Long Island, having been born in Manhattan; but, migrating across the East River at the age of five, I found the air so salubrious and inspiriting that I have never left since. Whereas Mr. Copland, who is also a Boys' High grad, has been tempted by the high life across the river, and for many years can boast only that he is *from* Brooklyn.

and Nadia Boulanger among others) I went through the usual difficulties of a young composer seeking to have his music played. My first "break" came when a bunch of us calling ourselves by the proud title "The Young Composers' Group" (we were a strange assortment) gave a concert at a downtown hall in 1932. Behold! the critics came and wrote not unfavorable reviews—even though one of the works on the program was "Five-and-Ten-Cent-Store Music," including in its instrumentation a milk bottle and a tin whistle. Performances by the various modern music societies followed, and gradually my music began to get around.

But in the early 1930's I found myself quite dissatisfied with performing for the narrow and oversophisticated audiences of the "élite" organizations, and turned to making music for the wider audience of people who never came to modern music concerts—never even heard of them, in fact. I organized a chorus of shipping clerks, house painters, stenographers, and college students (their enthusiasm was greater than their note-reading ability) and, together with another group of young composers, gave concerts of newly written American music in empty lofts and abandoned stores in Brooklyn, the Bronx—wherever we could get people to listen. Although the admission (usually 25 cents) was just about enough to pay the performers' carfares, contact with this fresh audience of common people was stimulating. They only paid a quarter to hear us, but always insisted on getting their money's worth. After the official program was over, the fireworks usually began. The members of the audience would rise and fire questions at the composers: "Where is the melody in your work?"—"Why did you write that composition?"—"What has your music to do with us?" Those questions sometimes made us pretty mad, but after it was all over, we realized that we had gotten the most honest and direct music criticism of all.

In this way, the people of Flatbush and Brighton Beach heard the first performances of compositions such as my *Strange Funeral in Braddock, North Pole Flight, Elegies for García Lorca,* and others later performed over radio chains and at concerts throughout the nation.

One day I was interviewed by the *Brooklyn Eagle,* and read in the paper the next day: BORO COMPOSER SEES MUSIC CLOSER TO PEOPLE, AWAY FROM HALLS. Although I had nothing against concert halls as such, that was in a way my direction in the late 1930's. Like many others, I too felt that good music should not stand off by itself, but should get out into all the activities of daily life; should go where the people were.

I eagerly sought the opportunity to write for the dance, theater, and radio, for schools, amateur performers, and children. At the same time, contact with these various agencies stimulated me to think along new lines, musically speaking. What might be called the "American" flavor in some of my scores: *American Holiday, Abraham Lincoln Walks at Midnight* (a cantata to words of Vachel Lindsay), and *Created Equal* (music for one of the Federal Theater's Living Newspapers), was probably a result.

I am not one of those who believe in any special formula for writing music, and I do not think folk music or any other kind of influence is necessary for the creation of great works. However, in the state of serious music in America about 1935—that of a rather abstruse, over-dissonant, and intellectualized art—contact with the simple, human quality of our folk tradition was a healthy, stimulating factor.

Like Mahomet and the mountain, I didn't come to folk music: it came to me. Walked up to me one day, as it were, in the person of Aunt Molly Jackson. It was after one of our downtown concerts that she cornered me and began forthwith to sing some of her Harlan (Kentucky) miners' songs. Then followed a whole series of blues, songs, ditties, and ballads that she garnered from her rich memory and imagination.

I liked Aunt Molly and her music. It seemed fresh and alive. When Lawrence Gellert invited me shortly afterwards to make notations of his collection of Negro folk music from the Deep South, I found that enjoyable, too. Charles Seeger and Henry Cowell played me more recordings of native American stuff at the New School (where I taught for a time) and roused my curiosity still more.

Since then I have played around with folk music, listening to it in various parts of the country, writing down some songs that hadn't been notated before, making several hundred arrangements and free fantasies on those that struck my fancy. Some of these have appeared on the programs of my American Ballad Singers on tour throughout the country, and in *The Treasury of American Song* which I brought out in collaboration with Olin Downes (whom I found a delightful person to work with, although we don't necessarily agree on many musical points).

The activity of a composer in America today carries him into many different fields. He finds himself giving concerts, teaching, writing books, performing over the radio, and heading towards the goal of making a living by his own music—surely a natural right. But there are few, if any, composers of "serious" music in America today who can do that. Perhaps it is our fault, perhaps the fault of the commercial-ism of Broadway and radio which tries to stick to musical clichés because they are sure sellers. I believe, however, that those composers who are heading towards a merger of the "serious" and the "popular" are going in the right direction. The old-time division of music into "fine art" and "common" music is growing less meaningful every day.

In the works I have written during the past few years, I think this tendency is noticeable. My *Walt Whitman Overture* and *American Folk Suite* for orchestra, the music for the play *Doodle Dandy of the U. S. A.* and the pageant *The Golden Doors,* the songs for Alfred Kreymborg's *Funnybone Alley* and the legendary ballads composed for my Ballad Singers have been written along these lines. I hope, in the orchestral and stage works which I look forward to writing, to make as good music as I possibly can, that will at the same time speak the language of all our people.

Other Americans

By Elie Siegmeister

AMERICAN music has grown at such a rate and on such a wide scale in the past decades that it is impossible to touch on even a fair proportion of its creators. However, in addition to those composers already dis-cussed, briefer mention must be made of another group of men whose contributions have been of great importance. Here again, some are eminent, and some very little known. The value of a man's work re-sides in the music itself, and not in how frequently it is played, how many honors its composer has won, or how much critical acclaim he has received. The following sixteen men are not members of any one school or coterie. In many ways they differ very strongly from each other. But, taken together with that of the composers already men-tioned, their music is a representative part of the American musical scene.

Ernest Bloch, although considered by many not an American composer at all (he was born in Geneva, Switzerland, in 1880), has lived and worked mainly in this country since 1916, and been an American citizen for many years. He has contributed greatly to the development of music in this country, and we should be more than proud to claim him as our own. For Bloch's music—a large part of it written, published, and first performed in the United States—has a grandeur, an emotional power, and a technical perfection equaled in the works of few other American composers. Outstanding among his works are the opera, *Macbeth;* the rhapsody for 'cello and orchestra, *Schelomo;* the Suite for Viola and Piano; the *Israel* Symphony; the Concerto Grosso; the String Quartet and Quintet; and the Violin Concerto. Much of his work has a rich and glowing Hebraic quality, an almost savage richness of color, a deep sincerity and conviction. Bloch's is a name known all over the world.

Edgar Varèse, born in Paris in 1885, is another foreign-born American whose influence has been strong in this country's musical circles. Although his music is little known (possibly with reason) to the broad concert public, he played an important part in introducing the "modern" idiom to the United States, and fought the good fight to secure recognition of contemporary composers and a contemporary style. Varèse was the founder and musical director of the International Composers' Guild, which was formed in 1922 and was the parent organization from which the League of Composers and the Pan American Association stemmed. His society was the earliest to introduce important works of Schönberg, Stravinsky, Milhaud, Hindemith, and other European modernists—and these had an incalculable influence on the growth of our own composers. As a composer, Varèse is of the "experimentalist" variety. The very titles of his works—*Hyperprism, Ionisation, Density 21.5, Arcanes*—show a preoccupation with the acoustical and scientific aspect of music. His star was highest in the "abstractionist" and "futurist" period. Although he apparently wished to bring music to the people, he never seemed to find a means of doing this in his own compositions.

Wallingford Riegger is one of the most reticent and least recognized figures in our musical Valhalla. Born in Georgia in 1885, he won the Paderewski and the Coolidge prizes in the 1920's; his works have figured on an occasional program; and he is fairly well known as a composer for the modern dance—but this is almost the extent of his recognition. Yet the sincerity and the solid, craftsmanlike qualities of his music entitle him to much more than that. Riegger has written a work called *Dichotomy,* and in a way he himself *is* a strange dichotomy.

Personally he is a simple, warm-hearted, humorous man, intensely pre-occupied with the fate of humanity about him; but his music is generally austere, violent, and esoteric. Unlike his early Trio in B Minor and *La Belle Dame Sans Merci,* which were tinged with romanticism, his more recent music is largely dissonant, harsh, atonal. Compositions such as the Rhapsody, *The Study in Sonority, Dichotomy,* and the String Quartet are not on the popular side. Riegger's dance music, however, especially the *New Dance* and *With My Red Fires,* have a more direct, down-to-earth quality. I should like to see more of the man's humor, simplicity, and kindly love of life come out in his music. In his recent Canon and Fugue for Strings and his Prelude and Fugue for Band there are signs that this is happening.

Deems Taylor is perhaps one of the best known of all American composers—not so much for his music as for the multifarious activities that have made his one of the biggest "names" in this country. President of ASCAP, music adviser to the Columbia Broadcasting System, commentator for the New York Philharmonic-Symphony Society's weekly broadcasts, author of clever books, and a frequent guest on "Information, Please," Taylor is a powerful influence in our musical life. Born in New York City in 1885, he has been music critic, editor, and writer of symphonic, theater, and ballet music. He is perhaps best known as the composer of *The King's Henchman* and *Peter Ibbetson,* both of them commissioned and performed by the Metropolitan Opera Company. Among his orchestral works are *Through the Looking Glass, Circus Days,* and *Marco Takes a Walk.*

Louis Gruenberg, born in Russia in 1884, was brought to this country at the age of one. He was among the first of his generation to turn to a distinctly American style in many of his works. He has written extensively for the orchestra, for the voice, and for various chamber-music combinations. Among his outstanding compositions in these fields have been the *Jazz-Suite, Daniel Jazz, Jazzettes, Enchanted Isle,* and *Creation,* a Negro preacher's sermon. Best of his works, however, have been his operas and film scores. *Emperor Jones,* based on the Eugene O'Neill play, was widely performed, as was also the children's opera *Jack and the Beanstalk.* Recently Mr. Gruenberg has been in Hollywood. Most impressive of all his film work was his score for a documentary on the question of infant mortality, *The Fight for Life.*

This was a dramatic and truly powerful score, integrated with the film in a deft and impressive manner.

Douglas Moore belongs to a younger generation than any of the above-mentioned composers. Born in Cutchogue, N. Y., in 1893, he grew up at a time when few were turning to American folk themes as material for their music. Mr. Moore, now Chairman of the Music Department at Columbia University, has expressed the American spirit in such works as the *Ballade of William Sycamore* for voice and four instruments; *Simon Legree* for men's voices and piano; *Moby Dick* and *The Pageant of P. T. Barnum* for orchestra. Best known and possibly most distinctive of his works is the opera *The Devil and Daniel Webster,* written to a text by Stephen Vincent Benét. This music has a sincere and authentic quality, and may be the forerunner of more operas in a distinctively American style.

Roy Harris, born in Lincoln County, Oklahoma, in 1898, is one of the most widely performed and successful of living American composers. He has written five symphonies, quite a number of overtures and other orchestral works, and much chamber music, choral works, sonatas, etc. He has won numerous awards and honors and is perhaps the most frequently commissioned of all contemporary Americans. His works have been played by every major symphony orchestra in the country and by all the radio networks, and there have been many critical discussions of his works and their meaning to America. His recent Fifth Symphony, dedicated to the people of Russia, was short-waved to that country, and the score was then sent on micro-film for performance there.

Lamar Stringfield is that rarity, a "regional" composer. Born in Raleigh, North Carolina, in 1897, he has been associated with many musical enterprises of his own state and has drawn richly on its native folk music. He organized the Institute of Folk Music at the University of North Carolina and was musical director of the North Carolina Symphony Society, the first state orchestra in the country. His orchestral works—especially *From the Southern Mountains, Moods of a Moonshiner, The Legend of John Henry, Cripple Creek,* and *A Negro Parade*—have a distinctive folk quality. They have been widely performed throughout the country.

Virgil Thomson, witty and acerb music critic of the New York *Herald Tribune,* is a composer with intentions all his own. Born in Kansas City, Missouri, in 1896, he held various positions and lived in Paris during 1925-32. There he acquired some of the mannerisms of the French group "Les Six" (especially of their prophet, Erik Satie), and the outlook of the "dadaists," including Gertrude Stein. It was to this writer's words that Mr. Thomson wrote his opera, *Four Saints in Three Acts,* performed in Hartford, New York, and Chicago under the auspices of the Friends and Enemies of Modern Music. Mr. Thomson's musical style is far less radical than are the titles and ideas with which he surrounds his music. Much of it is very simple. In his scores for *The River* and *The Plough That Broke the Plains,* he achieved a fresh and genuine treatment of native folk themes that added much to the enjoyable quality of those films.

Howard Hanson (born in Wahoo, Nebraska, in 1896) is one of the most vigorous exponents and defenders of all American composers. As Director of the Eastman School of Music, Dr. Hanson instituted the American Composers' Concerts, which over a course of years has given first performances to the music of many young and unknown American composers, in addition to those who are already established. His services to the development of our native style have been invaluable. As a composer, he has been equally active. Hanson's three symphonies are frequently performed; his opera *Merrymount* was given at the Metropolitan; his cantata *Lament for Beowulf* and many other works are widely known.

With Herbert Haufrecht we turn to the music of still another American generation. Born in New York City in 1909, Mr. Haufrecht has won great distinction as a writer of "functional" music—that is, music closely wedded to a given purpose or to another artistic medium. Thus, as staff composer for the late Federal Theater Project, he was commissioned to write a score for a puppet ballet on Ferdinand the Bull. As narration and movement had all been timed in advance, Haufrecht's task—to create within the narrowest restrictions—was no easy one. Yet the music he created for this puppet play was so delightful that it has become a favorite throughout the country as an independent orchestral composition and has been performed in more than a dozen cities. Other "functional" music written by Haufrecht include *Give Us This Day,* one of five pageant scores he has written for New

York's Madison Square Garden; and much music for the dance, for schools, and for amateur choruses. Among his outstanding works have been *Three Fantastic Marches* (programmed by Stokowski), the rollicking *Square Set* based on folk themes from the Catskill Mountains, the cantata *John Brown's Body,* and the recent *Call from Vilna,* a vigorous and moving challenge to the destroyers of humankind.

William Schuman, pupil and disciple of Roy Harris, has begun to rival his mentor in the number of performances and the distinctions attained by his compositions. Still comparatively young (he was born in New York City in 1910), he has won the first award of the New York Critics' Circle, the first Pulitzer Prize regularly given to a musician, and numerous commissions, and has to his credit important publications, recordings, orchestral performances, and radio broadcasts of his works. He has turned out four symphonies, numerous choral and chamber-music works, a score for a film, and considerable other music. His is a severe and elevated style, which some feel to be extremely powerful.

Robert McBride's music is in greatest possible contrast to that of Mr. Schuman. The latter's is austere; McBride's is simple, playful, easygoing. A westerner, Mr. McBride was born in Tucson, Arizona, in 1911. From the age of ten he played oboe, clarinet, saxophone, and piano in school bands, theater orchestras, and dance bands. His compositions reveal this early familiarity with popular music, both in their fresh, light-hearted manner and in their very titles. *Go Choruses, Hot Stuff, Swing Stuff, Workout for Chamber Orchestra, Jingle Jangle,* and *Wise-apple Five* are some of the works in which McBride has wedded "popular" and "serious" styles. His *Fugato on a Well-known Theme* has been recorded and many of his compositions have been broadcast. Mr. McBride teaches at Bennington College.

Bernard Herrmann is one of the comparatively few young American composers who have been strongly influenced by literary and pictorial sources. Born in 1911, he first won attention as staff conductor and composer for the Columbia Broadcasting System. He wrote much of the background music for the Columbia Workshop and the School of the Air and derived much of his orchestral skill and knowledge of special sound effects from his experiences in radio. Herrmann is a lover of massive and violent effects, as shown in his dramatic cantata,

Moby Dick. Together with his recent Symphony, and a new work, *The Fantasticks,* this composition has been performed by leading orchestras. Particularly effective in mood were his scores for Orson Welles's film *Citizen Kane* (from which Herrmann extracted a concert suite, called *Welles Raises Kane*), and for William Dieterle's *All That Money Can Buy,* which won the Motion Picture Academy award. Herrmann's latest film score is that for *Jane Eyre.*

Representative of a quite different type of American music from any mentioned above is Gian-Carlo Menotti. Born in Milan in 1911, Mr. Menotti grew up in a background of opera, and it is in opera that he has achieved his most distinctive work. His *Amelia Goes to the Ball* was an *opera buffa* in a more or less conventional style, successfully performed at the Metropolitan. In 1939 Mr. Menotti wrote an hour-long radio opera, *The Old Maid and the Thief,* on commission from the National Broadcasting Company. His more recent *Island God* was not quite so successful.

Youngest of all the composers here discussed is George Kleinsinger (born in California in 1914). Like McBride and many other Americans of their generation, Kleinsinger worked his way through college by playing in jazz bands. Arriving in New York in the depression years of the early '30s, he became musical director of a CCC camp, and worked with various unions and other organizations. Kleinsinger is best known for his Cantata to words of Walt Whitman, *I Hear America Singing,* which has received prominent radio and concert performances. His talent for satire and his ability to portray scenes of common city life are revealed in the operetta *A Day in the Life of a Secretary* and in the humorous *Baseball Cantata.* Besides these, Kleinsinger has written theater music, popular ballads, serious chamber music, and a *Western Rhapsody* for orchestra. At the moment of writing he is the director of a USO Service Club.

American Music and the Future

The chapter "A Final Word" in "Music Comes to America"

By David Ewen

A CONCATENATION of forces during the past few decades has made ours the greatest musical country in the world, from whatever point of view one may adopt. It is certain that we shall maintain that position for a long time to come. After the present war is ended, American musical life will be in flower, while that of Europe probably will be quiescent.

Yet our picture would not be complete if, in conclusion, I did not bring to light some of the less agreeable colors. We have gone far —and in an astonishingly brief period. But (let us make no mistake about it!) we have still much further to go.

We could, for example, adopt a greater generosity toward American composers. It is still impossible for even the greatest of our serious composers to acquire a livelihood exclusively from his compositions. Public performances of American works frequently pay nothing (recitalists, chamber-music groups, smaller orchestral and choral societies never pay for the right to play an American work). When payment *is* made—by the leading orchestras and opera houses—the fee is niggardly. An orchestral budget of approximately $600,000 will allot about ½ per cent as royalties to modern composers. Translated into other figures, this means that the performance of an orchestral work by a major symphony orchestra brings the composer between $20 and $50; if this work has previously been published, this sum must be divided between publisher and composer. A major opera house will pay about $100 per performance for a work by an American, frequently less than that.

A friend of mine, for example, wrote a large symphonic work which took him three years to prepare. It was accepted for performance by the New York Philharmonic—which, from the point of view of recognition, is possibly the equivalent of a Broadway production of a play by a young dramatist. His work, since it was performed on a Sunday afternoon, was also broadcast throughout the country over the Columbia network. His total earning from this work was $75. But he had expended about $250 for the copying out of the parts for the orchestra and for other incidental expenses connected with the performance. Thus the success of having one of the great orchestras of the world play his large work netted the composer a loss of $175.

This, unfortunately, is by no means an isolated example. Daniel Gregory Mason has told in his autobiography what extraordinary success was enjoyed by his Second Symphony. Within a short period it was performed by many of the leading orchestras in America—including the Chicago Symphony under Stock, the Cincinnati Symphony under Reiner, and the New York Philharmonic under Bruno Walter. His total earnings from royalties were $175. His expenses were $395. The net result of an unusually successful American work was, therefore, a net loss of $220.

What greater recognition can come to an American composer than to have an opera of his performed by the Metropolitan Opera House? Louis Gruenberg was such a successful composer, and his opera, *The Emperor Jones,* was sufficiently appealing to warrant eleven performances. From these eleven performances Gruenberg earned about $1,000 in royalties.

Such a situation makes it physically impossible for a composer, however brilliant or successful he may be, to devote all his time to creation. Most composers earn their living by teaching—either privately or in music schools or colleges. In this class are such outstanding composers as Roy Harris, Ernest Bloch, Carl Ruggles, Walter Piston, Quincy Porter, David Stanley Smith, Douglas Moore, and numerous others. Aaron Copland, besides teaching, also writes and lectures. Virgil Thomson is a music critic. Deems Taylor holds a radio job. Morton Gould and Robert Russell Bennett also work for the radio. Vladimir Dukelsky writes popular songs [as Vernon Duke]. Louis Gruenberg, Werner Janssen, and Richard Hagemann work for the movies. Lazare Saminsky is a choirmaster. Charles Ives is an insurance man.

In no other field of artistic endeavor is such a situation duplicated. The successful and gifted novelist, dramatist, critic, sculptor, painter can expect a sizable income from his most serious endeavors once he has achieved the necessary recognition. But the serious composer must through necessity scatter his energy and diffuse his efforts by spending innumerable hours in teaching, lecturing, hack work and other menial occupations in order to acquire the sheer necessities of comfortable living. Creation he must relegate to hours stolen from his many other activities. It is a luxury in which he can indulge once he has filled other occupations that earn him his bread. Such a situation is not likely to yield the best results, either in quality or in quantity, from any composer. There can be no question that American music has suffered in consequence.

We do not make the best possible use of the enormous supply of musical talent at our disposal. We are, for the most part, as ungenerous to the talented musical performer as we are to the great composer—though in this direction there are notable exceptions. The hallowed great of the concert hall—the Toscaninis, Heifetzes, Horowitzes, Kreislers, Menuhins, Rachmaninoffs—are, of course, paid fabulously for their performances. Each of these artists can gross from a quarter to a half million dollars a year from his concert and radio activities. But for most musicians of lesser stature—and splendid musicians!—the concert world is a losing battle. We may have wonderful agencies for educating our musically talented young people and giving them a comprehensive preparation for a professional career. But once we have trained them, we seem to remain sublimely indifferent to their art if they are not in the very front rank. Our concert life seems to have room only for immortals.

The truth is that failure on the concert platform is not always the result of incompetence. Even if a musician is a fine artist, with sensibility, taste, and culture, it is questionable if he can make a living through his art. Albert Spalding once said it took him almost twenty years of supposedly successful concert work before he could derive a profit from his concerts; and Spalding, during most of those years, was recognized everywhere as America's greatest violinist. It is a well-known fact that there are artists of world-wide reputation—artists who have repeatedly received the acclaim of critics—who draw little or no profit from their concerts. A friend of mine, a remarkably gifted pianist —frequently praised lavishly by the critics—once said that he would trade his gifts and his reputation for the income of a successful bookkeeper!

With the concert stage unprofitable for the young artist who is not in the front rank, there remains a desirable post in one of the leading American orchestras. The demand for musicians among symphony orchestras is, however, limited and fails to absorb even a fraction of prodigies who enter the professional class. At the beginning of the 1941-1942 symphony season there were fewer than fifty openings among all of the important symphony orchestras in this country.

To play in a symphony orchestra is not quite so desirable a goal as might appear at first glance. Artistically it promises small satisfaction. The young musician becomes a cog of a machine, losing his individuality and creative urge. But even financially there is small reward. Except for the first-desk men—and these positions are few and far between—the orchestra men barely earn a respectable salary. A violinist in one of our major orchestras draws between $70 and $125 a week. This is very good, indeed. But there is one drawback. Since the symphony season consists of no more than twenty-four weeks or so, his salary for the year is really $32 to $60 a week unless he plays in summer concerts.

But, as I have said, posts with symphony orchestras are limited in number. Where else can the young musician turn for a livelihood? The radio, of course, is in the market for musicians—but is not a particularly rich market. The average network has hardly more than one full-size orchestra to fulfill all its musical needs. Radio positions, too, are few and far between.

To what, then, can the young musician turn? The final answer, I suppose, is teaching. But even here the opportunities are scarce. The leading conservatories which can afford to pay excellent salaries employ mostly famous concert artists such as Zimbalist, Serkin, Lhevinne, and Salmond. With a position at a conservatory denied him, the young talented musician is left with only one avenue: he opens a studio in his neighborhood, charges three dollars a lesson, and hopes that enough pupils will study under him to enable him to earn a respectable living. But a respectable living is not the usual fate for the private music teacher. There are, it is estimated, no fewer than eighty thousand music teachers in the country who have an average of ten pupils each and more than a hundred thousand teachers who have less than that number of pupils. Ten pupils or fewer must spell, for the music teacher, continued struggle.

Music may be a billion-dollar industry in this country, but the paradox is that in this billion-dollar industry the one who makes the music is the one who, generally, derives the smallest profit. Still another paradox exists: While there is an abundance of excellent artists who find it difficult to make their way, there are also innumerable communities and universities that are starved for good concerts. These communities, which cannot afford the price for a Heifetz or a Rachmaninoff, could use the services of concert artists of lesser stature who, nevertheless, come bringing with them great music in intelligent and sensitive performances. What is needed in this country is an agency that will promote concerts of good music in smaller and less affluent communities. America is much more than New York, Chicago, and San Francisco. By creating an active concert life in small towns and cities —and at prices of admission that everyone can afford—we shall not only have a limitless extension of our concert horizon, but we shall also provide work and a decent livelihood for every good artist.

Perhaps the most plausible solution to this problem can be provided by the government. Government sponsorship of music is a sadly needed development if America is to expand musically to its fullest potentialities. It is well known that no great orchestra or opera house can be self-supporting. Why should great music be dependent on public charity, or on the beneficence of a few public-spirited millionaires? The Federal Music Project, when it functioned with full force, proved how powerful government-sponsored music projects could be in the spreading of good music. When music was made accessible to the masses at reasonable prices, the public did not ask for great performers or world-famous conductors; it was satisfied with good renditions of musical masterpieces. Never before in the history of concert music had there been such prodigious audiences as those that attended the performances of the Federal Music Project throughout the country. And never before had so many musicians found permanent employment for their talent.

From time to time there has been talk of the creation of a Federal Bureau of Fine Arts which would sponsor performances of great music everywhere. Thus far this ideal has not been realized. Now it must await serener days. But it *should* come. We shall then have opera houses not only in two or three key cities but in most of the smaller cities as well. We shall have not a hundred but a thousand large symphony orchestras. We shall have an active concert life—recitals, chamber-music concerts, choral performances—wherever there is an audience for it. We will, in short, have a place and a function for every talented musician.

Government subsidy was long ago accepted in Europe as a civic necessity. The time should come when it will also be accepted in this country. We shall then not only have solved the problem of the artist, but we shall also have done ourselves a permanent service. Then, truly, will America be a country of music lovers and music making—perhaps the greatest of its kind the world has ever known.

"I cannot be too optimistic about anything concerning America, and particularly about its music." So wrote the ex-Czech composer Jaromir Weinberger in a personal communication to me. No doubt the future belongs to us. We shall grow musically in more and more directions as time passes.

I should like to see development in a few other directions than those discussed in the preceding pages. I should like, for example, to see the emergence of a more dynamic form of music criticism in this country. Our music criticism has, thus far, been too much in the nature of newspaper reporting. It should be more creative than that. It should fill a much more vital need than the mere recording of the essential facts about each concert. Music criticism should fulfill its highest role, that of serving as a link between composer and performer and their audiences. It should educate audiences to a finer and more sensitive understanding of great music. At the same time it should serve as the guide for the artist, as his teacher and counselor. Our critics—the best of them at any rate—have the equipment and gifts to fulfill such a function; what they lack most is the proper facilities. They should not be made to attend a concert every day, sometimes two a day; that task should be relegated to well-equipped subordinates. Our principal critics should be concerned only with a few important performances a week —particularly those of new works. More than this, I should like to see each critic have the time in which to study each new score (or attend several rehearsals) before he attempts to discuss a new work performed for the first time.

What is probably the first important step in making music criticism in America a more dynamic and cogent force has recently been taken in the formation of the Music Critics Circle, headed by Virgil Thomson.* The leading New York music critics are thus banded together to select each season the leading new American work, and the most promising new artist.

I should like to see opera performed in the English language throughout the country. But before this is attempted, I should like to see opera librettos rewritten in English by qualified dramatists and poets, retaining the original context but bringing to it modernity and freshness of diction and viewpoint. Opera will become a more personal experience to the everyday music lover when it is presented to him in a language he understands. Experiments have been made in this

---

* The chairman for 1943 is Olin Downes.—E. S.

direction, principally by smaller opera groups. In an informal survey conducted by Mrs. John DeWitt Peltz for the National Committee for American Opera, it was disclosed that while the major operatic organizations prefer the presentation of opera in foreign languages, there have been in 1940 seventy-two different operas produced in English throughout the country. The most significant and successful experiment in this direction was the presentation of Smetana's *The Bartered Bride* at the Metropolitan Opera House, which proved once and for all how zestfully audiences react to opera when they understand what is being said and done. In its revival of *The Magic Flute* for the 1941-1942 season, the Metropolitan Opera decided to present it in English— incidentally, at the express wish of the conductor, Bruno Walter, who wished the audiences to be aware of the amusing proceedings on the stage. These are the beginnings of a movement that should spread throughout our opera world. Opera, after all, has been performed in French in France; and in German in Germany. There is no reason why in this country it should not be presented more generally in our own language.

I should like to see the birth of a music festival in this country which is the true approximation of Salzburg. Thus far not even the Berkshire Symphonic Festival is a realization in this country of what Salzburg was in Europe. In one respect, and in one respect alone, it will not be possible to duplicate Salzburg in America. It is obvious that a setting so imbued with musical associations, so drenched with historic glamour as Salzburg is, is not to be found in this country. Except for this, America could easily duplicate—and possibly surpass—anything that has been done in Salzburg. Never before was there in one single country such an assemblage of musical genius as there is in America today. Why not gather together some of these wonderful elements— singers, conductors, performers, stage directors, scenic designers, orchestras, choruses, chamber-music ensembles—into the coherent and integrated pattern of a summer festival which could easily become the artistic center of the world?

The idea of an American Salzburg suggests succulent possibilities. Imagine a music festival in which the orchestra is not the Vienna Philharmonic but a magnificent organization like the Boston Symphony, the New York Philharmonic, or the Philadelphia Orchestra. Imagine an orchestra such as this conducted not by any one man but by the major conductors in America—including Toscanini, Koussevitzky, Stokowski, Bruno Walter, Rodzinski—performing great symphonic music, and accompanying our great opera stars in cycles of operas by Wagner, Mozart, Verdi, or Richard Strauss. Imagine choral performances of music by Palestrina, Bach, Mozart, Handel in which the fresh voices of the Schola Cantorum are joined with the rich orchestral texture of a New York Philharmonic conducted by Toscanini. Imagine programs of modern music directed by Stokowski or Rodzinski. Imagine cycles of chamber music (perhaps in open air) by an organization like the Budapest String Quartet. Imagine these things, and you have but a suggestion of what could be accomplished in America with the proper organization and initiative.

The only music that can be heard in Europe today is the roar of the dive bomber, the cannon, the tank. While Europe is in cultural darkness the musical lights in this country are burning brighter than ever, even though we, too, are in the war. A confession that they can be made to burn still more brilliantly is not an indication of failure to recognize their present brightness. If the future of music rests in our hands, we must be true to our responsibility by displaying courage and imagination, wisdom and resourcefulness. What we have already accomplished should be merely the inspiration for further and more ambitious achievements. After all, to be the musical capital of the world carries with it not only a blessing but an obligation.

The Contributors

LAWRENCE ABBOTT, 1902–   . American musician and writer. He was Walter Damrosch's assistant at N.B.C., and worked for a time as music critic on *Time* magazine. Author of *Approach to Music*.

LOUIS ARMSTRONG, 1900–   . Celebrated Negro musician, the first of the great jazz trumpeters. See the autobiographical article, page 711.

ROBERT BAGAR. American music critic and composer, program annotator for the New York Philharmonic-Symphony Society and music critic on the *New York World-Telegram*.

BÉLA BARTÓK, 1881–   . Distinguished Hungarian composer and musician. See the biographical study of him, page 590.

MARION BAUER, 1887–   . American composer and educator; author of *Twentieth Century Music*, and (with Ethel Peyser) of *How Music Grew* and *Music Through the Ages;* associate professor of music at New York University.

LOUIS BIANCOLLI. American music critic, program annotator for the New York Philharmonic-Symphony Society, and music critic on the *New York World-Telegram*.

WILLIAM BILLINGS, 1746–1800. The earliest professional American composer. See the biographical study of him, page 662.

FELIX BOROWSKI, 1872–   . American educator, lecturer, critic, and composer, a leading figure in Chicago musical life. For many years program annotator for the Chicago Symphony Orchestra. Editor of the revised edition of George P. Upton's *Standard Operas* and *Standard Concert Guide*.

WALLACE BROCKWAY, 1905–   . American editor and writer on musical subjects. Co-author (with Herbert Weinstock) of *Men of Music* and *The Opera*. Compiler (with Bart Winer) of *A Second Treasury of the World's Great Letters*.

JOHN N. BURK, 1891–   . American musicologist and critic. Succeeded Philip Hale as program annotator for the Boston Symphony Orchestra, and edited a volume of Hale's program notes for book publication. Author of *Clara Schumann: A Romantic Biography* and of the *Life and Works of Beethoven*.

GILBERT CHASE, 1906–   . American musicologist and critic, authority on Spanish music. Born in Cuba of American parents, he was music critic and Paris correspondent in Europe for many years. In 1940 published *The Music of Spain*. Associate editor of the *International Cyclopedia of Music and Musicians*.

CARLOS CHÁVEZ, 1899–   . Mexican conductor and composer. In 1928 he organized the Mexican Symphony Orchestra, which he has since conducted. He was director of the National Conservatory of Music (Mexico City) and in 1933–34 served as Chief of the Mexican Department of Fine Arts. Has made many guest appearances as conductor in the United States, appearing with our leading orchestras. Author of *Toward a New Music*. Composer of numerous works, including a ballet, *The New Fire;* the ballet *H.P.; Sinfonia India; Sinfonia de Antigona;* and a piano concerto.

AARON COPLAND, 1900–   . Leading American composer. See the biographical study of him, page 757.

OLIN DOWNES, 1886–   . American music critic and author, authority on Sibelius. Since 1924, music critic of the *New York Times*. Author of *The Lure of Music, Symphonic Broadcasts,* and *Symphonic Masterpieces,* and co-author (with Elie Siegmeister) of the collection of American folk songs, *A Treasury of American Song*.

CARL ENGEL, 1883–   . American musician and writer. From 1922 to 1934, chief of the Music Division of the Library of Congress. Editor of *The Musical Quarterly* and president of G. Schirmer, Inc., music publishers.

DAVID EWEN, 1907–   . Author of *Twentieth Century Composers, Composers of Today, From Bach to Stravinsky, The Man With the Baton, Dictators of the Baton, The Book of Modern Composers, Music Comes to America, The Story of George Gershwin,* and other works.

GEORGE GERSHWIN, 1898–1937. Famous American composer. See the biographical study of him, page 753.

LAWRENCE GILMAN, 1878–1939. American music critic and author. Music editor of the *New York Herald Tribune* from 1923, and for ten years program annotator for the New York Philharmonic-Symphony Society and for the Philadelphia Orchestra. Author of many books on music, including *Wagner's Operas* and *Toscanini and Great Music*.

BENNY GOODMAN, 1909–   . American bandleader and clarinetist, the "King of Swing." See the autobiographical article, page 718.

HERBERT GRAF, 1904–   . Opera stage director. Born in Vienna, he came to this country after work in opera in Austria and Germany, and is an outstanding figure in American operatic production. Since 1936 he has been stage director at the Metropolitan Opera and since 1938 at the San Francisco Opera. Has been giving courses in opera at the Berkshire Music Center since 1940, and in 1942 organized the Herbert Graf Opera Productions to give assistance to local opera everywhere in the United States. Author of *The Opera and Its Future in America.*

JOHN TASKER HOWARD, 1890– . American composer, lecturer, and writer. Author of *Our American Music, The Music of George Washington's Time, Stephen Foster, America's Troubadour, Our Contemporary Composers,* and *Ethelbert Nevin.* Editor and compiler of *A Program of Early American Piano Music, A Program of Early and Mid-Nineteenth Century American Songs,* and *A Program of Stephen Foster Songs.*

ARTHUR EAGLEFIELD HULL, 1876–1928. English writer on music, music editor, and organist. Founder of the British Music Society, and editor of *Monthly Musical Record.* Author of several books on music and editor of *A Dictionary of Music and Musicians.*

SCHIMA KAUFMAN. Violinist and author of *Mendelssohn; a Second Elijah, Discovering Music,* and *Everybody's Music.*

LINCOLN KIRSTEIN, 1907– . American critic and authority on the dance. He was one of the founders of the Harvard Society for Contemporary Art, and of the School of the American Ballet. In 1936 he established the famous dance group known as the Ballet Caravan. He is the author of *Dance,* on the history of theatrical dancing. He is now an engineer in the United States Army.

PAUL LANDORMY, 1869– . French musicologist; author of many books on composers, including Brahms and Bizet, and of *A History of Music.*

HUGO LEICHTENTRITT, 1874– . German musicologist, teacher, and composer. Lectured on music at Harvard in 1891–1894, and returned there in 1933, also lecturing at Radcliffe and at New York University. Author of many books on music, including *Music, History and Ideas.*

EUGENIE LINEVA, 1854– ? . Russian folk-song collector and writer on music. In 1891 she toured the United States with a Russian chorus which she organized. Was a pioneer in the scientific collection of Russian folk songs, being the first to use the phonograph to make accurate recordings. Author of *The Peasant Songs of Great Russia.*

DANIEL GREGORY MASON, 1873– . American composer, author, and educator. Among his many works are three symphonies; a Quartet on Negro Themes; *Songs of Love and Life* (to words by William Vaughn Moody) ; and the *Chanticleer* Overture. In 1919 he became a member of the Columbia University faculty and for a number of years was chairman of the Music Department. Author of *From Grieg to Brahms, Beethoven and His Forerunners, The Romantic Composers, Contemporary Composers,* and *Music in My Time* (autobiography).

DOUGLAS MOORE, 1893– . American composer and educator. See the biographical sketch, page 777.

CHARLES HUBERT H. PARRY, 1848–1918. Eminent British writer and composer, best known for his choral works. He was on the faculty of the Royal College of Music, and Professor of Music at Oxford. Author of *Evolution of the Art of Music. Studies of Great Composers,* the third volume of *The Oxford History of Music,* and other works.

ETHEL PEYSER, 1887– . American writer and music critic. Author of *The House That Music Built* (a history of Carnegie Hall), and co-author (with Marion Bauer) of *Music Through the Ages* and *How Music Grew.*

SERGEI PROKOFIEV, 1891– . Eminent Russian composer. For the biographical study of him, see page 608.

ROMAIN ROLLAND, 1866– . French novelist and writer on music. Author of *Jean-Christophe.* An authority on Beethoven, on whom he has written several books. Has also written a life of Handel, a study of Goethe and Beethoven, and other works, including *Some Musicians of Former Days, Musicians of Today,* and *Musical Tour through the Land of the Past.*

PITTS SANBORN, 1879–1941. American music critic. For many years music editor of the *New York World-Telegram.* Author of *The Metropolitan Book of the Opera.*

WINTHROP SARGEANT, 1903– . American musician and critic. Music critic on the *Brooklyn Daily Eagle* and the *New York American;* since 1937, music editor of *Time* magazine. A violinist, he has been a member of the San Francisco Symphony, the New York Symphony, and the New York Philharmonic-Symphony. Head of the department of theory and composition at the New York Philharmonic-Symphony Scholarship School. Author of *Jazz, Hot and Hybrid.*

DOROTHY SCARBOROUGH. Specialist in American folk song, author of *On the Trail of Negro Folk Songs, A Song-Catcher in Southern Mountains,* and other works.

PERCY SCHOLES, 1877– . Distinguished English musicologist. Author of *The Listener's Guide to Music, The Listener's History of Music, The Beginner's Guide to Harmony, The Appreciation of Music, The Oxford Companion to Music,* and many other works.

HAROLD C. SCHONBERG. American writer and editor, associate editor of *The American Music Lover.*

CECIL SHARP, 1859–1924. English composer and educator, pioneer in the collecting of English folk songs; has also made studies of Appalachian folk songs. In 1911 founded the English Folk-Dance Society. Author of *The Dance: An Historical Survey of the Dance in Music,* and *The English Folk Song: Some Conclusions.*

GRIGORI SHNEERSON. Contemporary Russian music critic and writer. For several years music critic of the *Moscow Daily News.* Is active in the Union of Soviet Composers, and in charge of the music section of the

Anglo-American department of the Society for Cultural Relations with Foreign Countries.

DMITRI SHOSTAKOVICH, 1906–   . The leading figure among the younger Russian composers. See the biographical study of him, page 616.

ELIE SIEGMEISTER, 1909–   . American composer and writer. See the autobiographical article, page 771.

NICOLAS SLONIMSKY, 1894–   . Russian-American musicologist and composer; specialist in ultra-modern music and in the music of Latin America. Author of *Music Since 1900,* and one of the editors of the *International Cyclopedia of Music and Musicians.*

IGOR STRAVINSKY, 1882–   . One of the greatest living Russian composers. See the biographical study of him, page 579.

DAVIDSON TAYLOR, 1907–   . American radio executive. Coming to New York in 1933 from WHAS in Louisville, Ky., he became (in 1937) head of the Music Department of C.B.S., where he is now Assistant Director of Broadcasts.

DEEMS TAYLOR, 1885–   . American composer, author, and radio commentator. Musical adviser to C.B.S. Has been commentator for the Metropolitan Opera broadcasts, and now speaks on the Sunday afternoon broadcasts of the New York Philharmonic-Symphony. Among his compositions are *Through the Looking Glass,* and the operas *The King's Henchman* (with book by Edna St. Vincent Millay) and *Peter Ibbetson.* Author of *Of Men and Music* and *The Well-Tempered Listener.*

GEORGE P. UPTON, 1834–1919. American author and music critic. Wrote the first music reviews in Chicago, and was on the staff of the *Chicago Tribune* from 1861 to 1885. Edited the autobiography of Theodore Thomas, and wrote the *Standard Concert Guide* and *Standard Operas.*

RALPH VAUGHAN WILLIAMS, 1872–   . Eminent English composer and folk-song specialist. Has worked with Cecil Sharp on English folk songs and dances, and made many collections. Is professor of composition at the Royal College of Music, and author of *National Music.* Among his many compositions are a *Fantasia on a Theme by Tallis, Pastoral Symphony, London Symphony, Three Norfolk Rhapsodies, A Sea Symphony,* and a *Fantasy on Christmas Carols.*

HERBERT WEINSTOCK, 1905–   . American writer on music. Editor and translator of Carlos Chávez' *Toward a New Music* (1937) ; co-author (with Wallace Brockway) of *Men of Music* (1939) and *The Opera* (1941) ; and author of *Tchaikovsky* (1943).

Acknowledgments

The editor gratefully acknowledges the kindness of authors and publishers in giving permission to reproduce copyright material in *The Music Lover's Handbook* as follows:

THE AMERICAN MUSIC LOVER: for the article "Manuel de Falla" by Harold C. Schonberg; and the article "Aaron Copland" by Marion Bauer from the magazine *The American Music Lover*. Reprinted by permission.

AM-RUS MUSIC CORPORATION: for musical quotations from Prokofiev's Peter and the Wolf and Shostakovich's First, Fifth and Seventh Symphonies.

BÉLA BARTÓK: for extracts from the article "The Relation of Folk Song to the Development of the Art Music of Our Time" by Béla Bartók from the June, 1921 issue of the magazine *The Sackbut*. Reprinted by permission.

BOSTON SYMPHONY ORCHESTRA, INC.: for the article on Prokofiev's Lieutenant Kije by John N. Burk from the Boston Symphony Program Notes. Reprinted by permission of the Boston Symphony Orchestra, Inc.

THOMAS Y. CROWELL COMPANY: for the selections from *Everybody's Music* by Schima Kaufman; for the selections from *Twentieth Century Composers* by David Ewen; for the selections from *Music Comes to America* by David Ewen. Reprinted by permission of Thomas Y. Crowell Company.

THE DIAL PRESS, INC.: for the selections from *Symphonic Masterpieces* by Olin Downes, copyright 1935 by The Dial Press; for the selections from *Symphonic Broadcasts* by Olin Downes, copyright 1931 by The Dial Press. Reprinted by permission of The Dial Press, Inc.

DODD, MEAD & COMPANY, INC.: for the following selections from *The International Cyclopedia of Music and Musicians,* ed. by Oscar Thompson: "Ballet and Music" by Lincoln Kirstein, "Robert Schumann" by Daniel Gregory Mason, "Peter Ilyich Tchaikovsky" by Daniel Gregory Mason, "Stephen Foster" by John Tasker Howard; and for the following selections from *Great Modern Composers,* ed. by Oscar Thompson: "Maurice

Ravel" by Gilbert Chase, "Serge Prokofiev" by Nicolas Slonimsky, "Dmitri Shostakovich" by Nicolas Slonimsky. Reprinted by permission of Dodd, Mead & Company, Inc.

E. P. DUTTON & CO., INC.: for the selection from *Music, Classical, Romantic and Modern* by A. Eaglefield Hull, copyright by E. P. Dutton & Co., Inc. Reprinted by permission of E. P. Dutton & Co., Inc.

FARRAR & RINEHART, INC.: for the selections from *Approach to Music* by Lawrence Abbott, copyright 1940 by Lawrence Abbott. Reprinted by permission of Farrar & Rinehart, Inc.

HARPER & BROTHERS: for the selections from *Stories of Symphonic Music* by Lawrence Gilman, copyright 1907 by Harper & Brothers, copyright 1935 by Lawrence Gilman. Reprinted by permissison of Harper & Brothers, publishers.

HARVARD UNIVERSITY PRESS: for the selections from *Music, History, and Ideas* by Hugo Leichtentritt, copyright 1938 by the President and Fellows of Harvard College; and for the selection from *On the Trail of Negro Folk Songs* by Dorothy Scarborough, copyright 1925 by Harvard University Press. Reprinted by permission of the President and Fellows of Harvard College.

JOHN TASKER HOWARD: for the selections from *Our Contemporary Composers,* published by the Thomas Y. Crowell Company, copyright 1941 by John Tasker Howard. Reprinted by permission.

MAUD KARPELES: for the selection from *The English Folk Song: Some Conclusions* by Cecil Sharp, published by Barnicotts, Ltd. of Taunton, England. Reprinted by permission.

LONGMANS, GREEN AND CO., INC.: for the selection from *Swing That Music* by Louis Armstrong. Reprinted by permission of Longmans, Green and Co., Inc.

A. C. McCLURG & CO.: for the selection from *Standard Concert Guide* by George P. Upton and Felix Borowski. Reprinted by permission of A. C. McClurg & Co.

MODERN MUSIC: for the article "Why Not Try the Air?" by Davidson Taylor from the January, 1938 issue of the magazine *Modern Music,* copyright 1938 by The League of Composers. Reprinted by permission of Modern Music.

THE MUSEUM OF MODERN ART: for the selection from *Mexican Music* by Carlos Chávez and Herbert Weinstock. Reprinted by permission of The Museum of Modern Art, publishers.

NEW MASSES: for the articles by Dmitri Shostakovich from the October 28, 1941 and August 4, 1942 issues of the magazine *New Masses.* Reprinted by permission of New Masses.

W. W. NORTON & COMPANY, INC.: for the selections from *Listening to Music* by Douglas Moore; and for the selections from *The Opera and Its*

Future in America by Herbert Graf. Reprinted by permission of W. W. Norton & Company, Inc.

OXFORD UNIVERSITY PRESS, LONDON: for the selection "Hunting for English Ballads" by Cecil Sharp from *Cecil Sharp* by A. H. Fox-Strangways; and for the selections from *The Listener's Guide to Music* by Percy Scholes. Reprinted by permission of Oxford University Press.

OXFORD UNIVERSITY PRESS, NEW YORK: for the selections from *National Music* by Ralph Vaughan Williams. Reprinted by permission of Oxford University Press.

THE PHILHARMONIC-SYMPHONY SOCIETY OF NEW YORK: for the articles from the Philharmonic-Symphony Program Notes by Louis Biancolli on Haydn's Symphony in G Major; by Robert Bagar on Wagner's Tristan Prelude and Love-Death, and Mussorgsky's Pictures at an Exhibition; by Pitts Sanborn on Ravel's Daphnis and Chloe, and Mahler's Symphony No. 1; and by Robert Bagar and Louis Biancolli on Gould's Spirituals for Orchestra. Reprinted by permission of The Philharmonic-Symphony Society of New York.

G. P. PUTNAM'S SONS: for the selections from *How Music Grew* by Marion Bauer and Ethel Peyser. Reprinted by permission of G. P. Putnam's Sons.

GEORGE ROUTLEDGE & SONS LTD. (Kegan Paul, Trench, Trubner & Co. Ltd.): for the selections from *Studies of Great Composers* by C. Hubert H. Parry; for the selection from *Handel* by Romain Rolland; and for the selection from *Beethoven* by Romain Rolland. Reprinted by permission of George Routledge & Sons Ltd.

WINTHROP SARGEANT: for the selections from *Jazz, Hot and Hybrid,* published by Arrow Editions. Reprinted by permission.

G. SCHIRMER, INC.: for the selections from *Alla Breve* by Carl Engel, copyright 1921 by G. Schirmer, Inc. Reprinted by permission of G. Schirmer, Inc., publishers.

CHARLES SCRIBNER'S SONS: for the selections from *A History of Music* by Paul Landormy. Reprinted by permission of Charles Scribner's Sons.

SIMON AND SCHUSTER, INC.: for the selection from *The Well-Tempered Listener* by Deems Taylor, copyright 1940 by Deems Taylor; for the selections from *Men of Music* by Wallace Brockway and Herbert Weinstock, copyright 1939 by Wallace Brockway and Herbert Weinstock; for the selections from *Of Men and Music* by Deems Taylor, copyright 1937 by Deems Taylor; and for the selections from *Stravinsky: An Autobiography* by Igor Stravinsky, copyright 1936. Reprinted by permission of Simon and Schuster, Inc., publishers.

STACKPOLE SONS: for the selection from *Kingdom of Swing* by Benny Goodman and Irving Kolodin. Reprinted by permission of Stackpole Sons.

STANFORD UNIVERSITY PRESS: for the selection "The Relation of Jazz to American Music" by George Gershwin from *American Composers on American Music,* ed. by Henry Cowell. Reprinted by permission of the Stanford University Press.

WHITTLESEY HOUSE: for the selections from *What to Listen for in Music* by Aaron Copland; and for the selections from *Our New Music* by Aaron Copland. Reprinted by permission of Whittlesey House.

The editor wishes also to express grateful appreciation to those many friends who assisted in the selection and preparation of this book: in the first place to his wife, Hannah Siegmeister; to Jack Radunski, Sidney Madian, Rose and Jack Kabat, Herbert Barrett, Bernard and Elaine Krauss, Edwin and Ruth Goldberg, Harold Baumbach, Harlan Crippen, Eleanore Lane, and Arthur Berger; to Dr. Harold Spivacke of the Library of Congress for suggestions regarding the material on Thomas Jefferson; and, finally, to the staff of the New York Public Library for their patient and devoted service.

Index

Index

Note—Bold-face type indicates a leading article by or about the person listed, or about the subject listed. An (M) in parentheses indicates that a musical example is found on that page. Names of compositions are listed under their composers.

organ works, 364
passacaglias, 144; in C minor, 101
Passions, 132, 371, 440
suites, 143-45, 374
Toccata and Fugue in D minor, 108
Well-Tempered Clavichord, 63, 368,
374, 427, 457, 470
Bach, Karl Philipp Emmanuel, 43, 373,
375, 378, 379, 389, 395
Bach, Maria Barbara, 357, 362, 363, 368
Bach, Wilhelm Friedemann, 372-73
Bachet, Sydney, 713
Bagar, Robert, **193-94, 197-200, 234-35**
Balakirev, 527, 534, 535
Balanchine, 317
Balfe, *I Dreamt That I Dwelt,* 699 (M)
ballad, 29-30, 33, 38, 673
ballad-opera, 266-67, 289-90
ballet—in modern opera, 297; classic,
307; modern music for, 214, 225-32,
313-17, 581-84 (for general treatment,
see dance)
Ballet Comique de la Reine Louise, 306
"ballet" for "ballad," 38-39, 303
Ballet Russe—*see* Diaghilev
Ballo, 303
banjo in jazz, 703, 705
"Barbara Allen," 673
Barbirolli, 643
Bardi, Count, 254
Barjansky, Alexander, 223
Barlow, Howard, 640, 644
Barnum, P. T., 737
Bartók, **45-47,** 49, 51, **590-95,** 727, 730;
birth and boyhood, 592-93; music
studies, 593; early works, 593-94; re-
searches in Hungarian folk music,
590-92, 594; later works, 594-95, 730
Bagatelles, 594
Bluebeard's Castle, 283, 594
Kossuth, 594
*Music for Strings, Percussion, and
Celesta,* 643
quartets, 594-95
Rhapsody (piano and orch.), 593
Rhapsody (violin and orch.), 595
Two Portraits, 594
Wonderful Mandarin, 594
Woodcut Prince, 594
Basie, "Count," 729, 731
bass, 81-82
basso ostinato, 101 n.
bassoon, 86
Battle of Prague, 738
Bauer, Harold, 636
Bauer, Marion, **744-46, 757-61**
Bax, Arnold, 125
Bayreuth *Festspielhaus,* 278, 280-81, 501-
502
Beaumarchais, 271, 402, 408

Beecham, Sir Thomas, 315
Beethoven, 44, 128, 139, 352, 388, 394,
395, **409-26,** 531
childhood, 410-11; to Vienna, 411;
appearance and manner, 409-10; por-
trait of, 412; deafness, 412-13, 420-21;
health, 414; love affairs, 413-14;
Heiligenstadt Testament, 414; republican sympathies, 411, 415; tastes in
reading, 418 n., notebooks, 63, 418 n.,
423; trouble with nephew, 422, 425;
illness and death, 425-26, 453
Coriolanus, 415, 418 n.
Egmont, 111 n., 415
Emperor Concerto, 415
Fidelio, 271-72, 291, 415, 420
Leonore Overture, 111 n.
Missa Solemnis, 134, 424, 425 n.
Prometheus ballet, 157
Quartets, 41, 211, 415, 421, 423, 425
Septet, 413
sonatas—piano, 97, 121, 407, 413, 414,
415, 416, 417, 421; violin and piano,
414, 415
songs, 411, 414, 417
symphonies, 118-20, 489
First, 413
Second, 120, 414, 415
Third (*Eroica*), 49, 114, 119, **154-
58** (M), 415, 416
Fourth, 416
Fifth, 42, 111 (M), 114, 120, 141,
158-60 (M), 352, 415, 416
Sixth (*Pastoral*), 46-47 (M), 127,
140, **160-62** (M), 416, 430, 519
Seventh, 114, 120, **162-64** (M), 419
Eighth, 419
Ninth (*Choral*), 49 (M), 58, 114,
120, 121, **165-68** (M), 421, 422-23,
424, 518-19
Violin Concerto, 506
Beethoven monument at Bonn, 485
Beiderbecke, "Bix," 721, 729
bel canto, 247, 262-63
Bellini, 275, 479, 537
Norma, 275, 490
Puritani, 276
Sonnambula, 276
bells, 90, 543
Bennett, Robert Russell, 95 n., 644, 782
Benois, Alexandre, 229, 576, 582
Berezowsky, Nicolai, 644
Berg, Alban, 284, 316, 604-608; *Wozzeck,*
284, 602, **604-608**
Bériot, Charles de, 555
Berkshire Festival, 787
Berlin, Irving, 699, 701, 768
Berliner, Emil, 649
Berlioz, 63, 141, 166, 310, 325, 430,
432-33, 440, **480-84,** 486, 527